AN INTRODUCTION TO Cognitive Psychology

Processes and disorders

Third Edition

David Groome

With Nicola Brace, Graham Edgar, Helen Edgar,
Michael Eysenck, Tom Manly, Hayley Ness, Graham Pike,
Sophie Scott and Elizabeth Styles

Routledge
Taylor & Francis Group

LONDON AND NEW YORK

Published 2014 by Routledge
2 Park Square, Milton Park, Abingdon, Oxon
OX14 4RN
711 Third Avenue, New York, NY 10017, USA

First edition published by Psychology Press 1999
Second edition published by Psychology Press 2006

British Library Cataloguing in Publication Data
A catalogue record for this book is available from the British Library

Library of Congress Cataloging in Publication Data
A catalog record for this book has been requested

ISBN: 978-1-84872-091-6 (hbk)
ISBN: 978-1-84872-092-3 (pbk)
ISBN: 978-1-315-87155-4 (ebk)

Typeset in Sabon
by Book Now Ltd, London

Contents

7. DISORDERS OF MEMORY

David Groome

Illustrations

FIGURES

BOXES

Authors

David Groome was Senior Academic in the Psychology Department at the University of Westminster until 2011, when he retired. However, he retains a research connection with the University, and he continues to write cognitive psychology books. Despite all this he has always considered himself to be mainly a guitarist who does psychology in his spare time.

Michael Eysenck is Professorial Fellow at Roehampton University and Emeritus Professor at Royal Holloway University of London. He has produced 46 books and about 160 book chapters and journal articles leading some to accuse him of following the adage, "Never mind the quality, feel the width!"

Nicola Brace is a Senior Lecturer in Psychology at The Open University. She has taught and researched cognitive psychology for over 25 years, and has come to the conclusion that when it comes to solving Sudoku puzzles understanding the brain is not nearly as useful as a good cup of tea.

Graham Edgar is currently employed as a Reader in Psychology at the University of Gloucestershire. He has spent most of his career coming to appreciate that, although psychology can be applied to pretty much everything, the difficult bit is working out how. He is presently researching situation awareness in the military, health, fire-fighting and driving domains and trying to see if neuroscience can explain it. He is an optimist.

Helen Edgar worked as principal research scientist at BAE SYSTEMS for more years than she cares to remember. She now divides her time between writing and consultancy regarding road traffic collisions. Her spare time is spent trying to 'herd cats', or at least keep her Persian off the computer whist she is writing.

Tom Manly is a clinical psychologist and programme leader at the Medical Research Council Cognition and Brain Sciences Unit in Cambridge. His insatiable need for attention has led him to perform in one of the UK's least successful bands and to attempt stand-up comedy, only one of which has been routinely associated with audience laughter.

Hayley Ness is a Lecturer in Psychology at The Open University, where she chaired the largest cognitive psychology course in Europe.

She is particularly passionate about memory and face processing but has a terrible memory and can't remember people's names. Therefore confirming the adage that people study the thing they are least proficient at.

Graham Pike is Professor of Forensic Cognition at The Open University and researches eyewitness memory. He has many pet peeves, though the greatest is his hatred of name dropping… which is a real pity because he has worked with both William Shatner and Philip Glenister.

Sophie Scott is Professor of Cognitive Neuroscience at the Institute of Cognitive Neuroscience, which is part of University College London. Sophie carries out research on the neural basis of vocal communication. She is also interested in laughter, both in the research lab and in her own time. Long ago in another life she was one of David Groome's students.

Elizabeth Styles is lecturer in psychology at St. Edmund Hall, University of Oxford. She has taught and examined cognitive psychology for many years and has previously written text books on the psychology of attention for Psychology Press. She has written a highly regarded book on attention, which was good practice for her contribution to the present book. When not working she likes to travel and study archaeology.

Preface

We wrote this book because we felt that it filled an important gap. As far as we know it is the first textbook to cover all of the main aspects of cognitive psychology and all of their associated disorders too. We believe that an understanding of the disorders of cognition is an essential requirement for understanding the processes of normal cognition, and in fact the two approaches are so obviously complimentary that we are quite surprised that nobody had put them together in one book before. There are books about normal cognition, and there are books about cognitive disorders (usually referred to as "cognitive neuropsychology"), but there do not seem to be any other books which cover both topics in full. We feel that this combined approach offers a number of advantages. In the first place, combining normal and abnormal cognition in one book makes it possible to take an integrated approach to these two related fields. References can be made directly between the normal and abnormal chapters, and theories which are introduced in the normal chapters can be reconsidered later from a clinical perspective. We chose to keep the normal and abnormal aspects in separate chapters, as this seems clearer and also makes it more straightforward for those teaching separate normal and abnormal cognitive psychology courses. There is also one further advantage of a combined textbook, which is that students can use the same textbook for two different courses of study, thus saving the cost of buying an extra book.

Another reason for writing this book was that we found the other available cognitive psychology texts were rather difficult to read. Our students found these books were heavy going, and so did we. So we set about writing a more interesting and accessible book, by deliberately making more connections with real life and everyday experience. We also cut out some of the unnecessary anatomical detail that we found in rival texts. For example, most neuropsychology books include a large amount of detail about the structure of the brain, but most psychology students do not really need this. So we decided to concentrate instead on the psychological aspects of cognitive disorders rather than the anatomical details. And finally, we decided to put in lots of illustrations, because we think it makes the book clearer and more fun to read. And also we just happen to like books which have lots of pictures.

So here then is our textbook of cognitive psychology and cognitive disorders, made as simple as possible, and with lots of pictures. We enjoyed writing it, and we hope you will enjoy reading it.

David Groome

Acknowledgements

We would like to offer our sincere thanks to the reviewers who provided valuable comments and suggestions about our manuscript, especially Julie Blackwell Young, Rosalind Horowitz, Sam Hutton, Wido La Heij, Karla Lassonde, Wolfgang Minker, Erik Nilsen, Jane Oakhill, Fenna Poletiek, and Gezinus Wolters. Also our heartfelt thanks to Richard Kemp and Hazel Dewart, who both made valuable contributions to chapters 4 and 10 respectively. Thanks also to those at Psychology Press, and in particular Rebekah Edmondson, Michael Fenton, Ceri Griffiths, and Natalie Larkin. And finally thanks to Richard Cook and Jef Boys at Book Now.

Chapter 1

Contents

Introduction to cognitive psychology

David Groome

1

1.1 COGNITIVE PROCESSES

A DEFINITION OF COGNITIVE PSYCHOLOGY

Cognitive psychology has been defined as the psychology of mental processes. More specifically it has also been described as the study of understanding and knowing. However, these are rather vague terms, and whilst they do provide an indication of what cognition involves, they leave us asking exactly what is meant by 'knowing', 'understanding' and 'mental processes'. A more precise definition of cognitive psychology is that it is the study of the way in which the brain processes information. It concerns the way we take in information from the outside world, how we make sense of that information and what use we make of it. Cognition is thus a rather broad umbrella term, which includes many component processes, and this possibly explains why psychologists have found it so difficult to come up with a simple and unified definition of cognitive psychology. Clearly cognition involves various different kinds of information processing which occur at different stages.

STAGES OF COGNITIVE PROCESSING

The main stages of cognitive processing are shown in Figure 1.1, arranged in the sequential order in which they would typically be applied to a new piece of incoming sensory input.

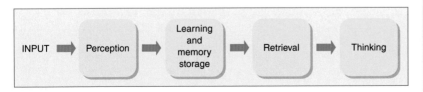

Figure 1.1   The main stages of cognitive processing.

Information taken in by the sense organs goes through an initial stage of perception, which involves the analysis of its content. Even at this early stage of processing the brain is already extracting meaning from the input, in an effort to make sense of the information it contains. The process of perception will often lead to the making of some kind of record of the input received, and this involves learning and memory storage. Once a memory has been created for some item of information, it can be retained for later use, to assist the individual in some other setting. This will normally require the retrieval of the information. Retrieval is sometimes carried out for its own sake, merely to access some information stored in the past. On the other hand, we sometimes retrieve information to provide the basis for further mental activities such as thinking. Thought processes often make use of memory retrieval, as for example when we use previous experience to help us deal with some new problem or situation. Sometimes this involves the rearrangement and manipulation of stored information to make it fit in with a new problem or task. Thinking is thus rather more than just the retrieval of old memories.

The cognitive processes shown in Figure 1.1 are in reality a good deal more complex and interactive than this simple diagram implies. The diagram suggests that the various stages of cognitive processing are clearly distinct from one another, each one in its own box. This is a drastic oversimplification, and it would be more accurate to show the different stages as merging and overlapping with one another. For example, there is no exact point at which perception ceases and memory storage begins, because the process of perception brings about learning and memory storage and thus in a sense these processes are continuous. In fact all of the stages of cognition shown in the diagram overlap and interact with one another, but a diagram showing all of these complex interactions would be far too confusing, and in any case a lot of the interactions would be speculative. Figure 1.1 should therefore be regarded as a greatly simplified representation of the general sequential order of the cognitive processes which typically occur, but it would be more realistic to think of cognition as a continuous flow of information from the input stage through to the output stage, undergoing different forms of processing along the way.

APPROACHES TO THE STUDY OF COGNITION

There have been four main approaches to the study of cognitive psychology (see Figure 1.2).

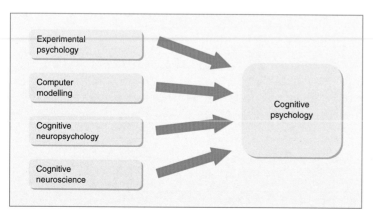

Figure 1.2   The four main approaches to studying cognitive psychology.

In the first place there is the approach known as experimental cognitive psychology, which involves the use of psychological experiments on human subjects to investigate the ways in which they perceive, learn, remember or think. A second approach to cognitive psychology is the use of computer modelling of cognitive processes. Typically this approach involves the simulation of certain aspects of human cognitive function by writing computer programs, in order to test out the feasibility of a model of possible brain function. The third approach is known as cognitive neuropsychology, which involves the study of individuals who have suffered some form of brain injury. We can discover a great deal about the working of the normal brain by studying the types of cognitive impairment which result from lesions (i.e. damage) in certain regions of the brain. Brain damage can impair information processing by disrupting one or more stages of cognition, or in some cases by breaking the links between different stages. The fourth approach to cognition is known as cognitive neuroscience, and this involves the use of techniques such as brain imaging (i.e. brain scans) to investigate the brain activities that underlie cognitive processing. The two most widely used brain-imaging techniques are PET scans (Positron Emission Tomography) and MRI scans (Magnetic Resonance Imaging, Figure 1.3). PET scans involve the detection of positrons emitted by radioactive chemicals injected into the bloodstream, whereas MRI scans detect responses to a powerful magnetic field. Both techniques can provide accurate images of brain structures, but MRI is better at detecting changes over a period of time, as for example in measuring the effect of applying a stimulus of some kind.

Key Term

Experimental psychology
The scientific testing of psychological processes in human and animal subjects.

Computer modelling
The simulation of human cognitive processes by computer. Often used as a method of testing the feasibility of an information-processing mechanism.

Cognitive neuropsychology
The study of the brain activities underlying cognitive processes, often by investigating cognitive impairment in brain-damaged patients.

Cognitive neuroscience
The investigation of human cognition by relating it to brain structure and function, normally obtained from brain-imaging techniques.

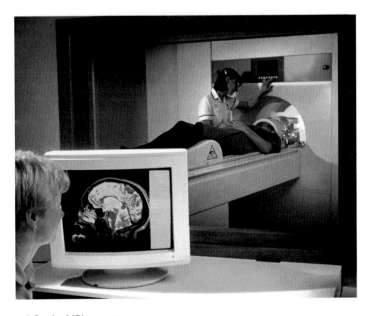

Figure 1.3   An MRI scanner.

Source: Science Photo Library.

These four approaches to cognition have all proved to be valuable, especially when it has been possible to combine different approaches to the same cognitive process. The rest of this chapter deals with these approaches to cognitive psychology, starting with experimental cognitive psychology (Section 1.2), then computer modelling (Section 1.3), and finally cognitive neuroscience and neuropsychology (Section 1.4). Subsequent chapters of the book will continue to apply the same basic approaches in a more detailed study of each of the main areas of cognition.

1.2 EXPERIMENTAL COGNITIVE PSYCHOLOGY

THE FIRST COGNITIVE PSYCHOLOGISTS

The scientific study of psychology began towards the end of the nineteenth century. Wilhelm Wundt set up the first psychology laboratory at Leipzig in 1879, where he carried out research on perception, including some of the earliest studies of visual illusions. In 1885 Hermann Ebbinghaus published the first experimental research on memory, and many subsequent researchers were to adopt his methods over the years that followed. Perhaps the most lasting work of this early period was a remarkable book written by William James (Figure 1.4) in 1890, entitled *Principles of Psychology*. In that book James proposed a number of theories which are still broadly accepted today, including (to give just one example) a theory distinguishing between short-term and long-term memory.

Figure 1.4   William James.

Source: Science Photo Library.

THE RISE AND FALL OF BEHAVIOURISM

Cognitive psychology made slow progress in the early years due to the growing influence of behaviourism, an approach which constrained psychologists to the investigation of externally observable behaviour. The behaviourist position was clearly stated by Watson (1913), who maintained that psychologists should consider only events that were observable, such as the stimulus presented and any consequent behavioural response to that stimulus. Watson argued that psychologists should not concern themselves with processes such as thought and other inner mental processes which could not be observed in a scientific manner. The behaviourists were essentially trying to establish psychology as a true science, comparable in status with other sciences such as physics or chemistry. This was a worthy aim, but like many worthy aims it was taken too far. The refusal to consider inner mental processes had the effect of restricting experimental psychology to the recording of observable responses, which were often of a rather trivial nature. Indeed, some behaviourists were so keen to eliminate inner mental processes from their studies that they preferred to work on rats rather than on human subjects. A human being brings a whole lifetime of personal experience to the laboratory, which cannot be observed or controlled by the experimenter. A rat presents rather fewer of these unknown and uncontrolled variables (Figure 1.5).

Figure 1.5   A rat learning to run through a maze.
Source: Shutterstock.

A good example of the behaviourist approach is the classic work carried out on learning by B.F. Skinner (1938), who trained rats to press a lever in order to obtain a food pellet as a reward (or 'reinforcement'). The work of Skinner and other behaviourists undoubtedly generated some important findings, but they completely disregarded the cognitive processes underlying the responses they were studying.

GESTALT AND SCHEMA THEORIES

Despite these restrictions on mainstream psychological research, some psychologists began to realise that a proper understanding of human cognition could only be achieved by investigating the mental processes which the behaviourists were so determined to eliminate from their studies. Among the first of these pioneers were the Gestalt psychologists in Germany, and the British psychologist Frederick Bartlett. Their work returned to the study of cognitive processes and it helped to lay the foundations of modern cognitive psychology.

It is very easy to demonstrate the importance of inner mental processes in human cognition. For example, a glance at Figure 1.6 will evoke the same clear response in almost any observer. It is a human face. However, a more objective analysis of the components of the figure reveals that it actually consists of a semi-circle and two straight lines. There is really no 'face' as such in the figure itself. If you see a face in this simple figure, then it is you, the observer, who has *added* the face from your own store of knowledge.

The idea that we contribute something to our perceptual input from our own knowledge and experience was actually proposed by a number of early theorists, notably the Gestalt group (Gestalt is German for 'shape' or 'form'). They suggested that we add something to what we perceive, so that the perception of a whole object will be something more than just the sum of its component parts (Wertheimer, 1912; Kohler, 1925). They argued that the perception of a figure depended on its 'pragnanz' (i.e. its meaningful content), which favoured the selection of the simplest and best interpretation available (Koffka,

Key Term

Behaviourism
An approach to psychology which constrains psychologists to the investigation of externally observable behaviour, and rejects any consideration of inner mental processes.

Gestalt psychology
An approach to psychology which emphasised the way in which the components of perceptual input became grouped and integrated into patterns and whole figures.

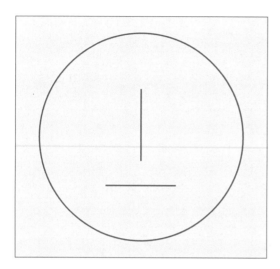

Figure 1.6   A shape recognised by most observers.

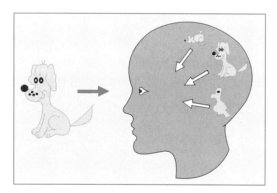

Figure 1.7   Schemas generated for comparison with new input.

Source: Drawing by David Groome.

1935). These theories were perhaps rather vague, but they did at least make an attempt to explain the perception of complex figures such as faces. The behaviourist approach, which refused to consider any influence other than the stimulus itself, could not offer any explanation at all for such phenomena.

The schema theory proposed by Bartlett (1932) was another early attempt to provide a plausible explanation for a person's ability to make sense of their perceptual input. The schema theory proposes that all new perceptual input is analysed by comparing it with items which are already in our memory store, such as shapes and sounds which are familiar from past experience. These items are referred to as 'schemas', and they include a huge variety of sensory patterns and concepts. Figure 1.7 illustrates the process of selection of an appropriate schema to match the incoming stimulus. (NB: This is purely diagrammatic. In reality there are probably millions of schemas available, but there was not enough space for me to draw the rest of them.)

The schema theory has some interesting implications, because it suggests that our perception and memory of an input may sometimes be changed and distorted to fit our existing schemas. Since our schemas are partly acquired from our personal experience, it follows that our perception and memory of any given stimulus will be unique to each individual person. Different people will therefore perceive the same input in different ways, depending on their own unique store of experience. Both of these phenomena were demonstrated by Bartlett's experiments (see Chapter 6 for more details), so the schema theory can be seen to have considerable explanatory value. The schema approach has much in common with the old saying that 'beauty lies in the eye of the beholder'. Perhaps we could adapt that saying to fit the more general requirements of schema theory by suggesting that 'perception lies in the brain of the perceiver'. As a summary of schema theory this is possibly an improvement, but I would concede that it possibly lacks the poetry of the original saying.

Schema and Gestalt theory had a major influence on the development of cognitive psychology, by emphasising the role played by inner mental processes and stored knowledge, rather than considering only stimulus and response. However, it would take many years for this viewpoint to take over from behaviourism as the mainstream approach to cognition.

TOP-DOWN AND BOTTOM-UP PROCESSING

Inspired by the schema theory, Neisser (1967) identified two main types of input processing, known as top-down and bottom-up processing. Top-down processing involves the generation of schemas by the higher cortical structures, and these schemas are sent down the nervous system for comparison with the incoming stimulus. Top-down processing is also sometimes referred to as schema-driven or conceptually driven processing.

Bottom-up processing is initiated by stimulation at the 'bottom end' of the nervous system (i.e. the sense organs), which then progresses up towards the higher cortical areas. Bottom-up processing is also known as stimulus-driven or data-driven processing, because it is the incoming stimulus which sets off some appropriate form of processing. One obvious difference between 'top-down' and 'bottom-up' processing is that their information flows in opposite directions, as shown in Figure 1.8.

Bottom-up processing theories can help to explain the fact that processing is often determined by the nature of the stimulus (Gibson, 1979). However, bottom-up theories have difficulty explaining the perception of complex stimuli, which can be more easily explained by top-down theories.

Although there have been disputes in the past about the relative importance of 'top-down' and 'bottom-up' processing, Neisser (1967) argues that both types of processing probably play a part in the analysis of perceptual input and that in most cases information processing will involve a combination of the two. We can thus think of input processing in terms of stimulus information coming up the system, where it meets and interacts with schemas travelling down in the opposite direction.

Key Term

Top-down (or schema-driven) processing
Processing which makes use of stored knowledge and schemas to interpret an incoming stimulus (contrasts with bottom-up processing).

Bottom-up (or stimulus-driven) processing
Processing which is directed by information contained within the stimulus (contrasts with top-down processing).

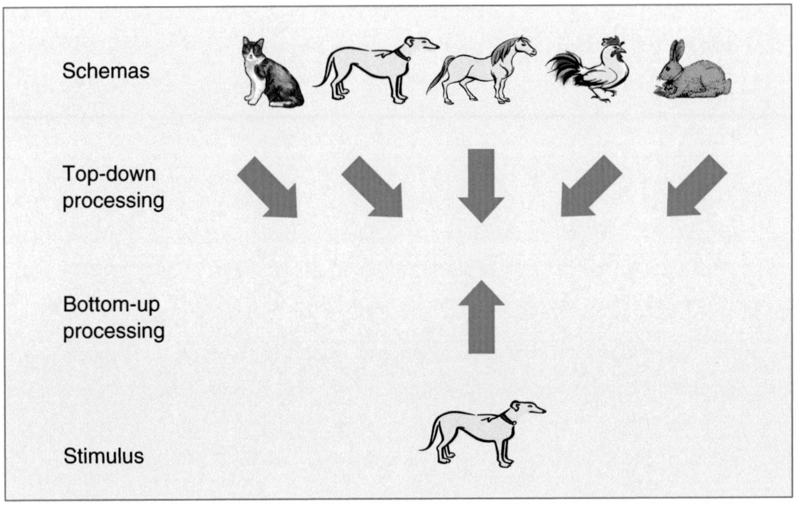

Figure 1.8   Top-down and bottom-up processing.

1.3 COMPUTER MODELS OF INFORMATION PROCESSING

COMPUTER ANALOGIES AND COMPUTER MODELLING OF BRAIN FUNCTIONS

A major shift towards the cognitive approach began in the 1950s, when the introduction of the electronic computer provided a new source of inspiration for cognitive psychologists. Computer systems offered some completely new ideas about information processing, providing a helpful analogy with possible brain mechanisms. Furthermore, computers could be used as a 'test-bed' for modelling possible human brain functions, providing a means of testing the feasibility of a particular processing mechanism. By separating out the various component stages of a cognitive process, it is possible to devise a sequential flow chart which can be written as a computer program and actually put to the test, to see whether it can process information as the brain would. Of course such experiments cannot prove that the programs and mechanisms operating within the computer are the same as the mechanisms which occur in the brain, but they can at least establish whether a processing system is feasible.

Among the first to apply computers in this way were Newell *et al.* (1958), who developed computer programs which were able to solve simple problems, suggesting a possible comparison with human problem-solving and thought. More recently programs have been developed which can tackle far more complex problems, such as playing a game of chess. Computer programs were also developed which could carry out perceptual processes, such as the recognition of complex stimuli. These programs usually make use of feature detector systems, which are explained in the next section.

FEATURE DETECTORS

Selfridge and Neisser (1960) devised a computer system which could identify shapes and patterns by means of feature detectors, tuned to distinguish certain specific components of the stimulus such as vertical or horizontal lines. This was achieved by wiring light sensors together in such a way that all those lying in a straight line at a particular angle converged on the same feature detector, as illustrated in Figure 1.9.

This system of convergent wiring will ensure that the feature detector will be automatically activated whenever a line at that particular angle is encountered. Simple feature detectors of this kind could be further combined higher up the system to activate complex feature detectors, capable of detecting more complicated shapes and patterns made up out of these simple components, as shown in Figure 1.10.

A hierarchy of feature detectors, continuing through many levels of increasing complexity, are able to identify very complex shapes such as faces. Selfridge and Neisser (1960) demonstrated that such a system

Key Term
Feature detectors
Mechanisms in an information-processing device (such as a brain or a computer) which respond to specific features in a pattern of stimulation, such as lines or corners.

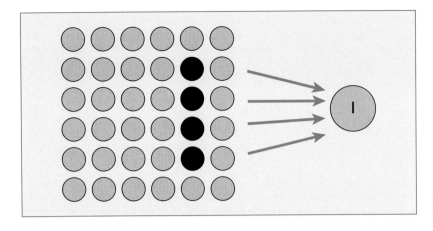

Figure 1.9 Wiring to a simple feature detector.

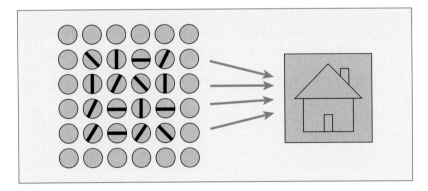

Figure 1.10 Wiring to a complex feature detector.

of simple and complex feature detectors could be made to work very effectively on a computer, which suggests that it does provide a feasible mechanism for the identification of shapes and patterns. This raised the possibility that human perception could involve similar feature-detecting systems, and indeed such feature detectors have been found in the brain. Hubel and Weisel (1959) found simple feature detector cells when carrying out microelectrode recordings in the brain of a cat, and more recently Haynes and Rees (2005) have used functional imaging techniques to identify similar feature detector cells in the human brain.

The discovery of feature detectors can be regarded as an example of different approaches to cognition being combined, with contributions from both neuroscience and computer modelling. The concept has also had a major influence on cognitive psychology, as feature detectors are thought to operate as 'mini-schemas' which detect specific shapes and patterns. This approach paved the way towards more advanced theories of perception and pattern recognition based on computer models, such as those of Marr (1982) and McClelland and Rumelhart (1986). A more detailed account of feature extraction theories can be found in Chapter 2.

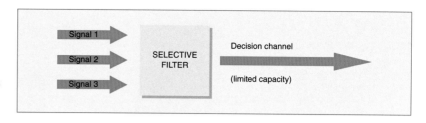

Figure 1.11 Broadbent's model of selective attention.

THE LIMITED-CAPACITY PROCESSOR MODEL

Broadbent (1958) carried out experiments on divided attention, which showed that people have difficulty in attending to two separate inputs at the same time. Broadbent explained his findings in terms of a sequence of processing stages which could be represented as a series of stages in a flow chart. Certain crucial stages were identified which acted as a 'bottleneck' to information flow, because of their limited processing capacity (see Figure 1.11).

This was an approach to information processing which owed its inspiration to telecommunications and computing technology. There is a clear parallel between the human brain faced with a large array of incoming information, and a telephone exchange faced with a large number of incoming calls, or alternatively a computer whose input has exceeded its processing capacity. In each case many inputs are competing with one another for limited processing resources, and the inputs must be prioritised and selectively processed if an information overload is to be avoided. Broadbent referred to this process as 'selective attention', and his theoretical model of the 'limited-capacity processor' provided cognitive psychology with an important new concept. This work on selective attention will be considered in more detail in Chapter 3. But for the moment these approaches are of interest chiefly for their role in the early development of cognitive psychology.

1.4 COGNITIVE NEUROSCIENCE AND NEUROPSYCHOLOGY

THE STRUCTURE AND FUNCTION OF THE BRAIN

Cognitive neuroscience is concerned with the relationship between brain function and cognition, and normally makes use of brain-imaging techniques. Cognitive neuropsychology is also concerned with the brain mechanisms underlying cognition, by studying individuals who have suffered brain damage. Both of these related approaches are now accepted as important components of cognitive psychology.

This is not a textbook of neurology, so it would not be appropriate here to deal with brain anatomy and function in detail. However, there will be references throughout this book to various regions of the brain, so it would be useful to consider a basic working map of the

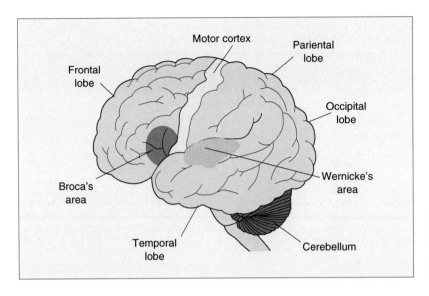

Figure 1.12 A side view of the human brain, showing the main lobes.

Source: Drawing by David Groome.

brain. Figure 1.12 shows a side view of the human brain, showing the position of its main structures.

The outer shell of the brain is known as the cerebral cortex, and it is responsible for most of the higher cognitive processes. The various lobes of the cortex are extensively interconnected, so that a single cognitive process may involve many different cortical areas. However, the brain is to some extent 'modular' in that certain brain areas do perform specific functions. We know this largely from the study of brain lesions, since damage to a certain part of the brain can often cause quite specific impairments. In recent years the introduction of brain scanning equipment has provided an additional source of knowledge to supplement the findings of brain lesion studies.

It has been established that the left and right hemispheres of the brain have particular specialisations. In right-handed people the left hemisphere is normally dominant (the nerves from the brain cross over to control the opposite side of the body), and the left hemisphere also tends to be particularly involved with language and speech. The right hemisphere seems to be more concerned with the processing of non-verbal input, such as the perception of patterns or faces. These functions may be reversed in left-handed people, though most have left hemisphere specialisation for language.

It would appear then (to borrow a football cliché) that it is a brain of two halves. But in addition to these specialisations of the right and left hemispheres, it has been argued that the front and the rear halves of the brain also have broadly different functions. Luria (1973) points out that the front half of the brain (in fact the area corresponding to the frontal lobes) is primarily concerned with output, such as for example the control of movements and speech. In contrast the rear half of the brain (the parietal, temporal and occipital lobes) tend to be more concerned with the processing of input, as for example in the analysis of visual and auditory perception.

> ### Key Term
>
> **Broca's area**
> A region of the brain normally located in the left frontal region, which controls motor speech production.
>
> **Wernicke's area**
> A region of the brain normally located in the left temporal region, which is concerned with the perception and comprehension of speech.

The frontal lobes include the motor region of the cortex, which controls movement. Damage to this area is likely to cause problems with the control of movement, or even paralysis. Also in the frontal lobes is Broca's area, which controls the production of speech, and it is normally in the left hemisphere of the brain. It was Broca (1861a), who first noted that damage to this region caused an impairment of speech production. Other parts of the frontal lobes are involved in the central executive system which controls conscious mental processes such as the making of conscious decisions. Recent neuro-imaging studies have shown that activation of the prefrontal cortex (the front-most region of the frontal lobes) is associated with intelligent reasoning (Jung and Haier, 2007), and prefrontal activation is also linked with the selective retrieval of memory items (Kuhl *et al.*, 2008).

The occipital lobes at the back of the brain are mainly concerned with the processing of visual input, and damage to the occipital lobes may impair visual perception (Weiskrantz *et al.*, 1974; Gazzaniga *et al.*, 2009).

The parietal lobes are also largely concerned with perception. They contain the somatic sensory cortex, which receives tactile input from the skin as well as feedback from the muscles and internal organs. This region is also important in the perception of pain, and other parts of the parietal lobes may be involved in some aspects of short-term memory. Recent studies using brain scans suggest that the parietal lobes are activated during the retrieval of contextual associations of retrieved memories (Simons *et al.*, 2008).

The temporal lobes are so called because they lie beneath the temples, and they are known to be particularly concerned with memory. Temporal lobe lesions are often associated with severe amnesia. For example, Milner (1966) reported that a patient called HM, whose temporal lobes had been extensively damaged by surgery, was unable to register any new memories. Aggleton (2008) concludes that there is now extensive evidence linking the temporal lobes to the encoding and retrieval of memories of past events. The temporal lobes also include the main auditory area of the cortex, and a language centre known as Wernicke's area (again usually in the left hemisphere), which is particularly concerned with memory for language and the understanding of speech (Wernicke, 1874).

Over the years lesion studies have not only established which areas of the brain carry out particular cognitive functions, but they have also shed some light on the nature of those functions. For example, as explained above, Milner (1966) reported that the temporal lobe amnesic patient HM was unable to remember any information for longer than a few seconds. However, his ability to retain information for a few seconds was found to be completely normal. From these observations it was deduced that HM's lesion had caused a severe impairment in his ability to store items in his long-term memory (LTM), but had caused no apparent impairment of his short-term memory (STM). This finding suggests a degree of independence (i.e. a 'dissociation') between STM and LTM. An interesting observation was made in a later study by Warrington and Shallice (1969), whose patient KF suffered an impairment of STM but with an intact LTM. This is an exact reversal of the pattern of impairment found in HM. It has thus been shown that either STM or LTM can be separately impaired while the other remains intact. This is known as a double dissociation, and it provides particularly convincing evidence for the view that STM and LTM involve separate processing and storage mechanisms. Later in this book there will be many references to dissociations of various kinds, but where a double dissociation can be demonstrated this is regarded as a particularly convincing argument for the independence of two functions.

The study of brain and cognition obviously overlap, and in recent years cognitive psychologists and neuropsychologists have been able to learn a lot from one another. A deliberate attempt has been made in this book to bring normal cognitive psychology and cognitive neuropsychology together, to take full advantage of this relationship.

INFORMATION STORAGE IN THE BRAIN

In order to operate as an information-processing system, the brain must obviously have some way of representing information, for both processing and storage purposes. Information must be encoded in some representational or symbolic form, which may bear no direct resemblance to the material being encoded. Consider, for example, how music may be encoded and stored as digital information on a silicon chip, as laser-readable pits on a CD, as electromagnetic fields on a tape, as grooves on a vinyl disc (remember them?), or even as notes written on a piece of paper. It does not matter what form of storage is used, so long as you have the equipment to encode and decode the information.

There have been many theories about the way information might be represented and stored in the brain, including early suggestions that information could be stored in magnetic form (Lashley, 1950) or in chemical form (Hyden, 1967). However, neither of these theories was very plausible because such mechanisms would be unable to offer the necessary storage capacity, accessibility, or durability over time. The most plausible explanation currently available for the neural basis of information storage is the proposal by Donald Hebb (1949) that memories are stored by creating new connections between neurons (see Figure 1.13).

The entire nervous system, including the brain, is composed of millions of neurons, which can activate one another by transmitting chemical substances called neurotransmitters across the gap separating them, which is known as the synapse. All forms of neural activity, including perception, speech, or even thought, work by transmitting a signal along a series of neurons in this way. These cognitive processes are therefore dependent on the ability of one neuron to activate another. Hebb's theory postulated that if two adjacent neurons (i.e. nerve cells) are fired off simultaneously, then the connection between them will be strengthened. Thus a synapse which has been frequently

Neuron (B)

Neuron (A)

Axon

Dendrites

Synapse

Neuron (C)

Figure 1.13 Neurons and their connecting synapses. Will neuron A succeed in firing neuron B, or neuron C? Whichever neuron is fired, this will strengthen the synaptic connection between the two neurons involved.

Source: Drawing by David Groome.

Key Term
Cell assembly A group of cells which have become linked to one another to form a single functional network. Proposed by Hebb as a possible biological mechanism underlying the representation and storage of a memory trace.

crossed in the past will be more easily crossed by future signals. It is as though a path is being worn through the nervous system, much as you would wear a path through a field of corn by repeatedly walking through it. In both cases, a path is left behind which can be more easily followed in future.

Hebb suggested that this mechanism of synaptic strengthening would make it possible to build up a network of interconnected neurons, which could represent a particular pattern of input. Hebb called this a cell assembly. Figure 1.14 shows a diagrammatic representation of such a cell assembly, though in practice there would probably be thousands of neurons involved in each cell assembly rather than half a dozen as shown here.

Hebb argued that a cell assembly such as this could come to represent a particular stimulus, such as an object or a face. If the stimulus had caused this particular group of neurons to fire simultaneously, then the neurons would become connected to one another more and more strongly with repeated exposure to the stimulus. Eventually the cell assembly would become a permanent structure, in fact a memory which could be activated by any similar stimulation in the future.

Hebb's theory has considerable explanatory value. In the first place it can explain how thoughts and memories may come to be associated with one another in memory. If two cell assemblies are activated simultaneously then some of the neurons in one assembly are likely to become connected to neurons in the other assembly, so that in future the activation of either cell assembly will activate the other. Hebb's theory can also explain the difference between short-term and long-term memory. Hebb speculated that the temporary activation of a cell assembly by active neural firing could be the mechanism underlying short-term memory, which is known to be fragile and short-lived. However, after repeated firing the synaptic connections between the neurons in a cell assembly undergo permanent changes, which are the basis of long-term memory storage.

When Donald Hebb first proposed the cell assembly theory in 1949, it was still largely speculative. However,

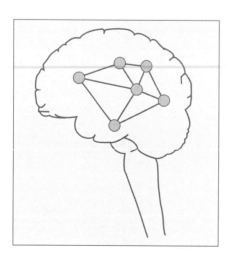

Figure 1.14   A cell assembly.

since that time a great deal of evidence has been gathered to confirm that the synapse does indeed change as a result of frequent firing of the neuron. Perhaps the most convincing evidence is the discovery that when electrical stimulation is applied to living tissue taken from the brain of a rat, the neurons do actually change in a lasting way, with their threshold of firing becoming much lower so they can be more easily activated by subsequent stimuli (Bliss and Lomo, 1973). This phenomenon is known as long-term potentiation (LTP). It has also been found that rats reared in a stimulating and enriched environment, with plenty of sensory input, develop more synaptic connections in their brains than rats reared in an impoverished environment where there is little to stimulate them (Greenough, 1987). More recent research has shown that short-term storage involves the strengthening of pre-existing synaptic connections, whereas long-term storage involves the growth of new synaptic connections between the neurons (Bailey and Kandel, 2004). Brain-imaging techniques such as PET scans have also confirmed that memory storage and retrieval do in fact coincide with the activation of large-scale neural networks spread diffusely through the brain (Habib *et al.*, 2003).

There is now plenty of evidence to confirm that memory storage depends on the growth and plasticity of neural connections (De Zeeuw, 2007), and recent reviews conclude that activity-dependent modification of synaptic strength has now been established as the probable mechanism of memory storage in the brain (Bailey and Kandel, 2004; Hart and Kraut, 2007). It has taken over half a century to collect the evidence, but it begins to look as if Donald Hebb got it right.

1.5 AUTOMATIC PROCESSING

AUTOMATIC VERSUS CONTROLLED PROCESSING

Some of the activities of the brain are under our conscious control, but many take place automatically and without our conscious awareness or intervention. Schneider and Shiffrin (1977) made a distinction between controlled cognitive processes, which are carried out consciously and intentionally, and automatic cognitive processes, which are not under conscious control. They suggested that because controlled processes require conscious attention they are subject to limitations in processing capacity, whereas automatic processes do not require attention and are not subject to such processing limits. Automatic processing will therefore take place far more rapidly than controlled processing, and will be relatively unaffected by distraction from a second task taking up attention. Another feature of automatic processing is that it is not a voluntary process, and it will take place regardless of the wishes and intentions of the individual. For a simple demonstration of automatic processing in a cognitive task, try looking at the words in Figure 1.15, taking care *not* to read them.

You will have found it impossible to obey the instruction not to read the message in Figure 1.15, because reading is a largely automatic process

Key Term

Long-term potentiation (LTP)
A lasting change in synaptic resistance following the application of electrical stimulation to living brain tissue. Possibly one of the biological mechanisms underlying the learning process.

Controlled processing
Processing that is under conscious control, and which is a relatively slow, voluntary process (contrasts with automatic processing).

Automatic processing
Processing that does not demand attention. It is not capacity limited or resource limited, and is not available for conscious inspection (contrasts with controlled processing).

> # DO NOT READ
> # THIS MESSAGE

Figure 1.15 A demonstration of automatic processing.

Figure 1.16 Driving a car involves many automatic responses for an experienced driver.

Source: Shutterstock.

(at least for practised readers) so if you attend to the message you cannot prevent yourself from reading it.

Schneider and Shiffrin suggested that cognitive processes become automatic as a result of frequent practice, as for example the skills involved in driving a car, in playing a piano, or in reading words from a page. However, we have the ability to override these automatic sequences when we need to, for example when we come across an unusual traffic situation while driving.

The automatic processing of words was first clearly demonstrated by Stroop (1935), who presented his subjects with colour words (e.g. red, blue, green) printed in different coloured inks (see Chapter 3, Figure 3.3). Subjects were instructed to name the ink colours as rapidly as possible, but they were not required to read the words. Stroop found that subjects could name the ink colour far more rapidly if it matched the word itself (e.g. the word 'red' printed in red ink) than if it did not (e.g. the word 'red' printed in blue ink). Since the words had a marked interfering effect on the colour-naming task despite the fact that subjects were not required to read them, it was assumed that they must have been read automatically. More recent theories about the Stroop effect are discussed in MacLeod (1998).

The distinction between controlled and automatic processing has been useful in many areas of cognitive psychology. One example is face familiarity. When you meet someone you have met before, you instantly and automatically recognise their face as familiar, but remembering where and when you have met them before requires conscious effort (Mandler, 1980).

Automatic processing has also been used to explain the occurrence of everyday 'action slips', which are basically examples of absentmindedness. For example, the author found during a recent car journey that instead of driving to his present house as he had intended, he had in fact driven to his previous address by force of habit. This was quite disturbing for the author, but probably even more disturbing for the owner of the house. Another of the author's action slips involved absentmindedly adding instant coffee to a mug which already contained a teabag, thus creating a rather unpalatable hybrid beverage. Action slips of this kind have been extensively documented and in most cases can be explained by the activation or perseveration of automatic processes which are not appropriate (Reason, 1979).

Norman and Shallice (1986) suggest that automatic processes can provide adequate control of our neural functions in most routine situations without needing to use up our attention, but they must be overridden by the conscious supervisory attention system when more complex or novel tasks require the flexibility of conscious control (see Figure 1.17).

Crick and Koch (1990) argue that the flexibility of the conscious control system stems largely from its capacity for binding together many different mental activities, such as thoughts and perceptions. Baddeley (1997) suggests that this conscious control may reside in the central executive component of the working memory (see Chapter 5), which is largely associated with frontal lobe function.

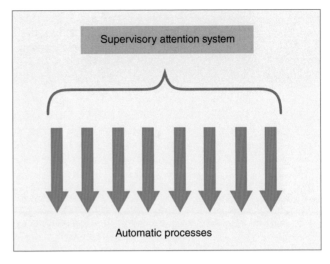

Figure 1.17   The supervisory attention system model.

Source: Adapted from Norman and Shallice (1986).

Johnson-Laird (1983) compares conscious control with the operating system that controls a computer. He suggests that consciousness is essentially a system which monitors a large number of hierarchically organised parallel processors. On occasion these processors may reach a state of deadlock, either because the instructions they generate conflict with one another, or possibly because they are mutually dependent on output from one another. Such 'pathological configurations' need to be overridden by some form of control system, and this may be the role of consciousness.

Such theories add an interesting perspective to our view of automatic processing. Automatic processes are obviously of great value to us, as they allow us to carry out routine tasks rapidly and without using up our limited attentional capacity. However, automatic processes lack flexibility, and when they fail to provide appropriate behaviour they need to be overridden by consciously controlled processing. There is some evidence that this override system may be located in the frontal lobes of the brain, since patients with frontal lesions are often found to exhibit perseveration of automatic behaviour and a lack of flexibility of response (Shallice and Burgess, 1991a; Parkin, 1997). Frontal lobe functions will be examined further in Chapters 8 and 9.

CONSCIOUS AWARENESS

We all have conscious awareness, but we do not really know what it is (Figure 1.18). I am quite certain that I am conscious because I experience things consciously, and you probably feel the same. We can all understand what is meant by the term consciousness as a subjective experience, yet no-one has yet been able to provide an explanation of what conscious awareness actually is, or how it might arise from neural activity. Indeed the very assumption that conscious awareness must somehow arise from the mere firing of neural circuits seems remarkable in itself. Crick (1994) calls it 'the astonishing hypothesis', yet it remains the only plausible hypothesis.

Consciousness remains the last unexplored frontier of psychology, and arguably one of the greatest mysteries of life itself. But although we do not understand what consciousness is, we are beginning to learn a bit about what consciousness does, and the part it plays in cognitive processes. As explained in the previous section, psychologists have recently devised methods of distinguishing between processes which are consciously controlled and those which are unconscious and automatic. For example, judging whether a person's face is familiar seems to occur automatically and unconsciously, but if we need to remember actual occasions when we have previously met them then a conscious recollection process is required (Mandler, 1980). This distinction will be considered in more detail in Chapter 6.

The study of patients with certain types of brain lesion has provided particularly valuable insights into the nature of conscious and unconscious cognitive processes. For example, amnesic patients often reveal evidence of previous learning of which they have no conscious recollection. Mandler (1989) has argued that it is usually not the memory trace which is lost, but the patient's ability to bring it into consciousness. These studies of amnesia will also be discussed further in Chapter 7. A similar phenomenon has been observed in some patients with visual agnosia (impaired perception), who can detect visual stimuli at an unconscious level but have no conscious awareness of seeing them (Weiskrantz, 1986; Persaud et al., 2007). This phenomenon is known as blindsight, and it will be examined in more detail in Chapter 4.

Autism is another disorder which has shed light on the nature of consciousness, because autistic individuals appear to lack some of the characteristics of conscious processing. Their behaviour tends to be highly inflexible and repetitive, and they usually lack the ability to form plans or generate new ideas spontaneously. Autistic individuals also tend to lack the ability to develop a normal rapport with other people, and they often tend to disregard other people as though they were merely objects. Observations of such symptoms have led Baron-Cohen (1992) to suggest that autistic people may lack a 'theory of mind', meaning that they are unable to understand the existence of mental processes in others. This may provide a clue about some of the possible benefits of having consciousness. An awareness of other peoples' thoughts and feelings seems to be crucial if we are to understand their behaviour, and it is an essential requirement for normal social interaction.

Another view of the function of consciousness has recently been proposed by Seligman et al. (2013), who point out that consciousness allows us to use information from the past and the present to make

Key Term

Blindsight
The ability of some functionally blind patients to detect visual stimuli at an unconscious level, despite having no conscious awareness of seeing them. Usually observed in patients with occipital lobe lesions.

plans for possible events in the future.

One interesting finding from an EEG study (Libet, 1985) is that when we make a conscious decision to act in some way, the conscious awareness of the decision appears to follow the actual decision, rather than preceding it. Recent fMRI research has added support to this finding (Soon *et al.*, 2008). In view of these findings Wegner (2003) has suggested that decisions may actually be made at an unconscious level, and conscious awareness of the decision only follows later when we observe its outcome. This is an interesting view, as it reverses the usual assumption that decisions arise from a conscious process. Indeed it is a view that questions the very existence of free will, suggesting that the impression we have of making conscious decisions may be illusory.

Figure 1.18   Does your dog have conscious awareness? And is he wondering the same about you?

Source: Drawing by David Groome.

Recently neuro-imaging studies have been used to compare the patterns of brain activation during conscious and unconscious types of perception, showing that conscious perception appears to make more use of the superior parietal cortex and the dorso-lateral prefrontal cortex (Rees, 2007). However, there is some evidence to suggest that conscious awareness may not be located in one specific area of the brain. Dehaene and Naccache (2001) argue that full conscious awareness is only achieved when several different brain areas are activated simultaneously, and possibly results from the integration of these separate inputs. It has also been pointed out that the brain areas activated during conscious activity do not necessarily indicate the location of conscious awareness in the brain, as they may just reflect a subsidiary process or prerequisite of conscious activity (De Graaf *et al.*, 2012).

The studies discussed above appear to shed some light on the nature of consciousness, but this too may be illusory. They may tell us a little about which processes involve consciousness, or which parts of the brain are involved, but we are no nearer to knowing what consciousness actually is, or how it arises. As philosopher David Chalmers (1995) puts it, we are addressing 'the easy questions' about consciousness, but making no progress at all with 'the hard question', which is the question of how conscious awareness actually arises from neural activity. McGinn (1999) suggests that human beings will never fully understand the nature of consciousness, because it may be beyond the capability of the human brain to do so. Blackmore (2003) takes a somewhat more optimistic view. She believes that understanding consciousness will one day be possible, but only if we can find a totally different way of thinking about consciousness, since there is apparently something fundamentally wrong with our present approach. For the moment I tend to side with the pessimists and the killjoys, if only because the best brains in the known universe have been working on the problem of consciousness for many centuries without making much progress. I hope that someone will one day prove me wrong.

1.6 MINDS, BRAINS AND COMPUTERS
INTEGRATING THE MAIN APPROACHES TO COGNITION

It has been argued in this chapter that our present understanding of cognitive psychology has arisen from the interaction between experimental cognitive psychology, cognitive neuroscience, cognitive neuropsychology, and computer modelling. These same four approaches provide the subject matter of the rest of this book, and they will be applied to each of the main areas of cognitive processing in turn. These areas are perception, attention, memory, thinking, and language, and there will be a separate chapter on each of these processes. A unique feature of this book is that each chapter (or pair of chapters) on a particular cognitive process is followed by a chapter dealing with its associated disorders. This approach is intended to provide you with a thorough understanding of both normal and abnormal cognition, and also an understanding of the relationship between them.

SUMMARY

- Cognitive psychology is the study of how information is processed by the brain. It includes the study of perception, learning, memory, thinking and language.
- Historically there have been four main strands of research which have all contributed to our present understanding of cognitive psychology. They are experimental cognitive psychology, cognitive neuroscience, cognitive neuropsychology and computer modelling of cognitive processes.
- Experimental cognitive psychology has provided theories to explain how the brain interprets incoming information, such as the schema theory which postulates that past experience is used to analyse new perceptual input.
- Computer modelling has provided models of human cognition based on information-processing principles, and it has introduced important new concepts such as feature detector systems and processors of limited channel capacity.
- Cognitive neuropsychology provides knowledge about brain function, based on the study of people who have suffered cognitive impairment as a result of brain lesions.

- Cognitive neuroscience makes use of brain-imaging techniques to investigate the relationship between brain function and cognition.
- The science of cognitive psychology has generated new concepts and theories, such as the distinction between top-down and bottom-up processing, and the distinction between automatic and controlled processing.
- The study of consciousness has yielded some interesting findings but at present we have no real understanding of what consciousness is, or how it arises from neural activity.

FURTHER READING

- Blackmore, S. (2003). *Consciousness*. London: Hodder Arnold. Susan Blackmore embarks on a search for human consciousness. She doesn't find it, but the search is interesting.
- Esgate, A. and Groome D. *et al.* (2005). *Introduction to Applied Cognitive Psychology*. Hove: Psychology Press. This book is about the applications of cognitive psychology in real-life settings. I have nothing but praise for this text, though this is possibly because I am one of the authors.
- Eysenck, M.W. and Keane, M. (2010). *Cognitive Psychology: A Student's Handbook*. Hove: Psychology Press. This book covers many of the same topics as our own book, but with a bit more detail and less emphasis on clinical disorders. In fact Eysenck and Keane has become something of a classic over the years, and it is a very thorough and well-written book.

Chapter 2

Contents

Perception

Graham Edgar, Helen Edgar and Graham Pike

2

2.1 INTRODUCTION

Our perception of the world is something that we often tend to take for granted. We detect the sights, sounds, smells, etc. of things around us, and (sometimes) recognise objects and make decisions about how we are going to interact with them. It all seems so simple – until you try to work out how the process of perception operates. There are many theories of perception and they can appear to be quite different and, indeed, sometimes contradictory. It is possible that some of the theories are right and any contradictory theories are wrong, but it is more likely that the various theories are just looking at different aspects of a very complicated process. As an analogy, imagine trying to produce a theory of how a car works. One theory could be based on which pedals need to be pressed to make the car go, another could present the theory of the internal combustion engine. Both theories would provide valuable insight into how the car works, but would appear to be quite different. This chapter will provide an overview of a number of theories and will attempt to reconcile the different theories to give an impression of how perception 'works'.

2.2 VISUAL PERCEPTION

THEORIES OF PERCEPTION – SCHEMAS AND TEMPLATE MATCHING

The Grimm's fairy tale of 'Little Red Riding Hood' (Grimm and Grimm, 1909; first published 1812), illustrated in Figure 2.1, is an excellent illustration of a problem that lies at the very heart of the process of perception. Little Red Riding Hood is fooled, and ultimately eaten (although there is a happy ending) by a wolf that tricks her, masquerading as her grandmother. So a key issue for perception (and for Little Red Riding Hood!) is how do we recognise an object such as a chair or our grandmother? Just as importantly, how do we recognise when an object has changed and granny has, for instance, been replaced by a scheming and very hungry wolf? Well, one way to recognise your grandmother would be to have an internal schema or 'template' that could be compared with incoming sensory information. If the incoming sensory information matches the grandmother template then

Figure 2.1 'But, Grandmother, what big teeth you've got.'

Source: Drawing by David Groome.

Figure 2.2 Stimuli of the kind used by Shepard and Metzler (1971). The participants' task was to judge whether or not the figure on the right was a rotated version of the one on the left (as in the top pair above) – or a different figure (as in the bottom pair).

Source: Adapted from Shepard and Metzler (1971).

Key Term

Templates
Stored representations of objects enabling object recognition.

she is recognised. The template theory is essentially a development of the schema theory introduced in Chapter 1, as it is a system which uses information from past experience to make sense of a new stimulus.

There is some evidence for the existence of internal templates. For instance, Shepard and Metzler (1971) did experiments that required people to say whether two shapes (such as those shown in Figure 2.2) were the same or different (e.g. mirror images). The more the picture of one shape was rotated from the other, the longer it took people to make a decision. This suggests that people could be rotating a template of one shape to see if the second shape fits it. This does suggest that people are able to form internal representations of an external figure and manipulate them. There is, however, a difference between generating an internal representation of a specific, and very simple, external stimulus, and having a stored template that is general enough for 'grandmother'. This issue will be considered in more detail later. However, template matching can only occur (if it occurs at all) after information from the outside world has been encoded in some way by the visual system. This, in itself, is not a trivial problem. For instance, in the Shepard and Metzler task, how do we pick the shape out from the background and work out just what we are going to compare with our template?

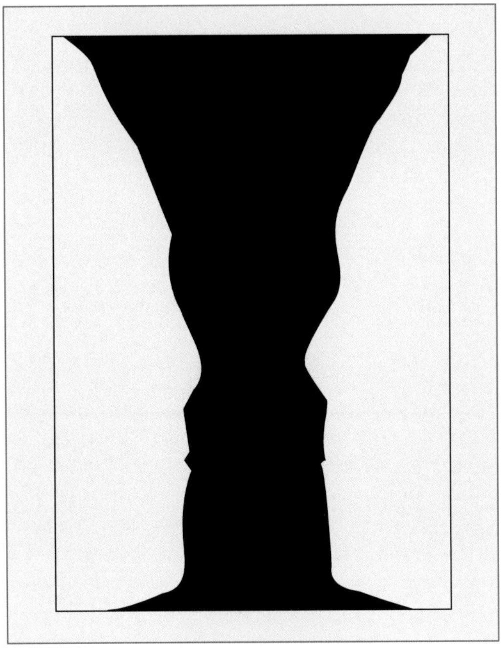

THE GESTALT APPROACH

The issue of how objects are defined was central to the theories developed by the Gestalt approach (Rubin, 1915; Wertheimer, 1923), which was introduced in Chapter 1. A key issue addressed by the Gestalt psychologists was the way that we might segregate the world into figures and the background against which they appear. This may sound trivial but is crucial as, if we are to recognise objects, we need to be able to tell them apart from everything else. The importance of figure and ground can be illustrated by one of the well-known reversible figures shown in Figure 2.3. If you consider the white area to be the 'figure' and the black area the 'ground' then you see a vase. If you consider the black area to be the figure and the white area to be the ground then you see two faces. The picture is the same, the pattern of light falling on the retina of the eye is the same, but it can be segregated into figure and ground in different ways. Being able to see the same stimulus in more than one way demonstrates the influence on perception that organising things into figure and ground can have. Before deciding which part of the scene is the figure and which parts are ground it is necessary to decide which parts of a visual scene constitute a single object. Gestalt psychologists proposed a number of laws of perceptual organisation that could be used to group parts of a visual scene into objects. Two of these laws are illustrated in Figure 2.4.

While appealing, the Gestalt approach only covers a small part of the process of visual perception. For instance, using Gestalt laws we could work out which parts of the visual scene are objects that we might be interested in, and compare them with a template to decide what they are. Both the Gestalt and template-matching theories are, however, rather vague in specifying how we might get information into the 'system' in the first place, although a possible mechanism is provided by feature-extraction theories.

Figure 2.3 A reversible figure. If you concentrate on the black area as the figure then you will see a vase, if you concentrate on the white areas then you will see a well-known person talking to himself.

Source: Adapted from Rubin (1915) by Helen Edgar.

Key Term

Reversible figure
A figure in which the object perceived depends on what is designated as 'figure' and what is designated as '(back)ground'.

Laws of perceptual organisation
Principles (such as proximity) by which parts of a visual scene can be resolved into different objects.

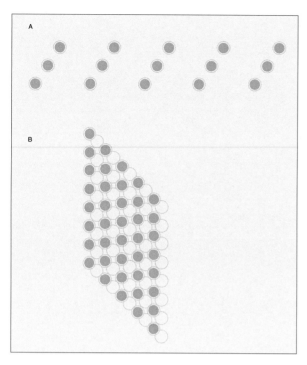

Figure 2.4 Examples of Gestalt laws of perceptual organisation. (A) Demonstrates the law of proximity. Items that are grouped close together tend to be considered as part of the same object and so (A) is usually perceived as five slanted lines of dots rather than three horizontal lines. (B) Demonstrates the law of similarity. Although the circles can be 'grouped' in many different ways it appears to be natural to group them on the basis of common colour.

FEATURE-EXTRACTION THEORIES

Feature detectors were introduced in Chapter 1 as a possible mechanism for extracting the features contained in an incoming stimulus. In many ways, feature-extraction theories are simply a variation on template theories; it is just the nature of the template that is different. Rather than trying to match an entire object (such as a grandmother) to a template, feature-extraction theories look to break objects down into their component features. The process is basically still template matching, but with *features* of the object rather than the whole thing at once. A key issue, of course, is just what constitutes a feature? Little Red Riding Hood appears (unsuccessfully) to have been applying a form of feature extraction in order to recognise her grandmother (picking out ears, eyes, hands and, finally, teeth). Perhaps one of the nicest conceptualisations of the feature-extraction approach was Selfridge's Pandemonium model (Selfridge, 1959) which is illustrated in Figure 2.5. The way that the model works is that there are layers of 'demons'. Demons at the lowest level in the system (remember this is essentially a bottom-up approach) look for very simple features (such as lines or angles). Each demon looks for only one feature. If they 'see' it, they shout. Demons at the next level up listen and only respond if certain combinations of demons shout. If this happens, then they have detected a more complex feature (such as a line-junction), and they will shout about that. So each level of demons detects more and more complex features, until the object is recognised. Of course, as many demons are likely to be shouting at once it will be pandemonium, hence the name.

Most people would probably not believe that we have little demons in our brain, but the feature-extracting computer model of Selfridge and Neisser (1960) discussed in Chapter 1 suggests that the general approach is workable. Furthermore, there has long been evidence to suggest that, at least at the lower levels of the visual system, there are cells that do the job of Selfridge's demons. For instance Kuffler (1953) demonstrated that cells in the cat retina (ganglion cells) responded to a spot of light at a particular position in the visual field. Hubel and Wiesel (1959) found cells in the cat's brain (in the visual cortex) that responded to edges and lines. These cells receive inputs arising from ganglion cells and, of course, you can construct relatively complex features such as edges and lines from simple features such as spots. Modern brain-imaging techniques also support the existence of 'feature detectors' in the human brain (Haynes and Rees, 2005). Thus

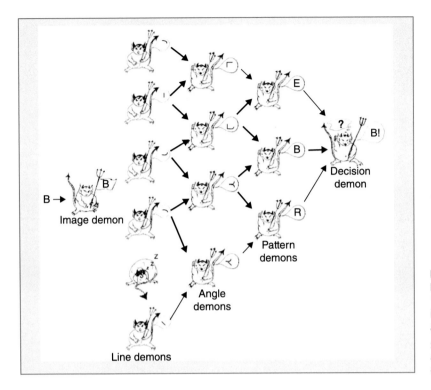

Figure 2.5
Pandemonium (Selfridge, 1959). The heavier arrows illustrate which demons are shouting the loudest!

Source: Adapted from Lindsay and Norman (1972). Demon artwork by Helen Edgar.

there is a physiological basis for feature-extraction theories, at least at the 'lower' levels of the visual system.

Breaking an image down into its component features is a useful way of coding information within the visual system, but the difficult part is working out how the different features can be interpreted and used to recognise an object. Essentially, they have to be put back together again.

MARR'S COMPUTATIONAL THEORY

Marr (1982) developed an approach that concentrated on the implementation of some of the processes discussed above, progressing through a number of stages until an internal representation of the viewed object is achieved. The first stage is called the raw primal sketch when features such as circles and lines are extracted from the image. In particular, Marr proposed that the visual system can use *natural constraints* to work out which features form the borders of an object. For instance, a border that is created by the edge of an object tends to have a greater and more sharply defined change in luminance than an edge caused by, for instance, a shadow. Once the features have been identified, they can be grouped according to Gestalt principles and these groups of features then define the surface of the object. This is referred to as the 2½-D sketch. This sketch is only 2½-D and not 3-D as it is a representation of an object – but only from the viewpoint of the person looking at it. From this 2½-D sketch a 3-D sketch can be constructed (although Marr was a little vague about the details of how this might be done) to give a 'full' representation of the object that is independent of the viewer (that is, there may be a representation of parts that the viewer cannot see directly). Marr and Nishihara (1978) suggest that this 3-D representation can then be compared against previously stored representations, and the object can be recognised. This approach thus rather nicely combines feature extraction and template matching into a plausible theory.

BIEDERMAN'S RECOGNITION-BY-COMPONENTS APPROACH

There have been many developments of Marr's general approach such as the theories developed by Biederman (1987) which, again, are based on feature extraction. In this case, however, the features are three-dimensional and are referred to as geons. Biederman devised a system using 36 basic geons such as cones, cylinders and blocks that could be used to construct a vast range of objects. The basic principle of Biederman's theory was that if we can identify the geons that make up an object, then we can recognise that object. One problem with this (and other feature-extraction theories) is that it is relatively easy to imagine that very different objects (such as a car and a tree) can be recognised and discriminated quite easily, but it is more difficult to imagine how the process might deal with more subtle distinctions (such as discriminating two different faces).

As well as the problem of discriminating between different objects, there is also the problem of how to recognise changes in the *same* object. This issue presents a particular difficulty for template-matching approaches. In the Shepard and Metzler (1971) study discussed earlier, the template matching is fairly simple. A clearly defined stimulus (the block shape) can, conceptually, be internalised as a template and used for comparison with another shape. Both shapes are relatively simple and fixed. But consider what happens with more complex and changeable stimuli, such as your grandmother. It is plausible that you could recognise your grandmother by comparing the incoming visual input with an internal 'grandmother template', and perhaps there is even one special cell, a 'grandmother cell' (for a discussion of the origin of this term see Rose, 1996), in your brain that fires when (and only when) you see your grandmother. The problem occurs if there is some change in your grandmother (such as being replaced by a wolf for instance). Would the template still work? What happens if she is facing away from you? Would you need a 'grandmother facing the other way' template as well? You may end up with the impossible situation of requiring a template for every possible view and orientation of your grandmother; and all other objects as well. While there are many neurons in the brain, this is still rather impractical.

PARALLEL DISTRIBUTED PROCESSING APPROACHES

One way of getting around the problem of needing an almost infinite number of 'grandmother cells' in the brain is provided by parallel distributed processing (PDP) models (Rumelhart and McClelland, 1986). PDP models are also sometimes referred to as connectionist or neural network models and these models, when implemented on computers, attempt to model the way in which the brain may work. In some ways, PDP approaches are still template approaches but the templates are much more flexible and, given that they represent stored knowledge, they are another conceptualisation of the schema described in Chapter 1. Crucially, any object can be represented not by the activation of a single neuron, but by the activation of many cells forming a *network*. Thus an object is represented not by the activity of a single cell, but by a *pattern* of activity across many cells. Initially, this may seem to make the problems discussed above worse. Now you need not just one cell to represent an object but many. The key point, however, is that any one cell can form a part of many *different* networks (as exemplified by the work of Hebb discussed in Chapter 1). It is the connections between cells that are important as much as the cells themselves.

Neural networks also have the ability to make the object recognition process much more 'fuzzy'. If the object doesn't quite match the template, not all the cells in the network may be activated, but many of them may be. Thus, the system can make a 'best guess' at what the object is *most likely* to be. Given feedback on whether the guess is right or wrong (this can be done in the real world by simply gathering more information) the system can *learn* and the networks can change and adapt. If your grandmother is replaced by a wolf, *some* parts of a grandmother network may be activated (by the clothes and bonnet, etc.) but, hopefully, so will some parts of a 'wolf network'. Given further feedback as to what the object is (getting eaten in Little Red Riding Hood's case – feedback in the truest sense) you will *learn* to recognise the wolf more easily.

The notion that the object recognition process can learn is an important one. Apart from anything else, without learning it would be impossible to recognise any new objects. Learning implies stored knowledge (whether as templates, within neural networks, or in some other form) and this is something that most of the theories discussed above do not address in detail. This is not a criticism of the theories but reflects the fact that the theories discussed so far mostly concentrate on bottom-up processing. They are thus attempting to explain how sensory information gets into the visual system to be processed further. All the theories do, however, have some aspect of top-down schema-driven processing incorporated into them (e.g. templates or neural networks). This reflects the fact that perception is essentially the interface between the physical world and our interpretation of it (more in the next section). Thus, at different levels of perception there is a changing balance, moving from simply encoding and transmitting information from the outside world to interpreting and making sense of it. It is often hard to appreciate the difference between these different aspects of perception, however, until something goes wrong. When something *does* go wrong with our perceptual system and what we perceive does not truly represent the outside world we usually refer to this as an illusion, and the study of such illusions provides valuable insights into how perception operates at different levels.

VISUAL ILLUSIONS

Richard Gregory (1997) has attempted a classification of illusions. One of the dimensions of this classification is essentially the contribution

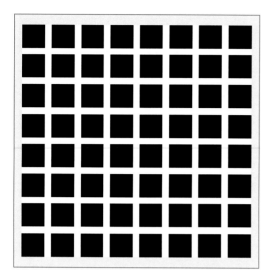

Figure 2.6 The Hermann grid. Illusory grey spots should be visible at the intersections of the white lines. Interestingly, the spot is usually not so obvious at the junction that you are fixating on.

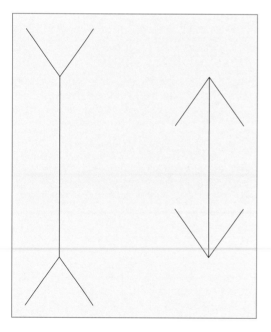

Figure 2.7 The Müller-Lyer illusion. The vertical line on the left appears to be longer than the one on the right, even though they are actually the same length.

of bottom-up and/or top-down processes to the generation of the illusion. This then gives a rather satisfying continuum running from those illusions that arise from the physical properties of the world to those that arise largely from the cognitive processes of the mind. For instance, at the 'lowest' level are illusions that are really nothing to do with the sensory processes at all, and these illusions would include such things as rainbows and mirages. They arise from physics, not perception. At the next level are the illusions that *do* arise from basic properties of the perceptual system but are really not influenced by cognitive processes. An example of an illusion of this type is provided by the Hermann grid, named after Ludimar Hermann in 1870, and shown in Figure 2.6. The illusory spots at the intersections are supposedly due to the lateral connections between cells in the retina, with no top-down influences evident.

Perhaps the most interesting illusions, however, are those that are generated as a result of top-down influences on perception. These illusions provide strong evidence for the notion that what we know affects what we perceive. One of the most well-known illusions of this type is shown in Figure 2.7. This is the Müller-Lyer illusion, first reported by Franz Müller-Lyer in 1889. The illusion is that, although the two vertical lines are actually the same length, the one on the left is perceived as being longer. The theories discussed so far cannot easily explain such an effect without reference to top-down influences. For instance, a simple feature-extraction approach should not be biased by the precise arrangement of the features (the left and right figures are both made up of the same features) so that this suggests that something beyond what is present in the image is influencing our perception of it. Richard Gregory (1966) (whose theories we will discuss in more detail later) suggested that, although the figure is just a two-dimensional arrangement of lines, we *interpret* them using our knowledge and experience of a three-dimensional world. Thus, Gregory suggests that we see the illusion as two corners (as shown in Figure 2.8) with one corner going away from us (and so appearing more distant) and the other coming towards us (and so appearing closer). To explain the illusion, we have to accept that we also 'know' that things that are further away give rise to a smaller image on our retina and we

Figure 2.8 A possible explanation for the Müller-Lyer illusion. The figures are perceived in three dimensions as illustrated here and this leads to distortions of perceived size.

Source: Drawing by David Groome.

scale them up to make allowances for this (we don't perceive people as shrinking in size as they walk away from us). This is an example of size constancy. In the illusion the two lines are actually the same length, but one *appears* to be further away and so is scaled up by our visual system, giving the impression that it is longer.

Support for the role of knowledge and experience in the interpretation of the Müller-Lyer illusion also comes from a study of the Bete people (Segall *et al.*, 1963) who live in a dense jungle environment with relatively few corners. The Bete people do not perceive the Müller-Lyer illusion as strongly as do Europeans, providing support for the role of knowledge and experience in the interpretation of the figure. It is possible to get an idea of the influence of our 'square world' on perception by considering another illusion, the Ames room (invented by one Adelbert Ames), which is shown in Figure 2.9.

The two figures in the room appear to be of vastly different size even though they are, in fact, identical in size. The explanation becomes clear when we see the shape of the room. The room is distorted so that from one viewpoint only (shown by the arrow in the figure) it *appears* to be a 'normal' square room. In actual fact, one corner is much further away than the other. Thus, although it appears that both the little figures are the same distance away from us (so we *do not* do any scaling up as we do in the Müller-Lyer illusion) one is actually much further away, giving rise to a much smaller retinal image. The distorted perspective cues mean that the viewer does not 'know' that one figure is further away than the other, and so no rescaling to maintain size constancy occurs. It is even possible to get the Ames room illusion without the room. In fact, all you need to do is to move something, such as the lighthouse in Figure 2.10, out of its 'normal' depth plane within a picture to reveal how much size constancy influences the perceived size of objects.

There is still some debate as to how much top-down influences are responsible for illusions. For instance, there are explanations of the Müller-Lyer illusion that do not rely on top-down processing (e.g. Day, 1989) It is, however, hard to explain all illusions without at least some reference to the influence of top-down cognitive processes

Key Term

Size constancy
The perceived size of objects is adjusted to allow for perceived distance.

Figure 2.9 The Ames room. Two identical figures (left) appear to be of very different sizes. This is due to the unusual shape of the room (right).

Source: Photographs by Graham Edgar.

Figure 2.10 When size constancy breaks down. Moving objects (or people) out of their natural position in a scene reveals how much our visual system automatically compensates for changes in retinal image size with object distance.

based on knowledge and experience, and there is evidence from brain-imaging studies (Hayashi *et al.*, 2007) that both bottom-up and top-down processes are involved in the perception of perspective illusions. As discussed previously, however, knowledge in this context should be interpreted rather more broadly than, for example, 'Something I learned in school.' Size constancy, for example, is based on an individual 'knowing' that objects that are further away generate a smaller retinal image. Individuals are, however, rarely aware that such knowledge is being used to influence their perceptions, or even of acquiring such knowledge in the first place. It is only when size constancy fails that we really become aware of how much top-down processing is influencing our perception. Pure bottom-up processes rely only on information gleaned from incoming sensory information, whereas top-down processes also use information that is not present within the sensory information, such as knowledge of the way the world usually is. So 'knowledge' could be broadly interpreted as any information that resides in the perceiver, rather than being contained within the stimulus that is being perceived. Thus the Gestalt laws could be considered to be a form of implicit knowledge, likewise the precise configuration of neural networks. They represent information held within the individual, and not the stimulus.

If knowledge is involved in the perception of illusions then certainly a definition beyond 'Things learned in school' is necessary, as the perception of illusions appears to be the preserve not only of humans. There is evidence, for example, that pigeons perceive the Müller-Lyer illusion (Nakamura *et al.*, 2006), although it is not clear whether jungle-dwelling pigeons would be less susceptible (see the Segall *et al.* (1963) study on the Bete people). Furthermore, there is evidence that some non-human species not only perceive illusions, they actively create them.

For example, some male bowerbirds build 'avenues' (where the female will stand to view the male mating display) using two parallel walls of sticks that lead onto a 'court' consisting of grey or whitish objects (pebbles, bones, etc.) on which the male will stand to display coloured objects (Figure 2.11). Remarkably, the grey and white objects are carefully arranged so that the larger objects are placed further away from the avenue, leading to a distortion of perspective rather like that in the Ames room. Essentially, the court will appear foreshortened (to humans and, presumably, to the female bowerbird). Such an arrangement appears to be quite deliberate. If the size gradient of the objects is reversed by curious humans (Endler *et al.*, 2010) the male bowerbird will move the objects to re-establish the original gradient. Of course, the illusion created by the male bowerbird can only work from one viewpoint (as does the Ames room). Probably not entirely by chance, the viewpoint of the female bowerbird is constrained by the avenue of twigs. Quite what effect the illusion has on the perception of the female is unclear but it seems likely that there is an effect, as there is evidence (Kelley and Endler, 2012) that the more regular the resulting pattern from the point of view of the female (and thus the better potential illusion), the greater the mating success of the male. Surely this is one of the more unusual applications of a visual illusion.

Returning again to humans, the use of knowledge as a part of top-down processing allows us to *interpret* incoming sensory information, rather than just encoding it. It also means that our final perception of the sensory information may (as we have already seen) be strongly influenced by what we already know. The rest of this section on visual perception will consider in more detail the role of knowledge in perception, particularly when considering perception

Figure 2.11 The avenue and court (strewn with brightly coloured ornaments) carefully constructed by the male bowerbird to woo the female.

Source: Shutterstock.

Figure 2.12 'Well I never expected that!'

Source: Drawing by Dianne Catherwood.

in the 'real world' (as opposed to the laboratory). Crucially, the distinction between sensation and perception will be considered and two further theories of perception will be discussed that differ markedly in the importance they place on the role of knowledge in perception.

THE DIFFERENCE BETWEEN SENSATION AND PERCEPTION

Imagine that you are in a car driving along a road that you do not know. The road disappears around a bend. What do you do? If it were not for your top-down processing, you would probably have to get out of the car and peer around the corner to check that the road does, in fact, continue and that there are no other unexpected occurrences such as that in Figure 2.12. In 'real life', however, you will almost certainly proceed round the bend, secure in the *knowledge* that roads tend to continue and do not simply terminate without warning. An example such as this, while superficially rather silly, emphasises just how much we rely on what we *know* to influence almost everything that we do.

It is now worth defining what we mean by sensation and perception. Sensation will be considered to be the 'raw' bottom-up input from the senses and *perception* will be considered to be the end result of the processing of that sensory material within the visual system. The individual may be consciously aware of the perception arising from incoming sensory information, or they may not (subliminal perception). Sensation and perception thus lie at opposite ends of the visual process and may well be quite different. That is, what pops out of the 'top' of the system as perception may be a highly modified version of what went in at the 'bottom' of the visual system as sensation. It is beyond the scope of this chapter to discuss subliminal perception, so the following discussion will focus on perception as a conscious awareness of the output of the visual system.

It is possible that not all the information that is sensed will reach perception at all. Some of the sensory information entering the visual system may be filtered out by attentional processes (discussed briefly in Chapter 1, and in detail in Chapter 3) and will not form a part of our perception. This chapter has also considered that what we already know may influence what we perceive and so perception may represent not only a filtered, but also a modified, version of the original sensation. A simple diagram of the route from sensation to perception is presented in Figure 2.13. Different parts of the process may also interact; what we know may influence the way that attentional filtering operates, *as well as* our final perception of the sensory information. It should thus be noted that the process described above is a very simplified version of what appears to be happening in the processing of visual input.

Key Term
Sensation The 'raw' sensory input (as compared with 'perception').

The philosopher Immanuel Kant refers to the objects or events that exist independently of the senses as numena and our experience of those objects and events as phenomena. Kant argued that we can never truly access the numena, only the phenomena. That is, we can never know the world as it truly is, only our perception of it after it has been filtered and modified by our senses and cognitive processes. There is a saying that is often attributed to Kant which sums up perception, and which runs, 'We see things not as they are, but as we are.'

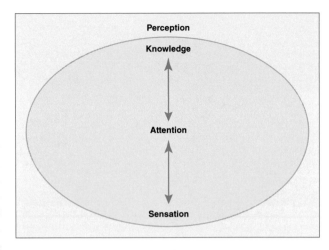

Figure 2.13   The components of perception. Raw sensory information is filtered and combined with knowledge to form the overall percept. Note that information is seen as flowing top-down as well as bottom-up at all stages.

To illustrate the difference between sensation and perception and the complex processes that operate in between, we will return to the discussion about driving and, in particular, accidents that occur while driving. Generally, those individuals who are most likely to have an accident while driving lie at the ends of the age range for drivers (Claret *et al.*, 2003). Young drivers (under 25) and older drivers (75+) tend to have an increased risk of accidents, whereas those drivers in between have a lower risk of being involved in an accident. This is the case for most types of accident, with one notable exception. These are accidents that are usually referred to as 'looked but failed to see' (LBFS) accidents (Sabey and Staughton, 1975).

Key Term

Numena
The world as it really is. See also 'phenomena'.

Phenomena
Numena as we perceive them.

'LOOKED BUT FAILED TO SEE' (LBFS) ACCIDENTS

'Looked but failed to see' accidents refer to occasions when drivers have crashed into something and claimed subsequently that they simply 'did not see it', even though the object they have just hit should be easily visible (see Figure 2.14). This is where the distinction between sensation and perception becomes particularly important. Undoubtedly, some accidents *are* due to a failure of sensation. Fairly obviously, if an object is not within a driver's field of view (for example they are not looking where they are going), they will not detect it visually and may crash into it. Sensing an object, however, involves more than just detecting the light coming from it. Even if light from

Figure 2.14   High sensory conspicuity does not guarantee accurate perception. . .

Source: Photograph courtesy of Gloucestershire Constabulary.

Figure 2.15　The effect of contrast on detectability. The pedestrian on the left of the picture is silhouetted against the oncoming headlights which increase the contrast between the pedestrian and the background; increasing detectability. The pedestrian on the right presents against a lower contrast background, and is harder to detect.

Source: Shutterstock.

Key Term

Sensory conspicuity
The extent to which aspects of a stimulus (such as colour and luminance) influence how easily it can be registered by the senses. See also 'attention conspicuity'.

Attention conspicuity
The interaction of aspects of a stimulus (such as colour, luminance, form) with aspects of an individual (such as attention, knowledge, pre-conceptions) that determine how likely a stimulus is to be consciously perceived. See also 'sensory conspicuity'.

the object does reach the eyes of a driver, this does not guarantee that they will become aware of it. Earlier in the chapter the Gestalt approach emphasised the importance of picking an object out from its background, and Marr provided a possible process by which this could be done. But what if it is difficult, or impossible, to discriminate an object from its background? The visual system may sense the light reflecting from that object (so you could argue that the system has 'detected' it) but the light from the object, and the light from the background, may be too similar to tell one from the other. For example, a pedestrian at night can be extremely difficult for a driver to pick out from the background (see Figure 2.15) because of the lack of contrast between the pedestrian and the background against which they are seen. The term used to describe how easily an object can be detected by the senses is sensory conspicuity, and refers to the intrinsic properties of an object (such as shape, colour, brightness, amount of noise that it is making) that are likely to be registered by the senses – usually as a result of increasing contrast with the background. Thus, a pedestrian can often increase their sensory conspicuity by carrying a torch, or wearing reflective material.

Research by Cole and Hughes (1984) has suggested that sensory conspicuity, although necessary for the detection of objects, may not always be sufficient for an individual to become *aware* of that object and take action to avoid it. Cole and Hughes suggest that in order to be able to consciously perceive (and react to) an object, it should also have high attention conspicuity. This term refers to the fact that to perceive something, the individual's senses need to detect that it is there and, *in addition*, the individual has to *attend* to the information provided by the senses. The discussion of attention above, and that in Chapter 3, suggests that much information that we sense is not attended to. There is an interesting distinction that can be made here between sensory conspicuity and attention conspicuity. As mentioned above, sensory conspicuity relates mainly to aspects of the object being perceived (brightness, etc.), whereas attention conspicuity is more likely to be influenced by aspects of the individual doing the observing (previous experience, expectations, etc.). Broadly speaking, sensory conspicuity relies primarily on bottom-up processing whereas attention conspicuity is more heavily influenced by top-down processes. At most road junctions, for example, the class of road user that a driver is most likely to have to avoid is other cars – and thus a driver may be biased towards searching for cars; their search for hazards is influenced by what they expect to be there (Hills, 1980; Theeuwes and Hagenzieker,

1993). Objects that do not conform to the size, shape and speed of a car (such as a cyclist) are therefore less likely to be attended to, and more likely to be hit (Räsänen and Summala, 1998).

Thus if a driver is not *expecting* a motorcyclist at a particular location they may drive into them, even if the motorcyclist has high sensory conspicuity. It is this class of accident that may be referred to as LBFS. In accidents of this kind the object that is hit may be of very high sensory conspicuity, and it appears almost certain that the driver would have looked in the general direction of the object and, at a sensory level, detected it. Unfortunately, although the driver looked in the region where the hazard was, they didn't 'see' it. That is, although the object was registered by the driver's senses, they did not attend to it, become consciously aware of it, or take action to avoid it.

Is there any evidence that accidents of this kind occur? Martin Langham and his co-workers (Langham *et al.*, 2002) looked at accidents involving vehicles that have perhaps the highest sensory conspicuity of any on the road – police cars. Despite having a full range of conspicuity enhancers (reflective and retro-reflective materials, flashing lights, cones) stationary police cars have been hit by drivers who subsequently claimed that they did not see them. In these cases it is hard to believe that the individuals' senses failed to register the police car, but something has gone wrong after the initial registration. The police car, while having high sensory conspicuity, has low attention conspicuity *for those individuals*.

Langham *et al.* were interested in establishing just what factors of the situation or the individual (or the interaction between them) would be likely to lead to LBFS accidents. To do this, they gathered survey data from a variety of sources, obtaining details of 29 vehicle accidents. This survey identified a number of interesting aspects of LBFS accidents that will now be considered in relation to the discussion above on the role of knowledge in perception. The factors that seemed to be important in LBFS accidents were:

1. *There were more accidents when the police vehicle was parked 'in-line' (stopped in a lane and facing in the same direction as the prevailing traffic flow) than when it was parked 'in echelon' (parked diagonally across a lane).* It is easy to speculate that the orientation of the car may influence the perception of that car. Experience tells us that most cars that we see on a road have the same orientation as the other cars and, crucially, that they are moving. Thus a car parked in-line may well be perceived as a moving car – until it is too late. There is much less ambiguity with a car that is parked in echelon; it is an unusual (or even impossible!) orientation for a moving car, and so it is perhaps much more likely to be perceived as stationary.
2. *Deployment of warning signs and cones did not guarantee detection.* The deployment of such aids would almost certainly raise the sensory conspicuity of the police car still further, but not enough to prevent an accident.

Key Term

Visual search
Experimental procedure of searching through a field of objects ('distractors') for a desired object ('target').

3. *Although the accidents usually occur on motorways and dual carriageways, 62 per cent of the accidents were close (within 15 km) to the perpetrators' homes.* Again, it is possible that this finding is the result of experience. Drivers are familiar with the environment and the roads around their home. They may have driven the same route every day for years – and never seen a police car parked in the road. Thus, when they do see a stationary police car, they assume it is moving, with disastrous consequences.

4. *The offenders were all, except one, over the age of 25.* As discussed above, this is highly unusual as it is usually the younger drivers that are more likely to be involved in accidents. The finding emphasises the role that knowledge and experience are likely to play in these accidents. More experienced drivers have learnt that cars on the motorway are nearly always moving, and so do not pay sufficient attention to cars that are not moving. It seems highly likely that they detect them, but they do not perceive them appropriately.

It would thus appear that one explanation for LBFS accidents is that more experienced drivers are placing more reliance on what they already know and this is affecting what they perceive (or do not perceive). Edgar *et al.* (2003) have also demonstrated that an overemphasis on using prior knowledge to guide perception may underlie serious accidents referred to as 'friendly fire' in which the military open fire on their own side (or on civilians) believing them to be the enemy, even though there are plenty of sensory cues to suggest that they are not (as illustrated in Figure 2.16).

Figure 2.16   Vehicles that had earlier been carrying members of a BBC TV team, hit by 'friendly fire' from an aircraft in the 2003 Iraq war. The pilot apparently believed that he was attacking enemy forces that were nearby. Note the clear markings on the side of the vehicle (and the top of the vehicle was also marked).

Source: http://news.bbc.co.uk/1/hi/in_depth/photo_gallery/3244305.stm.

THE INFLUENCE OF TOP-DOWN PROCESSING: AN EXAMPLE

There appear to be numerous, not to mention dramatic, examples of what we know influencing what we perceive. To try and drive (excuse the pun) the message home and to allow you to experience a clear example of knowledge influencing perception, have a look at Figure 2.17. What do you see? It is most interesting if you just see a pattern of light and dark shapes. Does it change your perception of the picture if you are told that it is, in fact, a picture of a cat? If you could not see the cat initially but now can after being provided with extra information about the picture, then this is a clear example of knowledge influencing perception. If you still cannot see the cat, have a look at the picture at the end of this chapter, which should give you even more information about where the cat is. The sensory aspects of the original picture have not changed *at all*. It is still a collection of light and dark blobs. What has changed is what you know about the picture, and this has changed your perception of it. Even if you did see the cat immediately, your perception of it will be forever changed (hopefully) by knowing that it has been used as an illustration in a textbook.

THE CONSTRUCTIVIST APPROACH: PERCEPTION FOR RECOGNITION

From the examples discussed above, and from your own experience, it should now be clear that what we know has huge (and sometimes detrimental) effects on what we perceive, even sometimes overruling apparently clear sensory information that may be telling us something different. Truly, 'We see things not as they are but as we are'. The next issue to consider is just why we make so much use of stored knowledge. Given that the consequences of using what we know can sometimes be somewhat detrimental, perhaps it would be better not to use it to such an extent. So why does stored knowledge appear to have such an influence on perception?

Figure 2.17   What do you see? (Answer at end of chapter.)

One of the theories of the way in which perception operates and which deals explicitly with why we make so much use of stored knowledge is the constructivist theory which was initially proposed by Irvin Rock (1977, 1983) and Richard Gregory (1980). It is called a constructivist theory because it is based on the notion that it is necessary for us to 'construct' our perception of what we see from *incomplete* sensory information. Thus we use what we already know to fill in the gaps and interpret the sensory information coming in. In order to do this Gregory suggests that we act as 'scientists', generating perceptual hypotheses (predictions) about what we may be seeing and testing those hypotheses against the sensory information coming in. The cat picture used previously can be used again to give an idea of how this works. The picture is not at all clear and may be difficult, at first, to resolve into anything that makes sense. You might thus generate a range of hypotheses about what it may be (horse, cow, battleship, chair, duck) which you can then check against the sensory information: 'It looks as though it has ears, so the hypothesis that it is a battleship is probably wrong.' Of course the process is not seen as occurring that consciously or that explicitly, but that is the general idea. Once the hypothesis fits the sensory information, the image is then recognised, hopefully correctly. The constructivist theories thus emphasise a strong interaction between sensory information moving 'bottom-up' (see Chapter 1) and knowledge moving 'top-down'. The interaction of the two determines what is perceived.

As we have already seen in this chapter, however, the end result of the perceptual process may be wrong (as with the Müller-Lyer illusion).

Key Term

Constructivist approach
Building up our perception of the world from incomplete sensory input. See also 'perceptual hypotheses'.

Perceptual hypotheses
An element of the constructivist approach, in which hypotheses as to the nature of a stimulus object are tested against incoming sensory information.

Figure 2.18 The faces of Einstein. The left-hand view of the mask is from the front showing a 'normal' convex face. Even though the right-hand panel shows a 'hollow' face (with the nose going away from you) the percept is of a normal face.

Source: Photographs courtesy of Graham Edgar.

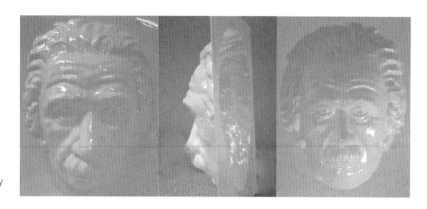

Gregory, in particular, has demonstrated that we can perhaps learn as much about the perceptual processes when things go wrong as when they go right. Once again, when things go wrong, it seems to be previous knowledge that is to blame. Gregory uses a nice demonstration that illustrates this point (Gregory, 1970, 1997). Look at the faces in Figure 2.18. The figure is a hollow mask of Einstein with the view from the 'normal' (convex) side on the left of the figure and the view from the (concave) back on the right. Under certain viewing conditions, whichever view of the mask we take, it still *looks* like a solid face – *not* a hollow face. Gregory suggests that this is because we are very familiar with faces as visual stimuli and we are used to seeing 'normal' faces with the nose sticking out towards us. A hollow face is a very unusual visual stimulus and we appear very resistant to accepting the hypothesis that what we are viewing is a face that is essentially the spatial 'negative' (the bits that normally stick out now go in) of those that we are used to. Although we can, at times, perceive the face as hollow, we are heavily biased toward seeing it as a 'normal' face. Some evidence for this perception being based on acquired knowledge is provided by studies (Tsuruhara *et al.*, 2011) that suggest that infants (5-8 months) appear less likely than adults to see a hollow face as 'solid'.

If what we know seems to have so much impact on what we perceive and, apparently, lead to so many errors (as discussed above), then the obvious question is, 'Why do we make so much use of what we already know in driving our perception of the world?'. It only seems to lead to trouble, so why not ignore what we already know? Apart from the obvious answer that we would not even be able to recognise our own grandmother, there are other reasons for involving knowledge in the process of perception. We have already touched on a possible answer when we first considered the constructivist theory. This is the notion that the sensory input is rather impoverished, and we need to 'construct' our perception aided by what we already know to make best use of the rather limited information coming in. The incoming information is limited in two ways. One way has been considered in Chapter 1 (and will be covered in much more detail in Chapter 3) and this is that our cognitive resources can only cope with a certain amount of incoming information, so that a proportion of it is filtered out by our attentional processes. Another factor limiting the completeness of the incoming sensory information (as already mentioned) is the fact that our senses may not provide a full picture in the first place. This is illustrated by the lower part of Figure 2.19. Our visual acuity is not constant across our field of view and the scene in the upper picture has been progressively blurred in the lower picture to represent the effect of the reducing acuity of the eye with increasing distance from the high-acuity centre (the fovea). What this means is that much of the visual information coming in is actually of quite poor quality. Thus the constructivist theory seems to be making a reasonable assumption in proposing that we need to use prior knowledge to help us to interpret the rather blurry image that we receive from our retina.

EVIDENCE FOR THE CONSTRUCTIVIST APPROACH: MASKING AND RE-ENTRANT PROCESSING

Although using stored knowledge to aid in the interpretation of incoming information is likely to make object recognition better and faster, the iterative process of generating hypotheses and testing them is going to take a certain amount of time. This is not a problem if the incoming sensory information remains constant (or if the observer is, at least, continuing to look at different bits of the same object), but what happens if it changes? The hypothesis testing constructivist approach would predict that a sudden change in the visual input would disrupt processing and make it more difficult to recognise an object, and this appears to be exactly what happens. Di Lollo *et al.* (2000) demonstrated that changing one stimulus rapidly for another disrupted processing of the first stimulus, a process referred to as masking. A typical target stimulus and mask are shown in Figure 2.20. In a masking paradigm, a second stimulus can prevent recognition of an earlier stimulus if the mask follows very soon after presentation of the stimulus. It is not even necessary for the stimulus and mask to be at the same position in the visual field (i.e. not spatially coincident). A mask that surrounds the stimulus (as in Figure 2.20) but does not appear in the same place can be effective in blocking recognition of a target (Enns and Di Lollo, 2000).

Figure 2.19   Demonstrating what we really see (below) as opposed to what we feel we see (above).

Source: Photograph courtesy of Graham Edgar. Photographic manipulation by David Brookes.

Key Term

Visual masking
Experimental procedure of following a briefly presented stimulus by random visual noise or fragments of other stimuli. Interferes with or interrupts visual processing.

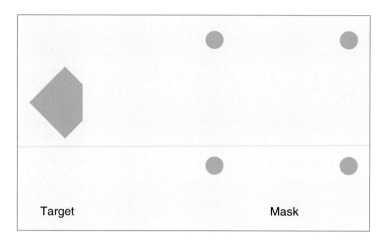

Target   Mask

Figure 2.20   A target and mask of the type used by Enns and Di Lollo (2000).

Source: Adapted from Enns and Di Lollo (2000).

Enns and co-workers (Enns and Di Lollo, 2000; Di Lollo *et al.*, 2000) suggest that the mask is effective because it disrupts re-entrant processing. This term is used to describe the finding in neuroscience research that communication between different areas of the brain is never in one direction only. If a signal goes from one area to another, then there is sure to be one coming back the other way (Felleman and Van Essen, 1991). Thus the flow of information diagrammed in Figure 2.13 could conceivably be a high-level representation of hypothesis testing using re-entrant processing. Indeed, masking could be conceptualised as drawing attention away from the initial target stimulus so that cognitive resources are no longer allocated to processing it. Certainly, masking provides support for the constructivist approach. Hupe *et al.* (1998) suggest that re-entrant processing could be the basis of the hypothesis testing postulated by Gregory. Incoming sensory information (flowing bottom-up) is used to generate an initial hypothesis. The accuracy of this hypothesis is then checked against the continuing sensory input using re-entrant pathways (flowing top-down) and the hypothesis can then be modified and rechecked.

The constructivist theory of vision is thus very appealing, elegantly combining bottom-up and top-down processing. One slight puzzle remains, however. If this approach is so good, why does it make so many mistakes? Much of the evidence used to support the constructivist approach, as already discussed, comes from examples of where it goes wrong and visual illusions such as the Müller-Lyer are good examples. Given that it seems to be so easy to 'fool' the perceptual system, why aren't such things as LBFS accidents far more common? They are, thankfully, quite rare. One criticism of the constructivist approach is that previous knowledge appears to be so important due to the kinds of methods and stimuli used to test perception. Many investigations of perception are done in the laboratory using deliberately simple, and often static, stimuli. Thus, the sensory input is a very impoverished version of what an individual would normally be exposed to in the real world. Some of the stimuli used to illustrate the use of knowledge are even deliberately difficult to recognise, such as the cat picture in Figure 2.17. Thus, it could be argued that if you ask people to view a static two-dimensional, impoverished, image under laboratory conditions, you will force them to use knowledge to try and make sense of it. If you allow people to move around in the world, with a rich flow of sensory information coming in and changing as the individual moves and looks around (and as objects in the world move around

Key Term

Re-entrant processing
Information flow between brain regions (bidirectional).

them), then it is possible that far less top-down information will be needed – or perhaps none at all! Thus the lower picture in Figure 2.19 only looks so poor because it represents what the world would look like if we were unable to move our eyes, or ourselves.

THE GIBSONIAN VIEW OF PERCEPTION: PERCEPTION FOR ACTION

The notion that studying perception in artificial conditions in a laboratory will give rise to false conclusions of how the system works was a notion championed vigorously by J.J. Gibson (1950, 1966). Gibson, rather than considering *how* perception operates, was much more concerned with what perception is *for*. That is, Gibson proposed that perception should be considered in terms of how it allows us to interact with the world we live in. Gibson's approach may be summed up by the term 'perception for action'. In the theories of Gibson there is a strong link between perception and action with perception being referred to as direct. The basis of direct perception is that the sensory information available in the environment is so rich that it provides sufficient information to allow a person to move around, and interact with, the environment without the need for any top-down processing. Gibson would claim that the results obtained in laboratory studies are misleading in that they are studying *indirect* perception of static 2-D representations of the world. That is, laboratory studies (and visual illusions) do not demonstrate how we interact with the world, merely how we react to impoverished representations of it.

For Gibson, moving within the environment and interacting with the environment are crucial aspects of perception. As Gibson (1979) put it, 'perceiving is an act, not a response'. One problem, of course, with denying the use of stored knowledge in perception is that it becomes rather difficult to work out how we can interact with objects in the world without recognising them in the way that would be proposed by the constructivist approach. Gibson (1979) developed his theories by suggesting that we are able to interact with objects in the world because they *afford* their use. For instance, consider Figure 2.21. It is a picture of a hammer, and Gibson would suggest that a hammer would afford hitting things. If you think this is an unreasonable assumption, try giving a hammer to a two-year-old who has never seen a hammer before, and see what they do with it. Actually *do not* try that, although it would almost certainly be a good example of an object affording its use.

> **Key Term**
>
> **Direct perception**
> Perception without the need for top-down processing.

Figure 2.21   What do you do with this?
Source: Photograph courtesy of Graham Edgar.

EVIDENCE FOR THE GIBSONIAN APPROACH

Although Gibson's theories may seem a little unreasonable there is evidence that at least some part of the perceptual process may act in a 'Gibsonian' manner. Handy *et al.* (2003) presented participants with pictures of two task-irrelevant objects while they were waiting for a target to be presented. One of the pictures was of a tool and the other was of a non-tool. Objects that could be grasped (such as hammers) drew attention and functional magnetic resonance imaging (fMRI) of brain function indicated activity in dorsal regions of premotor and prefrontal cortices. Also, as suggested by Bruce *et al.* (1996), direct perception would make sense in terms of instinctive, visually guided behaviour. For example, if a frog were trying to snare a fly with its tongue, it is not necessary for the frog to 'know' anything about flies, or even to recognise the small buzzing object *as* a fly. All it needs to do is to sense the small flying object and use that sensory information to guide its tongue to allow it to snare it (although it could be a nasty surprise if it is not a fly).

Thus the constructivist and Gibsonian theories seem to conflict, one emphasising the centrality of stored knowledge in the perceptual process, the other denying that it is necessary at all. The question, of course, is which one is right? Well, it is not giving too much away to say that it looks as though both theories could be right and that both types of processing could be occurring in perception. To illustrate this, we shall have a look at the structure of the visual system.

THE STRUCTURE OF THE VISUAL SYSTEM

Even very early in the visual system there appear to be (at least) two distinct streams of information flowing back from the retina (Shapley, 1995). These streams are referred to as the parvocellular and magnocellular pathways (e.g. Shapley, 1995), the names deriving from the relative sizes of the cells in the two pathways. These pathways carry information back to the primary visual cortex. You may already have an idea of where your visual cortex is if you have ever been hit on the back of the head (where the visual cortex is) and 'seen stars'. A blow to the back of the head can lead to spontaneous firings within the visual cortex – and the impression of 'stars'. After the visual cortex, the visual information is still maintained in (at least) two distinct streams (see Figure 2.22). One stream is termed the ventral stream and leads to inferotemporal cortex and the other, leading to parietal cortex, is known as the dorsal stream.

THE DORSAL AND VENTRAL STREAMS

While heavily interconnected and apparently converging in prefrontal cortex (Rao *et al.*, 1997), the dorsal and ventral streams seem to be specialised for different functions and to have different characteristics. For instance:

1. The ventral stream is primarily concerned with recognition and identification of visual input whereas the dorsal stream provides information to drive visually guided behaviour such as pointing, grasping, etc. (Ungerleider and Mishkin, 1982; Goodale and Milner, 1992).

Key Term

Ventral stream
A pathway in the brain that deals with the visual information for what objects are.

Dorsal stream
A pathway which carries visual information about the spatial location of an object.

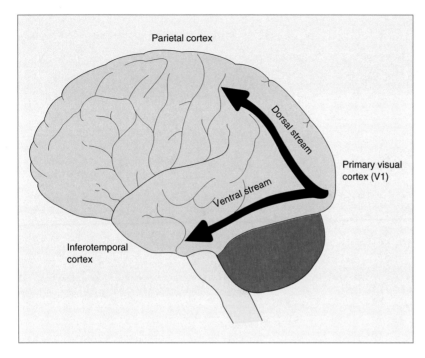

Figure 2.22 The dorsal and ventral streams.

Source: Drawing courtesy of David Groome.

2. The ventral system is better at processing fine detail (Baizer *et al.*, 1991) whereas the dorsal system is better at processing motion (Logothesis, 1994), although the differences are only relative as, for example, the ventral system can still carry motion information.
3. The ventral system appears to be knowledge-based using stored representations to recognise objects whilst the dorsal system appears to have only very short-term storage available (Milner and Goodale, 1995; Bridgeman *et al.*, 1997; Creem and Proffitt, 1998).
4. The dorsal system is faster (Bullier and Nowak, 1995).
5. We appear to be more conscious of ventral stream functioning than dorsal. For instance individuals may report awareness of ventral processing, while manifesting different dorsal processing. A good example of this is if people actually interact with visual illusions, such as the hollow-face illusion (Ho, 1998; Króliczak *et al.*, 2006). The perception is illusory, but the action (e.g. flicking a fly off the nose of the hollow face) does not appear to be influenced by the illusion. This difference in dorsal and ventral processing will be discussed in more detail below.
6. The ventral system aims to recognise and identify objects and is thus object-centred. The dorsal system is driving some action in relation to an object and thus uses a viewer-centred frame of reference (Goodale and Milner, 1992; Milner and Goodale, 1995).

These characteristics support earlier research (Schneider, 1967, 1969) which suggested that the ventral stream is concerned with the question, 'What is it?' whereas the dorsal stream is concerned with the question, 'Where is it?' Thus, the ventral pathway is often known as a 'what' system, and the dorsal pathway a 'where' system (Ungerleider and Mishkin, 1982).

Norman (2001, 2002), following on from similar suggestions by Bridgeman (1992) and Neisser (1994), has suggested a dual-process approach based on the characteristics of the two streams outlined above. In this approach, it is suggested (Goodale and Milner, 1992) that the dorsal and ventral streams act synergistically, with the dorsal stream largely concerned with *perception for action*, and the ventral stream with *perception for recognition*.

The function and characteristics of the two streams thus seem to fit rather nicely with the two theories of perception outlined above, with the dorsal stream appearing rather Gibsonian in the way that it operates, and the ventral stream rather constructivist. Thus, we appear to have a fast system ideally suited for driving action, but which makes relatively little use of stored information (the Gibsonian dorsal stream) combined with another slower system that uses stored knowledge to analyse fine detail and recognise objects (the constructivist ventral stream). A rather elegant study conducted by Króliczak *et al.* (2006) demonstrated the different modes of operation of the two streams. The study used a hollow face like the one in Figure 2.18. Participants were asked to estimate the position of targets placed on the hollow (but phenomenologically normal) face and then to use their finger to make a rapid motion to 'flick' the target off. Even though participants still saw the illusion of the face as solid and coming toward them, the flicking movements were directed to the 'real' position of the face; that is 'inside' the hollow face. The authors suggest that the ventral stream maintains the perception of the face as 'solid' (as it is fooled by the illusion) whereas the dorsal stream drives the flicking action and is *not* fooled. It is rather apt that, considering Gregory used illusions to illustrate the constructivist approach, that the 'constructivist' ventral stream 'sees' the illusion, whereas the Gibsonian dorsal stream apparently does not – especially as Gibson regarded visual illusions as mere artefacts of using unrealistic stimuli.

THE INTERACTION OF THE DORSAL AND VENTRAL STREAMS: PERCEPTION FOR RECOGNITION AND ACTION

Of course, just because the two streams appear to process the hollow face independently, it does not mean that the streams do not interact. It is interesting to speculate, as we finish this discussion of visual perception, just *how* these two types of processing may act together to allow us to perceive our world. To do this, it is worth considering our experience and consciousness of what we are perceiving, i.e. our phenomenological experience. The founder of the phenomenological tradition was a German philosopher-mathematician called Edmund Husserl (1931) who suggested the concept of *intentionality*, whereby the mind reaches out to the stimuli that make up the world and interprets them in terms of our own personal experience, which

Key Term
Phenomenological experience Our conscious experience of the world.

is a theme that has been developed throughout this chapter. As an example of this, consider once more the pictures in Figure 2.19. At any one moment the sensory information coming in from the world gives us a view of the world rather like that in the lower picture. Our phenomenological experience of the world, however, is more like that of the upper picture. We have the impression that we have a clear and accurate perception of the world surrounding us at any one time. An analogy for this is the light in your refrigerator (Thomas, 1999). It always appears to be on because whenever you go to the fridge and open the door, the light *is* on (the irreverent magazine *Viz* once suggested that it would be a good idea to drill a hole in the door of your refrigerator so you can really be sure that the light *does* go off when you close the door!). The experience of the real world is much the same. Whenever you look at any object in the real world it appears clear and sharp (assuming your eyesight is good) because as soon as you become interested in some part of the visual world, you tend to move your eyes so that the image of that part falls on the high-acuity central region of the retina. Thus, you tend not to be aware that the rest of the time that part of the world is just a blur (in the same way that you never see the refrigerator light off).

Stored knowledge allows us to maintain this phenomenological percept that the world is sharp and clear. Having looked at something, we can remember it as sharp and clear, even when we look away and the sensory information coming from that information is actually blurred. Essentially, we could build up an internal 'model' of the world around us at any time using our knowledge. This is not to suggest that we do have a little 'model' of the world inside our heads (although a template-matching model would certainly suggest that we have bits of it). We don't really need it as we can use our environment as an 'external memory' (O'Regan, 1992) that we can recall at any time just by looking around. The constructivist ventral stream would seem to be ideal for building up, and maintaining, our representation of the world, recognising objects as they appear in central vision and generating stored representations of those objects for when we are looking elsewhere. As long as everything remains unchanged, our perception of the world should be fairly accurate. To maintain that accuracy, however, we need a system that will warn us if some part of the visual world changes. This is one of the functions that the dorsal stream could serve.

Just as the ventral stream appears to be ideally suited for recognising objects, so the dorsal stream appears to be well suited to detecting change in the visual world (e.g. Zeki, 2003). Beck *et al.* (2001) demonstrated this function of the dorsal stream using a paradigm in which participants viewed (sequentially) two images of a face or a scene. Sometimes the two images were the same, and sometimes the second image had been changed in some way. A blank screen was presented between the two face/scene images to avoid participants simply detecting any 'flicker' caused by the change. Functional magnetic resonance imaging (fMRI) was used to examine the different brain activity when subjects noticed the change (change detection) as opposed to when they missed the change (change blindness). Beck *et al.* (2001) found enhanced activity in the parietal lobe (an element of the dorsal stream) when subjects were conscious of a change, but not when the change went unnoticed. Of course, fMRI studies of the sort conducted by Beck *et al.* only reveal an *association* between a region of brain activity and some behaviour on the part of the individual. Beck *et al.* (2005), however, used repetitive transcranial magnetic stimulation to disrupt activity in the right parietal cortex and found that the ability to detect changes in a visual stimulus was disrupted (no effect if the left parietal cortex was disrupted). There thus appears to be evidence that the dorsal stream is, indeed, well suited to a role of detecting change in the environment, so that the ventral stream can then be brought into play to see what has changed and how.

Given the evidence presented so far, there seems to be a rather elegant division of function in perception between 'perception for recognition' and 'perception for action', and this split in perception is supported by two functionally distinct processing streams in the brain, the dorsal and the ventral. It seems almost too simple to be true and, unfortunately, that may be the case. Singh-Curry and Husain (2009) suggest that the *inferior* parietal lobe (right hemisphere), amongst other functions, responds to salient *new* information in the environment. This response fits in well with one of the suggested roles for the dorsal stream; that of signalling the appearance of change. Singh-Curry and Husain, however, suggest that the inferior parietal lobe is *not* a part of either the, 'traditional' dorsal or ventral streams, and suggest that the original dorsal/ventral dichotomy is rather simplistic. Thus we need to bear in mind (excuse the pun) that the simple dorsal/ventral distinction may need to be tweaked a bit. For the moment, though, we can accept that no matter how many streams there may be, between them they can handle 'perception for recognition' and 'perception for action'. Thus, to return to the question earlier in this chapter, it may not be necessary to get out of your car every time you come to a sharp bend. If there is something unexpected around the corner, your visual system will probably detect it, recognise it, and guide your action appropriately – most of the time.

2.3 AUDITORY PERCEPTION

So far we have only considered one of the senses – vision. As we shall see (or hear!), there are many others, although perhaps the most researched sense after vision is that of hearing. Our sense of hearing serves many functions, not least in allowing us to hear speech. There is, however, insufficient space to consider the complexities of speech perception in this chapter, and good introductions to speech perception are provided in Banich and Compton (2010) and Goldstein (2009). This section will therefore consider the role of hearing in an area that we have already discussed: detecting change in the environment. Any sound occurring in the environment will, by definition, be the result

Figure 2.23 Sound localisation in the horizontal plane. Sounds to one side of the head will reach the nearest ear sooner and tend to sound louder in that ear. Individuals can use these cues to localise a sound and so orient towards it.

Source: Photographs courtesy of Graham Edgar.

of some change. To produce the transient changes in air pressure that form sound waves, something must have changed, even if only by a small amount. Thus one of the functions of our auditory system is to detect sounds resulting from changes in the environment and to give some indication of *where* those sounds are occurring.

A discussion of auditory localisation is useful here, in that it emphasises particularly strongly that the senses do not operate independently, but act *synergistically* to allow us to perceive the world around us.

AUDITORY LOCALISATION

Auditory localisation is usually described using the following three coordinate systems:

1. *Azimuth* (horizontal), determined primarily by binaural cues, specifically *time* and *intensity* differences between stimuli reaching the left and right ears (see Figure 2.23). Interaural intensity differences are largely due to the shadowing effect of the head that keeps high-frequency sounds from reaching the far ear. Long wavelengths (low-frequency sounds) are unaffected by the head, but shorter wavelengths (high-frequency sounds) are reflected back. This feature has been shown to be surprisingly useful in an evolutionary perspective. As a general rule, animals with smaller heads are sensitive to higher frequencies. Pheasant chicks have evolved a chirp that exploits this feature. The chicks emit chirps at roughly the same wavelength as a fox's head width, thus making it very difficult for their main predator to locate them by sound, whereas the chicks' mother (having a smaller head than a fox) can locate them easily (Naish, 2005).

2. *Elevation* (vertical), determined mainly by spectral cues which are generated by the way in which the head and outer ears (pinnae) affect the frequencies in the stimulus. Sound reflected from the pinnae can be used to give an idea of the elevation of a sound. Thus the pinnae play an active role in sound localisation, suggesting that they did not evolve solely to rest spectacles on. If you fill in the pinnae with modelling clay (do not try this at home, although if

> **Key Term**
>
> **Binaural cues**
> Cues that rely on comparing the input to both ears, as for example in judging sound direction.
>
> **Spectral cues**
> Auditory cues to, for example, distance provided by the distortion of the incoming stimulus by (e.g.) the pinnae (ear lobes).

you give the modelling clay to the two-year old that you gave the hammer to in Section 2.2, they will probably stick it in their ears without being asked; modelling clay is also likely to afford its use), sound localisation progressively worsens (Gardner and Gardner, 1973). Sound can also be reflected back off the torso ('shoulder bounce').

3. *Distance coordinate* (how far a sound source is from the listener). Generally, judgements of distance for sounds within an arm's length are good (interaural level difference (ILD) is large), but as sounds get further away, distance judgement is much more difficult, and distance to far-away sounds is generally underestimated. There are several mechanisms for auditory far-distance judgement, which are used together to determine perception of a sound's distance (much as with visual distance cues); they include:

- *Sound level* – just as light sources that are further away appear dimmer due to scattering and absorption of the light by the intervening atmosphere (assuming you're not in space of course), doubling the distance of a sound source can reduce sound pressure level (SPL) by around 6 dB (outside in the open with no echoes) – or to about a quarter of its original level. It is difficult, however, to make a judgement of distance based on sound pressure intensity without some *prior knowledge* of how loud the source should appear at different distances. Therefore the listener needs to be familiar with the sound source (e.g. a voice) or be making a comparative judgement of the distance of two identical sources.
- *Frequency* – short (blue) wavelengths of visible light tend to be more strongly absorbed and scattered by the atmosphere, and so the more atmosphere the light has to travel through, the redder it will appear (this is why sunsets and sunrises tend to appear reddish). Similarly, high frequencies of sound undergo more attenuation by the atmosphere than low frequencies. Sounds that are further away, therefore, become more dull and muffled.
- *Motion parallax* – see Figure 2.24. Nearby sounds appear to shift location faster than sounds that are further away. This is analogous to the visual depth cue of motion parallax.
- *Reflection* – Sound can reach the ears in two ways:
  - *direct sound*: an uninterrupted path from source to ear;
  - *indirect sound*: sound that is bounced off (reflected by) objects, e.g. walls or ground.

As distance increases, so does the ratio of indirect to direct sound and the change in sound quality provides a distance cue.

The differences in auditory processing result in differences in the accuracy with which the human listener can place sounds along these axes. Localisation accuracy is generally lower for elevation sources than for sources that differ in azimuth (Middlebrooks, 1992). Listeners can localise sounds directly in front of them most accurately (errors average 2–3.5°) and sounds that are off to the side and behind the head

Figure 2.24 Motion parallax. Moving sound stimuli that are closer will tend to shift location *with respect to the listener* faster than those that are further away. The same is true for visual stimuli.

Source: Drawing by Helen Edgar.

least accurately (errors up to 20°). For further discussion of auditory localisation acuity see Oldfield and Parker (1984a, 1984b).

One question of course is that, given there appears to be a processing stream (or streams) within the brain specialised for working out where visual stimuli are, is there a similar stream for auditory stimuli? The answer, unsurprisingly, is that there appears to be just such a stream (for a review of the evidence see Rauschecker and Scott, 2009) The postero-dorsal stream runs from primary auditory cortex to the parietal lobes (and then to the frontal lobes). It was originally proposed (Kaas and Hackett, 1999) that this postero-dorsal stream was involved in localising sounds, serving a function analogous to the original conceptualisation of the visual dorsal stream as a 'where' stream. Also, like vision, it is now suggested (e.g. Hickok and Poeppel, 2004, 2007) that the postero-dorsal auditory stream provides an interface with the motor system and is involved in, amongst (many!) other things, speech production, which would imply that the postero-dorsal stream is also a 'perception for action' stream (Hickok and Poeppel, 2007).

As you might expect, if there is a 'perception for action' stream in audition, there is also likely to be a 'perception for recognition' one too, and indeed this does seem to be the case. There is an antero-ventral stream running from primary auditory cortex to the temporal lobes and, again on into the frontal lobes. The role of this pathway appears to be similar to that of the visual ventral stream, and involves auditory object identification and speech perception (e.g. Hickok and Poeppel, 2007; Rauschecker and Scott, 2009).

Much of the work on auditory processing has concentrated on how a listener (often with fixed head position in a quiet room or an anechoic chamber) can hear sounds, and some interesting problems have been highlighted. For instance, for auditory stimuli that are equidistant from the two ears, confusion can occur as to whether the source is in front of or behind the observer. For most situations in the real world, however, the listener will be able to move freely and will have visual (and other) cues available that can be used to resolve any ambiguity. Under real-world conditions the sensory systems work together and accurate predictions of real-world responses are difficult to measure or generalise when considering, for example, the auditory system in isolation. So far, we have focused on vision and audition, and it can be seen (or heard!) that the auditory and visual systems interact in many ways to influence our final percept. For example, Vroomen and de Gelder (2000) demonstrated that the perceptual organisation of sound affects visual scene analysis. Links between auditory and visual systems can occur at the low-level bottom-up stages (Vroomen *et al.*, 2001), or through the influence of higher cognitive processes (top-down) such as the prior expectations of a participant (Egeth and Yantis, 1997). Sedda *et al.* (2011) found that, if participants heard the sound of a wooden block being placed on a table, it affected their grip aperture when they reached for it – whether or not they were able to see it as well. The participants appeared to be using auditory cues, and previous knowledge (such as what sound a block of wood of a certain size makes when it hits a table) to assist in their reaching, and these auditory cues were still utilised when visual cues were also present. When considering the cognitive psychology of auditory perception, it is therefore advisable to remember that, although a single aspect may be studied in order to isolate factors for investigation, these factors rarely act alone in the real world. Interactions can lead to rather different results to those found in the laboratory, for example improved auditory localisation with visual cues.

Cross-modal studies of auditory localisation have demonstrated that visual cues can improve the accuracy of auditory localisation both in azimuth and elevation, provided that the visual cues are congruent with the auditory stimulus (an inconsistent or mismatched visual cue is worse than no cue). The McGurk effect, where a listener hears a completely new sound 'da' when viewing mismatched lip movements 'ga' and sound 'ba' from a monitor, could be considered as an extreme example of incongruent auditory and visual stimuli.

In addition the *type* of visual stimulus will affect the degree of improvement. If the visual stimulus strongly matches the auditory stimulus, then participants perform more accurately. Thus if the visual stimuli are speaker icons, then performance is better than if a simple card marks the possible sound sources. Also, visual facilitation of auditory localisation is better if the source locations are marked with objects placed in actual 3-D positions, rather than represented on a 2-D grid. Auditory localisation performance is therefore improved if an auditory stimulus is accompanied with a meaningful (congruent) visual cue (Saliba, 2001).

These findings demonstrate once again the influence of knowledge on perception. For instance, we *know* that there has to be a source for a sound – such as a loudspeaker.

AUDITORY ATTENTION

Unlike our eyes, our ears cannot be directed to avoid registering material that we wish to ignore. In a busy setting we are swamped with simultaneous sounds. Principles of auditory grouping analogous to the Gestalt laws of visual perception can be utilised to solve this problem and help *direct* auditory attention to differentiate 'signal' from 'noise' and separate superimposed sounds:

- *Location:* Sounds created by a particular source usually come from one position in space or move in a slowly changing and/or continuous way (e.g. a passing car).
- *Similarity of timbre:* Sounds that have the same timbre are often produced by the same source, i.e. similar sounding stimuli are grouped together.
- Sounds with similar frequencies are often from the same source.
- *Temporal proximity:* Sounds that occur in rapid progression tend to be produced by the same source.

Treisman and Gelade (1980) suggest people must focus attention on a stimulus before they can synthesise its features into a pattern. This applies not only for visual stimuli, but also for auditory stimuli ... *you must focus your attention on complex incoming information in order to synthesise it into a meaningful pattern.* Thus, *meaning* is also important for deciding where an auditory stimulus is and whether it will be processed to the level of perception.

INTERACTIONS AND REAL-WORLD EXAMPLES

There is an important distinction between reductionist laboratory-based research and more applied areas such as auditory display research (Walker and Kramer, 2004). Psychophysical experiments that isolate particular aspects of a stimulus provide fundamental background information (from a carefully controlled environment) about how sound reaches the ears and how it is sensed. This approach, however, is just a starting-point for the study of auditory perception. Concentrating upon individual aspects of the (auditory) system and *not* the interactions that lead to the final percept can lead to some interesting (and expensive) problems.

Example – concert theatre design

The optimum reverberation time for a concert hall is considered to be 2 seconds. The New York Philharmonic Hall, which opened in 1962, was designed to replicate this single factor of '*ideal reverberation*'. Despite achieving a reverberation figure very close to the 'ideal', the musicians could not hear each other and the acoustics were obviously not as expected. This culminated in a complete rebuild of the interior. Current practice uses *multiple measures*, e.g. intimacy, spaciousness, timbre and tone colour (Beranek, 1996). The current approach recognises what has been termed a more *ecological* approach and attempts to consider the effects of sound as it is heard in the real world (natural sound). This is more akin to the approach of Gibson, discussed earlier in this chapter.

TOP-DOWN INFLUENCES ON AUDITORY PERCEPTION

A listener's experience and frame of mind can influence how a message is perceived. Diana Deutsch (2003) demonstrated, with phantom word illusions, that people often report 'hearing words related to what is on their minds'. The demonstration used simple words, e.g. 'Boris', 'Go back', 'Harvey' played repeatedly and continuously. Listeners reported hearing new words and phrases that were not present in the original recording. As with vision, there is an interaction of top-down and bottom-up processing.

> **Key Term**
>
> **Phantom word illusion**
> What we hear may be influenced by what we expect to hear.

A real-world example of how different individuals may extract very different meanings from the same stimulus is given by the following summary adapted from a report in the confidential human factors incident reporting (CHIRP) aviation bulletin of 2005.

Public announcement (PA) overload – a personal perspective?

- An early afternoon flight was slightly delayed due to maintenance.
- During boarding the cabin crew twice announced a welcome, apologised for a short maintenance delay and offered the opportunity to purchase scratch cards.
- Those on board tended to ignore the PA and continue to chat or read.
- When all were on board, the Captain made a PA (at a low volume) apologising for the delay. He gave a few details about the trip and asked passengers to pay attention to the safety brief.
- The safety brief was preceded by an announcement about the in-flight magazine, gift items and scratch cards.
- The aircraft pushed back and the safety brief commenced.
- Most people continued to chat or read and some revellers in the rear [of the cabin] continued to make a noise.
- The aircraft commenced take off; at the point of rotation (aircraft still on the ground but starting to pitch up) the aircraft lurched quite markedly.
- The aircraft became airborne and all seemed normal again.
- During the climb the cabin crew broadcast a PA about the imminent scratch-card sale.
- After the scratch-card sale was over, another PA informed passengers that snacks, drinks and gift items featured in the magazine would be offered for sale.
- The next PA was from the Captain, again at low volume. He announced details of the weather at the destination, the expected arrival time and a couple of features of interest visible from the left-hand side of the aircraft.
- Again most people were reading, chatting or being noisy. Most were not listening to the Captain's PA, which had by this stage been on air for a minute or so.

- The Captain then proceeded to quietly inform the passengers: 'Oh by the way, some of you may have noticed a roll on take-off, we may have a problem with the aircraft so just as a precaution we are going to prepare the cabin for an emergency landing.'
- The emergency brief was delivered by the cabin crew very quickly, but included a demonstration of the brace position (the position that passengers are advised to sit in for an emergency landing).
- There were still a significant number of passengers who were unaware that anything out of the ordinary was going on.
- The cabin crew hurriedly secured the cabin.
- The aircraft descended and there were no further PAs.
- The writer [of the report] was unsure whether or not to adopt brace position.
- The aircraft touched down normally and taxied onto the stand, followed by emergency vehicles.
- The next PA (low volume) came from the Captain, apologising for the emergency preparation and saying, 'Better safe than sorry.'
- Almost immediately a cabin crew PA thanked passengers for choosing their airline. After a brief pause the PA continued with information about car hire, bus tickets and hotel offers.
- In the baggage hall, one woman was openly crying, some people were excitedly talking about the incident whilst some seemed unaware that anything untoward had happened.

The writer concluded that the constant bombardment of PAs caused people to 'switch off' and not listen. 'If there had been a problem on landing and we did thump and skid across the airfield, there would have been a significant number of passengers who were not prepared for it.'

What is clear from this incident report is that different people came away from the same flight with widely different ideas about what was going on. Some passengers were so upset by the emergency landing, and what they considered to be a narrow escape, that they were reduced to tears, whereas others were totally unaware that there had been an emergency landing. So, how could this happen since they were all 'listening' to more-or-less the same auditory stimuli (messages) in the same environment (the aircraft cabin)? To answer this question, it is necessary to consider the aspects of both the stimulus and the listener that might lead to different percepts in different individuals:

- Each individual will not have received exactly the same auditory stimuli. There will have been variations in the level of sound due to the cabin *environment*.
- The individuals' mental model of what is going on or likely to happen could influence what they attended to.
- Sensory overload: A listener can be 'overloaded' with auditory messages or warnings (Meredith and Edworthy, 1994). In this example there were eleven PAs and two safety briefings containing information on at least twenty different topics.

- *Confusion*: Critical information embedded in messages with lots of trivial/irrelevant information (Edworthy *et al.*, 2003).

This example highlights the fact that, just because a stimulus is above threshold and is capable of being 'heard' does not mean that the listener will attend to the stimulus or that the information content can be extracted and assimilated into a meaningful percept ready for action. In effect, this is the auditory equivalent of the 'looked but failed to see' problem (listened but failed to hear?).

In order to study how a listener will respond to a particular auditory stimulus in the real world, be it music in a concert hall or an auditory warning display in a cockpit, it is essential that *multiple factors and interactions* are considered. After all, humans are not passive listeners in their environment, hearing has a function and that function is usually linked to action. For instance, if a person hears a loud bang, they will have some idea from their auditory system about where that bang has originated, they will probably orientate towards the bang in order to gather additional visual information to improve the accuracy (with which they can localise the source); if they have any previous knowledge of that type of sound, they may move towards the sound (if the mental model is of a two-year-old falling off a chair, possibly while trying to reach the hammer or the modelling clay…) or away from the sound (if the mental model is of a runaway truck approaching).

The example of a runaway vehicle highlights another important aspect of how auditory stimuli are perceived in the real world, that is the stimuli are by nature dynamic, transient (e.g. a clap) or changing (the source could be moving, or varying as in speech or music). In many cases the listener will also be moving, for example walking, travelling in a car, or simply turning or nodding their head. Thus, there are a myriad of links between action, vision, hearing and other senses, some of which will be discussed in the next section.

| Key Term |

Mental model
A representation that we construct according to what is described in the premises of a reasoning problem, which will depend on how we interpret these premises.

Sensory overload
A situation in which there is too much incoming sensory information to be adequately processed.

2.4 HAPTIC PERCEPTION

MORE THAN FIVE SENSES?

It is usual to think of humans as having five senses: vision, hearing, smell, taste and touch. However, can we not also sense whether we are standing upright or leaning forward, and if so, which sense is this? Similarly, if I close my eyes I can sense quite precisely where my arms and legs are, at least with respect to my body and to one another; but what sense am I using? When I touch an object I can discern whether it is smooth or rough, large or small and also whether it is hot or cold, but are all of these worked out using my sense of touch? If so, how is it I can sense the heat from a hot cup of tea as I move my hand above it or that I feel cold as I walk along the freezer aisle at my local supermarket, even though I'm not touching either the tea or the freezers? What about pain; is that the same thing as touch? If it is, am I somehow touching my intestines when I have indigestion? In addition,

Sensory modality	Conservative	Accepted	Radical	Sensory modality	Conservative	Accepted	Radical
Vision	✓			**Hearing**	✓	✓	✓
Light		✓	✓	**Mechanoreception**	✓		
Colour		✓		Balance	✓	✓	
Red			✓	Rotational acceleration			✓
Green			✓	Linear acceleration			✓
Blue			✓	Proprioception – joint position		✓	✓
Smell	✓	✓		Kineasthesis		✓	
2,000 or more receptor types			✓	Muscle strength – Golgi tendon organs			✓
Taste	✓			Muscle stretch			
Sweet		✓	✓	– muscle spindles			✓
Salt		✓	✓				
Sour		✓	✓	**Interoceptors**			
Bitter		✓	✓	Blood pressure	✓	✓	
Umami			✓	Arterial blood pressure			✓
				Central venous blood pressure			✓
Touch	✓	✓		Head blood temperature			✓
Light touch			✓	Blood oxygen content		✓	✓
Pressure			✓	Cerebrospinal fluid pH		✓	✓
				Plasma osmotic pressure (thirst?)		✓	✓
Pain	✓	✓		Artery–vein blood glucose difference (hunger?)		✓	✓
Cutaneous			✓				
Somatic			✓	Lung inflation		✓	✓
Visceral			✓	Bladder stretch			✓
				Full stomach			✓
Temperature	✓						
Heat		✓	✓	**Total**	10	21	33
Cold		✓	✓				

Figure 2.25   How many senses do we have?

Source: Adapted from Durie (2005).

I can somehow sense, for example, whether I am thirsty or hungry and whether my lungs are inflated.

From the above, it should be clear that five senses are not nearly enough to encompass the entire spectrum of information that we can detect. So, how many senses do we actually possess? Even excluding such phenomena as a sense of disappointment, a sense of achievement or a sense of belonging, and restricting the definition of a sense to detection of a specific form of information by a specific type of sensory cell which in turn is processed by a particular part of the brain, Durie (2005) suggests that there are at least 21 senses, possibly a lot more (see Figure 2.25). It should also be apparent that we have some senses, such as hearing and smell, that are primarily concerned with sensing information coming from our environment, and some senses, such as our sense of pain (we call this 'nociception') and senses such as thirst and hunger (which involve specific types of interoceptors) that provide information about the state of our own bodies.

Importantly, we can combine cues from these two broad categories of senses (i.e. internal and external senses) to provide more detailed information about the environment around us. For example, even without using my eyes I can determine where objects are and how large they are simply by moving my hands over their surface. In doing this I'm combining information about the relative position of my hands (where they are with respect to each other and my body) with information from the touch receptors in my fingers, that let me know when they are in contact with a surface, to determine exactly where my hands are when they come in contact with the surface. In the rest of this section we will be exploring in more depth how we can perceive the environment using senses such as 'touch' and looking at how we combine information from more than one sense.

PROPRIOCEPTION, KINESTHESIS AND HAPTIC INFORMATION

The sense that keeps track of the position of our body, limbs, fingers, etc. is known as proprioception and it operates through a system of nerve cell receptors (known as proprioceptors) that allow us to ascertain the angle of our various joints. A related sense, known as kinesthesis, allows us to discern how our body and limbs are moving and is a key element in such things as hand–eye coordination, and as such is a sense that can be improved through training and practice. Unfortunately there is considerable variability in exactly what the terms kinesthesis and proprioception are taken to mean (Owen, 1990). For example, Riccio and McDonald (1998) define kinesthesis as the perception of the change in the location of the whole body compared with the environment (thus movement of the whole body is necessary to generate kinesthetic information) and proprioception to mean the perception of where our body parts are in relation to each other and the environment. Proprioception is also sometimes used as a collective term encompassing all the information regarding the position of the body, including kinesthesis and our sense of balance. We will not concern ourselves with debating a precise definition here, but instead will stick to the key point, which is that we are able to sense the position and movement of our bodies and limbs without resorting to looking to see where they are.

If you try reaching out (with your eyes closed of course) and feeling an unknown object in front of you, you will quickly realise that to obtain any information that might be useful in recognising what the object is, you need to be able to sense when your fingers touch the object (through the touch receptors in your skin) and also where your fingers are when they touch it. As you move your fingers to explore the object, you need to sense whether or not they are still in contact with the object and also how far they are moving. Thus in exploring the environment we need to combine our sense of touch with proprioception and kinesthesis, and in so doing we produce what is referred to as haptic information.

Our ability to judge the position and movement of our hands seems to be quite accurate and compares well with the acuity of our visual system (Henriques and Soechting, 2003). There are some elementary judgements that are more accurately performed using visual rather than haptic information; we tend to mistake an inwardly spiralling movement as describing a circle for instance, but on the whole we can judge the geometry of any surface we touch very accurately without recourse to vision (Henriques and Soechting, 2003). Indeed, there is some evidence that the brain uses the same cognitive processes to categorise natural objects (e.g. seashells) regardless of whether the object was identified visually or haptically (Gaissert and Wallraven (2012).

However, unlike the visual system, which combines the sensory input from both eyes, there is some evidence that the brain does not work in a similar fashion with regard to the two hands. Squeri *et al.* (2012) used a robotic manipulation to move the hands of participants along curved contours and asked them to indicate which contour was the more curved. Their results showed that sensitivity was *not* increased when both hands were moved compared with when just one hand was moved. Instead, the results suggested that the brain uses a process of sensory selection, whereby information from the hand that is 'motorically dominant' (usually the right hand) is given preference over the other hand, even though this is often the hand that is more sensitive (usually the left).

As you might expect, given how similar our hands are and also our brains, there appears to be great similarity in how people explore the environment in order to generate haptic information. Klatzky *et al.* (1987) reported that their participants tended to employ a consistent series of exploratory procedures when asked to explore an object using their hands. Lederman and Klatzky (1990) found that each particular exploratory procedure seemed to be used in order to determine a specific aspect of the object, so that unsupported holding was used to ascertain the object's weight, whilst enclosing the object with one or both hands was used to tell what the overall shape of the object might be.

The use of the term 'exploratory procedure' suggests that the way we obtain haptic information has a lot in common with active perception and the ideas of Gibson that were discussed previously; in fact it was Gibson who first coined the phrase 'haptic information' (Gibson, 1966). If we just sat still and did not attempt to explore our environment using our hands, we would not gain very much new

> **Key Term**
>
> **Haptic perception**
> Tactile (touch) and kinaesthetic (awareness of position and movement of joints and muscles) perception.

> **Key Term**
>
> **Active perception**
> Perception as a function of interaction with the world.

information at all. Instead, on most occasions we have to interact with the environment actively to generate haptic information that will be of use. It is also the case that we can think about our sense of touch (and kinesthesis) in terms of 'bottom-up' and 'top-down' processing. A lot of haptic information is likely to be processed in a very bottom-up manner: for example the information about the texture and resistance of my keyboard keys and the relative position of my fingers can be said to flow from my senses upward through the perceptual system. However, haptic information can also have a top-down element and one excellent example of this is the parlour game where blindfolded people are asked to guess what object has been placed in their hand. Although this task involves considerable bottom-up processing, it is likely that the person would use their prior knowledge regarding the size, shape, weight and texture of objects to form and test hypotheses as to what the object might be.

USING ILLUSIONS TO EXPLORE HAPTIC INFORMATION

One of the key approaches to distinguishing between top-down and bottom-up processing is based on illusions. You may remember that the Müller-Lyer illusion provides evidence of top-down processing, as we use existing knowledge to interpret the lines and mistakenly decide that one is longer than the other. Interestingly, there is evidence that the Müller-Lyer illusion works for haptic as well as visual information. Heller *et al.* (2002) produced a version of the illusion in which the lines were 'raised' (in a similar fashion to Braille) to allow them to be felt and participants estimated the size of the key lines using a sliding ruler. Blindfolded-sighted, late-blind, congenitally blind, and low-vision participants completed the task and all were influenced by the illusion, i.e. they estimated the 'wings-in' line to be shorter than the 'wings-out' line. Not only does this experiment demonstrate that the Müller-Lyer illusion is not reliant on either visual imagery or experience, it also suggests that there is an element of top-down processing with haptic information, just as there is with visual information.

Previously, the concept was introduced that haptic information was generated by combining information from our sense of touch with proprioception and kinesthesis, but as we reach to feel or pick up an object we also need to take account of the information picked up by other senses, most notably vision. That both vision and haptic information are used to explore or pick up an object with our hands is obvious, otherwise it would be just as easy to pick something up with our eyes closed as it would with them open. As well as demonstrating visual top-down processing, illusion studies can also show the extent to which visual and haptic information is integrated.

Gallace and Spence (2005) constructed a task that involved participants looking at the Müller-Lyer illusion whilst at the same time attempting to tell which of two sticks hidden from view was the longer. The sticks were placed directly behind the Müller-Lyer illusion (see

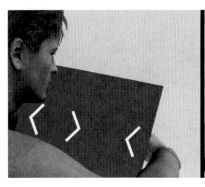

Figure 2.26 A (CGI) recreation of the task from the Gallace and Spence (2005) study in which a participant feels the length of two unseen sticks placed behind the Muller-Lyer illusion.

Source: Adapted from Gallace and Spence (2005).

Figure 2.26), which was presented in a horizontal '< > <' configuration with just the 'wings' and not the lines themselves drawn (this is known as the Brentano version of the illusion). This meant that the Müller-Lyer illusion was being presented visually, and at the same time as they were viewing it participants were performing a task utilising haptic information. The results of this experiment revealed that the visual illusion did interfere with the participant's ability to 'feel' the correct length of the line, so that the length of the sticks were either overestimated or underestimated as a result of the participant seeing the illusion. Thus, visual information was affecting the processing of haptic information.

Another distinction that was introduced earlier when discussing visual perception is that of perception for recognition and perception for action, and this distinction is particularly relevant to the processing of haptic information. If you remember, the idea is that the information from our retinas is processed through two separate, but interconnected, visual pathways in the brain: the ventral pathway appears to be used for processing information that is used to recognise objects, whilst the dorsal pathway is used for processing information used to guide the visual control of action (Milner and Goodale, 1995). Above, studies by Klatzky *et al.* (1987) and Lederman and Klatzky (1990) were described that examined how we can use our hands to generate haptic information in order to recognise objects. However, unless there is no light available or the person concerned has impaired vision, most of the time we rely very heavily on vision in order to recognise objects. Instead, we tend to make use of haptic information to interact with the environment around us in precise ways, i.e. haptic information is probably more useful in terms of guiding action than in recognising objects.

A key question, therefore, is whether there is a divide between perception for recognition and perception for action in the processing of haptic information? In attempting to answer this question, it is possible to make further use of evidence from studies that have utilised illusions. The Ebbinghaus illusion is an example of a size-contrast illusion (see Figure 2.27) in which two circles of equal size appear to be of different sizes due to the presence of surrounding circles. If you look

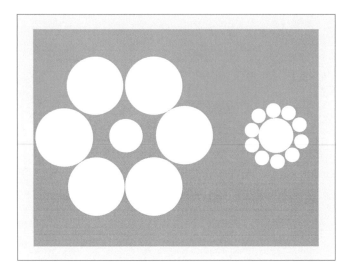

Figure 2.27   The Ebbinghaus illusion.

at Figure 2.27 and compare the two circles in the centre of the others (we call these the 'target' objects), the one on the right will appear to be larger than the one on the left even though both are exactly the same size. In judging the size of the two target circles your perceptual system is taking into account the contrast between their size and the size of the circles surrounding them (we call these 'flanker' objects). Thus a target object will appear smaller when placed next to flanker objects that are larger than it and will appear larger when placed next to flanker objects that are smaller than it.

Aglioti *et al.* (1995) found evidence to support the dissociation between ventral and dorsal processing by conducting an experiment in which participants were asked either to estimate the size (ventral processing) of the central circle in the size-contrast illusion described above or to reach out and pick it up (dorsal processing). When estimating the size of the circle the participants' judgements were affected by the illusion, but analysis of the size of their grip revealed that the action of picking-up the circle did not appear to be affected, a result similar to that in the study by Króliczak *et al.* (2006) described earlier (the one that involved flicking the mark off the hollow face).

Hu and Goodale (2000) conducted a series of studies utilising a different version of the size-contrast illusion in which participants were presented with two objects (the objects were actually 'virtual' as they were presented by reflecting a video image onto a mirror placed in front of the participant) and were asked either to pick up the target object or to indicate its size using a manual estimate (i.e. by separating their finger and thumb). These two tasks were both performed either immediately or after a five-second delay. The results showed that when performed immediately, the manual estimates were influenced by the size of the flanker object. However, analysis of the recording of the participants' hand movement in the 'pick-up' condition revealed that the size of their grip was not influenced (statistically significantly) by the size of the flanker. When providing the manual estimate, the participants must have been utilising 'perception for recognition' processing, as they would have had to generate a mental description of the object in order to estimate its size. When picking the target object up, the processing required would have been 'perception for action'. Further evidence that this task demonstrates dissociation between perception for action and recognition was provided by asking participants to perform both the manual estimate and pick-up tasks from memory. Here, both tasks necessitate the use of perception for recognition, as the participant has to create a mental description of the object in their memory. Analysis of this experiment did indeed show that both tasks were influenced by the size-contrast illusion, i.e. the size of the flanker influenced the perceived size of the target.

The Hu and Goodale (2000) study involved the processing of haptic information, as proprioception and kinesthesis were used in moving the participants' arm and fingers, and their touch receptors were used for detecting when the fingers came in contact with the target object. However, the actual illusion employed (the size-contrast illusion) was presented visually and therefore it was visual information and not haptic information that was responsible for the participants misjudging the size of the target object. So, whilst the study provides evidence that visual information is processed in a dissociated manner, through either perception for recognition or action, it does not tell us whether haptic information is also processed in this way.

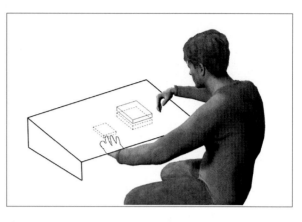

Figure 2.28   A (CGI) recreation of the task from the Westwood and Goodale (2003) study in which a participant feels unseen flanker and target objects with their left hand and indicates the size of the target with their right.

Source: Adapted from Westwood and Goodale (2003).

To explore this issue further, Westwood and Goodale (2003) conducted a similar study to that of Hu and Goodale (2000), except that they replaced the visual size-contrast illusion with a haptic version. Participants were asked first to feel an unseen flanker object and then to feel an unseen target object using their left hand. When they had done this they were asked to use their right hand either to provide a manual estimate (again using finger and thumb) of the size of the target object or to reach out and pick up an object placed in front of them (which was also not in view, as they were asked to keep their eyes closed) that was matched in size to the target (see Figure 2.28). The results of this experiment showed that the manual estimate task was affected by the illusion, in that participants tended to overestimate the size of the target when it was paired with a smaller flanker object and to underestimate the size of the target when it was paired with a larger flanker object. However, when the data from the pick-up task was analysed, the size of the participants' grip as they reached for the object did not appear to have been affected by the illusion, i.e. their grip was the same regardless of the size of the flanker object. This is evidence suggesting that haptic information is processed in a similarly dissociated manner as that of visual information, or indeed (as the authors themselves suggest) that all sensory processing might be organised according to a general principle.

In summary, the common notion that there are five human senses is somewhat inaccurate (to the tune of at least sixteen!) and we usually confuse several different senses (particularly kinesthesis and proprioception) when we talk about touch. Our ability to explore the environment with our hands is very well developed and by combining haptic and visual information we can interact with objects very accurately. In addition, the way in which we process haptic information seems very similar to visual information, in that both bottom-up and top-down processing are employed and there appears to be a dissociation between perception for recognition and perception for action.

APPLICATIONS OF HAPTIC INFORMATION TO DRIVING

When travelling, by whatever means, we are bombarded with signs, warnings and other information that is presented visually, and sometimes auditorily, but very rarely haptically. When on foot we have the time to stop and focus on one sign at a time, but when driving this can be problematic due to the need to pay attention to other visual stimuli, such as the road ahead! Modern technology means it is possible to build various safety features into vehicles to warn drivers about potential collisions, if their vehicle is drifting into a different lane, whether they are falling asleep and even if they are entering a bend or approaching an intersection too quickly. Presenting these various warnings using a visual signal is potentially problematic if it draws the driver's eyes and attention away from the road. Using an audible warning can overcome this issue, but there are other sounds the warning would need to compete with, including road/wind noise, music and conversations. In addition, audible warnings are not suitable for drivers with impaired hearing. So, a key question that has been looked at by researchers is whether haptic information offers a solution to warning drivers effectively without distracting them.

A variety of different devices that make use of haptic information have been studied: Navarro *et al.* (2007) found that using a steering wheel that vibrated whenever a driver began to deviate from their current lane improved steering performance; Janssen and Nilsson (1993) reported that reactions to potential collisions were improved by using an accelerator that pushed back on the driver's foot to warn them; and a study conducted by Scott and Gray (2008) found that a haptic seat belt was effective at reducing the time it took a driver to brake in order to avoid a potential collision ahead. In addition, Kozak *et al.* (2006) compared warnings aimed at preventing drowsy driving provided through either a visual head-up display, auditory signals or through a vibrating, turning steering wheel and found the haptic signal to be the most effective. Although all these technologies mean that the driver's visual attention can remain on the road and other vehicles, they do suffer from other problems. For example, vibrating the steering wheel might cause the driver to let go of it; not everyone wears their seatbelt; accelerators are not used when the car is in cruise control mode; and again, vibrating any of the pedals might cause an inappropriate reaction in the driver.

One solution that researchers have considered is to place pads in the driver's seat, which can vibrate in different ways and in different orders to alert the driver to different hazards. Using the driver's seat has the advantage that none of the vehicle's controls is being interfered with, the driver remains in continuous contact with their seat and the area involved is quite large, allowing the use of multiple areas of vibration. Although some studies have found drivers can get confused about which vibration is meant to be an alert for which problem (Sayer *et al.*, 2005), more recent research (Fitch *et al.*, 2011) has found results suggesting that multiple haptic signals can be presented through the driver's seat, as long as these alerts are in unique positions that are widely spaced and map to the appropriate response (e.g. pads at the front of the seat pulse when there is a potential collision in front of the car). Another study, conducted by Chang *et al.* (2011), compared a similar haptic warning system in the driver's seat with visual and auditory signals, and found the haptic interface performed the best; though the authors also noted that people need time to adjust to this new technology and can (subjectively) find it off-putting to begin with.

It is very likely that cars in the future will be equipped not only with new sensory technology that can detect a variety of hazards, but also with warning systems that make use of haptic information to not only alert the driver that there is a hazard, but what the hazard is and even in which direction it is located.

2.5 CONCLUSION

There are a number of points made throughout this chapter that will be drawn together here. One major theme is the distinction between 'perception for recognition' and 'perception for action'. How these two systems interact (or not) is an issue that runs throughout the chapter. The section on vision concluded with the supposition that the two perceptual systems operate synergistically to allow us to perceive the world. The sections on visual and haptic perception both end with the proposition that there can be a dissociation between perception for action and perception for recognition. The idea that there are pathways in the brain for supporting recognition and action, and that these pathways are functionally independent, is supported by studies such as the one that involving 'flicking the mark off the hollow face' (Króliczak *et al.*, 2006). Westwood and Goodale (2011) have drawn together a body of evidence to suggest that a clear recognition/action distinction is reasonable in perception. Others, however (e.g. Schenk *et al.*, 2011), argue that the two processes are not independent. Indeed, de Haan and Cowey (2011) argue that, given there is evidence for at least five 'subsections' of the dorsal stream, it is perhaps better to think in terms of a patchwork, or network of interconnecting and interacting brain areas rather than a clear stream. This is certainly consistent with the PDP approaches discussed earlier and suggests a greater level of interaction between the different processing streams and a greater sharing of function.

These apparently contradictory conclusions can perhaps be reconciled by appealing to the argument that is made particularly clearly in the section on auditory perception. It is possible to use sophisticated experimental techniques to study, for instance, the perception for action and perception for recognition systems in isolation. This approach is invaluable in that it gives an indication of how these systems operate. It does not, however, give a complete picture of how these systems operate in 'real life'. If this issue is considered, then there is evidence that the two systems are heavily interconnected and that perception results from an interaction of these two primary systems (and their many sub-systems!). So, perception for recognition and perception for action *can* work together, but whether they do or not will depend upon the circumstances. It may be time to move on from the analogy of clearly defined streams, as this seems to downplay the wider context in which these 'streams' operate, and the interactions between them. Perhaps 'perception for action' and 'perception for recognition' are more 'currents in a lake' than streams …

One theme that runs through the discussion of all the senses considered in this chapter and that is encapsulated in the notion of the functions of the dorsal and ventral streams, is the notion that perception consists of far more than the simple collection of sensory information. Perception involves building up a model of the world around us and the objects and people in it. We certainly use sensory information to do this, and to work out where and what things are at any particular time (and to interact with them), but we also use our knowledge, experience and expectations to build up our percept. This chapter could best be summed up by rewording a phrase that has already been used, namely: 'We *perceive* things not as they are, but as we are.'

SUMMARY

- There are a number of theories that attempt to explain how we encode incoming sensory information.
- Perception is not the same as sensation. We may detect something but not perceive it.
- Knowledge is crucial in our influencing our perception of the world – according to constructivist theories.
- Knowledge is unnecessary in our perception of the world – according to direct perception theories.
- Both approaches may operate in vision with the ventral stream operating primarily for perception for recognition and the dorsal stream operating primarily for perception for action.
- Knowledge is also crucial in auditory perception.
- There are strong interactions between auditory and visual perception.
- There may be at least twenty-one senses (not just five!).
- Knowledge also influences haptic perception.
- We sense things not as they are, but as we are.

FURTHER READING

- Banich, M. T. and Compton, R. J. (2010). *Cognitive Neuroscience, International Edition* (3rd edn). Pacific Grove, CA: Wadsworth. If you like the squishy stuff, then this is for you. An excellent introduction to the workings of the brain.
- Goldstein, E. B. (2009). *Sensation and Perception, International Edition* (8th edn). Pacific Grove, CA: Wadsworth. A highly readable and comprehensive discussion of aspects of perception.
- Mannoni, L., Nekes, W. and Warner, M. (2004). *Eyes, Lies and Illusions*. London and Aldershot: Hayward Gallery Publishing/Lund Humphries. If you are interested in illusions then this is the book for you. An entertaining read that covers the history of illusions rather than the explanations for them. Basically, all the bits that this chapter did not cover.

Figure 2.29 Answer to Figure 2.17. Now can you see the cat?

The well-known person silhouetted in Figure 2.3 is the ex-president of the USA, George W. Bush.

Chapter 3

Contents

Attention

Elizabeth Styles

3

3.1 WHAT IS ATTENTION?

Attention refers to systems involved in the selection and prioritisation of information processing, and it is intimately linked with perception and memory and is thus central to almost everything we do. We can direct attention intentionally, for example when we move our eyes around the environment to search the visual scene for something specific, or when we 'tune in' to listen to a conversation in a noisy room. Attention can also be captured unintentionally, for example when a sudden movement 'catches our eye', or when we hear a familiar sound such as our name being spoken, and it seems to 'pop out' from the noise in a crowd. Attention also refers to a more general, non-selective state of alertness or arousal. Experiments have shown that it is possible to distinguish these different aspects, and studies of brain activity have revealed that attention involves multiple areas of the brain working together.

The most characteristic property of attention is that it is limited. Desimone and Duncan (1995: 193) say 'The first basic phenomenon is limited capacity for processing information. At any given time only a small amount of information available on the retina can be processed and used.' William James (1890: 404) said that 'Everyone knows what attention is. It is the taking possession of mind in clear and vivid form of one out of what would seem several simultaneous possible objects or trains of thought.' James went on to say 'Focalisation, concentration of consciousness is of its essence. It implies the withdrawal from some things in order to deal effectively with others.' Here James adds some further properties of attention, in particular that attention may be given to external or internal stimuli and that what is attended becomes consciously available to us. When we are conscious of something, that information is held in short-term working memory, which can only maintain and manipulate a limited amount of information. We are also limited because we can only look in one direction at once, reach for one thing with one hand, or say one word at a time. These limitations necessitate the use of attention to select and prioritise which information to process. Everyday activities like supermarket shopping challenge our attention. What do we want? Where shall we look? Which one shall we reach for?

Key Term

Capture
The ability of one source of information to take processing priority from another. For example the sudden onset of novel information within a modality such as an apple falling may interrupt ongoing attentional processing.

Figure 3.1   Would you hear your name spoken from across a crowded room?

Source: Shutterstock.

Figure 3.2   Everyday tasks like shopping demand attention.

Source: Shutterstock.

> **Key Term**
>
> **Selection for action**
> The type of attention necessary for planning controlling and executing responses, or actions.
>
> **Selection for perception**
> The type of attention necessary for encoding and interpreting sensory data.

3.2 WHAT IS ATTENTION FOR?

Here I shall introduce many of the functions of attention to be addressed in detail later. An important question to ask is 'what is attention for?'. Schneider and Deubel (2002) identified two possible functions of selectivity in visual attention. First, there is selection for perception (i.e. detecting and selecting what to process from a visual display) and second, selection for action (i.e. detecting and selecting which response or action to make). For example when texting on your mobile you must select the correct letter from the keypad, then select and make an action to press the correct location. This involves not only knowing 'what' something is but also 'where' it is, or how to act upon it. As explained in Chapter 2, the brain has two visual pathways (Ungeleider and Mishkin, 1982; Corbetta and Schulman, 2002), a ventral pathway that computes colour, shape, category (or the 'what' properties of a stimulus), and a dorsal pathway that computes the spatial information required for a motor response to that stimulus (the 'where' properties, where to direct the action or how to respond). These two functions of attention, processed in the two brain pathways, allow the effective selection of actions in response to selected sensory stimuli.

However, in order to correctly combine *what* something is with *where* it is, these two sources of information must be correctly linked together. For example, if there is a red colour in the shape of a circle on the left, and a green colour in the shape of a square on the right, the colour, shape and position of each property must be correctly bound together. This is called the binding problem, and an important function of attention is to bind together what an object is, together with where it is and how to act on it. As we shall see later, some theories of attention aimed to explain the selective nature of attention, but other theories also aimed to account for the binding problem.

When we attend to an object, information associated with that object enters working memory (LaBar *et al.*, 1999), so the outcome of attention is a representation in working memory that enables us to consciously 'know about' what is attended. Unattended stimuli do not enter working memory, and so remain unconscious. Unless we become conscious of stimuli we do not act upon them, as is evident in some patients with attentional disorders such as blindsight and unilateral neglect (see Chapter 4).

When attention is driven by our intentions it is called controlled attention, or *executive* control, and is said to operate *top-down* because it is influenced by a goal we have set ourselves such as searching for something in particular. The source of control is endogenous, it comes from within us. According to Craik and Bialystock (2006), 'Control is the set of fluid operations that enable intentional processing and adaptive performance' (p. 131). In contrast, exogenous attention is *stimulus-driven,* where incoming or *bottom-up* stimuli trigger *automatic* processing which cannot be controlled intentionally. For example, while holding a conversation we might unexpectedly hear our name spoken elsewhere.

A good example of a selective attention task, and the relationship between controlled and automatic processing, is demonstrated by the Stroop effect, in which the task is to name the ink colour of a colour word. For example, using the list in Figure 3.3, try naming the colour of the ink for each word in the list as quickly as possible. Then do the same task whilst reading the words.

Stroop (1935) discovered that when reading the words, there is little effect of the incongruent ink colour on speed of word naming, but naming the ink colour is significantly slowed by the incongruent colour word. This shows that the written word activates its response automatically, so that when the goal is to name the ink colour (but *not* to name the word) the already active word response interferes with producing the name of the ink colour. In this example controlled attention is necessary to inhibit the unwanted response to the word, and to allow the response to the ink colour to be produced. Despite your best intentions you will have found that the written word cannot be ignored and interferes with naming the ink colour. Automatic processing and its distinction from controlled processing will be considered later in the chapter when we look at Shiffrin and Schneider's (1997) theory.

Patients with frontal lobe damage have difficulty inhibiting automatic responses and switching between tasks, as their mechanisms of attention appear to lack control (see Chapter 9). Theories of attentional control (e.g. Norman and Shallice, 1986; to be discussed later), aim to explain goal-directed behaviour and everyday slips of action.

It is evident that the term 'attention' is applied to a variety of cognitive processes and therefore attention cannot have either a single definition or be accounted for by a single theory. While most early research into the psychology of attention was based on behavioural experiments, it is now possible to look at underlying brain activity using *in*

Key Term
Binding problem The problem of how different properties of an item are correctly put together, or bound, into the correct combination.
Controlled attention Attention processing that is under conscious, intentional control. It requires attentional resources, or capacity, and is subject to interference.

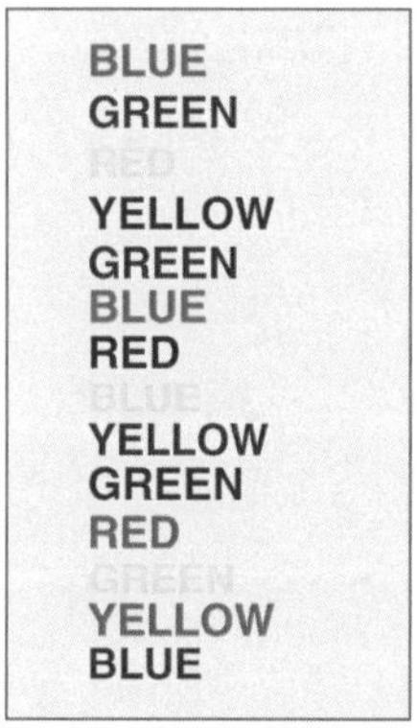

BLUE
GREEN
RED

YELLOW
GREEN
BLUE
RED

YELLOW
GREEN
RED

GREEN
YELLOW
BLUE

Figure 3.3 The Stroop test.

Key Term
Endogenous attention Attention that is controlled by the intention of a participant.
Exogenous attention Attention that is drawn automatically to a stimulus without the intention of the participant. Processing by exogenous attention cannot be ignored.

Key Term

Stroop effect
The effect of a well-learned response to a stimulus slowing the ability to make the less-well-learned response; for example, naming the ink colour of a colour word.

Slips of action
Errors in carrying out sequences of actions, e.g. where a step in the sequence is omitted, or an appropriate action is made, but to the wrong object.

Psychological refractory period
The time delay between the responses to two overlapping signals that reflects the time required for the first response to be organised before the response to the second signal can be organised.

Bottleneck
The point in processing where parallel processing becomes serial.

vivo imaging techniques such as positron emission tomography (PET) and functional magnetic resonance imaging (fMRI). These newer studies clearly demonstrate that attention involves multiple brain areas and that different areas are involved in different tasks. Corbetta and Schulman (2002), for example, provide imaging data which supports a clear distinction between stimulus-driven (automatic, bottom-up, exogenous) attention, and goal-directed (controlled, top-down, endogenous) attention.

3.3 WHERE IS THE LIMIT? THE SEARCH FOR THE BOTTLENECK

When two stimuli are presented in rapid succession and the participant must make a fast response to both, response time (RT) to the second stimulus depends upon the time interval between the presentation of the two stimuli (Welford, 1952). At short inter-stimulus intervals, RT to the second stimulus is slower than when there is a longer interval. Welford called this delay in responding to the second stimulus the psychological refractory period (PRP). He argued that the PRP demonstrated that there was a bottleneck in processing, so that at very short inter-stimulus intervals, processing of the second stimulus must wait until processing of the first stimulus is completed. According to this hypothesis some central cognitive processes cannot be carried out simultaneously in parallel. They are called 'central' because they occur after early perceptual processing but before later response selection. This concept of a central bottleneck in processing seemed to account for the limit on our ability to process more than one set of information concurrently, and the search began to determine the precise location of this limitation within the human information-processing system.

Most of the early studies investigated the basis on which auditory selective attention might operate. It was reasoned that if a stimulus property could guide selective attention then that property must have been available early on in processing, prior to selection; but if a property of the stimulus could not be used to guide selective attention, that property could not have been analysed, hence revealing where the bottleneck was located. Cherry (1953) used the dichotic listening task to discover which properties of auditory stimuli could guide selective attention. Cherry's task involved presenting two different messages at once over headphones, one message to the left ear and the other message to the right ear. The participant was instructed to attend to one of the messages and repeat it back as it arrived, a procedure known as shadowing. Cherry found that participants were able to use ear location (left or right) and voice quality (male or female) to select the message to be attended. However, at the end of the experiment, when participants were quizzed on the meaning of the unattended message they were unable to say what it had been about. So without attention there seemed to be no memory for the meaning of the unattended message, although people did notice if there was a change of voice from male to female, and they could detect a bleep in the ignored message. The results were interpreted as evidence that the perceptual properties of a message are processed without attention, and can guide selective attention. But the meaning (or semantics) of the ignored message was not processed. This finding suggested that the bottleneck was located at a point after perceptual processing had taken place, but before the meaning of the words became available.

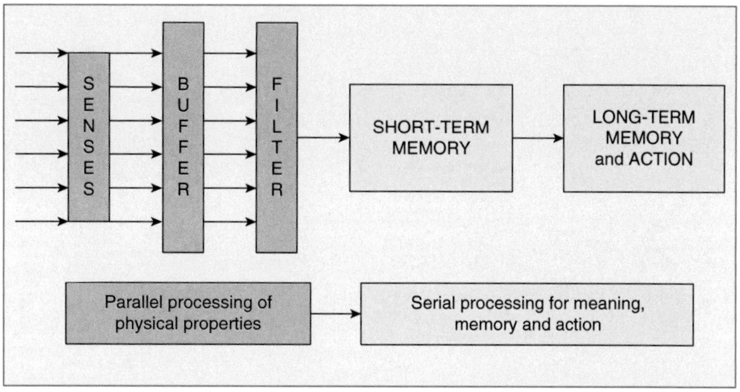

Figure 3.4   A simplified version of Broadbent's filter model. Information enters the senses in parallel and passes to the sensory buffer where its physical properties are available to the selective filter. The filter cannot pass on all the information at once, so just one source of information is selected for entry to the limited capacity channel of short-term memory. Unless information is selected from the buffer before its trace has decayed it will be lost.

The first complete conceptualisation of the flow of information processing from input to response was provided by Broadbent in 1958. It is often called the 'Filter model' because it assumes the existence of a selective filter between the perceptual input system (which processes sensory information in parallel) and a limited capacity channel (which can only process the meanings of words one at a time, serially, to provide semantic identification and transfer to short-term working memory). As stimuli can only be transferred one at a time from the parallel input to the serial stage this causes a bottleneck in processing (Figure 3.4).

According to Broadbent, the unselected stimuli must wait in a high-capacity, fast-decay sensory memory, and unless they are selected for transfer before decaying they will be lost. So, if unselected stimuli do not get passed on to the identification stage they remain unattended and nothing is known about their meaning. This is called an early selection theory of attention, because selection of information for further processing is made at an early processing stage. At first glance this model accounts well for the research results available at the time. However, evidence soon began to accumulate that revealed shortcomings in Broadbent's theory.

3.4 THE PROBLEM OF BREAKTHROUGH

Many experimenters began to discover evidence that the filter was not preventing the activation of semantics. For example, Moray (1959) found that some participants in dichotic listening tasks did notice if their name was presented in the unattended message. This effect is called breakthrough of the unattended message.

Treisman (1960) required participants to attend to a story (story 1) presented to one ear, and to ignore a different story (story 2) presented to the other ear. Treisman found that if story 1 was replaced by a new

Key Term

Shadowing
Used in a dichotic listening task in which participants must repeat aloud the to-be-attended message and ignore the other message.

Early selection
Selective attention that operates on the physical information available from early perceptual analysis.

Breakthrough
The ability of information to capture conscious awareness despite being unattended. Usually used with respect to the unattended channel in dichotic listening experiments.

Key Term

Late selection
An account of selective processing where attention operates after all stimuli have been analysed for their semantic properties.

Galvanic skin response
A measurable change in the electrical conductivity of the skin when emotionally significant stimuli are presented. Often used to detect the unconscious processing of stimuli.

Subliminal
Below the threshold for conscious awareness or confident report.

story (story 3) in the attended ear, and the attended story was switched over to the unattended ear, participants switched their attention to continue shadowing story 1 despite the fact that it had switched to the 'unattended' ear. To do this, participants must have known something about the meaning of the story, despite the fact that it was now heard in the 'unattended' ear. These results are clearly inconsistent with a selective filter that completely blocks all semantic processing.

A different way of accounting for semantic processing of the unattended message was proposed by Deutsch and Deutsch (1963). According to their theory, all inputs are analysed for meaning before selective attention operates. The bottleneck in processing is at the point of response selection, where only the most important signals switch in other processes such as memory storage or motor output. This is the classic late selection model.

In 1964, Treisman proposed a compromise that could account for how the meaning of some messages could break through the filter. Rather than the filter being an 'all or none' mechanism, she suggested that it acted as an attenuator, turning down the activation for the unattended message rather than completely blocking it. This meant that familiar or important words (such as a person's name), or words that followed on in a story, could break through the filter because although they were attenuated, their activation levels were still higher than for less familiar words, and so would still reach an activation level sufficient to be detected.

3.5 SUBLIMINAL PRIMING EFFECTS

In the early 1970s, experiments began to show semantic effects of 'unattended' stimuli using indirect measurements of stimuli that subjects were unable to consciously report. Corteen and Wood (1972 measured the galvanic skin response (GSR) to words presented in the unattended message using dichotic listening tasks. They conditioned participants to expect an electric shock in association with particular words, and found that although these words were not noticed when occasionally presented in the unattended message, shock-associated words still produced a GSR. Not only did conditioned words produce a GSR, but also words that were semantically associated. For example, if shock was conditioned to city names such as London, Rome, Prague, the presentation of a new city name (such as Paris) also produced a GSR despite having not been conditioned with a shock. It was therefore argued that all word meanings were processed unconsciously in parallel before selective attention operated, which thus supported a late selection theory of attention. These auditory experiments revealed evidence for semantic processing without attention, and below the level of conscious awareness. In visual experiments this is often called subliminal perception.

Some of the most impressive and controversial demonstrations of the subliminal perception of unattended visual stimuli came from the work of Marcel (1980, 1983). Marcel used an associative priming task, in which a briefly presented prime word was followed by a mask made from a pattern of letter fragments, which prevented participants from identifying the prime. When a prime word (such as BREAD) was followed by a semantically associated target word (such as BUTTER), Marcel found response to the target was faster than when it was preceded by a non-associated word (such as NURSE), even though subjects were completely unaware of the prime. When the prime was followed by a different type of mask, which did not contain letter fragments but was a pattern of random dots (a noise mask), there was no associative priming. Marcel argued that this result provided evidence for two different types of masking; one type produced by a noise mask which degrades the perceptual input at an 'early' stage of processing and prevents information being passed to an identification stage, and another type produced by the pattern mask which prevents passage to a conscious identification stage. Marcel proposed that the pattern mask did not prevent activation of semantics, but *did* prevent the binding together of the 'what' and 'where' information about the stimulus. Without this binding of the stimulus properties there was no conscious awareness of the physical presence of the prime word. However, as semantics had been activated the prime word could still produce semantic priming.

> **Key Term**
>
> **Masking**
> The disruptive effect of an auditory or visual pattern that is presented immediately after an auditory or visual stimulus. This is backward masking, but there are other types of masking.

3.6 OBJECT SELECTION, INHIBITION AND NEGATIVE PRIMING

Evidence for semantic processing of unattended stimuli is also found in experiments using *negative priming* (Tipper, 1985; Tipper and Cranston, 1985). Negative priming refers to the finding that the response time to categorise a target item will be slowed if that same item has been presented on the previous trial as a distractor item which was to be ignored. Clearly then, the distractor item must have been semantically processed despite the instruction to ignore it. In this type of experiment, participants are briefly presented with two overlapping pictures, for example a dog drawn in green ink and a spanner drawn in red ink. Since the stimuli are superimposed, spatial position cannot be used to select which object to attend to, and selection can only be made on the basis of colour. The task is to categorise the red object as quickly as possible, so if the spanner is red and the dog is green the response is 'tool' as opposed to 'animal'. When the target item on the priming trial was repeated as a target on the following trial (a condition known as 'attended repetition'), Tipper found that the response to the target was facilitated. However, he found that if the previously ignored distractor item was used as the target on the following trial, response time was slowed relative to control trials. Tipper reasoned that the activation of the distractor item must have been suppressed by inhibitory processes to allow the target to be selected. This inhibition results in a slower response to the item if it is presented as the target on the following trial, because its activation level has been significantly reduced. Consequently it will take longer to reach a level of activation at which it can be reported, so producing a 'negative priming' effect.

The phenomenon of negative priming suggests that one way of preventing irrelevant items from controlling response is to inhibit their representations in memory or their connections to the response system. Negative priming also provides evidence for late selection because the effect relates to the meaning of stimuli. So, is selectivity for attention 'early' or 'late'? There seems to be considerable evidence on both sides of this debate. A resolution of this problem was proposed by Lavie (1995) who found evidence that whether selection is early or late seems to depend on the overall attentional demand of a task. When the task does not use up all available attention there is spare capacity which can be used for other processing. We shall return to these ideas after we have considered how attention is directed in visual search and examined how attention is directed to environmental stimuli.

3.7 DIRECTING THE SPOTLIGHT OF VISUAL ATTENTION

The way that selective processing is directed and controlled has been addressed in numerous studies on vision. Posner (1980) said 'attention can be likened to a spotlight that enhances the efficiency of the detection of events within its beam' (p. 173). The spotlight analogy suggests that objects or events in the beam of visual attention will be highlighted for processing and easily detected, whereas those outside the beam will not be. When we search the visual environment we can make an eye movement, or saccade, to direct the focus of visual attention to a location if there is something there we wish to know about. This movement is overt, and it is obvious to others where you are looking. Usually where we are attending coincides with where we are looking, because when we fixate on an item the fovea (the most sensitive part of the eye) is directed to the area of interest. However, we may also attend to something 'out of the corner of our eye', without making an eye movement. If you fixate your gaze here – *** – you are still able to make judgements about the page layout, surrounding colours, shapes and so on. In this case you are intentionally directing, or orienting, your attention in an endogenous way, using top-down control. This type of orientation of attention is covert (hidden), because where your eyes are directed does not reveal where you are attending. However, sometimes, despite intentionally attending to something, for example reading in the garden, the attention spotlight may be captured exogenously by a sudden movement or change in the visual environment such as an apple falling from a nearby tree. Posner wanted to understand more about the way visual attention is controlled and directed.

Posner's original experiments (e.g. Posner *et al.*, 1980; Posner, 1980) were aimed at understanding the processes underlying the orienting of visual attention, and measured the effects of providing participants with a visual *cue* which indicated the probability of the location where

Key Term

Saccade
The movement of the eyes during which information uptake is suppressed. Between saccades the eye makes fixations during which there is information uptake at the fixated area.

Overt attentional orienting
Making an eye movement to attend to a location.

Fixation
When the fovea of the eye dwells on a location in visual space, during which time information is collected.

Orienting
In the spotlight model of visual attention this is attention to regions of space that does not depend upon eye movements.

Covert attentional orienting
Orienting attention without making any movement of the eyes.

a visual target would appear. Two types of cue were used; a *central cue*, presented at the central fixation point, which was an arrow pointing left or right; or a *peripheral cue*, which was a brief illumination of a box presented to the left or right, in peripheral vision away from the fixation point. The task was simple. Participants fixated the centre of the visual display and responded as quickly as possible when they detected a target which would be presented either to the left or right side of the fixation point. No eye movements were allowed, so attention would have to be covertly directed. Results showed that valid cues produced a faster response than neutral cues and invalid cues produced slower responses than neutral cues. This showed that attention could be covertly directed in the absence of eye movements. Posner *et al.* (1980) manipulated the likelihood that the cue was a valid indicator of target location. Participants were told that there was a 20 per cent, 50 per cent or 80 per cent chance that the cue was a valid indicator of which side the target would be presented. So, when participants knew the cued location was only 20 per cent valid they should have been able to voluntarily direct attention to the opposite side. Performance in trials with a central cue showed that participants could ignore cues likely to be invalid and direct attention to the other side of visual space. However, participants were unable to ignore the effect of peripheral cues; they could not voluntarily prevent attention being drawn to the cued location.

Posner (1980) interpreted these results as evidence for two attention systems. First, an endogenous system which can be controlled intentionally by the subjects' expectations and is used to direct attention in the central cueing condition, and second, an exogenous system which is not under intentional control that, whether a cue is valid or not, automatically draws attention to the location of a change in the visual environment, as in the peripheral cueing condition. The slowing of response due to an invalid peripheral cue suggests that because attention is automatically drawn to the position indicated by the cue it then has had to be intentionally shifted to the actual target location, which takes time.

Posner and Petersen (1990) extended Posner's original idea of separate endogenous and exogenous systems to include three components of controlling attention. To move attention from one location to another it is necessary to *disengage* it from the current location, *shift* it to the desired location and then *engage* it on the new visual stimulus. Studies of patients with visual neglect have shown that they have difficulty engaging attention on the neglected side of space (see Chapter 4). Extending the work of Posner and colleagues with the analysis of many other studies (including evidence from brain-scanning studies and neuropsychological patients), Corbetta and Schulman (2002) proposed two interacting attention systems. One a bottom-up, stimulus-driven pathway involved in exogenous attention which is specialised for detecting unexpected behaviourally relevant stimuli, such as the falling apple. This pathway can interrupt the other pathway which is involved in the top-down, goal-directed preparation and control of attention involved in endogenous attention. In this way attention can

Key Term

Gaze-mediated orienting
An exogenous shift of attention following the direction of gaze of a face presented at fixation.

be captured by environmental changes that might be important, and this is of obvious evolutionary advantage. Recent evidence has begun to suggest that central cueing by an arrow can sometimes trigger automatic attention shifts even if it is uninformative, and also that the orienting of visual attention can be triggered by the direction of gaze of a face presented at fixation (Galfano *et al.*, 2012). This phenomenon is known as gaze-mediated orienting and allows us to share attention with a person we see looking at something. Shared attention is one example of the role of orienting attention in everyday life (Box 3.1).

Box 3.1   Shared attention

When another person directs their gaze it provides information to those who observe it. A shift of the eyes may mean they have detected something of interest or importance. Infants are sensitive to gaze direction from only about four months old and, in monkeys, the superior temporal sulcus (STS) is known to respond to the orientation of the head and direction of gaze (Perret *et al.*, 1985). It seems that directing one's gaze to the location

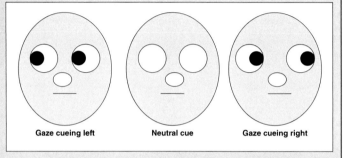

Figure 3.5   Schematic faces similar to those used by Friesen and Kingstone (1998) which triggered reflexive, automatic, exogenous orienting responses in the direction of eye gaze.

where one sees another move their eyes may be evolutionarily important; it enables sharing attention. To test this idea, Friesen and Kingstone (1998) used stimuli similar to those shown in Figure 3.5 in a modification of the standard Posner task, but participants were told that the direction of gaze was not in any way predictive of the location at which a target could appear. However, RT to targets congruent with gaze direction showed an early, short-lived facilitation. There was no cost when the target appeared at the uncued location.

Related experiments using photographed faces by Driver *et al.* (1999) also found an

effect of congruency and additionally that even when the participants were told that the target was four times more likely to appear in the opposite direction to gaze they were unable to ignore gaze direction. Only after about 700 ms could attention be intentionally redirected. These results suggest shared attention is based on gaze perception, and looking where another person looks is fully automatic because it is impossible to intentionally override the tendency to briefly attend to where another person looks. This has recently been confirmed by Galfano *et al.* (2012).

Key Term

Modality
The processing system specific to one of the senses, such as vision, hearing or touch.

3.8 CROSS-MODAL CUEING OF ATTENTION

So far we have been concerned with attention processes within a single modality, such as vision or hearing. However, we live in a world of objects that have both visual and auditory properties, as well as other properties such as what they feel, smell or taste like. Experiments on attention have investigated cross-modal effects on orienting spatial attention, for example between seeing and hearing. In an early experiment, Spence and Driver (1996) used a cross-modal version of Posner's cueing task. Results showed that participants could split auditory and visual attention in certain conditions, but when targets were expected on the same side of space for both modalities, the orienting effects were greatest.

In another experiment, Spence and Read (2003) asked participants to shadow triplets of two-syllable words, presented from either of two loudspeakers (placed either to the front or to the side), whilst trying to ignore speech from an irrelevant, intermediate location. At the same time, the participants were required to drive along a busy road using a driving simulator. Participants found it easier to shadow words coming from in front of them, that is when their visual attention was directed in the same location as the to-be-attended auditory message.

Clearly, this kind of research may have direct application to complex everyday monitoring situations. Ho and Spence (2005) investigated the possible benefits of using spatial auditory warning signals in another simulated driving task. They reasoned that cross-modal links in exogenous spatial attention between vision and audition would facilitate the orienting of attention to a cued direction in space. They discovered that drivers reacted more rapidly to a critical driving event behind them, although these were seen indirectly via the rear-view mirror, when they were preceded by a valid auditory warning cue from the rear, rather than when the warning signal came from the opposite direction (the front). The results suggest that drivers associate what they see in the rear-view mirror with space behind them rather than in front of them, although this is where the visual information is actually presented. Again, the lesser effect of auditory warning cues to a critical event happening in front may be due to the focus of visual attention being usually directed in front while driving.

Other studies of cross-modal links in orienting attention have shown that vision is usually the dominant sense. This can lead to illusions, such as the 'ventriloquist effect'. When the ventriloquist speaks without moving his mouth, but synchronises the movements of the dummy's mouth with the words, it appears as if the speech is coming from location of the dummy's mouth. Driver and Spence (1994) manipulated the spatial relationship between the words we see and the words we hear. They found that when lip-read and auditory words were at the same location, performance was better than when visual and auditory information came from opposite sides of space. It appears that when endogenous attention is oriented to a spatial location, selection of both modalities is enhanced. This effect is evident in the cinema when the voice of a speaking person appears to emanate from the lips of that person – as two characters converse, their voices seem to come from them in turn; however,

Figure 3.6 The ventriloquist effect. Vision tends to predominate over hearing in competing for our attention.

Source: Shutterstock.

if you look away from the screen, the voices come from the sound system.

Vision is usually the dominant sense and evidence from vision is taken as the most reliable, but in different circumstances other sensory modalities may be the most appropriate, for example, we feel to 'see' if there is a chip on the rim of a glass. Visual attention can also be directed to different levels of analysis (Box 3.2). Links across modalities have been demonstrated between all combinations of senses and affect both endogenous (voluntary, goal-driven) and exogenous (involuntary, stimulus-driven) orienting (see Spence, 2010, for a review).

Box 3.2　Local–global (seeing the wood for the trees)

Attention can be directed to either the global or local level of objects. We can attend to a tree or its leaves, but not both at once. Navon (1977) used compound letters in which the global and local elements were congruent or incongruent (Figure 3.7). He found that response to global identity was unaffected by congruency, but response to local (small letters) identity was interfered with by the global (large letter) identity, which suggests attention is directed to coarse global properties prior to fine-grain analysis of local properties. Try this for yourself.

EEEEE	HHHHHH
E	H
E	H
EEEE	HHHH
E	H
E	H
EEEEE	HHHHHH
Congruent	Incongruent

Figure 3.7　Stimuli of the type used by Navon (1977).

3.9 VISUAL SEARCH

What about searching a cluttered visual environment? Often we are looking for something specific, such as a product on the supermarket shelf or a familiar face in a crowded street. And although we are surrounded by multiple sources of sensory information we observe a coherent scene – the traffic may be moving around us but we see 'a red bus moving', 'green grass below', and 'blue sky above' rather than 'red sky moving' a 'blue bus above' and 'green sky below'. We shall now consider experiments addressed at understanding how attention is involved in visual search and that aim to explain how one object can be selected from amongst other distracting or irrelevant objects.

An important step toward understanding this was taken by Treisman and Gelade (1980) who proposed a feature integration theory (FIT) of attention. According to FIT, attention is the 'glue' that sticks the features of objects together. We have already mentioned the binding problem, which is concerned with how different properties of a stimulus are correctly combined in the introduction and in studies of subliminal priming. The initial assumption of FIT was that different sensory features are coded by specialised independent sub-systems or 'modules' and each module forms a feature map for the dimensions of the feature it encodes. Colours are represented on the feature map for colour, while lines of different orientations are represented on the orientation map. Detection of individual features that are represented on all the different maps takes place without the need for attention, in parallel, but if a conjunction (or binding) of features is required the separate features must be combined. A conjunction of features can be achieved three ways. First, features that have been encoded on the feature maps may fit into predicted object 'frames', according to stored knowledge; for example we know that buses are red and the sky is blue, so that if the colours red and blue are active at the same time, we are unlikely to combine red with sky and blue with bus. Second, attention may select within a 'master-map of locations' that represents where all the features are located but not which features are where. When attention is focused on one location in the master map, it allows retrieval of the features present at that location and creates a temporary representation of all the object's properties in an 'object file'. The contents of the object file are then used to recognise the object by matching it to stored knowledge in memory. Treisman (1988) assumed that conscious perception depends on matching the contents of the object file with stored descriptions in long-term memory, allowing recognition. Third, features may combine without attention on their own, but sometimes this conjunction may be inaccurate and give rise to an 'illusory conjunction', for example there may be a 'red X' and a 'green Y', but a 'red Y' reported. You can try feature search and conjunction search using the examples in Figure 3.8.

> **Key Term**
>
> **Conjunction**
> A term from feature integration theory of attention that describes a target defined by at least two separable features, such as a red O amongst green O's and red T's.

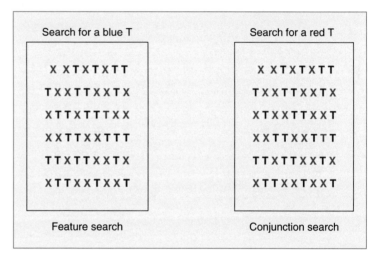

Figure 3.8 Examples of the kind of stimuli used in feature integration tasks.

3.10 EVIDENCE FOR AND AGAINST FIT

Treisman and Gelade (1980) found that for conjunction search the time taken to find a target increased linearly with the number of distractors in the display. However, if the target was defined by a unique feature, search time was independent of the number of

Key Term

Pop-out
An object will pop out from a display if it is detected in parallel and is different from all other items in the display.

distractors. This difference in search times was taken as evidence that when a conjunction is required to identify the target, a serial search is necessary in which focal attention moves to each object location in turn, conjoining features at each location until the target is found, when the search stops. This is called a serial self-terminating search. However, when a target is defined by just one distinctive feature, that feature is available on its feature map and calls attention to itself, resulting in pop-out. Treisman (1986) argued that if attention is necessary for detecting a conjunction of features, then a pre-cue for target location should eliminate the need for serial search of any other display locations. In contrast, as feature search is parallel across all display locations, a pre-cue to target location should provide no benefit. Results showed that a valid pre-cue speeded conjunction search, but had no effect on feature search. This evidence reinforced the suggestion that attention to location is important in conjunction search.

There are problems with the original conception of FIT. Attention is often directed to objects rather than a specific location. Neisser and Becklen (1975) superimposed two moving scenes and found that it was easy for participants to segregate the two movies, attending to one at the expense of the other. A similar effect can be observed when you watch the credits rolling at the end of a film – you can either watch the background scene or read the credits, but not both. Here attention is directed to different 'objects' at the same location – so, contrary to original FIT, location is not the sole factor important for selective attention. Furthermore, 'pop-out' can occur for groups of objects.

Duncan and Humphreys (1989, 1992) put forward attentional engagement theory, which stresses the importance of similarity not only between targets but also between distractors. They demonstrated that similarity is an important grouping factor and, depending on how easily targets and distractors form perceptual groups, visual search will be more or less efficient. For example Duncan and Humphreys manipulated the type of distractors and their relationship to the target – the participant might have to search for an upright L amongst rotated Ts, the Ts might be homogeneous (i.e. all rotated the same way), or heterogeneous (i.e. all at different rotations). According to FIT the elementary features of objects are coded pre-attentively in parallel, but the conjunctions necessary to determine if the features made up an L or a T would require serial search with focal attention. However, Duncan and Humphreys showed that in some conditions conjunction search was unaffected by display size, and when all distractors were homogeneous, thus allowing efficient texture segregation, absent responses could actually be faster than present responses. They proposed that selection was at the level of the whole display and that, in this case, visual search for the target is based in rejection of the complete non-target group.

Other experiments have shown that response relationship between targets and distractors is an important factor in the efficiency of target selection. The amount of interference depends on the spatial proximity of the distractor letters to the target letter and the nature of the task.

Laberge (1983) showed that the spotlight of attention could change its width depending on whether participants were told to focus on a specific letter within a word or to attend to the whole word. Eriksen and Eriksen (1974) showed that when letters flanking a target letter share a compatible response with the target there is less interference than when the flanking letters have an incompatible response. This result is evidence for parallel processing to the 'late' level of response selection. Further, they found that the amount of interference from incompatible distractors was dependent on the separation of the distractors from the target. Eriksen and St. James (1986) suggested that visual attention was like an adjustable zoom lens, taking in more or less information according to task demands. If the zoom was set wide, letters either side of the target would be processed and cause interference, but if set to a narrow beam, distractors would not be processed and so not interfere with the response to the target.

These results are inconsistent with the original FIT which proposed identification after serial search for conjunctions and a fixed-focus attention beam. Treisman (1999) proposed a broader conception of FIT. She suggested that pop-out and texture segregation occur when attention is distributed over large parts of the visual display, with a broad 'window' rather than a narrow spotlight. When the window is large, feature maps are integrated at a global level but for accurate localisation and for conjoining features the window must narrow its focus. If attention is narrowly focused then stimuli in the unattended areas will not be processed. Within this model the 'what' pathway includes the motion and colour maps and 'where' pathways are those coding location. Treisman also introduced the idea of connections that could inhibit non-target properties in a display. However, the more similarity there is between targets and distractors the less effective an inhibitory strategy becomes, and this would account for Duncan and Humphreys' results. Treisman (1993) also argued that selection could be early or late depending on the concurrent load on perception; when perceptual load is low, late selection can occur, but if perceptual load is high, selection will be early. This idea was developed by Lavie (1995) as we shall see next.

3.11 THE IMPORTANCE OF TASK DIFFERENCES

Kahneman and Treisman (1984) suggested that the difference between experiments supporting early selection and those suggesting late selection is due to differences in the overall demand for attention in an experimental task. They distinguished between selective filtering and selective set paradigms. Tasks such as dichotic listening or conjunction search involve selective filtering, which is more complex and attentionally demanding than a selective set task such as the experiments by Eriksen and Eriksen (1974), which only required detecting the presence or absence of a letter from a small target set.

> **Key Term**
>
> **Selective filtering**
> An attentional task that requires selection of one source of information for further processing and report in a difficult task such as dichotic listening or visual search for a conjunction of properties.
>
> **Selective set**
> An attentional task requiring detection of a target from a small set of possibilities.

As selective filtering tasks tend to provide evidence for early selection and selective set tasks tend to provide evidence for late selection, perhaps the nature of the task is an important factor in how attention seems to operate.

Lavie (1995) proposed that the ability to focus narrowly and exclusively on a target in visual search depends on the perceptual load, or overall demand on attention of the whole task. She suggested that 'a physical distinction is a necessary but not sufficient condition for selective processing' (Lavie, 1995: 452.) Although a clear physical distinction, such as colour or a particular voice, can allow relevant stimuli to be selected from amongst irrelevant stimuli, this differentiation does not necessarily prevent processing of irrelevant stimuli. If there is enough attention available, stimuli other than the target can be processed. So, depending on the demand, or perceptual load, of the overall task, more or less of the available information will be able to be processed. Once the limit of attention is exceeded, selection will be required. Here, Lavie is using a 'capacity' account of attention rather than thinking of attention as a bottleneck in a sequence of stages.

The capacity view of attention is similar to that proposed by Kahneman (1973) and is useful when considering how multiple tasks are simultaneously performed. According to the capacity view of attention, when high-priority, relevant stimuli do not use up all the available capacity, irrelevant stimuli will, unintentionally and automatically, capture any spare capacity. So, studies that show evidence of late selection such as those by Eriksen and colleagues discussed above, may do so because the overall task has low load. The task does not demand all the available processing capacity, so capacity is left over to process distractors through to the response stage and cause interference suggestive of late selection. In experiments where there is high load and all the attentional capacity is demanded for processing relevant information, there is no spare capacity remaining to process irrelevant distractors – producing an early selection result. Load theory has received much empirical support and not only appears to be a resolution to the 'early–late' debate, but also provides an important theoretical link between attention, perception and memory (see Lavie, 2005, 2006, for reviews).

3.12 ATTENTION, WORKING MEMORY AND DISTRACTION

De Fockert *et al.* (2001) combined two unrelated tasks, one requiring selective visual attention and the other a working-memory task. The selective attention task required the participants to classify written names as politicians or pop-stars while ignoring the face over which the word was written. Half the names and faces were congruent, for example the name of a pop-star written over the face of a pop-star. The other half were incongruent, for example the name of a pop-star written over the face of a politician. Participants were required to ignore the faces and respond only to the names, classifying them as pop-star or politician. The selective attention task was embedded in a working-memory task that required remembering five digits and then deciding if a specific digit had been in the memory list. The working-memory task had two levels of difficulty. When the selective attention task was combined with the difficult working-memory task, RT to the name was slower in the incongruent condition, showing that when working memory was more heavily loaded, selective visual attention was less efficient and unable to ignore the irrelevant stimulus dimension. Concurrent fMRI measuring activity in the fusiform face area of the brain showed that activity was greater in the high- than the low-memory-load condition. Similar evidence for the relationship between working memory and selective attention was found by Conway *et al.* (2001) who showed that people with a low digit span (a measure of short-term working memory capacity) are more likely to hear their name on the unattended channel in a replication of Moray's (1959) dichotic listening experiment. They also found that low memory span correlated with distractibility, and reasoned that breakthrough may result from inability to ignore the unattended channel.

More recently, Forster and Lavie (2007) investigated how this type of laboratory finding relates to everyday-life distractibility. Their participants completed a questionnaire which measured everyday slips of action and failures of attention. When tested for the effects of distractors on response competition in a visual search experiment, Forster and Lavie found that people who scored highly on the questionnaire experienced greater interference from distractors but only when it was combined with a low perceptual load. Under high perceptual load all people showed less distractor interference, even those who reported being highly distractible in everyday life. This shows that people fail to ignore distractors in conditions of low perceptual load and fail to recognise distractor objects in conditions of high perceptual load, which has implications for everyday behaviours (see Lavie, 2010, for a review).

3.13 ATTENTION AND COGNITIVE CONTROL

How do we prepare to detect or respond to some stimuli and ignore or suppress others? How do we carry out sequences of actions to achieve a goal? In everyday life we go about mundane activities such as making a cup of coffee without necessarily realising how complex they really are. This complexity is evident when we make errors, for example, in making coffee we may put sugar in the milk jug, or pour water on the coffee without boiling it. We may go upstairs to fetch something and do something else instead. In all these cases it is necessary to set goals, to monitor and update them as the actions are carried out and avoid being distracted by starting to do other things we had not planned. Norman and Shallice (1986) proposed a model for the 'willed' control of action that distinguishes between routine behaviours, which are largely automatic, such as making coffee and non-routine behaviours such as performing the Stroop task you did earlier. A routine behaviour requires little monitoring; we do it almost without thinking about it, with the completion of each step in the sequence automatically triggering the next step. However, the price paid for this low level of control is that we sometimes make a slip of action. Norman and Shallice's model can account for everyday slips of action. Reason (1979) studied the diaries of 35 volunteers who recorded their slips of action over a two-week period. He recorded 433 errors which he classified (Box 3.3). Such errors usually occurred

Box 3.3 Some everyday slips of action

Examples of action slips from Reason's (1979) diary study:

- 'I put my shaving cream on my toothbrush.'
- 'I put the butter on the draining board and two dirty plates in the fridge.'
- 'I was about to step into the bath when I discovered I still had my underclothes on.'

- 'I picked up my coat to go out when the phone rang. I answered it and then went out without my coat on.'
- 'I went upstairs to the bedroom but when I got there I couldn't remember what I came for.'

Can you think of situations where you have made action slips? How could you explain what caused them to happen?

when familiar, largely automatic tasks were being performed. Norman (1981) also studied 'actions not as planned' and argued they were a result of different types of failure in the triggering, selection and application of action schema. Errors could, for example arise from failing to form or remember an intention or to faulty activation of a schema when unintentional activation captures behaviour.

For non-routine behaviour, Norman and Shallice (1986) propose that attention is necessary to achieve the behavioural goal. Such situations include those that demand planning or decision making; situations that require error correction; situations where the responses are not well learned or contain novel sequences of actions; dangerous or technically difficult situations; and those that require overcoming a habitual response or temptation.

In this model, information from the perceptual system activates schema stored in long-term memory (LTM). The most active schema then takes control of the action system. Schema activation takes place unconsciously and is controlled by an automatic system, called the contention scheduler that allows automatic actions to run smoothly. However, the automatic system must be interrupted if our goal is to perform behaviour which is different from the one that is automatically activated. If the schema most strongly activated, bottom-up, by an environmental stimulus always took control of action, it would be impossible to enact goal-directed actions without being interrupted by

Key Term

Contention scheduler
A component of Norman and Shallice's (1986) model which is responsible for the semi-automatic control of schema activation to ensure that schema run off in an orderly way.

stimuli that activate well-learned responses. This is what has happened when you intend to do one task but find yourself doing something else – a slip of action has occurred. To allow goal-directed behaviour, Norman and Shallice propose a supervisory attentional system (SAS) that sends top-down activation to the goal-relevant schema that allows it to take control of action. Figure 3.9 illustrates how an SAS could intervene to explain performance of the Stroop task. As goals change, so too must the activation of the goal-relevant schema. In addition, once a goal has been achieved it must be cancelled so that it is not repeated.

If you return to the list of Stroop colour words in Figure 3.3 you can try goal switching by alternately naming the colour of the ink and naming the word on alternating trials. You should find that shifting goals between tasks, updating and monitoring are very demanding on attention and short-term working memory. Norman and Shallice's model can also account for the behaviour of patients with frontal damage, who demonstrate frontal lobe syndrome (Baddeley, 1993), also discussed in Chapters 7 and 9.

Miyake *et al.* (2000) proposed three executive functions; inhibition (as required when naming the ink colour in the Stroop task), shifting (required when switching attention rapidly between tasks), and updating (which refers to updating the contents of working memory and allows us to monitor progress of an ongoing task). Evidence from positron emission tomography (PET) has revealed that there are different patterns of pre-frontal cortex activity according to which aspects of control are being done. Collette *et al.* (2005) found that all tasks involved activity within different regions of pre-frontal cortex and that all tasks involved activation of the right intraparietal sulcus, which they propose

| **Key Term** |

Frontal lobe syndrome
The pattern of deficits exhibited by patients with damage to the frontal lobes. These patients are distractible, have difficulty setting, maintaining and changing behavioural goals, and are poor at planning sequences of actions.

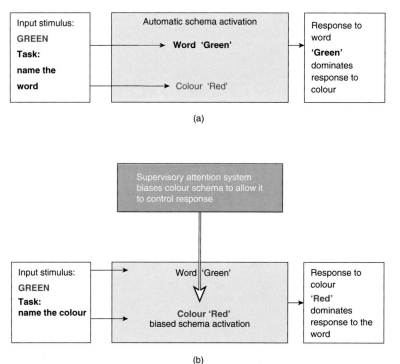

Figure 3.9 A simplified explanation of how Norman and Shallice's (1986) model explains automatic behaviour and behaviour controlled by the SAS in the Stroop task. (a) Automatic response. When the task is to read a word the activation for word naming is stronger than that for colour naming and automatically takes control of response. (b) Controlled response. When the task is to name the colour the SAS sends activation to the colour schema. This allows the colour schema to overcome the activation of the schema for word response and the colour is named.

Figure 3.10   Multitasking.

Source: Shutterstock.

is important for selection of relevant stimuli and the inhibition of irrelevant stimuli. The left superior parietal sulcus is involved in switching attention and integrating information and the left pre-frontal cortex is involved in monitoring ongoing activity and temporal organisation. Other experiments using transcranial magnetic stimulation (TMS) have indicated that dual task performance also activates the dorso-lateral prefrontal cortex (Johnson and Zartorre, 2006). The frontal lobes, where executive processing is located, are very complex and are important for many aspects of executive control.

3.14 COMBINING TASKS

In everyday life we are familiar with the problem of trying to do two tasks at once and know that sometimes we have to stop doing one task because it is impossible to do them both without making a mistake. Often we find ourselves having to 'multitask' (Figure 3.10).

We have already discussed a capacity view of attentional resources when we met Lavie's (1995) load theory. When we attempt to combine tasks, attentional capacity can be allocated alternately to one or other of the tasks or we can attempt to share it between the tasks. However, although some tasks are difficult to combine, others' combinations are much easier. Posner and Boies (1971) attempted to discover why this is so. In their experiment participants were required to combine a visual matching task, which required a key response, with a tone detection task, which also required pressing a key. Reaction time to detect a tone depended on when it was presented during the visual task. If the tone arrived while the warning signal was being presented or while the participant was waiting for the first letter, there was no effect on tone detection. However, if the tone was presented at the same time as either of the letters, participants were slower to respond to it. The slowest response was when the tone was presented during the interval between letter presentations while the participant was attending to the first letter in preparation for response to the second. It appeared that, in this case, both tasks were competing for the same attentional resource. During waiting times of the visual task, attention was free to deal with tone detection, but when the visual task also demanded attention, resources were shared leaving less attention for detecting or responding to the tone. These results appeared to show that the same resource was being shared between the visual and auditory task. To test this, Mcleod (1978) changed the response required to the tone from key-pressing to saying 'bip'. With this response combination there was no interference between tasks no matter when the tone was presented.

This result showed that when the response systems for the two tasks were different, interference disappeared, which is inconsistent with the idea that visual task and auditory task shared the same resource.

Rather than a general limitation on attentional resource capacity, the interference between tasks seemed to depend on how each stimulus was linked with its response, or *stimulus–response compatibility*. Shaffer (1975) showed that skilled typists could copy-type and simultaneously do a shadowing task, but could not audio-type and read aloud. In these experiments copy-typing could be combined with shadowing because the processing route from the shadowed input to the speech output used a different processing system to that used for mapping the visually presented words onto finger movements. It appeared that when there was no competition for specific processing resources or stimulus response mappings, tasks could be combined more easily. However, were all aspects of these tasks really being performed at once? Welford's (1952) experiments on the psychological refractory period (PRP) were taken as evidence for a central limit on processing. Greenwald and Shulman (1973) showed that the PRP, as in the experiments mentioned above, was also affected by stimulus response compatibility. However, further tightly controlled studies (e.g. Pashler, 1990, 1994; Lien *et al.*, 2002) have detected PRP effects even in tasks that do have stimulus response compatibility. The probability is that experiments that appear to show no interference between tasks are not sufficiently sensitive to detect small, but reliable costs in concurrent task performance. Tasks may more easily be combined when there is no requirement for absolute synchronicity, allowing attention to be rapidly switched between the tasks. This may have been happening in tasks such as typing while shadowing in Shaffer's (1975) experiment. What about other real-world activities, like driving?

Laboratory tasks are usually simple, presented in a predictable order and have simple responses. Levy *et al.* (2006) wanted to determine whether central-bottleneck phenomena, like PRP, would generalise to everyday tasks such as driving. Using a driving simulator, participants drove along a winding road, using a steering wheel and pedals, following a lead car that travelled at varying speeds. The lead car occasionally braked, requiring the participants to brake. This was the 'braking task'. This task is a simple reaction time task (SRT), as the only response to seeing the braking lights of the lead car is to press the simulator brake pedal – no choice is required. In addition, participants performed an intermittent choice response task (CRT) in which they had to indicate, with either a manual or vocal response, whether a brief auditory or visual stimulus was presented only once or twice. Manipulations of CRT task were the modality of presentation, visual or auditory; modality of response, vocal or manual; and stimulus onset asynchrony (SOA) between the choice and braking tasks in the dual-task condition. There were two types of trial: single-task trials, where each task was performed alone; and dual-task trials, where the tasks were performed concurrently.

Box 3.4   Attentional blink

Attentional blink (AB) is the phenomenon that the second of two targets cannot be detected when it appears close in time to the first. It is used to study the effects of attention distribution over time. In all AB experiments stimuli are presented at the same spatial location so that it is only time that differentiates one stimulus from the next. A typical experiment (e.g. Raymond *et al.*, 1992) uses an RSVP task in which a rapid series of visual presentations, at a rate of between 6 and 20 items per second, are shown to the participant. The target in the first half of the visual stream might be a white X, then the task is to detect if an X appears in the second half of the stream. Results show that when the first target is correctly identified participants are very likely to miss the second target if it is presented between 100 and 500 ms afterwards. At longer intervals the second target is much more likely to be detected. Originally AB was thought to be due to attentional resource limitations (Chun and Potter, 2001) or suppression of temporally close distractors (Olivers, 2007). However, Nieuwenstein *et al.* (2009) have evidence to suggest that AB results from difficulty in engaging attention twice within a short period of time. For an online demonstration of AB go to Shapiro *et al.* (2009).

The choice task showed large effects of stimulus and response modalities similar to those found by experiments mentioned previously. However, the most important finding in this experiment was that the braking task reaction times increased as SOA between the choice and braking tasks was reduced, showing that the standard PRP effect generalises even to a well-practised everyday task – braking in response to the onset of the leading car's brake lights. Although the choice task was easy, it still produced a dual-task decrement when combined with the braking task. This interference between tasks was interpreted by Levy *et al.* (2006) as evidence for a central bottleneck in processing and therefore that vehicle braking is not 'automatic'. It shows that even a 'trivial' additional task can slow the braking response and is consequently of importance for driving safety.

It is now well established that concurrent activities lead to deterioration in driving performance. For example Strayer and Drews (2007) using an event-related potential (ERP) measure found that the P300 wave, which is a neurophysiological indication of attentional activity, was reduced by 50 per cent when mobile phone use was combined with an urgent response to the onset of brake lights to the car in front. When two stimuli appear in rapid succession the second stimulus may be missed. This is called attentional blink (Box 3.4).

3.15 PRACTICE, AUTOMATICITY AND SKILL

Schafer's typists were highly skilled. Their ability to copy-type had become *automatic* through years of practice. So, what happens with practice? We have talked about automatic and controlled processes throughout this chapter but we have not yet discussed this distinction in detail. Shiffrin and Schneider (1977) proposed a two-process theory of controlled and automatic processing. They conducted a series of experiments in which participants were given thousands of trials using a multiple-frame visual search paradigm. In the first frame, one, two or four stimuli were presented, which were to be remembered – the memory set. Next there was a fixation dot followed by a succession of 20 frames in which one, or none of the memory set was presented and the participant was to decide whether any of the memory set was present in the display. The crucial experimental manipulation was the mapping between the stimuli of the memory set and their responses. In the consistent mapping condition, targets were always consonants and distractors were always digits. In the varied mapping condition, both the memory set and distractors were a mixture of letters and digits. Results showed that with consistent mapping, search time was virtually independent of both the number of items in the memory set and the number of items in the display, as if search is taking place in parallel – reflecting 'automatic processing'. By contrast, in the varied mapping condition, participants were slower to detect targets and RTs increased with the number of distractors in the display – reflecting attention demanding 'controlled processing'.

Letters and digits belong to different categorical groups and have well-learned habitual responses. To test if, with practice, it was possible for participants to develop automatic processing for a novel arbitrary distinction, Shiffrin and Schneider did another experiment. They divided the consonants into two groups, B to L and Q to Z. Using consistent mapping, one set of consonants was always the target set and the other set was always a distractor. After over 2,100 trials, performance began to resemble that of the letter–digit experiment. Search became fast and independent of the number of display items, the hallmark of automaticity. Now that automaticity was established the response mappings were reversed, i.e. letters that had once been targets became distractors and vice versa. There was a dramatic change in performance. To begin with, subjects were unable to 'change set', responses were very slow, error prone, with many intrusions from the distractor set and performance was limited by both memory set size and number of distractors. However, after a further 2,400 trials of practice, participants were performing at the same level as they had been after 1,500 trials in their original training. It was as if the previously learned automatic response had to be unlearned before the reversed set could become automatic. These experiments and many others provide support for two types of processes involving attention; one type that runs off automatically beyond conscious control and another that can be quickly adapted by conscious intentions. Furthermore, they show that, over thousands of trials, automaticity can gradually develop and that once a process has become automatic it does not draw on limited attentional resources. There are, however, some serious difficulties with this view and the distinction is not as

Key Term

Consistent mapping
A task in which distractors are never targets and targets are never distracters, so that there is a consistent relationship between the stimuli and the responses to be made to them.

Varied mapping
The condition in which a stimulus and its response are changed from trial to trial.

clear-cut as once thought. Also, there needs to be some explanation of what actually happens when automaticity develops.

Moors and De Houwer (2006) proposed that automatic processes have four features; they are goal unrelated, unconscious, fast and efficient, i.e. they place little or no demand on attentional resources or capacity. They suggest that rather than there being a clear-cut distinction between automatic and controlled processes, the difference is graded. This view is supported by a review of neuro-imaging studies. Saling and Phillips (2007) found that the development of automaticity involved a shift in brain activity from cortical areas towards sub-cortical areas. In particular, Jansma *et al.* (2001) showed, using fMRI, that during the development of automaticity in a consistent mapping task there is a reduction in activity in frontal areas associated with executive control. Despite problems of definition, the terms automatic and controlled processing are widely used, as they seem to capture some fundamental difference between processing types.

We have seen that, with practice, some tasks can become automatic and are involved in skilled performance. Skills can be cognitive, such as problem solving; perceptuo-motor, such as typing; or a combination of both cognitive and perceptuo-motor, such as driving. We may also use the term 'expert' to describe their performance. In all cases it is 'practice makes perfect'. Newell and Rosenbloom (1981) showed that the learning curve for skill can be described as a power law; although we never stop improving with practice the initial rapid improvement gradually becomes less and less as we become more skilled (Figure 3.11).

When an expert driver stops at a red light, the stimulus automatically triggers a sequence of actions that brings the car to a halt. The expert driver can drive and hold a conversation. However, for a novice driver the red light does not trigger a single process but rather a set of actions to do with braking – clutch control, brake control, gear disengagement, possibly with some verbal self-instruction. They cannot concurrently have a conversation. Often, when attempting a novel and difficult task we hold the instructions in working memory to tell ourselves what to do. So, as a skill is learned, performance changes both qualitatively and quantitatively. One way of thinking about how performance changes with practice

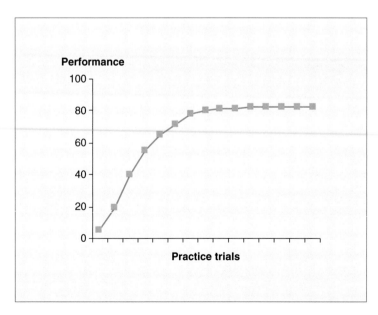

Figure 3.11   The power law of practice.

was proposed by Fitts and Posner (1973). In the first, 'cognitive phase', the learner tries to understand the task and follows instructions. During this phase, performance is error prone and feedback is needed to demonstrate where the learner went wrong. As the learner improves, they enter the 'associative' phase. Now the learner starts to rely more on self-monitoring, and the activity begins to form into larger units of performance and become fluent. At this stage, the task can begin to be combined with another task, like talking, because it has become more automatic. As the component processes of a task become more and more automatic they become less and less under direct conscious control and less likely to be interfered with by other activities or distractions.

Another influential account of expert performance is the 'adaptive control of thought – rational' (ACT-R), put forward by Anderson *et al.* (2004), based on Anderson's earlier ACT* model. This theoretical framework was developed and extended by Anderson *et al.* (2008). ACT-R has four modules, each of which performs its own operations: a retrieval module responsible for maintaining retrieval cues needed to access stored information; an imaginal module involved in transforming problem representations; a goal module that tracks intentions and controls processing; and a procedural module that uses production rules and is the heart of the system.

The procedural module works like a production system. The basic principle underlying production systems is that human cognition can be conceived of as a set of condition–action pairs called productions. The condition specifies a set of data patterns and IF (the condition) elements matching these patterns are in working memory THEN (the action) rule can be applied. For example IF the traffic light is red THEN stop the car. In ACT-R there are three memory types: procedural memory (to which we have no conscious access) and declarative and working memory (to which we do have conscious access). These types of memory are discussed further in Chapters 5 and 6. Working memory contains the information currently available to the system but because working memory has only a limited capacity, consciously maintaining all the steps involved in doing a complex task would overload it – as in the novice driver. However, if only a small amount of information needs to be represented in working memory the system can run more efficiently – as in the expert driver. With practice, rules of the task become procedures. New IF–THEN procedures are formed using knowledge gained in the initial stages of learning and new conditions can become embedded into them. For example, IF the traffic light is red AND it is icy THEN brake gently. This 'proceduralisation' frees up space in working memory because the declarative knowledge no longer needs to be explicitly retrieved. The rules governing behaviour are available to the processing system, but may no longer be available to consciousness. As we become more practised at a task, we gain expertise. We are able to perform the task fluently but cannot explain to someone else exactly how we do it.

Key Term
Production system A computational model based on numerous IF–THEN condition–action rules. IF the rule is represented in working memory THEN the production stored in long-term memory is applied.

Key Term
Procedural knowledge
Unconscious knowledge about how to do something. It includes skills and knowledge that cannot be made explicit but can be demonstrated by performance.

Eliciting knowledge from experts and skilled operators can be extremely difficult; when asked how they do something, they do not know – they 'just do it'. Logan and Crump (2009) found that skilled typists have little explicit knowledge of what their fingers are doing, and Liu *et al.* (2010) point out a paradox in skilled performance. 'Experts spend years acquiring knowledge about their skill, which they use very effectively to support their performance, but have little explicit access to that knowledge' (p. 474). They investigated skilled typists' ability to report knowledge about the layout of keys on a standard keyboard and found they had poor explicit knowledge of key locations. This result could be explained by assuming that years of practice have built up procedural knowledge which is implicit and allows performance of the task but cannot be made available to consciousness.

Once performance is automatic there is evidence that consciously attending to it can actually interfere with performance. Beilock *et al.* (2002) tested expert golfers' putting performance. The golfers were asked to focus their attention on components of the task, such as monitoring the swing and stopping the follow through, in a single task condition and in a dual-task condition in which the golfers putted while doing a tone detection task. Results showed that putting performance was better in the dual-task condition than under the skill-focused condition. The explanation for this is that directing attentional control interferes with the running-off of the automatic process. So, while most of the time we think we should 'pay attention' it appears that sometimes paying attention is detrimental to performance.

SUMMARY

- Attention is limited. It can be viewed as either a limiting step in information processing or as a limited capacity for processing. It comes in a variety of forms.
- Attention operates on functions that are widely distributed across the brain and functions to select prioritise and integrate perceptions and actions.
- Attention is involved in binding features and results in conscious awareness.
- A long debate over the locus at which selection took place, the 'early–late debate', has been resolved by assuming that attentional capacity is allocated flexibly according to overall task demand.
- Concurrent working-memory load interacts with selective attention. Attention may be intentionally controlled or captured automatically.
- With practice, tasks that initially demand attention can become automatic but attending to automatic processes involved in skills can interrupt them.

FURTHER READING

- Driver, J. (2001). A selective review of selective attention research from the past century. *British Journal of Psychology, 92,* 53–78.
- Styles E. A. (2005). *Attention Perception and Memory: an Integrated Introduction.* Hove: Psychology Press.
- Styles E. A. (2006). *The Psychology of Attention* (2nd edn). Hove: Psychology Press.

Chapter 4

Contents

Disorders of perception and attention

Tom Manly and Hayley Ness

4

4.1 INTRODUCTION

In the previous chapters we described the processes involved in perception and attention, and described how we construct an internal representation of the world around us. Given the complexity of these processes, it is not surprising that brain damage can disrupt perception and attention. These can have devastating consequences for peoples' everyday lives. Examining the range and nature of these impairments can also give us useful clues as to the beautiful computational complexity and efficiency of the unimpaired system. To adapt a well-used analogy, a television that is in perfect working order tells you little about *how* it works. When it malfunctions, however, it emits clues as to its underlying structure; if you can hear the sound but not see the picture you know immediately that, at some level, these two functions are handled differently within the system. The hope is that by studying disorders of perception that we can better understand normal function and find better ways to help patients cope with impairments. The emphasis in this chapter is to study the pattern of disorders with relatively little emphasis on the location of functions within particular brain regions. We have taken the view that it is more important to know *how* we perceive than *where* we perceive.

Before we proceed, we would like you to try a demonstration that you may well have done before. In the box below is a dot. Close your left eye and hold the book about 5 cm from your face and look straight at the dot. Then, *without moving your eyes to track the dot*, move the page slowly to the right (to the left if using your left eye).

At some point, the dot will disappear. You have found your blind-spot where your retina meets the optic nerve and is insensitive to light. Now, still with one eye, look back at the complex world around you. Where is the blind spot? How does the world look so complete? One of the most startling perspective shifts we undergo in studying the brain is knowing that all that is 'out there' (from a visual perspective) is light of different intensities and wavelengths bombarding the retina at 299,792,458 metres per second. The world of objects and people and faces and colours and textures that we see are actually reconstructions, or perhaps more accurately, *predictions* by the brain of objects that the light has bounced off on its journey to the retina, based on its knowledge of the world. The section on visual illusions in Chapter 2 provides other good examples.

Most of the disorders discussed in this chapter result from brain injury, which leaves the affected individual with a noticeable deficit. However, the first 'condition' we will consider is a little different. This is the extraordinary case of synaesthesia. Whilst it can begin following an injury to the brain (Fornazzari *et al.*, 2011), many people with synaesthesia have had it for as long as they can remember and regard it as a gift rather than a disability. For the remainder of the chapter we will study other syndromes which have an increasingly specific impact on perception and attention. We will first consider disorders which prevent conscious perception or distort attention, then we will consider disorders which affect the ability to recognise objects, and finally we will discuss disorders which appear to affect the ability to recognise one particular category of object or the ability to encode one particular type of information.

> **Key Term**
>
> **Synaesthesia**
> A condition in which individuals presented with sensory input of one modality consistently and automatically experience a sensory event in a different modality (for example seeing colour on hearing musical notes).

4.2 SYNAESTHESIA

What colour is Monday? How about the number 7? What does blue taste like? For most of us these are ludicrous questions. For a minority of you reading this chapter they will make perfect sense. These readers show synaesthesia, which literally means 'to perceive together'. When presented with a particular stimulus, a person with synaesthesia (synaesthete) will consistently and automatically experience another sensory event, sometimes in the same modality (e.g. both in vision), sometimes in another sense. The most common form is to experience a colour on seeing or hearing a letter, number or word. The triggers of synaesthetic experience are called inducers. Hence, Monday might be yellow, and 7 might be red. Other examples include linking colours with familiar faces, days, or weeks, but also feeling sounds, seeing musical notes, seeing tastes and tasting colours (Baron-Cohen *et al.*, 1996; Carpenter, 2001; Ward, 2013). Many synaesthetes also report that inducers which follow a reliable sequence (e.g. letters of the alphabet, days of the week, months of the year) are experienced in a particular spatial arrangement, for example as segments in an arc projected around the body (Figure 4.1).

The first known report of synaesthesia was in the 1812 dissertation of an Austrian doctor, George Sachs, who described his own colour sensations when exposed to letters and numbers (Jewanski *et al.*, 2009). Although

> **Key Term**
>
> **Synaesthete**
> A person who has the condition synaesthesia.

brought to greater prominence by Galton in the latter years of that century (Galton, 1883), with the rise of behaviourism and its scepticism about subjective reports, it largely fell from scientific favour. In the 1980s a landmark paper by Baron-Cohen *et al.* (1987) brought the topic back into mainstream cognitive psychology. Baron-Cohen responded to an advertisement placed in a psychology journal by a synaesthete called EP who described herself as 'an artist who has experienced the life-long condition of hearing words and sounds in colour'. First, they tested the replicability (reliability) of EP's synaesthetic experiences. She was asked to describe her response to 100 aurally presented words, letters, names and numbers, and a selection of non-words. Ten weeks later and without warning she was retested on the same list. In every case her description matched that on the first test. This 100 per cent replication contrasted with just 17 per cent in a non-synaesthete asked to remember her random responses over just a two-week period. EP's remarkable consistency was achieved despite the fact that the descriptions she provided were much more elaborate than those offered by the control participant (Figure 4.1). For many synaesthetes, the colour induced by the first letter determines the apparent colour of a word. However, when EP was presented with word-like letter strings (called pseudo-words, e.g. "bralbic") her synaesthetic experience was a mix of the colours induced by each letter.

Inducing Item	Description of the induced synaesthetic experience
Moscow	darkish grey with spinach-green, and a pale blue in places
Fear	Mottled light grey, with a touch of soft green and purple
Daniel	deep purple, blue and red, and is shiny
Maria	deep violet blue
Huk (non-word)	The combination of the colours of the component letters; dark red (H), yellow (U), and purple (K)
H	Dark red
M	Blue-black
Q	Greeny yellow

Part (a)
Some examples of the very consistent colour descriptions offered by synaesthete EP in response to the sound of words, names, non-words and letters.

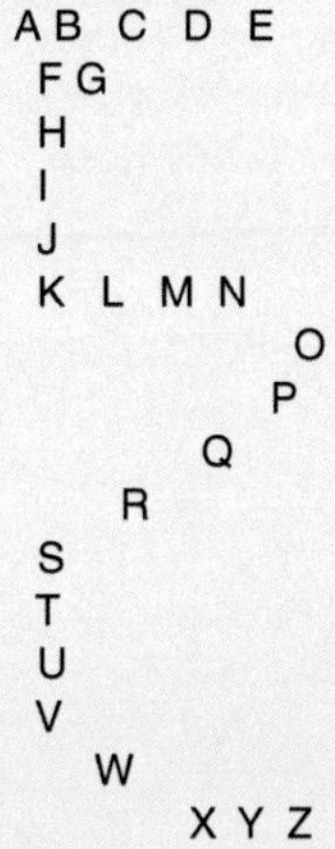

A B C D E
 F G
 H
 I
 J
 K L M N
             O
            P
          Q
        R
 S
 T
 U
 V
   W
      X Y Z

Part (b) The spatial arrangement of the letters of the alphabet as perceived by EP

Figure 4.1 Baron-Cohen's investigation of EP's synaesthesia.

Source: After Baron-Cohen *et al.* (1987).

THE NATURE OF SYNAESTHESIA

This high level of consistency over time is not unique to EP. In fact Mattingley *et al.* (2001) reported accuracy levels of 80-100 per cent in a group of fifteen synaesthetes compared with 30-50 per cent in fifteen non-synaesthete controls. The synaesthetes' reports were significantly more consistent over a three-month test–retest interval than were the controls after a delay of just one month. For some classes of items, such as Arabic numerals, the synaesthetes achieved a mean consistency of more than 90 per cent compared with less than 30 per cent consistency in the control participants.

Synaesthesia is usually a unidirectional process; the letter A may give rise to the perception of red but not vice versa. For most synaesthetes, simply imagining the inducer can be enough to produce the response. Synaesthetic experiences are limited to fairly low-level percepts such as colour or spatial location rather than the appearance of a face or an object (Grossenbacher and Lovelace, 2001). Curiously, a high number of inducers seem to be things that we learn as children, such as letters, numbers, or days, where the relationships between the perceptual form and the entity that it represents is arbitrary but fixed within a culture.

An interesting study (Witthoft and Winawer, 2013) linked consistent colour–letter associations in eleven synaesthetes to a specific Fisher-Price coloured letter set that had been manufactured between 1972 and 1990 (which all but one of the participants then reported being able to recall from their childhood). This result does not mean that all synaesthesia is based on such developmental experiences, but it is important in suggesting that learning can play a role.

Most synaesthetes regard their condition as a good thing (Carpenter, 2001). However, Baron-Cohen *et al.* (1996) describe one individual, JR, who experienced particularly strong colour and sound associations working in both directions. Each colour in a scene triggered a different musical note, each sound a different colour. Understandably, this was rather overwhelming and JR restricted her lifestyle to avoid excessive stimulation.

Steven and Blakemore (2004) reported the details of six synaesthetes who experienced seeing colours on hearing or thinking about letters or numbers, despite being blind for many years. All had experienced letter–colour synaesthesia for as long as they could remember and the condition persisted after they became blind. One of the six had been blind for thirty-five years. Another experienced colour when he touched the raised dots of Braille characters even though he had been without colour vision for ten years. As Steven and Blakemore comment, this suggests that synaesthesia 'persists for very long periods with little or no natural experience in the referred modality' (2004: 855).

There is a great deal of commonality to the subjective reports provided by synaesthetes. Almost all report that they have had the condition for as long as they can remember (Baron-Cohen *et al.*, 1993) and many have strong memories of the moment at which they discovered that they were different to other people (see Box 4.1). However, Dixon *et al.* (2004) distinguish two forms of synaesthetic experience.

Box 4.1   Discovering one is a synaesthete: A case history

Synaesthete Patricia Duffy provides a vivid account of the moment she first realised that her experience of coloured letters was unusual. Duffy recounts a conversation she had at age 16 in which she reminisced with her father about learning to write the letters of the alphabet (Duffy, 2001):

I said to my father, 'I realized that to make an "R", all I had to do was first write a "P" and then draw a line down from its loop. And I was so surprised that I could turn a yellow letter into an orange letter just by adding a line.'

'Yellow letter? Orange letter?' my father said. 'What do you mean?'

'Well, you know,' I said. ' "P" is a yellow letter, but "R" is an orange letter. You know – the colors of the letters.'

'The colors of the letters?' my father said.

It had never come up in any conversation before. I had never thought to mention it to anyone. For as long as I could remember, each letter of the alphabet had a different color. Each word had a different color too (generally, the same color as the first letter) and so did each number. The colors of letters, words and numbers were as intrinsic a part of them as their shapes, and like the shapes, the colors never changed. They appeared automatically whenever I saw or thought about letters or words, and I couldn't alter them.

I had taken it for granted that the whole world shared these perceptions with me, so my father's perplexed reaction was totally unexpected. From my point of view, I felt as if I'd made a statement as ordinary as 'apples are red' and 'leaves are green' and had elicited a thoroughly bewildered response.

They differentiate between 'projectors', who experience the colour as if it were 'out there' in the physical world superimposed on the stimulus, and 'associators', who see the colour in their 'mind's eye'. Dixon *et al.* report that about 90 per cent of synaesthetes in their sample were associators. We will return to this distinction later.

INCIDENCE AND FAMILIARITY

Based on response rates to newspaper adverts, Baron-Cohen *et al.* (1996) estimated the incidence of synaesthesia at about 1 in 2,000, with about 80 per cent being female. There are of course many problems with this sampling method, including how representative the readership are, the likelihood of responses from people who believe they are synaesthetic and those who do not, and possibly different propensities of men and women to respond. More reliable methods include screening with checks on the test–retest consistency of the subjective reports. Reviewing these studies, Ward (2013) cites prevalence rates from 0.2 per cent of the population for taste–shape synaesthetes, 1.4 per cent for letter/number–colour, and up to 20 per cent for those who image sequences into spatial arrays. These studies suggest that an approximately equal number of men and women have synaesthetic experiences.

In Baron-Cohen's newspaper survey, about one-third of synaesthete respondents reported having a relative who also had synaesthesia. This is higher than you would expect based on the general frequency in the population, and subsequent studies suggest a genetic component, though it is always important to keep in mind the possible influence of shared environment. Any genetic component is now thought to involve multiple genes and not a specific sex-linked (X-chromosome) component, as first suggested by Baron-Cohen (Smilek *et al.*, 2005; Asher *et al.*, 2009; Tomson *et al.*, 2011). What appears to be shared in families is not the precise manifestation in terms of particular inducer–modality pairings but rather a more general predisposition (Ward *et al.*, 2007). Even when family members do share, say, letter–colour synaesthesia, they are no more likely to agree on the colour of any particular letter than unrelated synaesthetes (Barnett *et al.*, 2008). A general predisposition account would also help explain why the majority of synaesthetes report more than one type of synaesthetic experience (Baron-Cohen *et al.*, 1996). We return to the idea of a predisposition to synaesthesia in the brief discussion of candidate neural mechanisms below. Before that we turn to what experimental psychology methods can tell us about this phenomenon.

EXPERIMENTAL INVESTIGATIONS OF SYNAESTHESIA

Several researchers (e.g. Mills *et al.*, 1999; Mattingley *et al.*, 2001) have used versions of the Stroop test (Stroop, 1935) to investigate synaesthesia (see Chapter 3 for details of the Stroop task). In these tasks, a synaesthete is asked to identify the actual colour of a series of stimuli, some of which are inducers and some not. It turns out that when the inducer colour matches the synaesthetic colour (is *congruent*), responses are significantly faster than on neutral, non-inducer, trials. When an inducer has a different (*incongruent*) colour, it interferes with performance and responses are significantly slower than neutral trials. Even when it is interfering with the task, therefore, it appears that synaesthesia cannot be 'switched off'; hence the responses are termed *mandatory* or *automatic*.

Mattingley *et al.* (2001) modified the Stroop technique to investigate whether conscious processing of an inducer is necessary for a synaesthetic response. Inducers were presented very briefly followed by a visual mask (visual masks are a scramble of lines etc. that disrupt the representation preserved after a picture has disappeared, reducing the time available to 'see' the image). We know that such brief, masked presentations are registered in the brain at some level because they can influence (or 'prime') responses to subsequent related material. However, this technique prevents conscious awareness, and neither the synaesthetes nor the control participants were able to report what they had seen. Under these conditions, no synaesthetic Stroop interference was found. It appears that conscious awareness is therefore necessary for synaesthetic responses to occur. This idea is supported by studies that used visual search paradigms. If you are asked to look out for the red letter F amongst lots of other red letters, the more other letters there are, the longer you will take to find it. If, however, you are asked to look for the red F amongst blue letters, the number of these extra distractors makes little difference; the distinctive red letter 'pops out' and can be detected at a glance (see Chapter 3). So, if synaesthetes cannot help but experience, say, a blue F as red, do they have a built-in advantage in separating it out from blue distractors? No such advantage was found (Edquist *et al.*, 2006) again suggesting that conscious attention to the inducer is necessary before the synaesthetic experience will occur.

Conscious attention to the inducer may be necessary but does the inducer actually need to be present? Dixon *et al.* (2000) worked with a number–colour synaesthete called C who completed a Stroop task. Each trial had the sequence: number, arithmetic operator (+, {min} etc.), number, colour patch (e.g. 2 ... + ... 5... [green]). C was asked to name the colour as quickly as possible. It turned out that when the colour patch was congruent with the colour induced in C by the *answer* to the sum (7), she was significantly faster than when it was incongruent, despite it never being presented. A similar conclusion follows from Myles *et al.* (2003). An ambiguous grapheme like 2 can appear as a number or letter depending on context (e.g. 1234, 2ebra). This enabled the researchers to use the same stimulus in both congruent and incongruent trials in a Stroop task. The results demonstrated that it was the synaesthete's *interpretation* rather than the physical properties of the stimulus, which predicted the synaesthesia.

Taken together, these careful experiments show that synaesthetic experiences are reliable over time, appear mandatory or automatic, occur whether the inducer is physically present or in the mind, but require conscious attention to the inducer.

BRAIN-IMAGING STUDIES OF SYNAESTHESIA

Functional brain-imaging techniques, such as functional magnetic resonance imaging (fMRI), allow researchers to examine changes in measures of brain function as volunteers perform different sorts of tasks, think different thoughts, remember different things and so on. It is important to remember that these techniques all have some limitations. fMRI, for example, takes advantage of detecting changes in the oxygen level of blood in different parts of the brain (the blood oxygen response level, or BOLD, signal). Areas that are working harder during a given task require more oxygen and this arrives via the blood a few seconds after the work is done and takes a few more seconds to dissipate. When we are looking at fMRI patterns, therefore, we are not looking directly at brain function but a map that is somewhat blurred, both spatially and in time, in a brain where blood is flowing in many directions for different reasons, creating a noisy signal.

Electroencephalography (EEG) records minute changes in voltage detectable from electrodes harmlessly resting on the scalp. These measures are very sensitive to millisecond-by-millisecond changes but give us only a crude idea about which parts of the brain (or combinations of parts) the signals are coming from. Very occasionally, it is possible to directly record electrical activity from a small group of brain cells, for example, when a volunteer is being prepared for essential brain

Key Term

Functional magnetic resonance imaging (fMRI)
A medical imaging technology that uses very strong magnetic fields to measure changes in the oxygenation of the blood in the brain and thus map levels of activity in the brain. It produces anatomical images of extremely high resolution.

Electroencephalography (EEG)
Recording the brain's electrical activity via electrodes placed against the scalp. Can be used to continuously record rhythmic patterns in brain function or particular responses to events (**event-related potentials**).

Key Term

Event-related potentials (ERP)
Systematic changes in the brain's electrical responses linked to the presentation of a stimulus. Typically the stimulus is presented numerous times with the EEG signals time-locked to its occurrence then being averaged to separate the signal from noise.

Transcranial magnetic stimulation (TMS)
This technique uses an electrical coil placed near the surface of the head to induce a rapid change in the magnetic field, which, in turn, produces a weak electrical current in underlying brain tissue. This can cause depolarisation or hyperpolarisation. The technique can use single bursts or repetitive stimulation. It can be used to support inferences about the role of that brain region in a particular task (e.g. by showing that repetitive stimulation slows responses in task *a* but not task *b*, that the region is involved in task *a*).

surgery. This gives you a very precise picture of the response to a given stimulus etc. *in that area* but no way of knowing how this links to what is happening in the rest of the brain. The methods described so far are observational-correlational, as an area may respond under certain conditions but we do not know exactly what it is doing or how it contributes to a behavioural response.

Transcranial magnetic stimulation (TMS) is a method that allows some inference about the *functional* involvement of a brain area in a process. In TMS an electromagnetic coil near the scalp is used to induce an electrical pulse in the underlying cortical region. This can cause excitation or, with repeated stimulation, a period of under-excitability, a little bit like a temporary brain lesion in that area. If inhibition worsens performance on a task, for example, it suggests that brain area was contributing to good performance. A limitation of this technique is that it is only really effective near to the cortical surface.

Understanding the limitations of these techniques is important, because the last few decades have seen many examples, particularly in the press, of the logical fallacy ('neurorealism') that something that has a detectable 'brain signal' is more real than something that does not. In the case of synaesthesia, it would be wrong to conclude that the synaesthesia is real because it was associated with activity in regions that are also sensitive to colour – perhaps simply imagining colour could have the same effect, or perhaps these regions are involved in some other way such as anticipating colour judgements. Similarly, it would be very dangerous to conclude that a synaesthetic experience was not real just because your method could not detect a reliable signal in a particular brain region. There are many ways of failing to discriminate real activity!

Functional imaging generally requires multiple participants to make generalised claims and most studies of synaesthesia have accordingly focused on the most frequently seen word–colour form. Nunn *et al.* (2002), using fMRI, reported that synaesthetes showed increased activity in V4, a region of the brain linked with colour perception, when listening to inducer compared with non-inducer words. This signal was not detectable in non-synaesthete control participants who had been asked to associate colours and words. Consistent findings were reported by Hubbard and Ramachandran (2005). These results were exciting because they suggested that synaesthetic colour was represented in exactly the same system as that based on 'real' colour. However, other studies have failed to detect this activity (Rouw *et al.*, 2011; Hupe *et al.*, 2012), and there are suggestions that different forms of synaesthesia may be associated with different patterns (Van Leeuwen *et al.*, 2011). Currently the brain regions most commonly activated in the critical synaesthesia response study conditions lie in the frontal and parietal lobes, particularly in a fold in the brain in this region called the intra-parietal sulcus (IPS). For the IPS in particular there is developing (and reassuring) convergence across different methods; it is more active in fMRI comparisons, differences in brain structure in this region (grey matter volume) between synaesthetes and control groups have been reported, and TMS to the area influences behavioural measures of synaesthesia effects (Weiss *et al.*, 2005; Weiss and Fink, 2009). It is also interesting because this region has been implicated in functional imaging and neuropsychological studies in integrating across multimodal sensory information.

MECHANISMS UNDERLYING SYNAESTHESIA

In some ways synaesthesia is less surprising than it first appears. We know from many sources that the brain integrates information from across modalities to develop a working, *useful* model of the world around us. We know that what we can see can influence what we hear and vice versa (Driver and Spence, 1998). We know that sensory feedback from muscles or from the vestibular (balance) system can influence how the world appears to us (Bottini *et al.*, 2001; Schmida *et al.*, 2005), and that priming and memory cues activate representations across modalities (think of an apple and you will get a shape, a colour, a smell, a taste, a crunching sound etc.). Perhaps the curious thing is that the associations are so strong for some people that the presence (or thought) of an inducer is enough to trigger a full perceptual experience in the same or different sensory modality, whilst for most of us it may activate related mental content, but not sufficiently to produce a percept.

Neural spiking is the brain's common currency. From the brain's point of view the colour red is a level of activity in and across particular neurons and, if this occurs, the brain cannot tell if this is due to an external or internal event (without other clues, at least). Most neural accounts of synaesthesia are based on the idea that regions related to the perception of the inducer (e.g. letter reading) become linked to regions related to the experience (e.g. colour perception) such that the occurrence of the former automatically activates the latter. Variants of this argument, which in truth do not tell us much more than the descriptions of synaesthesia presented above, are that these connections exist for everyone but they are functionally more active in synaesthetes or inhibited for the majority of the population who are non-synaesthetes.

An interesting theory is that we were all synaesthetes once but that the neural connections that supported this are usually pruned out in early childhood (the infant's brain has massively more connections than the adult's). By this account, a small group maintain enough of these connections to become adult synaesthetes (Maurer and Mondloch, 2006). Ramachandran and Hubbard (2002) note that brain areas involved in colour perception (V4 in the fusiform gyrus) are immediately adjacent to the areas active during letter reading. 'Can it be a coincidence', they comment, 'that the most common form of synaesthesia involves graphemes and colours and the brain areas corresponding to these are right next to each other?' (p. 9). It certainly could be coincidental and others have argued that there is no necessary argument for either local or long-range extra neural connections in synaesthesia. Grossenbacher and Lovelace (2001), for example, put forward a 'disinhibited-feedback' theory. This suggests that connections between different sensory pathways exist in 'normal' brains, but that the activity of these pathways is usually inhibited to prevent unadaptive cross-talk between sensory modalities. They point out that certain hallucinogenic drugs such as LSD can induce temporary synaesthetic experiences in non-synaesthetes, suggesting that the pathways connecting the different sensory modules exist in normal brains. The action of LSD could plausibly involve the disinhibition of existing pathways but is not likely to induce the 'growth' of new pathways. Interesting functional imaging evidence supporting disinhibition theory has been reported. Neufeld *et al.* (2012) found no difference between fourteen auditory–visual synaesthetes and non-synaesthete fMRI participants in terms of the functional connectivity (both being active) between auditory and visual areas but greater connectivity between sensory areas and the IPS in the synaesthetic group, suggesting that it may be links via this integration area that are supressed in non-synaesthetes.

SYNAESTHESIA – ADVANTAGE OR DISADVANTAGE?

We have seen that unbidden synaesthetic experiences were so overwhelming for JR that they had a detrimental effect on her quality of life (Baron-Cohen *et al.*, 1996). Survival and reproductive fitness will often depend on making quick, accurate decisions on what is 'out there' (can I eat it or will it eat me?). Interference with accurate perception from synaesthetic content, as we saw with the Stroop tasks, can impede rapid judgements. However, we have also seen how, in surveys, most synaesthetes do not view their condition as an impediment and there is growing evidence that synaesthesia may result in or stem from (or both) enhanced general perceptual skills in the relevant domain (Yaro and Ward, 2007). There is evidence too that some synaesthetes can use their elaborated representation of inducers to enhance memory and mathematical manipulations and that a disproportionate number may be drawn towards the creative arts (Ward, 2013). Synaesthesia may therefore form a useful example of the idea of 'neurodiversity' – individual differences in brain function that have advantages in some settings, disadvantages in others. There is a good argument that applying that idea to other characteristics currently seen as 'developmental disabilities' may have positive results.

CONCLUSIONS

Synaesthesia is an interesting example of the historical progress of cognitive psychology. As an inherently subjective state it received relatively little scientific interest at first. The application of appropriate scientific method to this area over the last 30 years has shown it to be both a 'real' phenomenon and one that offers a number of insights into normal cognition and perception, and human diversity. From the fraction of studies reviewed here we know that it takes many forms; it runs in families; it reflects an underlying propensity with many synaesthetes showing a number of manifestations; it is automatic but requires conscious awareness of the inducer; it may confer advantages in some circumstances; and it may be reflected in relative patterns of neural feedback on connections between inducer and synaesthetic response brain areas.

4.3 BLINDSIGHT

The striate cortex, or area V1 as it is now known, is central to visual perception. Damage to the left striate cortex will result in blindness in the right *visual field* of both eyes and damage to the right striate cortex will result in blindness in the left visual field of both eyes. These areas of blindness are called *scotomata* (plural of scotoma). In order to imagine the effect of such damage, look straight ahead, and cover the left half of each eye. The very restricted visual field you now experience is similar to that which you would experience following damage to your right striate cortex. To see anything to your left side you need to turn your head (the patient would be able to turn their eyes).

Now imagine that you were asked to point to a flash of light that had occurred somewhere to your 'blind' left side. If persuaded to take part in this puzzling experiment you would expect to perform at chance levels, sometimes guessing the correct location but more often being wrong. Poppel *et al.* (1973) studied a group of ex-servicemen who suffered visual field deficits as a result of gunshot wounds to the striate cortex, and asked the participants to make just such judgements. Lights were flashed in the defective area of the visual field of each participant. Because the servicemen could not see the flashes, the light was paired with the sound of a buzzer, and on hearing the buzzer the servicemen were asked to move their eyes in the direction of the light source. The servicemen found this a difficult task, but to their surprise, all were able to direct their gaze towards the light which they could not see.

In the following year, Weiskrantz *et al.* (1974) described a patient DB who seemed to demonstrate the same remarkable ability. DB was blind in his lower-left visual field following surgery to remove part of his right striate cortex to relieve very severe migraine headaches. What was remarkable about DB was the extent to which he could report details of objects appearing in the blind areas of his visual field despite having no conscious experience of seeing them. Weiskrantz coined the term 'blindsight' to describe this phenomenon.

In a series of experiments covering many years (see Weiskrantz, 1986), Weiskrantz and colleagues were able to systematically investigate the perceptual abilities preserved in the 'blind' areas of DB's visual field. DB was able to detect the presence of an object, and indicate its location in space by pointing. He could discriminate between moving and stationary objects, and between horizontal and vertical lines, and he could distinguish the letter X from the letter O. However, he was unable to distinguish between X and a triangle, suggesting that the ability to distinguish between X and O was dependent on some low-level characteristic of these stimuli rather than any residual ability to discriminate form. DB's inability to discriminate form is further demonstrated by his failure to distinguish between rectangles of various sizes or between straight- and curved-sided triangles.

> **Key Term**
>
> **Scotoma**
> A blind area within the visual field, resulting from damage to the visual system (plural = scotomata).

BLINDSIGHT – A SCEPTICAL PERSPECTIVE

Some scientists have questioned the existence of blindsight, arguing that there are several possible explanations which need to be considered carefully. Cowey (2004) summarised the arguments put forward by sceptics such as Campion *et al.* (1983). Three of these arguments are summarised below.

The stray light hypothesis

Campion *et al.* (1983) favoured the stray light explanation of blindsight, suggesting that blindsight patients were responding to light which was reflected from the object onto the functioning areas of the visual field (remember that patients such as DB are only partially blind, and can see normally in large areas of their visual field). Campion *et al.* described one patient who reported that he was using such a strategy to distinguish between vertical and horizontal bars presented to the blind areas of his visual field. This patient claimed that he could see a faint glow in the preserved areas of his visual field and used this cue to undertake the task. Campion *et al.* also demonstrated that such a strategy could lead to the accurate localisation of a light in a 'blind' area of the visual field of normal subjects whose vision had been masked. However, it is difficult to see how this stray light could explain DB's ability to distinguish letters such as X and O or two different spatial frequency gratings with the same average brightness. In addition, DB could locate objects even against a bright background, whereas Campion *et al.*'s normal subjects could only locate a light source against a low level of background illumination.

Paradoxically, the best evidence against the stray light explanation came from DB's *inability* to respond accurately to objects whose image fell onto his blindspot. The blindspot, where the optic nerve passes through the retina, is devoid of receptor cells so we are blind to images falling on this part of the retina. If DB's blindsight was explained by stray light, then we would expect him to perform equally well whether the image of the object fell on the blindspot or in the scotoma. In fact, DB showed no evidence of being able to detect the presence of objects or lights presented at his blindspot, yet could accurately detect objects or events occurring within the scotoma immediately adjacent to the blindspot (Figure 4.2).

More recently, some evidence has emerged to suggest that one form of the 'stray light' hypothesis might help to account for some reports of unexpected abilities in blindsight patients. Cowey (2004) noted that most research with blindsight patients uses 'raster displays' (television screens or computer monitors) to present the visual stimuli. Cowey demonstrated that a pattern displayed on one side of such a screen will often give rise to a faint 'ghost' image on the other side of the screen. Cowey and Azzopardi (2001) showed that in a display that included this artefact a normal participant could determine whether a grating presented in the masked area of the visual field was drifting up or down. However, once the display was modified to remove the artefact, this ability disappeared. Similarly, when the unmodified display

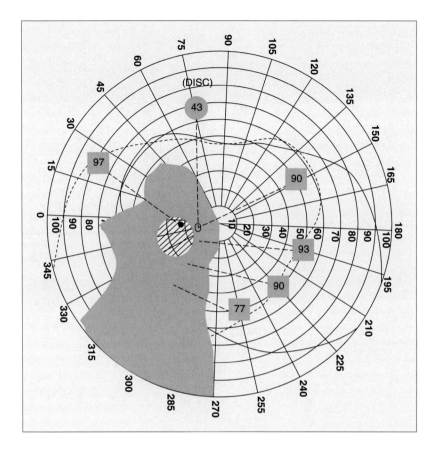

Figure 4.2 Weiskrantz's investigation of DB's blindsight.

Note: The dark area indicates the 'blind' area of DB's visual field. The hashed area indicates that region in which DB had some partial awareness of the presence of the light. When the light occurred at his blindspot (marked DISC) DB performed at chance level, correctly reporting the presence of the light on less than 50 per cent of occasions. However, performance at all other locations was well above chance. The stray light hypothesis would predict that performance at the blindspot should be well above chance.

Source: Weiskrantz (1986), reproduced by permission of Oxford University Press.

was used, three blindsight patients could detect both the presence of a moving pattern and the direction of movement, but once the artefact was removed they were sensitive to the presence of movement but not its direction. Thus, it seems that some, but not all of the apparent abilities of blindsight patients might be attributed to the presence of these artefacts.

Spared islands of residual vision

Wessinger *et al.* (1997) suggested that blindsight was attributable to small areas or 'islands' in the scotoma within which vision is spared, and that blindsight may be mediated by what is left of the primary visual pathway rather than other secondary pathways. This suggestion was tested by Kentridge *et al.* (1997) who looked for scattered regions of spared vision in one patient using a procedure which ensured that the effects of eye movements were abolished. Under these stringent testing conditions, Kentridge *et al.* noted that blindsight did not extend across the whole of the area of the scotoma, but was evident in some areas even after eye movements had been eliminated, leading to the conclusion that although there may be some spared islands within the scotoma, these cannot account for all blindsight. Furthermore, Cowey (2004) notes that the results of MRI scanning of several blindsight patients has shown 'not a shred of evidence' of any sparing of the striate cortex in the area of the scotoma.

A change in criterion to report the presence of the stimulus?

Another explanation offered by sceptics is that blindsight represents a change in response criterion but not in sensitivity, such that blindsight patients are equally sensitive to the presence of a stimulus but less willing to report conscious awareness than a normal subject. Cowey and Azzopardi (2001) employed a signal detection approach to determine whether performance in a two-alternative-forced-choice task (such as determining in which of two time intervals a stimulus has been presented) was determined by a change in sensitivity or a change in criterion. The results suggest that the performance of blindsight patients tested was characterised not only by a change in response criterion, but also by a different mode of processing. That is, blindsight is qualitatively and not just quantitatively different from normal vision. However, Cowey (2004) notes that we should not ignore the possibility that changes in response criteria might partially account for some aspects of the performance of blindsight patients. This is an area of continuing research interest.

THE SENSATION OF BLINDSIGHT

It is very difficult to imagine what a patient such as DB experiences when a stimulus is presented within the 'blind' regions of his visual field. It is clear that the experience is very different from that of normal vision. Weiskrantz records DB as saying that he 'felt' movement rather than saw it. As far as we can tell, blindsight patients are learning to respond to very subtle experiences which have little in common with the normal perceptual experience. As Cowey (2004) observes, it is important not to think of blindsight as 'normal vision stripped of conscious visual experience' (p. 588). Blindsight is a very poor substitute for normal vision with very significantly reduced sensitivity to fundamental aspects of the scene.

So how can we imagine the experience of blindsight? Suppose you are sitting reading this book when suddenly, in your peripheral vision ('out of the corner of your eye'), a spider scuttles across the floor. Before you are conscious of the motion, you move your head and eyes towards the spider. You did not 'see' the spider but your visual system was able to guide you towards it. Perhaps this is a reasonable analogy to the experience of blindsight. Patients such as DB do not have any conscious experience of perception, yet, at some level below that accessible to introspection, the visual system does have access to information about the outside world.

THE IMPLICATIONS OF BLINDSIGHT: ONE VISUAL SYSTEM OR TWO?

The most widely accepted explanation for blindsight is that we have two separate visual systems, one primitive non-striate system and a more advanced striate system. The primitive non-striate system might be sensitive to movement, speed, and other potentially important characteristics of a stimulus without giving rise to conscious perception. A frog can catch a fly because it can locate its position in space very accurately, but it is unlikely that the frog consciously perceives the fly. Perhaps blindsight represents the working of this primitive visual system whose functioning is normally masked by the conscious perception which results from the action of the striate visual system.

A slightly different explanation would be to see the striate and non-striate systems as having evolved to fulfil different roles. One possibility would be that the striate system has evolved to allow the identification of an object, whereas the non-striate system has evolved to allow the localisation of that object in space. There is some evidence from non-human animal studies to support this view. Based on a series of lesion studies in hamsters, Schneider (1969) suggested that there were two separate visual pathways: one responsible for the identification of objects, and the other for the location of objects in space.

Goodale and Milner (1992, 2004) suggested that the distinction might be between a system responsible for the recognition of objects and one responsible for the control of actions such as picking up an object. Goodale and Milner (1992) suggested that object recognition and the control of action might be mediated by different and mutually incompatible types of representation. In this case, they reasoned, it might be *necessary* to separate these two pathways and only allow one of them to have access to consciousness.

4.4 UNILATERAL SPATIAL NEGLECT

As we saw in the previous section, patients with blindsight are able to respond to a stimulus they cannot see. In unilateral spatial neglect the opposite seems to be true – patients fail to respond to stimuli which they can see. A patient may have normal vision yet fail to react to objects or events to one side of space – hence the terms *unilateral* (one-sided) *neglect* (ignoring rather than being blind to). The condition has a number of other names including *hemi-inattention, contralateral neglect* and simply *spatial neglect*. These represent terminological preferences rather than different conditions.

The main cause of unilateral spatial neglect (USN) is stroke, an interruption to the brain's blood supply. Because of its organisation, this interruption will primarily affect one or other hemisphere. Although USN may seem like an exotic neuropsychological phenomenon it is extremely common. Up to 84 per cent of patients with damage to the right hemisphere (RH) of the brain from stroke will show evidence on ignoring information on their left (the side opposite the lesion often called *contralateral* or *contralesional*). Similarly, up to 64 per cent of patients with left hemisphere damage can show the opposite pattern, ignoring information on their right (Stone *et al.*, 1993). One of the most robust and mysterious findings in neuropsychology is, however,

Key Term

Unilateral spatial neglect
A difficulty in noticing or acting on information from one side of space typically caused by a brain lesion to the opposite hemisphere (e.g. right-hemisphere damage producing lack of awareness for information on the left). Also called hemispatial neglect or hemispatial inattention.

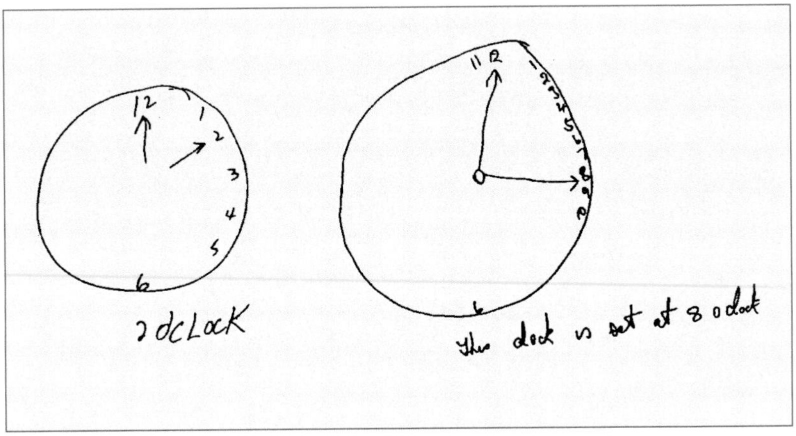

Figure 4.3 Examples of drawings of clock faces produced by patients with unilateral visual neglect.

Source: Halligan and Marshall (1993), by permission of Psychology Press Limited, Hove, UK.

that this fairly balanced picture is seen only very early on after the stroke. For some reason, left neglect following right hemisphere lesion is markedly more severe and persistent than its right neglect/left hemisphere equivalent (Bowen *et al.*, 1999). For that reason we will generally be talking about left-sided neglect in this chapter.

Patients with USN may fail to notice object in 'clear view' on the left, ignore people approaching from the left, eat food only from the right side of the plate, or wash and dress only the right side of their own body. A classic demonstration is to ask a patient to draw a clock face. USN patients will often omit the numbers between 7 and 11, or will try to squeeze these numbers onto the right side of the clock (Figure 4.3).

USN impacts upon many activities of daily living, can exclude people from rehabilitation and is associated with longer hospital stays and dependence on others. It is a serious clinical problem for patients and families. For science it also offers fascinating insights into the nature of awareness, consciousness, vision–action links and attention. A hope, as with other disorders, is that these insights will feed back into better targeted rehabilitation for the disorder.

A DISORDER OF ATTENTION?

A definition of USN is that it is a failure of or difficulty in responding to information on one side of space that we cannot explain by basic sensory loss. As we have seen, damage to primary visual areas can produce blindness for one half or portion of space. How does this differ from USN? This is an important question both because many patients with USN also have some loss of vision on the affected side (*hemianopia*) and because the rehabilitation implications of the two disorders may differ (Zihl, 1994).

The most obvious difference between USN and visual field loss is that the former can exert an influence across modalities whilst the later is restricted to vision. USN has been reported in audition (De Renzi *et al.*, 1989), tactile exploration, touch and body sensation (*haptic* and *somatosensory* perception (Vallar *et al.*, 1993; McIntosh *et al.*, 2002) imagery (Bisiach and Luzzatti, 1978; see below) and even smell! (Bellas *et al.*,

1988). However, many dissociations between modalities have been reported (meaning that a patient may show spatial bias in one modality but not the other). Assessment in non-visual modalities can be complex, and it is difficult to rule out non-visual sensory loss from stroke. Even in the visual domain, however, there are fundamental differences between visual field loss and USN, to which we now turn.

Visual field losses are strictly retinotopic – the blind area will move with the eyes. USN in contrast varies in different spatial frameworks, it may occur for objects to the left side of the body (*egocentric* space) or for objects on the left side of *something* (like a page or room) regardless of where this is in relation to the person (*allocentric* space). USN may occur for the left side of each object *within* a scene (Driver and Halligan, 1991). Marshall and Halligan (1993) for example, asked patients to copy pictures of plants. Bizarrely, a patient may miss leaves and petals on the left side of one plant and then go on to draw the right side of the next plant, which lies further into their neglected side. Perhaps the best way to think about this difference between visual field disorders and USN is to imagine looking around your room through a cardboard tube. At any given moment your view is greatly restricted and you will miss things happening outside of this narrow window. By scanning the tube around the room, however, you can see everything. With the important exception that you are consciously aware of the restricting tube, this is like visual field loss. Now imagine instead limiting your scans only to the left side of the room or the left side of each object in the room. This is more like neglect.

Another astonishing example of neglect was reported by Driver and Halligan (1991). To imagine this effect, hold this book upright and look at the words at the top-left side of the page. Driver and Halligan found, unsurprisingly, that USN led to insensitivity to differences between two stimuli in details at this location. Now rotate the book, but not your head, 45° to the right (sorry if this makes it difficult to read). Now the top-left words are on the 'right' side of the stimulus. Would this spare them from being neglected? No, remarkably, the neglect appeared to rotate with the page! It is as if the left side of *something* is first identified and then ignored.

So USN is different from basic visual loss, but is it a disorder of *attention*? This depends on quite what you mean by this notoriously difficult-to-define term. A key idea in lay uses of 'attention' is that you *could have* noticed something had you remembered to, or if it was pointed out to you. Both appear to be true in neglect. Patients *can* attend to the left if cued to do so or if particularly salient events draw attention there, although this often drifts quickly back to the right (Riddoch and Humphreys, 1983). In cognitive neuroscience the idea of *competition* is central to the study of attention; we have limited capacity resources, and objects, events etc. compete for access. If an object gains access, another is inevitably ignored, at least partially (Desimone and Duncan, 1995). This too seems to fit USN. A stimulus that appears in isolation in the neglected field will often be detected. When the same stimulus appears in competition with a rival on the good side, however, it is more likely to be missed (this is called *extinction* and is commonly assessed at the bedside by *confrontation testing* – the examiner wiggles one, other or both of two fingers in the patient's line or sight and asks what was seen). Another characteristic of attention, illustrated already in the cueing and extinction examples, is *variability*. It is tempting to think of USN as reflecting a clear border between left and right. Instead there is much more of a gradient stretching from the left to the right affecting the probability that a stimulus will be detected (Karnath, 1997). Patients' performance on spatial tasks can show a very high level of trial-to-trial variability (Anderson, B. *et al.*, 2000). We have seen a patient show severe USN on a clinical test and then perform the *same test* without obvious impairment moments later. Such volatility in a symptom, as we shall discuss, can be very useful in suggesting the potential for rehabilitation.

Attention can be to external stimuli or internal content (e.g. day-dreaming). A fascinating example of USN was reported by Bisiach and Luzzatti (1978). They asked two USN patients to describe a famous square in their native Milan (the *Piazza del Duomo*) from memory. When the patients imagined themselves at one end, looking into the square, they showed a marked tendency to report landmarks that would be to their right. When asked to now imagine themselves at the other end looking back, the previously neglected left landmarks, now on their imagined right, re-entered consciousness. We have observed similar striking effects in asking a man with USN to describe his house to us from the front- and back-garden perspectives. Again his access to memories of entire rooms was peculiarly determined by where he imagined himself to be with respect to them. Arguably, omissions in patients' drawings of clocks, flowers etc. from memory also reflect distorted mental imagery, although in these cases, concurrent perception and even motor neglect is hard to rule out.

With due caution regarding blindsight and the heterogeneity of USN, a further fascinating difference with a purely visual field loss concerns the level to which neglected stimuli may be processed. Marshall and Halligan (1988) showed a USN patient pairs of drawings of a house. The patient failed to notice when the house on the left was on fire, but was above chance in choosing the non-burning building when asked which would be preferable to live in. Berti and Rizzolatti (1992) showed that presenting a brief stimulus in USN's patients 'bad' left field primed subsequent responses to related information in the good field, despite patients reporting no conscious awareness of the prime. Manly *et al.* (2002) asked USN patients to perform a common clinical test in which they had to find and cross out small stars scattered over a page amid distractors (a *cancellation* test). Under normal conditions, in addition to missing many targets on the left the patients showed a strong tendency cross out the same targets on the right of the sheet over and over again (this tendency to repeat actions without obvious cause is called *perseveration* and is a noted feature of neglect (Na *et al.*, 1999; Manly *et al.*, 2002) and some other neurological conditions (Joseph, 1999). When, however, the ignored targets on the left of the sheet were replaced by non-targets, this re-marking of targets on the right dramatically declined. This suggests that on the standard version of the task the patients were aware, at some level, of the missing targets and this drove them to repeatedly cancel those on the right. Taken together the results suggest that neglected stimuli may be processed to quite a high level and yet fail to reach conscious awareness.

DO WE ALL SHOW NEGLECT?

A common clinical observation is that patients with persistent (chronic) left neglect tend to be drowsy and appear to have difficulty remaining focused on all sorts of tasks. This impression has been supported by research showing that such patients indeed tend to perform very poorly on non-spatial sustained attention measures (Robertson *et al.*, 1997; Samuelsson *et al.*, 1998). By itself this could reflect two independent consequences of overall stroke severity. However, Robertson *et al.* (1998b) showed that alerting patients with a loud tone temporarily but dramatically reduced or reversed their neglect, even when the tone was to their right. Subsequent studies have shown that stimulating medication (Malhotra *et al.*, 2006) or thoughts (George *et al.*, 2008) can cause similar gains.

If levels of alertness influence spatial biases in patients with USN, might this relationship also occur in other groups? A number of studies have now shown that some children with a diagnosis of attention deficit hyperactivity disorder (ADHD), who struggle to sustain their attention, can show a marked pattern of omissions reliably from one side of space. So far, this has always been the left (Voeller and Heilman, 1988; Manly *et al.*, 1997; Shepard *et al.*, 1999; Dobler *et al.*, 2003; George *et al.*, 2005). Healthy volunteers show significant rightward shifts in spatial attention after sleep deprivation (Manly *et al.*, 2005), when awake but sleepy in the early hours of the morning (Fimm *et al.*, 2006) and after long periods of repetitive task performance (Dobler *et al.*, 2005; Manly *et al.*, 2005; Dodds *et al.*, 2008). Whilst these biases are not generally as marked as in USN, they provide potential insights into why left neglect in particular may be so persistent.

REHABILITATION FOR UNILATERAL SPATIAL NEGLECT

USN is an area in which the results of studies primarily aimed at improving the outcome of patients have had direct relevance for our understanding of the disorder. This is perhaps because the most obvious form of rehabilitation, encouraging and training patients to look towards and be aware of the left, often produces rather disappointing results at practicable durations (Lawson, 1962; Weinberg *et al.*, 1977). An interesting example of a more positive effect came from Robertson *et al.*'s work (Robertson *et al.*, 1998a; Robertson and Hawkins, 1999; Robertson *et al.*, 2002). This showed that movements of the patients' left arm/hand could generally enhance visual awareness of the left, even if those movements occurred out of sight.

As we saw in the discussion of synaesthesia, parts of the brain integrate information from across the senses to form a coherent model of the world. Because this system is intolerant of discrepancy (you cannot be facing one way and another!) you can use input to one modality to bias perception in another. In caloric vestibular stimulation, for example, pouring cold water into one ear (and sometimes hot water into the other) disturbs the vestibular balance system and can produce involuntary eye movements to the left (and, of course, wet ears). Similarly, tricking the *proprioceptive* (body sense) system into believing that the trunk of one's body is rotated by mechanical vibration of the muscles can produce reflexive re-orienting to the left (Karnath *et al.*, 1993). These are not just interesting experimental effects. Fifteen sessions of 80 Hz neck muscle stimulation was linked with lasting improvements across a range of spatial tasks in USN patients (compared with a similar period of just practising tasks) (Schindler *et al.*, 2002). Training in adapting to rightward deviating prism lenses (that causes a rebound effect to the left) has also produced positive results (Rossetti *et al.*, 1998; Frassinetti *et al.*, 2002). Do these effects help us explain USN?

EXPLAINING UNILATERAL SPATIAL NEGLECT

As we have seen, USN occurs at a remarkably high frequency following stroke. It has also been reported following damage to a wide variety of brain areas including the parietal, temporal and frontal lobes and a good number of subcortical areas (Mort *et al.*, 2003). This has led to the idea that normal spatial attention may reflect a dynamic – and easily disrupted – competitive balance between the widely distributed networks in the hemispheres (Mesulam, 1999). In this view, the left hemisphere is pushing attention into right space and the right hemisphere pushing back to the left. In USN we are not seeing simply the effect of the lesioned hemisphere (which may have much residual function) but its exaggeration due to the supressing effects of its undamaged rival (Sprague, 1966; Kinsbourne, 1977).

We discussed how the idea of information 'competing' to gain access to limited capacity processing was useful in thinking about attention. This competition may occur at all sorts of cognitive/perceptual levels and in different modalities. However, it has been argued that, for coherent goal-directed action, this competition is integrated so that, for example, rather than being aware primarily of one event in the visual modality, another in audition, and thinking about a memory of the third – in general the levels will try to converge at any one time on a single target. An important factor influencing whether a given stimulus will win the competition for conscious awareness is therefore the state of activity relevant to that stimulus across all levels of the system (Desimone and Duncan, 1995; Driver and Spence, 1998; Duncan, 2006). Within this framework it is easier to see how unilateral brain damage could have cascading effects reducing the likely awareness of different sorts of information in contralesional space (be this based in egocentric, allocentric, object-based or imagery-based space). It also makes more sense of why a rather diverse set of rehabilitation interventions and experimental manipulations (in as much as these potentiate the representation of the left) appear to work.

4.5 VISUAL AGNOSIA

Agnosia is an ancient Greek word which means 'non-knowledge'. So visual agnosia roughly translates to 'not knowing through vision' and it refers to an impairment in the ability to visually recognise objects. Patients with visual agnosia aren't blind. In fact, sensory processes are usually intact. Patients can move around without bumping into things and they can reach for and pick up objects which they are unable to recognise. Generally, patients with visual agnosia can also recognise objects through touch, so they haven't lost their knowledge about objects; they just can't recognise them visually.

> **Key Term**
>
> **Agnosia**
> The failure to recognise or interpret stimuli despite adequate sensory function. It is usually classified by sensory modality, so visual agnosia is the failure to recognise objects that are seen.

APPERCEPTIVE AND ASSOCIATIVE AGNOSIA

This observation that people can be impaired in their ability to recognise objects without other sensory or global cognitive impairment was first discussed by Lissauer in 1890. In fact, Lissauer was one of the first people to study visual agnosia systematically and identified two broad patterns of impairment, which were termed *apperceptive* and *associative* agnosia. Someone suffering from apperceptive agnosia was thought to have normal visual acuity with an inability to draw an object (Figure 4.4), to say whether two similar objects were the same or different, or even to describe the component parts of an object. Someone suffering from associative agnosia *would* be able to draw an object, to match similar objects *and* be able to describe the component parts *but* they would be unable to recognise the objects they had just seen or drawn.

Lissauer proposed that these two stages were serial and hierarchical. So in the apperceptive stage the elements or components of the object

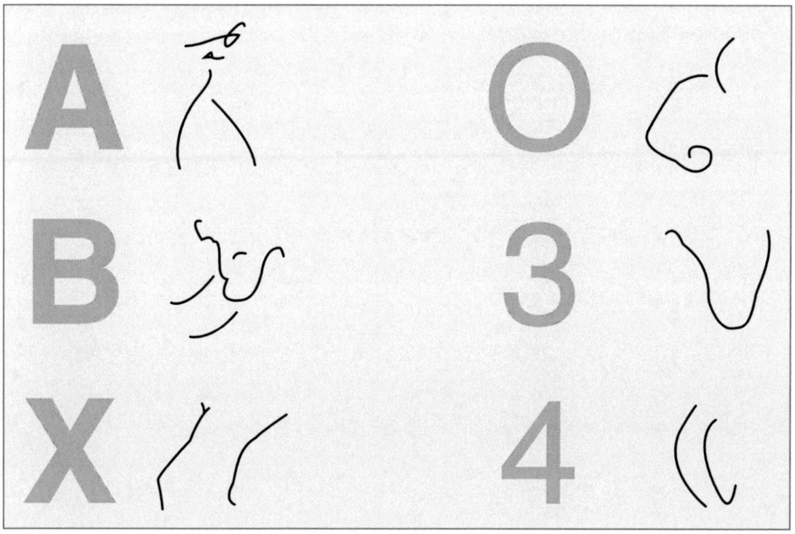

Figure 4.4 The attempts of a patient with apperceptive agnosia to copy six simple figures.

Source: Farah (1990), reproduced by permission of MIT Press.

are established, and then in the associative stage these elements are integrated into a representation of the whole object which is then linked to a store of object knowledge which enables recognition and identification. This means that patients with pure apperceptive agnosia have an intact store of knowledge about objects, but as they are unable to distinguish the shape of objects, they are unable to identify objects visually. In contrast, patients with pure associative agnosia are able to perceive objects but are often unable to identify them. In practical terms, the decision to categorise a patient as apperceptive or associative was often based on their ability to copy a drawing. If a patient could not copy a drawing, they would be classified as having apperceptive agnosia. If they could copy them but failed to recognise the objects in the drawings, they would be diagnosed as having associative agnosia.

Lissauer's broad classification of the impairments that are observed in visual agnosia are still useful today. However, research over the last 20 years has highlighted the difficulty in identifying and diagnosing 'pure' cases of visual agnosia. Furthermore, different sub-types of impairment have been identified which means that both Lissauer's original classification of visual agnosia and the processes that are involved in recognising objects have become fractionated (see Humphreys and Riddoch, 2006, for a review).

FORM AND INTEGRATIVE AGNOSIA

Form agnosia is now the generally accepted term for patients who are unable to discriminate between objects and are unable to copy line drawings of objects (apperceptive agnosia) (Farah, 2004). Similarly, integrative agnosia is the generally accepted term for associative agnosia as it more accurately reflects the processing difficulties that patients experience. So, it refers to patients who can perceive the individual shapes and elements of objects but are unable to integrate these into a representation of the whole object. Carbon monoxide poisoning seems to be a particularly common cause of form agnosia (for example patient 'Dee' described by Goodale and Milner, 2004), although other rarer incidents such as assault and cardiac events have been reported. In contrast, integrative agnosia has been reported with incidents of stroke, brain trauma and Alzheimer's disease where there are often bilateral lesions. In addition, patients with integrative agnosia appear to have more medial ventral lesions than patients with form agnosia (Riddoch *et al.,* 2008a).

LIVING WITH VISUAL AGNOSIA

It is very difficult to imagine just what it is like to suffer from a visual agnosia, and the experience must vary greatly with the type of agnosia. In order to gain a small insight into the difficulties that these two types of visual agnosia have on everyday functioning, it is helpful to draw on case studies. One such case study is patient HJA, who has integrative agnosia and has been studied extensively by Humphreys and Riddoch. In a captivating account of their work with HJA, Humphreys and Riddoch (1987) provide a valuable insight into the life of an individual with visual agnosia (Box 4.2).

Key Term

Form agnosia
This is now the generally accepted term for patients who are unable to discriminate between objects and are unable to copy line drawings of objects (this was previously termed apperceptive agnosia).

Integrative agnosia
This is the generally accepted term for associative agnosia. It refers to patients who can perceive the individual shapes and elements of objects but are unable to integrate these into a representation of the whole object.

Box 4.2   HJA: Living with visual integrative agnosia

After an operation, HJA suffered a stroke which caused damage to both of his occipital lobes and affected his posterior cerebral artery. When HJA first woke up in hospital he was unable to recognise his surroundings and he assumed that it must have been caused by a 'bang on the head' or a 'hangover'. While some improvement was observed over the following weeks, HJA was still unable to recognise many familiar objects. After a formal assessment, it was found that HJA was blind in the top half of both visual fields. However, this couldn't explain his inability to identify objects because the lower half of each visual field was undamaged, so a simple movement of the object or head would reveal aspects that were previously hidden by his visual field deficit. HJA could negotiate his environment well. He could walk around without bumping into objects and he could also reach for objects and pick them up. However, he had considerable difficulty in naming objects on the basis of their appearance alone. While he could recognise some objects, many were a mystery to him and he had particular difficulty in making within-category judgements (e.g. distinguishing between two types of animal or plant). This problem is illustrated by the fact that HJA could trim the garden hedge with shears, but he couldn't differentiate between the hedge and the roses, so he would decapitate them.

HJA's difficulties were not caused by memory difficulties. When he was given names of objects, he could eloquently describe their appearance and functions. However, when HJA was shown the same objects that he had just described he was unable to identify them (Figure 4.5). This pattern of spared and impaired processing suggests that while HJA could form a

HJA offered the following definition of a carrot:

'A carrot is a root vegetable cultivated and eaten as human consumption world wide. Grown from seed as an annual crop, the carrot produces long thin leaves growing from a root head; this is deep growing and large in comparison with the leaf growth, some times gaining a length of 12 inches under a leaf top of similar height when grown in good soil. Carrots may be eaten raw or cooked and can be harvested during any size or state of growth. The general shape of a carrot root is an elongated cone and its colour ranges between red and yellow.' (p. 64)

However, HJA was unable to identify a line drawing of a carrot, saying:

'I have not even the glimmerings of an idea. The bottom point seems solid, and the other bits are feathery. It does not seem to be logical unless it is some sort of a brush.' (p. 59)

Figure 4.5   HJA's definition of the word 'carrot' and his attempt to recognise a line drawing of a carrot (as recorded by Humphreys and Riddoch, 1987).

representation of the major elements of an object and extract shape and textural information from drawings, he was unable to integrate this information into a representation of the whole object. This means that as HJA doesn't know what the whole object is when he sees it, he is unable to 'match' it to his memory store of common objects and identify it. Importantly, when HJA was blindfolded and asked to identify objects by touch, he was able to name many objects which he could not identify by sight. This demonstrated that his impairment was not a form of anomia (loss of memory for the names of objects).

HJA spoke eloquently and insightfully about his processing difficulties. For example, while he could describe a favourite etching of London which had hung on his living room wall for many years, and he was still able to pick out some distinctive aspects (such as the dome of St Paul's cathedral), he commented:

> But now it does not 'fit' my memory of the picture nor of the reality. Knowing that I should be able to identify the general design of the

dome-headed, high circular central tower covering a particularly cruciform building, I can point out the expected detail but cannot recognise the whole structure. On the other hand, I am sure I could draw a reasonable copy of the picture.

(Humphreys and Riddoch, 1987: 33)

HJA also described a visit to an aircraft museum. During the war he had served in the RAF and at the museum he was able to describe the shape of his bomber to his friends, and was able to recount various stories and describe technical aspects of the aircraft. It is clear that he had a detailed memory for the aircraft and its appearance; however, HJA stated that 'in all honesty, I did not recognise the "whole"'.

When asked to copy a picture, such as the etching of London described above, HJA could produce a reasonable likeness (Figure 4.6), but this image took six hours to complete by a laborious process of line-by-line reproduction which did not seem to be guided by any knowledge of the form of the object. It was as if he was being set the task of copying a complex pattern of random lines. However, when drawing from memory rather than attempting to copy, HJA produced very recognisable and detailed drawings (Figure 4.7) indicating that he retained a good visual memory for the objects which he could no longer recognise. He stated:

I don't find [drawing from memory] too difficult, bearing in mind that I never

Figure 4.6 HJA's copy of his favourite etching showing St Paul's Cathedral, London, which took six hours to complete by a laborious process of line-by-line reproduction.

Source: Humphreys and Riddoch (1987), reproduced by permission of Psychology Press, Hove, UK.

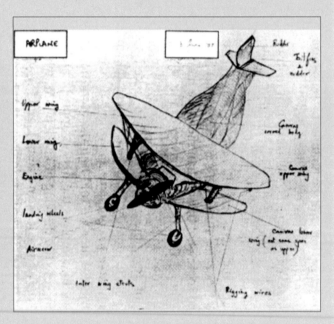

Figure 4.7 An example of one of HJA's drawings from memory.

Source: Humphreys and Riddoch (1987), reproduced by permission of Psychology Press, Hove, UK.

had much drawing ability .... My mind knows very clearly what I should like to draw and I can comprehend enough of my own handiwork to know if it is a reasonable representation of what I had in mind.

Patients with visual form agnosia experience a very confused and distorted visual world in which almost nothing seems familiar and even basic forms are indistinguishable from each other. Perhaps the best analogy would be to imagine looking at the world through a very powerful microscope. To look at an object you would have to scan the microscope around the object, trying to remember what each view of the object has revealed. To form a representation of the whole object you would need to assemble a mental picture of the overall structure of the object by piecing together the independent microscopic views. In this way, despite being able to see the component details of the object accurately you would find it very difficult to recognise the whole, and the more complex the local detail the harder the recognition task would become. These difficulties are evident with patient Dee (see Goodale and Milner, 2004, for a powerful description of the problems faced by Dee). She has severe visual form agnosia as a result of carbon monoxide poisoning which resulted in bilateral damage to her occipitotemporal visual system. Despite being unable to recognise objects or their shape, she can perceive the surface characteristics (texture and colour) and uses them as cues to help her to recognise the object. She can also identify familiar objects through touch. However, Dee cannot copy line drawings of objects or simple shapes. Interestingly, when Dee is asked to show how wide an object is (using her fingers) she is unable to. However, when she is asked to pick up an object that she cannot identify, Dee makes the correct hand movements. Furthermore when walking, Dee is able to negotiate her environment and can step over objects, even though she can't say what the objects are (Goodale, 2008). Dee can also move around her own home freely and she can undertake tasks such as making a cup of tea without help.

PERCEPTION AND ACTION

From Dee's pattern of spared and impaired processing we can see that she has retained her 'action' abilities (e.g. reaching, grasping and stepping over objects) but her recognition ability is impaired. Goodale and Milner (1992, 2004) suggested that these two unconscious processes might be facilitated by different brain areas. As the parietal cortex provides information about the orientation and structure of objects in order to help guide movement and the temporal lobe provides visual information, they suggested that these different types of information might give rise to different representations. This led Goodale and Milner (1992) to develop their two-streams account of visual processing as explained in Chapter 2 (see also Milner and Goodale, 1995, 2006). They suggested that visual information follows two main streams or routes; the ventral stream (sometimes informally called the 'what' pathway) travels to the temporal lobe and is thought not only to be responsible for identifying objects and events but also to help attach meaning and significance to them (along with other cognitive structures). The dorsal stream (sometimes informally called the 'where' pathway) travels to the parietal lobe and it does not involve visual information. Instead, it processes spatial information and works with the sensorimotor system to help generate skilled movements (Goodale, 2008). This provides a clear account of Dee's pattern of spared and impaired processing; her dorsal stream is intact (Dee can negotiate her environment well) but she cannot recognise objects visually, so her ventral stream is evidently damaged. While the two-streams account is a highly influential and widely accepted account, some researchers have questioned the nature of the dissociation between the two streams (e.g. Franz *et al.*, 2000). These issues and more are considered fully in an excellent review by Milner and Goodale (2008).

COMPARING FORM AND INTEGRATIVE AGNOSIA

While there are many benefits to examining the pattern of spared and impaired processing using patient case studies, it is often very difficult to make direct comparisons and draw conclusions from case studies for a number of reasons. One particular difficulty is that researchers often use different tests, stimuli and methods to assess the level of spared and impaired processing and these methodological differences can make direct comparisons very difficult. To help remedy this, Riddoch *et al.* (2008a) directly compared HJA (who has integrative agnosia) with another patient SA (who has form agnosia) using an extensive array of tests. Both patients had bilateral occipital lesions, though they involved the dorsal route (action) with SA and the ventral route (recognition) with HJA. The results provide evidence for qualitatively different types of processing in the two types of agnosia. In particular, it was found that patient SA tended to process more at a local level, while HJA processed at a more global level. This led Riddoch *et al.* (2008a) to propose that successful object recognition depends on the ability to code the global aspects of an object's shape with the fine, local detail at the same time. So, as HJA processed more globally, he could match shapes well, whereas SA was impaired at this task. Similarly, while HJA could copy drawings, SA's drawings often contained errors. Therefore, HJA's pattern of impairment clearly fits integrative agnosia. He can code the shapes of objects, but he is impaired in the ability to segment parts of objects and group them into a whole, whereas SA's pattern of impairment fits clearly with form agnosia.

RECOGNISING LIVING AND NON-LIVING OBJECTS

SA was much better at identifying animate objects rather than inanimate ones, whereas HJA showed the opposite pattern, as he was better at identifying inanimate rather than animate objects. This finding that identification varies depending on the category of object has also been reported by other researchers. For example, JBR could name drawings of many non-living objects (such as a spade or hairbrush), but he couldn't name drawings of living things (such as dog or fly), or musical instruments (such as a trumpet), according to Warrington and Shallice (1984). Researchers have also reported that other patients have difficulty in identifying living things (e.g. Farah *et al.*, 1989, patient LH; Farah *et al.*, 1991, patient MB; Stewart *et al.*, 1992, patient HO).

One of the difficulties in interpreting results such as these is that the distinction between living and non-living things is not perfect. For example, JBR also had difficulty naming musical instruments (as did HO). One possibility is that the living and non-living things used to demonstrate this effect may also differ in other characteristics. Stewart *et al.* (1992) pointed out that although the living and non-living pictures used to demonstrate this effect were matched for the familiarity of the object names, they were not matched for the familiarity of the pictures themselves. Furthermore they observed that there is a tendency for line drawings of living things to be more complex than drawings of non-living things. When Stewart *et al.* (1992) retested their patient HO with a new set of materials which were matched for familiarity of both name and picture as well as image complexity, they found that he no longer demonstrated a category-specific agnosia, and when Funnell and Sheridan (1992) retested Warrington and Shallice's patient JBR using materials which controlled for item familiarity, there was no evidence of the category-specific naming deficit that Warrington and Shallice had originally observed.

One additional difficulty of using line drawings is that they don't contain important surface characteristics (e.g. colour, texture and 3-D shape information) which are useful cues to aid identification. As Hiraoka *et al.* (2009) state, it is common in studies of visual agnosia to find an identification superiority for real objects over line drawings as they only contain basic 2-D shape information. Interestingly, Peru and Avesani (2008) reported that patient FB couldn't name most of the black-and-white line drawings that she was shown. However, she could identify more objects when the drawings were in colour. FB also couldn't identify coloured pictures of living things but she recognised 70 per cent of non-living things.

Farah and McClelland (1991) argue that this difference between identifying living versus non-living things may in fact be an artefact. They state that in most cases where there is impaired knowledge of perceptual attributes compared with intact knowledge of functional properties, there is also an impairment for inanimate objects. They suggest that this is because perceptual attributes (colour, size, shape etc.) are crucial for identifying animate objects, whereas the identification of inanimate objects relies mainly on functional attributes (e.g. a kettle is used to boil water). However, there is evidence that knowledge of perceptual attributes can be distinguished from functional attributes in semantic memory (Riddoch and Humphreys, 1987). Furthermore, while FB has impaired knowledge of object form, her knowledge of object colour remains relatively intact. Indeed, the findings from FB led Peru and Avesani (2008) to tentatively suggest that different properties may be stored discretely in semantic memory. What is clear is that while there are clearly methodological issues with the stimuli that have been used to assess the levels of impairment in visual agnosia, the finding that HJA and SA showed a converse pattern in their ability to identify animate and inanimate objects (Riddoch *et al.*, 2008a) using the *same* stimuli, suggests that this effect cannot be attributed to an artefact of the stimulus materials. Research in this area continues.

4.6 DISORDERS OF FACE PROCESSING

Prosopagnosia is a form of agnosia that relates to faces. As you read in the previous section, agnosia is an ancient Greek word which means 'non-knowledge'. The 'prosop' part of the term comes from another ancient Greek word 'prosopon' which means 'face'. The term prosopagnosia was first used by Bodamer (1947); he examined three patients who, he believed, showed a face-specific deficit, as they were apparently able to recognise non-face objects normally. So prosopagnosia roughly translates to 'not knowing' faces, or rather the inability to recognise faces. People with severe prosopagnosia cannot recognise family members, friends and even themselves in the mirror, and this cannot be explained by visual or sensory impairment. However, individuals with prosopagnosia are often able to use other cues such as voice to recognise familiar people. This means that identity and semantic information hasn't been lost. They still know who the people are, it's just that they can no longer recognise their faces. Bruce and Young (1986) used evidence gained from studying individuals with face processing deficits and from studies of normal individuals to propose a model of face processing (Figure 4.8). This model suggests that the recognition of identity, expression and facial speech analysis (e.g. lip reading) are independent processes, and subsequent evidence from brain-damaged patients largely supports this view.

Given that face recognition is one of the most demanding and sophisticated tasks that our visual system undertakes, it is unsurprising that an impairment in this ability can be acquired through brain damage. Faces are remarkably similar in appearance. They have the same first-order global configuration (eyes above nose above mouth etc.) and facial features are remarkably similar. Despite this, we are able to recognise thousands of faces with apparent ease. It is important to note that brain damage rarely leads to the complete destruction of this ability. Instead, research has demonstrated that there is considerable variation in the severity of the impairment, the associated deficits and types of face processing skills as well as in the location of and type of lesions that result in acquired prosopagnosia (Barton, 2008). Furthermore, prosopagnosia may present alongside other associated deficits and disorders such as autism or Alzheimer's disease, and recent research has demonstrated that it may be present in childhood. This part of the chapter focuses primarily on the evidence for prosopagnosia that has been acquired in adulthood but developmental and congenital prosopagnosia will be considered at the end of the chapter.

LIVING WITH PROSOPAGNOSIA

While the variation of spared and impaired processing in prosopagnosia may help to tell us a great deal about face processing and its underlying mechanisms, it tells us very little about what it is like to live with prosopagnosia. Our ability to communicate socially and professionally depends to a large extent on our ability to be able to converse

---

Key Term

Prosopagnosia
An inability to recognise faces despite adequate visual acuity.

Developmental prosopagnosia
This is thought to be a result of early neurological trauma that might be caused by accident or injury.

Congenital prosopagnosia
This is thought to be present from birth and is thought to occur without any apparent brain injury.

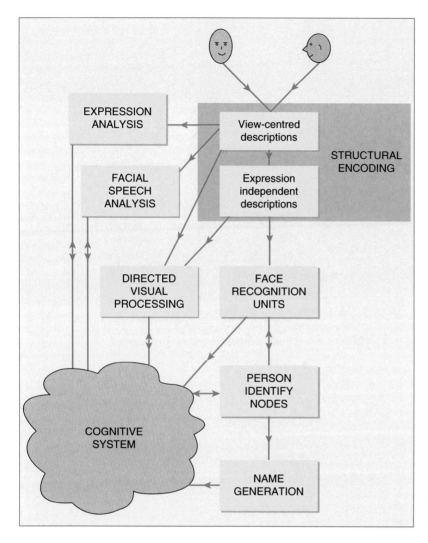

Figure 4.8   Bruce and Young's model of face processing showing independent pathways for face recognition, expression analysis and speech analysis.

Source: Bruce and Young (1986), reproduced by permission of the British Psychological Society.

and interact with our family, friends and colleagues. So what is it like to live with prosopagnosia? The material in Box 4.3 has been kindly provided by Jeff Hunt. I met Jeff while he was a cognitive psychology student with the Open University. Despite having prosopagnosia, Jeff was able to hold down jobs as both a lecturer and an IT manager for a large college. Here he provides just a few examples of how prosopagnosia impacts on his daily life.

WHAT KIND OF DAMAGE CAUSES ACQUIRED PROSOPAGNOSIA?

There is considerable variation in the type and location of lesion that results in prosopagnosia. Early autopsy studies (e.g. Damasio *et al.*, 1982) reported that prosopagnosia was caused by bilateral lesions in the occipito-temporal cortex. More recent reports have supported this

Box 4.3   Jeff: Living with prosopagnosia

Example 1

One day I was at home and the front door opened unexpectedly and a strange lady walked straight into my hall. I stared at her wondering what to do and what to say, especially as I was just dressed in a pair of boxer shorts. She said 'Oh you don't like it; I can tell by the way you are staring!' It was only when she spoke that I realised that it was my wife. She had been to the hairdressers and had her hair cut and dyed. I simply had not recognised her. The only reason I was staring was because I was trying to work out why this woman was in my hallway!

Example 2

The only lecturing incident that I clearly got wrong was when my lecture was moved from one lecture room to another. I was not told but the students were. So I went into my lecture and started talking about artificial intelligence and John Searle and his Chinese Room problem. After about 20 minutes another lecturer came in and asked me if I had his students – he was a geography lecturer. The students had decided not to say anything as they found my lecture interesting, which I guess is a compliment but I felt rather cross with myself that I had thought that I had recognised some of them.

Example 3

My youngest daughter was shopping with me and we have a lifelong habit of playing jokes on each other. She wanted to go and look at the chocolates so I let her wander while I found a few bits I needed. I went to find her and saw her looking at the sweets. She looked at me watching up the aisle and then pretended to ignore me and look away. So I crept around the other end of the aisle and ran up behind her and tickled her in the ribs. At that moment she turned round and to my horror it was not my daughter! To nicely compound my humiliation, her mum came up and tried to find out what was going on. Thankfully, as I was trying to explain, my daughter came along and I politely pointed out that her hair was similar to the child I'd tickled in the ribs. The mum very reluctantly accepted it.

Prosopagnosia also affects Jeff's life in other not so obvious ways. One is that it is very difficult for him to watch television and films. This is because actors often change clothing and hair styles during a film. The consequence of this is that Jeff can get the actors confused with each other, or it seems that a new character has been introduced when it is just an existing character with a new hairstyle. Jeff writes that 'the film *Fifth Element* is great for me as all of the characters look completely different'. With television though, 'I do struggle to believe that the character Brian Potter in *Phoenix Nights* is Peter Kay, the comedian.'

by showing that patients with prosopagnosia have bilateral lesions (e.g. Boutsen and Humphreys, 2002; Sorger *et al.*, 2007), suggesting that both hemispheres play an important role in face processing. However, in rarer cases it can also be caused by unilateral damage in the right hemisphere (De Renzi *et al.*, 1994; Barton, 2008) and even rarer still, by left-hemisphere lesions (Mattson *et al.*, 2000).

Data from imaging studies has also demonstrated that most cases of prosopagnosia have damage in the fusiform and lingual gyri, although there are also cases of damage in more anterior temporal areas (e.g. Gainotti *et al.*, 2003). The fusiform area has been shown to be a key structure in face and object processing, and numerous studies have shown that the fusiform gyrus contains an area dedicated to face processing called the fusiform face area (FFA) (e.g. Haxby *et al.*, 1994; Kanwisher *et al.*, 1997; McCarthy *et al.*, 1997). There is variability, however, in the location of the FFA across individuals, and this may help to explain why prosopagnosia sometimes seems to occur with damage in only one hemisphere (Bruce and Young, 2012). Given this individual variability, many imaging studies have adopted what has been termed a 'functional localiser' approach. Kanwisher *et al.* (1997) developed this technique by identifying functional areas of interest for each individual. Multiple tests are then performed and the activity within this pre-defined area is examined. Doing this allows for the fact that people's brains and brain structures are of different sizes, so it allows precise comparison across the same brain area in different people, without mistakenly measuring activity in a different brain area. Using this technique, it is possible to identify activity in structures such as the FFA.

While the FFA plays a key role in face processing, there is still variability in the type of brain damage that can result in prosopagnosia. This variation is consistent with current thinking regarding face processing – there is no single area in the brain that is responsible for processing faces. Instead, this highly developed and demanding process is underpinned by a distributed neural network that is made up of many bilateral regions (Haxby *et al.*, 2000). So how does this variability impact on the type of face-processing impairments that are observed in prosopagnosia? Barton (2008) examined this by reviewing the data from ten patients. It was reported that the most severe impairments were found in patients who had bilateral occipito-temporal lesions, involving the fusiform gyri. In particular, bilateral lesions in this area resulted in severe impairments in the ability to form an image of a face, to perceive and integrate configural information and also resulted in the lowest levels of familiarity to famous faces. This led Barton to conclude that the right fusiform gyrus was involved in configurational processing and that memory for faces was more severely disrupted when these bilateral lesions also included right anterior temporal lobe damage.

PROSOPAGNOSIA – A FACE-SPECIFIC DISORDER?

Riddoch *et al.* (2008b) studied FB and found that she was unable to identify faces of famous people that she was previously familiar with. She was also poor at saying whether two faces were the same or different when they were in different views. FB could, however, make age, sex

Key Term

Fusiform face area (FFA)

An area in the fusiform gyrus dedicated to face processing.

and expression judgements. She could learn object names faster than controls, and she scored within the normal range on an object-naming task. FB was also faster to respond to parts of faces than whole faces. This dissociation between FB's ability to process objects and faces indicates that her deficit is in the ability to perceive facial information. As the results provide support for face-specific processes, it indicates that FB demonstrates a relatively 'pure' form of prosopagnosia.

Does this mean that prosopagnosia is specific to faces? While there is clearly evidence for face-specificity (e.g. De Renzi and Pellegrino, 1998; Wada and Yakamoto, 2001; Riddoch *et al.*, 2008b) some people with prosopagnosia also have difficulty in processing objects (e.g. Farah *et al.*, 1995). One of the major difficulties in trying to draw conclusions regarding face specificity is that there are methodological issues surrounding the assessment of face and object processing. The main difficulty is that face recognition requires what is called a within-category judgement. That is, in order to successfully recognise a face, we have to recognise it from our 'pool' of all of the other faces that we know. So we need to be able to discriminate between a whole host of similar-looking faces – a remarkable feat which we generally perform with ease. In contrast, we rarely have to recognise an individual object amongst a whole host of other similar objects. Imagine that you had to select a Braeburn apple from a crate that also contained Cortland, McIntosh and Gala apples (they're all red ones!). This would seem to be an almost impossible task, unless you were an apple expert. Now, imagine that you are given a specific Braeburn apple to inspect, which is then put into the crate with all of the other apples. The task now requires you to identify and select the *same* apple that you originally inspected. This seems like an impossible task and yet we achieve it every day when we recognise an individual face. This difference in process between making a within-category judgement (as has just been described) and making a between-category judgement (recognising an apple in a crate of oranges, melons and plums) is what makes face recognition special. It is all about individuation, and we need to be able to recognise many individual faces in order to function successfully in society. The challenge for researchers is that in order to be able to clearly demonstrate whether prosopagnosia is face-specific or not, similar tasks need to be employed to examine object and face processing. So, this means comparing a face recognition task with an object recognition task where the set of stimuli are as similar to one another as the faces are to each other. Some researchers have used sets of similar manufactured items such as eyeglasses or cars (De Renzi *et al.*, 1991; Sergent and Signoret, 1992; Farah *et al.*, 1995; Tippett *et al.*, 2000) and on the whole these studies find that prosopagnosic patients are significantly more impaired with faces than these other non-face items. However, unlike faces, cars or eyeglasses are not natural biological objects, and for this reason some researchers have also attempted to study performance on tasks which require patients to identify individual members of non-human species, including cows and sheep. Bruyer *et al.* (1983) reported that Mr W, a prosopagnosic farmer, was still able

Key Term

Individuation
Recognising one specific item from other members of that class of item (e.g. recognising the face of a particular individual).

to recognise his cows. This is in contrast to the report by Bornstein *et al.* (1969) who described a prosopagnosic farmer who could not recognise either humans or his cows, and Assal *et al.* (1984) who describe a farmer who was initially unable to recognise either humans or cows but after six months recovered the ability to recognise human faces but not to individuate cows. Thus, almost unbelievably, we have evidence of a double dissociation between the ability to individuate humans and animals following brain injury. McNeil and Warrington (1993) describe the case of WJ, who took up farming after becoming prosopagnosic and remarkably showed evidence of being able to recognise his sheep, despite remaining profoundly prosopagnosic for human faces. This is an important case because it demonstrates that it is possible to learn to distinguish between very similar biological forms (sheep) despite being prosopagnosic and unable to identify even highly familiar human faces. This is in contrast to the patient described by Tippett *et al.* (2000) who could recognise faces and non-faces he had learned prior to his injury, and could learn new non-face objects but could not learn to identify new faces.

Figure 4.9   Would you recognise this cow if you saw her again?

Source: Shutterstock.

While there are clear dissociations in the literature, Duchaine and Garrido (2008) argue that dissociations are not enough to provide support for face specificity. They state that 'A network of areas is involved in face processing, but the role of these areas and their interactions remain poorly understood' (p. 767). Therefore, it is still unclear what conclusions should be drawn concerning the degree of face specificity in prosopagnosia. In part the problem lies with the fact that as faces are, in one sense at least, special – it is difficult to find suitable non-face control stimuli which can be individuated as well as faces by normal subjects.

COVERT RECOGNITION IN PROSOPAGNOSIA

Some, but not all prosopagnosic patients show evidence of covert recognition (Bruyer, 1991), that is, an indication that at some level their brains are discriminating between faces. Some of these patients demonstrate covert familiarity – for example showing differences in neural electrical responses (evoked potentials) produced by viewing familiar and unfamiliar faces (Renault *et al.*, 1989). In other cases it has been possible to demonstrate some retained knowledge about the person shown in a photograph, such as occupation or name. Interestingly, Bruyer *et al.* (1983) found that it was easier to teach a prosopagnosic patient to associate faces with their real names than with randomly assigned names, and de Haan *et al.* (1987) showed that this was true even for people that their patient (PH) had met after he had become prosopagnosic, suggesting that he continued to learn the names and faces of people he met despite having no conscious awareness of recognition.

Simon *et al.* (2011) examined covert processing of faces with patient PS. EEG and fMRI data were collected while PS performed a gender discrimination task for both familiar and unfamiliar faces. The results from both the EEG and fMRI data revealed that PS had different patterns of activity for faces that were previously known to PS compared with unfamiliar and famous faces, even though PS could not identify any of the faces and had no conscious feeling of familiarity. In particular, there was increased activation in the FFA for previously familiar faces, compared with unfamiliar faces. This difference wasn't found for famous faces and provides evidence that the FFA is involved in covert processing as well as in individuating faces.

There are different explanations for why covert recognition may occur. Bauer (1984) linked face processing to the two streams of processing proposed by Goodale and Milner (1992), suggesting that conscious, overt face recognition is facilitated by the ventral pathway, whereas covert recognition is mediated by the dorsal pathway. As the ventral route is damaged in acquired prosopagnosia, whereas the dorsal route is intact, this may explain why people with acquired prosopagnosia often show covert recognition but are unable to overtly recognise a face. Others, however, have suggested that the difference between overt and covert recognition in acquired prosopagnosia arises from a disconnection. De Haan *et al.* (1992) suggested that this disconnection occurs between an intact face-processing system and a higher system that facilitates conscious awareness. Burton and colleagues (Burton *et al.*, 1991), however, explain the disconnection in terms of connection weights. They developed the IAC (independent activation and competition) model of face recognition, which was based on the earlier Bruce and Young (1986) model and found that this model could simulate some of the covert recognition behaviours that have been observed in the literature. In this connectionist model, different units (e.g. face recognition units (FRUs); person identity nodes (PINS)) are linked together with bidirectional weighted connection links, and it was found that covert recognition could be simulated by halving the weight (or strength) of these links (Burton *et al.*, 1991; Young and Burton, 1999). This means that activation can still occur within the face recognition system, but this activation doesn't reach the level that is required for overt recognition. Bruce and Young (2012: 343) state that one implication of this is that 'covert recognition will not be an "all or none" phenomenon – effects will be graded according to the functional locus and severity of damage'.

CAN PROSOPAGNOSIA OCCUR WITHOUT BRAIN DAMAGE?

While the early literature on prosopagnosia described cases where it had been 'acquired' as a result of brain trauma in adulthood, more recently, it has been reported that prosopagnosia can occur much earlier and in some cases without acquired brain trauma. These cases have been called 'congenital' or 'developmental' prosopagnosia, and while these terms are often used interchangeably in the literature, they are quite different. Congenital prosopagnosia is thought to be present from birth and was traditionally thought to occur without any apparent brain injury. In contrast, developmental prosopagnosia is thought to be a result of early neurological trauma that might be caused by accident or injury (Avidan and Behrman, 2008). Recent MRI studies have, however, questioned the lack of brain abnormality in congenital prosopagnosia. While some have reported no brain abnormalities (e.g. Patient GA in Barton *et al.*, 2003) others have reported a range of abnormalities. For example, Behrmann *et al.* (2007) reported that the fusiform gyrus was smaller and that there was a relationship between size and impairment: the smaller the fusiform gyrus, the more severe the impairment. Therefore, the nature of the impairment in congenital prosopagnosia is at present, far from clear.

One of the reasons why the terms 'developmental' and 'congenital' prosopagnosia are often used interchangeably is that it is often extremely difficult to be sure if there has been early childhood injury or if the condition has been present from birth. For example, Duchaine *et al.* (2006) examined face processing in Edward, who was thought to have developmental prosopagnosia. However, the authors state that Edward's impairment has been lifelong and he is not aware of any childhood trauma, so he may in fact have congenital prosopagnosia. While tests have been developed to aid diagnosis of these two forms of prosopagnosia there are issues with them (see Bowles *et al.*, 2009, for a discussion), so at present diagnosing these two different types of prosopagnosia is extremely difficult.

TYPES OF IMPAIRMENT IN DEVELOPMENTAL AND CONGENITAL PROSOPAGNOSIA

Individuals with developmental prosopagnosia sometimes have impairments in the ability to process facial emotion (e.g. Duchaine, 2000) and the ability to make gender judgements (e.g. de Haan and Campbell, 1991). Furthermore, while many cases of developmental prosopagnosia seem to have impairments that are consistent with autism spectrum disorder (ASD) (Wilson *et al.*, 2010), developmental prosopagnosia does occur without ASD. For example, Wilson *et al.* (2010) examined six children between the ages of four and eight years who were thought to display prosopagnosic symptoms. Using a range of face-processing and cognitive tasks they found that four of the six children did not display any sign of ASD but they did exhibit a range of difficulties in processing faces and objects.

Patients with congenital prosopagnosia show considerable variability in face-processing impairment. However, it does seem that most have an associative or integrative impairment. That is, they can perceive a face as a face but are unable to link it to their stored representation of known faces. For example, Bentin *et al.* (2007) examined the face-processing abilities of KW who was unable to identify faces, had a bias towards local feature processing and had difficulty processing holistically, not just for faces. This suggested that KW had congenital integrative prosopagnosia.

Many patients with congenital prosopagnosia also show evidence of covert recognition, similar to acquired prosopagnosia (Avidan and Behrmann, 2008; Bate *et al.*, 2008). This finding is extremely interesting because it was traditionally thought that patients with congenital prosopagnosia could *not* show evidence of covert recognition because it is associated with patients who had previously been able to recognise faces and as such would have a store of intact face representations (Barton *et al.*, 2001). This questions many of the functional models of face processing and much more research is needed in order to fully understand the nature of covert processing in congenital prosopagnosia.

SUMMARY

- Damage to different brain regions can result in a variety of perceptual and attention disorders which display a surprising degree of specificity.
- The pattern of disorders observed suggests a highly modular system in which a series of independent processes each contribute towards the goal of perception.
- Synaesthesia is a phenomenon which seems to result from a breakdown in this modularity.
- Blindsight provides an example of this dissociation between conscious experience and the ability to respond appropriately to a stimulus.
- Prosopagnosia also provides evidence of this dissociation, as does unilateral neglect, where some patients show evidence of partial insight into the nature of neglected objects.
- There is some evidence that the nature of the representation formed might be dependent on the task to be performed, and in particular there may be an important distinction between the perceptual processes that mediate action and those which result in recognition.
- Two broad patterns of impairment in visual agnosia have been identified and these were originally termed *apperceptive agnosia* (now generally known as *form agnosia)* and *associative* agnosia (now known as *integrative agnosia*).
- In *form agnosia* patients are unable to discriminate between objects and cannot copy line drawings. *Integrative agnosia* is characterised by an ability to perceive the individual shapes and elements of objects with an inability to integrate these elements into a representation of the whole object.
- *Prosopagnosia* involves an impairment of face processing. It can be acquired or it can be developmental or congenital. In all forms of prosopagnosia there is considerable variation in the severity

Key Term

Modular system
A system in which different types of processing are carried out by separate and relatively independent sub-systems.

of impairment, associated deficits and types of face processing skills.

- In acquired prosopagnosia there is variability in the location and type of lesion, although impairment in areas such as the fusiform face area seems to be particularly important.
- Some patients with prosopagnosia show evidence of covert recognition even when the disorder appears to have been present from birth (congenital prosopagnosia). This finding challenges many functional models of face processing, and research in this area continues.

FURTHER READING

- Bruce, V. and Young, A. (2012) *Face Perception.* Hove: Psychology Press. A comprehensive and extremely accessible text covering all aspects of face perception.
- De Gelder, B., de Haan, E. H. F. and Heywood, C.A. (2001). *Out of Mind: Varieties of Unconscious Processes.* Oxford: Oxford University Press. This edited collection of papers examine the nature of blindsight and related conditions.
- Farah, M. J. (2004). *Visual Agnosia* (2nd edn). Cambridge, MA: MIT Press. A very readable account of disorders in object recognition written by one of the leading researchers in the field.
- Goodale, M. and Milner, D. (2004). *Sight Unseen.* Oxford: Oxford University Press. In this book Goodale and Milner provide a fascinating account of their work with patient 'Dee'.
- Harrison, J. (2001). *Synaesthesia: The Strangest Thing.* Oxford: Oxford University Press. This book provides a very accessible account of synaesthesia.
- Hole, G. and Bourne, V. (2010). *Face Processing: Psychological, Neuropsychological and Applied Perspectives.* Oxford: Oxford University Press. An extremely accessible text that contains several easy to read chapters on the neuropsychology of face processing.
- Karnath, H. O., Milner, A. D. and Vallar, G. (2002). *The Cognitive and Neural Bases of Spatial Neglect.* Oxford: Oxford University Press. This edited volume brings together some of the leading researchers in the field.
- Young, A. W. (ed.) (1998) *Face and Mind.* Oxford: Oxford University Press. Provides a fuller description of prosopagnosia, and related conditions including some not covered in this chapter.

Chapter 5

Contents

Short-term memory

David Groome

5.1 MULTISTORE MODELS OF MEMORY

THE DUAL-STORE THEORY OF MEMORY

Information which has been perceived and attended will sometimes be put into the memory store. Early cognitive psychologists assumed that there was just one memory store, but William James (1890) suggested that there were two separate stores, one for items being held briefly in conscious awareness and the other for items held for longer periods in unconscious storage. He called these two stores 'primary memory' and 'secondary memory' respectively, though they subsequently became known as short-term memory (STM) and long-term memory (LTM). STM refers to the memories which are currently receiving our conscious attention, and it is a store of fairly brief duration and limited capacity. LTM refers to the memories which are *not* presently in conscious awareness, but which are held in storage ready to be recalled. The LTM store has a very large capacity and can hold information for a lifetime. Atkinson and Shiffrin (1968) used these ideas to develop a theoretical model of memory, which is shown in Figure 5.1.

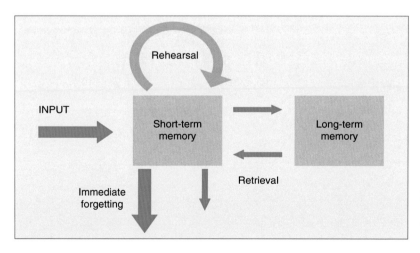

Figure 5.1 The dual-store model of memory.

Source: Atkinson and Shiffrin (1968).

Key Term

Long-term memory Memory held in permanent storage, available for retrieval at some time in the future (contrasts with short-term memory).

Short-term memory Memory held in conscious awareness, and which is currently receiving attention (contrasts with long-term memory).

According to the Atkinson and Shiffrin model, information is held in STM by continually rehearsing it, and without rehearsal it will be almost immediately forgotten. The LTM is seen as a more passive store of information which is available for retrieval but not kept in an activated form. Earlier models of memory storage had seen the STM as little more than a 'port of entry' into the LTM, but in the Atkinson and Shiffrin model the STM store is also used for retrieval of memories from storage. This notion of STM as a focus of both input and output of memories is of central importance to the more recent working memory model (Baddeley and Hitch, 1974), which has developed the concept of the STM as a conscious workspace.

The distinction between STM and LTM is sometimes referred to as the 'dual-store' theory of memory, because it proposes two distinct forms of memory storage. It therefore constitutes one of the first 'multistore' theories of memory, describing memory as a number of related structures rather than as a single entity. In fact the Atkinson and Shiffrin model included a third store, which was seen as a very brief preliminary store for unprocessed sensory information, essentially an after-image occurring in the sense organ itself. There is some evidence for such a brief sensory store (Sperling, 1960), but the STM and LTM are of far greater importance to cognition.

James made the distinction between the STM and LTM stores essentially on the basis of subjective experience. He felt that conscious memory seemed different to storage memory, and seemed to have different characteristics. James was a psychologist of great intuitive genius, and like many of his theories the distinction between primary and secondary memory remains plausible to this day. However, it was left to later psychologists to provide scientific evidence for the existence of two separate memory stores.

CLINICAL EVIDENCE FOR THE STM/LTM DISTINCTION

Over the years, evidence has gradually accumulated in support of the dual-store theory, the most convincing evidence coming from the study of amnesic patients. Those suffering from organic amnesia (a memory impairment caused by physical damage to the brain) have difficulty forming any new long-term memories, but their immediate short-term memory is usually unimpaired (Baddeley and Warrington, 1970). Such patients are able to remember what has been said to them during the previous few seconds, but not much else. The finding that STM can remain intact despite severe impairment of LTM suggests that they are separate and independent memory stores.

This view receives further support from the finding that a few patients have been studied who show the exact reverse of this dissociation, with an intact LTM but a severely impaired STM. For example, Warrington and Shallice (1969) described a patient known as KF who had suffered damage to the left parietal region of his brain in a motorcycle accident. KF had no LTM impairment but his STM was quite severely impaired. In fact he could only hold one or two digits in conscious STM at a particular moment in time, whereas most normal people can hold at least seven digits (this measure of STM is known as digit span, and it is further discussed in Section 5.2). Although this type of impairment is very rare, a few other patients have since been studied who show a similar pattern of impaired STM with an intact LTM (Basso *et al.*, 1982; Vallar and Baddeley, 1982). However, in recent years researchers have realised that these digit span impairments normally only affect one component of the STM, namely the phonological loop. This is explained more fully in Section 5.4.

Taking the two types of evidence together, it is apparent that either the STM or the LTM can be separately impaired whilst the other store remains intact. A 'double dissociation' of this kind is regarded as being far more convincing than evidence of a single dissociation, and it is the main reason why most cognitive psychologists today accept that STM and LTM are separate memory stores.

Key Term

Digit span
A measure of the largest number of digits which an individual can recall when tested immediately after their presentation. Widely used as a test of the capacity of the phonological component of the working memory.

Recency and primacy effects
The tendency for participants to show particularly good recall for items presented towards the end (recency) or the start (primacy) of a list.

THE RECENCY EFFECT

Ebbinghaus (1885) demonstrated that memory for a list of items is affected by the serial position of an item in a list. Items at the end of the list are particularly well remembered (the recency effect), and to a lesser extent items at the start of the list also tend to be remembered (the primacy effect). However, items in the middle of the list are more likely to be forgotten. This serial position curve is illustrated in Figure 5.2.

Ebbinghaus suggested that items in the middle of the list might suffer more interference from other adjacent items than would items at the start and end of the list, which could explain why the items in the middle are less easily remembered. However, a more likely explanation was subsequently put forward for the recency effect, which is that the last few items on the list are probably remembered because they are still in the STM at the time of recall. This theory received convincing support from the finding that the recency effect disappears when a delay is introduced between learning a wordlist and recalling it (Glanzer and Cunitz, 1966). A delay of 30 seconds, filled with a simple task (counting backwards) to prevent subjects from rehearsing the wordlist, was found to be sufficient to completely eliminate the recency effect. The results of this experiment are summarised in Figure 5.3.

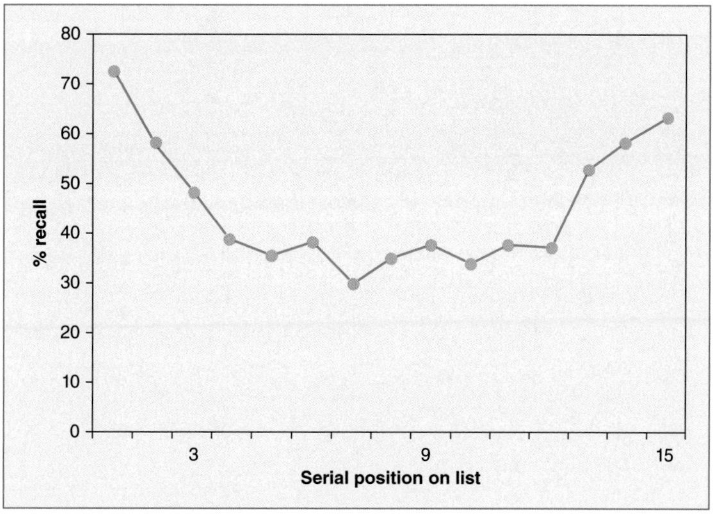

Figure 5.2 The serial position curve.

Glanzer and Cunitz concluded that the recency effect was explained by the fact that the last few items on the list were still being held in the

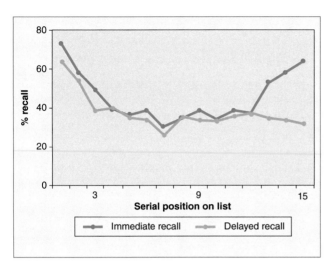

Figure 5.3   The effect of delayed recall on the recency effect.

Source: Glanzer and Cunitz (1966).

STM. Their findings add further support for the STM/LTM distinction, and they also suggest that information requires conscious rehearsal in order to maintain it in the STM store.

A number of different explanations have been suggested for the primacy effect. There is some evidence (Oberauer, 2003) that items at the beginning of the list benefit from greater attention than those later in the sequence. It has also been shown that the retrieval of the first items on the list may inhibit the retrieval of subsequent items (Cowan, 2005), a phenomenon known as output interference.

5.2 MEASURING STM PERFORMANCE

THE DURATION OF STM STORAGE

We can get a good indication of the duration of STM storage by studying amnesic individuals who are unable to transfer information to the LTM. This means that they can only store information in STM. For example, the severely amnesic patient CW has virtually no LTM, and consequently he can only retain new information for about seven seconds (Wilson and Wearing, 1995). Similar STM retention periods have been reported for other amnesics (Spiers *et al.*, 2001), so it would appear that STM can only hold on to information for a few seconds. The Brown–Peterson task (Brown, 1958; Peterson and Peterson, 1959) is a technique for measuring the duration of STM storage in normal individuals. The task requires them to retain a few test items whilst being prevented from repeating or rehearsing them, thus stopping them from transferring the items to LTM. The participant is presented with test items which are well below maximum span (such as three letters), which they are required to repeat back after a short retention interval. However, during this retention interval the participant is required to perform a distraction task (such as counting backwards in threes) to prevent rehearsal of the test items. The results obtained by Brown and the Petersons showed that, when rehearsal is prevented in this way, the test items are forgotten very rapidly. In fact most items had been forgotten within 5-10 seconds of being presented (Figure 5.4).

Two main conclusions can be drawn from these results. First, STM storage apparently requires rehearsal of some kind, to keep the item in conscious attention. Second, when rehearsal is prevented, items are lost from the STM very rapidly. In fact Muter (1980) showed that most items are forgotten within 3-4 seconds if the subject is not expecting to be tested. Muter claims that this is probably a more accurate estimation of STM duration, since the use of an unexpected test may help to eliminate the contribution of LTM.

STM CAPACITY

Most traditional tests of memory, such as the recall of wordlists or stories, provide what is predominantly a measure of LTM. Tests of STM are harder to devise, but one of the most popular tests of STM capacity is the immediate memory span. The subject is simply read a series of items (such as digits) and is then required to repeat them immediately, in the correct order. Since there is no time delay, immediate memory span is thought to depend largely on STM, and has become widely accepted as an approximate measure of STM performance.

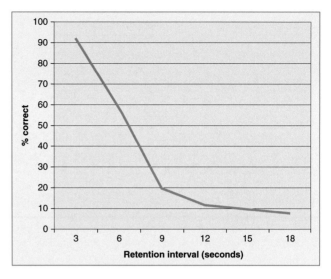

Figure 5.4   STM forgetting when rehearsal is prevented.
Source: Peterson and Peterson (1959).

If you wish to test your own digit span, you will find an example of the procedure in Figure 5.5. Read the five digits in the top row of the list, then cover up the list and try to write them down. If you get them all right, test yourself on to the next row, in which the number of digits is increased to six. Keep on going until you

71504
284936
8351609
25736184
940627135
2753180649

Figure 5.5   The digit span test. The first row of letters is read to the participant, who must repeat them immediately. If they get this row correct, move on to the next row, and so on until they make an error.

start getting some of the digits wrong. Your digit span is the largest number of digits you can get right in one trial.

Tests of this kind suggest that the average normal person has a maximum digit span of about seven digits, and in fact their maximum span for letters or words tends to be fairly similar (Miller, 1956). There is some variation among the general population, with scores varying typically from five to about nine items. However, immediate memory span is probably not a pure measure of STM, since there is evidence that LTM may make some contribution to span performance (Hulme *et al.*, 1991). In particular, information stored in LTM may facilitate the 'chunking' of several items into one meaningful item (Wolters and Raffone, 2008). This may explain why digit span tends to yield a higher estimate of STM capacity than other measures. An example of chunking is given in Chapter 6 (Section 6.3).

The recency effect (see Section 5.1) offers another possible means of measuring STM capacity. Based on the number of items in the 'recency' section of the serial position curve, Craik (1970) estimated the capacity of STM to be about three or four items. This is rather less than the estimate obtained with the digit span method. Cowan (2005) arrived at a similar estimate of STM capacity by using the running memory task. This involves listening to a sequence of digits which is suddenly ended, at which point the participant must try to remember as many of the digits as possible. Cowan found that about four digits would typically be recalled in this test, which is again fewer than would typically be achieved in a standard memory span test.

Based on these findings it is currently thought that the STM has a capacity of only about four items (Cowan, 2010), and the slightly higher measures produced by simple digit span tests are assumed to reflect an additional input from the long-term memory store.

Figure 5.6   Alan Baddeley.
Source: Google Images.

> **Key Term**
>
> **Working memory (WM)**
>
> A hypothetical short-term memory system which serves as a mental workspace in which a variety of processing operations are carried out on both new input and retrieved memories.

5.3 THE WORKING MEMORY MODEL

WORKING MEMORY

Early versions of the dual-store model tended to regard STM and LTM as two stores differing mainly in their duration. However, the working memory model (Baddeley and Hitch, 1974) emphasises the different functions of these stores. They argued that the STM was more than just a temporary storage space, and that it functioned as an active working memory (WM), a kind of mental workspace in which a variety of processing operations were carried out on both new and old memories. In contrast, the LTM was seen as a storage memory (SM), maintaining information in a fairly passive state for possible future retrieval. Baddeley and Hitch use the terms WM and SM because they emphasise the function of these systems rather than storage duration.

A possible analogy is to think of the working memory as resembling the screen of a computer, a space in which various tasks are performed on current data, whilst the storage memory serves a similar purpose to the computer's memory disks, holding large amounts of information in long-term storage (see Figure 5.7).

Baddeley and Hitch (1974) regarded the working memory as a workspace where analysis and processing of information would take place. They reasoned that such processing would require some means of storing information while it was being processed, but their research suggested that there were two short-term stores rather than just one. This research made use of the dual-task paradigm, in which the subject has to carry out two WM tasks at the same time. They found that two simultaneous WM tasks will disrupt one another severely if both tasks involve auditory input, or if both tasks involve visual input. However, a visual WM task and an auditory WM task can be carried out simultaneously without disrupting one another, suggesting that they are able to make use of two different stores. The disruption caused by one task to a second task involving the same sensory modality is assumed to result from competition for the same storage space.

Baddeley and Hitch concluded that the working memory must have separate stores for visual and auditory information. They proposed a model of working memory (Figure 5.8) comprising a central executive served by two short-term stores. These are the phonological loop, which holds auditory and speech-based information, and the visuo-spatial sketchpad, which holds visual information.

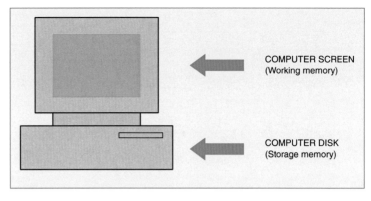

Figure 5.7   The computer as an analogy for WM/SM.

Source: Groome (1999).

The working memory model has been very influential over the last 30 years, and a great deal of research has been carried out on its components. Some of this research is described below.

Figure 5.8   The working memory model.

Source: Baddeley and Hitch (1974).

5.4 THE PHONOLOGICAL LOOP
EVIDENCE FOR THE PHONOLOGICAL LOOP
The phonological loop is assumed to provide brief storage for auditory input such as words, and it is assumed to be the mechanism underlying measures such as digit span. The main evidence for the existence of the phonological loop arises from the dual-task paradigm described above. For example, Baddeley and Lewis (1981) found that the immediate recall of a list of spoken words is severely disrupted by the simultaneous

Figure 5.9   If you must do two things at once, make sure they don't use the same WM loop.

Source: Shutterstock.

performance of a second verbal task, even one which requires no significant attention or processing. The second task in their experiment involved simply repeating 'the, the, the,' over and over again, a procedure known as articulatory suppression because despite its simplicity it uses up the subject's capacity for repetition of input. However, a task involving visual imagery does not disrupt the recall of spoken words. Baddeley and Lewis concluded that performing a second verbal task disrupts the first one because they are both competing for the limited storage space in the phonological loop.

Further evidence for the existence of two separate WM loops comes from the study of clinical patients with impaired STM. For example, Warrington and Shallice (1972) reported that their patient KF (referred to above) showed a severe impairment in the immediate recall of spoken items (e.g. digits, letters, or words), but performed quite well when items were presented visually.

THE WORD-LENGTH EFFECT

The phonological loop is seen as being the mechanism underlying tasks such as digit span or word span, which was previously believed to have a limit of about seven items (Miller, 1956). However, Baddeley et al. (1975) found that the word span limit is greater for short words than for long words, a phenomenon known as the word-length effect. This finding led them to suggest that the phonological loop is limited not by the number of items it can hold, but by the length of time taken to speak them. In fact the word span was found to be limited to the number of words that could be spoken in about two seconds. The phonological loop thus seems to work in a rather similar way to a short loop of recording tape, which explains how it got its name. Some recent findings suggest that the word-length effect may depend primarily on the complexity and distinctiveness of the items rather than merely their length, since the word-length effect disappears when very complex and distinctive test items are used (Hulme et al., 2004).

SUB-COMPONENTS OF THE PHONOLOGICAL LOOP

Baddeley (1986) suggested that the phonological loop contains two separate components. These are the *phonological store*, which stores auditory information, and the *articulatory control process*, which allows sub-vocal rehearsal of the information. The articulatory control process is seen as a kind of 'inner speech' mechanism, linked to actual speech production, and it also helps to maintain verbal information in the phonological store.

These two sub-components were postulated because they offered an explanation for a number of unexpected findings. In the first place, it had been found that during articulatory suppression subjects were still able to make phonological judgements (Besner et al., 1981), suggesting that there were separate systems to perform articulation and storage of auditory information.

Baddeley et al. (1984) discovered that, rather oddly, articulatory suppression eliminates the word-length effect for visually presented words but not for spoken words (Baddeley et al., 1984). In order to explain this

---

Key Term

Articulatory suppression
A task used to occupy the articulatory control process of the working memory, normally involving the repetition of a sound (such as "the") which requires articulation but little processing.

Word-length effect
The finding that word span in immediate recall is greater for short words than for long words.

finding Baddeley *et al.* suggested that the articulatory control process is required for registering visually presented words and transferring them into the phonological store, whereas auditorily presented words gain direct access to the phonological store since they are already in the appropriate format (see Figure 5.10). Thus visually presented words use the articulatory control process but auditorily presented words do not. This would explain why articulatory suppression will affect the input of visually presented words but not spoken ones. The word-length effect is seen as being a function of the limited space available in the articulatory rehearsal process, so this will also be eliminated by articulatory suppression.

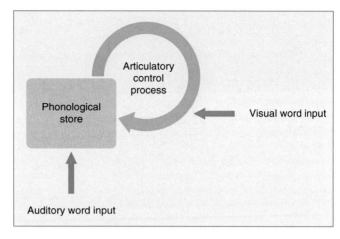

Figure 5.10   Access to the phonological loop.
Source: Baddeley (1986).

The phonological loop also offers a possible explanation for the 'irrelevant speech effect'. This is the finding that the retrieval of a sequence of visually presented items is disrupted by the simultaneous presentation of irrelevant spoken material (Salame and Baddeley, 1982). Again this can be explained by hypothesising that all spoken material automatically enters the phonological store, even background speech which is not being attended to.

The hypothesis that the phonological store has two components receives some additional support from clinical findings, as certain brain-injured patients appear to show impairment of either the phonological store or the articulatory control process in isolation, whilst the other sub-component remains intact (Vallar *et al.*, 1997).

NON-SPEECH SOUNDS

Whilst the phonological loop is assumed to hold verbal items, there is some uncertainty about whether it also deals with non-speech sounds, such as the sound of a dog barking or a telephone ringing. Shallice and Warrington (1974) reported that their patient KF had a WM impairment which was restricted to verbal items, whereas his WM recall for non-speech sounds was fairly normal, which suggests that verbal and non-verbal material appear to use different systems. In their study of the irrelevant speech effect (see previous section), Salame and Baddeley (1982) reported that background speech caused disruption of verbal memory, but non-speech sounds did not cause such disruption. They concluded from this that verbal material enters the phonological loop, but non-speech sounds do not. However, this view is disputed by Macken and Jones (1995), who found that unattended non-speech sounds did cause disruption in some circumstances. However, the exact mechanism involved in storage and retrieval of non-speech sounds remains uncertain.

THE PHONOLOGICAL LOOP AND LANGUAGE ACQUISITION

Much research has been directed towards investigating the function performed by the phonological loop in real life, and studies have suggested that its main function may involve the use and development of language. Baddeley and Lewis (1981) found that articulatory suppression interfered with a subject's ability to detect errors of logic or word order in a sentence, suggesting that the main function of the phonological loop may be to hold on to a sentence for long enough to analyse it for logic, word order and overall meaning. This view is supported by clinical studies, which show that patients with severe impairment of the phonological loop (indicated by a very small memory span), often have difficulty in understanding long and complex sentences, but have no trouble with short and simple sentences (Vallar and Baddeley, 1984). It therefore seems that the problem is not one of basic comprehension, but an inability to retain and examine a long sentence. Other studies have found evidence of reduced phonological memory performance in children with language problems (Raine *et al.*, 1992), and in normal children with poor linguistic ability (Gathercole and Baddeley, 1990).

Whilst these findings appear to suggest that the function of the phonological loop is concerned with language comprehension, in some cases patients with a severely impaired memory span have been found to exhibit normal language comprehension (Martin, 1993). This finding suggests that the phonological loop may be more important for the acquisition of language rather than for the subsequent use of that language (Baddeley *et al.*, 1998). Several studies offer support for this view. For example, children with specific language learning impairments have been found to have impaired phonological loop performance (Gathercole and Baddeley, 1989). It has also been found that a person's aptitude for learning a second language correlates with immediate memory span (Service, 1992; Gathercole *et al.*, 1999), and Baddeley *et al.* (1998) have reported a correlation between digit span and vocabulary. It has also been found that vocabulary size depends on the capacity of the phonological loop (Majerus *et al.*, 2006).

5.5 THE VISUO-SPATIAL SKETCHPAD

MEASURING THE CAPACITY OF THE VISUO-SPATIAL SKETCHPAD

Just as the capacity of the phonological loop can be measured approximately by the number of spoken digits you can hold consciously at one moment, so the capacity of the visuo-spatial sketchpad can be measured by the number of visually presented objects you can hold consciously at one moment. Try glancing briefly at the array of objects in Figure 5.11, then cover them up and try to remember the objects

Figure 5.11 Measuring the capacity of the visuo-spatial loop.

and their position on the page. Clearly there must be some short-term visual memory store which enables you to do this, and this store is referred to as the visuo-spatial sketchpad.

Your ability to remember the identity of each of the items probably also involves the use of the visuo-spatial sketchpad, but this task will also involve some input from the LTM, so testing the position of the objects is probably a purer measure of WM function.

There are several ways of testing the visuo-spatial sketchpad, most of which roughly follow the procedure described above. For example, one of the most widely used measures is the Corsi Blocks test (Corsi, 1972), in which the experimenter touches the blocks in a certain sequential order which must then be copied by the subject. The Corsi Blocks test provides a means of measuring visuo-spatial WM span which is analogous to the use of digit span for the measurement of phonological WM capacity.

EVIDENCE FOR THE VISUO-SPATIAL SKETCHPAD

As with the phonological loop, evidence for the existence of the visuo-spatial sketchpad comes from the dual-task paradigm. Alan Baddeley (1995) describes an interesting real-life example of how difficult it can be to perform two visual WM tasks at the same time. Whilst

Figure 5.12   If you are going for a drive, listen to the music station not the football.

Source: Shutterstock.

driving his car down an American freeway, Baddeley noticed that his steering became hopelessly erratic when he attempted to visualise the details of an American football game he was listening to on the radio. Since his car was weaving from side to side he decided that it would be safer to switch over to a music programme.

Subsequent experiments have confirmed that short-term visual recall is severely disrupted by performing a second visual task at the same time, but is not disrupted by performing a non-visual task. For example, Logie (1986) found that the ability to learn words by using imagery was greatly disrupted by a second visual task but not by a speech task, and Logie *et al.* (1989) reported that performance on a visual computer game was disrupted by a second visuo-spatial task. Robbins *et al.* (1996) found that the ability to recall positions on a chess board was disrupted by a secondary spatial task (manipulation of a keypad) but not by a task involving the repetition of words.

There is also some clinical evidence for the existence of the visuo-spatial sketchpad. There is a disorder called Williams syndrome in which the main symptom appears to be an impairment of visuo-spatial processing and the visuo-spatial loop, but with normal verbal processing (Bellugi *et al.*, 1994). An interesting recent finding is that although Williams syndrome individuals perform normally on tests of grammar comprehension, they do in fact exhibit an impairment for grammatical structures which denote spatial position, such as 'above', 'below', or 'shorter' (Phillips *et al.*, 2004).

SUB-COMPONENTS OF THE VISUO-SPATIAL SKETCHPAD

Logie (1995) suggests that, like the phonological loop, the visuo-spatial sketchpad also contains two sub-components. These are the *visual cache*, which stores visual information about shapes and colours, and the *inner scribe*, which holds spatial information and assists with the control of physical actions.

Some evidence for this distinction comes from clinical studies which suggest that some brain-injured patients show impairment of the visual cache but not the inner scribe. For example, Farah *et al.* (1988) described a patient who showed very poor judgements based on visual imagery of objects, despite showing a fairly normal performance on spatial tasks. It has also been demonstrated that normal participants carrying out two simultaneous WM tasks suffer considerable task disruption when both tasks are visual, or when both tasks are spatial, but show less disruption when simultaneously performing one visual task and one spatial task (Klauer and Zhao, 2004).

5.6 THE CENTRAL EXECUTIVE

INVESTIGATING THE CENTRAL EXECUTIVE

The central executive (CE) is thought to have overall control of cognitive processing, and it is probably the main focus of conscious awareness. It also controls the phonological and visuo-spatial loops, and uses them to help with processing. The CE was originally regarded as being essentially a single control system, but more recent research has shown that it actually performs several fairly distinct functions (Baddeley, 2007). Miyake *et al.* (2000) identified three main CE functions, by submitting scores on a large number of different executive tasks to a form of factor analysis involving the extraction of latent variables. These latent variables emerge from the analysis when several tests are found to correlate strongly with one another, suggesting that they all depend on the same underlying factor. The three factors identified by Miyake *et al.* were inhibition (suppression of a dominant response), shifting (switching attention between different tasks) and updating (monitoring stored information and new input). Although these three factors are fairly independent of one another, Miyake *et al.* found that they were slightly correlated, suggesting that there may be a general factor affecting all three. Recent research has shown that these factors show individual differences which remain fairly consistent throughout life, and that they predict many aspects of behaviour in real-life settings (Miyake and Friedman, 2012). These findings are considered in Section 5.7 (see 'Individual differences in WM').

IMPAIRMENT OF CENTRAL EXECUTIVE FUNCTION

Certain brain lesions appear to cause an impairment of central executive function, such that patients tend to have difficulty in producing controlled and flexible responses and instead rely on automatic processing and stereotyped responses. This type of impairment is known as dysexecutive syndrome (Baddeley and Wilson, 1988), and it has been found to be mainly associated with frontal lobe lesions (Shallice, 1988).

Impaired executive function has been described in a wide variety of different conditions, including Alzheimer's disease (Baddeley, 1996; Storandt, 2008), Tourette syndrome (Ozonoff *et al.*, 1994), Autism (Hill, 2004), and ADHD (Schulz *et al.*, 2004). Most of these conditions are known to involve frontal lobe dysfunction (see Chapter 9 for further details of executive dysfunction relating to thinking disorders).

Stuss and Alexander (2007) showed that the pattern of impairment in dysexecutive syndrome varies from one case to another, depending on which of the different CE functions was most affected. In view of this variability, they argued that dysexecutive syndrome should not be regarded as a single impairment but as a range of different CE impairments.

Key Term

Dysexecutive syndrome
A collection of deficits observed in frontal lobe patients which may include impaired concentration, impaired concept formation, disinhibition, inflexibility, perseveration, impaired cognitive estimation and impaired strategy formation.

5.7 WORKING MEMORY THEORY TODAY

THE EPISODIC BUFFER

Although the working memory model has been very influential, it has received a number of criticisms in recent years. One problem with the WM model is that, by fractionating the WM into a number of separate memory loops dedicated to specific sense modalities, it offers no clear explanation of how information from the visual and phonological loops can be combined and linked to multimodular information in the LTM. Baddeley (2000) has therefore postulated an additional loop called the episodic buffer, which is thought to integrate information from a variety of sense modalities, and which also provides a link between the WM and the LTM.

The episodic buffer also helps to explain the finding that some amnesic patients are able to retain lengthy prose passages for a brief period of time, despite having very poor retention of prose over longer periods (Baddeley and Wilson, 2002). It is well known that normal subjects can remember lengthy prose passages over long or short retention periods, but it is assumed that they use LTM to achieve this performance. However, this is clearly not possible for amnesic subjects, whose LTM is severely impaired. Baddeley and Wilson suggest that both normal and amnesic subjects can use the episodic buffer to store such passages over a short period. Baddeley and Wilson (2002) note that this capacity for immediate prose recall is not found in Alzheimer patients, suggesting that these patients may have an impairment of the episodic buffer itself. Baddeley (2003) also suggests that the episodic buffer may be involved in conscious awareness, previously thought to reside primarily in the central executive. His revised version of the WM model, incorporating the episodic buffer, is illustrated in Figure 5.13.

One further piece of evidence which supports the notion of the episodic buffer is the finding that Alzheimer patients have a specific impairment of feature binding. They can retain information about individual features (e.g. colour and shape) but they cannot integrate and combine them (Parra *et al.*, 2009). This is consistent with the assumed function of the episodic buffer as a mechanism for binding different features of the input.

> **Key Term**
>
> **Episodic buffer**
> A hypothetical component of working memory which integrates information from different sense modalities, and provides a link with the LTM.

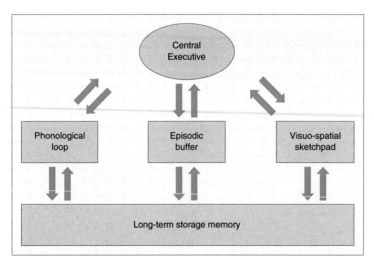

Figure 5.13   Revised version of the working memory model.

Source: Adapted from Baddeley (2000).

The WM model has generated a vast amount of research over the last 30 years, and continues to do so. It remains to be seen whether it can survive in the face of future research, but if so it seems likely that it will be a rather different WM model which eventually emerges.

UNITARY THEORIES OF MEMORY

Despite the popularity of the WM model, some theorists consider that the dual-store model is not justified, as the research findings can be equally well explained by a single memory store. Neath and Nairne (1995) argue that there is no need to postulate multiple storage loops as assumed by the WM model, as most findings are compatible with a single-store model. Their 'feature model' postulates that WM retrieval depends on matching the features of a WM trace with those of an SM (storage memory) trace, the main limitation being that the SM trace is degraded by interference.

Nairne (2002b) points out that whenever a new finding is reported which cannot be explained by the existing version of the WM model, a modification is made to the model (such as the proposal of a new WM loop), which enables it to cope with the new findings. But this process of continuous modification and patching makes the WM model impossible to falsify. More recent studies have confirmed that in most respects WM and SM operate on the same basic principles and processes, which questions the justification for making a distinction between these two stores (Suprenant and Neath, 2009).

CONTROLLED ATTENTION THEORY

Cowan (2005, 2010) argues that WM consists of the temporary activation of a part of the SM, rather than being a totally separate system. In this model, WM depends primarily on controlled attention, which temporarily activates one part of the SM before moving on to another part shortly afterwards. This controlled attention (CA) theory is consistent with most evidence, though it does have difficulty explaining the preservation of STM in temporal lobe amnesics.

Baddeley (2009b) considers that Cowan's view of WM is broadly compatible with the original WM model, and Logie (2011) points out that the two theories differ mainly in focusing on different aspects of WM. Whereas CA theory emphasises limits on attentional capacity, the standard WM theory focuses on the type of processing carried out. These can be seen as different and complimentary approaches to what is essentially the same WM mechanism, rather than as conflicting theories.

INDIVIDUAL DIFFERENCES IN WM

Turner and Engle (1989) demonstrated that there are consistent individual differences in the WM performance of different individuals, and that these differences prove to be a surprisingly good predictor of other types of cognitive performance. They found even stronger correlations with other cognitive measures when they employed complex

Figure 5.14 Measures of executive function can predict whether you are able to control your weight.

Source: Shutterstock.

WM span tasks (e.g. span tasks which require additional processing such as reading or calculating), instead of simple span measures. Complex span tasks have been found to correlate highly with cognitive abilities such as language comprehension, fluid intelligence and academic performance (Kane and Engle, 2002). For example, measures of visual WM account for more than 40 per cent of the variance in fluid intelligence (Fukuda *et al.*, 2010), and no less than 80 per cent of the variance in overall cognitive performance (Gold *et al.*, 2010).

Kane and Engle (2002) argue that the main feature of complex WM capacity which predicts such abilities is the ability to control the contents of consciousness. A low span indicates poor control of attention, and an inability to suppress unwanted items, and will thus impair performance on a wide range of cognitive tasks.

Miyake and Friedman (2012) have shown that several measures of central executive performance correlate with behaviour in real-life settings. As explained in Section 5.6, Miyake *et al.* (2000) identified three main CE factors, which are inhibition, shifting and updating. These three factors show reliable individual differences, which remain fairly consistent through life for a given individual and are partly determined by heredity (Miyake and Friedman, 2012). All three factors reflect the ability of an individual to control their cognitive processes, and it has been shown that measures of these factors provide a surprisingly accurate prediction of the degree of self-control and willpower that the individual will show in everyday life. For example, scores on the three CE factors predict successful control of diet, exercise and weight, and they even predict the likelihood of expressing racial prejudice or committing an act of infidelity to a spouse or partner (Miyake and Friedman, 2012).

Although individual differences in WM performance tend to be fairly consistent and reliable within a particular age cohort, recent work has shown that WM scores vary with age. For example, Brockmole and Logie (2013) reported that WM scores improve through childhood to reach a peak at about 20 years of age, after which they undergo a steady decline over the remainder of the lifespan.

In recent years there have been attempts to develop techniques for improving WM performance, mainly by practising various procedures involving the WM. However, there is no evidence that these techniques are effective, and a recent meta-analysis of 23 previous studies (Melby-Lervåg and Hulme, 2013) concluded that there were no lasting benefits.

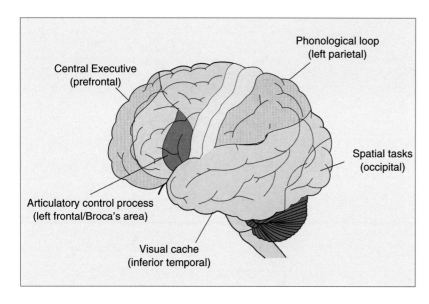

Figure 5.15 The main areas of the brain involved in working memory.

NEURO-IMAGING STUDIES AND WM

The development of brain-imaging technology (brain scans) has made it possible to investigate which parts of the brain are involved in the activities of the working memory and its various components. Smith *et al.* (1996) used PET-scan imaging to show that verbal WM tasks mainly produce activation in the left hemisphere, whereas visuo-spatial WM tasks activate regions in the right hemisphere. Further brain-imaging studies revealed that use of the phonological store leads to activation of a region at the edge of the left parietal lobe called the supramarginal gyrus (Smith and Jonides, 1999; Henson *et al.*, 2000), an area already known to be associated with language comprehension. The same studies found that use of the articulatory control process produces activation of a part of Broca's area in the left frontal cortex, an area known to be involved in speech production.

Brain scans carried out during the performance of visuo-spatial tasks show activation of quite different brain areas. It has been found (Smith and Jonides, 1999; Wager and Smith, 2003) that WM tasks involving object recognition produce activation of the left parietal and inferotemporal zones, associated with the ventral pathway. However, spatial WM tasks involve activation of the right dorsal prefrontal, parietal and occipital lobes, associated with the dorsal pathway. The ventral and dorsal pathways are known to be involved in 'what?' and 'where?' types of perceptual processing respectively, as explained in Chapter 2.

The central executive involves many different functions, so a variety of different brain areas are involved according to the task in question. However, brain scans suggest that most central executive tasks tend to involve activation of the prefrontal cortex, together with the parietal lobes in certain specific CE tasks (Collette and Van der Linden, 2002; Owen *et al.*, 2005).

These brain scan findings would therefore appear to lend support to the WM model, in so far as they show that different areas of the brain are activated during the use of different components of WM. Figure 5.15 summarises the brain areas which are mainly associated with the various different types of WM task.

However, recent brain-imaging studies have not provided clear support for the view that WM and SM involve completely separate stores. Oztekin *et al.* (2010) carried out fMRI imaging on participants while they were retrieving items from a recently presented list. Similar levels of temporal lobe activation were found for the later and therefore most recent items (assumed to be held in WM) and earlier items (assumed to be held in SM). This finding does not entirely refute the distinction between WM and SM, but it does suggest overlap between the mechanisms underlying the retrieval of items from these two stores.

SUMMARY

- Evidence suggests that there are two separate memory stores, known as 'short-term memory' (or 'working memory') and 'long-term memory' (or 'storage memory').
- Evidence for the distinction between these two stores arises from clinical studies showing that amnesics may suffer damage to one store whilst the other remains intact.
- The short-term working memory is assumed to function as an active mental workspace in which a variety of processing operations are carried out. In contrast, the long-term storage memory is seen as a passive storage space.
- Baddeley and Hitch (1974) have proposed a widely accepted model of working memory which comprises a central executive served by two short-term stores, the 'phonological loop' and the 'visuo-spatial sketchpad'.
- Evidence for the existence of these memory systems has come from experiments showing that two tasks will interfere with one another if they make use of the same WM component.
- The phonological loop is assumed to provide brief storage for auditory input, and it is thought to play a major role in the use and development of language.
- The visuo-spatial sketchpad holds visual images, and it is also thought to be involved in involved in visual pattern recognition, and in the perception and control of movement.
- The central executive is assumed to be the main focus of conscious awareness, and it appears to be involved in mental abilities such as decision making, planning and problem solving.
- Recently, an additional loop has been postulated called the 'episodic buffer', which integrates information from a variety of sense modalities, providing a link between the WM and the LTM.

- Impairment of the central executive is known as 'dysexecutive syndrome', and it has been found to be associated with frontal lobe lesions. It is considered to play a part in certain clinical disorders such as Alzheimer's disease, autism and schizophrenia.
- The development of neuro-imaging technology has made it possible to investigate which parts of the brain are involved in the activities of the working memory and its various components.
- The working memory model has been very influential, but in recent years it has received some criticism, and alternative models have been proposed.

FURTHER READING

- Baddeley, A. D. (2009). Working memory. In A. D. Baddeley, M. W. Eysenck and M. C. Anderson (eds) *Memory*. Hove: Psychology Press. An excellent review of recent research on working memory, written by one of the original creators of the working memory model.
- Heathcote, D. (2005). Working memory and performance limitations. In A. Esgate and D. Groome (eds) *An Introduction to Applied Cognitive Psychology*. Hove: Psychology Press. This chapter deals with applied aspects of working memory and its performance limitations in real-life settings, such as language learning, industrial tasks, and air-traffic control.

Chapter 6

Contents

Long-term memory

6

David Groome

6.1 THE NATURE AND FUNCTION OF MEMORY

MEMORY AND ITS IMPORTANCE IN EVERYDAY LIFE

Long-term memory is the mechanism which enables us to store information and experiences in a lasting fashion, for possible retrieval at some point in the future. This ability to create and retrieve memories is fundamental to all aspects of cognition, and it is crucial to our ability to function properly as human beings. Our memories allow us to store information about the world so that we can understand and deal with future situations on the basis of past experience. The processes of thinking and problem-solving also rely heavily on the use of previous experience, and memory also makes it possible for us to acquire language and to communicate with others. Memory also plays a very basic part in the process of perception, since we can only make sense of our perceptual input by making reference to our store of previous experiences. Even our social interactions with others are dependent upon what we remember. In a sense it can be said that our very identity relies on an intact memory, and the ability to remember who we are and the things that we have done. Almost everything we ever do depends on our ability to remember the past.

ENCODING, STORAGE AND RETRIEVAL OF MEMORY

The memory process can be divided into three main stages (Figure 6.1). First of all there is the *input* stage, where newly perceived information is being learned or encoded. Next comes the *storage* stage, where the information is held in preparation for some future occasion. Finally there is the *output* stage, where the information is retrieved from storage.

There are clear parallels between these three stages of human memory and the input/storage/output processes involved in storing a computer file onto disk. Perhaps the most important reason for

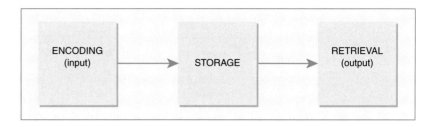

Figure 6.1 The encoding, storage and retrieval stages of memory.

distinguishing between these three stages is that each stage will need to be successfully completed before we can retrieve a memory. This means that when we find we are unable to recall some item, the cause could be either a failure at the input stage (i.e. faulty learning), a failure at the output stage (i.e. faulty retrieval), or even a failure of the storage mechanism. In practice, storage failures probably do not occur unless there is damage to the brain, so it is probable that most forgetting is caused by either learning failure or retrieval failure.

6.2 THE FIRST MEMORY EXPERIMENTS

EBBINGHAUS AND THE FORGETTING CURVE

The scientific study of memory began with the work of Hermann Ebbinghaus (1885), whose methods were to have a huge influence on memory research for many years. Using himself as the experimental subject, Ebbinghaus carried out a number of classic experiments in which he attempted to measure memory performance in a scientific and quantified manner, making an effort to eliminate all unwanted variables from his experimental design. For example, Ebbinghaus realised that the use of verbal items in a memory test would add an uncontrolled variable to the design, since the words used would vary in their meaningfulness and familiarity. He therefore decided to eliminate this variable by using nonsense material instead of meaningful words as his test items. Ebbinghaus compiled lists of test items known as 'nonsense syllables', so called because they are pronounceable syllables but have no meaning, such as VOP or TUV. Ebbinghaus considered that all nonsense syllables were roughly equivalent in their memorability, since they were meaningless.

Having devised lists of nonsense syllables, Ebbinghaus used them to investigate how forgetting occurs with the passage of time. A list of syllables would be learned, and then retested after a certain retention interval. The scores were plotted as a 'forgetting curve', as shown in Figure 6.2.

As the graph shows, forgetting was extremely rapid at first, but at longer retention intervals the rate of forgetting gradually levelled off. This same basic forgetting curve has been confirmed in many subsequent experimental studies. In fact Rubin and Wenzel (1996) reviewed no fewer than 210 studies of forgetting carried out over the years, all of which reported forgetting curves which were generally similar to that found by Ebbinghaus. Meeter *et al.* (2005) used an internet study to test the memories of 14,000 people for news items and other public events, and the results showed that their forgetting over time was essentially similar to the Ebbinghaus forgetting curve. However, autobiographical events of personal significance are remembered far more accurately over long periods of time than would be found in laboratory studies of memory (Bahrick *et al.*, 2008). See Section 6.8 for further details of these autobiographical memory studies.

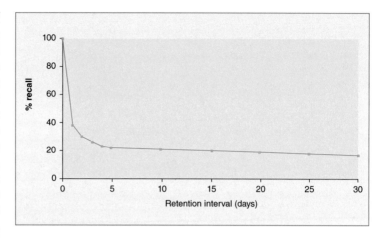

Figure 6.2   The forgetting curve.

Source: Ebbinghaus (1885).

INTERFERENCE AND DECAY

The forgetting curve demonstrates that memories tend to dissipate over a period of time, and Ebbinghaus suggested two main theories to explain why this might occur:

- *Decay* – memories fade away with the passage of time, regardless of other input.
- *Interference* – memories are actively disrupted by the influence of some other input.

Ebbinghaus was able to demonstrate experimentally that interference did indeed have a significant effect on memory. He showed that memory scores for the learning of one list were considerably reduced by the subsequent learning of a second list, a phenomenon known as retroactive interference. Another experiment showed that the memory for a list was also subject to interference from a previously learned list, a phenomenon known as proactive interference. In summary, the interference effect could be caused by any additional input occurring either before or after the target list. Many subsequent studies have confirmed the effects of interference, which has been shown to depend largely on the degree of similarity between the target item and the items interfering with it (McGeoch, 1932; Underwood and Postman, 1960).

Producing evidence for the occurrence of spontaneous decay has proved to be rather more difficult because of the difficulty of separating its effects from those of other forms of forgetting (including interference) which also inevitably take place with the passage of time. However, a recent review of previous research (Altmann and Schunn, 2012) concluded that both decay and interference probably play a part in the forgetting process.

Thorndike (1914) suggested that decay only affects memory traces which remain unused for a long period, an idea known as the 'decay with disuse' theory. This theory has recently been revived and updated by Bjork and Bjork (1992), who suggest that access to a memory trace is strengthened by frequent retrieval, whereas unretrieved memories become more inaccessible as time passes. Bjork and Bjork call this the 'New Theory of Disuse'. More recent research has suggested that there may be inhibitory mechanisms at work in the brain, which actively suppress unretrieved memories (Anderson, 2003). This phenomenon is known as retrieval-induced forgetting, and it may help to explain why memories fade over time. If so then this puts the whole concept of forgetting into a totally new perspective, because it suggests that forgetting may be caused by an inhibitory mechanism in the brain rather than by some failing or inadequacy of the memory system. The new theory of disuse and the retrieval-induced forgetting phenomenon will both be considered in more detail in Section 6.7.

The experiments carried out by Ebbinghaus over a century ago had a huge influence on subsequent memory research. However, although his basic findings (such as the forgetting curve) are still generally accepted, the theories that Ebbinghaus proposed to explain them have been revised in the light of subsequent research. One aspect of Ebbinghaus' approach which has been particularly criticised is his use of nonsense material, since it has become clear that meaning is a central factor in memory processing. This will be considered in the next section.

> **Key Term**
>
> **Retrieval-induced forgetting (RIF)**
> The phenomenon whereby the successful retrieval of a memory trace inhibits the retrieval of rival memory traces.

6.3 MEANING, KNOWLEDGE AND SCHEMAS

BARTLETT'S STORY RECALL EXPERIMENTS AND THE SCHEMA THEORY

The early memory experiments of Ebbinghaus influenced memory research for many years, but cognitive psychologists eventually came to question one very central feature of his research, namely his use of nonsense syllables as test items. By controlling out the effects of meaning and knowledge, Ebbinghaus had eliminated what is possibly the most important feature of memory function.

The first clear experimental demonstration of the importance of meaning and knowledge on memory was provided by Bartlett (1932), in a classic study regarded by many as the first step towards the modern cognitive approach to memory. Bartlett investigated the way that individuals remembered a short story. He deliberately chose stories which were unusual such as the one below, which is a Native American folk tale called 'The War of the Ghosts'. If you wish to try the experiment on yourself then you should read through the story once, then cover it over and write down as much of it as you can remember.

The War of the Ghosts

One night two young men from Egulac went down to the river to hunt seals, and while they were there it became foggy and calm. Then they heard war-cries, and they thought 'maybe this is a war party.' They escaped to the shore, and hid behind a log. Now canoes came up, and they heard the noise of paddles, and saw one canoe coming up to them. There were five men in the canoe, and they said 'What do you think? We are going up the river to make war on the people.' One of the young men said 'I have no arrows'. 'Arrows are in the canoe', they said.

'I will not go along. I might be killed. My relatives do not know where I have gone. 'But you', he said, turning to the other, 'may go with them.' So one of the young men went, but the other returned home. And the warriors went up the river to a town on the other side of Kalama. The people came down to the river, and they began to fight, and many were killed. But presently the young man heard one of the warriors say: 'Quick, let us go home: that Indian has been hit.' Now he thought 'Oh, they are ghosts.' He did not feel sick, but they said he had been shot. So the canoes went back to Egulac and the young man went ashore to his house, and made a fire.

And he told everybody and said: 'Behold I accompanied the ghosts, and we went to fight. Many of our fellows were killed, and many of those who attacked us were killed. They said I was hit, and I did not feel sick.' He told it all, and then he became quiet. When the sun rose he fell down. Something black came out of his mouth. His face became contorted. The people jumped up and cried. He was dead.

This story is rather strange to the average person from a western cultural background because it contains references to ghosts, magic and states of invulnerability, all concepts which are rather unfamiliar to most of us. Bartlett's most important finding was that his subjects tended to recall a changed and distorted version of the story. However, the changes noted by Bartlett were not random, but were systematically directed towards the creation of a more rational and sensible story. Bartlett concluded that subjects tended to rationalise the story to make it fit in with their expectations, based on their own past experience and understanding of the world. Typically the story recalled by Bartlett's (British) subjects would be a far more straightforward account of an expedition which was relatively free from ghostly or magical interventions. Some of the more strange and unfamiliar parts of the story tended to be left out altogether, whilst others would be distorted and changed to fit in with a more conventional and British view of the world.

Bartlett explained these findings in terms of his schema theory (see Chapter 1), which proposes that we perceive and encode information into our memories in terms of our past experience. Schemas are the mental representations that we have built up from all that we have experienced in the past, and according to Bartlett we compare our new perceptual input with our schemas in an effort to find something meaningful and familiar. Any input which does not match up with existing schemas will either be distorted to make it match the schemas, or else it will not be retained at all.

These findings have quite important implications for a variety of real-life situations, as they raise questions about whether we can rely on the accuracy of eyewitness testimony. We should expect, for example, that witnesses presenting evidence in a court of law will be likely to produce a distorted and rationalised version of events they have witnessed. We should also question the accuracy of any eyewitness accounts, such as news reports and accounts of historical events. Indeed we should even question the accuracy of our own memories of past events, since much of what we think has happened to us has probably been subjected to distortion of which we are completely unaware. On those rare occasions where we do actually get a chance to check the accuracy of our memories, as for example when chatting with a friend about some shared experience from the past, we often discover quite major discrepancies between two people's accounts of the same event. Bartlett's experiments showed that we should never expect memory to be entirely accurate, since it will tend to reflect our own efforts to make sense of its content. Bartlett also demonstrated that memory appears to be stored in terms of its meaningful content, and thus depends on the extent to which the individual's previous knowledge can be used to make sense of the incoming information.

THE EFFECT OF MEANING AND KNOWLEDGE ON MEMORY

Bartlett's theories were not widely accepted at first, partly because they concerned inner mental processes (such as schemas), which were unacceptable to the behaviourists who dominated mainstream psychology at that time. Moreover, Bartlett's experiments were not very scientifically designed. For example, the main variable in his story recall experiments was the meaningfulness of the story content, but as this was determined purely on the basis of subjective opinion it is perhaps not surprising that it met with some criticism.

In recent years a number of studies have provided a more scientific basis for some of Bartlett's theories, by providing an objective means of varying the meaningfulness of the narrative. For example, Bransford and Johnson (1972) tested their subjects' ability to recall a short passage which made relatively little sense unless the subject was provided with some kind of explanatory context, which in this case was provided by a picture (Figure 6.3).

Two groups of subjects were used in this experiment. One group was shown the helpful picture, but the other group was not. The group who had seen the picture were subsequently able to recall far more of the passage than the other group, probably because the picture helped them to make sense of the passage. The passage is reproduced below, and you may wish to try out the experiment on yourself.

The balloons passage

If the balloons popped the sound wouldn't be able to carry since then everything would be too far away from the correct floor. A closed window would also prevent the sound from carrying, since most buildings tend to be well insulated. Since the whole operation depends on the steady flow of electricity, a break in the middle of the wire would also cause problems. Of course, the fellow could shout, but the human voice is not loud enough to carry that far. An additional problem is that the string could break on the instrument. Then there would be no accompaniment to the message. It is clear that the best situation would involve less distance. Then there would be fewer potential problems. With face-to-face contact, the least number of things could go wrong.

In this experiment the subject's ability to find meaning in the passage was scientifically controlled by giving helpful information (i.e. the picture) to one group but not to the other. This method of controlling the variable of meaningfulness was thus quite objective and did not rely at all on the subjective opinion of the experimenter as it did in Bartlett's story recall experiments. Since the two groups of subjects were read exactly the same passage in exactly the same conditions, the only major variable was the degree of meaningfulness, which was systematically controlled by the experimenter.

These experiments on story recall suggest that a passage is more memorable if we can make use of our knowledge and experience to increase its meaningfulness. Other studies have shown that subjects who possess a great deal of expert knowledge about a subject are particularly good at remembering material which relates to their field of expertise. Chase and Simon (1973a) found that expert chess players were able to remember the positions of the pieces in an uncompleted chess game with great accuracy, whereas chess novices produced far less accurate recall. However, the chess experts only achieved superior recall when the test material consisted of real or plausible chess games, but not when the chess pieces were placed in random positions. This suggests that the real games were probably more memorable to the chess experts because they held more meaning and significance for the expert player, full of implications for the subsequent development of the game. Similar benefits of expert knowledge have been reported for the memories of experts on football (Morris *et al.*, 1981) and experts on TV soap operas (Reeve and Aggleton, 1998).

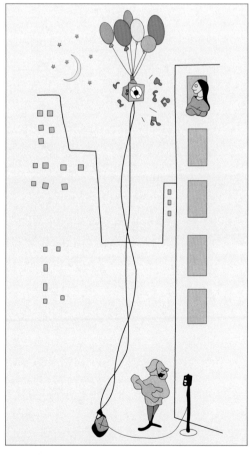

Figure 6.3 Picture used to make the balloons passage meaningful.

Source: Bransford and Johnson (1972).

SCHEMAS AND SCRIPTS

Schank and Abelson (1977) argued that schemas are also important in making sense of everyday events. They proposed a form of schema called a script, which combines a sequence of events which might normally be expected in a particular situation. Scripts can therefore guide our behaviour by enabling us to anticipate what will happen next. For example, a visit to a restaurant typically involves the following sequence of events and actions:

> *Enter restaurant / Find table / Choose seat / Sit down /*
>
> *Get menu / Choose food / Order from waiter / Wait for food /*
>
> *Food arrives / Eat food / Waiter brings bill / Pay bill / Leave restaurant.*

This sequence provides us with a general idea of what to expect when we go to a restaurant. It will therefore come as no great surprise when a bill is presented after the meal (though the size of the bill is often a surprise). Scripts may help us to organise our plans and our actions, by providing us with a general framework with which to organise them. They also help us to understand events and the behaviour of others.

SCHEMAS AND DISTORTION

Although there have been many studies demonstrating the effect of knowledge and schemas on memory, the phenomenon of distortion has not been so extensively studied. However, there have been a few such studies, and some of these have extended the study of distortion into real-life settings. For example, Hastorf and Cantril (1954) found that fans watching an American football match subsequently recalled a highly distorted and biased version of the game, with the supporters of each team somewhat predictably recalling more fouls being committed by the opposing team.

Distortion of eyewitness testimony by previous schemas has also been investigated. Tuckey and Brewer (2003) discovered that eyewitnesses were able to provide far more accurate information about events that were consistent with their existing schemas, such as a robbery involving masked criminals carrying guns and escaping in a getaway car. However, their memory was likely to be distorted for any events they had witnessed which were inconsistent with their previous knowledge and schemas. A number of other studies have shown that eyewitness testimony for a crime or accident can also be distorted by subsequent events as well as by previous knowledge, and these findings will be considered in Section 6.8.

Apart from the studies mentioned above, there have been relatively few studies of memory distortion since Bartlett's pioneering work. Koriat *et al.* (2001) suggest that the main reason for this is the fact that distortion cannot easily be quantified, so investigators are forced to find some qualitative means of assessment (i.e. observing the type of forgetting rather than the amount). Now that qualitative research methods are becoming more accepted it is possible that memory distortion will be studied more extensively.

MEANING AND MNEMONICS

As Bartlett showed, people are not very good at learning things which they find meaningless. The human brain does not appear to be well suited to rote-learning, or 'parrot learning' as it is sometimes called. However, this point was understood long before Bartlett's studies. For centuries people have made use of techniques known as mnemonics, which depend on adding meaning to an item in order to make it more memorable. For example, if you read the number 1984747365 just once, there is very little chance that you will still remember it in ten minutes' time. In fact you have probably forgotten it already. However, try looking at the number again and this time try to imagine George Orwell (1984) sitting on a jumbo jet (747) for one year (365). By adding these associations to the numbers they become more meaningful and thus more memorable. In addition, this mnemonic benefits from the principal of 'chunking' (Miller, 1956), since the original ten items have in effect been reduced to just three chunks of meaningful information. Consequently, you are not only likely to remember these numbers in ten minutes' time, but it is entirely possible that you will still remember them in ten years' time. I offer my apologies if this turns out to be the case.

Essentially what we have done here is to make use of knowledge that is (probably) already in your LTM store, to add meaning to a list of otherwise meaningless digits. Many other mnemonic techniques have been devised over the years to enable us to add some meaning to an otherwise meaningless list of numbers or words, and you probably already know and use several. One good example is the use of mnemonics to assist with the recall of the sequential order of the colours of the spectrum, by turning it into a sentence such as 'Richard Of York Gave Battle In Vain'. The first letters of these seven words may help retrieval of the colours of the spectrum in their correct order (red, orange, yellow, green, blue, indigo and violet). It will be noticed that in this case the colours themselves are not devoid of meaning, but their sequential order is. There are other popular mnemonics for remembering the notes on the musical scale, the number of days in each calendar month, the twelve cranial nerves, and many other items which are either meaningless or else occur in a meaningless sequence.

A number of books have been written about the use of mnemonic strategies to enhance memory performance (e.g. Lorayne and Lucas, 1974; Herrmann *et al.*, 2002), and there is a section on mnemonics in Esgate and Groome (2005). Mnemonics usually work by adding meaning to items which are otherwise fairly meaningless, and their effectiveness provides evidence for the view that people are much better at memorising meaningful information, which they are able to relate to their previous knowledge.

Key Term
Mnemonic
A technique or strategy used for improving the memorability of items, for example by adding meaningful associations.

6.4 INPUT PROCESSING AND ENCODING

LEVELS OF PROCESSING THEORY

Craik and Lockhart (1972) proposed a theory to explain the role of knowledge and meaning in memory, which in some ways borrows from schema theory in that it stresses the importance of extracting meaning from the perceptual input. However, their 'levels of processing' (LOP) theory suggests that the processing of new perceptual input involves the extraction of information at a series of levels of increasing depth of analysis, with more information being extracted at each new level (Figure 6.4).

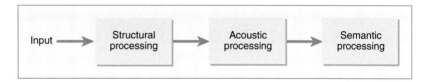

Figure 6.4 The levels of processing model.

Source: Craik and Lockhart (1972).

Thus initial processing will be shallow, extracting only the more superficial features of the input such as the shape of an object (structural processing) or the sound of a word (acoustic processing). However, the input may subsequently be processed at a deeper level where more complex features are analysed, such as the meaningful content of a word (semantic processing).

One crucial aspect of the LOP theory is that it emphasises the need to carry out extensive processing on incoming information in order to store it. Previously it had been widely assumed that information could gain entry into the long-term storage memory by merely being repeated or held in consciousness for a period of time. Craik and Lockhart argued that this is not enough, and that long-term storage can only be achieved by active processing of the input. In fact Craik and Lockhart argued that the memory trace is essentially a by-product of perceptual processing.

The main prediction of the LOP theory is that the retention of a memory trace will depend on the depth to which it has been processed during the encoding stage. Like schema theory, the LOP theory is able to explain the well-established finding that meaningful material is more memorable than non-meaningful material, by postulating that meaningful material can be more deeply processed. However, unlike schema theory, the LOP theory is readily testable, as it specifies a number of distinct stages in the processing sequence, and then makes a firm prediction that memory performance will depend on the level to which processing has progressed. Evidence supporting the LOP theory has mostly been obtained from the use of orienting tasks.

> ## Key Term
>
> **Orienting task**
> A set of instructions used to influence the type of cognitive processing employed.

ORIENTING TASKS

An orienting task is essentially a set of instructions which are intended to direct the subject towards a certain type of processing. For example, Craik and Tulving (1975) presented the same list of 60 words to three different groups of subjects, but gave each group a different orienting task to carry out. The orienting tasks were as follows:

1. *Structural orienting task* (e.g. is word in block capitals?)
2. *Acoustic orienting task* (e.g. does word rhyme with 'bat'?)
3. *Semantic orienting task* (e.g. does word fit the sentence 'the cat sat on the __'?)

Craik and Tulving's results are shown in Figure 6.5. They show that tasks which require deep processing tend to produce better retrieval than do tasks which involve

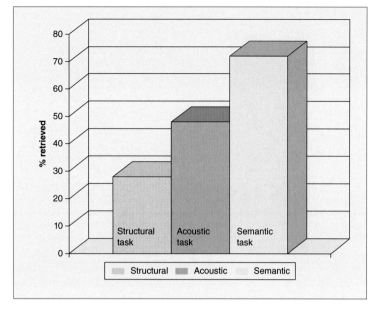

Figure 6.5   The effect of orienting task on retrieval.
Source: Craik and Tulving (1975).

shallower processing, and this general finding has been confirmed by other orienting task studies (e.g. Hyde and Jenkins, 1973; Parkin, 1983).

The effect of processing depth is not limited to verbal test items. For example, it has been found (Winograd, 1976; Burgess and Weaver, 2003) that face recognition scores were higher when faces were subjected to deep processing (e.g. rating the pleasantness of each face) rather than shallow processing (e.g. identifying a structural feature of each face, such as whether or not it had curly hair). It has also been found that recall scores are particularly high for test items which the subjects have used in reference to themselves (Rogers *et al.*, 1977), as for example when an orienting task requires subjects to decide whether adjectives can be used to describe them personally. This is known as the self-reference effect, and it suggests that personal involvement may lead to deeper processing.

The design used by Craik and Tulving for their orienting task experiment required the subjects to read through the wordlist without realising that their memory of it would later be tested. In other words it was a test of incidental learning rather than intentional learning. This technique was used in order to prevent subjects from deliberately trying to learn the wordlist, since subjects motivated to learn the words might tend to disregard the instructions to carry out a particular orienting task. It is interesting to note that when Craik (1977) instructed a group of subjects to try to learn the list deliberately, their recall scores were no better than those of the group performing incidental learning with a semantic orienting task. This suggests that even when we are deliberately trying to learn something we cannot improve on semantic processing, which is more important than making a deliberate effort to learn. This finding is entirely consistent with our experience of learning in real life. You can probably remember in considerable detail many of the things you did earlier today, despite the fact that you did not at any point say to yourself 'I must try hard to remember this'. You are likely to remember the events which you thought about and processed, perhaps because they held some meaning or significance for you.

LEVELS THEORY REVISED

In its original form the LOP theory proposed a strict sequential order of processing, beginning with structural processing and then proceeding to acoustic and finally semantic processing. However, this processing sequence is not entirely plausible, since the three types of processing are qualitatively different and thus discontinuous with one another. It is difficult to see how structural, acoustic and semantic processing might somehow blend into one another. Furthermore there is some evidence (e.g. the Stroop effect – see Chapter 3) that semantic processing can sometimes take place before the 'shallower' structural and acoustic stages are complete. It was partly in answer to these criticisms that the original sequential model of processing depth was replaced by a revised version (Lockhart and Craik, 1990), in which structural, acoustic and semantic forms of processing are assumed to take place simultaneously and in parallel rather than in sequence (Figure 6.6).

This revised version of the theory assumes that any new input will be subjected to several different types of processing at the same time, though semantic processing apparently creates a more effective and lasting memory trace than the non-semantic forms of processing.

The LOP theory has been subjected to plenty of criticism over the years, but research has generally supported the basic underlying principle that semantic processing is usually more effective than non-semantic processing (Rose and Craik, 2012). There is also evidence from PET scans showing that semantic and non-semantic processing involve different areas of the brain (Otten and Rugg, 2001), with semantic processing mainly activating the left prefrontal cortex whilst non-semantic processing mainly activates the posterior sensory cortex. However, whilst the LOP theory remains plausible, it is now considered that the effectiveness of deep processing probably reflects the fact that it facilitates elaborative encoding, whereby the new input becomes connected with previous memories.

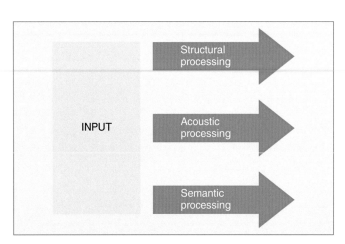

Figure 6.6   The revised levels of processing model.

Source: Lockhart and Craik (1990).

ELABORATIVE AND MAINTENANCE REHEARSAL

Rehearsal is commonly employed as a method of retaining a piece of information, as for example repeating a telephone number over and over to yourself until you have the chance to write it down. Craik and Lockhart (1972) made a clear distinction between 'maintenance rehearsal', in which the input is merely repeated without further processing, and 'elaborative rehearsal', in which links are created between the new input and previously stored information. They argued that only elaborative rehearsal would lead to long-term retention of the information, and that maintenance rehearsal served only to hold it temporarily in conscious awareness without actually strengthening the trace.

Whilst it has certainly been found that elaborative rehearsal tends to be more effective than maintenance rehearsal, research suggests that both forms of rehearsal can improve memory, but in different ways. Glenberg *et al.* (1977) found that recall tests benefit mainly from elaborative rehearsal, whereas recognition tests benefit more from maintenance rehearsal. Hunt and McDaniel (1993) explain such findings by suggesting that elaborative rehearsal assists with *relational processing* (i.e. forming new associative connections with other items), whereas maintenance rehearsal assists *item-specific processing* (i.e. increasing the strength of the memory for one item).

ELABORATIVE ENCODING AND ORGANISATION

Elaborative encoding refers to the formation of associative connections with other memory traces, and this occurs most effectively where meaningful associations can be found. A number of studies have confirmed that semantic elaboration does indeed create a stronger and more lasting trace (Craik and Tulving, 1975; Cherry *et al.*,1993). The elaborative encoding theory thus proposes that semantic processing creates a large number of associative links with other items in the memory store, so that the new trace becomes incorporated into an extensive network of interconnected memory traces, as illustrated in Figure 6.7.

Since each of these associative links can serve as a potential retrieval route, the trace will be more easily retrieved if there are many possible pathways leading back to it. Recent versions of LOP theory have therefore tended to place emphasis on the strengthening of inter-item associations and the

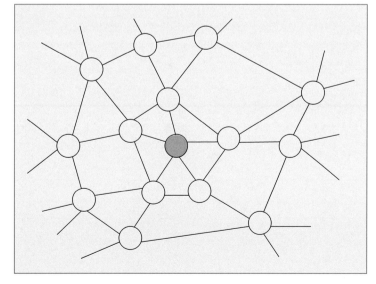

Figure 6.7   Elaborative connections between memory traces.

consequent creation of additional retrieval routes which are brought about by elaborative processing (Craik, 2007). An additional advantage of deep and elaborative processing is that it may produce a more distinctive and unique memory trace, which can be more easily distinguished from other stored items (Eysenck, 1979; Hunt, 2013). At the present time both the 'elaboration' and 'distinctiveness' accounts of processing depth remain plausible, and it is probable that both mechanisms operate together.

Mandler (1972) showed that retrieval was greatly improved when test items were organised into categories by the participant, which allowed the items to be incorporated into a network of related memories. Mandler's *organisation theory* suggests that memory is structured into a semantic network of related items, and accessing one item activates the whole network. Mandler suggests that this mechanism is consistent with the findings of LOP theory since it offers a possible explanation for the benefits of extensive semantic input processing (Mandler, 2002, 2011).

6.5 RETRIEVAL AND RETRIEVAL CUES

RECALL AND RECOGNITION

There are two main ways of testing retrieval, which are *recall* and *recognition*. In a recognition test, the original test material is presented again at the retrieval stage, whereas in a recall test they are not. However, there are two different types of recall test. In a test of *spontaneous recall* you are required to generate the test items without any assistance, but in a *cued recall* test you are given retrieval cues (i.e. reminders) of the target items, but not the actual items themselves. So in practice, retrieval tests usually involve one of the following three procedures:

1. *Spontaneous recall:* requires the generation of items from memory without any help.
2. *Cued recall:* retrieval cues are provided to remind us of the items to be recalled.
3. *Recognition:* the original test items are re-presented at the retrieval stage.

It is generally found that people can recognise far more items than they can recall. For example, Mandler *et al.* (1969) presented their subjects with a list of 100 words, which were repeated five times. The average spontaneous recall score obtained was only 38 per cent, whereas the average recognition score was 96 per cent. It is worth noting that cued recall performance usually tends to fall somewhere in between recall and recognition performance (Tulving, 1976), though the actual score will depend on the quality of the retrieval cues. The apparent superiority of recognition performance over recall performance is so striking that any theory of retrieval needs to provide an explanation for it.

GENERATE AND RECOGNISE THEORY

The 'generate and recognise' (GR) theory (Kintsch, 1968; Anderson and Bower, 1972) explains the superiority of recognition over recall performance by assuming that recall and recognition are fundamentally different processes, and that recall is more difficult because it involves an extra stage. According to GR theory, in a recall test the participant must first generate possible target items, after which the items thus generated are subjected to a recognition test in order to discriminate between correct and incorrect items. In a recognition test, however, there is no need for the subject to generate possible test items since the items are already in front of them. Thus recall is seen as having two stages (generate and recognise), whilst recognition has only one (recognise). This could explain why recall is more difficult than recognition.

An important feature of the GR theory is that it makes the assumption that recognition is actually one of the sub-processes of recall. This means that, in theory, any item that can be recalled should also be recognisable. However, it has been shown that in certain situations people are unable to recognise items which they can recall (Tulving and Thomson 1973). This phenomenon is known as 'recognition failure of recallable items' (often abbreviated to 'recognition failure'), and it provides evidence against the GR theory. Recognition failure is most easily demonstrated with a design in which strong retrieval cues are provided for recall but not for recognition. It has been demonstrated with a number of different experimental designs (for a review see Nilsson and Gardiner, 1993), and it is one of the main reasons why GR theory is no longer widely accepted. But in any case, more recent research has shown that recognition is not a single mechanism. It can be sub-divided into two distinct processes, which are familiarity and recollection (Mandler, 1980). This theory is discussed further in Section 6.6.

CUE-DEPENDENT FORGETTING AND THE ENCODING SPECIFICITY PRINCIPLE

Tulving (1972) argued that memory retrieval is largely cue-dependent. In other words, whether we can retrieve a memory or not will depend on the presence of suitable retrieval cues, which act as reminders and help reactivate the original memory trace. There is a considerable body of evidence confirming that retrieval success is closely related to the number and quality of the retrieval cues available (Tulving, 1972; Mantyla, 1986). In fact memory performance can be surprisingly good when suitable cues are provided. Mantyla (1986) asked people to read a list of 600 words, and to think of three things they knew about each word. When these three self-generated cues were employed in a subsequent recall test, the average retrieval score obtained for the target words was over 90 per cent. To recall about 550 words from a list of 600 is actually quite an impressive performance, and this finding demonstrates how good the human memory can be when given the right retrieval cues.

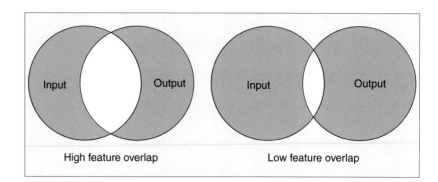

Figure 6.8   The overlap between features encoded at input and features available in the retrieval cue at output.

High feature overlap   Low feature overlap

Key Term

Encoding specificity principle (ESP)
The theory that retrieval cues will only be successful in accessing a memory trace if they contain some of the same items of information which were stored with the original trace.

Feature overlap
The extent to which features of the memory trace stored at input match those available in the retrieval cues. According to the ESP, successful retrieval requires extensive feature overlap.

Tulving (1972) proposed that the retrieval of an item from memory depends on the presence of retrieval cues that match up with specific aspects of the stored memory trace. Tulving called this the encoding specificity principle (ESP), since it states that retrieval cues will only be successful if they contain some of the same specific information which was encoded with the original input. Of course it is not necessary for *all* of the stored features of the item to be available in the retrieval cues too, but some of them must be there if retrieval is to be successful. Tulving argued that the chance of retrieving a memory trace depends on the amount of feature overlap between input and retrieval information, which is the extent to which features of the trace stored at input match those available at retrieval. The principle of feature overlap is illustrated in Figure 6.8.

An important aspect of Tulving's ESP theory is the assumption that successful retrieval depends on the interaction between encoding and retrieval information, rather than depending on either one alone. A useful analogy is the way in which a key fits a lock. Opening a locked door does not depend on either the key or the lock alone, but on whether they fit one another.

A number of studies have provided support for the ESP theory, by showing that retrieval of target items is far better when retrieval cues coincide with information encoded with the original trace (Tulving and Thomson, 1971; Klein and Murphy, 2001). For example, Tulving and Thomson (1971) showed that retrieval scores were dramatically increased when the retrieval cue was an item which had been present at the encoding stage. Their subjects were required to learn paired associates such as 'fast–river', word pairs that were deliberately chosen for their relatively weak association strength. When retrieval was tested later for the second word in each pair (e.g. river), cueing with the word presented at encoding (fast) proved to be far more effective than cueing with a stronger associate (e.g. lake) which had not been present at encoding.

In addition to these experimental studies, ESP theory also gains credibility from the fact that it can provide a convincing explanation for many of the observed phenomena of memory function. The ESP theory explains the superiority of recognition over recall by suggesting that recognition tests offer more feature overlap between input and output, since a recognition test provides more retrieval information than does a recall test (Tulving, 1976). ESP theory can also provide an explanation of the effects of processing depth and elaboration on retrieval (see Section 6.4), by assuming that the associative connections created by deep processing and trace elaboration can each serve as a potential retrieval route to that trace. For example, if we are trying to remember the name Winston Churchill, it would help if we have stored plenty of associations with that memory trace (Figure 6.9). Thus the use of elabora-

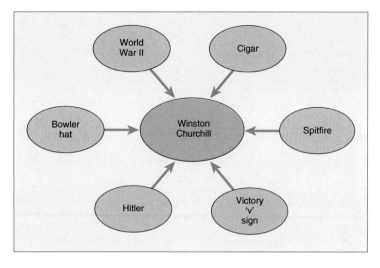

Figure 6.9 Retrieval cues leading to a memory trace (Churchill).

tive processing attaches the trace to an extensive network of other traces, which increases the chance of feature overlap between input and output information.

Although ESP theory has become widely accepted by memory theorists, Nairne (2002a) found evidence that increasing feature overlap between input and output information improves retrieval not through an encoding match but through enhanced cue distinctiveness. However, for the moment ESP remains a plausible explanation for the retrieval phenomena described above. ESP also receives support from two other important memory phenomena, transfer-appropriate processing and context-dependent memory, which will be considered in the following sections.

TRANSFER-APPROPRIATE PROCESSING

Transfer-appropriate processing (TAP) refers to the finding that the most effective type of input processing will be whatever offers the closest match with the available retrieval cues (i.e. processing transfers from input to output stage). TAP has been demonstrated in a number of studies (e.g. Fisher and Craik, 1977; Mulligan and Picklesimer, 2012), which show that when the retrieval cues are acoustic in nature (as for example when the subject is asked to recall a word similar in sound to a cue word), then acoustic orienting tasks are found to produce superior retrieval. On the other hand, when the retrieval cues are semantic, then a semantic orienting task will produce the best retrieval (Figure 6.10).

The most effective type of input processing is thus found to be that which best matches up with the processing at the retrieval stage. This finding clearly fits in well with ESP theory, and indeed TAP can be regarded as an example of ESP and feature overlap.

TAP was originally thought to challenge the LOP theory, since it shows that semantic processing does not always turn out to be

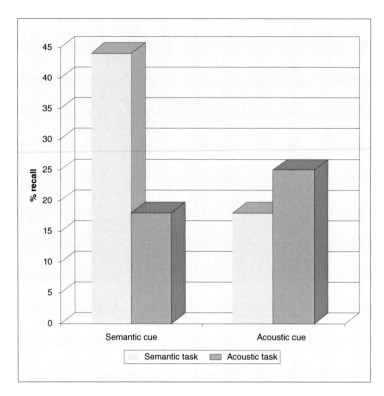

Figure 6.10   Transfer-appropriate processing.

Source: Fisher and Craik (1977).

superior to non-semantic forms of processing. However, Craik (2002) points out that that when the overall number of retrieved items is considered, semantic processing still produces better recall than non-semantic processing. Thus the TAP data are actually consistent with both the ESP theory and the levels of processing theory. Indeed TAP can be regarded as essentially a form of encoding specificity, as both emphasise the importance of a match between input and output information.

Brain-imaging studies have revealed that the same sensory areas of the brain which are activated during encoding are once again activated during retrieval (Nyberg, 2002), and this finding is consistent with the predictions of TAP and ESP theory.

CONTEXT-DEPENDENT MEMORY

It is a common observation in everyday life that returning to some earlier contextual setting can serve as a powerful cue for the retrieval of memories. You may have noticed that when you revisit some place where you spent part of your earlier life, old memories from that period tend to come flooding back, cued by the sight of a street or a building that you have not seen for many years. Sometimes a particular piece of music may bring back old memories. Even a smell or a taste can help to revive memories from the past. These are all examples of context-dependent memory, and they rely on revisiting or reinstating an earlier context which then serves as a retrieval cue.

In one of the first experimental studies of the effect of context on retrieval, Greenspoon and Ranyard (1957) tested the recall of two groups of children who had both learned the same test material in the same room. However, for the retrieval test one group returned to the room where they had carried out the learning, whereas the other group were tested in a different room. It was found that the group whose learning and retrieval took place in the same room showed better retrieval than those who were tested in a different room. This finding has been confirmed by subsequent studies (e.g. Smith, 1986), and it has been shown that merely imagining the original room and its contents can assist the recall of what was learned in that room (Jerabek and Standing, 1992).

One experiment which demonstrated the phenomenon of context-dependent memory in a particularly clear manner was that of Godden and Baddeley (1975), who carried out their research on divers. The divers were required to learn a list of 40 words, either in a 'wet' context (under the sea) or in a 'dry' context (on the seashore). Similarly, recall of the list of words could be tested in either the 'wet' or 'dry' settings (Figure 6.11).

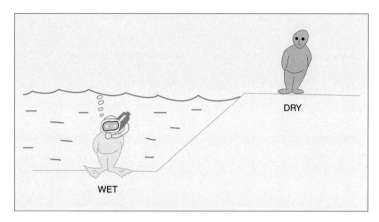

Figure 6.11 The 'wet' and 'dry' contexts.

Source: Godden and Baddeley (1975).

In comparison with previous studies, the two contexts used by Godden and Baddeley are very distinct and contrasting. One of the possible reasons why previous studies had produced a fairly modest context-dependent learning effect was that the contexts employed were rather similar (e.g. moving from one room to another similar room). On the other hand, there are very big differences between sitting under the sea in full diving equipment and sitting on the seashore without it.

The recall scores obtained by Godden and Baddeley are shown in Figure 6.12. It is clear from these findings that divers who learned the wordlist underwater recalled it best when they were also tested underwater, and those who learned on dry land also produced the best recall when they were tested on dry land. The main conclusion of this experiment was that recall of the wordlist was maximised when the context of learning (i.e. wet or dry) was reinstated for the recall test. However, a subsequent experiment suggested that context reinstatement tended to assist recall but not recognition (Godden and Baddeley, 1980), possibly because contextual

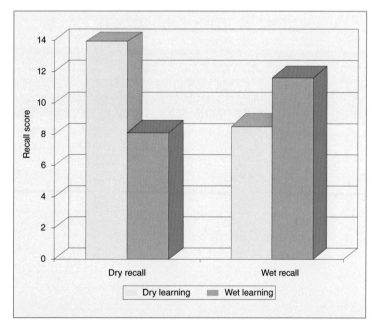

Figure 6.12 The recall of words by divers under 'wet' and 'dry' learning and retrieval conditions.

Source: Godden and Baddeley (1975).

Figure 6.13 Does that biscuit bring back memories?

Source: Shutterstock.

features act as retrieval cues, which are particularly scarce in a recall test.

The context reinstated in the above experiments was predominantly visual in nature, though clearly other sense modalities might also have made a contribution. Subsequent studies have shown that retrieval can be enhanced by the reinstatement of cues relating to specific odours. Chu and Downes (2000) found that odours could also act as strong cues to the retrieval of events from early life, a finding which has been referred to as the 'Proust phenomenon' as it parallels the observations of Marcel Proust about the evocative nature of odours. However, a more recent study has shown that although odours can certainly evoke memories from the past, they are no more effective than visual stimuli in this respect (Toffalo *et al.*, 2012). Perhaps the most valuable concept contributed by Proust was the observation that memory retrieval can often be involuntary, without requiring any effort or intention to retrieve them (Troscianko, 2013).

Smith and Vela (2001) found that context reinstatement is only effective when the participant is paying attention to their surroundings, and its effects may be masked by distraction or stress. For example, Thompson *et al.* (2001) compared wordlist recall for subjects who were either on the ground or skydiving during their learning and recall trials. In this case no significant context reinstatement effect was found, possibly because of the stressful and distracting nature of skydiving. Most of us would probably find it difficult to concentrate on a wordlist whilst falling freely from an aircraft at high altitude, so it is perhaps not surprising that recall scores were low and that context reinstatement did not significantly improve them. Interestingly, Thompson *et al.* did succeed in finding context effects when subjects merely watched a video of skydiving during learning and recall trials, rather than actually jumping out of an aircraft.

The occurrence of context-dependent memory clearly fits in very well with ESP theory, which predicts that retrieval depends on the amount of feature overlap, including feature overlap for contextual information. The effect of context reinstatement has also proved to be of great practical value in helping eyewitnesses to improve their retrieval of events such as crimes they have witnessed. This finding has led to the development of the cognitive interview, which is considered in more detail in Section 6.8.

STATE-DEPENDENT AND MOOD-DEPENDENT MEMORY

A phenomenon related to context-dependent learning is the finding that retrieval can be assisted by the reinstatement of a particular mental state

at retrieval which was also present at the learn
several studies have shown that subjects who we
intoxication at the learning stage of the experim
items more readily if they were again intoxicate
(e.g. Goodwin *et al.*, 1969). Apparently the exp
constitutes a form of inner context which can
This phenomenon is known as 'state-dependent m
been reported with other variations in mental sta
Bower *et al.* (1978) found that the retrieval of a
better if the subject was again in the same depresse
they had been in at the learning stage. It has also b
asked to recall autobiographical events from earlie
in a sad or depressed mood tended to recall a disp
of sad and depressing events, whereas people in a h
recall rather more of their happier experiences (Mi
2005). This phenomenon is more accurately refer

memory – mood dependant

Happy = Reliving Happier Times

(can lead to continual deppresion preception)

University of the Highlands and Islands Perth College

gruent memory rather than mood-dependent memory, since the subject retrieves words which are congruent with their present depressed mood but which are not actually known to have been present during a previous depressed phase.

The finding that memory can be mood-dependent has importance not only for theories of memory and retrieval but also for theories of depression. It has been suggested that some people are prone to depression because they have a cognitive bias to perceive the more negative and depressing aspects of their experience and not to notice the more positive aspects (Beck *et al.*, 1979). Mood-dependent retrieval might perpetuate this selective cognition, by making a depressed person more likely to recall experiences from previous periods of depression, thus trapping them in a cycle of selective cognition leading to further depression. Mood-dependent memory is discussed further in Chapter 12.

6.(

EPI

Selective cognition.

Brain focuses on specific memorys / Thought processes

Som ... number of sepa-
rate ... s made a distinction ... y for events and
episo ... ich is essentially
our ... ortant difference
betw ... emory involves
the ... ith a particular
cont ... hereas semantic
mem ... on (such as the
mea ... rticular context.
Tu ... in everyday life
and i ... lic memory. For
exam ... st of words, you
migh ... act you are not

University of the Highlands and Islands Perth College

Key Term

Episodic memory
Memory for specific episodes and events from personal experience, occurring in a particular context of time and place (contrasts with semantic memory).

Semantic memory
Memory for general knowledge, such as the meanings associated with particular words and shapes, without reference to any specific contextual episode (contrasts with episodic memory).

being asked to recall any information about dogs, or even what the word 'dog' means. You are being asked whether the word 'dog' was on that particular wordlist, presented in a particular place and time. In other words, you are being asked to recall the *context* in which you heard the word 'dog'. In contrast, there are occasions where we are required to retrieve general knowledge about some item, without reference to any specific context or event, as for example if you were asked to explain what a 'dog' is, or whether it has four legs and a tail. This type of retrieval involves semantic memory, and it is essentially context free. Other psychologists have come up with their own terms for episodic and semantic memory, notably Warrington (1986) who refers to 'memory for events' and 'memory for facts'.

Tulving points out that a semantic memory represents an item which has been experienced many times (e.g. eating food), so its retrieval may depend on repetition making the memory stronger. However, an episodic memory involves a specific event which has occurred only once (e.g. eating dinner last night), so its retrieval is likely to be mainly dependent on feature overlap, since a single event offers no opportunity to strengthen associative connections.

The distinction between semantic and episodic memory received some initial support from reports that patients suffering from organic amnesia appeared to be selectively impaired in their ability to recall specific episodes and events, whilst showing little impairment in their ability to recall semantic knowledge (Tulving, 1983). These conclusions have been questioned in recent years because most amnesics tend to show some impairment of semantic memory too, but certainly there are some amnesics who show episodic impairment with a relatively intact semantic memory (Tulving, 2001). This issue will be considered in more detail in Chapter 7.

The exact relationship between semantic and episodic memory remains uncertain. Tulving (1972) originally regarded them as two quite separate memory stores, but more recently he has suggested (Tulving, 2002) that semantic and episodic memories probably represent different processes within essentially the same memory storage system, with each semantic memory being derived from the combination of a series of memories for related episodic events. Tulving (2002) also argues that episodic memory involves a higher level of consciousness than semantic memory, one which makes it possible to perform 'mental time travel', consciously re-experiencing events from the past and imagining events in the future. Tulving argues that this remarkable ability probably represents a more recently evolved memory process, one that may be unique to humans. He speculates that non-human

Figure 6.14 Is this dog reminiscing about events from the past?

Source: Photo by Jennifer Law, with permission.

mammals, such as cats and dogs, may be restricted to recalling the general kind of knowledge available from semantic memory, and that they are probably unable to consciously recollect specific events from their past experience. Of course this hypothesis is entirely speculative, since dogs and cats are unable to describe their experiences to us.

Recent studies using brain-imaging techniques have provided some tentative evidence that episodic and semantic memories make use of some different brain areas but also share some areas of brain activation. Buckner (2000) found that the recall of semantic knowledge produces more activation in the left temporal lobe, whereas the recall of contextual episodes causes more activation of the right prefrontal area. However, there are some regions of the frontal cortex which are activated to a similar degree by both episodic and semantic retrieval (Prince *et al.*, 2007). It would therefore appear that the brain systems underlying episodic and semantic memory may overlap considerably, and possibly share a common underlying mechanism.

A recent study found that the pattern of activation of the hippocampus during episodic memory was repeated when participants were asked to imagine future events (Addis and Schacter, 2012). This suggests that the hippocampus may be involved in all forms of episodic memory which involve 'mental time travel', including representations of both past and future events.

FAMILIARITY AND RECOLLECTION

Another theory distinguishing between two memory systems is that of Mandler (1980), who pointed out that recognition involves two different retrieval processes. The first is a judgement of familiarity, which simply involves deciding whether or not an item has ever been encountered before. The second is the recollection of when and where the item was encountered, in other words the recollection of context. Mandler's main evidence for making this distinction was the observation that we can find someone's face familiar and yet be unable to recall the context in which we have met them before. This is actually a common experience in everyday life and all of us will have experienced it at some time, especially when we meet an acquaintance outside their usual context. For example, if you happen to meet your local butcher on the bus, you may find that although his face is very familiar you cannot remember who he is or where you have met him. At this stage the person's familiarity has been established but the setting from which they are familiar cannot be recollected. This may come to us later, but recollecting actual occasions when we have previously met the person usually requires some thought. This kind of experience has actually come to be known as the 'butcher on the bus' phenomenon (Cleary *et al.*, 2007), and it shows that it is possible to experience a feeling of familiarity even when we cannot achieve context recollection. This suggests that familiarity judgements and context recollection must involve separate retrieval processes (see Figure 6.15 for a demonstration).

Key Term

Familiarity
The recognition of an item as one that has been encountered on some previous occasion.

Recollection
Remembering a specific event or occasion on which an item was previously encountered.

Figure 6.15 Familiar faces – but who are they? (You can find their names at the end of this chapter.)

Mandler suggests that familiarity and recollection probably operate as two independent retrieval routes, which may either be used separately or in combination. The main distinction between familiarity and recollection is that recollection involves the effortful retrieval of context, whereas familiarity does not. This suggests some similarity with the episodic/semantic distinction.

Mandler (1980) pointed out that a familiarity judgement seems to be an automatic process, which occurs without any conscious effort or intention (see Chapter 1 for the differences between automatic and controlled processes). When you see a familiar face in a crowd, their familiarity seems to jump out at you automatically. No effort is required, and you cannot prevent yourself from making this familiarity judgement. Recollection, on the other hand, seems to be a controlled process, and one which requires some degree of volition, conscious attention, and effort. This theory receives further support from the finding (Parkin *et al.*, 1995a) that performing a second task during presentation of the faces has no effect on the accuracy of face familiarity judgements, whereas recollection scores are significantly reduced. Another interesting finding is that sleeping directly after a learning session leads to an improvement in contextual recollection but does not assist familiarity judgements (Drosopoulos *et al.*, 2005). It has also been found that amnesic patients show relatively unimpaired familiarity judgements but severely impaired context recollection (Huppert and Piercy, 1976; King *et al.*, 2004). These studies of amnesics will be discussed further in Chapter 7.

Recent brain-imaging studies suggest that recollection involves activation of the medial temporal lobes and hippocampus, whereas familiarity judgements are associated with activation of the perirhinal cortex (Eichenbaum *et al.*, 2007). The finding that familiarity and recollection appear to activate different brain areas adds support to the view that they involve separate retrieval processes. Eichenbaum *et al.* (2007) suggest that familiarity information (from the 'what' pathway) goes to the perirhinal cortex, whilst contextual information (from the 'where' pathway) goes to para-hippocampal cortex. These two streams of information (see Chapter 2) then converge and meet at the medial temporal lobes, where they are bound together. There is also evidence (Ranganath, 2010) that the binding of items encountered at different times involves activation of the prefrontal cortex.

THE R & K ('REMEMBER AND KNOW') PROCEDURE

One method which has been used to measure the relative contributions of familiarity and recollection is the 'remember and know' (R & K) procedure introduced by Tulving (1985). The R & K procedure involves asking subjects to indicate whether their recognition responses are based on consciously remembering the presentation of a test item (an 'R' response), or on simply knowing that the item is familiar without any specific memory of seeing it (a 'K' response).

Using the R & K procedure, Gardiner and Parkin (1990) found that 'remember' (R) scores for verbal items were significantly reduced when the participant was distracted by a second task during the learning of the list, but divided attention had no effect on the 'know' (K) scores. These findings suggest that 'remember' scores depend on giving full and undivided conscious attention at the learning stage, whereas 'know' scores do not. Another difference between 'R' and 'K' scores is that semantic orienting tasks produce higher 'R' scores than do non-semantic tasks, whereas 'K' scores are unaffected by processing depth (Gardiner and Java, 1993).

Based on such findings, Gardiner (2002) argues that 'R' and 'K' scores reflect two different underlying memory processes. However, there is some doubt over the question of whether the 'R' and 'K' scores really do provide separate measures of recollection and familiarity, and there is evidence that both the 'R' and the 'K' score may receive some contribution from both familiarity and recollection (Mandler, 2008).

IMPLICIT AND EXPLICIT MEMORY

Most tests of memory involve the direct testing of what the subject is able to consciously remember and report, which is known as explicit memory. Tests of recall and recognition are both examples of explicit memory, and for many years this was the only type of memory to be studied. However, recently there has been an increasing interest in the use of more indirect memory tests detecting implicit memory, which refers to memories for which the individual has no conscious awareness. Although such memories cannot be deliberately and consciously retrieved, their existence is implicit in the behaviour of the individual (hence the term 'implicit memory') because it affects their performance on certain tasks.

Jacoby and Dallas (1981) demonstrated the existence of implicit memory by showing that subjects who had been shown a list of words subsequently found those words easier to identify than unstudied words, even when they had lost any conscious memory of the words on the list. In another key experiment, Tulving *et al.* (1982) presented their subjects with a list of words, then after a lengthy delay (by which time the wordlist had been largely forgotten) they asked their subjects to produce the first word they could think of to complete a fragmented word. For example, if the original target word was 'telephone' then the fragmented word might be 't-l-p-o-e'. Half of the words in the

> **Key Term**
>
> **Explicit memory**
> Memory which a subject is able to report consciously and deliberately (contrasts with implicit memory).
>
> **Implicit memory**
> Memory whose influence can be detected by some indirect test of task performance, but which the subject is unable to report deliberately and consciously (contrasts with explicit memory).

test had been studied earlier, but the other half had not. Most subjects were able to complete far more of the fragmented words which had been previously shown, even though they were unable to identify those words in a recognition test. Indeed, subjects were found to be equally likely to complete a fragmented word with the previously primed target word regardless of whether that word could be recognised or not.

The initial presentation of the wordlist in these experiments was carried out in a way that involved presenting the words as part of some other task, so that the subject was not required to learn the words and was unaware that they would be tested later. This kind of presentation is known as 'priming', and it is a useful technique in an implicit memory experiment because although the subject is exposed to the words they do not attempt to learn them and thus tend to have no explicit memory of them later.

The significance of these experiments is that they demonstrated that priming a word could influence subsequent performance on a test of implicit memory, even when the word could not be retrieved explicitly. Similar effects have been obtained with a variety of implicit memory tests, including word-stem completion (e.g. complete the word 'tel____') and anagram solution (e.g. solve the anagram 'leopetneh'). Such tasks are used to guide recall towards the primed items, but subjects are not actually required to recall the primed words. They are simply asked to produce the first suitable word that comes into their head.

Parkin *et al.* (1990) investigated the effect of divided attention on implicit and explicit memory, by priming subjects with a list of target words whilst distracting them with a second task. They found that divided attention during priming caused a marked deterioration in a subsequent test of explicit memory (word recognition), but had no effect on the performance of an implicit task (fragment completion). These findings suggest that implicit memory does not require full conscious attention. Graf *et al.* (1984) found that implicit memory is also unaffected by the level of input processing carried out, whereas explicit memory benefits from semantic processing rather than non-semantic processing. These studies suggest that explicit memory requires full attention and deep semantic processing, but implicit memory does not. This finding is consistent with the suggestion (Hayman and Tulving, 1989) that implicit memory draws mainly on stimulus-driven processing (such as the identification of the perceptual features of the target item), whilst explicit memory may depend more on schema-driven processing (involving a more integrated whole target item).

Further evidence for the distinction between implicit and explicit memory arises from the finding that implicit memories seem to be more durable and lasting than explicit memories. Tulving *et al.* (1982) showed that implicit memory tends to survive for very long periods of time, often continuing to influence responses long after the subject has lost any ability to retrieve the target items explicitly. Their results are shown in Figure 6.16.

In another study, Mitchell (2006) found that individuals who had participated in an experiment still retained a significant amount of implicit memory for the test items 17 years later, despite showing no explicit memory for these items. It seems that memories can remain in store at an unconscious level for very long periods, long after people have lost the ability to recall them consciously.

The distinction between implicit and explicit memory has received further support from the finding that organic amnesic patients show impaired explicit memory but relatively intact implicit memory (Graf *et al.*, 1984; Conroy *et al.*, 2005). These findings will be examined in more detail in Chapter 7. Gopie *et al.* (2011) found that elderly people had worse explicit memory than younger people, but rather surprisingly the elderly actually scored higher than the young on tests of implicit memory. Gopie *et al.* suggested that older adults may have difficulty processing information conceptually, so that they will tend to process information at a perceptual level instead.

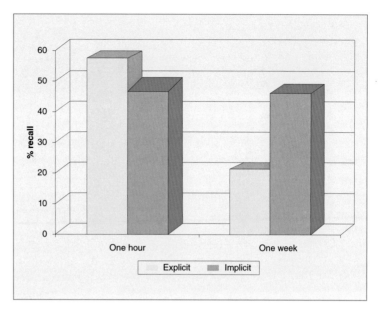

Figure 6.16   Scores for recognition (explicit) and fragment completion (implicit) after retention intervals of one hour and one week.

Source: Tulving *et al.* (1982).

Baddeley (2009a) argues that conscious explicit memory 'glues together' information about events which were experienced at the same time, thus creating a relatively rich and detailed memory for an entire episode in one's life. On the other hand, implicit memories merely consist of individual memory traces for features which remain essentially unconnected. Baddeley adds that implicit memory actually includes a number of fairly different and possibly unrelated processes, which are linked only by the *absence* of conscious episodic recall.

Schott *et al.* (2005) used an fMRI study to compare the effects of implicit and explicit memory retrieval. They found that the retrieval of explicit memories caused *increased* activation of the left and right parietal and temporal lobes, whereas the retrieval of implicit memories caused *reduced* activation in the frontal and occipital lobes and in the left fusiform gyrus. They attributed this reduction in brain activation to the fact that implicit memory is probably far easier to retrieve than explicit memory and thus requires less cortical activation.

IMPLICIT MEMORY IN EVERYDAY LIFE

The discovery of implicit memory has led to speculation about its possible influence in everyday life. For example, implicit memory is thought to be the mechanism underlying the phenomenon of 'conversational plagiarism' (Parkin, 1993), where someone unwittingly repeats a word they have just heard without being aware of having heard it. You have probably noticed this yourself at some time, as it occurs quite often in everyday conversation. One person happens to use an unusual word during a conversation, such as 'exquisite' or 'fortuitous', and shortly afterwards a different person will use that same word without being aware of having copied it. Hearing the word has presumably heightened its level of activation in the memory of the listener, so that they are more likely to use the word themselves despite having no conscious recollection of hearing it spoken. This phenomenon occurs frequently in everyday life, but it has also been demonstrated in experimental studies (Brown and Murphy, 1989). In fact it was first noted by Taylor (1965), who referred to it as 'cryptomnesia'.

Claxton (1998) suggests that implicit memory may also be the mechanism underlying intuition, or 'hunches'. Sometimes we may not be sure of the answer to a question, but we have a hunch that a certain answer is probably correct, possibly reflecting the retrieval of an implicit memory.

Brown (2004) suggests that implicit memory may also explain the occurrence of 'déjà vu', which is the feeling that you have experienced something before when in fact you have not. This is basically a mistaken judgement of familiarity, and although it is a rare occurrence most people will probably have experienced it a few times. Brown considers that the déjà vu experience occurs when some new situation triggers an implicit memory for some similar experience in the past, which can no longer be recalled in a conscious and explicit manner.

In recent years social psychologists have begun to develop theories which explain social interaction in terms of underlying cognitive processes. In particular it has been argued that our social interaction is strongly influenced by implicit memory (Greenwald and Banaji, 1995), such as our attitudes and responses to certain people and situations. Indeed, the possible involvement of implicit memory in social behaviour may help to explain why people often behave in ways that are contrary to their expressed views and attitudes (Amodio and Ratner, 2011).

In the clinical field it has been suggested that implicit memory may help to explain the occurrence of distressing intrusive memories in patients suffering from post-traumatic stress disorder (PTSD) , and possibly also the repressed traumatic memories which trouble many neurotic patients. Implicit memory shares certain characteristics with repressed traumatic memories, in that both are unconscious, cue-dependent and essentially perceptual in nature. Moreover, implicit memories are known to be very persistent and long-lasting, as noted in the previous section. One recent PTSD study (Amir et al., 2010) found that individuals suffering intrusive memories and PTSD symptoms showed an increased level of implicit memory for negative and trauma-related pictures, suggesting that heightened implicit memory could play a part in maintaining PTSD.

PROCESSES UNDERLYING DIFFERENT MEMORY SYSTEMS

It is interesting to note that the dissociations found between implicit and explicit memory resemble those found between familiarity and recollection. In both cases there are differential effects of divided attention, processing depth, and impairment in amnesic patients. Implicit memory and familiarity judgements appear to share a dependence on unconscious automatic retrieval processes, involving the activation of perceptual features of the trace rather than associative and contextual connections. In contrast, explicit memory and recollection seem to share a dependence on controlled effortful processes, and make use of associative or contextual links.

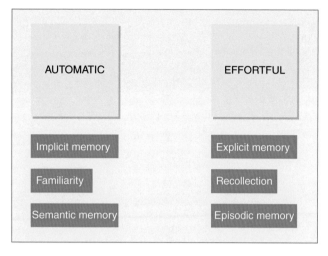

Figure 6.17   Automatic and effortful memory systems.

Some theorists have argued that the episodic/semantic distinction also resembles these two systems, as they once again seem to reflect a distinction between automatic and effortful processing. Schacter *et al.* (2000) argue that semantic memory is essentially a form of implicit memory, whilst episodic memory is explicit. Their classification of these memory systems is illustrated in Figure 6.17.

However, Squire *et al.* (1992) point out that the majority of amnesic patients suffer impairments of both episodic and semantic memory, suggesting that they probably reflect the same underlying memory mechanism rather than being entirely separate. Squire *et al.* therefore argue that episodic and semantic memory should both be classified as related forms of explicit memory (as shown in Chapter 7, Figure 7.9). This view will be considered in more detail in Chapter 7.

6.7 RETRIEVAL PRACTICE AND RETRIEVAL INHIBITION

RETRIEVAL PRACTICE AND THE TESTING EFFECT

It has been established that learning is far more effective if it involves testing and retrieval of the material you are trying to learn. This is known as the testing effect, and it has been demonstrated with a wide range of materials and conditions. The testing effect has been confirmed with the learning of wordlists (Allen *et al.*, 1969), general knowledge (McDaniel and Fisher, 1991), foreign language vocabulary (Carpenter *et al.*, 2008), and for visual tasks such as map learning (Carpenter and Pashler, 2007). Extending this research into a real-life setting,

Key Term

Testing effect
The finding that actively testing a memory improves its subsequent retrievability.

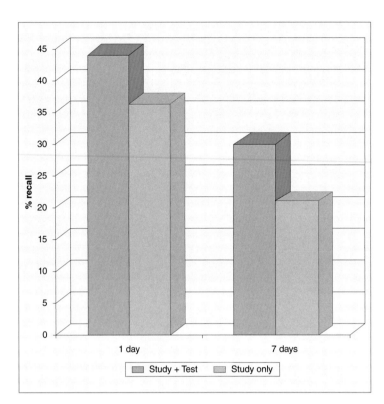

Figure 6.18   The effect of testing on subsequent retrieval of Swahili–English word pairs, after retrieval intervals of 1 day and 7 days.

Source: Carpenter *et al.* (2008).

McDaniel *et al.* (2007) found that students achieved higher exam marks if their revision focused on retrieval testing rather than mere re-reading of the exam material. Figure 6.18 presents the results of a typical experiment on the testing effect.

These findings have important implications for anyone who is revising for an exam, or indeed anyone who is trying to learn information for any purpose. Learning will be far more effective if it involves testing and retrieval of the material you are trying to learn, rather than merely re-reading it.

DECAY WITH DISUSE

The discovery of the testing effect has led some researchers to reconsider the reasons why memories tend to fade away with the passage of time. As explained in Section 6.2, early experiments by Ebbinghaus (1885) established that memories become weaker as time passes, and he hypothesized that memories decay spontaneously with time. However, Thorndike (1914) argued that decay only occurs when a memory is left unused for a long period, which is known as the 'decay with disuse' theory. An updated version of this theory has recently been proposed by Bjork and Bjork (1992), who argue that a memory trace which is not retrieved will eventually become inaccessible, whereas a frequently retrieved memory trace will be strengthened and becomes easier to retrieve in the future. They call this theory the New Theory of Disuse (NTD), and it receives strong support from the testing effect (see previous section), which demonstrates that retrieving an item makes it more retrievable in future.

Bjork and Bjork make a distinction between the storage strength and the retrieval strength of a memory. Storage strength depends how well the item has been learned and tends to be fairly permanent, whereas retrieval strength reflects the accessibility of the trace, which varies considerably from moment to moment. For example, the retrieval strength of an item increases when that item is retrieved and activated, but it is weakened by disuse and by the retrieval of rival items. Bjork and Bjork argue that the act of retrieval is in itself a learning event, which increases retrieval strength and makes the retrieved item easier to retrieve in the future. There is also evidence that the retrieval of a target item may cause the inhibition of rival items, which could explain the decay of disused items over time. This phenomenon is known as retrieval-induced forgetting (RIF), and it is discussed in the next section.

RETRIEVAL-INDUCED FORGETTING (RIF)

It has been discovered that practising the retrieval of a memory trace not only

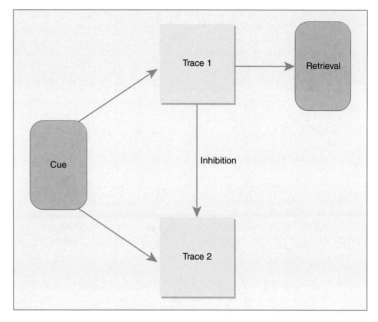

Figure 6.19 Retrieval-induced forgetting.

strengthens that trace, it also apparently inhibits the retrieval of rival memory traces (Anderson *et al.*, 1994). This phenomenon is known as retrieval-induced forgetting. Anderson *et al.* demonstrated the RIF effect by presenting their subjects with a series of word pairs, each consisting of a category word and an example of an item from that category (e.g. fruit–banana). Some of these items were subjected to repeated retrieval. It was found the retrieval of these practised items was greatly improved, as you would expect. But more surprisingly, the unpractised items from the same category as the practised items proved to be very difficult to recall. So, for example, retrieving 'banana' inhibited the recall of 'apple' (which also belongs to the 'fruit' category) but did not inhibit 'shirt' (which belongs to a different category). Anderson et al. concluded that the retrieval of an item somehow inhibits the retrieval of other items from the same category (Figure 6.19).

The RIF phenomenon has now been confirmed by a large number of studies (e.g. Anderson, M. C. *et al.*, 2000; MacLeod and Macrae, 2001; Groome and Sterkaj, 2010). It has been shown that RIF only occurs as a consequence of actually retrieving an item, and not from passive study such as re-reading test items (Anderson, M. C. *et al.*, 2000).

Anderson (2003) argues that RIF is caused by an inhibitory mechanism in the brain, which has evolved for the specific purpose of suppressing unwanted memories. Other researchers question this inhibitory account, as they consider that RIF might merely reflect the blocking of an unpractised response (Camp *et al.*, 2007). According to the blocking hypothesis, retrieval practice strengthens the connection between the practised item and the cue, thus preventing that cue from generating alternative items. However, the blocking account would predict that retrieval practice would create RIF only for one specific cue, whereas several studies suggest that RIF occurs with a range of different cues, including so-called 'independent' cues which are different to the one used for retrieval practice (Anderson, 2003). Moreover, Storm and White (2010) reported that individuals with attention deficit hyperactivity disorder (ADHD), which is characterised by impaired inhibitory control, also show an impaired RIF performance. Further support for the inhibitory account of RIF comes from the recent finding (Storm, 2011) that individuals with strong RIF are also are more capable of overcoming interference in other contexts too, for example in creative problem solving tasks.

Early studies suggested that the RIF effect created by a single retrieval practice session lasts for only about a day or so (MacLeod, 2002), but more recent studies have reported that RIF can still be detected one week after retrieval practice (Tandoh and Naka, 2007). It is possible that RIF could lead to more lasting memory inhibition if an item was subjected to repeated RIF inhibitions over a long period of time, raising the intriguing hypothesis (Anderson, 2003) that RIF could be responsible for the forgetting of disused memories over time.

RIF IN REAL-LIFE SETTINGS

The discovery of RIF raises an obvious question – what is this mechanism for? Anderson (2003) suggests that the purpose of RIF is to suppress unwanted memories, so that we can retrieve the items we actually require. RIF thus serves the function of helping memory to be more selective, by reducing interference from rival items. It is easy to see how such an inhibitory mechanism might have evolved, because selective retrieval of this kind would offer benefits in many real-life situations. For example, remembering where you left your car in a large multistorey car park would be extremely difficult if you had equally strong memories for every previous occasion on which you had ever parked your car (Figure 6.20). It would be very helpful to have a memory mechanism which activated the most recent memory of parking your car, whilst inhibiting the memories of all previous occasions (Anderson and Neely, 1996).

If the RIF mechanism really has evolved in order to facilitate selective retrieval, then we might expect RIF to produce benefits in real-life settings. Groome and Grant (2005) found that individuals showing a very strong RIF effect do appear to have better memories in everyday life, as measured by the Cognitive Failures Questionnaire (CFQ). There is also evidence that RIF affects exam revision. Students showed good recall of practised items, but very poor recall of

Figure 6.20   Where did you leave your car?

Source: Photo by Glenys Law.

related items which were unpractised (Macrae and MacLeod, 1999; Carroll *et al.*, 2007). These findings have possible implications for exam revision techniques, as they suggest that last-minute cramming before an examination may sometimes do more harm than good. Apparently it helps the recall of a few practised items at the expense of poorer recall for the others.

Shaw *et al.* (1995) have also demonstrated the occurrence of RIF in an experiment on eyewitness testimony. Their subjects watched a slide show about a crime, after which they were tested for their recall of what they had just seen. It was found that the successful retrieval of some details of the crime inhibited the retrieval of other items. Shaw *et al.* concluded that in real crime investigations there was a risk that police questioning of a witness could lead to the subsequent inhibition of any information not retrieved during the initial interview. However, MacLeod (2002) reported that these inhibitory effects tended to subside about 24 hours after the initial questioning, so a second interview with the same eyewitness might produce further retrieval so long as the two interviews were separated by at least 24 hours.

RETRIEVAL INHIBITION, DISUSE AND PSYCHIATRIC DISORDERS

Retrieval-induced forgetting and the New Theory of Disuse may have implications for the understanding and treatment of neurotic disorders. For example, victims of severe traumatic events such as wars and earthquakes often suffer later on from intrusive memories which can cause great distress for many years (Horowitz, 1976; Brewin, 1998), a condition known as post-traumatic stress disorder (PTSD). In fact unwanted intrusive memories are the main symptom of PTSD, which can therefore be seen as being to some extent a memory disorder. One possible factor in the causation of PTSD may be that distressing intrusive memories are strengthened by repeated retrieval, which may lead to the inhibition of other related memory traces due to RIF (Anderson, 2001). Amir *et al.* (2009) found an impaired RIF effect in individuals exposed to severe trauma, regardless of whether they showed symptoms of PTSD. This finding suggests that trauma may have a damaging effect on memory inhibition, possibly making the victims more vulnerable to intrusive memories. However, a subsequent study (Blix and Brennen, 2012) found normal RIF in trauma victims, so clearly there is a need for more research to clarify this issue.

Although neuroses have not traditionally been regarded as disorders of memory, most neuroses do involve unwanted memories which may trigger off a phobic response or an anxiety attack. It is therefore possible that memory mechanisms could play a part in causing or maintaining neurotic symptoms. Lang *et al.* (1999) argue, in accordance with the New Theory of Disuse and RIF research, that phobic responses may be strengthened by repeated retrieval, which might also suppress other less distressing memory responses to the same stimulus. Lang *et al.* suggest that phobic patients might benefit from practising the retrieval of alternative (non-fearful) responses to the stimulus, in order to inhibit the phobic response.

Recent studies have shown that RIF scores are impaired in those suffering from anxiety or depression. Groome and Sterkaj (2010) found that a group of individuals suffering from clinical depression showed greatly reduced RIF, though the direction of causality between depression and RIF was not established by this study. However, Bauml and Kuhbandner (2007) found that when they induced a sad mood state in normal participants this led to a reduction in their RIF scores, which suggests that RIF is affected by depression rather than the other way around. Reduced RIF scores have also been found in very anxious individuals (Law *et al.*, 2012). This finding is consistent with the predictions of the Attentional Control Theory (Eysenck *et al.*, 2007), which suggests that anxiety impairs the operation of cognitive inhibitory mechanisms (see Chapter 12). These findings may help to explain why RIF scores are not completely fixed and reliable for any given individual (Potts *et al.*, 2011), since the strength of the RIF effect goes up and down according to mood state.

DIRECTED FORGETTING

Retrieval-induced forgetting is thought to make use of automatic, non-effortful processing, which takes place at an unconscious level. However, there is evidence that people are able to deliberately suppress a memory if instructed to do so, and this is assumed to involve effortful and conscious processing. The procedure is known as directed forgetting (DF), and there are two different methods of demonstrating DF, the item method and the list method. The item method involves reading out a list of items with an instruction after each item to either 'remember' or 'forget' that item. Testing recall of the entire list afterwards shows that R (remember) items are better retrieved than F (forget) items (Bjork, 1972). The list method involves reading out a list of items, followed by a surprise instruction to forget them. A second list is then read out, this time followed by an instruction to remember. There is normally a control group who hear the same two lists, but without the 'forget' instruction after the first list. Once again the final recall test shows that the R items are better recalled than are the F items (Geiselman *et al.*, 1983).

A vital feature of the item method is that participants are given the R or F instruction directly after each item, so they are able to devote more processing effort to the R items. It is therefore assumed that, for the item method, inhibition mostly takes place at the encoding stage. However, with the list method inhibition must presumably occur at the retrieval stage, since the R/F instruction is not given until the entire list has been heard. There is some support for this theoretical viewpoint. Basden and Basden (1996) found that with the list method the suppression of F items occurs with recall tests but not with recognition tests, suggesting that the F items are actually encoded and available for recognition but encounter problems with the retrieval process. With the item method the DF effect is equally strong for recall and recognition tests, suggesting that item suppression occurs at the encoding stage.

Barnier *et al.* (2007) found that the DF effect occurs with more complex real-life memories, and not just with wordlists in an experimental setting. Delaney *et al.* (2009) also demonstrated the occurrence of DF with lists of meaningful sentences. These sentences each provided a piece of information about one of two people, named Tom and Alex. After seeing all of the sentences, participants were instructed to forget all of the sentences about Tom, but to remember the sentences about Alex. A subsequent recall test confirmed that participants did indeed remember more of the sentences about Alex, but the effect only worked when the sentences were separate and unrelated. When the sentences were related, and formed part of a continuous theme, the DF effect disappeared, probably because the sentences tended to cue one another.

Power *et al.* (2000) found that individuals suffering from depression did not show the usual DF effect for negative items, and in fact showed an increased retrieval of negative items which they were instructed to forget. A recent study by Aslan *et al.* (2010) found that the DF effect was stronger in individuals with a high working memory capacity, supporting the view that directed forgetting apparently involves effortful processing by the central executive.

RECONSOLIDATION

In the last few years researchers have made some exciting discoveries about the possibility of changing stored memories. Several studies have indicated that when an old memory is reactivated it becomes vulnerable to change. This means that the retrieval of a stored memory presents an opportunity to make that memory stronger or weaker before it is put back into storage. This phenomenon is known as reconsolidation, since it implies that a retrieved memory must be stored again, possibly in modified form.

In fact the first hint of the reconsolidation phenomenon was reported some 40 years ago. Misanin *et al.* (1968) were trying to find out whether electroconvulsive therapy (ECT) could harm stored memories. Using rats, they showed that an electric shock administered to the head had no significant effect on subsequent retrieval of a learned response. However, if the shock was administered after the rat had been given a reminder of their earlier training, that training was largely obliterated by the shock. It appeared to the researchers that by reactivating the memory they had made it more vulnerable to change. However, this rather intriguing finding was largely ignored for the next 30 years.

More recently, Nader *et al.* (2000) demonstrated that reactivated memories were also impaired by the effects of certain drugs (called protein-synthesis inhibitors), which prevent the formation of new memory traces. Once again, this research was carried out on rats, and it confirmed the earlier finding that the strength of a memory could be diminished by applying some form of suppression while the memory

Key Term

Reconsolidation
The finding that the reactivation of a memory makes it temporarily vulnerable to change.

was in an active state. These findings raised the possibility that such methods could be used to remove unwanted memories, such as the intrusive memories which plague PTSD sufferers. Unfortunately protein-synthesis inhibitors are not suitable for use on humans because of their toxic effects, but researchers have had some success in treating PTSD sufferers using interference from new learning to suppress an intrusive memory after first cueing its retrieval into an activated state (Hupbach *et al.*, 2007; Schiller *et al.*, 2010). Most importantly, they found that such intrusive memories were only suppressed if the extinction process was applied directly after retrieval, and when applied some time after memory retrieval there was no inhibitory effect.

Whilst these earlier reconsolidation studies all involved suppressing memories, a few recent studies have reported that activated memories can actually be strengthened. Blaiss and Janak (2006) reported that administering a stimulant drug to rats directly after retrieval of a memory increased the strength of that memory. Finn and Roediger (2011) found that the presentation of an emotionally arousing picture to human subjects directly after reactivating a memory caused that memory to be strengthened, whereas presenting an emotionally neutral picture had no such effect. Another recent study (St Jaques and Schacter, 2013) showed that reactivated memories could be enhanced or diminished in a real-life setting, involving memories for a museum visit.

These findings are still somewhat tentative, and they require further research and replication. However, if it is confirmed that existing memories can be strengthened or weakened by these reconsolidation techniques there could be many useful applications. Most obviously there is the possibility of removing unwanted memories in clinical conditions such as PTSD and depression, and a range of new therapeutic techniques could be developed as a result. The phenomenon of reconsolidation may also help to explain some of the established findings about memory, such as the misinformation effect and the testing effect. But all of this has yet to be investigated, so you will need to read journals yet to be published, or the next edition of this book, to find out what happened next.

> **Key Term**
>
> **Misinformation effect**
> The contamination of eyewitness testimony by information acquired after the witnessed event.

6.8 MEMORY IN EVERYDAY LIFE

ECOLOGICAL VALIDITY

One major criticism which can be directed at the majority of memory research is that it tends to involve rather artificial situations which are unlikely to occur outside a laboratory. You might like to consider when was the last time you were asked during your normal day-to-day life to retain three letters in your short-term memory whilst counting backwards in threes (Peterson and Peterson, 1959), or to complete a word stem with the first word that comes into your head following a word list priming that you can no longer remember (Tulving *et al.*, 1982). Unless your life is very different from mine, I suspect that these will not have been frequent experiences. These are tasks that do not occur in everyday life, but such laboratory experiments do have an important function, as they enable us to isolate processes like STM decay and implicit memory which are not otherwise seen in a pure form. Such processes probably do play a major part in everyday memory, but usually in combination with other processes, hence the need for artificial experiments to isolate them. However, whilst accepting the value of laboratory experiments, Neisser (1976) argued that memory should also be investigated in real-life settings where the conditions are completely natural. He describes this approach as seeking ecological validity. Since Neisser made this plea for ecological validity there has been an increasing amount of work on memory in real-life settings, including studies of autobiographical memory, flashbulb memory and eyewitness testimony.

> **Key Term**
>
> **Ecological validity**
> The extent to which the conditions of a research experiment resemble those encountered in real-life settings.

AUTOBIOGRAPHICAL MEMORY

How much can you remember about the events in your life up till now? How well can you remember your school days? How many of your teachers and schoolmates can you name? You might like to spend a few moments testing yourself on these questions. Better still, fish out an old school photograph (like the one showing the author in Figure 6.21), to provide a few retrieval cues. You will probably be surprised how much you can retrieve from the distant past, often about people and events you had not thought about for many years.

Figure 6.21   An old school photograph. (The author is on the front row, second from the right, next to the boy wearing a tie.)

Bahrick *et al.* (1975) investigated the ability of American adults to remember their old high-school classmates from an old school photograph, and found that most of their subjects could still match up the names and photos of more than 80 per cent of their college classmates even 25 years after graduation. In fact there was no significant decline in their performance over the years since the actual period when they had graduated. Although scores did drop off slightly at longer retention intervals, they still remained above 70 per cent despite an average time lapse of 47 years. Bahrick *et al.* concluded that memory for a real-life experience tends to be far more accurate and durable than memory for items tested in a laboratory experiment. This is probably because autobiographical memories have far greater personal significance to the individual than do the test items in a lab experiment. In a more recent study, Bahrick *et al.* (2008) asked people to try to recall their college grades at various times in their later lives. In fact participants performed surprisingly well, and on average they still recalled 80 per cent of their grades correctly even after an interval of 50 years. Forgetting mostly took place in the first few years and there was only a very slight

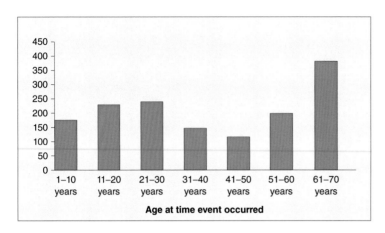

Figure 6.22   Retrieval scores for personal events from different times of an individual's life.

Source: After Rubin *et al.* (1986).

reduction after that. Again this study shows that with real-life memories of great personal significance there is far less forgetting than in lab studies of memory.

One problem with the study of autobiographical memory is that it is often difficult to check its accuracy. You may be quite sure that you remember the events of your 16th birthday clearly and accurately, but your memories may not be correct. A number of investigators, notably Linton (1975) and Wagenaar (1986), deliberately kept very detailed diaries of their own daily experiences over a period of many years, which could later be used to check the accuracy of their retrieval. Linton (1975) found that items which had been tested previously were far more likely to be retrieved later on, which is consistent with laboratory findings demonstrating the 'testing effect' (Allen *et al.*, 1969; Carpenter *et al.*, 2008).

Wagenaar (1986) kept a detailed diary over many years, but he also took the trouble to record retrieval cues for later use. By this means he was able to establish that the likelihood of retrieval depended on the number of retrieval cues available. With suitable cues Wagenaar recalled about half of the events recorded over the previous six years. Wagenaar's findings are therefore in broad agreement with the usual laboratory finding that successful retrieval depends on the availability of suitable retrieval cues (Tulving, 1972).

Rubin *et al.* (1986) found that most people tend to recall more autobiographical information from recent years than from the distant past, which is consistent with decay and interference theory (see Section 6.2), both of which predict that memories will become less accessible with the passing of time. However, one exception to these general findings is that older people tend to recall an increased amount from their early adult years (Rubin *et al.*, 1998), a phenomenon known as the 'reminiscence bump'. For example, Rubin *et al.* found that people in their seventies tended to recall a particularly large number of events from the period when they were aged 10-30 (see Figure 6.22).

A possible explanation for this effect is that their earlier years may have been more eventful or more pleasant, and thus more memorable. Berntsen and Rubin (2004) confirmed that the reminiscence bump does indeed peak at a time in life when important events are taking place. Young adulthood is a period in life when an individual is often experiencing something for the very first time, and people often have vivid memories for their first trip abroad or their first date. Unfortunately, subsequent dates and trips abroad tend to lose their novelty value and thus become less memorable.

Further evidence that the reminiscence bump reflects a favoured period of our lives comes from the work of Janssen *et al.* (2012), who asked people to choose their favourite footballers of all time. They found that most people chose players who were at their peak when the person choosing them was in their late teens, rather than picking more recent players.

Gluck and Bluck (2007) found that the reminiscence bump applies mainly to positive and happy memories. Since older people tend to enjoy remembering happy events from their younger days, this frequent retrieval might help to strengthen the retrieval routes to those early memories.

Most people remember very little from early childhood, and studies have confirmed that most people actually remember nothing at all from the first two or three years of their lives (Pillemer and White, 1989). This phenomenon is known as 'infantile amnesia'. One possible explanation for infantile amnesia is that the brain may not have completed its physical development in early infancy and is not yet able to store memories. Indeed it has been found that

Figure 6.23 Who is your favourite footballer of all time?
Source: Shutterstock.

the hippocampus (the brain area which is most important for memory storage) takes several years to become fully developed (Richmond and Nelson, 2007). However, there is also a possibility that during infancy memories may be stored in a form that is not retrievable in adulthood. Nelson and Ross (1980) showed that very young children are able to remember general facts (i.e. semantic memory) but not specific events (i.e. episodic memory). Their earliest memories thus tend to be based on schemas and scripts for general or typical events, but not for specific episodes of their own personal lives. Another possible reason why very young children cannot store memories may be their lack of language skills. Simcock and Hayne (2003) showed that young children perform very poorly on memory tests requiring verbalisation, but they do rather better on non-verbal tests.

One finding that has emerged from studies of autobiographical memory is that events which are shocking or emotionally charged tend to leave a particularly vivid and lasting memory trace. The most extreme cases of emotionally significant events are not only memorable themselves, but may leave a lasting memory of trivial aspects of the

Key Term

Flashbulb memory
A subject's recollection of details of what they were doing at the time of some major news event or dramatic incident.

context which happened to coincide with them. These are known as flashbulb memories.

FLASHBULB MEMORIES

Can you remember where you were and what you were doing when you heard the news of the World Trade Center attack? If so then this is an example of 'flashbulb memory', so called because the shock of hearing such news seems to illuminate the relatively trivial events of our own lives and makes them highly memorable. The significance of flashbulb memory is not that the major news event itself was well remembered (which you would expect), but that people are also able to remember trivial details of their own lives and their surroundings at the time of the event. Take a look at Figure 6.24 and you may find yourself remembering where you were on that day.

The first study of flashbulb memory was carried out by Brown and Kulik (1977), who decided to test out the widely held belief that all Americans could remember what they were doing when they heard the news of President Kennedy's assassination. Brown and Kulik found that all but one of their 80 subjects were indeed able to report some details of their circumstances and surroundings when they heard the news of Kennedy's death, despite the passage of 14 years since that event. Similar findings have been reported for a range of other major news events, including the explosion of the space shuttle 'Challenger' (Neisser and Harsch, 1992), the death of Princess Diana (Davidson and Glisky, 2002) and the terrorist attack on the World Trade Center (Talarico and Rubin, 2003).

Figure 6.24   The World Trade Center attack. Can you remember what were you doing when you first heard about it?

Source: Shutterstock.

In an effort to explain the occurrence of flashbulb memory, Brown and Kulik (1977) hypothesised that a special memory mechanism was involved, which could create a memory trace that was unusually accurate and immune to the normal processes of forgetting. This special mechanism was assumed to be brought into action only by events which were very emotionally shocking and which held great personal significance for the individual. It was argued that such a memory mechanism might have evolved because it would convey a survival advantage, by enabling an individual to remember vivid details of past catastrophes, which would help them to avoid similar dangers in the future.

However, the notion of flashbulb memory as a special process has been challenged by subsequent studies showing that flashbulb memories are far from infallible, and in fact seem to be no more accurate than any other type of memory. Neisser and Harsch (1992) used a questionnaire to record details of the circumstances in which a group of American subjects first heard news of the 'Challenger' disaster. They tested their subjects on the day after the disaster, and then tested them again three years later. In fact subjects showed a considerable amount of forgetting over the three years, and roughly half of the details recalled after three years disagreed with the information recalled the day after the crash. It was also found that flashbulb memories of the World Trade Center attack showed a decline in their accuracy over the months that followed (Talarico and Rubin, 2003; Wolters and Goudsmit, 2005), and were in fact no more accurate or lasting than the normal everyday memories of their subjects.

Whilst there is no doubt that flashbulb memory is unusually detailed and lasting, it can probably be adequately accounted for by the mechanisms underlying normal memory. For example, the memory for a very significant event would be likely to benefit from frequent recall and retelling of the memory, without requiring a special mechanism to explain it (Neisser, 1982). Davidson and Glisky (2002) also point out that the occurrence of a very dramatic event provides an exceptionally powerful contextual cue for otherwise trivial aspects of our surroundings and activities. Most researchers now agree that flashbulb memories probably do not involve a special mechanism, they are just normal memories for very emotional and shocking experiences (Talarico and Rubin, 2009).

It has been suggested that the powerful intrusive memories which occur in PTSD, and possibly those associated with phobias, depression, and drug-induced flashbacks, may arise from the same processes as those underlying flashbulb memory (Sierra and Berrios, 2000, Budson and Gold, 2009). However, this view remains speculative, so it is not yet clear whether flashbulb memory research can shed any light on the nature of these clinical disorders. There is further discussion of flashbulb memory in Chapter 12.

EYEWITNESS TESTIMONY

A courtroom is one place where memory can be of crucial importance, as the testimony given by an eyewitness frequently provides the decisive evidence which determines whether the defendant is convicted or not. But there is a great deal of evidence to suggest that eyewitness testimony is often unreliable and does not justify the faith placed in it by the courts. Indeed the introduction of DNA testing has revealed that many people have been convicted of crimes which they did not actually commit. Brewer and Wells (2011) reported that no less than 258 Americans convicted of serious crimes were subsequently freed as a result of DNA testing, and several of these individuals were on death row awaiting execution. The authors added that 200 of these individuals had been convicted on the basis of eyewitness testimony, which was

Figure 6.25   An eyewitness identifies the guilty person –
but could he be mistaken?

Source: Shutterstock.

evidently mistaken in all of these cases. It is clear that eyewitness testimony is not always reliable, and inaccurate testimony can have tragic consequences for those who are wrongly convicted.

The pioneering work of Bartlett (1932) demonstrated that recall is extremely inaccurate (see Section 6.3), and that it is particularly prone to distortion by the subject's prior knowledge and expectations. Research on eyewitness testimony has confirmed that eyewitnesses are indeed susceptible to reconstructive errors based on previous knowledge and expectations (Zaragoza and Lane, 1998). However, it has been found that eyewitness testimony is also prone to contamination from information acquired after the event, a phenomenon known as the 'misinformation effect'. This effect was clearly demonstrated by Loftus and Palmer (1974), who showed subjects a film of a car accident. When subjects were later asked to estimate how fast the cars had been travelling, their responses were found to vary significantly according to how the question was worded. Subjects who were asked how fast the cars were travelling when they 'smashed into one another' gave a higher estimate of speed on average than did subjects who were asked how fast the cars were travelling when they 'hit one another', and they were also more likely to report having seen broken glass, although in fact none was shown in the video. Merely changing a single word in the question was sufficient to influence subjects, essentially by making an implicit suggestion to them about what they must have seen.

Post-event contamination is now known to be an important influence on eyewitness testimony. Following the Oklahoma City bombing of 1995, in which 168 people were killed and over 600 injured by a massive car bomb, witnesses were found to have made errors in their description of events due to contamination from subsequent events. Timothy McVeigh, who was subsequently convicted of the bombing and executed in 2001, was described by three witnesses as having an accomplice when the hired the vehicle used for the bombing on the previous day. However, it was subsequently established that McVeigh had been alone. One of the witnesses had confused the memory of McVeigh's visit to the car-hire shop with that of two other men who came in to hire a vehicle later the same day, and that witness had later persuaded the other two that they had also seen two men rather than one. This case appears to demonstrate the occurrence of both post-event contamination and cross-witness contamination (Memon and Wright, 1999). Cross-witness contamination has since been demonstrated in a laboratory experiment designed to simulate aspects of the McVeigh case (Wright *et al.*, 2000), and it was found that witnesses were particularly likely to change their description of a crime after discussing it with another witness who expressed great confidence in what they had seen.

Like other forms of memory, eyewitness testimony becomes weaker and more fragmented with the passage of time, and consequently it becomes less reliable and more vulnerable to contamination from other sources. Flin *et al.* (1992) found that eyewitness reports became less accurate after a five-month delay, and although this applied to all age groups tested, small children were found to be particularly susceptible. In fact research has shown that child witnesses are generally more prone to suggestion and memory distortion (Davis and Loftus, 2005). It has also been found that elderly people tend to be fairly unreliable witnesses, despite showing more confidence than younger witnesses in the accuracy of their memories (Dodson and Krueger, 2006). Even among the younger adult population, individuals with lower intelligence and low working memory capacity are more vulnerable to misinformation and false memories (Zhu *et al.*, 2010).

A number of studies have shown that the retrieval of a particular piece of information can be inhibited by omitting it from a subsequent presentation (Wright *et al.*, 2001), or simply by failing to ask about it during a post-event interview (Williams *et al.*, 2002). Again, children seem to be particularly susceptible to this effect. It is even possible to create entirely false memories in the mind of a witness by the use of suggestion effects and 'memory implantation'. Loftus and Pickrell (1995) asked people to read and think about several descriptions of events which had happened to them in childhood, but they also included a description of one event which was actually fictitious (e.g. getting lost in a shopping mall). About a third of the participants subsequently described the fictitious event as having really happened to them, as though it had somehow been incorporated into their memory system. Many similar examples of false memories have been reported for real-life events, which can be elicited simply by questions that contain misleading information. For example, when asked whether they had seen TV footage of a bus exploding in the 2005 London terrorist attack, around 40 per cent of a UK sample reported that they had, despite the fact that no such footage existed (Ost *et al.*, 2008).

These false memory studies have important implications for the credibility of eyewitness accounts in real life, and they have played a particularly important part in resolving the 'recovered memory' debate. This debate concerns people who claim to have recovered previously repressed memories during psychotherapy, in some cases involving traumatic events such the experience of physical or sexual abuse during childhood (Andrews *et al.*, 1999; Lindsay and Read, 2001). Recovered memories of this kind obviously have important consequences, which might include accusations of abuse and even imprisonment of the alleged perpetrator, who may or may not actually be guilty. False memory studies offer a possible explanation of the way that recovered memories, or at least some of them, could have been created by misinformation and possibly even by the therapeutic process itself (Loftus and Davis, 2006; Geraerts *et al.*, 2007). Recovered memories are discussed in more detail in Chapter 12.

McLeod and Saunders (2005) suggest that the mechanism underlying the misinformation could involve retrieval-induced forgetting (see section 6.7). They showed that the misinformation effect was stronger for items which had been subjected to RIF inhibition. Indeed RIF could also be responsible for the tendency for witnesses to forget scenes which are omitted from a subsequent re-showing of the incident, as the strengthening of rival memory traces for items included in the re-showing would be likely to inhibit the memory traces of the omitted items.

From a consideration of these findings it is easy to see how easily a witness in a court case might be influenced by police questioning, or by information from other sources such as newspapers, lawyers, or other witnesses. There are obviously important lessons to be learned from these studies. In the first place, judges and juries should realise that witnesses cannot be expected to have infallible memories, and they should not place too much reliance on the evidence of eyewitness testimony alone. Statements should be taken from witnesses as soon as possible after the incident in question, and witnesses should be allowed to use notes when giving their evidence in court at a later date. Finally, police interviewers should be particularly careful about their methods of questioning, and should avoid the use of leading questions or suggestions which could implant misleading information in the witness's head. However, it cannot be assumed that such advice is currently being heeded. Research shows that most judges have little knowledge of research findings about eyewitness memory, and jurors know even less (Benton *et al.*, 2006).

THE COGNITIVE INTERVIEW

The interviewing of eyewitnesses has made extensive use of the findings of cognitive research. In particular, the principle of context-dependent memory has been found to be of value to police interviewers, who make use of context cues to jog the memories of witnesses. One way of achieving this is by creating a crime reconstruction, in which the original events and context of the crime are replicated as closely as possible. Actors play out the roles of the people involved in the crime, usually in the setting where the actual crime took place. Such reconstructions are often shown on television in the hope that witnesses may be reminded of some relevant piece of information by the use of contextual cues.

Similar principles are used in a technique known as the cognitive interview (CI), introduced by Geiselman *et al.* (1985). Unlike the traditional police interview, in which the witness is simply questioned about the actual crime, the witness undergoing a cognitive interview is encouraged to recall all aspects of the crime, including contextual details. The witness may be reminded of various aspects of the crime setting, such as what clothes they were wearing, what the weather was like, and even the newspaper headlines on that day. They may be shown photographs of the crime scene, or they may actually be taken back to it. There may also be an attempt to reinstate their mental state during the event, by asking them to try to remember how they felt at the time. An additional advantage of the CI is that it not only increases the amount of context reinstatement but also the variety of different retrieval cues, which may help to activate alternative retrieval routes. Geiselman *et al.* (1985) showed that the CI does in fact succeed in coaxing more information from the witness than does the traditional police interview (see Figure 6.26).

In addition to the basic principle of context reinstatement (CR), an additional technique used in the CI is to instruct the witness to report everything (RE), regardless of how trivial or irrelevant it might seem. Studies have confirmed that both the CR and the RE techniques add to the effectiveness of the interview and have been found to be useful in police work (Milne and Bull, 2002; Brown *et al.*, 2008).

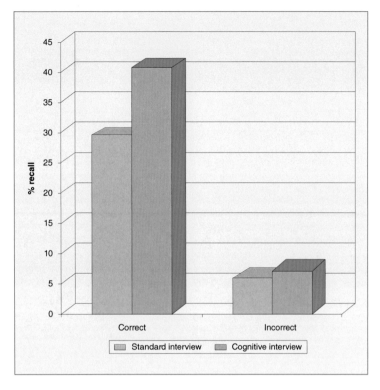

Figure 6.26   Recall performance with cognitive interview and standard interview procedures.

Source: Geiselman *et al.* (1985).

Fisher *et al.* (1990) demonstrated that the CI procedure was valuable in real-life police work, and that police detectives interviewing real crime witnesses found that the CI produced a significant increase in the amount of information recalled. Many subsequent studies have confirmed the effectiveness of the CI in both laboratory and real-life settings. In a review of 42 CI studies, Koehnken *et al.* (1999) concluded that the CI consistently elicited more correct pieces of information than a standard interview, for both adult and child witnesses. There is also evidence that the CI procedure can reduce the witness's susceptibility to misinformation effects and post-event contamination (Memon *et al.*, 2009).

One slight drawback of using the CI is that, whilst it does elicit more correct information from witnesses, it also elicits more incorrect information (Koehnken *et al.*, 1999), and this must be borne in mind by police officers making use of the CI procedure. Another limitation of the CI is that it does not seem to be very suitable for use on very small children, who often have difficulty understanding the instructions (Geiselman, 1999). However, the CI has been found to be reasonably effective for children aged eight years and above (Milne and Bull, 2003). One further problem with the CI procedure is that it becomes

Figure 6.27 'So what was the weather like when you saw this man robbing the bank?'

Source: Shutterstock.

less effective when very long retention intervals are involved (Geiselman and Fisher, 1997). However, in practice police officers do not always have the time to carry out a full CI procedure on all available witnesses directly after a crime, and for this reason a shortened form of the CI has been developed (Dando *et al.*, 2009). There is also a self-administered version of the CI in booklet form, which can be used to elicit responses from witnesses where interviewers are not immediately available (Gabbert *et al.*, 2009).

Although the limitations of the CI must be borne in mind when it is used in police work, research has shown that it can be an extremely valuable procedure. The CI is not yet in widespread use throughout the world, but it is now widely used by police forces in the UK, and most British police officers have now received formal CI training (Brown *et al.*, 2008; Fisher *et al.*, 2011). The CI is a shining example of how cognitive research is being applied in real-life settings.

SUMMARY

- Processing an input to a deep level, by making use of past experience to analyse its meaningful content, will increase the likelihood of retrieving that input in the future.
- Retrieval cues have a major effect on the success of retrieval, and are especially effective if there is extensive feature overlap between retrieval cues and stored information.
- The reinstatement of the context in which a memory trace was acquired can be of great assistance in retrieving the trace.
- Memory involves both automatic processes (such as implicit memory and familiarity judgements) and controlled processes (such as explicit memory and context recollection).
- The act of retrieving a memory makes it more retrievable in the future. This finding is known as the testing effect.
- Retrieval of a memory trace causes the inhibition of rival memory traces, a phenomenon known as retrieval-induced forgetting (RIF).
- The retrieval of a stored memory makes it vulnerable to change, and may result in a stronger or weaker trace. This phenomenon is known as reconsolidation.
- Studies of memory phenomena in real-life settings, such as eyewitness testimony and the cognitive interview, provide an important complementary approach to laboratory studies because of their greater ecological validity.

FURTHER READING

- Baddeley, A. D., Eysenck, M. W. and Anderson, M. C. (2009). *Memory*. Hove: Psychology Press. A very thorough account of memory research, written by three leading memory researchers.
- Esgate, A., Groome, D. H. *et al*. (2005). *An Introduction to Applied Cognitive Psychology*. Hove: Psychology Press. This book contains detailed chapters on most of the main areas of memory covered in the present chapter, but considered in the context of real-life applications.

Answer to Figure 6.15

The familiar faces were:

(a) Don Cheadle
(b) Angela Merkel
(c) Bradley Wiggins
(d) Freida Pinto

Contents

chapter 7

Disorders of memory

David Groome

7

7.1 AMNESIA AND ITS CAUSES

THE EFFECTS OF AMNESIA

Amnesia is the name given to disorders of memory. Amnesia normally involves severe forgetfulness which goes beyond the everyday forgetting observed in normal people, to the extent that it may interfere with the activities of normal life. We are all prone to moments of forgetfulness, but most people with intact cognitive functioning can remember quite a lot about the events in their lives, especially their most recent experiences and events which are important to them. However, a person suffering from amnesia may be quite unable to remember any recent events. You can probably recall quite easily where you were five minutes ago, or the person you just chatted with, or even what you did yesterday evening. Many amnesics would be unable to remember such things, and may have no idea of what they have done with their day so far. In severe cases they may be quite unable to commit any new experiences to memory, and this can be very disruptive to their lives. Without an intact memory it can become impossible to keep a job, to keep up relationships with family and friends, or even to look after oneself and maintain an independent existence. In fact it is clear from the study of severely amnesic patients that memory is quite crucial to our ability to function properly as human beings. Amnesia is a very disruptive and disabling condition. However, it is also a disorder from which a great deal can be learned about the nature of memory function.

CAUSES OF AMNESIA

Amnesia may arise from a number of different causes (also known as 'aetiologies'), which can be divided into two main groups, the organic amnesias and the psychogenic amnesias. Organic amnesias are caused by some form of physical damage (known as a lesion) inflicted on the brain. This may arise from a variety of different causes, including brain infections, strokes, head injuries, and degenerative disorders such as Alzheimer's disease (see below for a more detailed list). Organic amnesias tend to be severe and disabling, and they are

Key Term

Organic amnesia
An impairment of memory function caused by physical damage to the brain.

Psychogenic amnesia
A memory impairment of psychological origin.

Alzheimer's disease (AD)
A degenerative brain disorder usually (but not always) afflicting the elderly, which first appears as an impairment of memory but later develops into a more general dementia.

Korsakoff syndrome
A brain disease which usually results from chronic alcoholism, and which is mainly characterised by a memory impairment.

Herpes simplex encephalitis (HSE)
A virus infection of the brain, which in some cases leaves the patient severely amnesic.

also irreversible in the majority of cases because the brain lesion does not heal. Psychogenic amnesias are caused by psychological factors and usually involve the temporary suppression of disturbing memories which are unacceptable to the patient at some subconscious level. Psychogenic amnesias can be disorientating and disruptive to the patient, but they are rarely completely disabling, and as there is no actual brain damage they are reversible and in most cases will eventually disappear.

The organic amnesias are far more serious, and since they are also particularly instructive in helping us to understand the nature of memory function they will provide the main substance of this chapter. There are many different ways in which the brain can be damaged, and any of these may cause amnesia if the relevant brain regions are involved, most notably the temporal lobes. The main causes and origins (or 'aetiologies') of organic amnesia are listed below:

- Alzheimer's disease (AD) (Figure 7.1) is the most common cause of amnesia. It is a degenerative brain disorder which first appears as an impairment of memory, but later develops into a more general dementia, affecting all aspects of cognition. AD occurs mostly in the elderly, and in fact it is the main cause of senile dementia, eventually affecting as many as 20 per cent of elderly people. Although seen mainly in people who are at least 60 or 70 years old, in rare cases AD may affect younger people, when it is referred to as pre-senile dementia. AD was first identified by Alois Alzheimer (1907), though the cases he described in fact concerned the pre-senile form. It was only later realised that the same basic degenerative disorder, with its characteristic pattern of tangled neural fibres, was also responsible for most senile dementias too. Since the amnesic symptoms of AD patients are usually complicated by additional symptoms of general dementia (Storandt, 2008), they do not present a particularly pure form of amnesia and it is therefore quite difficult to investigate the nature of memory disorder in AD cases. For this reason they are not the most widely researched amnesic group. See Box 7.1 for a case study of Alzheimer's disease (Ronald Reagan).
- Korsakoff syndrome is a brain disease which usually results from chronic alcoholism, and it is mainly characterised by a memory impairment, which affects both recent memories and memories from the distant past. It was first described by Korsakoff (1887), and it has become one of the most frequently studied amnesic conditions, mainly because it usually presents as a relatively pure form of amnesia without the complication of extensive dementia or reduced intelligence. See Box 7.2 for a case study of Korsakoff syndrome.
- Herpes simplex encephalitis (HSE) is a virus infection of the brain, which can leave the patient severely amnesic. Fortunately cases of HSE are very rare. One important characteristic of HSE amnesia is its relatively sudden onset, which means that in many cases the date of onset of amnesic symptoms is known fairly precisely, in contrast

Box 7.1   Case study: Alzheimer's disease (Ronald Reagan)

Ronald Reagan was probably one of the most successful and famous people of all time. He first became famous as a film actor, appearing in many popular films. After retiring from the acting profession, Reagan began a new career in politics, and he was elected President of the United States in 1980. He remained in office until 1988, and during this eight-year period he was arguably the most powerful man in the world.

Source: Jacques M. Chenet/CORBIS.

As president of the United States Ronald Reagan came to be regarded as an outstanding communicator, the skills from his acting days clearly standing him in good stead in his new career as a politician. But in 1994, a few years after he had left office, he was told that he had the early signs of Alzheimer's disease, a progressive dementia which first destroys the memory and then all other cognitive abilities. Ronald Reagan announced the news in a brief handwritten letter to the American public. He wrote: 'I have recently been told that I am one of millions of Americans who will be afflicted with Alzheimer's disease. I now begin the journey that will lead me into the sunset of my life.' Within three years Ronald Reagan's memory had deteriorated so badly that he no longer remembered that he had once been the President of the United States. He was unable to understand why people waved at him in the street, and why strangers seemed to know him and wished to shake his hand. He was no longer able to recognise friends or former aides. In 1997 he received a visit from George Schultz, his former Secretary of State, but Mr Reagan did not seem to recognise his visitor despite their many years of working closely together. However, it is possible that some glimmer of recognition remained, perhaps a slight feeling of familiarity somewhere below the level of conscious recollection. At one point during the visit the former president had returned to the room where his wife Nancy was chatting with Mr Schultz. Mr Reagan turned to his nurse and asked: 'Who is that man sitting with Nancy on the couch? I know him. He is a very famous man.'

Ronald Reagan's dementia became increasingly severe over the next ten years, finally reaching a point where he no longer responded to any form of communication. In the spring of 2004 Nancy Reagan confirmed this, with the simple statement: 'Ronnie's long journey has taken him to a distant place where I can no longer reach him.' He died a few weeks later, on 5 June 2004.

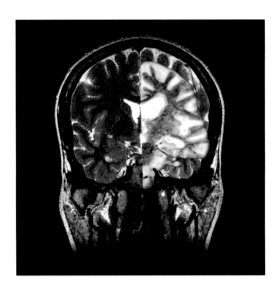

Figure 7.1 MRI scan of a normal brain (left) compared with the brain of an Alzheimer patient (right). The diseased brain is shown superimposed on a normal brain image, and it shows pronounced atrophy (shrinkage) especially affecting the temporal lobe.

Source: Science Photo Library.

Key Term

Electroconvulsive therapy (ECT)
A treatment used to alleviate depression which involves passing an electric current through the front of the patient's head.

---

to the very gradual onset of degenerative disorders such as Korsakoff and Alzheimer cases. See Box 7.4 for a case study of HSE amnesia, the patient CW (Wilson and Wearing, 1995).

- *Temporal lobe surgery.* A very small number of patients have become amnesic as a result of brain lesions caused by deliberate surgical procedures, usually involving the temporal lobes. Such cases are fortunately very rare, but they have been extensively studied because they provide a particularly valuable source of knowledge about memory. This is because the precise moment of onset of their amnesia is known, and furthermore the location and extent of their lesions is also known fairly accurately. See Box 7.3 for a case study of temporal lobe amnesia, the patient HM (Scoville and Milner, 1957).

- *Post-ECT amnesia.* Electroconvulsive therapy (ECT) is a treatment used to alleviate depression, usually in patients who have failed to respond to any alternative form of therapy. ECT involves the administering of an electric shock across the front of the patient's head. It has been found that a period of amnesia may follow the administering of the shock, and in some cases this amnesia may persist over longer periods. ECT-induced amnesia has been extensively studied because it represents a serious side-effect of a deliberately administered treatment. It is therefore important to establish the severity and duration of post-ECT amnesia in order to evaluate the usefulness of the treatment.

- *Other causes of organic amnesia.* Since any condition which damages the appropriate areas of the brain can cause amnesia, there are many other possible causes, though none of them has been as widely studied as those listed above. For example, strokes and tumours can sometimes lead to amnesia, as can head injuries, brain damage caused by cardiac arrest, HIV infection and degenerative conditions such as Huntington's chorea and Parkinson's disease.

AMNESIA AS AN IMPAIRMENT OF LONG-TERM MEMORY

The distinction between short-term memory (STM) and long-term memory (LTM) was explained in Chapter 5. The main symptom of the organic amnesic syndrome is an impairment of long-term memory, so that organic amnesics have difficulty in consolidating new information into their long-term memory store, and they often also have problems retrieving old memories from storage. However, despite this LTM impairment, organic amnesics usually have an intact short-term working memory. One clear indication of their intact STM is the fact that most organic amnesics are able to carry on a fairly normal conversation. Their conversation will of course be somewhat limited by

Box 7.2   Case study: Korsakoff syndrome

Whitty and Zangwill (1976) describe the case of a pub manager who developed amnesic symptoms following many years of excessive alcohol consumption. He was brought into hospital at the age of 60, as his wife had noticed a severe deterioration in his memory and a number of other signs of neurological disorder. These included slurring of speech, unsteadiness when walking, and occasional fits.

Memory tests revealed that he was unable to learn any new material presented to him. For example, when a short story was read to him he was unable to recall any of it five minutes later, and when the story was read to him a second time he denied ever having heard it before. He also performed very poorly on several other memory tests, including tests of sentence recall and picture recognition. He was unable to recollect any events or experiences from the previous seven or eight years. For example, he had no recollection at all of his recent work as a publican, which he had done for the previous five years. Instead he described himself as a

newsagent, which he had in fact been several years earlier. He also gave his address as one from which he had moved many years before. He gave his age as 52 (in fact he was 60), and he gave the year as 1956 (in fact it was 1963). It was as though seven years of his life had completely disappeared.

The patient also had no recollection of his second marriage, which had taken place two years earlier. However, when visited in hospital by his present wife he seemed to recognise her and he treated her as though she was familiar to him. In a similar way, he began to show a sense of familiarity with the nurses and clinicians in the hospital, although he claimed not to recognise them. Two further observations were made about this patient, both of which are characteristic of Korsakoff syndrome. First, he had a strong tendency to confabulation, claiming to recall events which had apparently not really taken place. Second, he showed no awareness or understanding of his condition, and in fact denied that he had any problems with his memory.

their inability to recall earlier events, but they are able to reply to questions, and they can complete sentences in a coherent fashion. This demonstrates that they are able to remember what has been said in the last few seconds, which is consistent with a normal short-term memory. Their problem seems to lie primarily in consolidating their memories into a permanent form for long-term storage.

Such observations have been confirmed by more objective measurements of STM function, such as digit span. Talland (1965) carried out a study involving no fewer than 29 Korsakoff patients, all of whom proved to be significantly impaired on a whole battery of long-term memory tests such as story recall, wordlist recall and picture recognition. However, their digit span scores were similar to those of normal individuals, averaging about seven items. Baddeley and Warrington (1970) again reported apparently normal STM span in Korsakoff patients, and in addition they found a normal recency effect in a test of free recall. As explained in Chapter 5, the recency effect is thought to reflect the STM component of free recall, so this finding provided further confirmation of the apparent preservation of STM. Reviewing such studies, Pujol and Kopelman (2003) conclude that Korsakoffs show normal performance on tests of both verbal and non-verbal STM.

A patient known as HM (see Box 7.3), whose amnesia was brought about by temporal lobe surgery, was found to retain a normal digit span despite his extremely dense amnesia (Wickelgren, 1968). Patients suffering from HSE amnesia again tend to have normal STM function (including normal functioning of the WM loops and the central executive), in contrast to their severe LTM impairment (Starr and Phillips, 1970; Wilson and Wearing, 1995). Similar findings of preserved STM span have been obtained with patients in the early stages of Alzheimer's disease (Miller, 1977), though in the later stages Alzheimer patients do show a deterioration of STM performance reflecting the general dementia which eventually pervades all aspects of their cognitive functioning. Morris and Baddeley (1988) reported that Alzheimer patients usually have no impairment of the phonological and articulatory loops, but they show increasing impairment of central executive function (Becker and Overman, 2004; Storandt, 2008).

From a consideration of the studies reviewed in the present section, it would appear that in virtually every type of organic amnesia there is severe LTM impairment, but a relatively unimpaired STM. This finding helps to explain the nature of organic amnesia, but it also tells us something about the structure of memory in normal individuals. It suggests that LTM and STM are essentially separate memory systems, since one can be impaired while the other is unaffected. Amnesic patients also provide us with an indication of the duration of STM storage, which has been estimated at approximately seven seconds, the length of time for which information can be retained by most severely amnesic patients. In fact Clive W, who is one of the most severely amnesic patients ever studied, was described in a recent TV documentary as 'the man with the seven-second memory' (see Box 7.4).

7.2 ANTEROGRADE AND RETROGRADE AMNESIA

DISTINGUISHING ANTEROGRADE FROM RETROGRADE AMNESIA

Korsakoff (1887) provided one of the first descriptions of organic amnesia. Having studied about 30 cases of severe amnesia associated with alcoholic abuse, Korsakoff concluded that the main impairment was an impairment of 'the memory of recent events'. However, he added that in many cases there was also an impairment of memory 'for the long past', which could extend back as far as 30 years. These two types of amnesia roughly correspond to the definitions of 'anterograde' and 'retrograde' amnesia, which are the two main types of memory loss. They are defined as follows:

- Anterograde amnesia (AA): impairment of memory for events occurring *since* the onset of amnesia.
- Retrograde amnesia (RA): impairment of memory for events occurring *before* the onset of amnesia.

Key Term

Anterograde amnesia (AA)
Impaired memory for events which have occurred since the onset of the disorder (contrasts with retrograde amnesia).

Retrograde amnesia (RA)
Impaired memory for events which occurred prior to the onset of amnesia (contrasts with anterograde amnesia).

The relationship between anterograde and retrograde amnesia is illustrated in Figure 7.2.

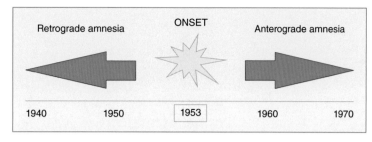

The distinction between AA and RA is most important, because it offers a possible means of distinguishing between learning disorders and retrieval disorders. A patient suffering from a disorder of learning would be expected to have AA but not RA, since they should have no difficulty in retrieving memories from the period before onset when their learning ability was unimpaired. On the other hand, a patient suffering from a disorder of retrieval would have difficulty in retrieving memories from any period in the past, and would thus be expected to have both AA and RA. It is possible that learning and retrieval disorders could occur together in the same patient, in which case both AA and RA would be expected but with the AA component probably being more severe.

Figure 7.2   Anterograde and retrograde amnesia shown in relation to the moment of onset (in this case for patient HM).

A common observation, first noted by Ribot (1882), is that amnesic patients often have clear memories of childhood and early adulthood, despite being unable to remember more recent periods in their lives. Ribot concluded that their RA showed a 'temporal gradient', since the degree of impairment increased with the recency of the event. This observation has become known as 'Ribot's law', though more recent studies have shown that it does not apply universally since some amnesic patients have a uniformly dense RA without any obvious temporal gradient.

TESTING ANTEROGRADE AND RETROGRADE AMNESIA

AA is essentially an impairment of new learning, so testing for AA is fairly easy and straightforward. The patient can simply be asked to learn some form of test material (words, stories, pictures, etc.) and they are then tested for the retrieval of these items at some later time. However, tests of RA are more problematic, since they involve testing items learned prior to the onset of amnesia. The presentation of the test material is therefore beyond the control of the tester, who must instead try to think of test items that the patient is likely to have encountered earlier in their life. This normally involves testing the patient's memory for events which happened many years before the test session, often referred to as 'remote memory', as opposed to the testing of 'recent memory' in more typical AA test procedures.

Remote memory tests can either involve the testing of past *public* events, which are likely to have been familiar to most people, or past *personal* events, which tend to be unique to each individual. Tests of past public events, such as major news events from the past, allow the same test items to be given to many different people. This makes it possible to devise a standardised test with known performance norms, so that amnesic and control subjects can be compared on exactly the same test. Various different test materials have been used for this purpose, which usually attempt to sample different time periods by selecting items that were widely publicised at a particular period, but which have received no subsequent publicity. One widely used battery of tests for past public events is the Boston Remote Memory Test (Albert *et al.*, 1979), which includes tests of famous faces and news events from the past. More recently, Steinvorth *et al.* (2005) have devised tests and interview procedures for the assessment of memory for public events and famous people.

Tests of past personal events tend to focus on autobiographical memory, for example asking the subject about events from their school days. Because of the unique and personal nature of these items, the scores of different individuals are not directly comparable, since they will be recalling different events. Another problem is that it is often difficult to check the accuracy of the responses given. Some refinement of this approach has been achieved by using a standard questionnaire to sample specific events in a typical person's life (Kopelman *et al.*, 1990), which are confirmed where possible by interviewing relatives. An autobiographical interview procedure has also been devised by Levine *et al.* (2002).

It is important to bear in mind that tests of past personal memory tend to involve specific events from an individual's autobiographical memory, which consist mainly of episodic memories. Past public memories, on the other hand, may sometimes involve semantic memory, in which items of general knowledge are retrieved without any specific episodic context (see Chapter 6 for the distinction between episodic and semantic memory). This distinction has not always been recognised in the past, and some earlier investigators made the mistake of comparing episodic measures of anterograde amnesia (e.g. 'Where did you go yesterday morning?') with semantic measures of retrograde amnesia (e.g. 'What was the name of your primary school?') without realising that they were not comparing like with like. In order to avoid such pitfalls, most recent studies have used the same test procedure (e.g. news events) to sample both anterograde and retrograde impairments. A further point which has confused researchers in the past is that tests of autobiographical memory are not necessarily restricted to episodic memory. Autobiographical memory includes both episodic memories (e.g. 'What did you do on your 21st birthday?') and semantic memories (e.g. 'What was the name of your primary school?') and it is important to distinguish between these two components (Rosenbaum *et al.*, 2005).

ANTEROGRADE AND RETROGRADE IMPAIRMENT IN ORGANIC AMNESIA

Early studies such as those of Ribot (1882) and Korsakoff (1887) suggested that most amnesic patients suffer from both AA and RA, and more recent studies have generally confirmed this finding. A pattern of AA together with

RA has been observed in dementing Alzheimer patients (Wilson *et al.*, 1981), and in Korsakoff patients (Albert *et al.*, 1979), and HSE patients usually show a similar pattern (Wilson and Wearing, 1995). In many cases RA extends back over a very long time period. For example, in Korsakoff patients RA typically extends back over a period of 30 years or more before onset (Pujol and Kopelman, 2003), and usually shows a marked temporal gradient in accordance with Ribot's law. Some typical results are presented in Figure 7.3.

However, this general pattern of severe anterograde and retrograde amnesia is not found universally. Some patients show severe AA but their RA is limited to a very short time period. For example, the temporal lobe surgery patient HM (see Box 7.3) had very severe AA, but his RA was mostly limited to the three years or so before onset (Ogden and Corkin, 1991). However, his amnesia for specific autobiographical memories extended back over a far longer period (Steinvorth *et al.*, 2005).

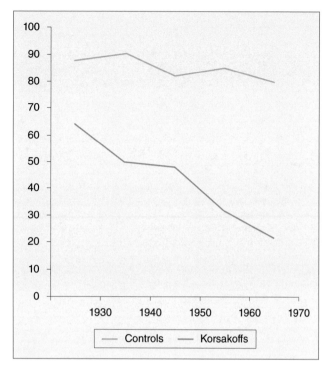

Figure 7.3 Memory performance for different periods from the past.

Source: Albert *et al.* (1979).

A few rather untypical Korsakoff patients have also been studied whose RA was limited to the few years before onset, and these patients have usually been found to lack the frontal lesions which are otherwise typical of Korsakoff patients (Mair *et al.*, 1979).

FOCAL RETROGRADE AND FOCAL ANTEROGRADE AMNESIA

Although most amnesics exhibit both AA and RA, a few cases have been studied who show either AA or RA in isolation. A number of studies have reported cases of 'focal AA' (AA without RA). Mair *et al.* (1979) studied two rather unusual Korsakoff patients with focal AA, and Cohen and Squire (1981) also reported focal AA in their patient NA, who was injured in a freak accident. Whilst sitting at his desk, NA was accidentally stabbed with a fencing foil. A friend thrust the foil at NA as a joke, intending to stop short. Unfortunately the foil entered NA's nostril and penetrated his brain, with devastating effects. The area chiefly damaged was NA's thalamus, and it left him with severe AA but without any significant amount of RA. Other studies of focal AA have confirmed that damage is mostly restricted to the anterior thalamus (Kapur *et al.*, 1996).

Examples of 'focal RA' (RA without AA) are extremely rare, but a few such cases have been reported in patients who have suffered head

Box 7.3   Case study: Temporal lobe surgery (HM)

On 23 August 1953, a 27-year-old man, referred to in the literature by his initials 'HM', underwent a surgical operation to remove both of the medial temporal lobes of his brain in an effort to alleviate his severe epilepsy. Although the surgeon did not realise it at the time, this operation was to have a devastating effect on HM's memory. Since that fateful day he was unable to learn anything new, and consequently held no intact memories for any of the events of his life since 1953.

Despite his inability to register any new experiences in his long-term memory, HM had an intact short-term memory and his STM span was completely normal (Wickelgren, 1968). However, this only allowed him to hold on to his experiences for a few seconds. HM could carry on a fairly normal conversation, but he could only remember the last sentence or so, which obviously restricted his conversational range. He also had a tendency to repeat something he had just said a few moments earlier.

HM proved to be virtually untestable on most measures of LTM, and it was reported that he 'forgets the events of his daily life as fast as they occur' (Scoville and Milner, 1957). Because of this HM would watch the same TV program several times without recognising it, and he did the same crossword puzzle many times without realising he had done it before. Even after several years of regular visits from clinicians such as Brenda Milner, he was still unable to identify them. HM's inability to create new memories is known as anterograde amnesia.

Although HM remembered nothing that had happened to him since 1953, his memory was reasonably good for events preceding that date. This means that HM had severe anterograde amnesia, but had relatively little retrograde amnesia. Ogden and Corkin (1991) reported that HM actually had a fairly severe retrograde impairment for a period extending about three years before the date of his surgery, but had fairly good retrieval of events from earlier years.

However, a more recent study of HM showed that his RA was actually far more extensive for autobiographical events (Steinvorth *et al.*, 2005). HM was a particularly interesting case for the comparison of anterograde and retrograde amnesia, since the date of onset of his amnesia is known precisely. We can therefore be confident about estimating of the extent of his anterograde and retrograde impairments.

Because of his severe amnesia, HM was unable to live a normal life, and he required continual care. However, he did retain some memory capabilities. Apart from his intact STM and childhood memories mentioned above, he also retained the ability to learn new motor skills such as mirror drawing, though he had no recollection of actually learning them. He also showed some learning on tests of implicit memory, such as completing the stems of previously primed words. In addition, he showed a vague familiarity with a few major news events from the period since 1953, such as the assassination of President Kennedy (Ogden and Corkin, 1991). These findings suggest that HM's amnesia was actually quite selective, an observation which has important implications for our understanding of the modular nature of memory processes.

HM (whose real name has now been revealed to be Henry Molaison) died in 2008 at the age of 82. He had spent most of his life trapped in the brief moment of time that is amnesia.

injuries (Kapur *et al.*, 1992; Sellal *et al.*, 2002), following HSE infection (O'Connor *et al.*, 1992), and following an epileptic seizure (Sehm *et al.*, 2011). Mayes (2002) suggests that in some cases focal RA may be of psychogenic origin, but the existence of focal RA of organic origin also seems to be clearly established. Focal RA has been associated with lesions to various different brain areas, but most commonly it tends to involve lesions in the temporal cortex (Sehm *et al.*, 2011). From these admittedly rather rare and unusual cases it would appear that deficits of learning and retrieval can occur separately, and thus they appear to be largely independent disorders.

EXPLAINING THE TEMPORAL GRADIENT IN RETROGRADE AMNESIA

Ribot (1882) noted that amnesics tend to retrieve older memories better than they can retrieve recent memories, and more recent studies have confirmed this temporal gradient in most types of organic amnesia. More recently Brown (2002) reviewed 61 separate studies of RA covering a wide range of aetiologies, and found that nearly all of them had reported a temporal gradient.

A number of possible explanations have been put forward for the occurrence of a temporal gradient in RA, some of which have already been mentioned above. One theory (Squire, 1982) is that older memories may be more durable than recent memories, possibly because they have developed more retrieval routes as a result of frequent retrieval over the years.

As explained earlier, some amnesics have RA which is limited to the three or four years preceding onset. In an effort to explain this finding, Squire (1992) suggests that the consolidation of a new memory may take several years to complete, and that it becomes increasingly resilient during this time. This theory has become known as the standard model of consolidation. The multiple trace theory (Moscovitch *et al.*, 1999) suggests that memories for recent events remain vulnerable because they are still held as individual episodic memories. As time passes these episodic memories combine with others to produce a semantic memory, which is more lasting and does not depend on hippocampal activity. Older semantic memories will thus tend to be more robust than recent ones. The standard model of consolidation and the multiple trace theory are discussed further in Section 7.4.

BRAIN LESIONS ASSOCIATED WITH ANTEROGRADE AND RETROGRADE AMNESIA

The brains of amnesic patients have been extensively studied in an effort to identify the main sites where **lesions** (i.e. injuries) have occurred. Traditionally this was done by post mortem examination, but in recent years a variety of brain-imaging techniques have been developed which make it possible to examine the brains of living patients. Brain scans of this kind have been able to detect a number of lesion sites which had not previously been identified by post mortem studies. Several areas of the brain have been identified where lesions tend to be found in cases of organic amnesia. These include the *temporal lobes*, the hippocampus

> **Key Term**
>
> **Hippocampus**
> A structure lying within the temporal lobes, which is involved in the creation of new memories. Hippocampal lesions usually cause impairment of memory, especially the storage of new memories.

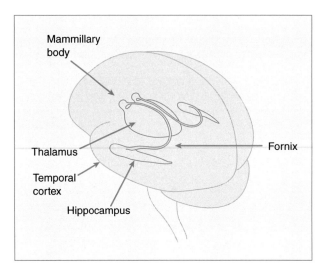

Figure 7.4 Brain structures involved in memory storage and consolidation.

(which lies within the temporal lobes), the *thalamus* and the *prefrontal lobes*. Their location in the brain is illustrated in Figure 7.4).

The temporal lobes contain the hippocampus, and this structure is of particular importance to the creation of new memories. Surgical removal of the hippocampus and parts of the medial temporal lobes of the patient HM was found to have a devastating effect on his memory, especially his ability to acquire and consolidate new memories (Scoville and Milner, 1957). Subsequent scanning techniques confirmed HM's hippocampal lesions, but showed that his lesions also extend into the temporal cortex (Corkin *et al.*, 1997).

The temporal lobes and hippocampus are also damaged in most cases of HSE (Colchester *et al.*, 2001), though their lesions are usually more extensive and may involve most of the temporal cortex (Figure 7.5). Similar temporal lobe lesions are found in the early stages of Alzheimer's disease (West *et al.*, 1994), though in the later stages of this progressive condition there are more extensive lesions, extending into the forebrain at first and later affecting most areas of the brain.

The other main area of the brain where lesions tend to produce AA is the diencephalon, a region which includes the thalamus and the *mammillary bodies*. These are the areas which are usually damaged in Korsakoff patients (Victor *et al.*, 1989), a finding confirmed by more recent PET scan studies (Reed *et al.*, 2003). Although Korsakoff patients tend to suffer damage to much of the diencephalon, their amnesic symptoms are mainly associated with lesions in the *anterior thalamic nuclei* (Harding *et al.*, 2000). Research on animal brains has shown that the hippocampus, anterior thalamus, and mammillary bodies are interconnected, and appear to work as a single system (Aggleton and Saunders, 1997). This system is known as the extended hippocampal complex, and it appears to operate as a linked circuit which carries out the encoding and consolidation processes.

The retrieval of old memories seems to involve different regions of the brain, notably the *temporal cortex* and the *prefrontal cortex*. Some Korsakoff patients have prefrontal lesions in addition to their diencephalic lesions, and these patients are more likely to exhibit retrieval problems than those without such lesions (Victor *et al.*, 1989; Reed *et al.*, 2003). In fact Kopelman *et al.* (2001) established that in Korsakoff patients the severity of AA is correlated with the extent of thalamic damage, whereas the severity of RA is correlated with the extent of prefrontal damage.

Box 7.4   Case study: Herpes simplex encephalitis (Clive W)

The case of Clive W is extremely well known, as he has been the subject of two television documentaries. Before his illness, Clive was a professional musician, and his energy and brilliance had made him extremely successful. He was chorus master to the London Sinfonietta, and he worked as a music producer for the BBC. But in March 1985, Clive developed a flu-like illness, complaining of a severe headache and fever. The illness was eventually identified as herpes simplex encephalitis (HSE), a rare viral infection of the brain. Unfortunately by the time a diagnosis had been made, Clive's brain had already sustained terrible damage, and he would never be able to return to his previous life again.

Brain scans have subsequently revealed that Clive's left temporal lobe has been completely destroyed, together with some damage to his right temporal lobe and parts of his frontal lobes. These lesions have robbed Clive of his memory, in fact making him one of the most severely amnesic patients ever studied. Clive suffers both anterograde and retrograde amnesia, and both are very severe. In fact his anterograde impairment is virtually total, so that he is completely unable to acquire any new memories. In the words of his wife, 'Clive's world now consists of just a moment. He sees what is right in front of him, but as soon as that information hits the brain it fades. Nothing registers'. This makes life extremely confusing for Clive. Any conversation he has with another person is immediately forgotten, as though it had never taken place. A visitor who leaves the room for a few minutes will be greeted afresh by Clive on re-entering the room, as if they were a new visitor. If Clive is allowed to go out into the street alone, he rapidly becomes lost. This is a risky situation for him, since he cannot find his

way back and he cannot ask for assistance as he does not remember where he lives.

Unlike some amnesics, Clive also suffers from a very severe retrograde amnesia. He cannot remember any specific episodes from his life prior to the onset of his amnesia, and he no longer recognises most of his former friends. This retrograde impairment even extends to famous public figures. Clive says that he has never heard of John F. Kennedy or John Lennon. He was also unable to recognise a photo of the Queen and Prince Philip, though when pressed he suggested that they might have been singers. However, Clive's retrograde amnesia is not total. He does remember a few facts about his childhood (such as the fact that he grew up in Birmingham), though he cannot remember any specific events from that period. In contrast to these limited recollections, Clive still clearly recognises his wife and he treats her with the same familiarity and affection as in earlier times.

In addition to his episodic memory impairments Clive also shows clear evidence of a semantic memory disorder. He is unable to provide definitions of a number of common words such as 'tree' and 'eyelid'. He also has difficulty in recognising some common objects, for example jam and honey, which he cannot distinguish from one another.

One aspect of Clive's memory which does seem to have remained surprisingly intact is his musical ability. He is still able to play the piano and sight-read music with great skill, despite the fact that he has virtually no memory of his previous career as a musician.

Before he became amnesic, Clive was a person of considerable intelligence, and he remains highly intelligent despite his lost memory. Perhaps this is why he is so acutely aware of the limitations of his present

(Continued)

(Continued)

state. Clive does not know what has caused his problems, because when it is explained to him he immediately forgets. However, he is very well aware that there is something wrong with his ability to remember, and he has tried hard to find explanations for it. One of his conclusions is that he must have been unconscious until the last few seconds. At every moment of his life he feels as though he has just woken up, and his diary contains repeated entries of the same observation: 'I am now fully awake for the first time'.

For most of us it is difficult to imagine what it must be like to experience such a state of mind, trapped in a few seconds of existence.

For a more detailed account of Clive's memory disorder see Wilson and Wearing (1995). Clive's wife Deborah has also recently written a book about their life together (Wearing, 2005), in which she reports that Clive's memory has actually improved slightly in recent years. From a neurological viewpoint this is a remarkable and unexpected turn of events.

Lesions in the temporal cortex (i.e. the cortical area surrounding the hippocampus) are also associated with retrieval problems (Reed and Squire, 1998). HSE patients whose lesions extend beyond the hippocampus to include large areas of the temporal cortex are usually found to exhibit severe RA in addition to their dense AA (Cermak and O'Connor, 1983). Stefanacci *et al.* (2001) reported that in HSE patients AA correlated with the extent of hippocampal lesions whilst RA correlated with the extent of lateral temporal lobe lesions. Focal retrograde amnesia (i.e. severe RA without AA) is also associated with lesions in the temporal cortex but not in the hippocampus (Sehm *et al.*, 2011).

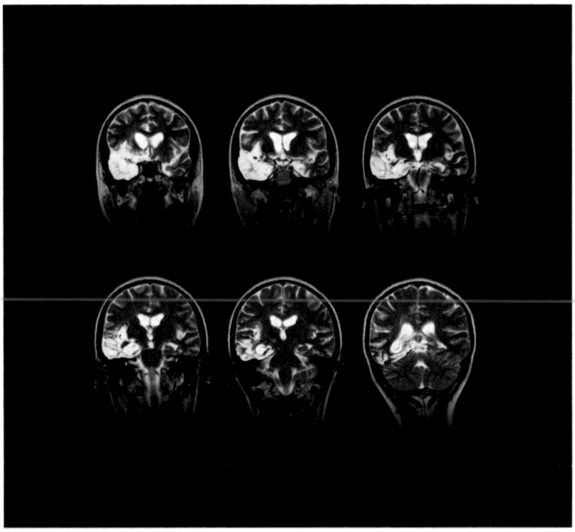

7.3 INTACT AND IMPAIRED MEMORY SYSTEMS

Perhaps the most interesting feature of organic amnesia is that it does not involve a universal impairment of memory function, as there are many aspects of memory which seem to remain largely unimpaired in organic amnesics. These areas of intact memory functioning are of great interest because they not only tell us a great deal about the nature of the underlying memory disorder, but they also shed light on the mechanisms underlying normal memory.

Figure 7.5 MRI brain scans of a patient with lesions in the right temporal lobe caused by HSE. These scans are seen from the front of the brain, and the images run the front (upper left image) to the back of the brain (lower right image).

Source: Science Photo Library.

MOTOR SKILLS

They say you never forget how to ride a bike. Certainly motor skills tend to be very durable in normal people, and there is considerable evidence that motor skills are also preserved in organic amnesics. Not only do amnesics tend to retain their old skills from before onset, they can also learn new skills and procedures, even in patients who find most other forms of learning impossible. This suggests that skill learning is fundamentally different to other forms of learning, perhaps because skills are performed in an automatic way without any need for conscious recollection.

For example, the HSE patient Clive W has retained most of his musical skills, both in conducting and in playing the piano (Wilson and Wearing, 1995), though he is totally unaware that he possesses these skills. Starr and Phillips (1970) also described a patient known as PQ, who had been a concert pianist before becoming amnesic as a result of an HSE infection. PQ not only retained his ability to play the piano, but proved to be quite capable of learning to play new pieces of music, though again he remained quite unaware that he was able to play them.

Corkin (1968) reported that HM was able to learn a number of new motor skills such as mirror drawing. Mirror drawing involves drawing a shape on a piece of paper viewed through a mirror, which is a very difficult skill to learn since all of the normal visual feedback is reversed. HM succeeded in learning this new skill to a high level of competence and he retained this expertise over a long period of time, yet he remained unaware that he had learned it and he did not recognise the mirror apparatus when it was shown to him on a later occasion. This ability to learn skills and procedures without being aware of having learned them seems to be a common finding in studies of amnesics.

Glisky *et al.* (1986) reported that amnesics had been successfully trained to carry out simple computer tasks, though the training had required a great deal of time and patience. It was also noted that although these patients had been able to learn how to use several computer commands, these skills were restricted to the computer program used for training and showed no generalisation to other computer applications. This suggests that skill learning in amnesics is highly inflexible, possibly because it is learned at an automatic and unconscious level.

Cavaco *et al.* (2004) investigated the motor skills of 10 amnesic patients, mostly with temporal lobe lesions caused by HSE. All of these patients displayed completely normal performance on a wide range of skills, including weaving, figure-tracing and target-tracking.

In view of the many studies showing intact skill learning in amnesics, Cohen and Squire (1980) suggested a distinction between procedural memory, which can be demonstrated by performing some skilled procedure, and declarative memory, which can actually be stated in a deliberate and conscious way. Cohen and Squire suggest that amnesics have

Key Term

Procedural memory
Memory which can be demonstrated by performing some skilled procedure such as a motor task, but which the subject is not necessarily able to report consciously (contrasts with declarative memory).

Declarative memory
Memory which can be reported in a deliberate and conscious way (contrasts with procedural memory).

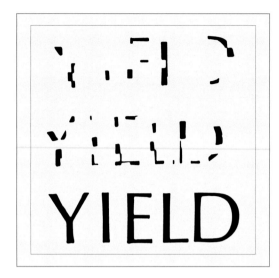

Figure 7.6   An example of a fragmented word stimulus.

Source: Warrington and Weiskrantz (1968), reproduced with permission of Macmillan.

an intact procedural memory, but an impaired declarative memory. This would explain the fact that amnesics can learn new skills and procedures but reveal no conscious awareness of having this expertise.

IMPLICIT MEMORY

In addition to motor skills, there are a number of other types of behaviour which most amnesics seem to be able to learn, though again without any conscious memory of the learning event. Such learning can sometimes be demonstrated by tests of implicit memory (see Chapter 6), in which the individual's behaviour is shown to have been influenced by some previous experience despite their inability to consciously recall it. An early demonstration of this phenomenon was reported by Claparede (1911), who carried out a rather bizarre experiment in which he greeted an amnesic patient with a handshake, made rather painful for them by the presence of a pin concealed in Claparede's hand. Claparede noted that the patient who had fallen foul of this trick refused to shake hands with him the following day, although she could not explain why she was unwilling to do so. The cautious behaviour of this patient thus revealed evidence of learning without any conscious awareness of the learning episode.

Another demonstration of the preservation of implicit memory in amnesics was performed by Warrington and Weiskrantz (1968). They showed Korsakoff patients a series of degraded pictures of common objects or words (see Figure. 7.6 for an example), starting with the most incomplete version and then showing increasingly complete versions until the word or object was correctly identified.

When the same procedure was repeated at a later time, the Korsakoff patients showed a marked improvement in their ability to identify the object, thus providing evidence of learning. A similar study was carried out on the patient HM, who also showed an improvement in the identification of degraded pictures following such repetition priming (Milner *et al.*, 1968).

Graf *et al.* (1984) used the priming of verbal material to demonstrate intact implicit memory in Korsakoff patients. Following a word-priming task, subjects were presented with word fragments and asked to complete them with the first word that came into their heads. In most cases the Korsakoff patients were found to respond with previously primed words, even though they revealed no conscious memory of those words in a test of explicit recall or recognition. In fact the Korsakoff patients achieved similar word fragment completion scores to the control subjects. Graf *et al.* concluded that implicit memory was unimpaired in Korsakoff patients, whereas explicit memory was severely impaired (see Figure 7.7).

Several other studies have confirmed that implicit memory, but not explicit memory, appears to be preserved in amnesics (Graf and Schacter, 1985; Conroy *et al.*, 2005). Although implicit memory is usually intact in organic amnesics, in occasional cases some impairment of implicit memory performance has been reported (Whitlow *et al.*, 1995). Brain scan studies suggest that impaired retrieval of implicit memory is associated with lesions in the occipital lobes (Schachter *et al.*, 1996) and in the left dorsolateral area of the frontal lobes (Eskes *et al.*, 2003).

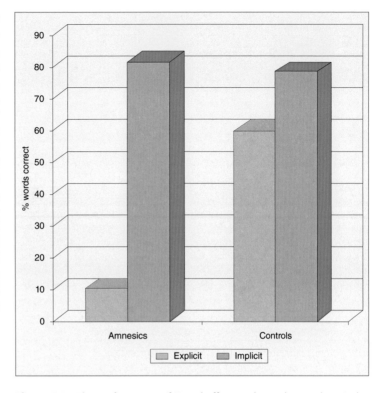

Figure 7.7   The performance of Korsakoff amnesics and normal control subjects on tests of explicit and implicit memory.

Source: Graf *et al.* (1984).

FAMILIARITY AND CONTEXT RECOLLECTION

As explained in Chapter 6, Mandler (1980) suggested that familiarity and recollection represent two alternative routes to recognition. An item may be judged familiar when we feel that we have seen it before, without necessarily remembering where or when. Recollection involves remembering the actual occasion on which the item was encountered. Recollection therefore involves the retrieval of context, whereas a familiarity judgement does not. Mandler argued that a familiarity judgement is an automatic process, which occurs without conscious effort or volition. Recollection, on the other hand, is considered to be a controlled process, which requires conscious effort and is carried out deliberately.

A number of studies have suggested that organic amnesics retain the ability to detect the familiarity of a previously encountered item, but have particular difficulty recollecting the context from which it is familiar. For example, the HSE patient Clive W clearly found his old friends and fellow-musicians familiar when he was reintroduced to them. He greeted them with warmth and happiness, even though he was unable to name them and had no idea where he had met them before (Wilson and Wearing, 1995).

Huppert and Piercy (1976) devised an experimental procedure to measure the accuracy of familiarity judgements. They showed Korsakoff and control subjects two sets of pictures, the first set being shown on day 1 of the experiment and the second set on day 2. Shortly

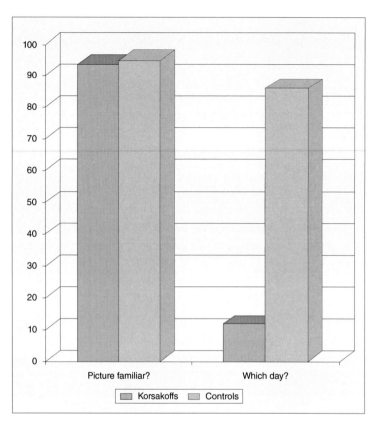

Figure 7.8 Familiarity judgements and context recollection for pictures in Korsakoffs and normal control subjects.

Source: Huppert and Piercy (1976).

Note: Scores shown are numbers of correct responses minus number of incorrect responses.

after the presentation of the second set, the subjects were tested for their ability to recognise pictures they had seen before, by distinguishing between previously presented and unpresented pictures. They were then asked to indicate which day they had seen each of the pictures. As Figure 7.8 shows, both the amnesics and the normal control subjects proved to be very good at identifying which pictures they had seen before. However, when asked to discriminate the pictures shown on day 1 from those shown on day 2, the performance of the amnesics fell to little more than chance level, whilst the control subjects still achieved a high level of accuracy. Most of us would have little difficulty in distinguishing between something we saw yesterday and something we saw today, but contextual judgements of this type seem to be particularly difficult for amnesics.

Huppert and Piercy (1978) carried out a follow-up experiment which showed that the recognition performance of the Korsakoff patients was mainly based on a judgement of the general familiarity of the pictures. The experiment was basically similar to their previous one, except that this time some of the pictures presented on day 1 were presented three times, in order to increase the strength of their familiarity. When requested on day 2 to pick out the recently presented (day 2) pictures, the amnesic subjects often chose pictures which had been presented three times on day 1, and in fact were just as likely to pick them as they were to pick out pictures presented once only on day 2. These results suggest that Korsakoff patients respond to a recognition test by making a judgement of the general familiarity of a test item, without knowing whether that familiarity arose from recent presentation or from frequent presentation.

A number of subsequent studies have suggested that familiarity-based recognition is relatively unimpaired in amnesics (King et al., 2004; Gardiner et al., 2008), but others have reported a small impairment (Zola-Morgan and Squire, 2000; Song et al., 2011). This discrepancy may reflect differences in the degree to which the test material allowed the use of familiarity judgements. King *et al.* (2004) reported unimpaired object recognition in amnesics, so long as the same stimulus was used for the learning and the test stages. However, any change in the viewpoint or even the background of the stimulus led to a significant impairment. Brandt *et al.* (2009) studied an amnesic called Jon, who suffered temporal lobe lesions following an episode of anoxia in early infancy. They found that Jon has very poor recall but almost normal recognition. Using the 'remember and know' (R & K) procedure (see Chapter 6), they showed that Jon's recognition performance was based on the use of familiarity judgements rather than recollection of the learning event.

Although the judgement of familiarity is spared in most cases of organic amnesia, impaired familiarity judgements are found in patients with lesions in the perirhinal cortex (Simons *et al.*, 2001; Lee *et al.*, 2005), which is a small region of the medial temporal lobe lying underneath the brain.

EPISODIC AND SEMANTIC MEMORY

The distinction between semantic and episodic memory (Tulving, 1972) was explained in Chapter 6. Episodic memory refers to memory for specific events in our lives, and it therefore involves the conscious retrieval of the event and its context (i.e. where and when the event took place). Semantic memory refers to the store of knowledge we possess (such as the meaning of a word), and requires no contextual retrieval and no conscious re-experiencing of an event.

Tulving (1989) suggested that amnesics exhibit a selective impairment of episodic memory, whilst their semantic memory remains intact. This theory is consistent with the general observation that amnesics usually retain a normal vocabulary despite their inability to remember any recent events in their lives. However, although a person's vocabulary is certainly part of their semantic memory, it is mostly acquired in very early childhood, which could explain why it is preserved in amnesic patients. Language is also unlike most normal memories in that it is practised continually throughout life.

Certainly it has been found that episodic memory tends to be far more severely impaired than semantic memory in most organic amnesics (Spiers *et al.*, 2001), but semantic memory can also be impaired to some degree. Studies of Korsakoff patients have shown that they tend to have severely impaired episodic memory but with some semantic impairment too, as shown by their poor ability to learn new vocabulary (Verfaillie and Roth, 1996). Studies of retrograde amnesia in Korsakoffs (Kopelman 1989) have also revealed an impairment of semantic memory (e.g. identifying famous people) as well as episodic memory (e.g. retrieval of personal autobiographical events). Similar impairments of both semantic memory and episodic memory have been reported in HSE amnesics (Wilson *et al.*, 1995).

Alzheimer patients are generally found to show impairments of both episodic and semantic memory, though the episodic impairment is usually more severe. Addis and Tippett (2004) reported that Alzheimer patients tend to suffer impaired autobiographical memory extending back over their entire lifespan, but their semantic memory impairment is usually more limited. Indeed their relatively intact semantic memory has been successfully used in rehabilitation strategies (Clare *et al.*, 2003).

The temporal lobe patient HM had no recollection of any events of his life since onset, and in addition to this AA he also had RA for most autobiographical events from his earlier life too (Steinvorth *et al.*, 2005). HM retained a considerable amount of semantic knowledge acquired before onset, but he had difficulty in learning new words (Gabrielli *et al.*, 1988). For example, he was usually unable to define words and phrases introduced since the onset of his amnesia in 1953, such as 'Jacuzzi'. HM succeeded in learning some new semantic information after the onset of his amnesia, which he used to help him solve crosswords. But this new learning was apparently restricted to items that he could relate to knowledge acquired before onset (Scotko *et al.*, 2004).

In view of these findings it would appear that both semantic and episodic memory are impaired in most organic amnesics, so there is no clear support for Tulving's original hypothesis that organic amnesia involves a selective impairment of episodic memory with a sparing of semantic memory. However, some individual patients have been studied who have focal episodic amnesia without any discernable semantic impairment. One example is the patient KC studied by Tulving and his colleagues (Tulving, 2001; Rosenbaum *et al.*, 2005). KC has lesions which are largely restricted to the hippocampus, and he has no episodic memories at all but retains good semantic memory for the period before onset. This pattern of impairment has been called 'episodic amnesia' (Rosenbaum *et al.*, 2005). Other cases of episodic amnesia have since been identified, including the temporal lobe patient 'Jon' (Gardiner *et al.*, 2008).

Just as there are patients with episodic amnesia, some patients have also been studied who have semantic amnesia. These individuals are unable to remember the meanings of words, but they can still recall episodic memories (Hodges *et al.*, 1994; Corbett *et al.*, 2009). For example, Hodges *et al.* (1994) described a patient known as 'PP', who no longer knew the meanings of the words 'food' and 'queen'. Although episodic memory is usually unimpaired in such semantic amnesias, Graham *et al.* (2003) report some impairment of early autobiographical memory in such patients. Corbett *et al.* (2009) found that semantic amnesia is associated with lesions in the anterior temporal lobe. It normally occurs as part of a more general condition known as semantic dementia (SD), which is a progressive degenerative disease. Semantic dementia is characterised by impaired semantic knowledge, and it can be distinguished from aphasia by the fact that SD involves an impairment of 'core knowledge' about the identity of objects. In other words, an individual with SD does not know what the object is, whereas those with aphasia understand what the object is but cannot produce appropriate words. Corbett *et al.* reported that aphasics can often mime the use of an object (e.g. using a hammer) even if they cannot name it, but SD patients are usually unable to mime the action.

Brain scan studies have generally suggested that the encoding of episodic memory is impaired by lesions to the hippocampus, whereas semantic memory impairment is associated with lesions in the temporal cortex (Verfaillie *et al.*, 2000). Steinvorth *et al.* (2005) noted that HM (whose lesions are restricted to the hippocampus and a small area of the temporal cortex) had extensive RA for episodic memory but not for semantic memory. On the other hand, he had AA for both semantic and episodic memory. A similar pattern of amnesia has been reported in an HSE patient (McCarthy *et al.*, 2005), who again has very similar lesions to those found in HM. These cases suggest that semantic and episodic memory do show differential degrees of impairment, though for most amnesic patients episodic memory is more severely impaired than semantic memory.

EXPLAINING PRESERVED MEMORY FUNCTION IN AMNESIA

The findings reported so far in this section suggest that amnesia is not usually an all-pervasive memory impairment, but tends to affect certain specific memory functions whilst leaving others intact. Figure 7.9 summarises the main memory systems, indicating those which are prone to severe impairment and those which are not (based on Squire, 1992).

As shown in the figure, there is evidence that procedural skill memory, implicit memory and familiarity judgements all tend to remain largely unimpaired in typical cases of organic amnesia.

In view of the fact that several memory systems remain unimpaired in most amnesics, it is tempting to look for some common underlying factor uniting them which might explain all of these findings with a single overall theory. One such approach (Squire, 1992) argues that the three most frequently preserved functions (i.e. procedural memory, implicit memory and familiarity judgements) all involve memories which can be demonstrated without requiring any conscious awareness or verbal declaration. Squire calls this type of memory 'non-declarative' memory. In fact it is normally demonstrated by some activity or behaviour which

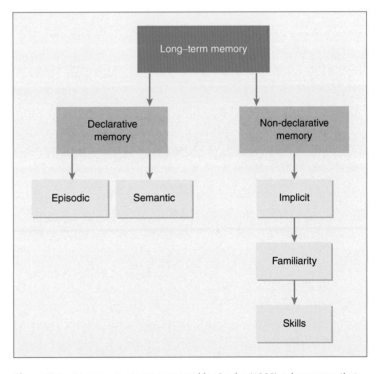

Figure 7.9 Memory systems proposed by Squire (1992), who argues that declarative memory is impaired in organic amnesics whilst non-declarative memory remains intact.

proves the presence of a memory even though the patient is not aware of possessing it. Squire argues that amnesics suffer an impairment of 'declarative' memory, which refers to the type of memory which requires conscious retrieval and usually some kind of spoken response.

There is some disagreement about how the episodic/semantic distinction fits into this general theory of amnesia. Schacter *et al.* (2000) suggest that episodic and semantic memory can also be differentiated in a similar way to the other memory systems. They argue that episodic memory is a form of explicit memory, whereas semantic memory is implicit (see Figure 6.17 in Chapter 6). However, Squire (1992) argues that episodic and semantic memory should both be considered as sub-categories of declarative memory, since both episodic and semantic memory tend to be impaired in most cases of organic amnesia. This viewpoint is now widely accepted (Bayley and Squire, 2003), and it is incorporated into Figure 7.9.

Baddeley (2004) argues that theories postulating a single underlying memory process to explain all aspects of amnesic impairment have not been supported by recent research findings. His view is that all of the different memory mechanisms can suffer impairment in certain cases. Although procedural memory, implicit memory and familiarity remain intact in most typical cases of organic amnesia, in fact all of these memory mechanisms can be impaired by certain types of lesion. For example, a few patients have been found to show impaired implicit memory (Whitlow *et al.*, 1995), and a few patients have been found to have impaired familiarity judgements (Lee *et al.*, 2005), as explained earlier in this section. Perhaps the simplest theory to fit all of these findings might postulate a number of independent memory systems, any one of which may be separately impaired.

7.4 THEORIES OF AMNESIA

A number of theories have been put forward over the years to explain organic amnesia. Earlier theories attempted to identify a single underlying cause which could explain all amnesias, but it soon became clear that this was an over-simplified view of what is a complex and very variable disorder. More recent theories tend to offer explanations for certain key aspects of amnesia, but do not attempt to provide a universal explanation for all aspects and types of amnesic disorder. The main theories of amnesia are summarised below.

ENCODING DEFICIT THEORIES OF AMNESIA

The early studies of HM suggested that he suffered a profound AA but very little RA (Scoville and Milner, 1957). On the basis of this observation, Milner (1966) argued that HM's impairment was essentially a failure to learn new information. More specifically, Milner hypothesised that HM was unable to consolidate memories from a temporary STM trace into a permanent LTM trace, bearing in mind his intact STM. This hypothesis raised the interesting possibility that other amnesias (such as Korsakoff) might also be explained by the same underlying consolidation problem. It was argued that the apparent occurrence of RA in Korsakoff patients might actually be an anterograde (learning) impairment which had simply gone undetected in earlier years (Piercy, 1977). Since the onset of Korsakoff's disease is slow and insidious, AA could well remain undetected for many years and might thus be mistaken later for retrograde amnesia. This would also provide an explanation for the temporal gradient of RA, since the increasing impairment would reflect the gradual onset of the condition. However, the encoding-deficit theory lacks credibility as a general theory of amnesia, because it cannot explain the occurrence of RA. Extensive RA is often found in patients whose amnesia had a sudden onset, for example HSE patients (Wilson and Wearing, 1995; McCarthy *et al.*, 2005). Indeed HM is also now known to have had fairly extensive retrograde amnesia (Steinvorth *et al.*, 2005). As the date of onset of amnesia is known with reasonable accuracy in these cases, it can be established beyond doubt that there is a genuine retrograde amnesia for events preceding that date.

RETRIEVAL DEFICIT THEORIES OF AMNESIA

In contrast to Milner's consolidation deficit theory, Warrington and Weiskrantz (1970) proposed retrieval impairment as the basis of organic amnesia. An impairment of retrieval could explain both the anterograde and the retrograde components of amnesia, since a failure of the retrieval mechanism would be expected to affect all previous memories regardless of when they were acquired. However, a retrieval deficit theory would predict equally severe AA and RA, whereas most amnesics suffer far more severe AA than RA. This could possibly be explained by the fact that earlier memories are for some reason more durable, perhaps because they have benefited from many years of rehearsal. This hypothesis also offers a possible explanation for the occurrence of a temporal gradient in RA, since the earliest memories would be the most rehearsed (Squire *et al.*, 1984). Whilst this remains a possible explanation for the occurrence of temporal gradients, the retrieval deficit theory does not provide an adequate general explanation for all organic amnesias. It cannot readily explain the dramatic variations in the relative severity of AA and RA between different patients, and why some amnesics have virtually no RA at all. Nor can it explain how anterograde and retrograde impairments can sometimes occur in isolation, as in the case of focal AA and RA. These findings suggest that AA and RA are probably separate and independent impairments.

SEPARATE IMPAIRMENTS OF ENCODING AND RETRIEVAL

Attempts to explain both anterograde and retrograde amnesia in terms of a single mechanism have not been supported by research

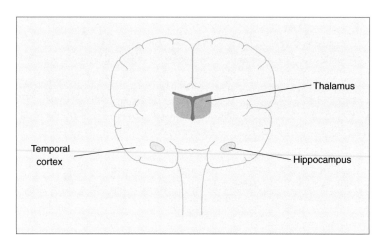

Figure 7.10   A cross-section through the human brain, viewed from the front, showing areas involved in memory function.

findings. It seems more likely that impairments of encoding and impairments of retrieval are essentially separate and independent of one another (Parkin, 1996). The finding that impairments of learning and retrieval are associated with lesions in different areas of the brain adds support to this view, as does the finding that both AA and RA can occur in isolation. In fact most amnesics exhibit both AA and RA to some degree, possibly because the brain regions mainly involved in learning and retrieval (the hippocampus and temporal cortex respectively) are actually quite close to one another and are extensively interconnected (see Figure 7.10). Damage to one of these regions is therefore likely to be accompanied by damage to the other. In summary it would appear that most amnesics suffer from both encoding and retrieval impairments, though their relative severity varies considerably from one patient to another.

THE STANDARD MODEL OF CONSOLIDATION

One problem for theories of amnesia is that some amnesics (e.g. typical Korsakoffs) tend to have RA periods extending back 30 years or more, whilst others (e.g. temporal lobe patient HM) have RA periods of only about two or three years. Squire (1992) has put forward a theory to explain this finding, which is now known as the standard model of consolidation. Squire postulates that in addition to the STM consolidation process (which takes only a few seconds to create a LTM trace) there is also a slower form of consolidation which continues to strengthen the trace for two or three years after its initial acquisition. The trace would thus remain vulnerable for a few years after input, since it has still not been fully consolidated. Squire argues that this long-term consolidation process probably involves the hippocampus, since patients with isolated hippocampal damage (such as HM) appear to have a relatively short RA period. According to Squire's theory, the hippocampus plays a role in both the initial encoding of a new trace and in its subsequent strengthening over the next few years. The relatively limited RA in patients such as HM may thus result from disruption of this slow consolidation process, whereas the far longer period of RA found in typical Korsakoff patients may have a quite different cause, involving an impairment of the retrieval mechanism.

MULTIPLE TRACE THEORY

An alternative explanation of RA is offered by the multiple trace theory (Moscovitch *et al.*, 1999), which suggests that each time an item is retrieved it creates new memory traces and new connections. In the years immediately following the acquisition of a new memory trace, this process causes episodic memories to be bound together to create semantic memories. This binding is assumed to be carried out by the hippocampus, but once the semantic memory is complete it becomes independent of the hippocampus. However, the retrieval of episodic memories always requires the hippocampus. This theory can explain the finding that hippocampal lesions usually disrupt episodic memories from all time periods, but will only disrupt the most recently acquired semantic memories. Supporting evidence has been provided by a recent study of two amnesics (HM and WR) with temporal lobe lesions, who had episodic RA extending back over their entire lifetime, whereas their semantic RA was limited to the few years prior to onset (Steinvorth *et al.*, 2005)

IMPAIRED DECLARATIVE MEMORY

In Section 7.3, evidence was presented to show that most organic amnesics show no impairment in their learning of procedural skills, implicit memory, and familiarity judgements.

These three types of memory have certain features in common, chiefly the fact that they appear to involve automatic processing, and that they do not require deliberate and conscious retrieval. Squire (1992) described this type of memory as 'non-declarative' memory, as opposed to the 'declarative' memories which characterise the conscious and deliberate recollection of some past event. Squire argues that organic amnesia is chiefly characterised by an impairment of declarative memory. Indeed, Mandler (1989) argues that amnesia is essentially 'a disease of consciousness', since the memory functions which are impaired are those which require conscious retrieval. However, Cohen and Eichenbaum (1993) emphasise that the impaired functions are mainly characterised by the binding together of separate memory traces, as explained below.

IMPAIRED BINDING

Cohen and Eichenbaum (1993) argue that the main feature of declarative memory is that it involves the creation of associative connections between memories (such as linking two memories together, or linking an item with its context). This process of connecting memories to one another is known as *binding*. In contrast, non-declarative memory seems to be restricted to the strengthening of a single response (such as a motor skill or the level of activation and familiarity of a word). Eichenbaum (2004) suggests that the hippocampus performs the associative binding function of declarative memory, whereas non-declarative memory involves the cortex and cerebellum. This view has received some support from MRI brain-imaging studies. Rosenbaum *et al.* (2009) found that the amnesic patient KC (who has hippocampal lesions) has severe retrograde amnesia for episodic memories and also for some autobiographical memories, but can still retrieve semantic memories from before onset. Interestingly, KC was able to retrieve autobiographical memories involving semantic information but not those which involved extensive contextual connections. Rosenbaum *et al.* concluded from these findings that the main function of the hippocampus is to bind memories together rather than just to store information.

IMPAIRED PERCEPTUAL PROCESSING

It has long been assumed that the function of the hippocampus is to carry out memory storage (see Section 7.2). However, animal studies (chiefly involving rodents and primate apes) suggest that the hippocampus also plays a major role in visual perception (Gaffan *et al.*, 2001). Graham *et al* (2008) have presented some evidence which suggests that the hippocampus may also have a perceptual function in humans, which may underlie some of the apparent memory problems of amnesic patients. Graham *et al.* suggest that memory storage involves a network of perceptual representations which are distributed throughout the cortex, which are controlled and activated by the hippocampus. Damage to the hippocampus would therefore impair the retrieval of old memories as well as the processing of new input. One problem for this theory is that studies of amnesics have mostly failed to identify a major perceptual impairment. For example, Hartley *et al.* (2007) tested four amnesics with focal hippocampal lesions and found that only two of them showed any evidence of perceptual impairment, and even that was relatively slight. Interestingly, all four individuals showed a marked impairment of spatial memory, even at retention intervals of just a few seconds. However, in a recent review of neuro-imaging studies, Lee *et al.* (2012) found evidence for the involvement of the hippocampus in the visual discrimination of complex scene stimuli. There is therefore some evidence to suggest that the hippocampus does apparently play a role in both memory encoding and perception. The processes underlying perception and memory may possibly overlap and interact, but the precise nature of this interaction remains uncertain.

7.5 OTHER TYPES OF MEMORY DISORDER

IMPAIRMENT OF SHORT-TERM MEMORY

It was pointed out in Section 7.1 that organic amnesia normally involves an impairment of long-term memory, whereas the short-term memory of amnesics usually remains completely intact. Impairments of short-term memory do occasionally occur, though they are associated with a quite different pattern of brain lesions to those found in typical organic amnesia. Alzheimer patients in particular may show severe WM impairments, chiefly involving executive function (Storandt, 2008). However, as STM impairment was covered in Chapter 5 it will not be discussed further here.

CONCUSSION AMNESIA

Concussion is one of the most common causes of amnesia, though fortunately the memory disturbance is usually temporary. A person who is knocked unconscious by a blow on the head will typically suffer from both anterograde and retrograde amnesia, which may be extensive at first but which then usually diminishes with time, to leave only a very limited period from which memories are permanently lost. For example, a footballer concussed by a collision with another player will probably be unable to remember the events immediately following the collision (e.g. being taken off the pitch and driven to hospital), and they will also frequently be unable to remember the events immediately preceding the collision (such as the actual tackle or the play leading up to it). Amnesias of this kind are known as concussion amnesias, and they fall within a broader category known as post-traumatic amnesias (PTA), which include all types of closed-head injury.

Russell (1971) surveyed a large number of concussion victims and found that typically retrograde amnesia affected memories for a period extending only a minute or two before the accident, though in a few cases it extended back over a period of days or even weeks. In all probability these rare cases of very extensive retrograde amnesia reflect some other form of memory disturbance in addition to the temporary effects of concussion, and may involve either a brain lesion or a psychogenic amnesia.

In some respects the characteristics of concussion amnesia resemble a temporary version of the pattern found in organic amnesia. For example, during the period immediately following the concussive accident, the patient is likely to show impairment in LTM tasks, but will perform normally on tests of STM such as digit span (Regard and Landis, 1984). However, the very limited extent of retrograde amnesia suggests that there is usually no lasting impairment to the patient's retrieval. The most likely explanation of this pattern of amnesia is that the patient is temporarily unable to consolidate memories from the STM (working memory) into the LTM store. This would explain why events following the concussive injury are not stored, but it also explains why events held in STM immediately before the injury may also be lost, because they have not yet been transferred to the LTM.

Although the effects of concussion on memory are usually temporary, a minority of mild to moderate head injuries may leave a more lasting impairment, referred to as post-concussive syndrome. Lasting cognitive impairment is rare with childhood concussive injuries, but it is more common in the elderly (King and Kirwilliam, 2011).

Figure 7.11 Frequent blows to the head can sometimes lead to brain injury and cognitive impairment.
Source: Shutterstock.

There is some concern that sports involving frequent head impacts may produce a permanent cognitive impairment, and there is evidence that this may occur in sports such as boxing (Galetta *et al.*, 2011) and football (Kirdendall and Garrett, 2001). In cases of post-concussive syndrome, brain lesions can often be detected by scanning techniques (Hofman *et al.*, 2002). Specialised screening tests have also been devised which provide a fairly accurate assessment of the cognitive effects of mild traumatic brain injury (De Monte *et al.*, 2005; Galetta *et al.*, 2011).

ECT AND MEMORY LOSS

ECT (electroconvulsive therapy) involves the passing of an electric current through the brain in an effort to alleviate depression. This treatment has been in fairly widespread use for over 50 years, though its use in the treatment of depression remains controversial. Although ECT has been shown to reduce depression in some patients, the benefits of ECT typically only last for a few weeks (Johnstone *et al.*, 1980; Read and Bentall, 2010). The benefits of ECT thus appear to be temporary, and these benefits must be weighed up against the evidence that ECT may cause lasting brain damage.

The main evidence for such brain damage is the observation that ECT can apparently cause memory impairment. In the period immediately following the administration of an ECT shock, the patient typically shows a temporary amnesia rather similar to that seen following concussion. There is usually both anterograde and retrograde amnesia (Squire *et al.*, 1981), which may be extensive at first but which usually then shrinks to leave only a fairly limited amnesia for the treatment period. It therefore appears that for most patients there is only a temporary impairment of memory, and follow-up tests of memory performance a few weeks after the completion of ECT treatment have often failed to detect any lasting memory impairment (Weeks *et al.*, 1980; Warren and Groome, 1984; Meeter *et al.*, 2011). Warren and Groome (1984) actually found that patients showed an improvement in their memory scores over the period of their ECT treatment, probably due to the alleviation of their depression over this period. However, it remains possible that this general improvement may be masking an underlying memory impairment. The memory tests employed in such studies are not sufficiently sensitive to detect small changes in real-life memory performance, and in any case the patients' original level of memory performance is often unknown. Despite the fact that memory tests usually fail to detect any lasting memory impairment following ECT treatment, patients often report that they

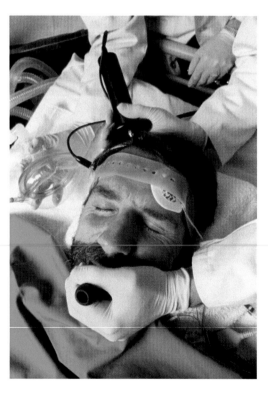

Figure 7.12   Patient receiving electroconvulsive therapy.

Source: Science Photo Library.

still feel subjectively that their memories have been damaged (Rogers *et al.*, 1993). A recent review of previous ECT studies (Read and Bentall, 2010) concluded that ECT treatment produces no lasting benefits, but it does cause significant memory loss in some patients. The authors therefore conclude that the use of ECT cannot be justified.

In recent years there has been increasing concern about the use of ECT. Some researchers insist that ECT is valuable in the treatment of depression, since many patients report an improvement in their quality of life following treatment (McCall, 2004). But a growing number of researchers argue that the limited benefits of ECT cannot be justified in view of its damaging effects on memory and cognition (Johnstone, 2003; Read and Bentall, 2010).

FRONTAL LOBE LESIONS

Patients with frontal lobe lesions often show some impairment of memory, though these tend to be rather different in nature to those associated with temporal lobe or thalamic lesions, and they seem to mainly involve impaired retrieval. More specifically, patients with frontal lobe lesions tend to have particular difficulty in retrieving contextual information (Parkin *et al.*, 1995b), and they therefore have difficulty in recalling the source of any information they recall. When tested a few days after learning a list of new facts, frontal lobe patients showed no impairment in their recall of the facts, but unlike normal individuals they could not remember where or when they had learned them (Schacter *et al.*, 1984). One possible explanation for this defect of context discrimination in frontal lobe patients is that they often have an impairment of the central executive of their working memory (Shallice, 1988). The central executive (which was discussed in Chapter 5) is assumed to be responsible for conscious processing and decision-making, possibly including decisions about the source of a retrieved memory. There is evidence that frontal lobe lesions do cause an impairment of the central executive (Ruggeri *et al.*, 2009). Such executive impairments also tend to affect thinking and problem-solving, and this will be considered in Chapter 9.

Another characteristic of patients with frontal lobe lesions is a tendency to confabulation (Moscovitch, 1989), which means that the patient describes memories for events which did not really take place and which are apparently invented. Confabulation is associated with impaired executive function, and with the consequent loss of mental flexibility (Nys *et al.*, 2004). Confabulation often leads to misunderstandings, especially when other people believe what the patient tells them. For example, if a patient wrongly claims to have been attacked by another person this can have serious consequences. Sometimes confabulation is mistakenly seen as lying. A patient who claims to have spent the morning talking to the Pope may appear to be lying (assuming of course that the Pope is unable to confirm their story). However, confabulation is not deliberate dishonesty, it is merely an error of retrieval. Andrewes (2001) points out that patients with frontal lobe lesions have difficulty in judging the validity of their memories, as they are unable to recall the source or context of the

> **Key Term**
>
> **Confabulation**
> The reporting of memories which are incorrect and apparently fabricated, but which the patient believes to be true.

remembered event. Consequently the patient may be unable to distinguish between memories for real and imagined events.

The impairments which have been described in this section are those which are associated with frontal lobe lesions, but it is important to bear in mind that frontal lobe lesions frequently co-exist with other types of lesion. For example, it has been found that many Korsakoff patients have frontal lobe lesions in addition to their diencephalic lesions (Shimamura *et al.*, 1988), and these particular individuals often exhibit a marked tendency to confabulation and retrieval problems in addition to the more usual amnesic symptoms found in Korsakoff syndrome. On the other hand, Korsakoff patients without frontal lesions often show neither retrieval problems nor confabulation (Pujol and Kopelman, 2003). An impairment of frontal lobe functioning is also thought to occur in many otherwise normal elderly people, and this will be considered in the next section.

MEMORY LOSS IN THE NORMAL ELDERLY

It is generally assumed that memory tends to decline in older people. However, although there is some evidence for such an age-related decline, it is not readily detectable until the age of about 65 or 70. Even then the degree of impairment is not usually very great, at least not among the normal elderly (Verhaeghen, 2011). So the popular view of old age leading inevitably to dementia is certainly not supported, and it is important to recognise the clear distinction between the dementing elderly (such as those with Alzheimer's disease), and the normal elderly who show only a relatively small memory impairment.

Studies have indicated that the normal elderly tend to show a decline in recall ability but not in recognition (Craik and McDowd, 1987). Furthermore, elderly subjects tend to show a deterioration of explicit memory, but their implicit memory for previously primed items remains unimpaired (Fleischman *et al.*, 2004). Elderly people also seem to have particular problems in retrieving contextual information. For example, Parkin *et al.* (1995b) found that older people had difficulty in remembering the temporal context of events. Parkin and Walter (1992) used the R & K procedure (as described chapter 6), to demonstrate that elderly people (mean age 81) were able to recognise an item as familiar but had poor recall of context compared with younger subjects. An interesting feature of these results was that the amount of decline in context recollection correlated with measures of frontal lobe impairment, such as the Wisconsin card-sorting test. These findings are similar to those observed in patients with frontal lobe damage, which is consistent with the finding that neural loss and degeneration in the elderly tends to affect mainly the frontal lobes (Tisserand and Jolles, 2003).

One possible explanation of age-related memory decline consistent with the above findings is that the elderly lose some of their capacity for consciously controlled processing and attention, and have to rely more heavily on automatic processes (Craik and McDowd, 1987). Elderly people also show a reduction in their processing speed (Salthouse,

1994). A recent study showed that memory deterioration in the normal elderly reflects impairment of learning and input processing, but there is no further impairment of retrieval at later test sessions even when they occur several years later (Salthouse, 2011).

One widely held assumption is that elderly people show a decline in their central executive functions, such as selective attention and task shifting. However, a recent meta-analysis concluded that the actual decline in executive function in the normal elderly is very slight (Verhaeghen, 2011). For those of us who are ageing this is very reassuring news.

PSYCHOGENIC AMNESIA

Some amnesias occur without any evidence of brain lesions, and these are assumed to be of psychogenic origin. In most cases they appear to be brought on by stress, and they are usually temporary, typically disappearing within a few days (Khilstrom and Schacter, 2000). Psychogenic amnesias usually involve loss of memory for past events, in other words retrograde amnesia, and anterograde amnesia is fairly unusual (Kopelman, 1995). The pattern of impairment found in psychogenic amnesias varies widely from case to case. Kopelman (2010) points out

Figure 7.13 Elderly people normally show very little memory impairment.

Source: Shutterstock.

that psychogenic amnesias may be 'global' (a complete loss of all memories) or 'situation specific' (amnesia for one specific event only). The global form may cause amnesia for the person's entire previous life, and may be accompanied by a loss of the sense of personal identity. Situation-specific amnesia involves a small gap in a person's memory, usually related to a traumatic episode.

A major problem with psychogenic amnesia is that it is difficult to distinguish it from faking (Kopelman, 2002). It is likely that many cases diagnosed as psychogenic amnesia may in reality involve faking amnesic symptoms, for example to support an insurance claim or to avoid conviction for a crime. Indeed it has been reported that more than 30 per cent of convicted murderers claim to have no memory of their crime (Kopelman, 2002), and some of these cases probably involve simulated amnesic symptoms. Kopelman (1995) describes a case of a man who stabbed his wife to death after discovering that she was having an affair, but he later claimed to have no recollection of killing her. He did recall having a furious argument with his wife, and then going to another room to say goodnight to his daughter, but could recall no further events of that evening. During his trial it emerged that he had not only murdered his wife, but he had then telephoned the police to report her death. He therefore had little to gain by faking amnesia, though as with many such cases there is some uncertainty as to whether his amnesia was genuine.

The main feature which enables clinicians to distinguish between psychogenic and organic amnesias is that those of psychogenic origin do not usually match up with the usual pattern of impairment found in organic patients. Indeed the memory symptoms may be very unusual and even quite inexplicable. For example, Smith *et al.* (2010) describe the case of a woman known as FL, who had developed an odd and highly unusual form of amnesia following a car accident. FL had normal recall of the events of each day until she went to sleep that night. On waking each morning, she discovered that all of her memories for the events of the previous day had been completely erased. This pattern of memory loss does not accord with any known type of organic amnesia, nor with any known memory consolidation mechanism. Since MRI scans revealed no lesions of any kind, FL's amnesia was assumed to be psychogenic. This was subsequently confirmed by a further test, in which events and items from the previous day were secretly added to a test for memory of the current day. The fact that FL remembered these items from the previous day suggested that the memories were still available. It was concluded that FL was probably suffering from a psychogenic amnesia, though the possibility that she was deliberately feigning amnesia cannot be completely ruled out. The authors also suggested that FL's amnesia may have been influenced by a popular film of the period called *50 First Dates*, in which the character played by Drew Barrymore suffers from a similar amnesic disorder. FL has since made a recovery from her amnesic symptoms.

7.6 REHABILITATION

HELPING PATIENTS TO COPE WITH AMNESIA

The effects of brain damage are usually irreversible, so it is not normally possible to restore normal memory function to those who suffer organic amnesia. However, this does not mean that nothing can be done to help them. There are a number of ways in which the lives of organic amnesics can be significantly improved by helping them to cope with their impairment and helping them to function as effectively as possible within the limitations of their condition. This approach is known as rehabilitation. Some rehabilitation strategies involve the use of techniques for maximising the performance of those memory functions which remain intact. Other strategies aim to bypass the impairment by finding alternative ways of carrying out a particular task. This may involve the use of other types of memory process which remain intact, or alternatively makes use of external memory aids such as lists or electronic reminders.

MAXIMISING MEMORY PERFORMANCE

Most of the techniques used to maximise memory function in amnesia are based on methods which also help to improve normal memory. For example, it can be helpful to encourage amnesic patients to pay more

Key Term

Rehabilitation
Strategies used to help patients to cope with an impairment or disability, enabling them to function as effectively as possible within the limitations created by the impairment.

attention to input, to repeat what is said to them, to organise items in memory, and to make meaningful associations between new input and the items already in memory. In one study (Milders *et al.*, 1995) a group of amnesics who were trained to use these strategies achieved a significant improvement in memory performance compared with a control group of untrained amnesics, though their advantage gradually disappeared over the next few years.

Wilson (2004) suggests a number of additional strategies. For example, it is helpful to ensure that an amnesic is only required to learn one thing at a time, and it is important to keep the input simple, avoiding jargon or long words. Amnesics also perform better if their learning is not context-specific. For example, a patient who has learned a memory technique in one setting may not use it in other settings, unless deliberately trained to do so. There is also evidence that amnesics can benefit from the use of 'spaced' rather than 'massed' learning sessions, especially when expanding retrieval practice intervals are employed (Broman, 2001). Mnemonic techniques have also proved to be helpful to many amnesics (Wilson, 1987; Clare *et al.*, 1999), and they can be devised specifically to suit the memory requirements of an individual patient.

One type of memory which usually remains intact in amnesic patients is procedural skill learning, and this type of learning can be used in amnesic patients who are otherwise unable to learn new information consciously. For example, Glisky *et al.* (1986) were able to teach amnesic patients to operate computer packages which were previously unknown to them. Procedural skill learning can also be used to help amnesic patients to perform everyday skills despite their lack of conscious awareness of the procedures involved. These methods have been used to help amnesics carry out tasks such as washing, dressing, or making tea (Zanetti *et al.*, 2001).

Baddeley and Wilson (1994) demonstrated that amnesics derive particular benefit from 'errorless learning', in which various strategies are employed in an effort to eliminate the possibility of errors occurring. For example, the patient's response can be restricted or guided in some way, or they may be told the correct information directly before testing, or provided with a very strong retrieval cue. This approach contrasts with most learning situations, where responses are learned by trial and error. There are a number of possible reasons for the effectiveness of errorless learning, but Baddeley and Wilson suggest that errorless learning may facilitate the retrieval of implicit or fragmented memory traces. Another possible benefit of errorless learning is that it ensures that incorrect responses are not produced so that they will not therefore be reinforced or strengthened.

EXTERNAL MEMORY AIDS

In addition to these techniques for improving memory function in amnesics, external aids can be used to assist memory. One useful approach is to change the immediate environment and living conditions of the amnesic patient so as to minimise their dependence on memory. For example, putting big labels on cupboards, or labelling doors as a reminder of which is the kitchen or the toilet. Environmental adaptations of this kind can help to make the amnesic's life safer and easier. For a more detailed discussion of environmental adaptations see Kapur *et al.* (2004).

Electronic devices and computerised systems have also been devised which can be programmed to produce a reminder to carry out some action at a particular time, usually by emitting a warning 'beep' which draws attention to an instruction on screen. The first successful device of this kind was an electronic pager called the 'Neuropage' (Hersh and Treadgold, 1994), which can be programmed to remind the user to perform a variety of tasks such as taking medicine, keeping appointments, or going to work. Neuropage has been found to be of great assistance to most amnesics who have used it (Wilson, 2004).

Another electronic memory aid has recently been developed called 'SenseCam', which makes use of a digital camera attached to the user's belt to take photos of events experienced each day in order to provide a reminder which can be viewed later on. The user can thus 'relive' each event many times to help strengthen the memory, and because the camera is triggered automatically by a movement sensor they do not need to remember to take photos of key events. Loveday and Conway (2011) reported that SenseCam can significantly enhance an amnesic's personal memories, and it can also improve their sense of wellbeing and general happiness. Reviewing events recorded on SenseCam at the end of each day also helps to improve the vividness of recall, and it helps to add context to an event. For example, by reminding the amnesic patient of the things they were doing and thinking, and their interactions with other people, SenseCam adds a richness to the memory which provides a sense of re-experiencing events. Loveday and Conway reported that SenseCam produced a significant and lasting improvement in subsequent memory for personal experiences and events, and this improvement was still evident nine months later.

A variety of memory strategies and aids are now in use, and many of them have been found to be of benefit to amnesic patients. Those who wish to know more about rehabilitation should see Wilson *et al.* (2009) for a review of current techniques.

SUMMARY

- Organic amnesia is caused by brain damage, usually affecting the temporal lobes, hippocampus and anterior thalamic nuclei.
- Such brain lesions may arise from a variety of different causes, such as Alzheimer's disease, Korsakoff syndrome, herpes simplex encephalitis, strokes and tumours.
- Organic amnesia is characterised by an impairment of long-term memory, but the short-term working memory usually remains intact.
- Most amnesics suffer from anterograde amnesia, so that they have difficulty in learning new information from the time period subsequent to onset.

- Many amnesics also suffer from retrograde amnesia, in which memories are also lost from the period preceding onset. However, the retrograde impairment may be fairly limited, and memories for earlier time periods such as childhood often remain intact.
- The anterograde and retrograde components of amnesia appear to be fairly independent of one another, so that their relative severity can vary considerably from patient to patient. In rare cases either retrograde or anterograde amnesia may occur in isolation.
- Most amnesics suffer a severe impairment of conscious declarative and explicit memory processes such as event and context recollection, but there is usually no impairment of non-declarative and implicit memory processes such as motor skill learning, priming and familiarity judgements.
- In addition to the amnesias which are characteristic of the organic amnesic syndrome, memory impairment may also be caused by other factors, such as ageing, concussion, ECT and psychogenic causes. However, these impairments tend to have their own distinct characteristics, and differ somewhat from the pattern of organic amnesic symptoms.
- Although brain lesions are usually irreversible, many rehabilitation strategies have been devised to help organic amnesics to cope with their memory impairment.

FURTHER READING

- Baddeley, A. D., Kopelman, M. D. and Wilson, B. A. (2004). *The Essential Handbook of Memory Disorders for Clinicians*. Chichester: Wiley. Offers detailed cover of all types and aspects of amnesia for the specialist. Aimed primarily at clinicians and researchers, but useful as a reference book for undergraduate students.
- Campbell, R. and Conway, M. A. (1995). *Broken Memories*. Oxford: Blackwell. A book of individual case studies. Each chapter contains a detailed study of a single patient with some kind of memory disorder, including a detailed acount of the HSE patient Clive W.
- Wilson, B. A., Gracey, F., Evans, J. J. and Bateman, A. (2009). *Neuropsychological Rehabilitation: Theory, Models, Therapy and Outcome*. Cambridge University Press. This book covers the main approaches to rehabilitation in current use.

Chapter 8

Contents

Thinking and problem-solving

Nicola Brace

8

8.1 INTRODUCTION

Most would agree that 'thinking' covers a range of different mental activities, such as reflecting on ideas, having new ideas, theorising, arguing, making decisions and solving problems. An important feature common to all of these particular activities is that they are under our own control and we can run through actions symbolically in our minds. Also common to most of these activities is that our thinking is directed towards specific goals, for example doing crossword puzzles or composing the answers to questions. However, other types of thinking do not have these characteristics; when imagining or daydreaming there is often a feeling of an uncontrolled drifting of our thoughts.

This chapter will confine itself to providing a selective overview of the key findings of research into problem-solving and reasoning. Other main research areas on judgement and decision-making and on the psychology of creativity are not covered here. It should be noted that whilst many have used problem-solving as an operational definition of thinking, such a narrow definition does restrict discussion to findings of research on goal-directed thought processes. However, as problem-solving takes time, involves several cognitive processes and mental representations, even constructing a theory of problem-solving alone is comparable with trying to provide a theory of art broad enough to cover everything from ceramics to opera (Cohen, 1983).

8.2 EARLY RESEARCH ON PROBLEM-SOLVING

Thought processes have been studied from many different theoretical points of view. Oswald Külpe was one of the first to examine thought processes, such as the making of judgements, using specially trained adult human participants and the classical introspective report as his research methodology (Külpe, 1895). Introspection involves self-examining one's thoughts and feelings, and Külpe's participants were asked to focus on their mental experiences and any component sensations whilst at different stages of solving a problem. This included observations before and after a problem was solved. This led him to believe that some thoughts could be imageless. Gilhooly (1996) comments that in particular the issue of thinking without images led to considerable controversy, with some introspectionists reporting imageless thought and others claiming that thought was always accompanied by imagery, albeit very faint images.

Frequently, we are conscious of the products of thinking rather than the processes themselves and the behaviourists offered a completely different approach, which of course focused on observable behaviour and 'learning' rather than 'thought'. Thorndike (1898) (Figure 8.1) argued that the process of problem solution occurred through trial and error; in other words responses to the problem are simply random responses until one of them proves successful. A cat placed in a box with a trapdoor was not observed to show behaviour approximating thinking, but instead performed all kinds of behaviours until the appropriate responses were made accidentally, the trapdoor would then open and food was available as a reward. With practice, the cat would escape quite quickly by reproducing these learned responses. Whilst some problem-solving may indeed occur through trial and error, alternative means of arriving at problem solution were investigated by the Gestalt psychologists, who conducted a number of well-known and widely cited experiments in this field of research. Their research revealed some of the reasons why people can have difficulty in finding the correct solution to a problem.

Figure 8.1   Edward Lee Thorndike.
Source: Science Photo Library.

THE GESTALT APPROACH TO PROBLEM-SOLVING

Research conducted by Wolfgang Köhler, one of the three founder members of the Gestalt school, took place on the island of Tenerife. He was trapped there during World War I and became the director of an animal research station. He founded a colony of chimpanzees and studied their problem-solving behaviour. For example, one chimp named Sultan was able to use a stick to obtain some bananas that were placed on the outside of his cage. When provided with two poles, neither of which was long enough to reach the bananas, the ape first 'sulked' then eventually put one pole inside the other to create a longer pole. Köhler (1925) used the term insight to refer to the ape's discovery. Other apes were observed when provided with bananas hanging from the ceiling out of their reach. Again, intense thinking typically preceded a flash of insight (the 'aha') and the apes would stack crates on top of each other to provide a staircase to the bananas. According to the Gestaltists, the process of some problem-solving requires the reorganising or restructuring of the elements of the problem situation in such a way as to provide a solution. This is known as productive thinking or insight. Reproductive thinking, on the other hand, relies on the rote application of past solutions to a problem.

The Gestalt ideas inspired the work of Maier, Duncker and Luchins. Maier (1930, 1931) investigated the 'two-string' problem (Figure 8.2). This involved human participants who were introduced to a room that had two strings hanging from the ceiling. Other objects in the room included pliers and poles. The participants were told to tie the two strings together, which was not easy as it was not possible to reach one string whilst holding the end of the other string. One solution is to attach the pliers to the end of one string so that it can swing like a pendulum. Maier waited until participants were obviously stuck and then brushed against the string to make it swing. Although not necessarily noticing his action, many went on to arrive at the pendulum solution and Maier claimed that his subtle hint resulted in a reorganisation or restructuring of the problem.

Some participants were unable to solve Maier's problem, even if he handed them the pair of pliers and explicitly told them that by using the pliers and no other object they could solve the problem. This was because they were unable to shift from seeing pliers as a tool for gripping things to seeing it as a weighty object. Duncker (1945) termed this functional fixedness and defined it as the inability to use an object appropriately in a given situation because of prior experience of using the

Figure 8.2   The Maier (1930, 1931) two-string problem.

object in a different way. Functional fixedness is a good example of stereotypical thinking and is a 'block' to problem solution.

A well-known study conducted by Duncker (1945) concerns a problem where individuals are handed a candle, a box of nails and other objects. The task is to fix the candle to a wall by a table, in such a way that it does not drip on the table. His observations revealed that few thought of using the box which contained the nails as a candle holder and were therefore considered to be fixated on the usual function of the box, namely to hold the nails.

A different potential block to problem-solving is referred to as mental set, which is the rote application of learned rules. Luchins (1942) asked participants to imagine that they had an unlimited supply of water and three jugs with which to measure out a certain quantity of water (see Figure 8.3). The volumes of the three jugs are specified for each separate problem. Participants were trained on a series of problems which either had the same complex solution method (the set condition) or on a series of problems that were solved using different methods (the control condition). Participants were then presented with critical problems, which could be solved either with the complex solution method or with a shorter, simpler method. To solve the critical problems, those in the control condition chose the simpler method. In contrast, those in the set condition used the complex method, providing evidence of reproductive thinking, even though in this case it hindered problem solution.

The nine-dot problem is another famous Gestalt problem. Scheerer (1963) presented participants with nine dots arranged in a 3 × 3 matrix. The task is to join all the dots in four straight lines without lifting the pencil from the paper, a task most participants could not do. The traditional Gestalt explanation is that this is a further example of a type of set effect, but this time produced by the way the task is arranged which means that participants attempt to keep their lines within the matrix or square created by the dots. The solution to the problem requires that they draw lines beyond the matrix (Figure 8.4). However, explicitly informing participants of this does not necessarily lead to an improvement in performance (Weisberg and Alba, 1981).

The research inspired by the Gestalt ideas demonstrates that some problems cannot be solved through reproductive thinking (i.e. the rote application of past solutions to a problem) and that instead our past experience may hinder problem solution. However, this early research did

Key Term

Mental set

A term to describe the rote application of one successful method to solve a problem which makes one 'blind' to an alternative and possibly much simpler method.

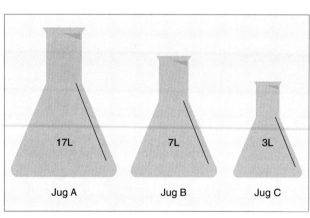

Figure 8.3   An example of the water jug problem.

Source: Adapted from Luchins (1942).

Note: The problem requires a quantity of water to be measured out. For example, to measure out 4 litres of water, you can either fill B and then pour 3 litres into C or follow a more complicated method, used in the set condition, which is to fill A, pour 7 litres of water into B and then two lots of 3 litres into C.

not provide us with an explicit account of the processes underlying productive thinking, that is, insight; such attempts arose later with research conducted within the information-processing framework.

8.3 THE INFORMATION-PROCESSING APPROACH TO PROBLEM-SOLVING

In the 1960s, Newell and Simon initiated research that resulted in the information-processing view of problem-solving (e.g. Newell and Simon, 1961). Their work also involved creating a computer program called the General Problem Solver (GPS). They demonstrated that most simple problems consisted of a number of possible solutions and each of these solutions could be broken down into a series of discrete steps or stages. The stages they identified included:

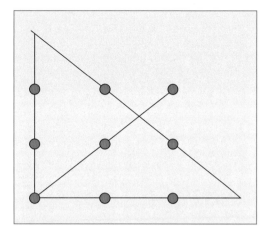

Figure 8.4   A solution to the nine-dot problem. Source: Adapted from Scheerer (1963).

1. Representing the problem – a problem space is constructed which includes both the initial state and the goal state, the instructions and the constraints on the problem and all relevant information retrieved from long-term memory. To assist such representation, symbols, lists, matrices, tree diagrams, graphs and visual imagery can all be used. This first stage reflects the assumption that problem-solving can be regarded as a form of search in a space consisting of all possible states of the problem.
2. Selection of operators – operators are actions that will achieve a goal, and are used for transforming the initial state.
3. Implementation of the selected operators – this results in a new current state within the problem space.
4. Evaluation of the current state – if it corresponds to the goal, a solution is reached.

Newell and Simon claimed that the key features of GPS were also characteristics of human problem-solving. They asked participants to solve problems whilst thinking out loud (a method known as 'protocol analysis') and when comparing the verbal protocols with the way GPS solved these same problems they found remarkable similarities.

PROBLEM-SOLVING STRATEGIES

According to Newell and Simon (1972) most problems are solved by the use of a small number of general-purpose heuristics, which are basically 'rules of thumb'. Heuristics are methods or strategies which often lead to problem solution but are not guaranteed to succeed. They

> **Key Term**
>
> **Problem space**
> A term introduced by Newell and Simon to describe the first stage in problem-solving; represented in the problem space are the initial state, the goal state, the instructions, the constraints on the problem and all relevant information retrieved from long-term memory.
>
> **Heuristics**
> Methods or strategies which often lead to a problem solution but are not guaranteed to succeed.

can be distinguished from algorithms, which are methods or procedures that will always produce a solution sooner or later. Our knowledge of the rules of arithmetic provides us with algorithms to solve problems such as 998 multiplied by 21. However, in certain situations we might estimate the solution to be in the region of 20,000. There are many situations in real life where we use heuristics, as either our memory constraints or other processing limitations do not allow us to use algorithms, or simply because there are no algorithms available.

To explore the different kinds of strategies that might be used, researchers have presented participants with well-defined problems. These are problems where all aspects are clearly outlined: the initial state, the available operators and the goal state are clearly specified. Although we might not encounter such problems very often in everyday life, studying how people attempt to solve well-defined problems allows us to identify the strategies they use and the sorts of errors they make.

Well-defined problems can be solved by deciding which moves are possible, starting from that initial state, and thinking through the consequences of each of these moves. A diagram showing all the possible sequences of actions and intermediate states can be constructed and this is called a state–action tree. Such a tree will allow one to find a sequence of actions that leads from the initial state to the goal state. Applying such a 'check-every-state' algorithm is, however, very time-consuming and impossible for complex problem-solving activities such as playing chess. Instead, many problems can be solved through problem reduction, a sort of 'divide-and-conquer' approach. The problem is converted into a number of sub-problems and each of these is further sub-divided unless it can be solved by the available operators.

The most important methods or heuristics for developing sub-problem structures are *hill-climbing* and means–ends analysis. In hill-climbing, operators are selected which make the current state of the problem as similar as possible to the goal state, so the problem-solver is likely to choose moves that reduce the distance between the current and goal states. More complex is means–ends analysis. First, the difference between the current state and the goal state is noted and, by working backwards from the goal, a sub-goal is identified that will reduce this difference and a mental operator is selected to achieve the sub-goal. Choosing appropriate sub-goals to achieve the main goal is important to successful problem-solving, and search processes are believed to involve the holding of these, and any intermediate results, in the limited-capacity working memory. An example of real-life means–ends analysis is making travel plans (Gilhooly, 1996). The desire to travel from London to New York will require one to note the large distance between the two and select air travel as the operator to reduce the difference. The initial sub-goal of 'ticket purchase' is then constructed which in turn leads to the sub-goal 'choose travel agent'. Clearly, a number of subsidiary problems have to be resolved in order to arrive at the desired destination.

Several well-defined problems that have been researched include the Tower of Hanoi and the Hobbits and Orcs; both are 'move' problems

Key Term

State–action tree
A diagram showing all the possible sequences of actions and intermediate states which can be constructed if the problem is well-defined.

Problem reduction
An approach to problem solving that converts the problem into a number of sub-problems, each of which can be solved separately.

Means–ends analysis
A general heuristic where a sub-problem is selected that will reduce the difference between the current state and the goal state.

(problems of transformation). The GPS program, which incorporated means–ends analysis, was able to solve these problems. The Tower of Hanoi problem consists of three discs placed in order of size on the first of three pegs (see Figure 8.5). The goal state is for these three discs to be placed in the same order on the last peg. Only one disc can be moved at a time and a larger disc cannot be placed on top of a smaller disc. These two rules restrict

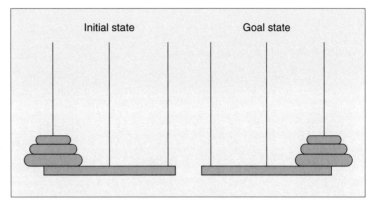

Figure 8.5   The Tower of Hanoi problem.

Note: Only one disc can be removed at a time and a larger disc cannot be placed on top of a smaller disc.

which mental operator can be selected so that, for example, there are only two possible first moves: to place the smallest disc on the middle or on the last peg. According to means–ends analysis, a reasonable sub-goal is to place the largest disc on the last peg. Karat (1982) found that even though participants did not have a complete understanding of the problem before initiating their solution, they would solve this problem by using the heuristic of means–ends analysis. The Tower of London task is a very similar task (which has been used to investigate the effects of frontal lesions, see in Chapter 9) and when Gilhooly *et al.* (1999) asked individuals to solve this task whilst thinking aloud, they also found that generally the strategy of means–ends analysis was employed.

DIFFICULTIES IN APPLYING PROBLEM-SOLVING STRATEGIES

One difficulty that we face when attempting to solve certain problems is that we need to be flexible in our choice of strategies and be prepared to depart from strategies that entail moving towards closer approximations of the goal. This was demonstrated in the Hobbits and Orcs problem, where three hobbits and three orcs need to be transported across a river in a boat. The constraints are that the boat can only hold two creatures and the number of orcs on either bank of the river must never exceed the number of hobbits (as the orcs want to eat the hobbits). At one point the problem-solver has to transfer one orc and one hobbit back to the starting point (Figure 8.6), and this move increases the difference between the current state and the goal state. Thomas (1974) found that participants experienced difficulty in making this move. However, participants also took longer and made more mistakes when there were a number of alternative moves that were possible. They were also observed to perform a sequence of moves quite rapidly, then pause for a while, and then perform another sequence of moves, suggesting that to solve the problem several major planning decisions were required.

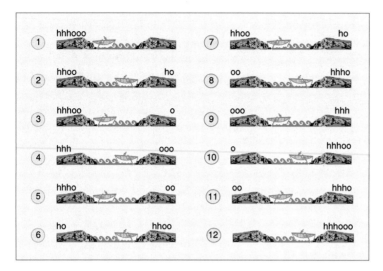

Figure 8.6   The Hobbits (h) and Orcs (o) problem.

Note: Moving from step 6 to step 7 often causes difficulty for problem-solvers as this involves transferring one orc and one hobbit back to the starting point, hence moving away rather than towards the goal.

Simon and Reed (1976) asked their participants to solve a more complex version of the problem and, unlike Thomas (1974), they did not observe extensive forward planning. Participants were observed to make 'local' move-by-move decisions and to shift strategy. They found that initially a balancing strategy was employed, ensuring that there were equal numbers of the creatures being transported on each side of the river. Since this strategy could not result in successful problem solution, participants then switched to a means–ends strategy to move as many to the goal side of the river and, finally, to an anti-looping heuristic which involved avoiding any moves that reversed the immediately preceding move. Thus, to solve this complex version of the problem successfully, participants needed to be flexible and prepared to shift from one strategy to a different strategy.

Another difficulty we face is that we may apply heuristics inappropriately in our attempts to solve a problem (MacGregor *et al.*, 2001; Ormerod *et al.*, 2002; Chronicle *et al.*, 2004). Problem-solvers may adopt a hill-climbing heuristic and therefore select moves that appear to make progress towards the goal state; however, goal properties inferred from the description of the problem may prevent them from making moves that will lead to the solution. For example, in the nine-dot problem (Figure 8.4) the goal inferred is that dots must be cancelled so individuals may evaluate potential moves according to the criterion that each line must cancel a number of dots given by ratio of dots remaining to lines available. This is easy for the first three moves as it is possible to cross out three dots with the first line and two with the next two lines, and because these criterion-meeting moves are available within the square shape of the dot array, solution attempts then stay within that square shape. Only by looking several moves ahead, and realising that by the fourth move the criterion cannot be met, might problem-solvers realise that alternative moves have to be selected, ones which involve extending some lines beyond the nine-dot square. This progress-monitoring explanation, involving the assessment of criterion-meeting moves, therefore provides one explanation for the processes underlying insight.

Problem solution is not, however, simply dependent on our choice of strategy. Asking individuals to verbalise their thoughts as they undertake such problem-solving tasks appears to have a positive effect, and different explanations for this have been put forward, including that it causes participants to 'stop and think' about the problem and that it focuses their attention on salient features of the problem. Davies (2000) found that unless directed at specific evaluation of moves, verbalisation *per se* did not lead to improvements in problem-solving performance (and such evaluation processes could take place non-verbally). Furthermore, explicitly asking participants to evaluate the success of a move immediately after making that move did not just enhance problem-solving performance (when the task was well-structured) but also appeared to help problem-solvers develop an explicit representation of the task. Next, the importance of problem representation is explored in more detail.

PROBLEM REPRESENTATION

How individuals represent the problem initially is an important factor influencing solution. They are influenced by the language used to describe the problem as there is evidence suggesting that participants construct a representation of a problem that is very similar to the wording of the problem's instructions (Hayes and Simon, 1974). Past experience can be of benefit as it may bias the initial representation of a problem in particular ways and, in turn, this initial representation will activate potentially useful knowledge, for example about strategies, operators and constraints (Ohlsson, 1992). However, sometimes the initial (and often unconscious) activitation of prior knowledge can be hindrance. One explanation for this is that it leads to a representation of the problem that does not permit a workable solution. Then an impasse will occur, a sort of mental 'blank' or block that is accompanied by a subjective feeling of not knowing what to do. This impasse can be broken by altering the representation of the problem. This may sound familiar as earlier it was noted that the Gestalt approach saw the process of some problem-solving as requiring the reorganising or restructuring of the elements of the problem situation, known as insight. This explanation is referred to as the representational-change account of insight, and is an alternative to the progress-monitoring explanation described earlier. As you will read next, this representational-change explanation proposes that insight involves unique processes.

Ohlsson (1992) made several proposals regarding how restructuring might occur and these have been tested and developed further by Knoblich *et al.* (1999). For example, 'chunk decomposition' and 'constraint relaxation' are two processes by which problem representations can be changed. Familiarity with certain objects or events can result in the abstraction of a pattern or chunk of components or features, and to solve a problem we may need to change the way this information has been encoded. Knoblich *et al.* suggest that the probability of re-encoding a piece of information is an inverse function of how tightly the information is chunked in the current representation; if the chunks are loose then it is possible to decompose the inappropriate chunks into their component features. Familiarity with a task or event can

Key Term
Impasse A sort of mental 'blank' experienced when trying to solve a problem, which is accompanied by a subjective feeling of not knowing what to do.

also mean that constraints are inferred which may hinder problem solution. Knoblich *et al.* (1999: 1535) suggest that

> *to understand a problem is, in part, to understand what does and does not count as a solution .... For example, opening a door is normally subject to the constraint that the door should not become damaged in the process.*

Therefore, constraint relaxation can help overcome an impasse by making the requirements of the task less restrictive than initially assumed.

Knoblich *et al.* (1999) devised matchstick algebra problems to test their predictions. Each problem is presented in Roman numerals using matchsticks and these make up a numerical equation which can be made equal by moving a single matchstick. Some were predicted to be easier than others because they required the relaxation of fewer constraints and the decomposition of relatively loose chunks, and indeed the results were consistent with their predictions in terms of both solution times and rates.

An example of a problem requiring chunk decomposition is VI = VII + I. This could be solved by moving one matchstick from VII to VI to produce VII = VI + I. More difficult is XI = III + III, because here the 'X' has to be broken into two slanted matchsticks to form the 'V' to make VI = III + III. An example of a problem requiring constraint relaxation is when more is required than just a change to a number value: I = II + II. This could be solved by removing one stick from the plus sign and hence changing addition into subtraction and then adding that stick to the first term to the right of the equal sign, thus producing I = III {min} II. Eye movement data have provided support for these two processes (Knoblich *et al.*, 2001) and further research has confirmed that the difficulty in solving these problems is due to constraint relaxation and the degree of representational change rather than the use of inappropriate heuristics (Öllinger *et al.*, 2006). Oddly enough, patients with damage to the lateral frontal cortex performed better than healthy control participants at solving matchstick problems requiring a constraint relaxation (Reverberi *et al.*, 2005b); the explanation provided is that this part of the brain is involved in defining responses suitable for a task and then biasing them for selection. The involvement of the frontal lobes in problem-solving is discussed in detail in Chapter 9.

Öllinger *et al.* (2008) have used the matchstick problems to explore the interplay between mental set and insight. As mentioned earlier, mental set occurs when applying repeatedly a successful method makes one 'blind' to an alternative and possibly much simpler method. Öllinger *et al.* looked at the effects of set using the two types of matchstick insight problems described earlier, one requiring chunk decomposition and the other constraint relaxation, and non-insight matchstick problems that could be solved without representational change by manipulating what they refer to as a 'loose chunk' that conforms to prior knowledge, for example VIII = VI + IV can be solved by moving the vertical stick from 'VI' to the left side, producing the solution VIII = IV + IV. They found that solving problems using prior knowledge which did not require a representational change (the non-insight problems) did not hinder the solution of those that did require a representational change (the insight problems). However, repeatedly solving problems requiring a chunk decomposition representational change impeded the solution of problems that required a constraint relaxation representational change. Also, repeatedly solving problems involving constraint relaxation inhibited the solution of both non-insight problems and those involving chunk decomposition. Therefore mental set effects were found only when the first set of problems to be solved required a different representational change to the later problems.

Öllinger *et al.* argued that a two-process model is necessary to account for this interplay between mental set and insight. The first process involves representational change which leads to a particular procedure being selected to solve a problem. The second process then takes place where the selection of the procedure is reinforced when it is used repeatedly, assuming it is successful. When non-insight problems are encountered, the first process is skipped and if an insight problem follows the representational change process will have to be applied first. Therefore first solving non-insight problems will not hinder the subsequent solution of insight problems. However, solving insight problems using one particular representational change process will inhibit the solution of subsequent insight problems if these need to be solved via a different form of representational change.

In summary, research on problem-solving has revealed that well-defined problems are often solved strategically by the use of certain heuristics. Studies have also sought to understand the difficulties that may arise when applying these heuristics. Past experience may benefit or hinder problem solution, and in the case of the latter an impasse or block will occur. The representational change approach provides a way of bringing together the Gestalt notion of restructuring with the information-processing notion of representing a problem in a problem space; by amending or adding new information about the problem to the problem space the constraints about what is permissible are relaxed and an impasse can be broken. The role that past experience can play is considered further in the next section.

8.4 PROBLEM-SOLVING BY ANALOGY

The discussion of problem-solving has so far focused on well-defined problems, where the problems are well specified and, like puzzles, the knowledge required to find the solution is present in the instructions given. The heuristics used to solve them have been termed 'general-purpose' or 'domain-independent' in that they can be applied to a wide range of situations or domains and do not involve specific knowledge of the domain. Frequently, in everyday life, the problems

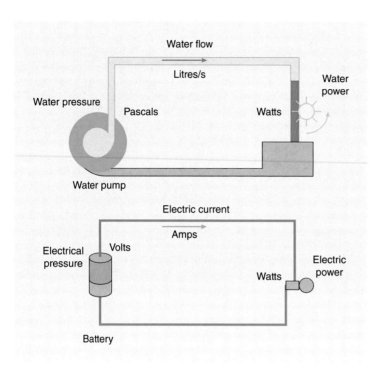

Figure 8.7   Analogy of electricity and water flow.

we face are either new or not well defined, but may resemble in some way a problem that we have previously encountered, and drawing on that by analogy may help us. The use of analogy in solving problems has been of considerable interest since the early 1980s, and understanding how useful knowledge might be transferred from one task to another is important for educational purposes.

Gentner and Gentner (1983) were among the first to consider how analogies might assist the way problems are solved. Participants learning how electricity flowed through the wires of an electrical circuit were taught either with a water-flow analogy or with a moving-crowd analogy. Then, they were presented with battery and resistor problems. In the water-flow analogy (Figure 8.7), participants were told that the flow of electricity was like water flowing through pipes, with water pressure acting like voltage and flow rate like current. They were able to use this analogy to understand the effects of combining batteries, as separate batteries could be modelled by separate sources of water pressure. In the moving-crowd analogy, participants were told that the flow of electricity was like a crowd of people moving through a passage and this group subsequently showed a better understanding when presented with resistor problems than with battery problems. They could see a resistor as analogous to a turnstile and the electric current as analogous to the rate of movement of people.

The processes of analogy or analogical mapping can be broken down into three phases (see Anolli *et al.*, 2001). First, the problem to be solved, the target problem, has to be interpreted and represented and here language comprehension plays a role. Second, a possibly useful source analogue has to be selected and retrieved from long-term memory. Third, some similarity between source analogue and target problem has to be noted and the elements of the source analogue mapped onto the target problem. This mapping is most successful when the best set of correspondences is found between source analogue and target problem. The novel information provided by the source allows inferences to be drawn and transferred. It might be the case that the target problem is in an unfamiliar domain, so that the problem-solver will transfer as much as possible. Alternatively, the mapping may involve matching relationships rather than conveying new knowledge. A final phase in which schema induction takes place has also been hypothesised. Gick and Holyoak (1983) proposed that when we are provided with two examples of one type of problem, we will extract a schema based on their similarity or dissimilarity; this schema then assists analogical transfer and hence the successful solving of similar problems in the future.

ARE ANALOGIES SPONTANEOUSLY USED TO SOLVE PROBLEMS?

The key problem identified in the literature is that unfortunately this potentially very helpful analogical transfer does not always occur. Providing source information is, in itself, not sufficient to induce participants to solve a new problem analogically. For example, Gick and Holyoak (1980) used Duncker's (1945) tumour problem. To solve this problem medical knowledge is not useful. The problem concerns a patient who has a malignant tumour that cannot be operated on. The tumour can only be removed by radiation, but radiation destroys healthy tissue at the same rate as diseased tissue. The solution is to direct a number of weaker rays towards the tumour so that they combine to destroy only the tumour. Gick and Holyoak (1980) found that presenting a completely different story, from a completely different domain of knowledge, could facilitate solution by analogy as both stories were structurally similar. In the General story, a General is attempting to attack a fortress which is well defended and can only be reached by a number of different roads. Each of these roads is mined and can only be crossed safely by a small group of men. The General splits his force into small groups, which approach simultaneously from different directions to converge at the fortress and win the battle. There was, however, little spontaneous use of the analogy; participants had to be provided with a cue as to how this different story was relevant. Similarly, Anolli *et al.* (2001) found in seven experiments that unless invited to relate the previously presented information to the target problem, by way of a 'hint', participants do not spontaneously transfer information from the source analogue to the target problem, even when this source has been activated. They conclude 'it seems that analogical problem-solving is not an automatic process, but it requires controlled attempts to relate the target to a prior source' (p. 258).

Structural similarity, which refers to the underlying relations among the objects shared by the source and target problems (such as Duncker's tumour problem and the General story), has been contrasted with superficial similarity, which refers to objects and their properties, story protagonists or story lines that are common to both the source and target problems. Many laboratory studies have shown that participants tend to draw on source analogues that are superficially similar to the target and have difficulty when they are structurally similar. For example, Keane (1987) found that when presented with a problem about a stomach tumour, participants were more likely to benefit from a story about destroying a brain tumour than the General story. More recent findings, however, suggest that people can and do use analogical sources that do not have superficial features in common with the target. In a naturalistic study, Blanchette and Dunbar (2001) identified 234 analogies when looking in newspapers during the final week of a referendum campaign in Canada, suggesting that analogy is prevalent in political discourse. Over 75 per cent of the source analogues were based on higher-order relationships and structural features rather than on superficial features, and were taken from a range of source categories (including family, agriculture, sport and magic) with only 24 per cent from politics. As analogy appeared twice as many times in opinion articles than in news reports, they suggest analogies are often used in argumentative political discourse. Using a 'generation paradigm', Blanchette and Dunbar (2000) gave participants a target political problem (relating to cuts in public spending) and asked them to produce the source analogues themselves. They found that not only were most of the analogies generated (80 per cent) non-political or non-financial, but also relatively few were based on superficial similarities and instead had structural similarities. Asking people to generate analogies therefore appears to encourage participants to search their memory for relational, structurally similar sources.

Using a naturalistic context, Chen et al. (2004) found that people can use a source analogue even after a substantial time interval and that there was both explicit and implicit retrieval and use of the remote analogy. Their participants were able to draw on folk tales heard during their childhood to solve a target problem; even those participants who claimed that they were not reminded of the source tale outperformed a control group. They also noted that when a common solution tool is shared by both problems, then it was easier for participants to choose this tool to solve a target problem by mapping it to the source analogue. Other studies have shown that there are indeed pragmatic constraints which influence the use of a source analogue. For example, Keane (1990) provided participants with one of two versions of a story about a fire and then asked them to solve Maier's two-string problem. The story describes two ways in which a helicopter was used to save people trapped on the upper floors of a burning skyscraper. Which method failed and which was successful was reversed in the two versions. Participants typically used the successful method as a source analogue for the string problem, irrespective of its specific content, confirming the importance of pragmatic goals in problem-solving.

COMPARING EXPERTS AND NOVICES

Bearman et al. (2007) looked to see if there was a difference in the extent to which domain experts and novices would show evidence of problem-solving by analogy. See Box 8.1, which outlines some early findings on expertise.

Box 8.1   Expertise

Summarised here are the findings of several early widely cited studies suggesting that expertise might depend upon the acquisition and organisation in long-term memory of domain-relevant knowledge. This knowledge allows experts to process information at a deeper level than novices and make use of the underlying relational structure of information in their problem-solving.

Studies have looked at chess and examined why grandmasters play chess better than others. De Groot (1965) collected protocols from some of the best chess players and examined their memories for chess positions. De Groot found that rather than spend time considering and discarding alternative moves, the grandmasters usually selected the best move within the first five seconds of looking at the board, and then spent fifteen minutes checking the correctness of the move. Their prior knowledge allowed them to avoid considering irrelevant moves. This contrasts with weaker players who selected their best move after much thought, a move which

was not as good as that of the grandmaster. The two groups of players seemed to differ in the way they perceived the chess positions, as grandmasters were found to accurately reconstruct a chess position from memory after only five seconds of study. When doing so they repositioned the pieces in small groups, placing four or five pieces on the board, then pausing and then positioning another four or five pieces. In other words, the grandmasters seemed to remember the chess board in chunks. Other research has shown that the grandmasters do not simply have better memories. If the pieces were arranged in a random way, in non-legal configurations of chess pieces, then the performance of the grandmasters and weaker players was comparable (Chase and Simon, 1973a).

Studies of novices and experts solving physics problems have also demonstrated the importance of specific knowledge structures or schematic knowledge. Chi *et al.* (1981) gave expert physicists and novices the task of categorising problems in mechanics. They found that novices tended to group problems together that shared the same key words or objects, for example pulleys, springs, friction or ramps. Experts, on the other hand, classified problems according to the principles involved, for example the conservation of energy principle or Newton's laws. The experts would solve the problems four times faster than novices despite the fact that they would spend more time analysing and understanding the problems by drawing on their available knowledge.

Bearman *et al.* (2007) were interested in seeing whether experts, given their larger pool of domain-relevant knowledge, would more readily than novices draw on source analogues to solve a new problem. The domain chosen was management science, and the participants included undergraduates as management novices and postdoctoral academics as management experts. The frequency with which each group used analogies to tackle business-case problems was compared, alongside the structural complexity of these analogies. Each group was solving these problems either as part of their studies (the novices) or as part of a workshop (the experts). The findings showed no major differences between the two groups of participants. Both novices and experts used analogies spontaneously in their problem-solving to a similar extent, and in both groups the analogies tended to be of similar structural complexity. They also revealed that the analogies used when tackling the business cases served two main functions, one of which was problem-solving and the other illustration (e.g. to draw parallels between two companies). Moreover, the structure of the analogical mapping tended to change depending on the function. Those used for illustration often involved the mapping of more superficial features, whereas those used to solve problems tended to involve relational mapping, with the higher-order relationships involving 'cause' being the most dominant (e.g. 'If A sells B, then this causes X to increase Y').

Based on their findings, Bearman *et al.* (2007) suggest that in the real world unprompted analogising may be a generic problem-solving strategy that all (both novices and experts) are able to use. However, they point out that it is possible that some real-world domains allow us to more usefully draw on everyday knowledge than others. Their study, and those of Blanchette and Dunbar described earlier, looked at the fields of business management and political science where a considerable amount of non-specialist knowledge can be used to help the problem- solvers arrive at solutions. Further research is needed to explore the extent to which spontaneous analogical reasoning occurs across the range of applied domains.

ENCOURAGING THE USE OF ANALOGIES TO SOLVE PROBLEMS

Another line of research has focused on how to promote the use of analogies in problem-solving. Loewenstein *et al.* (2003) asked masters of management (MBA) students and middle-level sales managers to compare two analogous negotiation training cases and found they were more likely to transfer a useful strategy to a novel negotiation situation than a similar group who were asked to look at these cases separately. One possible explanation is that comparison helps to reveal the common relational structure, leading to schema abstraction, whereas studying cases one at a time promotes a more concrete, context-specific encoding which then obscures the deeper similarities to the novel situation. Similar findings have been observed in a number of other studies, for example one involving novices learning negotiation strategies (Gentner *et al.*, 2003).

To explore the effects of comparison further, Kurtz and Loewenstein (2007) asked participants to compare two structurally similar unsolved problems to see if that helped them to retrieve an analogous previously read story. They established that undertaking this comparison was beneficial in terms of facilitating analogical retrieval, and a control group who engaged in comparison but did not receive the analogous story were less successful. Their findings showed that comparison was indeed crucial as asking participants to solve the two problems separately was found to be ineffective. The authors suggest that comparison leads to a more abstract understanding of the two problems to be solved and to the formation of a problem schema, which in turn allows access to the story encoded in memory that matched the two problems structurally. So here the schema acted as a memory probe helping to retrieve a relevant example from memory.

Bearman *et al.* (2011) have also explored how knowledge transfer might be promoted, but rather than ask participants to engage in *comparison* they asked them to undertake *evaluation*. They expected evaluation to have a similar beneficial effect, particularly as previous research has shown that asking participants to *explain* material to either themselves or others has both a beneficial effect on later recall and use of that material (e.g. Chi *et al.*, 1989). However, the findings from all four experiments reported pointed to a consistently detrimental effect. The explanation they offered is that participants who were asked to evaluate over-elaborated and thereby produced more extraneous information, for example on wider issues beyond the information provided, which then impaired recall of the useful analogous information. As the authors point out such a negative effect of evaluation has implications for techniques used to encourage successful problem-solving.

In summary, research on problem-solving by analogy has provided some clues as to how we might benefit from drawing on stored knowledge. Unprompted analogising may well be another generic problem-solving strategy available to us all and not just experts, at least in certain domains, and research has begun to reveal how best to encourage the use of analogies to solve problems. The remainder of this chapter will now focus on a particular set of problems that are reasoning problems.

8.5 DEDUCTIVE AND INDUCTIVE REASONING

There are three main criteria for deciding that an individual is engaging in problem-solving activities (Anderson, 1980), and a great variety of tasks meet these:

1. The activities must be goal-directed, i.e. the individual attempts to attain a particular end state.
2. The attainment of the goal or solution must involve a sequence of mental processes rather than just one.
3. These processes should be discernibly cognitive.

In most research on reasoning, participants are asked to solve problems which have a well-defined structure based on formal logic. This qualifies as problem-solving, since the behaviour of anyone tackling these problem is goal-directed and the task solution requires a number of intervening cognitive processes.

Key Term

Deductive reasoning task
A problem that has a well-defined structure in a system of formal logic where the conclusion is certain.

Inductive reasoning task
A problem that has a well-defined structure in a system of formal logic where the conclusion is highly probable but not necessarily true.

Research has looked at both deductive and inductive reasoning. The distinction between these is that whereas with deductive reasoning the conclusion is certain, with inductive reasoning the conclusion is highly probable. Inductive reasoning entails reaching conclusions which the participant cannot be certain are true, and in this sense the conclusion may be regarded as a hypothesis, the validity of which would have to be tested. For example, participants are often presented with specific instances to come up with a generalised or universal statement that would apply to *all* unknown instances. Deductive reasoning entails problems for which a normative solution is available, namely that required by the logical systems, and the participants' responses can be measured as either correct or incorrect against such a criterion. For example, participants are given certain statements or premises and the task is to decide whether the conclusion that follows is valid according to the laws of deductive logic. Consider the following where the conclusion is valid as this follows logically from the premises, the first of which is a universal statement:

Premise 1   All dogs are animals.
Premise 2   The Border Collie is a dog.
Conclusion   The Border Collie is an animal.

Much of the research that was conducted in the 1970s sought to examine whether individuals reason using formal rules such as logical calculus and to identify the particular rules that were used. In general, research found our reasoning to differ from that prescribed by a system of formal logic and that according to logic we make errors, although not always if the content is drawn from everyday life. Before examining the key studies that were conducted and the type of errors that have been revealed, it is worth noting that the errors should not be considered to reflect unintelligent behaviour. Evans (1989) wrote that

> *errors of thinking occur because of, rather than in spite of, the nature of our intelligence. In other words, they are an inevitable consequence of the way in which we think and a price to be paid for the extraordinary effectiveness with which we routinely deal with the massive information-processing requirements of everyday life.*

(p. 111)

INDUCTIVE REASONING: HYPOTHESIS GENERATION

Most of the reasoning in our daily lives would be classed as inductive rather than deductive reasoning. Inductive reasoning has been investigated by looking at the processes of hypothesis generation. One area of research relates to concept learning, which does not entail concept formation (how classes or categories are constructed) but concept attainment or identification, the search for attributes or qualities that are associated with a particular concept. In experiments, several stimuli will be identified as either positive or negative instances of the concept. The participant has to use the accumulating information from the positive and negative instances to decide what the concept is. Bruner *et al.* (1956) were the first to conduct research on concept learning, which demonstrated that we seem to select logical strategies when confronted with an inductive reasoning task. Which strategy is adopted, however, will depend on a range of factors, including the complexity of the problem and the cognitive skills of the person adopting the strategy. A tendency towards verifying rather than falsifying was initially observed in the way we seek to test the hypotheses we form.

In a classic study, Wason (1960) informed participants that the three numbers '2 4 6' conformed to a simple relational rule (three numbers in increasing order of magnitude). Participants were then asked to generate sets of three numbers and to explain why they had chosen that set of three numbers. The experimenter in turn indicated whether each set conformed to the rule. Participants were told that when they thought they had discovered the correct rule, they were to reveal it. Wason found that most participants would generate a hypothesis, often a less general one such as 'increasing even numbers', and then seek to generate sets of numbers that were consistent with the hypothesis. Only 21 per cent of participants guessed the rule correctly with their first attempt. Most participants did not attempt to disconfirm the hypothesis, even though doing so would allow them to test its correctness. In a later study, Wason (1968) asked participants how they would determine whether or not their hypotheses were incorrect and only one quarter gave the correct answer. Wason went on to suggest that this confirmation bias is a very general tendency in human thought, and one possible explanation for why prejudices and false beliefs are maintained.

IS CONFIRMATION BIAS A GENERAL TENDENCY?

Support for such a bias has come from studies looking at how evidence might be evaluated or gathered in real-life settings. Wagenaar (1994) looked at how guilt was determined in criminal courts and found evidence of the confirmation bias in operation as he found a preference for verification of guilt rather than falsification. For example, the positive identifications in a line-up by a few witnesses are likely to be believed even though the suspect was not recognised by a large number of other witnesses. Hill *et al.* (2008) looked at the effect of expectations of guilt on how an interviewer might question a suspect, building on earlier studies which had indicated that most interviewers assume suspects to be guilty (e.g. Mortimer and Shepherd, 1999). Hill *et al.* argued that if police officers presume suspects to be guilty, then their questioning may be directed towards finding information to confirm rather than disconfirm this assumption. They explored this possibility in studies with a student population and found that those holding expectations of guilt asked significantly more guilt-presumptive questions than those holding expectations of innocence. They concluded that confirmation bias was evident which in turn could lead to a self-fulfilling prophecy effect.

Does it therefore follow that performance on a reasoning task will improve if participants are taught to engage in disconfirmation? Gorman and Gorman (1984) found that when participants were instructed to use a disconfirmatory strategy using Wason's '2 4 6' task, they performed significantly better than participants instructed to use a confirmatory strategy or no strategy. This was because they tested their hypotheses with a set of three numbers they predicted would be incorrect. Poletiek (1996) also found that asking participants to falsify their hypothesis resulted in them producing number sets that did *not* conform to their hypothesis, however, argues that this (and the findings of Gorman and Gorman, 1984) should be interpreted as actually involving confirmation as the participants were expecting a 'No' response. Poletiek (1996) points out that a successful disconfirming strategy involves confirming rather than falsifying the hypothesis. Wetherick (1962) was the first to point out that choice of strategy should not be confused with confirmation or falsification. If participants choose a set of numbers that would be predicted by their hypothesis then this is confirmatory if participants believe their hypothesis to be correct. Selecting numbers that would not be predicted by their hypothesis and finding that these numbers do not conform to their hypothesis is also confirmatory if participants believe their hypothesis to be correct.

Other research has shown that simply modifying the '2 4 6' task can improve participants' performance considerably, and it is difficult to account for these findings in terms of a general bias towards confirmation. When the task was altered so that participants were provided with a diagram representing each set of numbers they generated, then the success rate on the problem increased to 44 per cent, compared with 21 per cent for those who solved the problem as in the original study (Vallée-Tourangeau and Payton, 2008). A difference in performance was also observed when participants were presented with '2 4 6', and told either that this is an *example* or a *counter-example* of the experimenter's rule ('increasing numbers' vs 'decreasing numbers' respectively): 54 per cent in the counter-example condition discovered the rule with their first attempt compared with only 4 per cent in the other standard example condition (Rossi *et al.*, 2001). It is thought that this is because participants focused on the salient features of the triple number set. The most frequent rule generated by participants in the example condition was 'ascending even numbers', which when tested would elicit positive feedback. In the counter-example condition it was 'ascending odd numbers', which when tested would elicit negative feedback (that the triples they generated did not conform to the experimenter's rule) and this negative feedback was more likely to lead them to revise their hypotheses and solve the problem.

However, the manipulation that altered performance the most was observed by Tweney *et al.* (1980) when asking participants to discover not one but two rules. One rule was 'increasing numbers' and the triple number sets that fitted this rule were named DAX. The other rule was 'any other number sequence' and the triple number sets that fitted this rule were named MED. The number of participants producing the correct answer on their first attempt rose considerably and this finding has been replicated by others, with the dual goal manipulation typically leading to success rates of above 60 per cent. However, whilst the finding is robust there is debate over the reasons that account for this. Gale and Ball (2009) considered three theories offering an explanation and report results supportive of two of these. What is, however, clear now is that a bias towards confirmation is not a sufficient explanation, and instead inductive reasoning is influenced by factors such as working memory constraints and encouragement to test multiple hypotheses.

DEDUCTIVE REASONING

Research on deductive reasoning involves presenting participants with logically valid or invalid arguments. The information required to perform these reasoning tasks is provided in the stimulus material so there is no need for participants to draw on any stored information from long-term memory. An inference is made in the conclusion, and this entails making explicit something that was initially implicit in the premises. The following is one example of a valid deductive inference:

Premise 1	Hannah is older than Francesca.
Premise 2	Joseph is younger than Francesca.
Conclusion	Therefore, Hannah is older than Joseph.

This example simply requires us to know that the relation older–younger is *transitive*, which means that objects can be ordered in a single line (other transitive relations are smaller–larger, warmer–colder and darker–lighter). Another example of a valid deductive inference is:

Premise 1	The kettle will only work if it is switched on.
Premise 2	The kettle is not switched on.
Conclusion	Therefore, the kettle will not work.

This second example simply requires us to understand the connective 'only if' (there are other connectives, for example 'not' and 'and'). The point to note here is that in a logically valid argument only the form of the argument and *not* the actual content is important.

With this sort of deductive reasoning, known as *conditional reasoning*, there are different rules of inference which are described in Box 8.2. The first two show conclusions that are valid and the second two conclusions that are invalid.

So, how accurate are we at responding according to these rules of inference? Research has shown that most of us do not make errors with MP; however, the error rate for MT can exceed 30 per cent, and participants frequently suggest that AC and DA are valid even though

Box 8.2   Rules of inference

Two logically *valid* inferences:

1. *Modus ponens* (MP):

If p then q	If the bell is ringing, then the dog is barking.
p	The bell is ringing.
Therefore q	Therefore, the dog is barking.

2. *Modus tollens* (MT):

If p then q	If the bell is ringing, then the dog is barking.
Not q	The dog is not barking.
Therefore not p	Therefore, the bell is not ringing.

Two logically *invalid* inference patterns:

1. *Affirming the consequent* (AC):

If p then q	If the bell is ringing, then the dog is barking.
q	The dog is barking.
Therefore	p Therefore, the bell is ringing.

2. *Denying the antecedent* (DA):

If p then q	If the bell is ringing, then the dog is barking.
Not p	The bell is not ringing.
Therefore not q	Therefore, the dog is not barking.

both are invalid (Evans, 1989). In relation to AC, the bell does not have to be ringing for the dog to be barking; a letter might have been delivered instead. In relation to DA, equally, just because the bell is not ringing, does not mean the dog is not barking. Schroyens and Schaeken (2003) combined the data from a large number of experiments showing participants 'if p, then q' statements. They found that 97 per cent of participants endorsed the conclusion when the inference type was MP and 72 per cent when the inference type was MT. However, 63 per cent of participants erroneously endorsed the conclusion when the inference type was AC and 55 per cent when it was DA.

One key reason why people make errors is that they go beyond the information provided and draw on their existing knowledge and personal beliefs about whether and to what extent p is necessary or sufficient for q. Byrne (1989) found that additional information can reduce acceptance of MP. The classic example is provided next, showing three rather than two premises:

A   If she has an essay to write, she will study late in the library.
B   If the library stays open, she will study late in the library.
C   She has an essay to write.

People know that when the library does not stay open late, her having an essay to write is a moot consideration, so adding B lowers the certainty of A and so lowers the acceptance of the MP conclusion 'She will study late in the library'. Byrne's findings have been replicated and extended in later research.

Other research has also highlighted the importance of the content of the problem and how this is interpreted. For example: Evans *et al.* (1983) found that 71 per cent of participants accepted invalid arguments when the conclusion was believable. Newstead *et al.* (1997) found that type of content, whether the conditional statements were expressed in the form of promises, tips, threats or warnings, had a marked influence on how participants responded respond to rules of inference. Stevenson and Over (2001) found that when a premise was provided by an expert, it was perceived as more likely and as more believable than when provided by a novice. These findings suggest people do not reason according to formal rules and this issue is explored further in relation to a particular deductive reasoning task that has been the subject of much research.

WASON'S FOUR-CARD SELECTION TASK

Another very famous task devised by Wason (1960) is known as the four-card selection task (Figure 8.8). Four cards are shown with A, K, 2 and 7 printed on them. The following rule is given: 'If there is an A on one side of the card, then there is a 2 on the other side of the card.' Participants are told to select only those cards that would need to be turned over in order to decide whether or not the rule is correct. The A card (*modus ponens*) and the 7 card (*modus tollens*) is the correct answer which was selected by very few. There is nothing to be gained by turning the 2 card over (affirmation of the consequent), since the rule does not claim that an A must be on the other side of a 2. The robustness of these findings has been demonstrated in subsequent work and typical results are that as few as 4 per cent of participants choose the correct answer, 46 per cent choose A and 2 cards, 33 per cent choose the A card only and 7 per cent choose A, 2 and 7 cards (Johnson-Laird and Wason, 1970).

Sometimes the selection of cards follows closely that which logic would prescribe. Reasoning is facilitated by the use of concrete and meaningful material (e.g. Wason and Shapiro, 1971; Johnson-Laird *et al.*, 1972), when the problem relates directly to the participant's own experience (Griggs and Cox, 1982), and by analogous rather than direct experience (Griggs and Cox, 1983). There are also individual differences among participants, with those following the logically correct solution having the highest general ability scores (Newstead *et al.*, 2004). However, a key focus

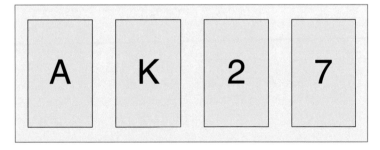

Figure 8.8   The Wason selection task.

Source: Adapted from Wason (1960).

Note: The rule is 'If there is an A on one side of the card, then there is a 2 on the other side of the card.' Select only those cards that would need to be turned over in order to decide whether or not the rule is correct. Each card has a letter on one side and a number on the other.

for many studies has been on uncovering what determines the selection of cards. Originally, Wason explained the choice of cards in terms of a confirmation bias; that participants were trying to confirm rather than disconfirm the rule. However, an alternative explanation is that participants selected A and 2 because they were biased towards those items mentioned in the rule, i.e. there was a 'matching bias' (Evans and Lynch, 1973). Linguistic cues to relevance determine which cards the participants attend to and hence those they will consider for selection. Support for the explanation was offered by modifying the rule as follows: 'If there is an A on one side of the card, then there is NOT a 2 on the other side of the card.' Most participants would correctly select A and 2. They also incorrectly selected these cards when the rule was: 'If there is not an A on one side of the card, then there is a 2 on the other side of the card.' The correct response is K and 7.

Evans and Over (2004) combined the data from several experiments that attempted to disentangle a matching bias from the use of logic, and found evidence for matching bias, but also evidence for an effect of logic too. So, a single explanation is insufficient. Evans and Ball (2010) reanalysed eye-movement tracking data which showed the cards participants were inspecting. Again these showed that whilst those cards that matched the items mentioned in the rule were inspected for approximately equal lengths of time, their selection rates were strongly affected by their logical status too. Participants were not always selecting the card they looked at. Evans and Ball conclude that the findings from their reanalysis provides support for a particular account of reasoning that involves both analytic reasoning processes as well as heuristic processes. This account, along with other key theories of reasoning, are outlined next.

8.6 THEORETICAL APPROACHES TO REASONING

There is a considerable number of theoretical approaches that have been proposed to explain reasoning. Outlined next are the key approaches, which vary in a number of different ways. They differ in their emphasis on linguistic/syntactic as opposed to visuo-spatial factors; some focus on conditional reasoning, whereas others provide a more general explanation of deductive and inductive reasoning, and the extent to which the theories address reasoning in everyday life also varies. Also, as you will read, some advocate more than one set of processes.

MENTAL LOGIC THEORIES

Mental logic theories (e.g. Braine and O'Brien, 1991), also known as formal rule theories, assume that our reasoning when making inferences is underpinned by the use of mental rules. Three parts are proposed: a set of inference schemas, a reasoning program that selects the appropriate inference schemas to be used at each point during reasoning, and a set of pragmatic principles that influence how the problem statements are interpreted and which are therefore important when the problems are not neutral in content. The inference schema selected will identify the conclusion that can be drawn from the information provided, for example when presented with *modus ponens*: if *p* then *q* and *p*. These schemas are therefore similar to some of the rules of formal logic, although the theories allow for the fact that we make errors and accept erroneous conclusions, and may not possess all the formal logical rules.

Braine *et al.* (1984) suggested that errors may also occur because of failures of comprehension; we expect to find all the information we need to know. If we are told, 'If the bell is ringing, then the dog is barking' then we will assume that it is just a bell ringing that makes the dog bark. Braine *et al.* (1984) showed that if we are provided with an additional premise, then we are less likely to consider the following affirmation of the consequent valid:

Premise 1   If the bell is ringing, then the dog is barking.
Premise 2   If the child is laughing, then the dog is barking.
Premise 3   The dog is barking.
Conclusion   Therefore, the bell is ringing.

Although all people are thought to have a repertory of abstract rules that they can use, additional schemas can be acquired through experience or when tutored in standard logic, accounting for individual differences. In the Wason selection task, participants will try to apply logical inference rules to the sides of the cards that are visible to predict what logically should be on the non-visible side. If they do not possess the *modus tollens* rule, then they would only select card A and typically 33 per cent select just card A.

As described earlier, Byrne (1989) found that providing additional information can reduce acceptance of *modus ponens* – that information about additional requirements can *suppress* logically valid inferences is known as the suppression effect – and although mental logic theories can provide explanations for such findings, it does not seem to be the case that our everyday conclusions are either endorsed or not. Instead, they appear to have a property known as 'non-monotonicity', which refers to how we constantly revise our everyday conclusions when we get new evidence.

PRAGMATIC REASONING SCHEMATA

The idea that we reason not according to formal deductive criteria, but instead on the basis of what we know or believe, is encapsulated in the notion of pragmatic reasoning schemata. Cheng and colleagues (Cheng and Holyoak, 1985; Cheng *et al.*, 1986) have argued that we develop abstract rules for reasoning from our experiences in many different domains, but these are not at a logical or syntactic level but at a pragmatic level. People often reason using pragmatic reasoning schemata, which are clusters of rules that are highly generalised and abstracted but defined with respect to different types of relationships and goals. For example, in our everyday lives we are exposed to situations involving permission (we need certain qualifications for certain professions), and these are situations in which some action A may be taken only if some precondition B is satisfied. Cheng *et al.* (1986) explain that if we encounter a problem where the semantic aspects suggest that this is a permission situation then all of the rules about permissions in general can be called on, including 'If action A is to be taken, then precondition B must be satisfied', 'Action A is to be taken only if precondition B is satisfied', 'If precondition B is not satisfied, then action A must not be taken', and so on. We are also exposed to situations involving obligation (if our child is ill for a while, we must inform the school they attend), and from these we note that the occurrence of some condition A incurs the necessity of taking some action B. Cheng *et al.* (1986) point out that rules about obligations are not quite the same but similar to rules about permissions. The rule 'If condition A occurs, then obligation B arises' implies 'If obligation B does not arise, then condition A must not have occurred', but not 'Condition A occurs only if obligation B arises'.

The rules of some of the pragmatic reasoning schemata will lead to the same solution as the rules of standard logic. Therefore, we will *appear* to provide responses that would be classified as logical. However, the underlying process has not entailed the application of logical rules, and errors will arise when the rules of the schemata differ from those that follow from standard logic. Of relevance here is that the 'abstract permission rule' will allow us to solve Wason's selection task, but this rule needs to be invoked by the rules stated in the task, and this is unlikely to occur with the standard abstract version of the task. Instead, we can solve versions of the task even if we do not have the direct experience of the rules, as long as the rules can be rationalised as giving permissions. Pragmatic reasoning schemata can also account for why the content and context of the reasoning task is important. Although this approach has been explored in research looking at a number of different issues including training and rule acquisition, in contrast to the remaining approaches discussed here it has not received much attention over the last decade.

MENTAL MODELS

Another theory that provides an alternative account to the mental logic theories is that of mental models. Rather than argue that our deductive reasoning is logical when we find the correct solution and illogical when we find the wrong one, Johnson-Laird (1983) suggested that we either use the appropriate mental model or an inappropriate one. We construct the mental model or representation according to what is described in the premises and this will depend on how these are interpreted. We can use imagery to create this representation, imagining possibilities or models. For example, according to the following set of premises:

The milk is to the right of the margarine.
The yoghurt is to the left of the milk.
The cheese is in front of the milk.
The cream is to the left of the cheese.

We could imagine the food on a shelf in a fridge laid out as:

margarine	yoghurt	milk
	cream	cheese

From this mental model we could conclude that the cream is in front of the yoghurt, even though this is not explicitly stated in the premises. To test this we would need to search for an alternative model that would also fit these premises; if none is found then we can stick with that conclusion. However, a search would yield an alternative model, namely:

yoghurt	margarine	milk
	cream	cheese

We would have to conclude that we are not sure whether the margarine or the yoghurt is behind the cream.

This approach distinguishes between first comprehending the premises, and secondly reasoning with the models. If we are not trained in logic, then we will find it difficult to reason with negation. Johnson-Laird *et al.* (1992) found that negation could either affect comprehension or it could affect reasoning. The statement 'It is not the case that there is no cream in the fridge' is difficult to comprehend and takes longer to comprehend than its logical equivalent 'There is cream in the fridge'. However, once the premises have been understood and represented as mental models, then reasoning will depend on whether you have searched for all possible models. For example, 'It is not the case there is cheese or there is yoghurt' only needs one mental model:

no cheese	no yoghurt

However, the statement: 'It is not the case that there is both cheese and yoghurt' actually yields three models:

1. no cheese yoghurt	2. cheese no yoghurt	3. no cheese no yoghurt

So although negation makes comprehension difficult, it is the number of mental models which have to be considered that makes reasoning more difficult. The limits of our working memory restrict the number of models that we can construct and hold in our working memory.

Errors occur if more than one model has to be constructed to allow us to reach a valid conclusion and it is suggested that we shy away from doing so, providing instead a conclusion that is true according to our initial model. Also, to minimise the load on working memory, the mental models we construct will tend to represent the what is true and not what is false, and there is evidence to support this (e.g. Legrenzi *et al.*, 2003).

The mental models theory has been refined and extended, increasing its explanatory power (Schaeken *et al.*, 2007), with many researchers applying it to different domains of reasoning and everyday reasoning, and indeed other areas of cognition such as language comprehension, and the notion that we reason by constructing concrete internal representations of situations has intuitive plausibility.

THE PROBABILISTIC APPROACH

Oaksford and Chater (1994, 1998) also proposed that logic does not provide us with an appropriate framework with which to understand people's everyday inferences. They argued that our everyday reasoning is probabilistic and we make errors when presented with logical tasks in the laboratory because we draw on the strategies we use in everyday life. For example, rather than use logical rules to ascertain an inference, we draw on our beliefs and prior experience and assess the likelihood, i.e. the conditional probability, that a certain conclusion is true. In relation to the following: 'If John has a runny nose then he has a cold', Oaksford (2005) explained that accepting this requires

> the belief that John's having a runny nose makes it very likely that he has a cold. This involves assessing the conditional probability that John has a cold given that he has a runny nose. So if you have noticed John having a runny nose on say 100 occasions, 95 of which involved him having a cold, then the relevant conditional probability is 0.95.
>
> (p. 425)

Oaksford and Chater have shown that probabilistic approach can account for participants' performances on deductive inference tasks as well as on Wason's selection task (Oaksford and Chater, 2001), as well as for suppression effects and biases (Oaksford and Chater, 2007). Importantly, this approach to reasoning departs from other explanations in the way it accounts for human rationality. Rather than define rationality as logical reasoning and explain departures from rationality (errors in our reasoning) in terms of performance limitations (e.g. the limited nature of short-term memory), the probabilistic approach defines rationality in terms of probabilistic reasoning. It has recently been extended and revised (Oaksford and Chater, 2009) and will undoubtedly continue to attract attention and stimulate future research.

DUAL-PROCESS ACCOUNTS

There have been attempts to integrate theories of reasoning by proposing a two-way partition in reasoning abilities. where one kind of thinking is often described as fast and intuitive and the other slow and deliberative. Dual-process accounts have been applied not only to reasoning (Evans and Over, 1996; Stanovich and West, 2000) but also to judgement and decision-making (Kahneman and Frederick, 2002) as well as other areas such as learning and social cognition. Those relating to reasoning propose that we do have an (albeit limited) capacity for explicit logical reasoning which is embodied either in mental logic, mental models or probability theory. However, much of our reasoning takes place implicitly and is independent of such logical processes.

How the two-way partition is described has changed as more research has been undertaken. For example, Evans and Over (1996) distinguished between two kinds of rationality; a personal rationality (rationality$_1$), when we are successful in achieving our goals, and an impersonal rationality (rationality$_2$), when we reason according to normative theory (formal logic or probability theory). They argued that whilst we have a considerable amount of the former, we have only a restricted capacity for the latter. Stanovich and West (2000) made a similar distinction between what they termed System 1 and System 2 reasoning processes. The former are automatic, unconscious and based on implicitly acquired world knowledge, whereas the latter are controlled, analytic and based on explicitly acquired formal rules. Using the terms introduced by Stanovich and West, Evans (2003) described System 1 as a form of universal cognition shared by humans and animals. In contrast, System 2 has evolved more recently and is considered to be uniquely human: 'System 2 provides the basis for hypothetical thinking that endows modern humans with unique potential for a higher level of rationality in their reasoning and decision-making' (p. 458). More recently, both Evans and Stanovich have moved away from using the terms System 1 and 2 (to avoid any suggestion that the two systems map explicitly onto two distinct brain systems), and instead they refer to Type 1 and 2 processing or at a higher level to two or more *minds*, and cognitive biases can be attributed to both types of cognition (Evans, 2011).

Importantly, there appears to be some consensus amongst theorists in that most are suggesting we have one form of cognition which is old as it evolved early, is innate or based on experiential learning, and this form operates largely automatically. Research suggests that it functions independently of general intelligence, and by manipulating instructions, time limits and working memory loads, experiments have shown that that it operates independently of working memory. The other form of cognition is newer, is distinctively human, and permits us to engage in rule-based forms of thinking that can solve novel problems. According to experimental research this form of cognition is heavily dependent on working memory and psychometric studies have shown it to be limited by cognitive ability. Studies using neuroscience methods have found that different brain regions are activated depending on the processes in operation. There has also been some discussion as to how these two systems might interact, and how conflict and competition between the two types of processing might be resolved, for example Evans (2009) has described a third type of processing: cognitive control processing, and Thompson (2009) has suggested that metacognitive processes act as a link between the two. However, although dual-process accounts have been developed further over the last decade, and have become increasingly influential, like the other theoretical accounts they have also received a fair amount of criticism. It is also important to note there have been alternative dual-process accounts to those described above where the probabilistic and the mental model accounts have been brought together (Verschueren *et al.*, 2005; Oaksford and Chater, 2010). Fuzzy-trace theory has also been described as being a dual-process approach that is relevant to reasoning and decision-making, and which can account for specific biases and the effects of emotion (Reyna and Brainerd, 2011). So, dual-process accounts are a family of theories concerned with different aspects of cognition and development, and even within the field of reasoning there is no single definitive version.

In summary, research undertaken on reasoning has distinguished between inductive reasoning and deductive reasoning, and has revealed that although we make mistakes on a range of reasoning problems, this does not mean that our thinking is irrational. Instead we may use heuristics or base our reasoning on what is probable drawing on our experience, particularly when dealing with less abstract problems or in our everyday reasoning. The range of theoretical approaches draw attention to different issues and the growth of dual-process accounts reflect the complexity of the findings.

SUMMARY

- This chapter has introduced you to some of the research on problem-solving and reasoning.
- The study of problem-solving has shown that we use a limited number of strategies and heuristics to solve a range of problems and these allow us to work within the limitations of our memory system.
- Successful problem-solving is dependent on how the problem is represented and on prior knowledge as well as the strategies used.
- Our existing knowledge may allow us to solve new problems through analogy; a source analogue is mapped onto the target problem.
- Naturalistic studies have shown that people will use structurally similar source analogues, although when tested in the laboratory analogical problem-solving may not be an automatic process.
- When assessed on tasks involving both inductive and deductive reasoning, often participants do not appear to reason according

to formal logic. Instead, the use of strategies and heuristics is also evident in how we solve reasoning tasks.

- Theories vary with some suggesting that we reason according to formal deductive criteria. Alternative explanations suggest that we use of pragmatic reasoning schemata, or construct mental models or reason using conditional probability.
- Dual-process accounts incorporate several different types of reasoning processes and can account for why some of our reasoning appears to be independent of logical processes and some appears to follow rule-based forms of thinking.

FURTHER READING

- Davidson, J. E. and Sternberg, R. J. (eds) (2003). *The Psychology of Problem Solving*. New York: Cambridge University Press. This edited book includes contributions on a wide range of issues within the specific area of problem-solving, including the representation of problems, expert performance and analogical transfer.
- Evans, J. St. B. T. (2007). *Hypothetical Thinking: Dual Processes in Reasoning and Judgement*. Hove: Psychology Press. This book brings together research on thinking and provides an integrated account of the different phenomena including confirmation bias in hypothesis testing and belief biases in reasoning and judgement. It also looks at characteristic findings in the study of decision-making which is not covered here in this chapter.
- Hastie, R. and Dawes, R. M. (2010). *Rational Choice in an Uncertain World*. Thousand Oaks, CA: Sage. This book will provide you with an insight into the area of decision-making which is not covered in this chapter and which reveals that we do not always use make rational decisions.
- Manktelow, K. I., Over, D. E. and Elqayam, S. (eds) (2011). *The Science of Reason: a Festschrift in Honour of Jonathan St. B. T. Evans*. Hove: Psychology Press. This edited book includes chapters by experts in the field of reasoning, covering probabilistic and causal reasoning, dual-process theory of thought and the nature of human rationality. The volume is in tribute to Jonathan St. B. T. Evans.

Chapter 9

Contents

Disorders of thinking and problem-solving

9

Nicola Brace

9.1 INTRODUCTION

The last chapter looked at research focused on how we solve problems and carry out reasoning tasks. What became clear is that this activity involves a number of operations such as searching, matching, deciding, evaluating and transforming, and successful problem solution sometimes requires the way the problem itself is represented to be restructured. However, it is not just these different problem-solving processes that need to monitored and controlled when we encounter a problem, many of our everyday tasks involve us overseeing a whole range of well-established routines. Think for a moment about all the steps involved in making coffee or cleaning the bath. Exactly how the more complex operations involved in problem-solving and the more routine everyday tasks are controlled is still open to debate; however, it is thought that the frontal lobes play an important role. Luria (1966) suggested that it was the responsibility of the frontal lobes to program and regulate behaviour, and Baddeley (1986) saw the frontal lobes as having a coordinating, monitoring and organising role in working memory. This chapter will consider how damage to the frontal lobes may affect problem-solving, but it will do so by looking more broadly at the role the frontal lobes play in relation to executive functions. These functions are thought to encompass meta-abilities necessary for appropriate social functioning and everyday problem-solving: namely the deployment of attention, the initiation of non-habitual action, goal-directed behaviour, planning, insight, foresight and self-regulation.

A major part of this chapter will outline research looking at the effects of frontal lobe damage on tests involving attention, abstract

> **Key Term**
>
> **Executive functions**
> Meta-abilities necessary for appropriate social functioning and everyday problem-solving, for example the deployment of attention, self-regulation, insight, planning and goal-directed behaviour.

and conceptual thinking, cognitive estimation and strategy formation. First, however, the chapter will look at the anatomy of the frontal lobes and consider the different behavioural deficits seen in patients with frontal lesions. In this first part of the chapter you will be introduced to one of the most famous case studies in psychology, namely that of Phineas Gage.

9.2 ANATOMY AND PHYSIOLOGY OF THE FRONTAL LOBES

The frontal lobes constitute approximately one-third of the mass of each cerebral hemisphere, encompassing all tissue anterior to the central sulcus. It is not surprising, therefore, that patients with damage to the frontal lobes area show a great diversity of impairments that may affect motor, emotional, social or cognitive processes. The lobes comprise a variety of areas which are functionally and anatomically distinct (Figure 9.1) and which can be grouped into three broad categories (Kolb and Whishaw, 1996). The first category is the motor cortex, which was classified by Brodmann as area 4. The second category is the premotor cortex (area 6 and some of area 8), and in humans the lateral premotor area includes Broca's area (area 44). The motor and premotor areas play an important role in the control of limb, hand, foot and digit movements as well as influencing the control of face and eye movements.

The third category is the prefrontal cortex, which in primates can be sub-divided into the dorsolateral prefrontal cortex (areas 9, 46); the ventral (or inferior) prefrontal cortex (areas 11, 12, 13, 14); and the medial frontal cortex (areas 25, 32). Studies conducted in the early decades of the twentieth century revealed rich and complex afferent and efferent connections to a variety of other areas of the brain. The prefrontal cortex receives afferent pathways from the auditory, visual, gustatory, olfactory and somatosensory areas. There are connections to and from many subcortical areas including the limbic system (which plays an important role in arousal, motivation and affect), the caudate nucleus (the part of the basal

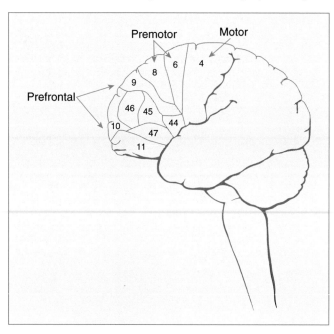

Figure 9.1 The frontal lobes. Lateral view of the brain illustrating the major subdivisions of the frontal lobes.

Note: Areas 12–14, 25 and 32 are not included because they are not visible in a lateral view of the brain.

ganglia involved in the integration, programming, inception and ter-
mination of motor activity) and the amygdala (which is implicated in
the control of fear, rage and aggression).

9.3 THE IMPACT OF FRONTAL LOBE DAMAGE ON BEHAVIOUR

Before looking at specific cognitive deficits that have been linked with
frontal lobe functioning, this section provides an overview of the case
histories of individuals who sustained frontal damage and the range of
behavioural deficits that have been observed. There is great variation
in the functional results of frontal lobe damage, and this was apparent
in studies conducted in the nineteenth and early twentieth centuries.
Many of the changes in behaviour are actually related to lesions in the
prefrontal cortex, and variation is hardly surprising given the size and
complexity of the prefrontal cortex and its many connections to most
brain areas. Some of these early studies will now be described and
these serve to highlight how damage to the frontal lobes can impact
on personality and bring about affective changes.

EARLY CLINICAL STUDIES

Early clinical work revealed wide-ranging changes in personality as a
result of frontal lobe damage. Some found a pattern of aggression, bad
temper and viciousness, whereas others described a lack of concern and
inappropriate cheerfulness. The most famous case is that of
Phineas Gage, described by Harlow (1848, 1868). Prior to
injury, Phineas Gage was a conscientious and industrious
railroad engineer, whose responsibilities included placing and
detonating explosives. A fuse and a tamping iron, an iron bar
3.5 feet long and 13.25 pounds in weight, were used to set
off the explosive. Accidentally, Gage placed the tamping iron
on the explosive, prematurely detonating the explosive, and
the result was that the tamping iron penetrated his skull. It
entered through the side of his face, passed through the left
frontal lobe and exited from the right frontal bone (Figures
9.2 and 9.3; also Macmillan, 1986). Gage survived and the
injury did not appear to have any major long-term effects,
with the exception of a change in his personality. Following
the accident he was no longer reliable or considerate and
showed poor judgement and poor social skills. Harlow (1868)
suggested that these changes in behaviour were a result of the
frontal lobe's responsibility for planning and the maintenance
of socially acceptable behaviour.

A change in personality was noted by Welt (1888) when
reporting the case of a 37-year-old man, presumed drunk,
who had fallen from a fourth-storey window. He suffered a
severe penetrating frontal fracture. Five days after sustaining

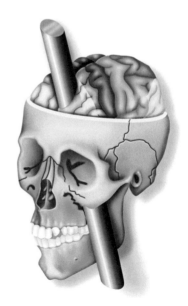

Figure 9.2 Phineas Gage's skull. The entry and exit of the tamping iron are shown here.

Figure 9.3   Phineas Gage.

this injury he showed a change in personality. He went from being an honest, hard-working and cheerful man to being aggressive, malicious and prone to making bad jokes (the term '*Witzelsucht*' was used to describe this addiction to joking). He teased other patients and played mean tricks on the hospital staff. After about a month of such objectionable behaviour, he became his old self, only to die some months later from an infection.

In contrast, Jastrowitz (1888) reported a form of dementia in patients with tumours of the frontal lobe, which was characterised by an oddly cheerful agitation. He used the term '*moria*' (meaning stupidity) to describe this behaviour. Others, including Zacher (1901) and Campbell (1909), emphasised the apathy and lack of concern shown by their patients. Brickner (1936) described a patient whose prefrontal region was almost completely excised in an operation. The fundamental disability that emerged appeared to be a problem with synthesising essentially intact cognitive processes. Ackerly (1937) found no decline in 'general intelligence' in a 37-year-old woman whose entire right prefrontal region had been amputated and left prefrontal region damaged. She also continued to be the same sociable, likeable and kind-hearted person; instead the key change in her behaviour was an abnormal lack of distractibility, so that once she had started a task she had to complete it and could not be made to even temporarily abandon it.

EARLY ANIMAL STUDIES

Early experimental work by physiologists on animals, investigating neural mechanisms, led to a variety of conclusions. Goltz (1892) experimented with dogs and, together with his assistant Loeb (1902), concluded that the prefrontal region did not contain the neural mechanisms underlying intelligence or personality traits. Ferrier (1876) found ablations of the prefrontal region in monkeys to result in changes that were difficult to describe precisely. Despite appearing normal, they seemed more apathetic and less attentive and intelligent. Bianchi (1922) conducted experimental studies on monkeys and dogs across three decades. He found unilateral prefrontal ablations to be without effect and, whilst bilateral ablations did not result in any sensory or motor defects, they did result in marked changes in character. The animals became less affectionate and sociable and more fearful and agitated; furthermore, they tended to perform repetitive, aimless movements rather than purposeful actions. Bianchi suggested that these changes were linked to the disintegration of the total personality rather than to a loss of 'general intelligence' or of a specific ability.

With the rise of animal psychology, many other studies examining the effects of experimentally produced prefrontal lesions were conducted during the first half of the twentieth century. These confirmed that unilateral ablation had no significant effect. Bilateral lesions were found to impair animals on tasks where they were required to keep in mind an environmental event for a short period of time. Jacobsen *et al.* (1935) found in one female chimpanzee a change in personality and behaviour as a result of a bilateral prefrontal ablation. Previously, the chimpanzee had become upset to the point of having temper tantrums when she made mistakes on complex tasks. After the bilateral lobectomy, she no longer showed such behaviour, and alongside this change in her affective reactions, behaviour suggestive of *Witzelsucht* was observed.

LATER CLINICAL STUDIES AND THE EFFECT ON 'EXECUTIVE' FUNCTIONS

More recent clinical studies also describe changes to personality and, in addition, highlight that decision-making can be affected, despite the fact that there is no indication of any significant impairment in any specific cognitive skill. For example, Eslinger and Damasio (1985) described the case of an accountant who underwent an operation to remove part of his frontal lobes. Afterwards, he was very poor at organising his life, even though he performed extremely well on a wide range of neuropsychological tests and achieved an IQ of over 130. He was unable to hold down a job, went bankrupt and was twice divorced. He was frequently unable to make decisions over relatively simple matters such as which restaurants to dine in or which clothes to wear. A similar effect of frontal lobe damage was described by Schindler *et al.* (1995), when reporting on two cases. Both patients showed a change in personality and, despite having intact language, memory and perceptual skills, each showed impaired decisional capacity. Both patients were able to describe their medical problems and their need for treatment, and both felt they could provide adequate self-care. Neither patient wanted to give up their familiar surroundings and change their way of living. However, on several occasions one patient had been found in her house lying on the floor with inadequate heating and rubbish filling some of the rooms. The other patient had failed to prepare meals for herself, despite the fact that her son ensured that food was available in her apartment. The patients appeared to be competent, demonstrating verbal fluency and intact memory, but in reality were unable to care for themselves.

The studies described so far demonstrate that damage to the frontal lobes can result in a range of different behavioural deficits, pertaining to humour, affect and personality as well as aspects of decision-making behaviour (Box 9.1). Della Sala *et al.* (1998) comment that although not all patients show personality change, certain recurring themes were observed, sometimes referred to as 'frontal lobishness' or 'frontal lobe syndrome'. One patient may show a higher level of apathy, another may display a contrasting picture of practical joking and disinhibited social behaviour, and a third may display, at different

Box 9.1 Three key aspects affected

Frontal lobe damage has been found to impact upon several different aspects of behaviour which are not necessarily mutually exclusive (Andrewes, 2001):

1. *Drive:* typically a patient fails to complete tasks on time, despite knowing that the task needs to be undertaken, she or he will not quite get round to doing it.
2. *Impaired social skills:* patients are frequently described as behaving inappropriately in social settings. In the more extreme cases, she or he may make inappropriate sexual advances and show aggressive behaviour. In less extreme cases, the patient may make inappropriate and hurtful comments.
3. *Lack of insight:* patients do not monitor their own behaviour or the reactions of others and this may hamper rehabilitation as they may not accept that they are performing poorly on tasks or in their social relationships.

times, both of these patterns. Benton (1991: 26) noted that the term frontal lobe syndrome 'was adopted to refer to this aggregation of deficits, perhaps as much as a convenient label as from any conviction that it represented a true syndrome, i.e., a conjunction of inherently related symptoms'. To avoid making assumptions about the area of the brain responsible, the term 'dysexecutive syndrome' is often used instead; alternatively some use the term 'executive dysfunction' to avoid the implications associated with the word 'syndrome'.

The case histories of those who have sustained frontal damage are rather perplexing in that any cognitive effects are often by no means immediately apparent and there is little or no obvious mental deterioration. In the past 30 years though, a considerable body of evidence has appeared which suggests that rather than being implicated in specific cognitive operations, such as memorising, the frontal lobes are concerned with the deployment and coordination of cognitive operation. Hence, as mentioned in the introduction, the frontal lobes have come to be regarded as being responsible for the highest forms of human thought, for the 'executive' or 'supervisory' functions of cognition, which refer to a range of related abilities, including our ability to plan and regulate goal-directed behaviour, to deploy attention and to use information flexibly.

The next section will review empirical findings concerning these executive functions. It will become apparent that there is no single test that will be failed by all frontal patients but instead a range of tests that appear to tap these so-called 'executive' tasks. It is also worth bearing in mind that although impairments on these tasks can be attributed to dysfunction of the frontal lobes, there are many different kinds of damage as the frontal lobes are large structures. Therefore, frontal patients are heterogeneous in terms of both the site of damage and their behavioural symptoms.

9.4 IMPAIRMENTS IN THE DEPLOYMENT OF ATTENTION

Successful problem-solving requires both goal-directed thinking and an ability to correctly direct and sustain attention. The ability of brain-damaged patients to monitor what is happening in the environment, and their ability to sustain their concentration and not be distracted, has been examined using a variety of tests. Characteristically, patients with lesions to the frontal lobes show impaired performance.

SUSTAINING AND CONCENTRATING ATTENTION

Salmaso and Denes (1982) asked participants to perform a vigilance task, namely to detect a target stimulus which was interspersed infrequently among repeated presentations of other stimuli (a signal detection task). The stimuli were either pairs of sloping lines or pairs of letters that were presented only briefly. Participants were required to respond on those occasional trials when the pairs of lines or letters were different. Some of the patients with bilateral frontal lobe damage could not reliably detect the targets. This suggests that their ability to sustain their attention was adversely affected.

An impairment in concentration in a simple counting task was observed in patients with right frontal lobe damage (Wilkins *et al.*, 1987). In particular, patients had difficulty in counting either auditory clicks or tactile pulse stimuli when they were presented at a rate of one per second. The involvement of the right frontal lobe in sustaining attention has also been reported in a more recent study. Rueckert and Grafman (1996) gave patients with left and right frontal lobe lesions three sustained attention tasks. The first was a simple reaction time task requiring participants to respond when they saw an X. The second was a Continuous Performance Test asking patients to respond to an X but not to any other letter. The third required them to respond to a specified target when reading a story. For all three tests, patients with right frontal lobe lesions missed more targets and showed longer reaction times compared with matched control participants. Furthermore, their performance on the Continuous Performance Test got worse with time.

SUPPRESSING ATTENTION

The reduction in the ability of patients with frontal lobe damage to sustain their attention is complemented by evidence of their distractibility and their inability to inhibit automatic or habitual responses. During testing, their attention frequently wanders and they will often report irrelevant things. Frontal patients have been observed to grasp or use objects placed near them (Lhermitte, 1983), providing evidence that the patient's habitual responses are being triggered even in situations where they are not required. Lhermitte (1986) describes one incident when a patient was brought to an apartment and shown around. When introduced to the bedroom, where the bedspread had been removed from the bed and the top sheet turned back, the patient got undressed and climbed into bed. This behaviour is termed 'utilisation behaviour' and is dependent on external environmental cues which capture the attentional resources available to the patient. The patient is often conscious of this behavioural dependence but is unable to control it even when the patient has been instructed to do something else, such as complete a psychometric test. One patient, LE, was observed to pick up and deal out a pack of cards appropriately for the number of people present in the room (Shallice *et al.*, 1989). The pack of cards present in the clinical interview acted as an environmental trigger. Balani *et al.* (2009) explored the factors that determined such stimulus-driven responses. In a single-case study, they found that FK would often select an item in a visual search task that matched an irrelevant cue rather than the target, and this seemed to be because of a failure to keep apart memory representations of the cue and the target. Also top-down constraints on the search were weaker so that FK was vulnerable to the activation from the irrelevant cue. When drawing attention away from the cue, for example by including a secondary task, then FK's responses to the search target were improved.

An inability to suppress the most salient response was observed when frontal patients were administered the Stroop Colour Word task. If shown the word 'red' written in 'blue' (in the incongruent condition), we usually have no trouble in saying what the word is, but find naming the colour of the ink more problematic because we need to suppress our habitual reading response (see Chapter 3 for further information). In one study, patients with left frontal lesions were found to perform very poorly on the Stroop test (Perret, 1974) and in another only bilateral frontal damage was found to be associated with increased errors and slowness in response time for the incongruent condition (Stuss *et al.*, 2001). The involvement of the frontal structures in this task has been confirmed in an experiment using normal volunteers; activation of anterior right hemisphere and medial frontal structures were observed using positron emission tomography (Bench *et al.*, 1993). Perret (1974) found that those patients performing poorly on the Stroop test also failed to perform well on a verbal fluency test (to search for words beginning with a certain initial letter). He suggested that this could be because the verbal fluency test makes similar cognitive processing demands, namely to suppress the habitual response of searching for words according to their meaning. Burgess and Shallice (1996a) considered this issue further, using a task which allowed them to examine both verbal response inhibition as well as response initiation. They presented a task involving sentences in which the last word was missing (the Hayling test). The missing word is strongly cued by the rest of the sentence, for example the word 'stamp' is cued by 'He mailed the letter without a ...'. For the first half of these sentences, patients were asked to provide the word which they thought could fit at the end of the sentence (response initiation condition). For the second half they were asked to provide a word which made no sense at all in the context of the sentence (response suppression or inhibition condition). In comparison with patients with posterior lesions, patients with frontal lobe lesions took longer to complete the sentences in the response *initiation* condition. They also performed worse in the response *inhibition* condition, providing significantly more straightforward completions of the sentence. Even when the answers were not completions, the words they selected were more likely to be semantically related to the sentence. An inability to suppress a current response is also a possible reason for frontal lobe patients' failure on other tasks, for example the Wisconsin Card Sorting Test described in the next section.

9.5 IMPAIRMENTS IN ABSTRACT AND CONCEPTUAL THINKING

Successful problem-solving requires us to go beyond the information provided and engage in abstract thinking. One commonly used method of assessing abstraction involves classification or sorting tasks. Such tasks require participants to abstract the concept or rule used for sorting. These are similar to the inductive reasoning tasks described in Chapter 8. The ability of frontal patients to formulate and test hypotheses as to what the correct rule may be is usually impaired; however, the cognitive nature of this impairment has been linked to other processes as well as the inductive one. As you will read, many of the tasks tap ability to shift response strategy as well as use of negative feedback to inform a change in response strategy.

SORTING TASKS

An early study by Halstead (1940) asked patients with bilateral frontal lesions to perform a fairly simple sorting task, namely to sort the items that were similar amongst 62 miscellaneous objects into separate groups. Some patients did not include all the items in their groupings, and the groupings themselves were not meaningful; there was no apparent coherent organising principle.

Other sorting tasks use an array of tokens which vary in dimensions such as shape and colour. In a study by Cicerone *et al.* (1983) patients with bilateral frontal lobe lesions were shown stimuli that varied on four dimensions, namely

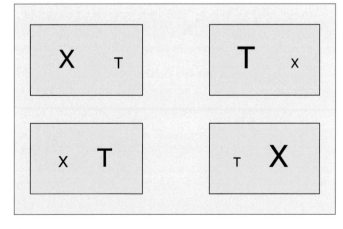

Figure 9.4   Card sorting task.

Source: Adapted from Cicerone *et al.* (1983).

Note: The task is to abstract a single critical dimension from stimuli varying on four dimensions: size, colour, form and position.

size, colour, form and position. The task was to abstract the critical dimension. On each trial, patients were shown four pairs of stimuli and asked to choose one according to what they thought the critical dimension might be (Figure 9.4).

On specified trials, they were told if their choice was right or wrong, and negative feedback would require them to switch to a different hypothesis and select a different dimension. Results showed that patients with tumours of the frontal lobe were impaired on this task compared with participants with posterior tumours. Those with frontal lobe lesions used fewer hypotheses and frequently failed to shift from an irrelevant hypothesis, even when told their choice was incorrect. They continued to select the stimulus using the same dimension on subsequent trials despite negative feedback, as if they were failing to attend to all of the relevant dimensions.

Failure to make effective use of feedback was also noted in earlier research using the Wisconsin Card Sorting Test. Here, patients are presented with four cards, which can vary along three dimensions, namely number, colour and shape (Figure 9.5). The number of items on the card ranges from 1 to 4, the shape of the items on the card is either a circle, triangle, cross or star and the colour of the items on the card is either red, green, yellow or blue. The task is to sort a stack of cards into four piles, with one pile below each card on the table.

As with the previous test, the participant has to hypothesise the rule, for example sort according to colour, and the experimenter provides feedback as to whether each card is being placed correctly in one of the four piles. So, if the card is red, the participant must sort the card with the pile that has red objects. After a spe-

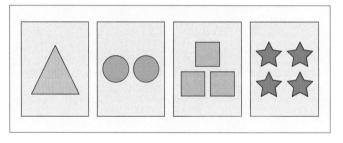

Figure 9.5   Wisconsin Card Sorting Test.

Note: The cards vary along three dimensions: number, colour and shape, and the task is to sort a stack of cards according to a rule.

cific number of cards have been correctly placed (for example ten consecutive correct responses), the experimenter changes the rule without warning and only sorts that accord with the new category will result in positive feedback. Neurologically intact individuals quickly detect such rule changes and switch to a new hypothesis accordingly. Patients with frontal lobe damage have been found to continue with their original rule despite the negative feedback they were receiving (Milner, 1964). This has been called a 'stuck-in-set' tendency; a change in rule involves a shift from the colour dimension to the number dimension but the patient still sticks with the colour dimension. They may continue to sort according to their first hypothesis for as many as 100 cards, showing an inability to shift response strategy, known as perseveration, and a lack of flexibility in their behaviour.

Key Term

Perseveration
An inability to shift response strategy, characteristic of frontal lobe patients.

EVIDENCE CONCERNING PERSEVERATION

Perseverative responses were also observed in a recent study by Miller and Tippett (1996), when employing the Matchstick Test of Cognitive Flexibility. This test is a visual problem-solving task and therefore a very different task to the sorting tasks described previously. It requires the participant to show different ways of removing sticks from a two-dimensional geometric figure so that a particular shape emerges (Figure 9.6). Their results showed that patients with damage to the right frontal lobe were impaired in their ability to shift strategy. Those with left frontal lobe damage displayed no significant difficulty. These results are consistent with earlier research that has found the right frontal lobe to be more important than the left when the tasks entail minimal verbal requirements.

Other research has attempted to identify the extent to which the perseveration observed in concept formation tasks is a result of not attending to the feedback provided. Findings have revealed that when a modified version of the Wisconsin Card Sorting Test is used, so that patients are warned and explicitly told of a change in the rule (Nelson, 1976), or are told explicitly which dimension to use to sort the cards (Delis *et al.*, 1992), a significant number of frontal patients still continued to show perseveration. Although patients are able to abstract a rule or formulate an hypothesis when presented with the Wisconsin Card Sorting Test, they do not use the feedback they are given to modulate their behaviour and shift to a different rule. The results of Delis *et al.* suggest that patients are impaired both in their ability to use the feedback provided *and* in their ability to shift to a different rule. Delis *et al.* used a new sorting task requiring participants in one condition to sort six cards spontaneously and to report the rule they employed; in a second condition to report the rules for correct sorts performed by the examiner; and in a third condition to sort the cards according to abstract cues or explicit information provided by the examiner. Their results revealed

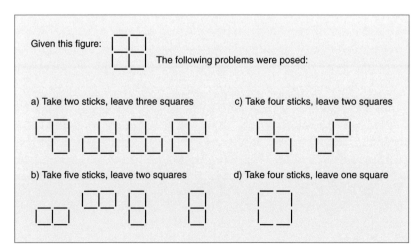

Figure 9.6 Matchstick Test of Cognitive Flexibility.

Source: Adapted from Miller and Tippett (1996).

Note: The four problems associated with one of the geometric designs used in the Matchstick Test of Cognitive Flexibility are shown here.

that no single deficit, such as perseveration, could account for their findings. The authors concluded that although impaired abstract thinking was not the primary deficit, it is one of several 'higher-level' functions that collectively disrupt the problem-solving ability of frontal patients. This notion is explored further in Section 9.8.

GOING BEYOND PERSEVERATION

Matters are complicated further by the findings of Owen *et al.* (1991). They found frontal patients were not impaired if the shift involved the same dimension. This is termed an intra-dimensional shift and occurs when a participant is required to transfer a rule involving a stimulus dimension such as colour or shape to a novel set of exemplars of that same stimulus dimension. Patients were impaired, however, when they were required to shift response set to an alternative, previously irrelevant dimension. This is termed an extradimensional shift and is a core component of the Wisconsin Card Sorting Test. The authors wrote that 'The behaviour of the frontal lobe group ... was observed to be characterized by a total disregard for the correct, previously irrelevant dimension' (p. 1003). Barceló *et al.* (1997) suggested that frontal lobe patients may be impaired mostly in making extradimensional shifts because of their inability to suppress previous incorrect responses; thus the poor performance of frontal patients on the Wisconsin Card Sorting Test may be linked to problems in inhibitory control. Helmstaedter *et al.* (1996) found impaired response inhibition (known as disinhibition) to be one characteristic of patients with frontal lobe epilepsy that differentiated them from patients with temporal lobe epilepsy.

In order to understand better the cognitive nature of impairments in the Wisconsin Card Sorting Test, Barceló and Knight (2002) sought to analyse the nature of non-perseverative errors as these will reduce the total amount of achieved categories. Using a modified version of the Wisconsin Card Sorting Test, their earlier research had found that normal participants are forced to make non-perseverative errors early in the series in order to find the new sorting rule (e.g. Barceló, 1999); and this was because participants undertake a trial-and-error process whereby they keep track of past incorrect rules to obtain the correct new rule quickly. Barceló and Knight termed these 'efficient errors' as they entail the efficient use of recent contextual information to optimise set shifting, and one would expect someone to make these errors following a shift in the rule. Another type of non-perseverative errors are those that involve a shift in set but entail inefficient use of past contextual information; these were termed 'random errors'. Compared with age-matched controls, their prefrontal patients made more perseverative errors and this is in line with the studies outlined previously. However, their patients also made a larger number of random errors. Indeed, in 52 per cent of the series patients produced more random errors than perseverative errors. When describing their observations, Barceló and Knight wrote:

Key Term

Disinhibition
Impaired response inhibition, an inability to suppress previous incorrect responses observed in patients with frontal lobe epilepsy.

Most patients described their problems sorting cards by saying that they were "confused" or "baffled" by the cards. One patient (WE) used to repeat aloud to himself the three categories when attempting a new shift in category. It appeared as if he had problems in keeping online all the information needed to shift category. As a result of these difficulties, patients took an average of 2.6 seconds longer than controls to sort each card.

(p. 355)

Using a different rule-detection task, Burgess and Shallice (1996b) failed to find significant differences in the incidence of perseverative responses when comparing patients with different cerebral lesions. They designed the Brixton Spatial Anticipation Test which, unlike the Wisconsin Card Sorting Test, allows the amount of guessing to be estimated. Patients were presented with a booklet containing 56 pages, with each page showing a 2 × 5 array of circles numbered 1–10 (Figure 9.7). Pages differed in terms of which circle was filled. The task was to predict which circle would be filled on the next page. The rule would apply to a certain number of pages, and this number would vary in an unsystematic way from 3 to 8. Therefore, changes in the rule could not be anticipated. The errors made by participants were scored either as perseverations, or as applications of other incorrect rules, or as bizarre responses and guesses. Patients with anterior lesions made more errors overall, with a significantly higher absolute number and proportion of the third type of errors. Also, having detected a correct rule, they were more likely to abandon it. However, their performance did not demonstrate a greater tendency to perseverate. These observations have been confirmed by Reverberi *et al.* (2005a) who distinguished between two different types of perseveration responses and found that frontal patients did not show an increase in either type. However, they did find that only patients with left lateral frontal lesions and not those with right lateral frontal lesions were significantly impaired in their performance on the Brixton test.

Although the Brixton Spatial Anticipation Test resembles the Wisconsin Card Sorting Test in that the participant has to learn arbitrary rules which change, there are important differences. Relevant rules can be abstracted from the perceptual display in the sorting task, for instance sort by colour or sort by shape; this

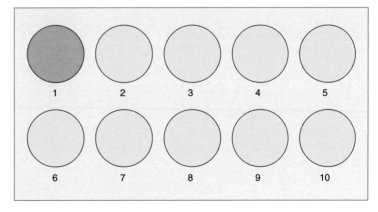

Figure 9.7 Brixton Spatial Anticipation Test.

Source: Adapted from Burgess and Shallice (1996b).

Note: Each page of the test shows a 2 × 5 array of circles. The task is to predict which circle will be filled on the next page.

is not the case in the spatial anticipation test. One possible explanation for their results, one of the three offered by Burgess and Shallice, is that the creation of an appropriate rule is a more abstract process in the Brixton test. Alternatively, one of their other suggestions is consistent with findings from studies involving cognitive estimation which are described in the next section, namely that anterior patients are more willing to think of bizarre hypotheses which they do not disconfirm.

Reverberi *et al.* (2005a) ruled out a number of different explanations for their findings and suggested that for their left frontal lateral group the fundamental process that is impaired is that of induction. They suggest that localised in the left frontal cortex is a key process necessary to carry out inductive inference, and point out that this proposal is in line with the findings of some of the imaging studies that have looked at brain activation whilst participants undertake inductive reasoning tasks (e.g. Parsons and Osherson, 2001).

A clinical test of concept formation is the Twenty Questions Test which is based on a game where one player asks yes/no questions to identify which famous person or object the other player is thinking of. Like the Wisconsin Card Sorting Test, it requires participants to abstract categories, utilise feedback to modify their responses as well as keep track of previous responses. They are shown an array of 30 line drawings and told to ask examinees the fewest number of yes/no questions in order to identify a target from the array. The advantage of this test is that it measures concept-formation skills directly from the patients' verbal responses rather than inferring them from card sorting responses. Baldo *et al.* (2004) found frontal patients to perform poorly on this test compared with control participants, largely due to ineffective categorisation strategies; rather than narrowing down their search, patients predominantly asked single-item questions (e.g. 'Is it the owl?'). Baldo *et al.* conclude that the ability to abstract conceptual categories is supported by the frontal cortex.

9.6 IMPAIRED STRATEGY FORMATION
COGNITIVE ESTIMATION TASKS

A different kind of reasoning is employed in tasks involving cognitive estimates, where deductions or inferences about the world are drawn from known information. Shallice and Evans (1978) asked questions such as 'What is the largest object normally found in a house?', 'How fast do racehorses gallop?', 'What is the height of the Post Office Tower?' and 'What is the length of the average woman's spine?' – in other words questions that cannot be answered directly from information stored in memory. Instead, a realistic estimate can be inferred from other knowledge. For example, a reasonable answer to the last question can be arrived at by first using knowledge about the average height of a woman, then realising that the spine runs about one-third to one half the length of the body, allowing one to judge the answer to be somewhere between 22 and 33 inches. Shallice and Evans found that patients with frontal lesions would perform worse than those with posterior lesions, sometimes providing absurd or outrageous values, for example that the spine is about '5 feet long' and that the largest object in the house is 'a ceramic toilet seat'. Shallice and Evans suggested that poor performance was a result of poor strategy formation – although the questions could be answered by drawing upon general knowledge, no immediate obvious strategy was available.

Poor cognitive estimation has also been observed in a task involving the price of goods. Smith and Milner (1984) showed individuals with frontal lobe damage miniature replicas of real-life products, such as a sewing machine and a car. Results showed that patients with right frontal lobectomies responded with bizarre estimates of price on about 25 per cent of trials. Again, poor performance is hypothesised to result from poor strategy formation.

In a later study, Smith and Milner (1988) asked patients to estimate the frequency of an event or item. A series of nonsense items was shown and some of the items appeared only once, whereas others appeared 3, 5, 7 or 9 times non-consecutively. A series of test items followed and for each test item the patient had to state whether or not it was included in the initial sequence and furthermore, if this response was positive, they were asked to estimate how often it had been shown. Whilst patients with lesions in both left and right frontal lobes were able to remember accurately the presence or absence of the test item in the initial sequence, they had difficulty estimating its frequency of occurrence. So, although these patients showed a normal ability to recognise an abstract design, they could not estimate accurately how many times they had seen that particular design. Closer inspection of the results reveals that their estimates were not significantly different at lower frequency levels; differences only emerged when the design had been shown at least seven times. Smith and Milner suggest that the patients' performance may reflect a difficulty in cognitive estimation; alternatively, frontal patients may find it difficult to carry out an orderly search for the representations of the designs in memory or in remembering information with a temporal component.

Wagner et al. (2011) reviewed the use of the cognitive estimation test devised by Shallice and Evans (1978) in healthy and clinical populations. They conclude that some studies have shown estimation abilities to be associated with frontal lobe injury and executive dysfunction, although a specific area in the frontal lobes has yet to be identified. They note that Taylor and O'Carroll (1995) failed to find a significant difference in the performance on this test between groups with anterior and posterior lesions, and that other studies have not found performance on the cognitive estimation test to be related with other measures of executive functions; the lack of associations between different measures of executive functions is explored in Section 9.8.

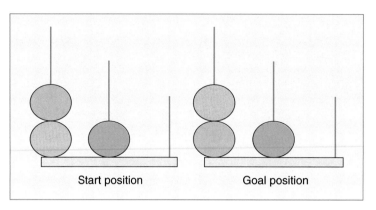

Start position   Goal position

Figure 9.8   An example of a problem from the Tower of London task.

Source: Adapted from Shallice (1982).

GOAL-ORIENTED PROBLEM-SOLVING

Other tests have been developed to investigate how well frontal patients can formulate a strategy to obtain a goal, and performance on such tests is a good indication of how well the individual can produce a plan of action, which can involve sub-goals, suited to the particular task presented. Shallice (1982) devised the 'Tower of London' task (a task related to the 'Tower of Hanoi' problem described in Chapter 8). The problem involves an apparatus with three beads and three pegs of varying heights so that each peg can hold one, two or all three beads. The task requires one to move the three beads which are placed on one part of the apparatus to a different position (e.g. Figure 9.8). These beads can only be moved one at a time and can only be moved to a different peg. The task is graded according to the number of moves necessary to achieve the solution. Frontal patients, specifically those with left frontal damage, were found to be both inefficient and ineffective at performing this task. In particular, they engaged in moves that only directly led towards their goal. Owen *et al.* (1990) used a computerised version of this task and found no differences between left and right frontal lobe patients. However, whereas normal participants and both groups of frontal patients spent the same amount of time planning their first move, the frontal patients spent considerably longer planning subsequent moves. Not only were they observed to have significantly longer thinking times overall, they needed more moves to solve the problem.

Morris *et al.* (1993) provided corroborative evidence of the involvement of the frontal regions in the Tower of London task by measuring regional blood flow in neurologically intact individuals. Participants performed a computerised touch-screen version of the task that entailed two conditions. In the first they were guided by the computer to solve the problem (a control task that requires no planning activity) whereas in the second they were asked to perform the task without guidance. Morris *et al.* found significantly higher levels of activation, i.e. a greater increase in regional cerebral blood flow, in the left frontal cortex in the second condition, when participants had to actively plan the moves. Furthermore, a relatively greater increase was shown by those participants who spent more time planning the solution and also in those who solved the problem in fewer moves.

The evidence presented so far implicates the frontal lobes in 'planning', at least in the case of the Tower of London task. Goel and

Grafman (1995) presented twenty patients who had lesions in the prefrontal cortex with a computerised five-disc version of the Tower of Hanoi puzzle and found them to be impaired on this task in comparison with normal controls. Their individual moves to solve the problems were analysed and both patients and controls were found to use the same strategy. However, the patients' poor performance could be attributed to a failure to spot and/or resolve the counterintuitive backward move. To achieve the goal, a move has to be made that takes you away from the goal and the conflict between the sub-goal and goal has to be acknowledged. This counterintuitive backward move was discussed in Chapter 8 in relation to the Hobbits and Orcs problem; many of us experience difficulty in implementing this move as it contravenes our favourite heuristic, to reduce the difference between the current state and the goal state. Goel and Grafman suggest that the patients are seeking to satisfy the goal rather than a conflicting sub-goal, and this is consistent with explanations of impaired performance on other tasks, namely that frontal patients have a particular problem with suppressing their current, salient or habitual response.

Goel and Grafman also stress that the Tower of Hanoi problem does not test planning ability in the sense of constructing and evaluating a particular plan, because unless the counterintuitive backward move is spotted the problem cannot be solved. The next section outlines research that considers planning ability in relation to real-life problems and, in line with the case studies described earlier, supports the notion that planning ability is impaired as a result of frontal lobe damage.

9.7 DEFICITS IN EVERYDAY HIGHER-ORDER PLANNING

It should be evident from the research outlined in the previous sections that a range of neuropsychological tests have been used to investigate the nature of the cognitive processes underlying the impaired performance of patients with frontal lobe damage. Failure on these is usually interpreted as suggesting that the cognitive processes involved in successfully completing the task are damaged. Burgess *et al.* (1998) make the point that with many of the tests, such as the Wisconsin Card Sorting Test, an assumption is made that the test itself taps into processes that are used to cope with many real-life situations. However, there may be little correspondence between the cognitive resources tapped by such tests and those tapped in real-world situations. For example, real-life problem-solving is usually open-ended in nature and different courses of action have to be considered and evaluated. It is rare that all the relevant pieces of information are available together and frequently solutions to real-life problems require a juggling of priorities which differ in importance according to the specific context. Therefore, there is a need to assess performance using tests that involve formalised versions of real-world activities and hence are more ecologically valid.

Shallice and Burgess (1991a) have developed tests that specifically explore higher-order planning deficits, and these mimic everyday problem-solving. The 'Six Element Test' is undertaken in a standard hospital office. It requires the patient to complete three different but not difficult tasks, each with two components, within a specified time period of fifteen minutes. The tasks are: dictating a route into a recorder; carrying out arithmetic problems and writing down the names of approximately one hundred pictures of objects. One key aspect of the instructions given to participants is that all the tasks should be completed and that the important thing is to do a little of each of the components of each of the tasks.

The 'Multiple Errands Test' requires the patient to carry out certain tasks in situations where minor unforeseen events can arise. The patient is given a card with eight tasks written on it and then sent to a shopping precinct to carry out these tasks. There are six simple requests (for example, buy a lettuce), the seventh tasks requires the patient to be somewhere in fifteen minutes and the eighth task requires the recording of four pieces of information during the errands (for example, the price of tomatoes or the rate of exchange of the euro yesterday). Patients are instructed to spend as little money as possible (within reason) and take as little time as possible (without rushing excessively). They are told to enter a shop only when wanting to buy something, and to tell the experimenter when they leave the shop what they have bought. They are informed that they cannot use anything not bought on the street, other than a watch, to help them. Finally, they are told that they can do the tasks in any order.

These tests were used in a study of three frontal head-injury patients (AP, DN and FS) described in Box 9.2. All three had Wechsler Adult Intelligence Scale (WAIS) IQs between 120 and 130, and on thirteen tests considered to be sensitive to frontal lobe damage, for instance the Wisconsin Card Sorting, Stroop and Cognitive Estimation tests, the performance of two of the patients (AP and DN) fell within the normal range. The performance of the third patient FS was impaired on four of these tests. In daily life, the three patients planned few activities and showed little spontaneous organisation; two had lost jobs because of gross oversights. When asked to complete the Six Element Test, all three patients performed at below the normal range; not only were their scores quantitatively lower, their performance was qualitatively different also when compared with that of control participants. AP started by making notes for four minutes, which were then never used. DN spent ten minutes on one task and did not even attempt a second task that was very similar. FS only tackled three of the six subtasks.

The three patients performed equally poorly on the Multiple Errands Test. They made more than three times as many inefficient actions and broke three times as many rules in comparison with

Box 9.2 The case histories of AP, DN and FS

In a paper by Shallice and Burgess (1991a), three patients with traumatic injuries to the prefrontal structures are described. All three found the organisation and planning of everyday-life activities problematic and their specific difficulties are described here.

AP was 23 years of age when he was involved in a road traffic accident. A CT scan revealed considerable bifrontal damage. He was unable to return to his job and a year later he attended a hospital as a day patient for rehabilitation. Although he was well-motivated and keen, he was unable to complete the simplest of activities as he could not maintain his concentration on the task at hand. For example, instead of returning to the therapy room after fetching coffee, he was found on the local golf course. Shopping was impossible because he was unable to buy more than one item before returning to his car. As soon as three months later he was transferred to a different rehabilitation clinic as an in-patient, where he remained for a year. Although there was some improvement in his ability to organise daily activities, he went home to live with his parents. He later reported in a clinical interview that he was unable to keep his room tidy, to file his magazines or to carry out shopping, cleaning and laundry duties. He was not able to plan ahead for his social life or provide any example of organising something in advance.

DN was 26 years of age when he was involved in a road traffic accident. Six months after sustaining his injuries, he found that he was unable to continue with his previous employment. Despite some success at studying and obtaining a teacher's certificate, he spent five years doing a variety of jobs and being dismissed from most of them. A CT scan performed 22 years later, when he was 48 years of age, revealed considerable damage to the right frontal lobe and some to the left frontal lobe. It emerged in a clinical interview that he was untidy and shaved, washed his hair and changed his clothes only when told to do so by his wife, bathing only if going out somewhere special. Domestic chores were rarely undertaken spontaneously and if his wife went out he would usually leave the food preparation to his 10-year-old son. When asked to do something by his wife, she had to give specific instructions and even then he might only complete some aspects of the task. The organisation of their social life was left to his wife. He was rarely successful at buying items needed, despite his wife preparing a shopping list, and she reported that he was occasionally irresponsible with money.

FS sustained injuries in two separate incidents. She suffered a skull fracture when thrown from a horse in her twenties and then at the age of 53 years she was knocked off her bicycle by a car, hitting her head on the road. A CT scan conducted two years later revealed a large lesion to the left frontal lobe and some atrophy to the left temporal lobe. It was revealed that she had kept the same job for the previous 25 years and lived by herself in a single room. In a clinical interview she reported that she was very untidy, that she shopped every day to buy just a few things and never visited the supermarket. She seldom went out in the evenings and almost never travelled away from her home town. She generally did not undertake inessential or novel activities and in the interview reported no plans for the following weekend. She could not recall an incident where someone relied on her to do something, and reported leaving the organising of any joint activity to others.

normal controls. Again, their behaviour was qualitatively different. Two of the patients experienced difficulties with shopkeepers. AP asked for the previous day's newspaper and on obtaining it angered the shopkeeper by leaving the shop without paying for it, breaking the rule that only bought items can be used. DN asked a shop assistant to give him a birthday card free, breaking the buying rule and resulting in a heated argument. FS broke the rule that no shop should be entered other than to buy something because the shop, a chemist, did not stock the soap she especially liked. She would not buy other cheap soap even though this would have been adequate for the task.

Shallice and Burgess proposed that these patients were able to generate intentions but not reactivate these intentions later on, when these were not directly signalled or primed by the stimulus situation. The patients lost the facility to activate or trigger markers. Normally, when intentions are created or rules are temporarily created, markers are activated which are then triggered if a relevant situation occurs. This triggering will interrupt ongoing behaviour to ensure that the intention or rule is realised. They explain that 'a marker is basically a message that some future behaviour or event should not be treated as routine and instead, some particular aspect of the situation should be viewed as especially relevant for action' (p. 737). The patients performed poorly on the Six Element and the Multiple Errands Tests, not because of motivational or retrospective memory impairments, but because of processes that bridge these; processes which assist the realisation of goals and intentions.

These findings shed light on why patients with frontal lobe damage can perform well in many laboratory tests that supposedly tap frontal lobe function and yet fail in everyday activities. The situations where these patients have problems are those that can be approached in a number of different ways and require decisions about how to allocate resources, and that tap subtle planning and prospective memory. Duncan *et al.* (1996) wrote

> In the laboratory it is often the rule to give strong verbal prompts to task requirements, to repeat these until performance is correct, to gather data over a long series of stereotyped trials, and to have only a modest set of concurrent task requirements. In all these respects, the activities of daily life may often be different: there are no explicit verbal prompts, no stereotyped repetition of closely similar 'trials', and sometimes multiple, concurrent concerns.
>
> (p. 296)

Research since has confirmed the value of a simplified version of the Multiple Errands Test for use in clinical practice. Alderman *et al.* (2003) found that although many patients passed the traditional tests of executive frontal lobe function, they made more and different types of errors than control participants on the new test, and patients' performance was characterised either by rule-breaking because they failed to act upon the information they received or misunderstood the instructions or by failure to achieve tasks, usually because the tasks were not initiated.

9.8 CONCEPTUAL ISSUES

It is apparent from the earlier sections of this chapter that a number of distinct processes have been related to the frontal lobes, including abstract/conceptual thinking and planning, and these processes can be classified as 'supervisory' or 'executive' functions. Apart from cognitive processes, damage to the frontal lobes can influence behaviour, emotion and motivation as well as impact on personality. The twenty most commonly reported symptoms of the 'frontal lobe' or 'dysexecutive' syndrome are reported in Box 9.3.

The development of a model of executive functioning is still in its infancy (Andrewes, 2001) and the oldest and most developed model is described next.

SUPERVISORY ATTENTIONAL SYSTEM

Norman and Shallice (1986) adopted an information-processing approach to explain these deficits of executive function. Complex but well-established patterns of behaviour are controlled by hierarchically organised schemas or memory representations. High-level schemas can call up subordinate programmes or subroutines, so, for example, 'making dinner' will have component schemas containing at the lowest-level instructions on how to use the oven and at higher levels how to make a cheesecake. Fundamental to their approach is the distinction between habitual and novel action routines. They suggested that each of these are selected and integrated in different ways.

Box 9.3   Characteristics of the dysexecutive syndrome (from Burgess *et al.*, 1998)

1. Abstract thinking problems
2. Impulsivity
3. Confabulation
4. Planning problems
5. Euphoria
6. Temporal sequencing deficits
7. Lack of insight and social awareness
8. Apathy and lack of drive
9. Disinhibition
10. Variable motivation
11. Shallowing of affective responses
12. Aggression
13. Lack of concern
14. Perseveration
15. Restlessness–hyperkinesis
16. Inability to inhibit responses
17. Knowing–doing dissociation
18. Distractibility
19. Poor decision-making ability
20. No concern for social rules

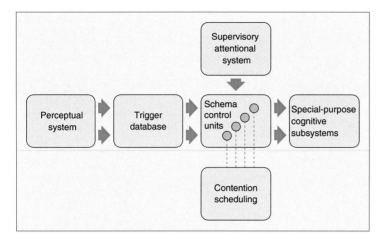

Figure 9.9   A diagram of the Norman and Shallice model.

Source: Adapted from Shallice (1982).

Norman and Shallice suggested that we frequently function on 'auto pilot', selecting and integrating cognitive or behavioural skills on the basis of established schemas. Environmental cues trigger certain responses which in turn trigger specific schemas, for instance a kettle may trigger your 'make a cup of tea' schema. Once triggered, a schema competes for dominance and control of action by inhibiting other schemas which might conflict with it. When there is a clash between two routine activities, an operation they call *contention scheduling* prevents two competing activated schemas from being selected through lateral inhibition. However, it is not always desirable to select schemas on the basis of the strength of their initial activation. Norman and Shallice argued that coping with novelty involves the selection of schemas that are modulated by the operation of a supervisory attentional system (similar to Baddeley's concept of a central executive, see Chapter 5). This system can heighten a schema's level of activation, allowing it to be in a better position to compete with other schemas for dominance and thus increasing its probability of being selected in contention scheduling (Figure 9.9).

Norman and Shallice indicated five types of situations that would involve the operation of this system:

1. situations that involve planning or decision-making (e.g. Tower of London test);
2. situations that involve error-correction or troubleshooting (e.g. Wisconsin Card Sorting Test);
3. situations that require less well-learned responses or require the involvement of a new pattern of actions (e.g. tasks involving cognitive estimates);
4. situations that are considered to be dangerous or technically difficult;
5. situations that require us not to suppress a strong habitual response or to resist temptation (e.g. Stroop test).

Their approach assumes that we might operate in one mode where potentially demanding but routine action or thought processes are selected by well-learned triggering procedures. When these routine operations will not allow us to achieve our goal then some form of explicit modulation or novel activity must take place, involving

> ### Key Term
>
> **Supervisory attentional system**
> A term used by Norman and Shallice to describe a system that can heighten a schema's level of activation, allowing it to be in a better position to compete with other schemas for dominance and thus increasing its probability of being selected in contention scheduling.

higher-level processes and the supervisory system. The notion that our cognitive processes might operate on different levels or modes (routine versus non-routine processing) is also contained in artificial intelligence models of problem-solving, e.g. SOAR (Laird *et al.*, 1987). Their use of the concept of 'schema' is also apparent in other explanations of cognitive behaviour (see Chapter 6).

Shallice (1988) explains how this approach can account for impairments of problem-solving. Lesions to the frontal lobes impair the functioning of the supervisory system so that contention scheduling operates unmodulated. The deficits in sustained attention and distractibility described earlier arise because unless strong trigger-schema contingencies are present, the patient is unable to inhibit irrelevant input. Observations of utilisation behaviour, the tendency to pick up and use objects in close proximity, are consistent with this. Perseveration will be observed when the situation triggers a well-learned set of responses. One schema would gain abnormal levels of dominance over others and it would be difficult to switch to a different set of responses. Perseveration has been observed in the performance of frontal patients on the Wisconsin Card Sorting Test. Tasks or situations that require a 'novel' response, for example those involving cognitive estimates, will be problematic as there is no routine procedure that allows the patient to produce an appropriate response.

ALTERNATIVE APPROACHES

Others have proposed accounts of frontal lobe dysfunction that do not specify a damaged central executive mechanism. Goldman-Rakic (1987) conducted extensive research with non-human primates and proposed that the dorsolateral prefrontal cortex is crucial for working memory, called 'representational memory' by that author. This framework has been extended by Kimberg and Farah (1993) to account for the range of human cognitive impairments following frontal lobe damage. They proposed that the strength of associations among working memory representations are weakened, specifically those representations of goals, environmental stimuli and stored declarative knowledge. The representations themselves are unaffected; instead the associations among these different working memory representations are deficient. Kimberg and Farah went on to simulate the weakening of working memory associations using a computer model. They selected four tasks that frontal patients had been found to fail, and found that their 'damaged' model also failed all four tasks in the same ways as frontal-damaged patients.

Duncan *et al.* (1996) argued that there is considerable overlap between the functions reflected in Spearman's concept of general intelligence ('*g*') and the executive functioning of the frontal lobes. This is based partly on the finding that some tests providing good estimates of overall intelligence also tap executive function. Based on the results of four experiments on goal neglect, they suggested that failure to satisfy a stated task requirement was the predominant finding in frontal patients and was closely related to Spearman's *g* in the normal population. They wrote that the conventional view that frontal patients show normal intelligence, as measured by psychometric tests such as the Wechsler Adult Intelligence Scale, is misleading. It is important to distinguish between tests of fluid intelligence, which assess ability for abstract thought and reasoning, and tests of crystallized intelligence that relate to prior knowledge acquired partly through fluid intelligence but also through education, culture and other experiences. As acquired knowledge may be less sensitive to frontal damage than fluid reasoning, frontal patients may show deficits on tests of fluid intelligence but not on standard intelligence tests which measure in part crystallized intelligence. Crinella and Yu (2000) failed to replicate the findings of Duncan *et al.*; their results did not find frontal lobe lesions to affect fluid intelligence, although performance on tests of executive functions was affected. It is possible though that the relationship between *g*, fluid intelligence in particular, and executive function differs according to the tests used. Roca *et al.* (2010) examined the role of fluid intelligence in executive deficits using a range of different tasks, comparing patients with focal frontal lesions with controls matched to patients in terms of age and National Adult Reading Test-estimated IQ. They found for some widely used tasks, including the Wisconsin Card Sorting Test, fluid intelligence could account entirely for frontal deficits. Furthermore, they found that these tasks were not related to a particular lesion location within the frontal lobe. However, for a second group of tasks that were associated with lesions in the right anterior frontal cortex, deficits were not fully explained by fluid intelligence. This second group of tasks were therefore more successful in tapping specific executive functions associated with these prefrontal region. These findings suggest that different tests may be tapping different types of executive functions and this is explored next.

FRACTIONATION OF THE EXECUTIVE FUNCTIONS OF THE FRONTAL LOBES

Other theoretical developments have sought to clarify the extent to which the executive functions are unitary in nature. Shallice and Burgess (1991b) suggested that the supervisory system should not be considered to act as a single resource and this view is supported by Stuss and Alexander (2000: 289), who wrote that 'there is no unitary executive function. Rather, distinct processes related to the frontal lobes can be differentiated which converge on a general concept of control functions'.

Burgess *et al.* (1998) performed factor analysis on patients' dysexecutive symptoms and reported that the twenty symptoms (Box 9.3) could be grouped into five orthogonal factors; two of these relate to the emotional and personality changes that can be seen in patients with frontal lobe damage. The remaining three are:

- inhibition or the ability to suppress a habitual response, assuming that impulsivity and disinhibition are the behavioural consequences of such a cognitive problem;

- intentionality, which is related to the creation and maintenance of goal-related behaviour;
- executive memory, which is related to confabulation and inability to recall the correct order of events.

These findings provide support that at the behavioural level the dysexecutive syndrome can be fractionated.

By fractionating the supervisory processes, it is possible to account for dissociations of deficits in problem-solving, and explain why a patient may be impaired on a scheduling test such as the Multiple Errands Test and not on other more standard tests of frontal lobe functioning. For example, Bamdad *et al.* (2003) found only a weak relationship between traditional measures of executive function and a newly developed measure of real-world planning/problem-solving abilities. Rueckert and Grafman (1996) failed to find significant correlations between any of the three measures of sustained attention and performance on the Tower of Hanoi or the Wisconsin Card Sorting Test. The authors suggest that the regions of the frontal lobe subserving sustained attention may not be the same regions involved in the problem-solving tasks. In the Burgess and Shallice (1996a) study that employed the Hayling Sentence Completion Test, analysis revealed extremely low correlations between the patients' performance in the response initiation and response inhibition conditions. Such results suggest that initiation and inhibition may be impaired singly and that the two processes are separable. Burgess and Shallice (1994) also reported low correlations between patients' performance on the Hayling Test and the Brixton Spatial Anticipation Test and concluded that the two tests are tapping either differing executive processes or dedicated supervisory resources.

Further evidence for fractionation emerged when Stuss and Alexander (2007) analysed the effects of focal lesions of the frontal lobes. They argued that the evidence points to at least three separate 'supervisory' processes each related to a different region within the frontal lobes:

1. *Energization* – a function involved in the initiation and sustaining a response; this is associated with the superior medial region of the frontal lobes.
2. *Task-setting* – a function involved in setting up stimulus–response relationships, such as in the early stages of learning to drive a car; this is associated with the left lateral region of the frontal lobes.
3. *Monitoring* – a function involved in checking a task over time and adjusting behaviour as appropriate, for example when timing an activity or detecting when errors occur; this is associated with the right lateral regions of the frontal lobes.

These three processes are anatomically and functionally independent, and are 'supervisory' as they are important for controlling lower-order processes. Stuss and Alexander consider them to be domain-general and to operate as required by task context and complexity in different networks, both within the frontal regions and also between frontal and posterior regions. There is no overarching supervisory system such as an undifferentiated central executive higher in the hierarchy; instead the functioning of such a system is carried out by the flexible assembly of these individual processes.

DIVERSITY AND UNITY OF EXECUTIVE FUNCTIONS

Although the finding of low correlations among executive tasks seems to be robust, Miyake *et al.* (2000) noted that it is not completely clear that these are indeed a reflection of distinct dissociable underlying executive functions (see also Chapters 3 and 5 for discussion of Miyake's findings). Non-executive processing requirements (for example ones that tap perceptual or motor abilities) may instead obscure the existence of underlying commonalities among the different executive tasks. In their study, Miyake *et al.* sought to extract what might be common among different tasks of executive function and then used this extracted factor to explore how different executive functions related to each other. They chose three executive functions: shifting between tasks, updating and monitoring working memory representations, and inhibition of dominant responses. They then selected a number of simple tasks that are believed to tap each function and a more complex, conventional executive task that is thought to tap several of these three functions. One hundred and thirty-seven college students performed each task. Miyake *et al.* concluded that their results 'suggest that the three often postulated executive functions of Shifting, Updating, and Inhibition are separable but moderately correlated constructs, thus indicating both unity and diversity of executive functions' (p. 87). They also found that each function contributed differently to participants' performance on the more complex executive test, highlighting the multifactorial nature of certain executive tasks that are often used in cognitive and neuropsychological studies.

More recently, the relationship between intelligence and these three executive functions, shifting mental sets, updating working memory and inhibiting prepotent responses, has been investigated in normal young adults. Friedman *et al.* (2006) found that 'updating' correlated with intelligence on the WAIS IQ, and on measures of fluid and crystallized intelligence. However, 'shifting' and 'inhibition' were not statistically significantly related to intelligence once their relationship with 'updating' was taken into account. These findings support those of Roca *et al.* (2010) described earlier, highlighting that intelligence measures do not relate in the same way to different executive functions. Friedman *et al.* (2008) have conducted a twin study and shown that individual differences in these three executive functions are almost entirely due to genetic rather than environmental influences. The unity of the executive functions was associated with a common factor that was 99 per cent heritable and that operated on all three functions; however, there were also genetic influences unique to particular executive functions highlighting their diversity. Finally, Collette *et al.* (2005) conducted a neuroimaging study to examine the brain areas that are common to, and also unique to, the three executive functions of shifting, updating and inhibition. They found common frontal and parietal areas activitated with all three functions suggesting that they are not subserved by the frontal lobes alone, however there were specific prefrontal areas associated with each executive process. These findings highlight again both the unity and diversity of these three particular functions.

A FINAL NOTE

The aim of this chapter was to introduce you to disorders associated with the frontal lobes, with a particular focus on what are referred to as executive functions which encompass processes associated with problem-solving. It is important, however, to acknowledge that the term 'executive functions' is a psychological construct, not to be confused with functions specifically associated with the frontal lobes. There are two reasons for this: first, impairment on tests of executive function may arise without focal frontal damage and after damage to non-frontal brain areas, and second, not all frontal lobe functions are executive ones; for example, as indicated in Section 9.3, some are related to behavioural or emotional self-regulation (Stuss, 2006). It is also important to note that although there are many tasks that are thought to tap executive function, not all of which have been described in this chapter, traditional tests such as the Wisconsin Card Sorting Test were not originally designed as a test of executive function in patient populations, and furthermore it is not entirely clear what they actually measure. Burgess *et al.* (2009) make the point that our understanding in this area is hampered by the fact that we do not have defining features for a test of 'abstract reasoning' that will reliably distinguish it from other executive functions such as 'planning'. However, it is important to seek an understanding of the specific deficits of patients with frontal lesions, as this knowledge can assist in the design of appropriate assessment tools and inform rehabilitation strategies. That fluid intelligence may account for performance on some of the measures of executive function suggests that separation from *g* could be an important step towards improving assessment.

SUMMARY

- Executive functions encompass the deployment of attention, the initiation of non-habitual action, goal-directed behaviour, planning, insight, foresight and self-regulation, and hence processes that are associated with problem-solving, an operational definition of thinking.

- Frontal lobe damage can affect performance on a wide range of tasks that are thought to tap executive functions.
- Case histories show that frontal damage may also result in changes to personality and affective behaviour.
- Neuropsychological studies have shown that impairments in the deployment of attention, in abstract and conceptual thinking and in strategy formation can follow frontal lobe damage, and these processes are important for successful problem solution.
- Findings suggest that laboratory tests may not be suitable for tapping those social problem-solving activities that frontal patients find difficult to perform in everyday life.
- Norman and Shallice have provided a theory of frontal lobe function that specifies damage to the central executive of working memory, however alternative accounts have identified weakening memory associations and an overlap with fluid intelligence.
- The executive functions appear separable but they also seem to share some underlying commonality.
- Research in this area is problematic, partly because many tests of executive functions are complex tasks which make demands on a variety of cognitive skills.

FURTHER READING

- Fellows, L. K. (2010). Damaged self, damaged control: a component process analysis of the effects of frontal lobe damage on human decision making. In R. R. Hassin, K. N. Ochsner and Y. Trope eds. *Self Control in Society, Mind, and Brain,* Oxford: Oxford University Press. This chapter looks at the effects of frontal lobe damage on decision-making; however, the focus is on self-control, exploring why a model suggesting 'top-down' control over 'instinctive/impulsive' behaviour is unsatisfactory, an issue not addressed in the current chapter.
- Goldberg, E. (2009). *The New Executive Brain.* Oxford: Oxford University Press. This is not a textbook and so provides an easy to read introduction to the different executive functions the frontal lobes perform.
- Jurado, M. B. and Rosselli, M. (2007). The elusive nature of executive functions: a review of ourcurrent understanding. *Neuropsychological Review,* 17, 213–233. This review paper covers many of the issues raised towards the end of this chapter and also ones not covered here, including the evolution of executive functions, the development of executive functions and their vulnerability to the effects of age.

- Levine, B., Turner, G. R. and Stuss, D. T. (2008). Rehabilitation of frontal lobe functions. In D. T. Stuss, G. Winocur and I. H. Robertson eds. *Cognitive Neurorehabilitation*. Cambridge: Cambridge University Press. This chapter provides an accessible overview of the effects of frontal lobe damage and extends this chapter by looking at the disorders affecting the frontal lobes and rehabilitation.

Contents

Language

Sophie Scott

10.1 INTRODUCTION

Human speech and language are arguably unique: no other animals regularly make sounds in the way that we do when we speak, and none of them uses those sounds to express an communication system as rich and as structured as human language. Despite this complexity, we rarely experience language use as 'difficult', perhaps because much of our use of language is supported by automatic, unconscious processes. For example, the reflex-like processing of syntax was the starting point of Fodor's interest in the modularity of human information processing (Fodor, 1983).[1] Furthermore, humans process linguistic information in a way that has certain, distinct differences from the perceptual and cognitive processing of other kinds of information, and this has been argued to reflect a mode of linguistic processing which may be fundamentally unlike other kinds of knowledge. Thus although language may interact with many of the other processes described in this book – such as working memory and attention – there are theoretical reasons to suspect that language may utilise a distinct and specialised set of perceptual and cognitive functions. Indeed, it has even been argued that cognitive phenomena such as verbal working memory do not represent distinct, natural cognitive faculties, instead reflecting interactions between the (pre-existing) speech perception and speech production systems (Jacquemot and Scott, 2006).

Language is perhaps the predominant system we have of encoding and describing our world, as well as forming a basis for the majority of our social interactions: language can also form an important code for thoughts and conscious experiences (although thought need not be linguistic in nature). This chapter will address the perception and production of language, via speech, writing and signing. This will include the ways that language is understood, and interactional use of language, for example in conversation. This chapter will outline these systems in the neurotypical brain, and Chapter 11 will explore the ways that we have learnt about language from working with people who have suffered different kinds of brain damage.

10.2 THE LANGUAGE SYSTEM

Spoken human language is generally considered to contain structure at a number of different levels. The 'lowest' level that is generally addressed

Key Term

Speech
Spoken form of a language: a way of conveying linguistic information with the human voice.

Syntax
Grammatical rules of a language. These rules govern the ways that words can be combined (and declined). Syntax can be independent of meaning: a sentence can be syntactically correct but meaningless (e.g. 'colourless green dreams sleep furiously').

Writing
A visual system for representing a language. Writing systems can be alphabetic (where one symbol corresponds roughly to one speech sound), syllabic (where one symbol corresponds to one syllable), or ideographic/logographic (where individual symbols correspond to one word).

Key Term

Phoneme
The smallest unit of speech which contributes to its linguistic meaning: changing a phoneme will change the meaning of a word.

Word
A word is a lexical unit which can stand alone in terms of its use in a language and its meaning. Words have meanings which map onto things and ideas: words are the level at which languages convey meaning.

Morphemes
Units of meaning within words. A word like 'descendant' contains a number of morphemes which contribute to its meaning ('de-' = from, '-scend-' = climb, '-ant' = person with the property of).

Semantics
The meanings of words and the ways that this knowledge is structured and interpreted. Sentences can be ungrammatical but fully semantically comprehensible (e.g. I don't want you to turn me down! I want you to turn me yes!).

is in terms of the acoustics of the speech, followed by phonetic information. Phonemes are the building blocks of spoken language: getting the right phonemes in the right order is often considered to give words their individual lexical identity. The next levels of structure are lexical and morphological structure, which refers to words and sub-structures of words respectively. If words refer to distinct conceptual entities, then the morphemes can be considered to form the units within words which alter the meanings and status of words. These can be thought of often as forming stems and affixes (e.g. walk, walk-ed, walk-ing, walk-er). Semantic representation refers to the meanings of words and syntax refers to the grammatical rules that delineate how words can be combined to make sentences. There are also pragmatic aspects of language, as well as specific uses of language, such as metaphor, and the use of language in discourse. Spoken language has further distinctive properties such as speech rhythm and intonation. Though we typically consider these different levels of language to form qualitatively distinct stages, there is considerable interaction between some of these levels.

SPEECH SOUNDS

Phonemes are a way of describing the smallest meaningful units of spoken language, such that changing a phoneme will change the meaning of a word: 'p' and 'b' are similar phonemes, but 'pit' and 'bit' are two different words with distinctly different meanings. The phonetic repertoire of any one language reflects the range of possible speech sounds that could be used to make up a word, and languages vary considerably in their phonetic repertoires: Mandarin is the official spoken language in China, and contains a wider range of fricatives and affricates than English, for example, while some sub-Saharan African languages (e.g. !Xhosa) use ingressive speech sounds (where air is sucked into the mouth, like a 'giddy-up' sound) as phonemes.

Within a language. any single 'phoneme' can be quite an abstract concept: for example, for Southern British English speakers the 'l' in 'leaf' and the 'l' in 'bell' are different in a great many ways acoustically, yet they are both examples of the phoneme /l/. Try saying these aloud and feel how your tongue is in a different position for both. The leaf 'l' is called a clear /l/ and the bell 'l' is called a dark /l/. These two very different /l/ sounds are described as allophones of the same phoneme – different sounding versions of the same phoneme. In English, clear /l/ is typically found at the onsets of syllables, and dark /l/ at the offsets: to complicate matters, however, phonemes can also vary considerably with regional accents. Thus in several Welsh accents of English, clear /l/ sounds are found at towards the ends of syllables and words.

Different languages carve up the range of possible sounds we can make into different phonetic identities: We are familiar with the idea that native speakers of Japanese have difficulty distinguishing English 'r' from 'l' sounds. This is not because these are not common sounds in Japanese, but instead because 'r' and 'l' are both different manifestations of the same phoneme (the 'allophones' described above) in spoken Japanese. Japanese listeners can find it hard to hear the difference

between the two as they are typically grouped together as one phoneme. If English speakers were confronted with a language where clear
and dark /l/ sounds were different phonemes we would find this hard
and we would make a lot of mistakes, although the /l/ sounds themselves are very familiar to us.

Phonemes are often described as being made up of constellations
of phonetic features, associated with place of articulation, manner of
articulation and presence/absence of voicing. Place of articulation is
where the smallest constriction is produced in the mouth (or larynx):
a 'k' has a velar place of articulation (i.e. the back of the roof of the
mouth, and a 's' has an alveolar place of articulation (the ridge just
behind the teeth). Manner of articulation refers to how the sounds
are made: is there a complete closure of the vocal tract, followed by
a release of sound as in a plosive sound such as 'b'? Is there a noisy
rattling of air, as in a fricative such as 'sh'? Is there a noisy sound combined with a movement of the tongue as in the affricate 'ch'? Voicing
refers to whether or not the vocal folds are vibrated together to give
the voice a strong sense of pitch. Phonetically, the difference between
'pit' and 'bit' are that the vocal folds are vibrated during the 'b' in 'bit'
but not during the 'p' in 'pit'. Minimal pairs, in phonetic terms, are
where two different words are made by changing one phonetic feature,
such as voicing: 'sue'/'zoo'; place of articulation: 'pit'/'kit'; or manner
of articulation: 'sat'/'tat'.

There are also rules about the ways that phonemes can be combined: in English, we can have the combination /dw/ at the start of a
syllable, but not the combination /pw/. This 'phonotactic legality' varies across languages, with different combinations of phonemes being
possible in some languages but not others. Thus words can start with
the phonemes /bw/ in some African languages but not in English.

The phonotactic legality of combinations of phonemes can also
have profound influences on the ways that syllables are structured
in different languages. Syllables are a way of describing structured
sequences of phonemes, which are always arranged around a vowel. In
many languages (e.g. Japanese) syllable structure is very constrained,
such that only one consonant is possible before a vowel, and the only
consonant possible after a vowel is a nasal such as 'n' or 'ng'. In contrast, English allows an extravagant array of consonants before and
after a vowel, yet still forming one syllable (though there are still
rules about how those consonants can be combined). Syllables can
start with up to three phonemes before the vowel in English, such as
'splash', and up to four afterwards, such as in 'lengths': this means that
the word 'strengths' forms only one syllable in English. A word like
'strengths' would not be phontactically legal in Japanese, and Japanese
listeners have been shown to hear an illusory (epenthetic) vowel in
between consonants in these illegal clusters, so that they become legal
in Japanese (Dupoux et al., 1999).

We also 'assimilate' speech sounds when we produce real speech –
most English people saying the words 'sweet girl' in connected speech
actually say 'sweek girl'. This is because English speakers use place

> **Key Term**
>
> **Phonotactics**
> Rules which govern
> how phonemes can
> be combined and
> sequenced in any
> one language – for
> example, a syllable
> can start with 'dw-' in
> English, but a syllable
> cannot end '-dw'.

assimilation: we anticipate the place of articulation of upcoming speech sounds and this can affect the sounds we are currently making. In 'sweek girl' the 't' at the end of sweet is produced further back in the mouth, anticipating the velar place of articulation of the 'g' at the start of 'girl'. Again, there are language differences in this phenomenon – French speakers don't show place assimilation, but they do show voicing assimilation, so upcoming voicing affects speech sounds. In French connected speech, 'football' is often said as 'foodball', as the 't' at the end of foot is voiced and becomes a 'd', in anticipation of the voicing of /b/. In contrast, English speakers often say 'foopball', as the 't' becomes a 'p' in anticipation of the bilabial place of articulation of /b/.

These anticipation effects, where one speech sound affects another, have influences over most of what we say, and mean that speech sounds are not produced in a context independent way, like beads on a string. Instead, they affect one another, and listeners use this information to help decode what they are hearing. If you say the words 'see', 'sue', 'sew', the 's' sounds are very different, depending on the next vowel sound (Bailey and Summerfield, 1980). This is not specific to speech sounds, and has been shown for handwriting and finger-spelling: when humans produce sequences of actions, we cannot produce fully separate, discrete acts. This means that our perceptual systems can and do derive information about the sequences by how these elements interact.

VISUAL LANGUAGES – BRITISH SIGN LANGUAGE

The precise way that language expresses information varies with the nature of that language. In British Sign Language (BSL), for example, the main articulators are the hands, and signs can be characterised by the shape of the hand, the movements of the hands and the location where the hand(s) are held. A word in BSL therefore corresponds to the combination of the hand shape, hand movements made and the hand location. This means that words in BSL thus do not have the same kinds of sequential segmental structure found in speech, but instead exploit positional detail in a way that speech does not.

Minimal pairs in speech are seen when a word changes by altering one phonetic feature – 'got' and 'cot' for example vary in terms of the presence or absence of voicing of the initial plosive. Minimal pairs in BSL occur when words differ in one feature – hand shape, movement or location. In Figure 10.1, the BSL words for 'name' and 'afternoon' are identical in terms of hand shape and movement, but the locations are different.

It is important to stress that sign languages are true languages – they are not simply pantomimed gestures but have complex syntactic structure, semantics and phonology (where phonology corresponds to details of the hand movements, shapes and locations). A second factor that is important to understand is that signed languages are not visual variants of spoken languages – British Sign Language is not a visual version of British English: the grammar is very different, for example. Indeed, BSL uses space in a very interesting way – signers will assign

Key Term

Sign language
A visual language, normally arising in deaf communities, in which the hands are used to express linguistic information. Sign languages are not just sequences of pantomimed gestures, nor are they typically visual forms of existing spoken languages – for example, British Sign Language has very little in common with spoken British English, having a very different syntax and rules for combining words. In sign language, the face is often used to replace the role of prosody and intonation in spoken language, being used to convey emphasis and emotion.

a spatial location to the things or people they are talking about, and will refer
back to that place when they refer to
that person or thing. Strikingly, there are
many similarities in how BSL and spoken
English are processed in the brain, suggesting that at higher-order linguistic levels of
representation, there are fewer differences
between spoken and signed language than
these overt surface differences would suggest (MacSweeney *et al.*, 2008).

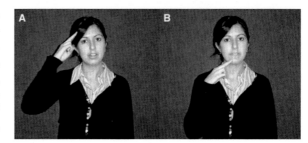

Figure 10.1   These BSL signs, (A) 'name' and (B)
'afternoon' differ only in location. Hand shape and
movement are the same.

Finger-spelling, in contrast, is a way of
signing information in which the letters of
the alphabet are mapped onto different finger shapes. Finger-spelling
thus represents a way to express information about the orthography
(written form) of a language with the hands.

WORDS AND MORPHEMES

Words are the psychological linguistic structures that relate directly to
our experience. We use words as representations that map onto the things
and events that we want to describe. Words are arguably the basic units
with which we engage with language: once we have learnt to read, we can
decompose words into phonemes, but if we have not learnt to read, this
kind of detail is much harder to grasp. Words are also the level at which
babies start to engage with the elements of spoken language.

Morphemes are syntactic structural units within a word, and can be
considered to refer to the smallest possible unit of meaning, but which
is not necessarily a word. The base, or stem of a morpheme assigns
meaning to the word – for example 'bee' is the stem or base of 'bees'.
Bee is also a 'free' or unbound morpheme – it can appear without elaboration as a stand-alone word. Prefixes are morphemes which come
before a stem, such as 'pre- in 'prefigure' or 'ex-' in 'export'. Suffixes
are morphemes which come after the stem, like the '-s' in 'bees' or the
'-ed' in 'carpeted'. These suffixes and prefixes are bound morphemes –
they cannot appear on their own as individual words. There is a lot of
interest in the extent to which morphological information is decoded
in the perception of language. It has been stressed that in speech, there
is a strong overlap between morphological structure and suprasyllabic
structure such as lexical stress and prosody.

Words also vary in terms of their role in speech, such as the difference between content words and form words. Form words (such as
'the', 'on', 'and', 'for') give sentences their structure, and content words
(such as 'dog', 'Peter', 'black', 'nine', 'taken') give the sentence structure referential meaning. Sentences such as those below share their
form words, and the underlying relationships between the content
words in the sentence can be seen to have similarities:

The cup was on the table.
The dog eats on the floor.

However, if we keep the form words the same and swap the content words around then the meaning gets radically altered:

The cup was on the table.
The table was on the cup.

Further distinctions can be made within the content words, for example, into nouns versus verbs. While these break down somewhat into 'things' versus 'actions', the boundary is blurred quite lot in languages, like English, where many nouns can be used as verbs. There are in fact few nouns in English which cannot be used as a verb. There are, however, differences in the processing of nouns and verbs if people are parsing them as nouns and verbs: verbs typically are longer to process than nouns (Kousta *et al.*, 2011), perhaps because a verb frequently involves associated information about not just the action, but the object which is performing it – it may be less complex to access and represent information about a *rabbit*, for example, than about *running*.

Learning a language means that we acquire new words – all the words anyone knows are words that they have learnt. The words that we know can be thought of as our vocabulary, and this is not fixed – we continue to acquire new words and new word meaning at the rate of around 1,000 a year, which is around three per day! These words make up our mental lexicon, which may nor may not form a separable linguistic store. As we will see later, some models of word access posit separate store of lexical items and others do not.

SENTENCE LEVEL

Sentences contain structure at a number of different levels. Thematically, for example, sentences can be described as having different components, such as the subject and object: in a sentence like 'Carolyn opened the present', Carolyn is the subject, the theme of the sentence – the sentence is about Carolyn. The present is the object, one of the things and events that are part of the sentence about Carolyn.

The syntactic structure – determining the different parts in the sentence depending on their grammatical relationship to one another – is the kind of structure that has been discussed most thoroughly in cognitive psychology, and is discussed later in the chapter. There are other kinds of structure, for example, thematic structure, which refers to the relationships between the meanings of the words in a sentence (Fillmore, 1968). This is well captured by the case of the words: for example, in the sentence 'Philip gave the cheese to David', Philip is the person doing something in the sentence, David is the person who receives something and the cheese is transferred. In terms of case, the different roles in the sentence would be: Philip is the agent; David takes the dative role (affected by the action named in the verb); and the cheese is the object (Schlesinger, 1995). The strength of case analysis of sentences is that it allows us to characterise a relationship between higher-order semantic relationships at a sentence level.

THE LEVEL OF DISCOURSE

Speech and language are used to build narratives and stories across sentences, and pragmatics is the term which describes the constraints on language use at this discourse level. Conversation is a linguistic universal – wherever you go in the world, whatever language is spoken or signed, the conversations will have common characteristics. It is also the case that most of us acquire our first spoken language in the context of conversation, and conversation is thus a linguistic universal which bridges between the development and the social use of communication.

10.3 PSYCHOLOGY AND LINGUISTICS

The study of psycholonguistics is traditionally associated with the latter half of the twentieth century, as epitomised by the work of Chomsky. Actually there have been psychologically motivated studies of human language for a couple of centuries (Levelt, 2012), including a great vogue for diary studies of children's language development and the neuropsychological insights of European neurologists in the mid-1800s (see Chapter 11). Of course, all of these different approaches embody very different approaches and intellectual traditions, the effects of many of which we still benefit from. However, the psycholinguistic approach of Chomsky and colleagues deserves more lengthy attention, not least because it has led to a number of developments in the study of language and cognition.

Chomsky noted that we are able to generate and understand entirely novel sentences, and his insight came from a hypothesis that this capacity must result from an underlying application of linguistic rules. A further development of this hypothesis holds that the ability to use these rules must reflect an innate, pre-potent ability, which does not need to be learnt. This approach was formulated in opposition to theories of human behaviour which were popular in the 1950s and which emphasised learning as a key property of human behaviour (Skinner, 1938). Chomsky considered that human language could not be acquired by learning alone, since the kinds of learning paradigms (e.g. operant conditioning) that Skinner addressed did not account for how children learn spoken language – for example, they are rarely rewarded overtly for this.

Key to Chomsky's approach, and congruent with a developing interest in cognitive processes in the field of psychology at the time, was the concept of an underlying, deeper structure to the surface expression of a sentence. For example, these sentences look very similar but are very different in meaning:

Phil is easy to understand.
Phil is eager to understand.

In contrast, these sentences look very different but have similar meanings:

Tom watched the film.
The film was watched by Tom.
It was Tom who watched the film.
It was this film that was watched by Tom.

As people frequently do not speak in 'proper sentences', with real speech being littered with slang, errors and corrections, Chomsky addressed the difference between the possibilities of language use and the actual ways that people speak by considering that there were differences between linguistic competence (the syntax of speech) and linguistic performance – the ways that people actually talk.

Some early work in psycholinguistics found links between syntactic structure and cognitive measures – for example, passive constructions:

Rebecca was followed by Carolyn.

have been identified as being harder to understand than active constructions:

Carolyn followed Rebecca.

This has been demonstrated in terms of processing speed and recall, where passive sentences take longer to read and are less well remembered than active sentences (Harley, 2001). However, Slobin (1966) showed that the slower processing of more complex passive sentences was held only for *reversible* sentences like the ones above, where the either noun could be the object and subject of the sentence. In contrast, when Slobin presented sentences like:

The chemist grasped the test tube.

where reversing the subject and object results in a nonsense sentences, the effect disappeared. Slobin found that non-reversible sentences were judged to be true or false faster than reversible sentences, which suggested that people use the semantic plausibility of a sentence to help constrain their interpretation. Developments of this perspective will be discussed in a later section.

It must be noted that studies of learning have made considerable inroads to the study of how spoken language can be acquired. Chomsky's original hypothesis was that the rules governing language must be innate, as they are not learnt: children are not presented with examples of all the possible ways that rules can be combined such that the underlying rules can be divined, and children are not rewarded (negatively or positively) for their syntactic behaviour; furthermore, children go through stages where they over apply syntactic rules and make errors, suggesting that the rules are 'real'. However, learning theories now acknowledge that learning does not require rewards, and that babies and children are exceptionally skilled at statistical learning, both for the phonetic regularities that underlie words (or possible words) in spoken language, and for the syntactic regularities that underlie the structure of sentences. Thus in English, the word 'the' predicts an upcoming noun, and a preposition predicts an upcoming noun phrase (Saffran, 2003). The development of this work to show that these sensitivities to statistical regularities in non-linguistic sequences suggests that syntactic rules may themselves be constrained by the kinds of statistical dependencies that human beings can learn.

TASKS IN THE STUDY OF LANGUAGE

Over the years, many different tasks have been employed to help shed light on the cognitive processing involved in language. These tasks are necessary because for behavioural studies of language, we need a behavioural correlate of the cognitive and linguistic processes underlying language. Of course, normal linguistic processing can be entirely passive – people can understand a sentence they hear without making any overt responses. The tasks used therefore aim to be performable in a relatively simple way, so as to avoid task effects, but to involve normal linguistic processes, such that manipulations we think will affect linguistic processes will also affect performance of these overt tasks. The tasks include asking people whether a sentence is true or false in the sentence verification task used by Slobin, asking people if a target item is a real word or a non-word in the lexical decision task, and asking people to name aloud a read word (speeded naming) or repeat a heard word (repetition task). In all the tasks both reaction times and errors are used as direct indices of cognitive processing of lexical items. People have also used measures such as eye movements to shed light on what kind of information a participant is using to perform a task. More recently, people have started to use functional imaging methods (Chapter 11) which show the neural systems recruited when people deal with linguistic information (e.g. listen to speech they understand).

> **Key Term**
>
> **Lexical decision task**
> An experiment in which participants are given a target item (typically written), and asked to decide whether it is a real word or not. Lexical decision tasks are used as the amount of time taken to give a response can indicate how the target item is being processed: this response can be used in combination with other tasks, e.g. priming.

10.4 RECOGNISING SPOKEN AND WRITTEN WORDS

HOW DO WE RECOGNISE SPOKEN WORDS?

When we hear someone speaking continuously in our language, we hear sequences of spoken words; however, the 'gaps' between the words we hear are illusory – in continuous speech, there is no silence between words. In Figure 10.2, the spectrogram of a sentence is shown – time is on the x-axis, frequency is on the y-axis, and where the colour is darker, there is more energy in the signal. From this, we can see that where there does appear to be silence, this is where the mouth is closed before the words that start with a 'b'. There is also silence when the mouth is closed to release the final 'd' in 'bread', and this does not sound like the start of a new word.

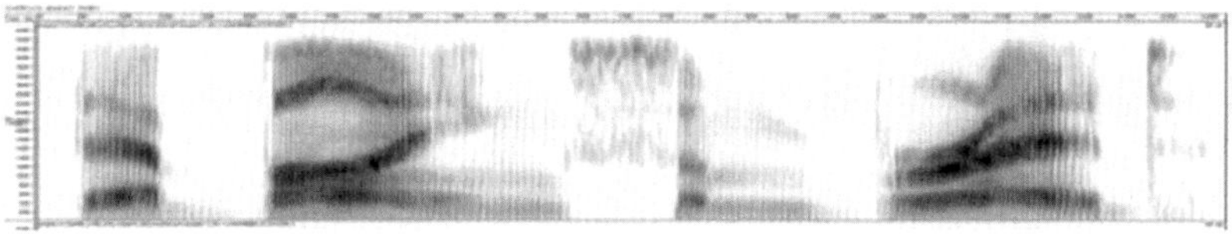

Figure 10.2
Spectrogram of a spoken sentence.

They're   buying   some   bread

Thus the identification and recognition of spoken words is not supported by those words themselves being acoustically separable. In terms of processing, when we hear a word, there are at least two ways that spoken word recognition can occur: using segmental, speech sound information (i.e. sub-lexical phonetic information), or looking for structure across the whole word – that is, matching for information at the level of words. There has been a lot of support for the latter position: using priming, Zwitserlood (1989) showed that both the words *captain* and *capital* are primed by the word cap, suggesting that part of speech perception entails the matching of lexical items. Not all 'words-in-words' prime other words, however: in Dutch, the word *zwijn* does not prime *wijn* (Vroomen and de Gelder, 1997). This research suggests that that lexical activation during speech perception depends on syllable onsets that are aligned with word onsets.

However, as described earlier in this chapter, we know that the actual phonetic realisation of the speech sounds in words is influenced by the context: try holding your hand in front of your mouth as you say 'port' and 'sport' and you'll notice that there is a big puff of air when you say 'port' that is not there for 'sport': the 'p' in 'port' is aspirated, i.e. produced with a big release of air, which the 'p' in 'sport' is not. There are other acoustic and phonetic differences – the 'p' in 'sport' is typically produced as a 'b' as the voicing of the vowel is anticipated. Speech sounds can have relatively long-range effects on one another in speech – the 'l' at the start of 'let' is different from the 'l' at the start of 'led', as the voicing of the syllable final 'd' 'darkens' the 'l' (Kelly and Local, 1986). Indeed, the phonetic features like voicing have multiple acoustic factors: the sequences 'apa' and 'aba' differ phonetically in just the voicing of the medial 'p' or 'b': however, there are more than sixteen separate, independent acoustic differences that underlie this phonetic difference (Lisker, 1977). Listeners are very sensitive to these differences so it would seem likely that acoustic/phonetic factors (e.g. those between the word 'cap' spoken in isolation and in the context of 'captain') could influence word recognition.

This is indeed the case. Davis *et al.* (2002), using a cross-model repetition priming paradigm, looked at the priming of a word in isolation and as part of a longer word. They presented morphemes in two different contexts, such as 'cap' in the sentence 'The soldier saluted the flag with his [cap tucked in] [captain]'. Priming was stronger in trials in which the visual probe matched the speech, even when the written probe appeared before the end of 'cap'. This indicates that listeners use the acoustic/phonetic differences that arise from the context in which words are said to help them understand the speech. This may take the form of speakers using subtle acoustic cues to constrain lexical search space.

Listeners will also use other cues if they are available: in English, metrical stress tends to follow a strong–weak profile, and listeners will use this, if they can, to segment out words. In Finnish, there is a property called vowel harmony, in which the properties of the initial vowel in a word govern which vowels can follow. My middle name is *Kerttu*, a Finnish name, and the Finnish vowel harmony principle means that *Kerttie* is not a legal word. Finnish listeners use this property to constrain lexical possibilities of what they are hearing, and to predict what is coming next.

Phonotactic rules are also used to segment words. As we saw earlier, there are 'legal' combinations of phonemes in any language – for example, English syllables can start 'sp' but not 'ps', although 'ps' is a legal way of ending a syllable like 'lips'.

These phonotactic regularities and probabilities are used by listeners: in word spotting experiments, it is easier to identify a word if its position in a non-word is aligned with a phonotactic cue to a syllable onset than if it is not. Thus listeners are faster to identify 'lips' in the non-word 'venlips' than the non-word 'veglips', as 'nl' is not a phonotactically possibly syllable onset in many languages (Dumay *et al.*, 2002; McQueen, 1998).

Lexical effects also influence the recognition of words: people can take longer to recognise words that come from dense lexical neighbourhoods, i.e. that have many similar sounding words (Luce and Pisoni,1998). Thus 'start', 'part' and 'hard' are close phonological neighbours. As spoken words evolve over time, the density of the phonological neighbourhood is related to the uniqueness point of a word – more unique words such as 'moccasin' typically have more sparse phonological neighbourhoods. The ways that sublexical and lexical processing affects speech recognition can be counterintuitive: we can see that phontactically more common profiles are faster to produce, but there is a cost to matching a word in a dense phonological neighbourhood, and this cost can be sensitive to the precise task required of the participants: people are faster to repeat non-words that have a high phonotactic probability and come from dense neighbourhoods, but this effect is reversed for real words (Vitevitch and Luce, 1998, 1999, 2005). This suggests that the repetition of non-words benefits from their being like many real words through priming of the response, while there is a cost to repeating real words with many phonological neighbours, through competition processes.

There is also evidence that the kinds of information used by listeners to understand speech can be quite flexible. In a study varying lexical stress and phontactic probabilities, Mattys *et al.* (2005) showed that sentential and lexical information dominated over phonotactic and lexical stress, in terms of speech processing. However, when they presented the same stimuli in noise, the rank ordering of the cues reversed. This suggests that the speech recognition system is a highly plastic and flexible set of processes and that listeners will utilise the information available to them in a way which will maximise their speech processing. This is necessary to process speech outside of the lab, where environments can be noisy, and speakers can vary hugely in how they actually produce the sounds of speech, both as a function of accent, and as a function of context. A lot of causal, connected speech is highly underarticulated.

Normal speech can vary a lot from speaker to speaker, and we do not all speak on the same way, either due to our accents or more personal factors. It is not at all uncommon in English, for example, to encounter people who produce the 'r' sound in a variety of ways: some people saying a 'w' sound instead, some producing a sort of 'v' sound. However, people do not typically find their speech hard to understand, and there is evidence that listeners will adapt rapidly to overtly different speech idiosyncrasies, and do so in a talker-specific way. Eisner and McQueen (2005, 2006) played people a story in which the talker's speech was manipulated such that their /f/ sounds were more like /s/ sounds, or their /s/ sounds were more like /f/ sounds. Although the listeners were simply listening to these stories, when their perception of f/s sounds was tested afterwards, they nonetheless showed a shift in perception, which was interpreted as an alteration in the way that the f/s boundary was represented. Crucially, however, this shift only occurred if the *same talker's voice* was used. This indicates that the perceptual remapping has not generally affected the whole speech perception system, but that it is an exemplar, or talker-specific adaptation.

HOW DO WE RECOGNISE WRITTEN WORDS?

To a large extent, reading written words is parasitic upon speech perception (and production) skills, although it is a visual skill. Thus, children who are good at parsing a spoken word into chunks (i.e. onset-rhyme) are also those who find it easier to learn to read (e.g. Goswami *et al.*, 2002).

Written words in English do not have a simple, lawful mapping between the ways that they are spelt, and the ways that they are spoken. Thus the sequence of letters '-ough' can rhyme with 'cow' (as in 'plough'), or 'toe' (as in 'though'), or 'port' (as in 'thought'), or 'shoe' (as in 'through'). Not all written languages have this weak relationship between spelling and pronunciation – Finnish, for example, has a direct one-to-one mapping between letters and speech sounds, and anecdotally it is not unusual to meet Finnish individuals who taught themselves to read. These regular spelling systems are termed transparent or regular orthographies, and spelling systems with less consistent spelling-to-sound rules are termed opaque or irregular orthographies.

Several different factors have been shown to affect visual word recognition. One important factor is familiarity, a measure of the frequency with which one encounters a word: lexical decisions, for example, can be faster for words which are encountered with high frequency (e.g. Balota *et al.*, 2004). However, familiarity has been argued to not be a stable measure (Gernsbacher, 1984), and it has been shown that familiarity correlates with semantic properties of words, such as their perceived meaningfulness (Balota *et al.*, 1999). Instead of straightforward frequency effects, it has been argued that we need to address the age at which words were acquired, known as age of acquisition (AOA) either because words that were learnt first have a special status, or because the amount of time one can be exposed to a word is longer if we learnt it earlier (Morrison and Ellis, 1995; Juhasz, 2005). There are also issues about the extent to which AOA is an outcome measure or a standard predictor variable – should we regard the AOA effects as arising due to the ways that AOA affects the representations of words, or is it having a post-lexical, task-based effect (Zevin and Seidenberg, 2002, 2004)?

Properties of the written words also affect their processing. Orthographic length (the number of letters) in a written word has a big effect on the processing and recognition of written words, and the effect is more marked for non-words than words (Coltheart, 2001). The regularity and consistency of written words both affect their processing and their recognition (Baron and Strawson, 1976; Gough and Cosky, 1977): people take longer to read irregularly spelled words like 'yacht' than regular words. The position and the kind of inconsistency may be important. Orthographic neighbourhood size refers, for example, to the density of the numbers of visually similar words that any one word has: a work like 'loot' has many orthographic neighbours ('boot', 'hoot', 'shoot' etc.) and comes from a dense orthographic neighbourhood, while the word 'shoe' has fewer orthographic neighbours, and comes from a sparser orthographic neighbourhood (Coltheart *et al.*, 1977). Orthographic neighbourhood is often called 'N', so a high N refers to a dense orthographic neighbourhood and a low N to a sparse orthographic neighbourhood. A high N has a facilitating effect on reaction times, and this is effect larger for naming than for lexical decision (Balota *et al.*, 2004). However, non-words with a large N (e.g. 'floot') are processed more slowly because the task of deciding whether the word is a real word or not is adversely affected if the non-word is visually similar to many real words (Coltheart *et al.*, 1977; Andrews, 1997). The effects of the high N on the non-word processing may thus be more associated with the task used than with the non-word itself. Indeed, the precise experimental task used does have an impact on the ways that words are apparently processed. For example, in lexical decision tasks the other words and non-words included can influence the results, and the use of illegal or legal non-words affect performance – a non-word like 'xci' may be more easily dismissed as a non-word than a non-word like 'cix'.

In word naming, N interacts with word frequency – low-frequency words show a higher effect of N than high-frequency words. In lexical decision, high N leads to faster responses for low-frequency words and slower responses for high-frequency words.

Influences of the phonological, spoken form of written words can be seen on word recognition. Pseudohomophones are words like *ranes* which can be said aloud to produce a real word, but which have an unfamiliar orthographical form. People can be slower to decide that *ranes* is a non-word in a lexical decision task, it might suggest that there are phonological influences on visual word recognition, and that the meaning has been accessed via phonology (Rubenstein *et al.*, 1971).

MORPHEMES AND WORD RECOGNITION

Semantically transparent complex words have morphological constituents, which have a clear relation to the meaning of the word, e.g. 'hunter' = 'hunt' + 'er'. Semantically opaque complex words have no semantic relation to their apparent morphological constituents. However, derived words only prime their stems if there is a semantic relationship, which may mean that the priming is semantic rather than orthographic. This was the argument made by Rastle and colleagues (2004), who used a priming paradigm to identify the extent to which lexical decision tasks are facilitated by morphological structure in masked primes. Masking a prime means that people do not consciously see the prime; however, lexical decisions were faster for words which were preceded by masked primes which were morphologically related to the target words (e.g. 'cleaner' – 'clean'). This was interpreted as showing a role for morphological processing in the visual recognition of words.

Some models of word recognition (e.g. parallel distributed models) do not use morphemes as explicit structures, instead allowing them to emerge as factors of the interaction of phonological and semantic representations – the more overlap there is between the two kinds of representation, the more priming there will be of a word. Consistent with this approach, 'sneer' primes 'snarl' as much as 'teacher' primes 'teach' (Gonnerman *et al.* (2007).

DATABASE APPROACHES

The classic approach in cognitive psychology is to control as many factors as constant as possible and then manipulate one factor in isolation, for example, to match word frequencies and imagability and vary phonological neighbourhoods and then identify the effect on lexical decision. However, it has been pointed out that this approach is unlikely to allow us to interrogate the complex processes which occur, likely in parallel, during normal word recognition (Balota *et al.*, 2004; Cutler, 1981). Furthermore, it can be very difficult to really control one factor while varying another:

> *The influence of spelling-to-sound correspondence will depend on a number of factors such as the frequency of the target word, the number and frequency of neighbors with similar spelling-to-sound correspondences (friends), the number and frequency of neighbors with different spelling-to- sound correspondences (enemies), and probably a host of other variables (see, e.g., Jared, McRae, & Seidenberg, 1990).*
>
> (Balota *et al.*, 2004: 284)

It is also the case that researchers may unconsciously bias the lists with the kinds of words they use: it has been shown that researchers are good at predicting which words will lead to a long RT in a lexical decision task. Small arrays of words in a stimulus set may therefore be prone to bias. As noted earlier, the use of different list contexts can have a great deal of an influence on lexical decision responses, and it has been argued that much of the variation in the role of orthographic neighbourhood effects in visual word recognition across experiments result from the use of legal versus non-legal non-words (where a legal non-word fits with the orthographic structure of real words – e.g. 'thurp' versus 'pthru') (Andrews, 1997). Finally, Balota and colleagues (2004) point out that almost all the visual word recognition research uses monosyllabic words, which has prevented many of the proper-ties associated with multisyllabic words from being studied, such as stress and prosody, syllable structures/boundaries and different kinds of length effects. Balota and colleagues have developed a very large database of responses to words and non-words (40,481 of each), with both lexical decision responses and speeded naming responses for all the stimuli, called the English Lexicon Project (ELP, http://elexicon. wustl.edu/) (Balota *et al.*, 2007). Over 1,200 participants were tested, with an average of 3,400 responses per participant on lexical decision and 2,500 on speeded naming. The advantage of this approach, in addition to the reduction of confounding factors due to the poten-tial use of a wide range of words, is that a multivariate approach can be used, instead of a factorial design. Thus the relative contribu-tion of different factors on a speeded naming task can be explicitly determined. By examining the lexical decision and naming latencies to 2,428 words (Balota and Spieler, 1998; Spieler and Balota, 1997), Balota *et al.* (2004) demonstrated that standard psycholinguistic vari-ables (e.g., length, frequency, orthographic neighborhood size) were able to account for nearly half the variance in the behavioural data.

From factorial studies we know that the semantic information asso-ciated with written words influences their recognition, and has larger effects on lexical decision than naming: both naming and lexical deci-sion are affected by imagability. Using a multiple regression analysis of the influence of different stimulus parameters on the responses, a role was identified for both imagability and semantic connectivity – a measure of how much a word is semantically related to other words. If AOA is included, imagability drops out as a factor, suggesting that age of acquisition and imagability of a word may account for similar kinds of variance in word recognition (Balota *et al.*, 2007).

10.5 UNDERSTANDING THE MEANINGS OF WORDS

How do we understand the meanings of words? In a completely modular system, it has been argued, semantic information is entirely encoded in terms of abstract representations. Within this, there is considerable debate about the nature of those representations – do we store exemplars, or hierarchies of information, or prototypes?

There has also been a long-standing view that semantic knowledge is not encapsulated – that there is a more distributed quality to semantic representations. There are several varieties of this argument, but all would fall broadly into the category of embodied semantics – that is, the semantic representations of words can exploit sensory-motor information associated with those words. These associations can vary with the kinds of words we are dealing with. Thus the words 'glove' and love are both nouns, but 'glove' is considered to be a concrete noun – gloves exist in the world, you can pick up a glove and you can describe its properties. 'Love' in contrast is an abstract noun – it's much harder to get a mental image of love, and the whole concept feels harder to define, though the precise sense of love can remain crystal clear. In the context of an embodied semantics, concrete nouns generally have many more sensory associations – I can imagine what a glove looks like and I can imagine what a glove feels like as I put it on. Other concrete words like 'carpet', 'cheese', 'crash' or 'tinkle' have somatosensory, olfactory, motoric or acoustic associations, or combinations of sensory-motor qualities. Indeed, since words have an acoustic realisation, English has a whole class of words that we call onomatopoeic words, where the word sounds 'like' the acoustic event ('whoosh', 'splash', 'splat', 'jingle'). Abstract nouns like 'government', 'affair' or 'allowance' are much less rich in sensory motor associations and have been held to lead to a greater reliance on their acoustic form when processing them than concrete words. However, it has recently been demonstrated that abstract words do have associations, but that these may be affective, rather than sensory-motor (Kousta *et al.*, 2011). Thus abstract words like 'government' or 'distinction' have relatively consistent emotional connotations for people. They may not therefore be represented in an entirely disembodied semantic or acoustic code.

Patterson *et al.* (2007) posit a model of semantic representations, the hub model, where there are pure, amodal representations of word meanings in the hub, and this is supported by links with embodied semantic information in distributed associated networks – for example, relevant areas of motor cortex (leg, arm or mouth) for different kinds of action words, and high-order visual cortex for highly imagable words. This model allows for both amodal semantic representations and less abstract perceptual-affective properties of the objects and items to be represented.

10.6 EXPLAINING LEXICAL ACCESS IN LANGUAGE COMPREHENSION

We can see that several factors are involved in the recognition of words, both written and heard, and there is also considerable interest in the ways that we can build cognitive models that capture properties of how our mental lexicon – all the words we know – is represented. The most influential of these is John Morton's Logogen Model (Morton 1969, 1970, 1979; Morton and Patterson, 1980). In this model, every word is represented by a unit, called a logogen, and each logogen represents characteristics (called features) about that word. As the perceptual system(s) processes incoming words, logogens increase in activity as evidence accumulates for each one. Contextual evidence can also add to this activation, so if the incoming phonetic evidence for a word starting 'ta' and the contextual evidence is for a piece of furniture, the logogen for 'table' will increase and the logogen for 'title' will decrease, although both will have been increased in activation by a word starting with a 't' sound. When the threshold for that particular logogen is reached, the logogen fires, and the word is recognised, and the threshold for any one logogen is sensitive to context. This means that a logogen which has recently fired will have its threshold temporarily lowered. The baseline frequency with which any one word is encountered affects the resting activation of the associated logogen, with more common words having higher resting baselines, such that a frequently encountered word needs less activation of its logogen to fire (and to be recognised). The strengths of the logogen model lie in the ways that different factors can influence the firing of the logogens, and thus different aspects of word recognition are well captured. Words which have just been recognised are processed faster a second time, and this repetition priming is modelled by the transitory lowering of the logogen thresholds. We recognise more common words more quickly, and the higher baseline activity of the logogens for more frequent words means that they need less activity to be fired. I notice when I am around people speaking French that I am often distracted when someone says the word 'sauf' – which means 'except', but which is phonetically identical to most English pronunciations of my name, Sophie. By Morton's account, my name is a very frequently encountered word (by me) and the baseline activity for my 'Sophie' logogen must be high enough that it is easily fired, even in error.

The logogen model has been hugely influential, being recently described as the patriarch of computational models of word reading (Seidenberg, 2012), who notes that 'it is worth pausing . . . to recognise the sheer number of essential concepts that were introduced in this pioneering work' (p. 187). As Seidenberg stresses, many later models of reading incorporate aspects of the logogen model, sometimes in a modified form, which is a testament to its power. In Chapter 11, for example, we will see several links to current connectionist models of reading.

An important alternative to the logogen model is the cohort model (Marslen-Wilson, 1973, 1975, 1987, 1989), which is focused specifically on the recognition of spoken words. This model involves the activation of particular candidate words by hearing the first two phonemes of a word – these candidate words are the 'word initial cohort', and this cohort declines in size as more of the incoming word is heard,

Key Term

Comprehension
Refers to the outcome of a range of linguistic processes, from acoustic to semantic and syntactic, which contribute to the way that a linguistic message is understood.

and the recognition units for words which have been ruled out by the incoming activation decline in activation and leave the cohort. Like the logogen model, the cohort model allows for multiple words to be co-activated, and for changes in activity to drive whether the words stay in the competition or not: unlike the logogen model in which the accumulation of activity for any one logogen is a passive process, the activated word units in the cohort model actively try to stay or leave the competition. This was tested in a study of evoked response potentials (ERPs) – measures of brain activity yoked to temporal aspects of the stimuli presented (O'Rourke and Holcomb, 2002). ERPs were measured while participants made lexical decisions about words and non-words, and the uniqueness point – the point in a word where it becomes different from all other words, and the point in a non-word where it becomes unlike any existing lexical item – was varied. An ERP component called the N400 varied in size, depending on whether the items had early or late uniqueness points, as did the lexical decision reaction times. This supports the incremental aspects of the cohort model and is a demonstration of the kinds of evidence that brain response data can provide.

HOW SHOULD WE MODEL LINGUISTIC PROCESSING – RULES OR REGULARITIES? THE CASE OF REGULAR AND IRREGULAR PAST-TENSE VERBS

Many of the cognitive models you will encounter in this book will fall into connectionist, parallel-distributed models, and more rule-based systems. This is the case for cognitive-linguistic models – for example, models of reading can be connectionist (Seidenberg and McClelland, 1989) or symbolic (e.g. the Dual-Route Cascade model, Coltheart, 2001). While both approaches have strengths, they also each have limitations, and debate remains as to the best way to characterise human cognitive processes. Within the realm of language, the inflection of past-tense verbs has been identified as an ideal system for investigating this topic (Pinker, 1997).

Although not as complex as other systems of inflection (e.g. Polish and Czech) English words are inflected to denote aspects of their syntactic or semantic status: nouns can be singular or plural, verbs can be in different tenses. In English, some verbs are inflected to have a past-tense meaning by the addition of the bound morpheme '-ed'; thus 'jump' > 'jumped', 'hand' > 'handed', 'hum' > 'hummed'. These are termed regular past-tense inflections, as the bound morpheme is added in an identical way for each verb morpheme (although their pronunciation can differ – try saying 'jumped', 'handed' and 'hummed' and you will note that the '-ed' ending sounds different in each, coming out more like a '-t' in 'jumpt', '-ed' in 'hand-ed' and a '-d' in 'hummd').

There are a great many of these regular past-tense verbs, at least 10,000 in English. These regular inflections can be contrasted with past-tense verbs like 'eat' > 'ate', 'have' > 'had', 'run' > 'ran'. For these irregular verbs, the past-tense verbs cannot be simply predicted from the present-tense form, and they can be phonetically very dissimilar (e.g. 'tell' > 'told'). There are many fewer irregular verbs, around 106 in English, and they typically are very high in frequency – that is, they are very commonly used verbs.

There is considerable debate about the ways that these two forms of past-tense verbs are represented cognitively: do we encode and represent this information in a symbolic, rule-like fashion, or can a distributed cognition account adequately explain the existence and processing of these regular and irregular forms? These two positions have very different theoretical imports: the symbolic processing model accounting for an explicit syntax in the construction of past-tense verbs. Following on from the conceptual position of Chomsky, Pinker (1999) proposed that regular verbs were formed by rule-based processes, while irregular verbs are formed by lexical mechanisms, which bear more in common with semantic processing than with rule-based mechanisms. In contrast a parallel-processing account of regular and irregular verbs does not require any explicit rules or syntax.

From the symbolic representation position, the regular verbs have been described as a 'paradigm example' of a rule-based system: a very simple bound morpheme is added to a verb to make the past-tense form. Although the phonetic realisation of the '-ed' ending can differ, this is still predictable from the form of the original verb morpheme. Pinker identified three predictions of this approach which support this two-stage process: first, that the acquisition of the past-tense regularisation rule should be very rapid, even instant; second, that the application of the rule be uniform in its application (e.g. not be influenced by semantic information) and third, that the rule-based regular system is distinct from the lexically mediated irregular system.

There is a lot of evidence to support this position. First, many children use past tenses (both regular and irregular) correctly at first, and then go through a stage where they over regularise, producing statements like 'we goed to the zoo' or 'I eated that'. Simple association learning is held to be unable to account for this, as the children will not have (generally) been exposed to these incorrect versions, and they had previously been producing the correct version. Pinker has identified this as a sudden 'eureka' moment, where children come up with the rule which they then start to apply both accurately and inaccurately. The uniformity of the regular rules is seen, according to the Pinker approach, by the use of regular inflections as a default construction of the past tense – if no irregular construction is formed (by the lexical mechanism) a regular form will be produced.

There has remained considerable debate about the extent to which a symbolic, rule-based system is necessary to model the past-tense inflections of English. For example, an early parallel distributed processing model by Rumelhart and McClelland (1986) with modifiable connections between verb root representations and the phonological form of the past-tense verbs, was not only able to learn both regular and irregular past-tense verbs, but also showed the same pattern of early, correct application of regular and irregular inflections, followed by a period of over- regularisation. This demonstrated that apparently 'rule-like' behaviour can arise from a non-symbolic system which has no rules built into it.

There are some other specific criticisms of some of the central assumptions of the Pinker model. The suddenness with which children acquire the regular past-tense rule has been queried: since any one child's profile of verb productions, both correct and incorrect, can be very noisy and infrequent, it is possible to identify both patterns of immediate rule gaining (e.g. an increase of regularisations from 0 to 100 per cent over three months), and of slow rule acquisition (22–44 per cent over 6 months) from the same child's data. Notably, for example, the 100 per cent profile was based on eight observations (McClelland and Patterson 2002). It is certainly not the case that a clear and unambiguous onset of a rule use is seen in the data.

There are also problems with the way that the regular rule is considered to apply in a uniform way, that is, that the application of this rule is not influenced by semantic or phonetic information. Thus both regular and irregular inflections of past-tense non-words are judged to be more acceptable if they are phontactically well formed and come from a higher 'island of reliability', which is similar to orthographic and phonological neighbourhood density, and forms a measure of how many real words are similar to the non-word.

Thus, the use of the regular rule can be influenced by phonological properties – the application is not necessarily uniform. Likewise, if a non-word like 'flink' is produced in a context where is could be more semantically linked to 'drink' it will be more likely to be inflected as 'flank' than if it were semantically linked to 'blink'. This is an indication that the regularisation rule is not insensitive to semantic properties.

In English there is a tremendous dominance of regular verbs – 86 per cent of the most frequent 1000 verbs in English are regularly inflected (McClelland and Patterson 2002). However, it is not clear that regularisation – application of the regularity rule – is the default way of generating past tenses when no lexical irregular form is available. The Pinker argument requires that the default use of regular rules is not a consequence of their frequency, but because they reflect a truly linguistic mechanism. It is thus necessary to identify languages in which there are both regular and irregular inflections, but where the regular inflections are less common than the irregular. There are few of these, comprising the regular German past tense '-t', the Arabic broken plural and the German '+s' plural. It transpires that both the regular German past tense '-t' and the Arabic broken plural are both in fact less frequent than has been claimed (McClelland and Patterson, 2002). Furthermore, the German plural '+s', while less frequent, is not applied as the default inflection in language use. It may thus not be possible to make the claim that the rule-based mechanism is the default mechanism, even when it is less frequent than the irregular, lexical mechanism.

In contrast to the two-stage rule-based mechanism, McClelland and Patterson identify a connectionist model by Joanisse and Seidenberg (1999) as a likely, parallel distributed processing alternative. Unlike the original Rumelhart and McClelland (1986) model, this model of verb inflection has a route for semantic as well as phonetic influences on the learning of correct inflections.

McClelland and Patterson make the point that a connectionist model, which can exploit any regularities in the input, can learn the quasi-regularities which are found in the vast majority of irregularly inflected verbs (e.g. fall and fell). In other words, 'irregular' verbs are typically somewhat regular, and are part of a family of similarly declined verbs: indeed, in English only 'be' and 'go' are fully irregular and can neither be predicted, nor share commonalities with other verbs. It has been argued that quasi-regularity may actually be the norm in linguistic systems, and a model of past-tense verbs which can learn about these statistical relationships between phonological forms and past-tense declensions will have strengths over models which do not (McClelland and Patterson, 2002).

10.7 SENTENCE COMPREHENSION

We are continually confronted with ambiguity in language, though we read the sentence 'Time flies like an arrow' we are seldom aware that there are more than 100 legal syntactic interpretations (Altmann, 1998). However, we do consistently find certain grammatically correct sentences confusing, and will often find them to be ungrammatical. These may shed light on how we are dealing with ambiguity in sentences. Take for example:

The car raced past the crowd crashed.
The car driven past the crowd crashed.

Although both sentences are grammatically correct, the first is often considered to be ungrammatical. The problem is that 'raced' is ambiguous – it can be processed either as the main verb of the sentence, or as a past participle – a past-tense passive form of a verb, used here to describe something about the car in the sentence. If 'raced' is processed as the main verb, then 'the crowd crashed' becomes hard to process and the sentence feels ungrammatical. In contrast, 'driven' can only be a past participle, not a part-tense version of a verb (which would be 'drove'). This makes the second sentence considerably more acceptable. We also experience problems with sentences like this:

I will read the paper that you submitted tomorrow.

We tend to associate the word 'tomorrow' with the immediately previous phrase 'that you submitted'. This immediately feels wrong as there is a clash between the past-tense of 'you submitted' and the word 'tomorrow' (Altmann, 1998). For a long while, the explanation for this is that certain syntactic structures are more easily processed than others, and that certain syntactic processing principles can lead us consistently into confusion. Two particular syntactic preferences have been identified as important in this respect (Kimball, 1973; Frazier, 1979).

The first principle is associated with a preference for a simple syntactic structure rather than a complex one. As the perception of 'raced' as a past participle requires a sub-clause in the sentence, this makes for a more complex syntactic structure than the perception of 'raced' as the main verb of the sentence. The second principle, as in the sentence 'I will read the paper that you submitted tomorrow' is called 'late closure' and refers to a tendency to associated incoming information with the most recent information acquired. These two principles mean that we will consistently misunderstand certain syntactic frameworks, where the construction is not simple and words associated with earlier noun phrases are found towards the end of a sentence.

This perspective was very consonant with a psycholinguistic emphasis of the role of syntactic structure on human language processing, where a syntactic processor which is informationally encapsulated (i.e. not influenced by other kinds of information) works through the incoming sentence. However, a more recent view, strongly influenced by models of word recognition, has been put forward in opposition to this, which uses probability and context as ways of driving the interpretation of words in sentences (Altmann, 1998). In this model, as words are read, multiple meanings are activated, with the activation weighted by probability of that particular meaning. The context in which the sentence appears also affects the weighting of the activation of any one meaning. This means that word meaning that is normally high probability can become lower in activation because of the semantic context in which it appears (Altmann, 1998).

According to this approach, a sentence like 'The car raced past the crowd crashed' is harder to understand because the verb 'raced' is ambiguous – it can be either transitive (someone is racing something) or intransitive (someone is racing). As we have seen, this verb can also form the main verb of the sentence, or form a past participle, where it is defining aspects of the meaning of one of the words in the sentence but is not the main phrase. These two properties of verbs interact: a past participle must be transitive (as something is being raced by someone), while a main verb can be either transitive or intransitive (Altmann, 1998).

As Altmann points out, verbs vary a lot in these probabilities, with some verbs appearing as past participles very often (e.g. 'enjoyed') and some less often (e.g. 'received'), and readers will use this information to interpret the meaning of the sentence. Readers will also use semantics to constrain the interpretation of words: In a sentence starting with 'the chef fed', readers will use the semantic knowledge that chefs are generally cooking for other people to interpret 'fed' as a main verb, not a past participle. People will also use the plausibility of whether the subject of a sentence is animate or inanimate to interpret sentences. Take for example:

The page ripped by the toddler was mended.
The page that was ripped by the toddler was mended.

The phrase 'by the toddler' takes longer to read in the first sentence than if the same phrase appears after 'that' in the second sentence (Trueswell, 1996). This has been interpreted to show that although inanimate objects rarely rip things, the readers are trying to process 'ripped' as the main verb of the sentence, in the absence of cues like 'that' which indicate sub-clauses to the sentence. This indicates that the main constraint on the processing of this sentence concerns the plausibility of 'ripped' being a main verb or a past participle (Altmann, 1998).

People will also use a wider context to help understand a sentence, as in the following:

Put the orange on the plate in the bag.

People hearing the sentence will often assume that 'put the orange on the plate' is the start of the instruction, and have difficulty with 'in the bag'. In an experiment testing whether this effect can be modulated, participants were played sentences with instructions in, and shown pictures like those in Figure 10.3. Experiments have shown that this kind of visual context leads people to interpret 'on the plate' as a description of which orange is being discussed, not as part of the action to perform upon the orange (Tanenhaus *et al.*, 1995). Importantly, this kind of research is performed with data about eye movements being collected as people process the sentences, and these studies have shown that as soon as 'on the plate' is heard, the participants look at the picture of the orange on the plate.

In terms of constraint satisfaction as a model of sentence processing, the influences of these different sources of variability in interpretation will vary depending on their probability. Thus the stronger one kind of cue is (e.g. the probability of certain argument structures, like main verbs occurring early in the sentence), the weaker the influence of other kinds of cues (e.g. the likelihood of pages ripping things).

In normal speech perception, it must be stressed that prosodic and intonational cues are another highly important way that talkers cue listeners into their intended meaning, with the result that these kinds of confusions are harder to establish in informal speech. Indeed, in

Figure 10.3 Testing the effect of visual context on interpretation of a sentence.

normal reading, the job of punctuation is to help readers deal with this kind of complex structure (often by explicitly implying aspects of speech intonation and timing). This does not take away the importance of these constraint-based models of sentence comprehension but it does mean that language has a structural context (prosodic or derived from punctuation) which also facilitates comprehension.

10.8 LANGUAGE PRODUCTION

Speech production – deciding what we want to say, and articulating this accurately and fluently – is a behaviour which we take very much for granted, and which we typically do extremely well – it has been estimated that any one talker uses a production vocabulary of around 20,000 words, but that we make mistakes of word selection in only around every one in a million words produced.

The processes involved in turning thoughts into spoken words are called lexicalisation, and two main stages have been hypothesised (Levelt, 1989, 1992). The first stage comprises a link between conceptual thoughts and word forms which include semantic and syntactic information, but not phonological detail. This is called the 'lemma' and the processes of identifying and choosing the correct word is called lemma selection. In the second stage, the lemma makes contact with the phonetic representation of the word, called the lexeme, and the specifying of this form is called lexeme selection. Much of the evidence for this two-stage form of word selection in speech production comes from a frustrating state that many people have experienced, called *tip-of-the-tongue state*. When in this condition, people have an absolute certainty that they know a word that they want to say, combined with a lack of sensation of how they should say it. In this state, people can often access a lot of information about a word, such as what it means and aspects of its syntax, and this has been ascribed to being able to access lemma information, without being able to make contact with the lexeme detail (Harley, 2001).

There is also experimental evidence for these stages from studies of priming, for example, participants name pictures more quickly if they had previously named or defined the word, but not if they had produced a homophone which sounds the same but has a different meaning. This suggests that priming at the lemma level (semantic and syntax) can operate separately from lexeme (phonological) priming.

Historically, another influence on our understanding of speech production processes comes from studies of speech errors, or 'slips of the tongue'. Fromkin (1973) said these errors 'provide a window into linguistic processes' (pp. 43–44), although it has also been pointed out that these errors rely on accurate acoustic and phonetic decoding by the listener, which comprise a complex set of psychological processes (Boucher, 1994).

There are consistencies in the kinds of errors speakers make, where the errors occur at the level of phonemes, morphemes or words, rather than random noisy patterns of errors. This gives weight to the suggestion that they result from specific kinds of errors in the speech production system (Fromkin, 1971, 1973; Garrett, 1975; Dell, 1986; Harley, 2001).

Garrett developed a model of speech production based on a set of speech errors which he considered to be particularly informative:

- *Word substitutions* – these affect content words, not (typically) form words, such as 'man' for 'woman' or 'day' for 'night'.
- *Word exchanges* in which words from the same category swap positions with each other, such that nouns swap with nouns, verbs with verbs, etc.
- *Sound exchange errors* such as classic spoonerisms such as 'wastey term' for 'tasty worm', where the onsets of words swap positions with each other, commonly over words which are next to each other.
- *Morpheme exchange* – this is where word endings (morphological inflections) move to other points in the sentence, such as 'Have you seen Hector Easter's egg?' for 'Have you seen Hector's Easter egg?'. Morpheme exchange errors can also include 'stranding' errors such as "Have you seen Easter's Hector egg?".

In Garrett's model of speech production there are several, independent levels involved in speech production:

1. *the message level,* which represents the concepts and thoughts that the speaker wants to express;
2. *the functional level,* at which these concepts are expressed as semantic lexical representations, and thematic aspects of the sentence (the subject and object, for example) are also represented – i.e. the roles that these semantic items will take in the sentence;
3. *the positional level,* at which the semantic-lexical representations are implemented as phonological items, with a syntactic structure;
4. *the phonetic level,* at which the phonological and syntactic representations are realised as detailed phonetic sequences, precisely articulating the word forms and inflections specific by the positional level;
5. *the articulation level,* which form control of the vocal apparatus to express the

In Garrett's model, the semantic information about content words is specified at the functional level, while function words and bound morphemes (such as '-ing' endings) are added to the sentence structure at the positional level, where they are associated with their phonetic forms: in contrast, the phonological forms of the content words needs to be generated within the sentence at the positional level. This kind of constraint in the model allows for word substitution errors, which are generated at the functional level (or the lexical level in Levelt's model), and which infrequently affect form words. Likewise, sound exchange errors arise when content words are being phonologically constructed at the positional level, and again, affect form words much less (as they are phonologically prespecified at this level). Stranding errors occur when the content words are being positioned in the sentence, which occurs before syntactic structure and inflections are added to the sentence.

This is a serial model of speech production: speech production is a result of a series of independent output stages in which there are distinct computational processes specified in a serial, non-interacting fashion; this is also true of the Levelt model. There are other approaches to modelling speech production which proceed along more parallel lines, and which are typically modelled within the connectionist, interactive framework – for example, the speech production model of Gary Dell (Dell, 1986; Dell and O'Seaghdha, 1991; Dell *et al.*, 1997). In this model, a spoken sentence is represented as a sentence frame, and is planned simultaneously across semantic, syntactic, morphological and phonological levels, with *spreading activation* permitting different levels to affect each other. This allows speech errors to be 'mixed': as Dell has pointed out, many speech errors (such as 'The wind is strowing strongly') represent several different kinds of errors.

Functionally the Dell model works via different points in the sentence frame activating items in a lexicon – for example when a verb is specified, there will be activation across interconnected nodes for concepts, words, morphemes and phonemes. When a node is activated, there is a spread of activation across all the nodes connected to it. Thus if the node for the verb 'run' is activated, there will also be activation for the verb 'walk'. Selection is based on the node with the highest activation, and after a node has been selected its activation is reset to zero (to prevent the same word from be continuously produced). In this way, word substitution errors occur when the wrong word becomes more highly activated than the correct target word. The model contains categorical rules which act as constraints on the types of items which are activated at each level in the model, and these rules place limits on the kinds of errors that can be made – nouns swapping places with nouns, for example. In contrast, exchange errors occur as a result of the increases in activation, which means that a lexical element (a phoneme, or a word) can appear earlier in a sentence than was intended, if its activation unexpectedly increased: as the activation is immediately set to zero once an item has been selected, another highly activated item is likely to take its place in the intended part of the sentence frame.

As in other areas of cognitive psychology, there has been a lively debate about the extent to which speech production is well modelled by interactive connectionist models, or by more rule-based, serial, symbolic models. The two-stage model of Levelt was developed into a more complex six-stage model of spoken word production (Levelt, 1989; Bock and Levelt, 1994; Levelt *et al.*, 1999 called WEAVER++ (Word-form Encoding by Activation and VERification). The stages are:

1. conceptual preparation;
2. lexical selection (the stage at which the abstract lemma is selected);
3. morphological encoding;
4. phonological encoding;
5. phonetic encoding;
6. articulation.

Like Dell's model, WEAVER++ is a spreading activation model, but unlike Dell's model, activation is fed forward in one direction only, from concepts to articulation: furthermore, the WEAVER++ model is truly serial, as each stage is completed before the next stage is started.

In an experimental attempt to generate speech errors, Levelt *et al.* (1991) required participants to name pictures while also listening to words, and pressing a button when they recognised a word. The relationships between the seen objects and heard words varied – there were semantic relationships, phonological relationships and unrelated pairs, and some had a 'mediated' relationship to the picture, that is, linked through a semantic and phonological connection. If the picture was a dog, a mediated relationship word could be 'cot', which is phonologically similar to 'cat', which in turn has a semantic relationship with 'dog'. The study was specifically designed to test the hypothesis, inferred from Dell's model, that a model of speech production in which different levels can interact would predict a facilitation of naming 'dog' when 'cot' is heard (Levelt *et al.*, 1991). Experimentally, this predicted facilitation was not found: there was no phonological activation of semantically related items. In contrast, the results supported a sequential model. Specifically, there was priming of lexical decisions to the heard word from semantically related words only at very short intervals (around 70 ms), while priming of lexical decisions from phonologically related words was only significant at longer intervals (around 600 ms). These results were taken to support a sequential, stage-based implementation of word naming.

There is evidence in favour of the Dell model, however: Morsella and Miozzo (2002) asked participants to name pictures in the presence of other (distractor) pictures: there was facilitation of picture naming when there was a phonological relationship between the target and distractor pictures. This was taken to show a beneficial effect of phonological information at an earlier stage in word selection and production than would be predicted by a feed-forward, sequential model like Levelt's.

Speech production has been somewhat less closely studied than other aspects of language in cognitive psychology (especially when compared with the detailed investigations of speech production seen in the aphasia literature as will be seen in Chapter 11); however, that profile is changing rapidly as a range of experimental techniques are becoming available to researchers (Griffin and Crew, 2012).

10.9 DISCOURSE LEVEL

Human language is not just an extraordinarily complex system for representing and processing information; it is also the dominant system within which we communicate with each other. Discourse is the term that refers to the higher-order aspects of language use, both in terms of how connected ideas are expressed (e.g. over the course of sentences) and in conversation, which is the shared use of language in interactions (be those interactions spoken, signed or written).

Conversation is an extremely interesting and complex use of language for several different reasons. It is the context in which we acquire spoken language – all of us learn to speak (or sign) in interactions with others. Conversation also represents an extremely good example of well-coordinated behaviour; a verbal behaviour which relies on very high-order use on intentions and thought, and our main social tool for interactions.

COORDINATING CONVERSATIONS

When we have conversations with people, certain universal rules are followed. These have been summarised by Sacks *et al.* (1974) as:

1. Speaker change occurs.
2. One person speaks at a time.
3. Simultaneous speech is common but brief.
4. Transitions with no gap and no overlap are common.
5. Turn order is not fixed, nor is turn size, duration of a turn or content.
6. Number of talkers can vary.
7. Talk can be continuous or discontinuous.

Speakers in a conversation are generally excellent at following these rules, and if you've ever had the unpleasant experience of talking to someone who won't let you take your turn, you'll be struck how infrequently this happens. The principles exist probably because they form a natural framework in which relatively unconstrained conversation can be easily managed. It has been observed that the maximum limit on conversational partners is around four to five people – if a social group gets larger than this, separate sub-groups of conversational partners will emerge (Dunbar *et al.*, 1995). The exact reason for this has yet to be determined; however, it may well be a result of following the principles of Sacks *et al.* with larger numbers of people: that is, it may be relatively simple for two to four people to negotiate the acceptable boundaries of conversation (e.g. managing who speaks next) but much harder for six to seven people.

The management of turn-taking in conversation is very important: even in phone conversations, complete strangers, who cannot see each other, manage to take turns in the conversation very smoothly. The vast majority of intervals between talker turns in conversation fall within a range of ±150 ms (e.g. De Ruiter *et al.*, 2006). This speed is far faster than one would expect to see if turns were entirely reactive, that is, the preparation for a turn were to start when the prior talker has finished their turn, which would be associated with far longer reaction times. Instead it has been suggested that talkers in a conversation start to entrain their behaviour with each other, speaking at the same rates as each other, and that talkers time their turns based on the speech rhythm and prosody of the other talkers during their turns (Wilson and Wilson, 2005). Indeed, conversation has been described as an incredibly detailed exercise in coordinating our verbal behaviour with that other our co-talkers: when we talk to other people, we start to coordinate our breathing and speech rate with each other. We also start to coordinate the language that we use: when we talk to each other, we will start to use the same words and the same grammatical constructions (Garrod and Pickering, 2004).

MEANING AND INTENTION IN CONVERSATION

One of the intriguing facts about conversational speech is that we almost never say exactly what we mean: if my partner comes into the room and says 'have you seen my phone' he is hugely unlikely to be pleased if I respond 'yes, you had it when you rang your mother this morning'. On the face of it, his question was about my having visual experience of his phone but in the context of his uttering it, it is of course an indication to me that (a) he is looking for his phone and (b) he wants to know if I know where his phone is. For me to understand his question accurately, I need to decode not simply the words that he says but his underlying intentions. This is a *pragmatic* use of language and it means going beyond the words someone says.

One of the first people to explore this topic was Grice (1975), who established that when a someone talks, it important to decode their intentions in addition to their words. Grice described talkers as implying much if the information in their statements: if I say that 'I am not going to the party, I'm feeling tired', one can interpret my meaning by assuming the reason why I am not going to the party is *because* I am feeling tired. Grice identified differences of implied meaning – which he termed *implicatures* – which ways if describing the meaning implied in speech acts. He identified different kinds of implicatures:

1. *Conventional implicatures* – these arise through semantic representations of the meanings of particular 'turns of phrase' which are used in conversational speech. Thus someone may use the phrase 'I have to say …' at the start of a sentence and not be understood to mean that they are being forced to say anything.
2. *Conversational implicatures* – these arise from the concept that there is implied meaning in how sentences are constructed in speech; if a talker says, 'I would take fish pie to the party but I think Jane is allergic', the use of 'but' is drawing a contrast between the two statements. This kind of meaning is operating at a pragmatic level.
3. *Cooperative principle* – this principle entails that you should 'Make your conversational contribution such as is required, at the stage

of the conversation at which it occurs, by the accepted purpose of direction of the talk exchange in which you find yourself.' This principle leads to four maxims (Grice, 1975):

the maxim of quantity – say what is informative for the discussion but no more (and no less);
the maxim of quality – don't say what is untrue (or what you consider to be untrue);
the maxim of relation – which means, in short, that what you say should be relevant, or germane, to what is being discussed;
the maxim of manner – try not to be ambiguous or hard to understand.
In Grice's theory, it is the operative use of these maxims that makes the conversational implicatures comprehensible to talkers in a conversation.

Grice's great insight was that in conversation, as we hardly ever specify exactly what we mean by the words we say, the important job for a listener is to understand a talker's intentions. In conversations, the speech acts produced by a talker set up expectations in a listener that they infer on the basis of the implicatures in order to derive the meaning of what is being said: his perspective therefore is a highly active, inferential model of communication (as opposed to a more passive decoding strategy). This aspect of Grice's work was developed by Sperber and Wilson (1985) who picked up on this active inferential model to explore the concept of relevance in communication. Essentially, Wilson and Sperber questioned the need for the maxims, principles and implicatures which Grice specified, and posited that the expectation of relevance was sufficient for the listener to start interpreting the utterances. Relevance, in this context, refers to a property of utterances, but also as a property of any piece of verbal information, from a thought to any observable phenomena. In this framework, relevance is considered to mean that uttrerances are assumed to be relevant, to be meaningful, to have a sense that we will be able to follow. Relevance is thus a property not of linguistic mechanisms that are recruited to understand speech, but of human cognition: we can understand spoken language because the quest for understanding, and the corresponding belief that information is meaningful, is an omnipresent property of human thought, and the ways that we engage with the world. In this light, I can understand what my partner means when he asks 'Have you seen my phone?' because I can also understand what an ominous clunk means when I hear my son drop his dad's phone onto a flagged stone floor. Indeed, in more recent implementations of their theory, Wilson and Sperber have been extending relevance to properties of human cognition (Wilson and Sperber, 2002).

SOCIAL CONVERSATIONS
In psychology textbooks we tend to give examples of conversations which include lots of people marching around looking for lost

phones and uttering excuses not to go to parties. However, human language is not only the main way that we share information with each other, it is also the main way that we make and maintain our social connections, and when we talk to each other in this way, our conversation is rarely composed of demands for information or statements of intent. Instead, the main thing we do when we talk to our friends is to discuss other people (Dunbar *et al.*, 1997). As we are social primates, it is not perhaps too surprising that the most interesting things we have to talk about are other people. It has even been suggested that human language has replaced social grooming for humans: for non-human primates, an individual's position in the social hierarchy is made manifest by whom they groom and whom they allow to groom them, and social grooming is a very important aspect of primate life, for this reason. In humans, social language has been hypothesised as the main way that we show with whom we have our important social links. In line with this, humans have exploited other forms of communication than face-to-face conversations since we have been able to write to one another, and over the centuries this has exploded with communication on phones and text, from SMS and email to online social media like Facebook and Twitter. Notably, however, we enjoy face-to-face conversation most of all, even if that face-to-face conversation takes place on a computer: studies have shown that we rate ourselves as happier, say that we have laughed more, and keep the conversation going for longer for face-to-face conversations (both in the presence of the other talkers and online) than phone conversations, text messaging or email interactions (Vlahovic *et al.*, 2012). Indeed, the precise linguistic aspects of our spoken language are influenced by social context: if my partner indirectly asks if I've seen his phone, and I respond (with very reduced articulation) 'dunno', this might be acceptable in a way that it would not be if he was asking me directly if I let our son drop his phone on the stone floor (when a more fully fledged speech act would be required in response) (Hawkins, 2003). When we speak with people we like, all the processes of alignment that we saw in the earlier section are enhanced, such that we will use the same words and syntax as someone else, the more we like them. We not only learnt to speak in conversations, we have those conversations with the people close to us, emotionally and physically, and this may lead to a lifelong enjoyment in talking to the people we want to be with, which in turn influences our own speech.

NOTE

1. In the dedication to *The Modularity of Mind*, Fodor writes: '[...] Merrill Garrett made what seems to me the deepest remark that I have yet heard about the psychological mechanisms that mediate the perception of speech. "What you have to remember about parsing," Merrill said, "is that basically it's a reflex".'

SUMMARY

- Speech is an extremely complex sound and way of expressing language: other ways include written language and sign language.
- Languages have structure at a number of different levels from phonetic, morphological, lexical, semantic and syntactic, through to pragmatic meaning.
- Linguistics aims to understand language as a complex system, and psychologists have been interested in identifying how this can inform human language use. There may be some important differences in these approaches, not least because linguists have historically tended to underplay a role for learning.
- Several different factors have been implicated in how we recognise written and spoken words, and database approaches have opened up the possibility of analyses these influences in a complex multifactorial way.
- Sentence comprehension has been strongly influenced by models from psycholinguistics; however, approaches influenced by research into word recognition have shown important roles for biasing effects of probabilities and contexts in sentence comprehension.
- In models of language processing, there is a tension between approaches which favour symbolic, rule-based processing models, and approaches which favour a more interactive, connectionist approach. Past-tense verbs in English have been identified as key in testing claims in this debate.
- Speech production involves a number of different kinds of representation and the extent to which these may or may not interact when speaking is debated.
- Using speech in conversation is highly complex, and social and affiliative behaviours start to interact with cognitive and linguistic processes at this level.

FURTHER READING

- Berko-Gleason, J. and Ratner, N. (1997). *Psycholinguistics,* 2nd edn. Orlando, FA: Harcourt Brace College Publishers. An excellent introductory text, very well presented.
- Carroll, D. W. (2003). *Psychology of Language,* 3rd edn. Belmont, CA: Brooks/Cole. This is a good introductory textbook covering a wide range of topics in an accessible way.
- Clark, H. H. (1996). *Using Language.* New York: Cambridge University Press. A stimulating account of the way people cooperate together in speaking and listening, participating in the joint enterprise of using language for conversational interaction.

- Harley, T. A. (2001). *The Psychology of Language: From Data to Theory,* 2nd edn. Hove: Psychology Press. This is a very comprehensive textbook on the psychology of language, more advanced than the Carroll or Whitney texts and with more coverage of UK-based research. Highly recommended.
- Pinker, S. (1994). *The Language Instinct: The New Science of Language and Mind.* Harmondsworth: Penguin. A fascinating and exceptionally well-written exploration of the nature of language and its role in our mental makeup. A really good read.
- Whitney, P. (1997). *The Psychology of Language.* Boston, MA: Houghton Mifflin. A good introductory text.

Contents

Disorders of language

Sophie Scott

11.1 INTRODUCTION

How is language represented in the human brain, and how can linguistic functions be impaired? This chapter will outline the historical background of these studies and also address more recent developments in the ways that these linguistic processes can be investigated. There are two different general ways in which human brain function can be disrupted, which are acquired damage and developmental disorders. In acquired damage, a healthy brain is lesioned, for example, via a stroke (where the blood supply to the brain is disrupted), disease (e.g. encephalitis), a tumour, trauma (e.g. a penetrating object), or a progressive disease such as Pick's disease. These causes of brain damage are all different in terms of what leads to them, what kinds of damage they cause and what kinds of recovery are possible, but all lead to a non-transient disruption in brain function. The second route is via a developmental disorder, such as autism, or specific language impairment, where the brain is affected either during its development in utero (e.g. due to genetic factors) or during birth. The emphasis here is less on how the brain is damaged, and more on how a child's behaviour and brain function is affected over the course of development. Much of the history of language disorders has been based on acquired disorders, but there are also several developmental disorders which affect language, and I will address these towards the end of this chapter.

The first cognitive functions to be localised in the human brain were associated with language. In the 1860s, following influential theories about whether or not the human brain was organised with different specific functions associated with different anatomical locations, there was a developing consensus that areas in the left frontal cortex might be critical for the production of speech (see Levelt, 2012). A neurologist called Paul Broca was specifically interested in such cases, when he was introduced to a patient known as 'Tan', an adult Frenchman with an expressive disorder of spoken language (i.e. acquired brain damage). Over the previous 21 years, Tan's speech had worsened, although his general mental abilities remained intact. By the time he came to

Broca's attention, Tan could no longer produce any intelligible speech, uttering only 'tan' and some swearwords (Broca, 1861b). Broca was keen to know which brain areas might be damaged in Tan. However, relating behavioural changes to brain damage was not easy at the time; until the late twentieth century, when techniques such as CT scans and MRI scans became available, neurologists were limited to post-mortem analyses to investigate the human brain. Tan died shortly after meeting Broca, and a post-mortem was conducted at which Tan was found to have brain damage (typically called a brain lesion), caused by a tumour associated with syphilis in the front half of the left side of his brain. Specifically, the lesion lay in the posterior (back) third of the left inferior frontal gyrus (Figure 11.1). Over the next century, this brain area became known as Broca's area, and associated with a disorder of speech production called Broca's aphasia. Broca's aphasia is characterised by halting, non-fluent speech, with many grammatical errors. Broca's aphasia was considered to result from a loss of motor memories for speech, and nowadays it is often associated with difficulties in selecting and planning the control of speech acts.

Shortly after Broca's influential paper, Karl Wernicke (1881) described patients with disorders of speech comprehension, that is, people who developed difficulties understanding spoken language: this is typically described as a sensory, or receptive aphasia. Wernicke determined that patients with a sudden onset of speech comprehension difficulties had damage to the left superior temporal gyrus (Figure 11.2). A deficit in understanding spoken language after brain damage became known as Wernicke's aphasia. Speech production can be intact in people with Wernicke's aphasia. However, in some cases people's speech can be disordered in content, such that their speech is difficult to understand; it can be made up of random words, a so-called 'word salad', or consist of made up words (known as neologisms).

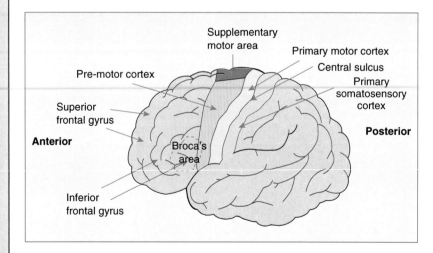

Figure 11.1 Diagram of the brain showing the position of Broca's area (Broca, 1861b).

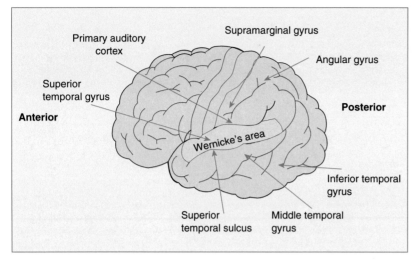

Figure 11.2   Diagram of the brain showing Wernicke's area (Wernicke, 1881).

11.2 MODELS OF APHASIA

THE WERNICKE–LICHTHEIM MODEL OF APHASIA AND ITS MODIFICATIONS

Wernicke used his insights into the problems of patients who had difficulties in understanding spoken language, and the ways their problems differed from individuals with Broca's aphasia, to develop a model of speech perception and production (Figure 11.3). In terms of cognitive processes, Wernicke realised that the two different profiles of the ways that language could be affected by brain damage indicated that there were some underlying differences in how these processes and representations must be implemented in the human brain. In terms of modern cognitive neuropsychology, the findings that speech perception and speech production can be differentially and separably affected by brain damage is evidence for a 'double dissociation' (Shallice, 1988); double dissociations became a central feature of cognitive neuropsychology and cognitive science over the twentieth century, especially with the rise of cognitive psychology in the second half of the century.

From the outset, these diagrams were both very popular and controversial: Levelt (2012) has recently outlined exactly how popular diagrams (or cognitive models as we would now call them) were, and also how critical people were: Henry Head, for example, considered that researchers would twist the clinical cases they observed to try and fit their models (Head, 1926). However, from the outset these models had the power of being testable and of being used to generate hypotheses. In terms of predictions, Wernicke predicted conduction aphasia as a consequence of his model, if there were a disconnection of the phonetic lexicon from the speech motor planning centre (lesion of line C in Figure 11.3), resulting in a problem where patients can

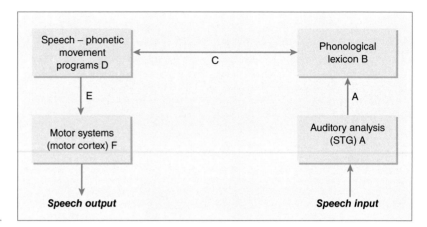

Figure 11.3 Wernicke's (1881) model of speech perception and production.

understand speech, but make errors in repetition. Wernicke's model was tested by Lichtheim, who identified a potential kind of speech problem which the model could not account for. In transcortical sensory aphasia, patients have problems understanding speech, and fluent speech output (though their speech production can be confused). Unlike Wernicke's patients, however, these patients can repeat accurately. In Wernicke's model, there is no route for speech comprehension to be compromised, but for repetition to be intact. Lichtheim proposed the addition of a semantic-conceptual module to the Wernicke model. This model (Lichtheim, 1885) has been described as the first cognitive model that identified different subsystems in an information processing framework (Figure 11.4).

Lichtheim's modified model identified an output, motor module (D), an input store of phonological lexical information (B) and a

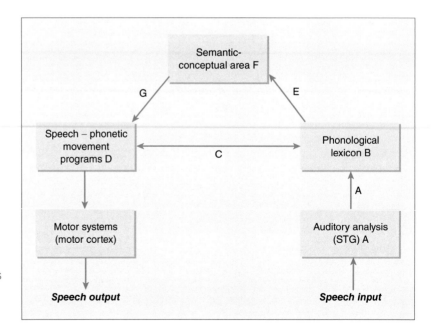

Figure 11.4 Lichtheim's (1885) model of speech perception and production.

conceptual centre (F). Lesions which disconnect or damage elements of this model lead to different profiles of aphasic problems. For example, Broca's aphasia would result from damage to D, and Wernicke's aphasia from damage to B. Damage to the connection between B and D would lead to a problem in connecting from sounds to speech output, and indeed in conduction aphasia, as predicted by Wernicke, affected individuals can produce speech, and can understand speech, but cannot repeat heard words. Further disruptions to speech production/perception following brain damage within this model of aphasia are classified in the Boston Aphasia Classification System (Goodglass and Kaplan, 1972).

THE BOSTON APHASIA CLASSIFICATION SYSTEM

The Lichtheim model of language (and the associated predicted patterns of language breakdown) led to the Boston Aphasia Classification System, often called the classical, or neoclassical classification system of aphasia. These aphasic syndromes are categorised by their symptoms, and by the ways that they are considered to be indicative of different kinds of damage to the Lichtheim model of language. These aphasic syndromes can be considered to be the first application of the study of disordered function to test predictions of a cognitive model. Note that some of these aphasias are considered to be caused by damage to particular brain areas which underpin certain functions (e.g. Broca's aphasia), and others are considered to result from damage to the pathways connecting different brain areas which are important in language – these are considered to be 'disconnection' syndromes. Thus, this approach distinguishes between damage to function and damage to connections between brain areas, which may mean that functioning brain areas can no longer contribute to a language task, because they have been disconnected by the damage. The Boston system is as follows:

1. *Broca's aphasia.* Speech production is laborious and grammar can be incorrect. This is caused by a lesion involving the expressive speech centre (D).
2. *Wernicke's aphasia.* Speech comprehension is impaired: patients find it hard to understand what is said to them. This is caused by a lesion of the audio-verbal centre, also referred to as the phonological lexicon (B).
3. *Conduction aphasia.* Patients can understand speech, and produce speech accurately, but they have specific difficulties with the repetition of heard words. This is caused by a lesion of the pathways connecting the audio-verbal and expressive speech areas (line C).
4. *Global aphasia.* Patients can neither understand or produce speech. This profile is produced by an extensive lesion involving both the audio-verbal centre (B) and the expressive speech centre (D).
5. *Transcortical motor aphasia.* Similar in symptoms to Broca's aphasia, but the patient's repetition skills are intact. The disorder is

Key Term

Boston Aphasia Classification System
A systematic classification of aphasic profiles which can be used to identify aphasia and to predict what profiles of damage a patients might be expected to show when assessing their damage. The Boston Classification System builds on the models of aphasia which were developed by Broca, Wernicke and Lichtheim. Implicit in this approach is the concept that language can be localised in the human brain, and that different profiles of language deficits are related to distinctly different patterns of brain damage.

associated with disruption of the pathways (shown in Figure 11.4 as line G) connecting the concept area (F) to the expressive speech area (D).

6. *Transcortical sensory aphasia* is similar to Wernicke's, or receptive aphasia, except that repetition is preserved. Indeed, patients can show *echolalia*, where there is an obligatory repetition of heard words. This is a result of lesions of the pathways (shown in Figure 11.4 as line E) connecting the audio-verbal centre (B) to the concept centre (F).

7. *Isolation aphasia*, also known as mixed transcortical aphasia, is a disorder in which the patient cannot understand heard speech, and cannot produce speech, but can still repeat words. This disorder is caused by lesions, which disconnect the concept centre from the audio-verbal centre and the expressive speech centre (in Figure 11.4, these are disconnections of line E between B and F, and line G, between F and D).

8. *Anomic aphasia* is a disorder associated with a problem in naming objects, across modalities (e.g. patient cannot name a cow by seeing a picture of a cow, or hearing 'moo'). Anomic aphasia can be caused either by a lesion involving the pathways which connect the concept centre to the expressive speech centre (line G in Figure 11.4), or if comprehension is also disrupted, a lesion of the concept centre itself (F).

The problem with the definition of anomic aphasia, as Lichtheim himself noted, was that anomic aphasia and transcortical motor aphasia are caused by very similar damage in the Wernicke–Lichtheim model, but are clinically quite distinct (Heilman, 2006). There are several other issues with the Wernicke–Lichtheim model of aphasia – for example, as Sigmund Freud pointed out, there is no account in this model of why a patient with Wernicke's aphasia might make (and fail to notice, let alone correct) frequent errors in their speech output, as they commonly do (Butterworth, 1993). A slightly different model was developed by Kussmaul (1877) who hypothesised connections from the semantic-conceptual area back to the phonological input lexicon: evidence from Feinberg *et al.* (1986) showed that people with conduction aphasia were able to tell whether or not pictures of words were pronounced the same way, even if they could not say those words aloud. This was evidence in support of Kussmaul's claim. Lichtheim had also described a patient who could repeat words, but who had great difficulty in speech comprehension: the patient also produced errors when speaking (e.g. using the wrong words) and had problems naming. This profile of problems was hard to account for in the Wernicke–Lichtheim model, since a disconnection of the acoustic-phonetic processing field from the conceptual system would not produce these deficits (Heilman, 2006). If there are reciprocal connections between the acoustic-phonetic input lexicon and the semantic-conceptual system, then a disruption of these will produce the profile that Lichtheim had described. Figure 11.5 shows Kussmaul's adaptations to the Wernicke–Lichtheim model. In this model there is no direct link

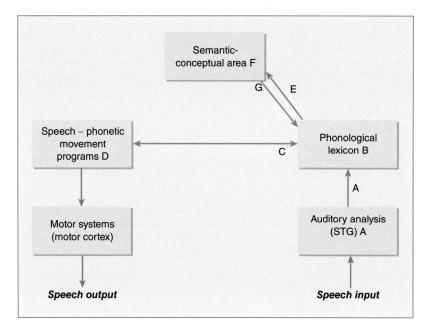

Figure 11.5 Kussmaul's (1877) model of speech perception and production.

between the semantic-onceptual system and speech output planning in Broca's area.

Further support for the reciprocal connections between the semantic-conceptual system and the phonetic analysis/phonological lexicon came when a patient was discovered who had transcortical sensory aphasia – that is, impaired speech comprehension but intact repetition with intact naming and clear speech production (Heilman *et al.*, 1981). The patient was unable to access semantic representations from phonological representations, but could access their phonological representations via intact processing from their semantic-conceptual module.

The Wernicke–Lichtheim model had a link from semantic-conceptual representations to speech output systems to provide a system for the production of normal, spontaneous speech. This enables the model to explain transcortical motor aphasia, where patients can understand speech, but have great difficulties in production: unlike Broca's aphasia, the patients can repeat words accurately. If the patients have a suspected deficit in activating semantic-conceptual models of what they want to say, this profile of aphasia is sometimes called adynamic aphasia: transcortical motor aphasia can also be associated with a specific problem in initiating speech output and the patients can be described as having a motor akinesia (a specific problem in initiating motor acts) (Heilman, 2006). The retention of the Wernicke–Lichtheim link between conceptual representations and speech motor planning would allow this profile of disorder to be accounted for, as would the inclusions of a module to represent the control of intentional speech production (Figure 11.6).

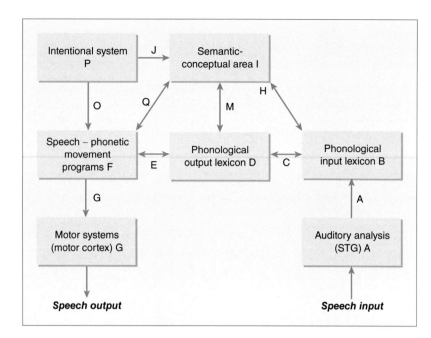

Figure 11.6 Heilman's (2006) model of speech perception and production.

Another patient group that is hard for the Kussmal–Wernicke–Lichtheim model to account for is deep dysphasia (Michel and Andreewsky, 1983; Katz and Goodglass, 1990). In deep dysphasia the patients, as in conduction aphasia, make speech production mistakes that include many phonetic errors. The deep dysphasic patients also make errors when repeating, as in conduction aphasia; however, unlike the people with conduction aphasia, who make phonetic errors when repeating words, the people with deep dysphasia make semantic errors. Thus, when repeating 'duck', someone with conduction aphasia might say 'duff', whereas someone with deep dysphasia might say 'goose'. When asked to repeat non-words, people with deep dysphasia produce real words that are phonetically similar to the target real words. The original Wernicke–Lichtheim model can account for this profile, as there is a route from conceptual representations to speech motor output control. However, to account for both conduction aphasia and deep dysphasia, it has been suggested that the Kussmal–Wernicke–Lichtheim model needs to split the phonological input lexicon and the phonological output lexicon (Figure 11.6) (Heilman, 2006).

The inclusion of separate phonological input and output lexicons provides a way to discriminate between the profiles of problems seen in people who have deep dysphasia and conduction aphasia: in conduction aphasia, people have a potential lesion of line E (Figure 11.6), connecting the phonological output lexicon to the expressive speech output centre (D): this would lead to phonetic errors in speech production and problems with repetition, as in conduction aphasia (Heilman, 2006). In contrast, a lesion of the connections (line C in Figure 11.6) between the phonological input and output lexicons would not prevent repetition, as the input and output lexicons could be connected

via the semantic-conceptual centre (I in Figure 11.6). As the semantic-conceptual route is based on 'real' words, non-word repetition
becomes difficult, as in deep dysphasia. Furthermore, as the semantic-conceptual system does not have access to phonology, frequent
semantic errors are made in speech production, as the words selected
for output are constrained by semantic, not phonetic representations
(Heilman, 2006).

The separation of the input and output phonological lexicons also
allowed people to account for the problems experienced by a patient
(Roth *et al.* 2006) who made many errors during speech production,
with the words produced often being semantically related to the target
words. When naming objects, he would often make errors, and was
not helped by semantic cues. In contrast, phonetic cues would often
help him name more accurately, but he would now make frequent
phonological errors. It was suggested that this patient had damage to
both whole word and phonetic methods of naming items – and that
furthermore, in normal language use, people would use both routes
when naming objects. This would link the models to a parallel-distributed
processing framework, rather than being limited to serial processing
(Heilman, 2006).

However, there is a further group of patients who have deficits of
confrontation naming – problems in identifying objects by name via
prompts. In anomic aphasia, these problems are independent of the
modality in which the patients are tested; in optic aphasia, patients
have a specific problem when given visual objects to name (Freund,
1889). In visual agnosia, patients have great difficulty not just in recognising and naming objects, but in retrieving semantic information
about the objects (e.g. describing how they would be used). In optic
aphasia, the problems are limited to naming the object from visual
presentation: that is, they might not be able to name a pair of scissors,
but they could mimic how they would be used, and describe situations
in which they would be used. Their problem can thus be considered
a form of aphasia rather than of visual processing or visual knowledge, and has been described as a problem in the link between visual
object knowledge and the phonological output lexicon. This has led
to a modification of the Kussmaul–Wernicke–Lichtheim model where
a module for visual object processing has been included (Figure 11.7)
(Heilman, 2006). The opposite profile of deficits has been described
in some patients with dementia, who can name objects that they are
shown, but not from verbal definitions: this has been termed non-optic
aphasia. The patients can repeat words without mistakes, and can
name objects correctly because the output lexicon and speech motor
systems are intact, as are their object recognition units and their access
to the phonological output lexicon. In contrast, normal speech production and comprehension were impaired, including their naming to
definitions and their non-optic aphasia was thus linked to degraded
semantic representations. This may link to semantic dementia, a focal
dementia where the first symptoms are associated with loss of the ability to map between heard words and their meaning.

Key Term

Dementia
A persistent
impairment
in intellectual
function due to
brain dysfunction,
which commonly
is associated with
a progressive loss
of function. It is
mainly a disease of
ageing, being more
common in more
elderly populations.
Dementias can be
relatively focal in their
effects (e.g. semantic
dementia) or more
widespread and
'global' in their effects
(e.g. Alzheimer's
disease). Some
dementias primarily
affect subcortical
regions (e.g.
Parkinson's disease)
and others have a
more cortical effect
(e.g. Pick's disease).

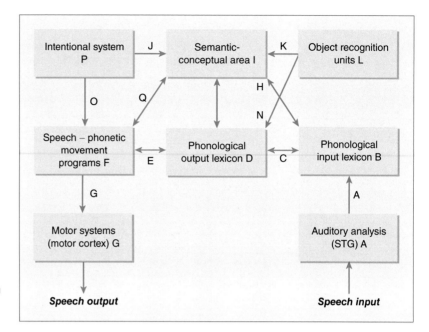

Figure 11.7 Heilman's (2006) revised model with additional module for visual object processing.

The cognitive neuropsychology approach to aphasia has been tremendously influential in the understanding of aphasia and the ways that human language is implemented in the human brain. There are some limitations to the uncritical application of some of these concepts, however, that are worth considering. In the next section, more detailed aspects of aphasic profiles are considered.

11.3 DETAILED SYMPTOMS OF APHASIC PROFILES

BROCA'S APHASIA

Patients with Broca's aphasia have highly non-fluent speech, with difficulties in repetition. There are typically long pauses between words when they speak, and their speech sounds effortful. There is very often a motor speech problem (apraxia) or dysarthria accompanying this. Their comprehension of speech, however, is not compromised. Broca's aphasia is often associated with damage that extends out of the posterior inferior frontal cortex into surrounding cortex. As primary motor cortex lies next to Broca's area, patients often have a muscle weakness or paralysis. This typically affects the right (opposite side of the body from the lesion – *contralesional*) side of the body, as the motor areas on the left side of the brain control the right side of the body, and vice versa.

There is not necessarily a correspondence between Broca's area and Broca's aphasia. 'Classical' Broca's area, as described by Broca, lies in the posterior third of the inferior frontal gyrus, and encompasses

Brodmann's areas 44/45 (Figure 11.1). However, to have a full clinical profile of Broca's aphasia, more extensive damage is required. Mohr *et al.* (1978) looked at twenty lesions at autopsy, and related the clinical speech problems that the people suffered in life to their acquired brain damage. A lesion to Broca's area itself caused transient speech mutism – a loss of all speech production. This may well have been transient, because of plasticity in the brain, or because the right hemisphere regions start to be recruited. For full Broca's aphasia, the lesion needed to encompass a lot of the Sylvian region including left opercula, insula, and subjacent white matter in the territory of the middle cerebral artery including Broca's area. Broca's original case, which involved damage due to a neoplasm (tumour), which arose due to syphilis, involved these areas. Functionally, the cell structure and anatomy of BA 44 corresponds to premotor cortex, and BA 45 to prefrontal cortex, so it is unlikely that they perform the same processing functions. It is therefore almost certainly the case that Broca's area is involved in a variety of processes, some motoric, some not. Since the development of functional imaging enabled the investigation of language (and other cognitive, perceptual and motoric functions) in intact, healthy human brains, it has become clear that Broca's area is engaged by a range of non-linguistic tasks, for example in the representation of task-relevant information, or in non-linguistic aspects of syntax. It is possible that the critical importance of Broca's area in speech production may therefore result from it having important general cognitive functions in the planning and control of behaviour, for example, response selection (Schnur *et al.,* 2009).

WERNICKE'S APHASIA

Wernicke's aphasia is a disorder of the comprehension of spoken language, and patients can also show poor naming and repetition. Speech output is fluent, although some patients speak with many paraphasias and neologisms, and speech can be (though is not necessarily) highly incoherent. Notably, these patients rarely if ever correct their errors, which suggests they are unaware of their problem, or that their speech makes little sense (the term for this is anosognosia). The patients don't normally have a hemiparesis, though they may have cortical blindness, which occurs when primary visual cortex is damaged, leading to a visual field defect (e.g. a hemianopia). This indicates a lesion which lies towards the back of the brain. Generally posterior damage means damage to the brain which lies behind the central sulcus (Figure 11.1). Wernicke's original papers indicate that he was describing the importance of the left superior temporal gyrus (STG) in speech perception. Over the years, however, papers started to especially emphasise the left posterior superior temporal sulcus (STS) as the location of Broca's area (e.g. Bogen and Bogen, 1976): this perspective almost certainly reflects the fact that most receptive aphasia cases are caused by cardiovascular disease, that is, stroke: strokes follow the anatomy of the blood supply, and in the temporal lobes, the blood supply runs back to front, meaning that strokes are more common at the back end of the temporal lobes than the front. This means that the posterior STS may be emphasised in Wernicke's aphasia because of how strokes happen, rather than because of its functional significance in speech perception. It is also the case that a full profile of Wernicke's aphasia arises from a more widespread left tempero-parietal lesion – and the larger the lesion, the more severe the speech comprehension deficit (Naeser *et al., 1987)*

CONDUCTION APHASIA

In conduction aphasia, there is a disruption of repetition, with preserved (relatively) comprehension and spontaneous speech, though there may be phonemic errors, and the patients can have problems with confrontation naming. There tends to be no associated neurological problem, e.g. hemiparesis is rare; this likely reflects the fact the conduction aphasia is generally caused by small lesions rather than by other problems (e.g. Wernicke's aphasia). Some patients have a limited right hemianasthesia, or visual field defect, and these patients may have difficulty with moving their face or limbs to command.

Following the conventions of the Boston Aphasia Classification System and the Wernicke–Lichtheim model, conduction aphasia is known as a disconnection syndrome because it is assumed to reflect damage to connections between brain areas connecting, for example, the phonological output lexicon to the expressive speech control centre (Figure 11.7). Not long after Wernicke's original prediction of the existence of conduction aphasia (as a prediction of his model), the arcuate fasiculus (AF) was discovered, and it appeared to be good candidate route for this pathway: the AF is a white-matter tract running from the posterior STG to Broca's area and this may represent a connection between B and D in the original Wernicke model (Figure 11.3). However, other reports have implicated the cortex in this condition, especially in Wernicke's area (Mendez and Benson, 1985). More recent electrical stimulation studies have confirmed this cortical involvement. Anderson *et al.* (1999) worked with an epileptic patient who, when her posterior STG was stimulated, made speech sound errors when speaking, and had impaired repetition, with preserved semantic comprehension. Conduction aphasia may this reflect a disorder of cortical areas important in repetition, rather than a disconnection syndrome. This, in turn, may mean that the left STG is important in speech-motor links as well as acoustic-phonetic processing of speech.

GLOBAL APHASIA

In global aphasia, all major language functions are impaired, both in output and comprehension. This tends to follow an extensive left-hemisphere lesion involving Broca's area and Wernicke's area. Such large-scale brain damage involves many associated neurological signs: hemiplegia, sensory loss, visual field defects and attentional disturbances such as extinction or neglect. The lesions need not necessarily be large, and they can often spare Wernicke's area. However, both cortical and subcortical regions tend to be involved.

TRANSCORTICAL MOTOR APHASIA

In this disorder, repetition is preserved but comprehension and spontaneous speech compromised, the latter strikingly so. The repetitions can be mandatory, which is termed echolalia, and can lead to rather disturbing speech patterns. The patients can correct errors in what they are asked to repeat. Spontaneous speech is stumbling, and stuttering, agrammatical and simple. These neurological signs are similar to Broca's aphasia. The locations of the underlying lesions are variable, and are frequently found anterior and superior to Broca's area, in the superior anterior frontal lobe. If the patients have problems with accessing semantic-conceptual representations when speaking, their lesions are associated with lateral prefrontal cortex, superior to Broca's area: if they have more of a problem in initiating the motor act of speech, their lesions are associated with midline premotor speech areas (Heilman, 2006).

TRANSCORTICAL SENSORY APHASIA (TSA)

In this disorder there is impaired comprehension, preserved repetition and fluent output. Words can be included in the speech output which have been overheard, but which have not been understood. Such 'repetition' is again often mandatory, i.e. the patients are echolalic. Kertesz *et al.* (1982) carried out a study into the localisation of the lesions, and found two sites associated with TSA, in the medial inferior ventral temporal lobe, and anterior STG.

MIXED TRANSCORTICAL APHASIA (ISOLATION APHASIA)

In this disorder only repetition is preserved – both comprehension and spontaneous speech are compromised. There is no voluntary language use, and the associated neurological signs are very variable. Some have a bilateral paralysis, leading to quadriplegia or quadriparesis, or unilateral signs, such as a right hemiplegia. There is often a sensory loss. A post-mortem study indicated that anterior and posterior brain damage was involved (Geschwind *et al.*, 1968), and a study by Ross (1980) showed involvement of the left motor and sensory cortices, as well as parietal lobe involvement.

ANOMIC APHASIA

Word-finding difficulties are the most prominent feature, leading to speech which can be 'vague' and imprecise in content. Most cases of anomic aphasia have no associated neurological signs, and it has been regarded as non-localising as no one area is shown to be implicated in patient studies. Gloning *et al.* (1963) found that 60 per cent of their patients had temporal-parietal lesions, but the other 40 per cent were wide ranging, though all in the left hemisphere.

PURE WORD DEAFNESS

Pure word deafness is very rare. Patients can sometimes tell spoken words from non-speech sounds, others cannot, but none of them can understand spoken words at all. Speech output can be disordered, and patients cannot repeat or write to dictation. Pure word deafness was first described as a lesion of white-matter tracts into the left auditory cortex (e.g. into A in Figure 11.3). However, more recent work has shown that cortical areas, often on both the left and right sides of the brain, are strongly implicated in pure word deafness. Auerbach *et al.* (1982) suggested that word deafness due to loss of prephonological auditory processing is associated with bilateral temporal lobe lesions, but that a unilateral left temporal lesion causes word deafness due to a deficit in phoneme discrimination and identification. Another clinical and psychophysical study of a patient does not support this, however; the patient had an initial infarction of the left dorsolateral temporal lobe and presented with Wernicke's aphasia, but subsequently developed word deafness after a right temporal infarct (Praamstra *et al.*, 1991). Loss of spoken word comprehension only occurred after the second, right-hemisphere infarct. Thus bilateral damage seems to be necessary for 'pure' word deafness – this may be a result of plasticity processes in the right hemisphere which support the recovery of some spoken word comprehension. Consistent with this view, more recent overviews have indicated that pure word deafness is seen after unilateral left temporal lobe damage, and bilateral temporal lobe damage, but not after unilateral right temporal lobe damage (Griffiths *et al.*, 1999).

PHONAGNOSIA

Phonagnosia is a disorder in which people are unable to recognise other people by their voices. This is not a speech perception problem per se, but as we saw in Chapter 10, we do adapt to idiosyncracies of speech production in a speaker-specific way, so it is not irrelevant to consider this issue. Phonoagnosia is rare, though this may reflect the fact that we are not good at recognising speakers by their voices alone. It may also reflect the fact that many interactions we have with other people are face to face, and hence other sources of information are available; if the voice alone is presented (e.g. on the phone) people commonly introduce themselves.

Patients with phonagnosia can recognise people by their faces, and do not have a more general problem with person identity knowledge. They do not have a disorder of speech perception, instead having a specific difficulty in recognising people from their voices. Phonagnosia associated with damage to the brain has been linked to damage to the right temporal lobe. A recent description of a developmental case of phonagnosia – someone with no known brain damage, who had experienced difficulties with identifying voices all her life – revealed no lower-level auditory-processing deficits, nor problems with the perception of other kinds of information from the voice, for example, emotional vocalisations. Instead her problem seemed to be limited to detecting speaker identity cues from the voice (Garrido *et al.*, 2009).

DYSARTHRIA

Dysarthria is an acquired disorder of speech production, and refers to a difficulty in the implementation of speech plans, when these are applied to the movement of muscles. Dysarthria is a specific problem with moving the articulators, due either to problems in the brain in the areas which directly control articulatory movements (e.g. damage to primary motor cortex) or to the cranial nerves which directly activate the muscles (the nerves which are sending the messages from the brain to the muscles). Either of these are routes to muscle weakness in the articulators, and dysarthria. In dysarthria, speech can be mumbled or indistinct, or slurred.

SPEECH APRAXIA

Speech apraxia is a disorder of the motor control of speech, in the absence of motor weakness. People with speech apraxia have great difficulty saying what they want to say, and they can be very inconsistent in their speech – a word may be accurately produced on one occasion but not on the next. Patients may be visibly groping for the right word. Their speech can have disordered rhythm and prosody. Patients with speech apraxia commonly have damage to the left anterior insula, which lies medial to Broca's area in the left inferior frontal gyrus (Dronkers, 1996).

PROSODY PRODUCTION AND PERCEPTION

Ross and Mesulam (1979) described two patients who had problems not with the production of spoken language per se, but with the production of appropriate melodic inflections to their speech: this had negative effects on their interpersonal interactions and relationships (Ross, 2000). In contrast, their ability to perceive prosody in speech was not affected. Both patients had right fronto-parietal lesions, and a role for the right frontal lobe in the control of speech prosody has been confirmed since (Gorelick and Ross, 1987; Ross, 1981; Ross and Monnot, 2008). In contrast, patients with damage to the right temporal lobe often have difficulty understanding the meaning of melody in heard speech. It is not unusual for right temporal lobe lesions to be relatively 'silent', because they do not often lead to frank language problems. However, on direct testing, patients with right temporal lobe lesions often show problems understanding the melody of spoken language, and this can extend to problems with other kinds of melody processing, for example in music.

11.4 PSYCHOLOGICAL AND PSYCHOLINGUISTIC ASPECTS OF APHASIA

The clinical basis of aphasia studies has necessarily focused on issues of symptoms and diagnosis, rather than on more conceptual aspects of language use. However, we know that speech perception and production, as discussed in Chapter 10, involve phonetic, lexical, semantic and syntactic aspects. Can we see these selectively damaged in clinical language problems?

PHONETIC DEFICITS

A problem of phonetic processing has direct and dire consequences for the comprehension of spoken language – a patient will be unlikely to have a deficit in perceptual speech processing that does not impact on lexical and semantic/syntactic processing. However, the locus of phonetic processing seems to correspond to lesions to the STG/STS (i.e. Wernicke's area).

SYNTACTIC DEFICITS

Agrammatical patients, who have a problem producing grammatically correct sentences, often have speech which is telegraphic and in which function words are omitted. They can have specific problems with passive constructions. Many of these patients (but by no means all) may have a Broca-like aphasic profile. Notably, patients with agrammatical speech also always have a motor speech problem – an apraxia or dysarthria of speech, for example, or (more rarely) foreign accent syndrome, where people's accents sound very changed to their fellow countrymen (due to the way we listen to and label accents, rather than the acquisition of a new accent). This suggests that syntactic processing and representations in speech production are closely linked to speech motor acts. Importantly, Varley and colleagues (Varley *et al.*, 2005; Varley and Siegal, 2000) have demonstrated that densely agrammatical patients can still perform other kinds of tasks accurately, including logical, mathematical and social cognitions (theory of mind tasks), suggesting that the disorder of syntax does not necessarily affect other kinds of complex cognitive processes.

SEMANTIC DEFICITS

As can be seen in aphasia, there is a variety of different ways that semantic processing can be compromised; however, the purest form seems to be seen in semantic dementia (see also Chapter 7), a focal dementing disorder which, unlike more global dementias like Alzheimer's disease, is associated with specific loss of grey matter in (initially) quite restricted cortical fields. In semantic dementia, the first symptom is a difficulty understanding the meaning of spoken words, and the damage is seen in the left anterior and ventral temporal lobe. The patients can understand what objects are, and use them appropriately, and their phonetic and syntactic performance is unimpaired. As the disease progresses, the patients start to make phonetic errors, suggesting that phonological processing is being compromised, and it has been suggested that severe problems in speech output are seen when the disease spreads to the right temporal lobe. Semantic dementia has therefore, in its initial stages, been identified as a selective semantic-processing deficit, and the left anterior temporal lobe has therefore been identified as a candidate location for amodal semantic representations, and thus potentially the central 'hub' in the hub model of semantic representations (Patterson *et al.*, 2007).

11.5 FUNCTIONAL IMAGING OF HUMAN LANGUAGE PROCESSING

We now have access to functional-imaging data, which complements our understanding of the neural basis of language processes based on patient studies. Functional-imaging techniques such as positron emission tomography (PET) and functional magnetic resonance imaging (fMRI) allow one to identify activity associated with a particular activity (e.g. speech perception) and also to localise the activity at the level of gyral anatomy, rather than neurons. This makes PET and fMRI particularly useful for investigating language processing in the healthy human brain, and to compare these results with the profiles seen in patients.

SPEECH PERCEPTION

Possibly because of the long established use of neurocognitive models in the study of aphasia, and the links between structure and function which have been made from patient studies, speech and language were two of the first phenomena to be studied with functional-imaging techniques, such a PET or fMRI. Importantly, all functional-imaging studies show patterns of relative activation, where the activation seen is relative to that seen in some kind of baseline contrast, so it is always important to identify what the contrasted conditions are in a PET or fMRI study.

A STUDY OF SPEECH PERCEPTION USING PET

Early functional-imaging studies showed that the perception of speech led to extensive bilateral activation in both the left and right superior temporal gyri compared with silent rest. Of course, heard speech is an acoustic signal, so to see activation specifically associated with speech, we need to control for activation associated simply with 'hearing a sound', for example, in primary auditory cortex. In addition, speech is an immensely complex acoustic signal, so we need to control for some aspects of acoustic complexity, without making a sound that is in any way intelligible. A study by Scott *et al.* (2000) attempted to do this with two forms of comprehensible speech. The design was a conjunction design, where the aim was to identify cortical responses to speech in a way that was independent of what the speech sounded like, while controlling for the complexity of the speech signal.

1. *Non-speech stimuli.* Spectrally rotated speech was used, in which the speech signal is 'turned upside down' in the frequency domain, creating a stimulus which contains all of the original speech signal, but which cannot be understood. Spectral rotation preserves the amplitude envelope and the pitch of speech sounds, so these rotated stimuli have preserved prosody, rhythm and syllabicity of the speech without comprehension being possible (Blesser, 1972); it thus forms an appropriately complex non-speech contrast.
2. *Intelligible speech.* Two forms were used: normal, clear speech and noise-vocoded speech, which sounds like a harsh whisper, and

---

Key Term

Positron emission tomography (PET)
A method of imaging structure and function in the human brain by directly tracking blood flow using radioactive tracers. PET can be used to form structural images of blood flow in the brain, as the brain is richly supplied with blood. PET can also be used to look at neural activity by tracking local changes in regional cerebral blood flow, which are seen when there is local increased in neural activity. Because the power of PET is limited by the number of scans, and because the number of scans is limited by the amount of radioactivity which can safely be administered, PET is becoming less commonly used for functional imaging studies.

Functional magnetic resonance imaging (fMRI)
A medical imaging technology that uses very strong magnetic fields to measure changes in the oxygenation of the blood in the brain and thus map levels of activity in the brain. It produces anatomical images of extremely high resolution.

which is a simulation of what someone who uses a cochlear implant can hear. The noise-vocoded speech does not sound like a recognisable person: it is intelligible but the listener cannot tell if they are listening to a man, a woman or a robot. Essentially, noise-vocoded speech lets us create a speech stimulus with little associated speaker information (of course, this is an obligatory aspect of normal speech, where we hear speech but also hear someone speaking, their gender, their age, their mood etc.).

3. *Conditions.* The conjunction design meant that there were four conditions: clear speech, noise-vocoded speech, rotated speech and rotated noise-vocoded speech. The design aimed to identify brain areas which were activated by both speech over rotated speech, and noise-vocoded speech over rotated noise-vocoded speech. The task was passive listening, and the eight subjects were all familiar with the stimuli.

The left superior temporal gyrus was strongly activated by the rotated speech as well as the intelligible clear and rotated speech. This is consistent with other studies implicating the STG in the processing of acoustic structure (e.g. Hall and Johnsrude, 2002). Other studies have indicated that there is complex processing of phonetic information in the left STG, with sensitivity here to linguistically relevant changes, relative to acoustic changes (e.g. Jacquemot *et al.,* 2003). Further studies have indicated that properties of phonemes are represented in the left STG (Obleser *et al.,* 2006), and that consonant-vowel combinations are selectively represented just below this, in the left STS (Liebenthal *et al.,* 2005). There is also evidence that syntactic and semantic information is processed in the left STG: a study explicitly contrasting semantic and syntactic violations in spoken sentences reported common activations to semantic and syntactic violations in the left STG (Friederici *et al.,* 2003). It is thus likely that there is massively parallel processing of spoken language in the superior temporal gyrus and sulcus, including semantic and syntactic processing as well as phonetic processing. This would be consistent with some of the evidence shown in Chapter 10 that the phonetic and acoustic realisations of spoken language vary systematically with semantic and syntactic features.

When the intelligibility conjunction was performed, to isolate cortical responses to speech which can be understood, over and above any processing dependent on the acoustic structure of the stimuli, a region in the left anterior superior temporal sulcus was identified as sensitive to intelligible spoken sentences, whether or not they were noise-vocoded or clear (see also Evans *et al.,* 2013). This indicated that we can identify a cortical response in the left anterior temporal lobe to comprehensible speech, over and about its acoustic complexity. However, as whole sentences were used, we cannot dissociate which elements (phonetic, semantic, syntactic, lexical) have contributed to this response, although it is almost certain that all factors do.

A further fMRI study (Cohen *et al.,* 2004) used the repetition of spoken words to investigate where the 'auditory word form' area lies:

auditory word forms are representations of the heard speech which are speech specific and not driven entirely by the acoustic signal. In this study, repetition suppression was used – the fact that a repeated stimulus will result in a reduction in the cortical response, while a change in stimulus properties to which a particular brain area is sensitive will not result in reduced activation. This study played people words, either novel or repeated, and found that the left anterior STS is the first point in the temporal lobes where there is significant suppression to repeated words, and enhanced responses to novel words (Cohen *et al.*, 2004). The left anterior STS is well placed between auditory areas and the left anterior lobe 'hub' for semantic representations (Patterson *et al.*, 2007), to form well-specified auditory representations of heard speech.

In contrast to a left anterior dominance in processing speech for meaning, posterior superior temporal lobe regions appear to be important in the processes subserving repetition, with posterior temporal lobe (and inferior parietal) fields being selectively involved in verbal fluency tasks (Price *et al.*, 1996), the silent rehearsal of non-words (McGettigan *et al.*, 2011) and vocal sound-to-action links (Hickok *et al.*, 2000; Warren *et al.*, 2005). This is consistent with an anatomical focus for the posterior STS in conduction aphasia, which is a specific disorder of verbal repetition.

The striking factor about all of these complex processes which translate between the sounds of speech and words in the brain is that they are all, anatomically, falling within the regions in the left STG originally described by Wernicke (Figure 11.8). Thus 'Wernicke's area' subsumes a range of different anatomical areas and functional properties, from acoustic/phonetic to semantic and syntactic, all of which underlie normal 'speech comprehension'. This probably results from considerable parallel processing of the properties of heard speech input. Outstanding questions concern the extent to which these processes involve the identification of phonemic structure, or of higher-order sequential structure over groups of phonemes. There is also

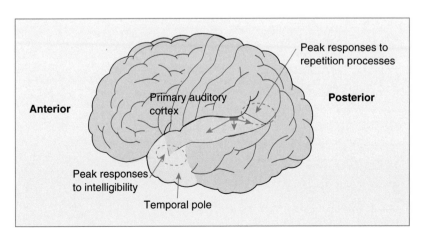

Figure 11.8 Diagram of the brain showing areas responding to repetition and intelligibility.

considerable interest in the extent to which there may be phoneme 'maps' in the STG, where phonemes are coded in terms of their features (e.g. Obleser *et al.*, 2006).

THE NEURAL BASIS OF CONTEXT EFFECTS IN SPEECH PERCEPTION

Context has a huge effect on speech processing. People find it easier to identify phonemes in a word than in a non-word, to recognise a word if it is in a sentence, and to understand a sentence if it is predictable than if it is unpredictable in content. Obleser *et al.* (2007) used fMRI to identify how linguistic context supports speech comprehension. They contrasted sentences like:

> The ship sailed across the bay.
> Sue discussed the bruise.

The former is very easy to understand, as there is a lot of contextual support, both semantic and syntactic, for the sentence. The second sentence is harder to understand, as there is no contextual support to help, unless one knows Sue and her particular tendencies to discuss these things. These effects can be seen in clear speech comprehension, and become very important if the speech is presented in noise, or if the listener has a hearing impairment.

Obleser *et al.* degraded spoken sentences to make them harder to understand, such that context could have an effect, and presented these to people whose neural activity was monitored using fMRI. When the conditions where the effects of context had the greatest impact on comprehension were investigated, the contrast of predictable sentences over unpredictable sentences revealed a distributed left-hemisphere system, all outside the left temporal lobe, with activation in the inferior and superior frontal gyri, angular gyrus and posterior cingulate. This suggests that a wide sematic network is recruited to support speech comprehension, and that this has great impact when context can be used to enhance understanding.

REHEARSING NON-WORDS VERSUS LISTENING TO NON-WORDS

One of the most basic findings in working memory research is the word length effect – the longer the verbal items being transiently stored, the fewer the items that can be stored accurately (e.g. Caplan *et al.*, 1992). McGettigan *et al.* (2011) addressed this in a study of the rehearsal of non-words, which varied both in duration (two or four syllables) and in phonetic complexity (no consonant clusters versus two consonant clusters). This led to four conditions: two syllables, no consonant clusters (e.g. *fipul*); two syllables, two consonant clusters (e.g. *frispul*); four syllables, no consonant clusters (e.g. *fotumipul*); and four syllables, two consonant clusters (e.g. *frotumispul*). In two separate fMRI experiments, two different sets of participants were asked to either rehearse the non-word prior to repeating it, or to listen to it passively, with no overt response.

In the passive perception task, the increasing duration of the non-words was associated with bilateral activity in the superior temporal gyri, running back from the primary auditory cortex into the posterior temporal lobes. This difference from the responses normally seen to speech may reflect the fact that these non-words have no (or little) semantic or syntactic content. Unlike the strong response to non-word duration (in syllables), there was no sensitivity to the consonant clusters in the STG responses, suggesting that there is a less marked sensitivity to individual phonemes in STG than to syllables. In the rehearsal experiment, there was also bilateral STG activation to the four-syllable non-words relative to the two-syllable non-words: this activation extended into left premotor cortex, and towards Broca's area on the left. During silent rehearsal of non-words, motor systems are recruited. Furthermore, these premotor fields were sensitive to the presence of consonant clusters, indicating a role of individual phonemes in the planning of motor speech output.

In addition to showing the relationship between the articulatory loop and brain regions critical to articulation during the rehearsal of non-words, this study shows different sensitivities in perceptual and motor systems to aspects of spoken words. Phonemes may thus form distinct segmental representations in speech production processes, rather than in speech perception processes.

NEURAL BASIS OF SPEECH PRODUCTION

The neuroanatomy of speech production varies, as might be expected, with the kinds of speech production tasks used. Simple repetition, for example, has been shown to be associated with activation of the left anterior insula, but not Broca's area. This is consistent with a role for the left anterior insula as the locus of damage in speech apraxia (Dronkers, 1996), and suggests that when speech production is simple (one word) and completely specified (the participant is told the word to repeat directly before it is repeated) then Broca's area need not be recruited (Wise *et al.*, 1999). This finding is consistent with the left anterior insula being closely associated with the control of the articulators, and Broca's area being associated with higher-order functions, including response selection and grammatical sequencing of output.

Consistent with this suggestion, Broca's area increases in activity if the speech task is made more complex. Another study of speech production contrasted counting aloud, reciting a well-learnt nursery rhyme, and generating propositional speech (responding to questions) with a baseline condition in which participants listened out for occasional noises (Blank *et al.*, 2002). Counting aloud involves producing words according to simple grammatical principles, as the numbers increase: the spoken numbers themselves form normal speech production, but with a highly constrained semantic and syntactic palate. The very familiar nursery rhymes are similarly constrained (there is no room for improvisation), though there is a far wider range of semantic and syntactic structure. The propositional speech, in which people generated speech in response to questions such as 'tell me about a relative you know well but do not live with', is relatively unconstrained: while the participant might be reasonably expected not to start to discuss the economic state of the euro, it is up to them if they discuss a brother, parent or cousin, and beyond that, whatever aspect of that person that they've decided to discuss. This means that in generating the speech, in addition to having a yet wider possible range of semantic and syntactic content than either nursery rhymes or counting, the participant has a lot of pragmatic decisions to make about what would constitute an appropriate answer. A portion of Broca's area, the pars opercularis, was least activated by the counting condition, more activated by the nursery rhymes condition, and most activated of all by the propositional speech.

The contrast of propositional speech over the counting and nursery rhymes conditions showed extensive activations, beyond Broca's area. There was activation in the left anterior temporal lobe, medial prefrontal cortex, left angular gyrus and posterior cingulate. These indicate the recruitment of a distributed semantic system to support the linguistic and memory components of normal conversational speech. It is striking that these activations are extremely similar to those seen in the study of the use of context in speech comprehension (Obleser *et al.*, 2007): this suggests that the same semantic/memory system is implicated both in speech production and perception, as would be predicted by the Kussmaul–Lichtheim–Wernicke model of aphasia (Figure 11.7).

During speech production, there is commonly a deactivation in the left mid STG/STS associated with listening to one's own voice. This may reflect a general reduction in sensory responses to self-generated stimulation – a very similar reduction in self-generated touch sensations has been suggested to underlie the fact that you cannot tickle yourself (Blakemore *et al.*, 1998).

11.6 READING

Both functional-imaging and patient studies indicate a distributed network of activations associated with reading, and these can be distinguished by their involvement in either word recognition and comprehension, or eye movements.

VISUAL WORD RECOGNITION

The primary visual cortex nestles in the calcerine sulcus, on the medial aspects of the occipital lobes. Lateral and ventral to this, is a cortical field on the inferior surface of the left occipital lobe which has been associated with the visual processing of words – a visual word form area (VWFA) (Figure 11.9). This region, if damaged, is associated with a dense alexia – a problem of reading words. Patients can typically use other kinds of visual symbols, e.g. do maths. The precise function of

---

Key Term

Alexia/dyslexia
Both refer to problems in reading written language. Alexia always refers to acquired difficulties in reading, while dyslexia is used to refer to developmental difficulties in reading. However, dyslexia is also used to refer to particular profiles of acquired reading problems, e.g. deep versus surface dyslexia.

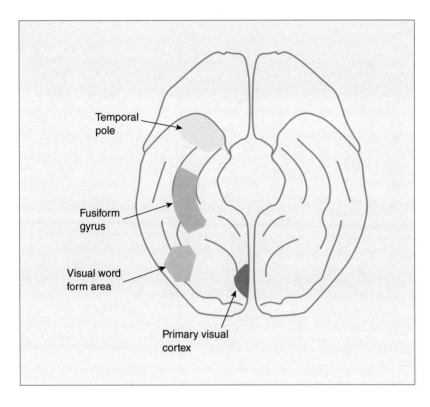

Figure 11.9 Diagram of the brain showing area associate with visual processing of words.

the VWFA remains controversial – for example, subtle problems with visual object processing can be seen in patients who have reading deficits following a lesion to this area, and it has been argued that reading is such a recent human development that it is unlikely that evolutionary processes have affected the brain's processing in this way (Price and Devlin, 2003). However, it is clear that the left inferior occipital lobe is important, indeed critical, to the early perceptual processing of written language.

NEURAL CONTROL OF EYE MOVEMENTS

The movements of the eyes (called saccades) across text are extremely precise and reflect a great deal of processing of the upcoming visual information – i.e. the upcoming text, which is to the left of the word currently fixated upon during reading (Rayner and Bertera, 1979). This is processed in such a way that, not only are the following saccades accurate, but they are not made onto every word – typically, for example, people do not saccade to a function word.

I LOVE TO SEE THE

THE RED SUN AND THE

THE NEW DAWN OF

OF ANOTHER MORNING

'Illusions' like the paragraph above (ask someone to read it aloud and see how many times they say 'the') occur precisely because we do not saccade onto every word in a sentence, so we don't notice if a function word is repeated.

Likewise, count the Fs in the following sentence:

FRIENDS OF MINE HAVE FOUND FINE COMFORT FROM THE SIGHT OF HOME

It's not unusual for people to report back three or four F's, but in fact there are seven Fs in that sentence. The illusion occurs because when reading we do not saccade to every word, but skip the function words such as 'of'. It is therefore harder to see the Fs in these words.

The planning of saccades is based on visual information in the right visual field (Figure 11.10), in the surrounding parafoveal regions where there is less precise resolution of the visual world, while the word which is being fixated upon (and onto which the last saccade landed) is being read (Rayner and Bertera, 1979).

There thus has been interest in the extent to which reading requires letter-by-letter processing, or whole-word processing, and the general consensus is that whole-word processing dominates. This means that sentences such as the following can be read:

FI YOU ASY HTAT OT EM AIGAN TEHN I HVAE ON OTPOIN BTU OT LAEVE

The role of parafoveal space in planning upcoming saccades across text means that there is a second kind of alexia, which is associated with problems reading words in a sentence. This is seen in patients

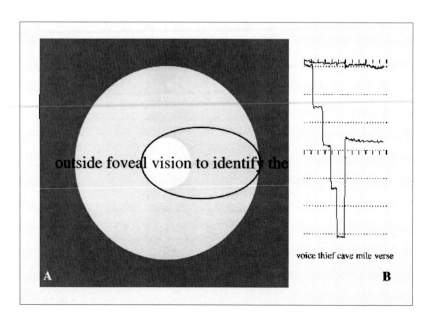

Figure 11.10 The control of saccades.

who have a deficit in their right visual fields, and a consequent lack of
visual information about the upcoming words that can be used to plan
saccades. These patients can often read a word presented to them in
a letter-by-letter fashion, sounding out 'cat' as C, A and T. They have
tremendous problems in reading connected text, because they cannot
see the upcoming words. Thus a motor problem (difficulty planning
eye movements to the next words in text) can result in a frank reading
difficulty (Zihl, 1995).

ROUTES TO READING

Research has established the important concept of different potential
routes for reading – for example, skilled adult readers can either read
a word by sounding out the letters or by recognising the whole word,
and when they encounter a new or a difficult word they may emphasise one way of reading more than another. The early diagrams incorporating the disorders of spoken language that we saw earlier in this
chapter have also been developed to account for acquired problems in
reading and writing. Acquired dyslexia (sometimes called alexia) refers
to a problem in reading which has its onset after the skill of reading
has been achieved, and acquired agraphia refers to a problem in writing which occurs after people have learnt to read. Both agraphia and
acquired dyslexia are associated with brain damage, often stroke or
dementia.

> **Key Term**
>
> **Dyslexia**
> Developmental
> difficulties in reading
> (see also **alexia**
> above).

As in spoken language, acquired problems with writing tend to
group into non-random profiles of difficulties, and these have been
specifically modelled along similar lines to the models of aphasia discussed earlier: some models even manage to encompass both speech
and writing disorders in the same model (Ellis and Young, 1996)
(Figure 11.11). Tests of reading often focus on whether words are
'real' words or non-words, or whether they are regularly spelled, or
whether they are frequently encountered (high or low frequency), and
their grammatical status (e.g. function words versus content words).

SURFACE DYSLEXIA

Some patients can only read words if they can sound them out first,
and tend to be better with regular than irregular words – for example, they might produce an irregular word like 'pint' as if it was pronounced like 'hint'. Only after they have said the word aloud do the
patients understand the meaning. This is known as surface dyslexia
and is associated with damage to the temporal lobes (Deloche et al.,
1982). In surface dyslexia, there is considered to be damage between
the visual representations – the visual word forms – and the wider
semantic system. This means that the patient cannot rely on a mapping
between the visual word form and semantics to access the meaning of
a word, but will need to utilise the connections between graphemic and
phonemic representations. This can be considered as a problem dealing with the 'whole word' route for reading, which forces the patients
to rely on sequences of individual letter to access the pronunciations,
and then the meanings, of the words.

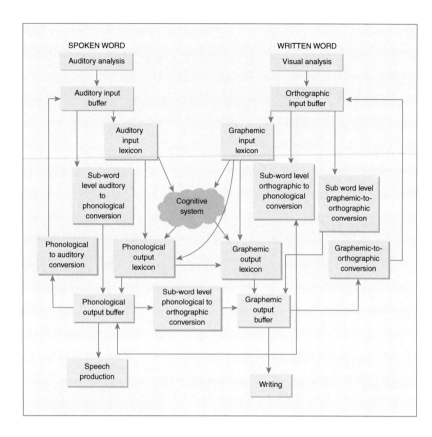

Figure 11.11 A neuropsychological model of the processing of spoken and written language.

Source: Adapted from Ellis and Young (1996).

PHONOLOGICAL DYSLEXIA

In phonological dyslexia, patients can read words which are both real words and familiar words (i.e. words known to them) but struggle with non-words (Shallice and Warrington, 1980; Ellis and Young, 1996). One such patient could read a list of content words with high levels of accuracy (95 per cent correct, including uncommon words like 'decree' and 'phrase', but was able to read only 8 per cent of a list of matched non-words (Patterson, 1982). When confronted with a non-word, for example 'soof', he would often read it as a real word (e.g. 'soot') – importantly, these errors with non-words typically involved the production of a visually similar real word. Unlike the surface dyslexia patients, who have damage to the lexical-semantic route for reading, but access to grapheme-to-phoneme conversion routes, patients with phonological dyslexia are thought to have damage to grapheme-to-phoneme conversion routes, which forces them to read via lexical-semantic pathways. This works well when they encounter familiar words, but causes problems when a word is unfamiliar, as they cannot use grapheme-to-phoneme conversion strategies to support reading these new words accurately.

DEEP DYSLEXIA

Marshall and Newcome (1966) described a patient with 'deep' dyslexia, who when reading made a large number of errors – around 50 per cent - but these errors were often semantically related to the target word (e.g. reading 'abroad' as 'overseas'). Other errors made by patients with deep dyslexia include reading non-words as real words (e.g. reading 'tweeps' as 'sweet'), and visual errors (e.g. reading 'nightmare' as 'night'); the list of errors seen is longer (up to twelve different kinds of errors have been described) (Plaut and Shallice, 1993). In contrast, these patients can be surprisingly good at some other kinds of tasks – for example, many patients can perform lexical decision tasks quite accurately (Coltheart, 1980).

Deep dyslexia has been described as arising from damage to both grapheme-to-phoneme routes, and to lexical-semantic pathways, as well as visual-processing problems (Morton and Patterson, 1987). Unlike many of the other kinds of language problems discussed in neuropsychological research, the variety of problems seen in deep dyslexia is harder to account for by referring to relatively simple ways of damaging a 'box and arrow' model of language (Coltheart *et al.*, 1987). That being said, the profile of problems associated with deep dyslexia co-occur with such consistency that the disorder reflects a consistent and coherent kind of language problem.

One account for deep dyslexia, which often follows left temporal lobe damage, is that it reflects the reading capabilities of the right hemisphere (Coltheart 1980, 1987; Saffran *et al.*, 1987). In this approach, left-hemisphere systems underlying lexico-semantic and grapheme-to-phoneme conversion have been damaged, but right-hemispheric mechanisms can still process some aspects of words and associate the words with semantic representations. This is argued to account for the semantic errors, as the right hemisphere is considered to be less precise in its semantic associations: it also accounts for the problems with function words and abstract words, as these are considered to be less well represented in the right hemisphere. Non-words cannot be read as they cannot access the intact semantic system(s). Following semantic activation, preserved speech output systems in the left hemisphere are recruited to support speech production.

Another approach to deep dyslexia is a connectionist model, developed by Hinton and Shallice (1991) (see also Plaut and Shallice, 1993). This model (Figure 11.12) used three processing levels (grapheme, intermediate and semantic, plus a 'cleanup' level)

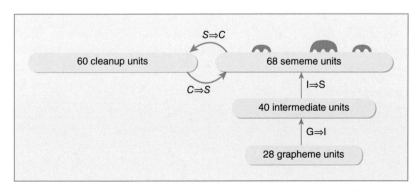

Figure 11.12 The network used by Hinton and Shallice. Notice that sets of connections are named with the initials of the names of the source and destination unit groups (e.g. G–I for grapheme-to-intermediate connections).

The model contained a semantic network in which semantic associations between words (from a limited possible set of words) was represented, across a number of different semantic parameters: the network was trained (using back propagation) on a set of words, after which it could map between written words to the correct semantic meaning. Plaut and Shallice then systematically lesioned the model, in terms of location of damage and severity, to identify patterns of errors that arose. They classified four different error types:

1. visual (cat > cot);
2. semantic (cat > kitten);
3. visual-semantic (cat > rat);
4. other (cat > mug).

All lesions were noted to lead to visual, semantic and visual-semantic errors at higher rates than random variation would predict. There was also a tendency for damage nearer the input layer to lead to visual errors, and damage nearer to the semantic layer to lead to semantic errors. However, errors characteristic of deep dyslexia were found following all the lesions. Thus deep dyslexia was an early demonstration of the power of a connectionist approach in accounting for patterns of damage in neuropsychological research.

FUNCTIONAL-IMAGING STUDIES OF WRITTEN LANGUAGE

As might be expected from the above sections, functional-imaging studies have shown the activation of the 'visual word form area' in the left lateral occipital lobe when visual words are silently read, and the recruitment of posterior parietal areas and frontal eye fields associated with the control of eye movements during the reading of text. These seem to be brain areas specifically associated with written language rather than heard speech, although they may not be specific to only written language (Price and Devlin, 2003). The acquisition of written language is parasitic on speech perception and production: while we learn to understand and produce spoken language without overt instruction, learning to read and write is something we need explicit instruction in, and which is something which is much harder for us to do it we had not learnt to understand a spoken language first. We might therefore expect considerable overlap between neural regions that support the processing of visual and spoken language perception. Functional-imaging studies have confirmed this relationship, by showing, for example, that both heard and read stories (each relative to a complex perceptual baseline) are associated with activation in the left superior temporal sulcus, and with activation in areas associated with amodal semantic representations running along the bottom of the left temporal lobe, and the left anterior temporal pole (Spitsyna *et al.*, 2006). If the reading task requires people to sound out the letters, then this can result in extra activation in premotor and supplementary speech areas; indeed, if readers are commonly reading by sounding out the letters, this will be often indexed by activity in the midline supplementary speech area. This represents ways of using articulations to access word forms, letter by letter.

11.7 DEVELOPMENTAL DISORDERS OF LANGUAGE

In addition to speech and language problems that are associated with damage to the brain – known as acquired disorders of speech and language – there are a variety of language problems that are a result of difficulties which are present from very early in life, and which are not associated with known incidents of acquired brain damage. These are generally known as developmental disorders, and they have some similarities and some important differences from the profiles seen in acquired damage. Key to the concept of developmental disorders is the need for the identified problem to be relatively more severe than the child's other abilities – for example, if the child has poor verbal IQ on tests, they will only be considered to have a specific language problem if their verbal IQ score is much poorer than their non-verbal IQ score.

DEVELOPMENTAL DISORDERS OF SPEECH PERCEPTION AND PRODUCTION – SPECIFIC LANGUAGE IMPAIRMENT

Specific language impairment (SLI) is a developmental disorder of language in which children show problems with spoken language comprehension and production, problems that are disproportionate to their non-verbal IQ. Furthermore, their language problems are not a consequence of brain damage, hearing loss, or deprivation. The speech of children with SLI can be hard to follow, as they can find it hard to express their ideas, and their speech can sound muddled and underarticulated; they use sentences but what they say can be difficult to understand. When they listen to other people, children with SLI can themselves find it hard to understand what is said, and find it hard to do what someone asks them to do. Their vocabulary can be restricted to a relatively small set of words, and they can find it hard to repeat words and sentences. These difficulties make it hard for children with SLI to cope, both in formal educational settings, and in interactions with their peers (e.g. when playing), unless support is provided for them. The condition can vary in severity, with some children experiencing relatively mild problems, and other children having much more severe difficulties: an eight-year-old child with relatively severe SLI might be producing speech typical of a three-year-old (e.g. 'me go there' rather than 'I went there') (Bishop 2006).

In terms of the underlying problem, there are three general theories of SLI. The first is that the children have an underlying auditory processing deficit, and their problems in processing sounds (e.g. in telling the order in which two sounds are played) can have a profound impact on their ability to hear speech, and a knock-on effect on their ability to produce speech. The second theory is that they have a particular problem with verbal short-term memory, and can find it hard to repeat non-words; this problem would lead to the children finding it hard to say and learn new words accurately. The third theory is that the children have a specific deficit in processing syntax, which leads to them having particular problems in hearing and producing syntactic properties of speech. The idea of a developmental disorder of syntax attracted a great deal of interest from people interested in the ideas of Chomsky and a universal grammar (Chapter 10). Similarly, there was a lot of interest in the auditory processing deficit model, since it would avoid the positing of specific linguistic mechanisms. If a general auditory-processing deficit were primarily manifest as a language deficit, this might be evidence against a universal grammar perspective.

Specific language impairment has a strong genetic component, being highly heritable; however, it has a complex profile of heritability, like asthma or diabetes, and does not show a simple pattern characteristic of a dominant or recessive genetic contribution. Instead, multiple genes seem to be involved. Work by Dorothy Bishop has indicated that there are separable genetic contributions to the problems with syntax and non-word repetition tasks shown by children with SLI. In contrast, their problems with rapid auditory processing have a strong environmental contribution, being primarily associated with whether or not there is a musical instrument in the home. These data suggest that SLI is not only a complex and variable disorder, but that there are separable contributions of problems with syntax processing and verbal working memory, as well as potential environmental issues. SLI may form an extremely important case for investigating the ways that genes and environment interact in language development and disorders (Bishop, 2006).

DEVELOPMENTAL DISORDERS OF READING – DYSLEXIA

In developmental dyslexia, children have a reading age which is lower than their chronological age, and the children have particular difficulties in reading and writing, both in terms of accuracy and fluency. The difficulties are out of proportion to their non-verbal IQ measures. Although children with dyslexia will learn to read and write, they will often show persistent problems, for example with spelling. They will also show 'phonological' problems – for example, difficulties in segmenting heard words around the onset/rhyme distinction. Children and adults with dyslexia often have problems, for example, with swapping onsets and rhymes around to make spoonerisms, for example turning 'windy day' into 'dindy way'.

There are more possible accounts of dyslexia than can be done justice to in a book about dyslexia, let alone a section in a chapter on language disorders. There have been accounts based on visual-processing deficits, problems in general task learning, and auditory processing. One important factor is that 'normal' reading and writing development involves use of 'phonological' information, which typically refers to aspects of the sound structure of words rather than to their phonetic construction (Snowling,

1998). Thus the ability to learn to read is predicted by children's ability to tell that two words have the same onset, or rhyme; this ability is predictive of reading/writing development, even if a child is learning to read a non-alphabetic script, such a written Chinese. Once children have learnt to read, they can break words down into phonemes, such that cat becomes C, A and T; this skill is a consequence of learning to read, however, and it is important in dyslexia research to identify problems which are a result of the dyslexia, rather than due to the child's slower acquisition of reading and reading-related skills.

The causes of these phonological deficits, which seem to hinder reading and writing in dyslexia, are still unknown, and there is a lot of interest in the possible role of auditory-processing deficits (Goswami, 2010) or deficits in the ways that children can access motor representations when performing 'phonological' tasks (Snowling, 1998).

DEVELOPMENTAL DISORDERS OF SPEECH PRODUCTION

In terms of speech production, one of the most difficult developmental disorders is a developmental dysfluency, commonly known as stammering or stuttering (Wingate, 1976). In stuttering, children have tremendous difficulties in speaking aloud, and can get stuck (known as 'blocking') on the start of a word, or repeating the start of a word, or prolong (stretch out) their speech sounds. Around 80 per cent of children with a developmental dysfluency will develop fluent speech production by the end of puberty; however, 20 per cent of children have a persistent problem which persists into adulthood. Despite the severity of the disorder – humans tend to strongly value fluency in verbal behaviour, and can be very intolerant of speakers whose speech is slow or hesitant, and the social anxiety associated with this knowledge can make a stammer much worse – we still do not have a unifying theory about stammering, nor any predictive information about why some people's stammers resolve while others are left with a life-long difficulty. Strikingly, a variety of different ways of altering someone's auditory environment and what their speech sounds like can improve developmental dysfluencies. Thus altering the acoustic consequences of spoken language by changing the pitch of someone's voice, or playing their speech back with a noticeable delay typically improves people's stuttering: several of these techniques have been incorporated into devices (e.g. built into phones, or as apps) that people who stutter can use to help them communicate. Strikingly, these techniques (e.g. introducing a delay) adversely affects the speech of fluent talkers, and can lead to them producing very dysfluent speech. Whispering also commonly improves stuttering. Altering the acoustic environment – for example, by putting people in noisy rooms, or getting them to talk in concert with someone else – also improves fluency. All of these improvements are transient, meaning that the improvements do not persist once the devices have been turned off (Howell, 2011). However, the fact that they all improve speech fluency suggests strongly that stuttering may not be a straightforward disorder of speech motor control, but may reflect a disordered processing of the dynamic perceptual control and guidance of speech production.

DISORDERS OF LANGUAGE USE IN AUTISM

Autism is a term covering a spectrum of developmental disorders, which can vary in severity from people who have profound learning disabilities through to people who can lead independent lives, but who may still experience considerable difficulties in their social interactions (Happé, 1999). Over the spectrum of autistic issues, there is considerable heterogeneity, with two main features, which seem to separately contribute to the profile. The first difference is one of perceptual processing, and can be crudely characterised as a problem of 'seeing the wood for the trees': people on the autistic spectrum can show an enhanced ability to focus on finer perceptual details, across sensory modalities. This means that they can do better at detecting embedded figures that a neurotypical control group, but it comes at the cost of poorer sensitivity to higher-order structure. Thus in speech perception and auditory processing, people with autism can be better at detecting pitch changes than a control group, but worse at understanding profiles of pitch that lead to prosody differences. The second common difference is one of perspective taking. It can be very hard for someone on the autistic spectrum to understand that someone else can know or believe something other than what they themselves know; this has been called a problem with 'theory of mind'. In practical terms, one of the most problematic aspects of difficulties in seeing the world from someone else's perspective is in social interactions, especially in conversation, where (as we saw in Chapter 10) people rarely say absolutely everything they mean, and trust that those they are talking to will understand the context in which their words are said. If, as we're unpacking the shopping and I'm about to start cooking lunch in something of a hurry, I say to my sister 'there were eggs on the kitchen table', then she is likely to interpret this as a request to know where the eggs are now, as only she and I are putting the shopping away. If she does not use context however, she might well reply 'yes I know there were' or 'why are you telling me that?' as without the use of context, it is a mystifying comment to make. While language acquisition can be delayed for people who have autistic symptoms, it has been argued that the lasting problem is not one of a language deficit per se, and more of a problem in the *use* of language. This can make social interactions even harder for people who are already experiencing considerable problems.

SUMMARY

* When we discuss language in the brain, we are discussing a wide range of representations and processes across perceptual, motoric, conceptual and syntactic levels. Language use incorporates both linguistic and non-linguistic processes, and it can be disturbed and disrupted in a wide variety of ways.

- Despite Henry Head's distaste for 'diagram-makers' (Head, 1926), considerable developments have been made by using cognitive models to reflect both on the different ways that acquired brain damage can affect language, and also how language is processed in the normal, healthy brain.
- Many aspects of the Kussmaul–Wernicke–Lichtheim model have subsequently been supported by functional-imaging studies, including a dissociation between speech motor control, speech perception centres, and the wider semantic-conceptual system.
- In the distinction between anterior cortical temporal lobe areas which support the processing of intelligibility in speech, and posterior cortical temporal lobe areas which are important in repetition, there is some support for the concept that the phonological input lexicon may be distinct from the phonological output lexicon.
- When the field is extended to include reading, we can see both reading-specific profiles (e.g. in the visual work form area) and activations common to reading and speech comprehension (e.g. in the anterior temporal lobe, STS and fusiform gyrus).
- Finally, developmental disorders of language reveal the potential impact of phonological deficits on reading development, and separable contributions of syntactic deficits and verbal working memory on specific language impairments. We can see a potential role for auditory processing in stuttering, and a problem of the social use of language in autism.

FURTHER READING

- Harley, T. A. (2007). *The Psychology of Language: From Data to Theory*. Hove: Psychology Press.
- Ward, J. (2006). *The Student's Guide to Cognitive Neuroscience*. Hove: Psychology Press.
- Hulme, C. and Snowling, M. J. (2009). *Developmental Disorders of Language Learning and Cognition*. Chichester: Wiley-Blackwell.

Chapter 12

Contents

Cognition and emotion

Michael Eysenck

12

12.1 INTRODUCTION

As the previous chapters in this book have revealed, psychologists have made considerable progress in understanding human cognition. In spite of that success, there is still some scepticism concerning the value of cognitive psychology. More specifically, it is sometimes doubted whether most research in cognitive psychology possesses ecological validity, which refers to the extent to which experimental findings are applicable in the real world.

How does cognitive psychology research lack ecological validity? One of the most important ways relates to participants' mood state when taking part in experiments. Experimenters typically try to ensure that participants are in a fairly neutral mood state. Note, however, that there are several exceptions. For example, participants in studies on eyewitness testimony are often exposed to emotionally threatening scenes that generate fear and anxiety (see Chapter 6).

The neutral mood state of most laboratory participants contrasts very much with everyday life with its pleasures, frustrations and disappointments. In the real world, thinking, problem-solving and decision-making often occur when we are happy, anxious, sad or angry. This difference between the laboratory and everyday life is important, because it is indisputable that our cognitive processes and performance are influenced by our current mood state.

Why have numerous researchers focused so strongly on human cognition in unemotional states? Part of the answer is that cognitive psychology for many years was much influenced by the computer analogy – the notion that information processing in humans resembles that in computers. Since it appears improbable that computers have mood states, use of the computer analogy led to limited interest in the effects of emotion on cognition.

There is accumulating evidence that mood states influence important aspects of everyday life. Consider, for example, a study by Pecher *et al.* (2009) on the effects of music on car driving in a simulator. Drivers listening to sad music found it as easy as those listening to neutral music to keep the car in its lane, but there was a slight reduction in speed. In contrast, drivers found happy music to be distracting. It reduced drivers' ability to keep the car in lane and there was an 8 mph decrease in speed compared with the neutral music condition.

The good news is that (rather late in the day!) there has recently been a substantial increase in research on emotion and cognition. This research has focused on the effects of mood state on cognitive processes such as perception, attention, interpretation, learning, memory, judgement, decision- making and reasoning. As we will see, positive mood states and negative mood states as diverse as anxiety, sadness and anger typically influence all of these cognitive processes.

As indicated above, most of the research in this area has focused on mood states. There is a distinction between mood and emotion. In general terms, mood states are typically fairly long-lasting and lacking in intensity. In contrast, emotional states are usually fairly short-lasting but intense. Note, however, that there is substantial overlap between mood and emotions, and the distinction is often somewhat arbitrary. The emphasis in research has been on mood states because they are easier to manipulate and the induction of mild mood states poses fewer ethical issues than the induction of intense emotions (especially negative ones).

MANIPULATING MOOD STATES

In much of the research on cognition and emotion, researchers have used various techniques to manipulate the mood states of their participants. One of the most effective techniques involves having participants write about personal events that created intense emotion in their lives. For example, Young *et al.* (2011) used this technique to create angry or sad mood states. Griskevicius *et al.* (2010) told their participants to write about a situation 'when another person really took care of you and made you feel better' to create feelings of attachment love.

Another technique is to use music to manipulate mood state, as was done in the study by Pecher *et al.* (2009) discussed above. A further technique was devised by Velten (1968). It involves participants reading emotional sentences that are intended to produce progressively more intense positive or negative feelings. This technique changes individuals' mood states. However, it often produces changes in various moods in addition to the one intended (Polivy, 1981).

12.2 MOOD AND ATTENTION

In this section, we will be mostly concerned with the effects of mood state on attention. Do various mood states lead to a narrowing or a broadening of attention? Answering this question is of relevance to an understanding of mood effects on memory, because what we remember is strongly influenced by what we attend to at the time of learning.

ATTENTIONAL NARROWING

One of the first systematic attempts to understand emotional effects on attention and performance was put forward by Easterbrook (1959). According to Easterbrook's hypothesis, the range of cues (i.e.

Key Term
Easterbrook's hypothesis The notion that high levels of arousal or anxiety cause a narrowing of attention.

the environmental features receiving attention) reduces as arousal or anxiety increases, which 'will reduce the proportion of irrelevant cues employed, and so improve performance ... further reduction in the number of cues employed can only affected relevant cues, and proficiency will fall' (Easterbrook, 1959: 193). In essence, Easterbrook was arguing that anxiety or arousal creates what is popularly known as 'tunnel vision' (excessive focusing of attention).

Most of the research has supported the hypothesis by finding that anxiety leads to a narrowing of attention (Eysenck, 1992). In other words, anxiety reduces the spatial area to which attention is paid. Why does anxiety cause attention to become narrower? According to Gable and Harmon-Jones (2010), anxiety is a negative emotional state high in motivational intensity. Individuals become anxious when in threatening situations, and so they are motivated to attend (and respond) to the source of the threat.

What are the effects on breadth of attention of the negative emotional state of sadness? Gable and Harmon-Jones (2010) argued that we become sad when we discover that some goal is unattainable. Sad individuals need to be open to new possibilities and this might cause broadened attention. As predicted, they found that sadness was associated with attentional broadening rather than narrowing. Thus, the presence or absence of high motivational intensity is important in determining whether there is attentional narrowing.

ATTENTION AND MEMORY

Attentional narrowing helps to determine the effects of mood on memory. Levine and Edelstein (2009) argued that a slightly modified version of Easterbrook's hypothesis could account for many of the effects of anxiety or stress on long-term memory. According to them, emotion enhances our memory for information central to our current goals but impairs it for peripheral or unimportant information.

There is reasonable support for the above hypothesis. For example, Cavenett and Nixon (2006) studied the effects on memory of anxiety created by having skydivers learn words while on a plane just before they jumped out of it. In the control condition, the skydivers did their learning on the ground.

When tested on the ground, the total number of words recalled was similar in the two conditions. However, the *balance* of what was recalled differed. Those skydivers who had learned under stressful conditions recognised more skydiving-relevant words than those in the control group. However, they recognised fewer words irrelevant to skydiving. These findings suggest that anxiety increases the focus on relevant stimuli at the expense of non-relevant ones.

Easterbrook's hypothesis is of some relevance to eyewitness testimony (Chapter 6). Consider what happens when an eyewitness is confronted by someone with a gun or other weapon. Loftus *et al.* (1987) found that memory for details was poor when eyewitnesses watched a person pointing a gun at a cashier and receiving some money. Memory for details of the same scene was better in the unemotional situation

Key Term

Weapon focus
The finding that
eyewitnesses pay so
much attention to
some crucial aspect
of the situation (e.g.
a weapon) that they
ignore other details.

in which the person handed a cheque to the cashier. Loftus *et al.* used the term weapon focus to refer to the way in which a weapon attracts attention and thus reduces attention to (and memory of) peripheral details.

Talarico *et al.* (2009) asked their participants to recall eight emotional autobiographical memories. These memories covered four positive emotions (happy; calm; in love; positive surprise) and four negative ones (negative surprise; angry; sad; afraid). There was poor memory for peripheral details with memories of anger, fear and negative surprise, as might be expected on Easterbrook's hypothesis (Figure 12.1). In contrast, sad memories were associated with reasonably good recall of peripheral details, which is consistent with the findings of Gable and Harmon-Jones (2010) discussed earlier.

What did Talarico *et al.* (2009) find with respect to the recall of positive autobiographical memories? There was good recall of peripheral details for all categories of positive memories. This suggests that individuals in a positive mood state show a broadening of attention.

12.3 MOOD AND MEMORY

Learning and memory are affected in several ways by mood. Two main approaches can be taken to assess these effects. First, researchers can manipulate participants' mood state at learning and/or retrieval. Second, researchers can consider the effects on memory of intensely emotional events in the world at large or in an individual's personal life. We will be considering both approaches in what follows. After that, we will focus on the amygdala, a part of the brain that plays a central role in emotional processing.

Figure 12.1 Mean proportion of total details of autobiographical memories that were rated as peripheral for four positive and four negative emotions. The emotions are ordered on the basis of the proportion of peripheral details.

Source: Talarico *et al.* (2009).

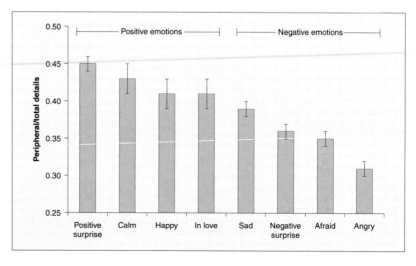

MOOD MANIPULATIONS AND MEMORY

Think of times in which you have experienced a negative mood state perhaps because something has just gone wrong in your life. What kinds of memories spring to mind at such times? Most people find themselves recalling far more negative or unpleasant than pleasant memories. Conversely, when we are in a good mood, we naturally find ourselves recalling happy personal memories. These are examples of mood-congruent memory – memory is better when the learner's (or rememberer's) mood state matches the emotional content of the material.

Many studies have obtained evidence of mood congruity effects on memory. Some of this research has focused on autobiographical memories. Miranda and Kihlstrom (2005) asked adult participants to recall autobiographical memories from childhood and adulthood when presented with pleasant, unpleasant and neutral cues. Music was used to produce a happy, sad or neutral mood. There was good evidence of mood congruity – retrieval of sad memories was facilitated by a sad mood and retrieval of happy memories was enhanced by a happy mood.

Holland and Kensinger (2010) reviewed the literature on mood and autobiographical memory. They concluded that there is a reliable mood-congruent memory effect when people are in a positive mood. However, mood-congruent memory is found less reliably when people are in a negative mood. That is also the case in studies of mood congruity with positive and negative emotional material not of an auto-biographical nature (Rusting and DeHart, 2000).

Why is mood-congruent memory relatively elusive with negative mood? Negative mood states are unpleasant and so individuals in such a mood state are motivated to change their mood into a more positive one. Any reduction in negative mood state is likely to reduce the accessibility of negative memories.

Support for the above explanation was reported by Rusting and DeHart (2000). In their study, participants wrote sentences about negative, positive and neutral words. After that, the participants were put into a negative mood state by thinking about experiencing distressing events. Next the participants were assigned to three conditions. In one condition, they were told to continue focusing on negative thoughts, whereas in another condition they engaged in positive reappraisal of the distressing events (e.g. 'List some good things that could happen as a result of any of the negative events in the stories'). Finally, there was an unexpected test of free recall for all the words presented initially.

What did Rusting and DeHart (2000) find? The typical mood-congruency effect was found in the continued focus condition, whereas participants in the positive reappraisal condition showed mood incongruity (i.e. better recall of positive than of negative words). These effects were much stronger among participants who had indicated previously that they were generally successful at regulating negative mood states. These findings suggest that the reason that mood-congruency effects are hard to find with negative mood states is because people strive to improve their mood.

> **Key Term**
>
> **Mood-congruent memory**
> The finding that learning and retrieval are better when the learner's (or rememberer's) mood state is the same as (or congruent with) the affective value of the to-be-remembered material.

There are two possible explanations of most mood-congruity effects (Fiedler *et al.*, 2001). First, they may be due to a genuine memorial advantage for mood-congruent material. Second, they may be due to a response bias with individuals being more willing to report memories matching their current mood state even if they are not genuine ones. Fiedler *et al.* obtained no evidence that mood-congruity effects are due to response bias. In other words, incorrect memories were not more likely when they matched participants' current mood state than when they did not. As a result, Fiedler *et al.* (2001) concluded that mood congruity is a genuine memory effect.

Another effect of mood on memory is mood-state-dependent memory. It occurs when memory is better when the mood state at retrieval *matches* that at learning than when the two mood states are different. There is some similarity between the notion of mood-state-dependent memory and that of mood-congruent memory. However, one important difference is that mood-state-dependent memory is not necessarily linked to the emotional content of the to-be-remembered information, whereas there is such a link with mood-congruent memory.

Ucros (1989) found in a review of forty studies that there was moderate support for the phenomenon of mood-state-dependent memory. The effects were greater when participants were in a positive mood than a negative one, which resembles the findings for mood-congruent memory. The explanation is the same – individuals in a negative mood state are motivated to change it in a positive direction.

Eich (1995) argued that mood-state-dependent effects on memory can be explained in terms of a 'do-it-yourself' principle. In essence, such effects are much more likely to be found when participants have to generate crucial information (i.e. the to-be-remembered material or the retrieval cues) for themselves (e.g. in free recall) rather than having it explicitly presented (e.g. in recognition memory).

We can see the value of Eich's do-it-yourself principle by considering the findings of a study reported by Pamela Kenealy (1997). Participants learned instructions concerning a given map route in happy or sad conditions and then had their memory tested the following day in happy or sad conditions. Two memory tests were used: (1) free recall, in which participants had to generate their own retrieval cues; and (2) cued recall, in which the visual outline of the map was present to facilitate retrieval.

What did Kenealy (1997) find? The results are shown in Figure 12.2. There was a strong mood-state-dependent effect in free recall. When retrieval cues were presented (i.e. in cued recall), there was no evidence of mood-state-dependent memory.

What causes mood-state-dependent memory? Information about the to-be-remembered material and contextual information (often including information about mood state) are encoded at the time of learning. At the time of retrieval, various kinds of information (including information about current mood state) are available. According to the encoding specificity principle (Tulving, 1979; see Chapter 6), memory is better when there is much *overlap* of the information available at learning and

Key Term

Mood-state-dependent memory
The finding that memory performance is better when the individual's mood state is the same at learning and retrieval than when it differs.

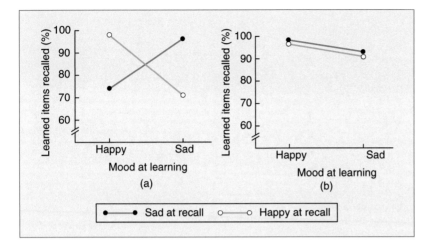

Figure 12.2 (a) Free recall and (b) cued recall as a function of mood state (happy or sad) at learning and at retrieval. (Based on data in Kenealy, 1997.)

Source: Eysenck and Keane (2010).

at test than when there is little overlap. This overlap is greater when participants are in the same mood state at learning and at test than when the mood state changes.

FLASHBULB MEMORIES

How good is your memory for dramatic world events (e.g. 9/11)? Most people believe they have very good memory for such events. Interest in flashbulb memories (vivid and detailed memories of dramatic events) goes back to Brown and Kulik (1977). According to them, dramatic events that are surprising and have genuine consequences for the individual trigger a special neural mechanism. This mechanism 'prints' the details of such events more or less permanently in long-term memory.

There is some evidence for strong and long-lasting flashbulb memories (Eysenck, 2012). However, such memories are often surprisingly inaccurate. Talarico and Rubin (2009) reviewed research on flashbulb memories, and they concluded that there is nothing special about flashbulb memories in terms of the underlying processes. Flashbulb memories seem especially vivid because they typically refer to distinctive events and so suffer little interference from other memories. Flashbulb memories are discussed in detail in Chapter 6.

RECOVERED MEMORIES

Most of the evidence suggests that memories formed in strong emotional states are well remembered. However, the bearded Austrian psychologist Sigmund Freud argued that precisely the opposite is sometimes the case. More specifically, he claimed that memories of traumatic events (e.g. childhood sexual abuse) often cannot be recalled because they are subject to motivated forgetting and are relegated to the unconscious mind. Freud used the term repression to refer to this phenomenon.

Key Term
Flashbulb memories Apparently vivid detailed memories of dramatic and significant events (e.g. 9/11).
Repression Motivated forgetting of traumatic or other very threatening events (e.g. childhood abuse).

How do we know that people have repressed memories if they are unable to recall them? What sometimes happens is that traumatic memories that had been forgotten for many years are suddenly remembered in adult life. Freud found that these so-called recovered memories were often recalled in the course of therapy.

The notion of recovered memories has proved very controversial. Many experts (e.g. Davis and Loftus, 2007) argue that most recovered memories are actually false memories, meaning they refer to events that did not actually happen. As you can imagine, this is an area in which it is extremely difficult to obtain convincing evidence. One reason is that there are rarely independent witnesses of traumatic events such as childhood sexual abuse.

It is probable that some recovered memories are genuine, whereas others are false. How can we decide which memories belong in each category? An important clue was provided by Lief and Feltowicz (1995) in a study on adult patients who admitted they had reported false memories. In 80 per cent of the cases, their therapists had suggested to them that they had been the victims of childhood sexual abuse. This happened because many therapists (especially psychoanalysts influenced by Freudian theory) believe strongly in the existence of recovered memories.

Geraerts *et al.* (2007) explored the genuineness of recovered memories in a study on three adult groups who had suffered childhood sexual abuse. One group consisted of those whose recovered memories had been recalled initially *inside* therapy (suggestive therapy group). A second group consisted of those whose recovered memories had been recalled initially *outside* therapy (spontaneous recovery group). The third group consisted of those who had had continuous memories of abuse from childhood onwards (continuous memory group).

Geraerts *et al.* (2007) obtained an approximate measure of the genuineness of each group's memories by finding out how many had corroborating evidence (e.g. the person responsible had confessed). Such corroborating evidence was present for 45 per cent of the continuous memory group and 37 per cent of the outside-therapy group, but for 0 per cent of the inside-therapy group. These findings suggest that recovered memories recalled inside therapy are often false memories. In contrast, most recovered memories recalled spontaneously outside therapy are probably genuine (see Geraerts, 2012, for a review).

How can we explain spontaneous recovered memories produced outside therapy? According to Freud, what happens here is the return of repressed traumatic memories. In fact, that is very unlikely to be the correct explanation. Clancy and McNally (2005/06) found that the great majority of adults reporting recovered memories described them as confusing or uncomfortable. Indeed, only 8 per cent described them as traumatic.

An alternative (and much simpler) explanation is more likely. Many spontaneously recovered memories are recalled because of the presence of relevant retrieval cues. Clancy and McNally (2005/06) obtained support for this explanation. Examples of relevant retrieval cues included returning to the location at which the abuse took place or seeing a movie about childhood sexual abuse.

In sum, there is very little support for Freud's repression account (McNally and Geraerts, 2009). Many recovered memories (especially those recalled within therapy) are false memories. Of those recalled spontaneously outside therapy, very few possess the traumatic quality emphasised by Freud. Most spontaneous recovered memories can be explained by simple mechanisms such as the presence of powerful retrieval cues.

AMYGDALA

The effects of emotion on long-term memory depend on several different regions of the brain. However, the brain area most involved is the amygdala. The amygdala is buried in the front part of the temporal lobe (Figure 12.3), and is associated with several emotions (especially fear). Note that the amygdala doesn't operate in isolation. A crucial reason for its importance is that it acts as a *hub* with numerous connections to other brain regions including 90 per cent of all cortical areas (Sander, 2009).

There is plentiful evidence that the amygdala is much involved in our processing of emotional stimuli. For example, Suslow *et al.* (2010) presented pictures of happy and sad faces so they couldn't be perceived at the conscious level. In spite of that, there was activation of the amygdala. Patients suffering from major depression had a greater amygdala response to sad faces than to happy ones, whereas healthy controls showed the opposite pattern. Thus, both groups of participants showed greater amygdala activation to faces that matched their mood state.

How can we show that the amygdala plays an important role in determining long-term memory for emotional material? One way is by assessing brain activity during the learning of such material. The prediction is that the probability of emotional items being remembered will be greater when they are associated with high levels of amygdala activation at the time of learning.

Murty *et al.* (2010) conducted a meta-analysis (a form of statistical analysis based on combining the findings from numerous studies). They

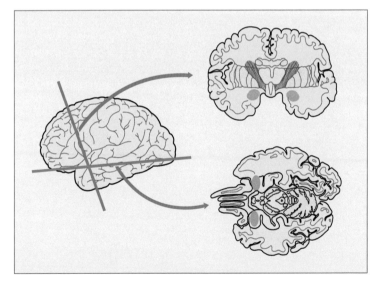

Figure 12.3   Image of the amygdala, a structure that forms part of the limbic system and that is activated in many emotional states.

Source: Ward (2010).

obtained reasonable support for the above prediction. What they actually found was that good long-term memory for emotional material was associated with greater activation during learning in a network of brain regions including the amygdala and parts of the temporal lobe involved in memory.

Other research suggests that the effects of being in an emotional state at the time of learning are especially great on subjective vividness. Kensinger *et al.* (2011) assessed amygdala activity while participants studied emotional and neutral objects. Amygdala activity at learning predicted the vividness of subsequent memory for the objects presented but did not predict the number of details recalled.

URBACH–WIETHE DISEASE

An alternative way of assessing the role played by the amygdala in emotional learning and memory involves the study of patients with Urbach–Wiethe disease. This is a disease in which the amygdala and adjacent areas are destroyed and there is a reduction in the intensity of emotional experience.

Cahill *et al.* (1995) studied BP, a patient suffering from Urbach–Wiethe disease. He was told a story, in the middle of which was a very emotional event (a boy is severely injured after being involved in a traffic accident). Healthy controls showed much better recall of this emotional event than of the preceding emotionally neutral part of the story one week after learning. In contrast, BP recalled the emotional event *less* well than the preceding part of the story.

The amygdala is involved in memory for positive information as well as negative information. Siebert *et al.* (2003) compared long-term memory for positive, negative and neutral pictures in healthy controls and in ten Urbach–Wiethe patients. The patients had poorer recognition memory than the controls for all picture categories, but their memory impairment was greatest for positive pictures and least for neutral ones.

SUMMARY AND CONCLUSIONS

In sum, similar findings have been reported in studies on patients with Urbach–Wiethe disease and on healthy individuals in brain-imaging studies. In both cases, there is much evidence that the amygdala plays an important role in enhanced memory for emotional information. This happens in part because the amygdala has connections to brain regions (e.g. hippocampus; prefrontal cortex) strongly involved in memory processes (LaBar and Cabeza, 2006).

12.4 JUDGEMENT AND DECISION-MAKING: MOOD EFFECTS

Our everyday lives are full of decisions of one sort or another. Most of these decisions are trivial (e.g. which programme will I watch on

> **Key Term**
>
> **Meta-analysis**
> A form of statistical analysis based on combining all the findings in a specific area to obtain an overall picture.
>
> **Urbach–Wiethe disease**
> A disease in which the amygdala and adjacent areas are destroyed; it leads to the impairment of emotional processing and memory for emotional material.

television?) but others are very important (e.g. do I want to become a psychologist?). The essence of decision-making is that it involves choosing among various options by expressing a preference for one option over all the others.

Judgement plays an important role in decision-making. We make judgements about the likelihood of various events occurring and then judge how we would feel if each event were to occur. Of particular importance to decision-making is whether our judgements about the future are optimistic or pessimistic. For example, your decision whether to become a psychologist might well be influenced by how optimistic or pessimistic you are that there will be plenty of well-paid and interesting jobs available for psychologists in the future.

This section focuses primarily on the effects of various mood states on judgement and decision-making. As we will see, mood states influence an individual's attitude towards risk-taking and this in turn affects his/her decision. What effect do you think negative mood states have on judgement and risk-taking? Many people predict that individuals experiencing negative affect will tend to be pessimistic in their judgements and risk-averse (i.e. making safe and cautious decisions). In contrast, it seems likely that individuals in a positive mood state will be optimistic about the future and so will tend to take risks. Experimental findings often support these predictions. Intriguingly, however, many findings fail to adhere to prediction.

Much of the research in this area has focused on the effects of any given mood state on performance or behaviour. For example, does a particular mood state enhance or impair the quality of decision-making? The emphasis here is on *outcome*. While it is necessary to assess outcome effects, it is also important to consider the effects of mood state on the cognitive strategies used. The emphasis here is on *processes*. The take-home message is that a full understanding of the effects of a given mood state on judgement and decision-making requires a consideration of the performance outcomes and of the underlying processes leading to those outcomes.

ANXIETY

We will start by considering the negative mood state of anxiety. One reason for doing so is because the findings are generally reasonably clear-cut and in line with the commonsensical predictions described above.

Anxiety is associated with concerns and worries about future threats (Eysenck, 1997). For example, Eysenck *et al.* (2006) used scenarios referring to very negative events (e.g. serious illness). The event in question could be a past event, a future possible event, or an future probable event. The participants indicated that they would have experienced more anxiety with the future events (possible or probable) than with the past events) thus indicating the future orientation of anxiety (Figure 12.4). In contrast, participants reported more depression or sadness for past negative events than for future ones.

Since anxiety involves worry about future threats, it is not surprising to find that it is associated with pessimistic judgements about the

> **Key Term**
>
> **Decision-making**
> This involves making a selection from various options, often in the absence of full information.
>
> **Judgement**
> This involves an assessment of the likelihood of an event occurring on the basis of incomplete information; it often forms the initial process in decision-making.

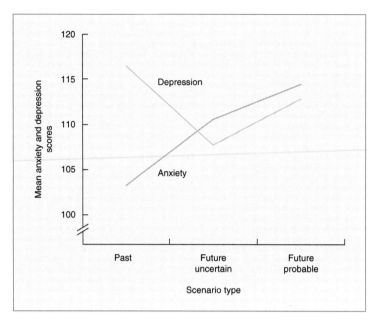

Figure 12.4   Mean anxiety and depression scores (max. = 140) as a function of scenario type (past; future uncertain; future probable) (*N* = 120). (From Eysenck *et al.*, 2006.)

Source: Eysenck and Keane (2010).

future to a greater extent than any other negative emotional state. Lerner *et al.* (2003) asked American participants very shortly after the terrorist attacks of 9/11 to focus on the aspects of those attacks that made them afraid, angry or sad. The key finding was that those participants who focused on what made them afraid estimated the probability of future terrorist attacks as greater than did those in the other two groups.

Most people have what is known as an optimistic bias. This bias involves exaggerating the likelihood of positive events happening to them in the future but minimising the likelihood of negative events happening. This optimistic bias seems to occur automatically and is still found even when people are offered rewards for making accurate predictions (Lench and Ditto, 2008).

Lench and Levine (2005) studied optimistic bias. College participants judged whether various positive and negative events were more or less likely to happen to them than to the average college students. Participants put into a fearful mood were less optimistic about future events than were those who had been put into a happy or neutral mood.

Decision-making

We turn now to the effects of anxiety on decision-making. Anxiety is generally associated with impaired decision-making. For example, Starcke *et al.* (2008) found that anxious participants had worse performance than neutral controls on a decision-making task (Game of Dice Task) that requires the use of various executive processes. This research was extended by Starcke *et al.* (2011). They found that decision-making on the Game of Dice Task was worse when participants performed an additional task requiring executive processes at the same time.

There are undoubtedly various reasons why anxiety impairs decision-making. However, one of the main reasons is because anxiety impairs the efficiency with which executive functions are used during the performance of complex cognitive tasks (Eysenck *et al.*, 2007).

We have seen that anxious individuals are generally pessimistic about the future and show impaired decision-making. In addition, anxiety is typically associated with the avoidance of risky decision-making (see Blanchette and Richards, 2010, for a review). Maner *et al.* (2007) made use of a computer-based balloon task on which participants gained rewards for blowing up a balloon provided it did not burst. Anxious individuals were more risk-averse than non-anxious ones – they blew up the balloon less.

Lorian and Grisham (2011) studied risk taking in patients suffering from various anxiety disorders. These patients (and healthy controls) completed the Domain-Specific Risk-Taking Scale. This scale consists of thirty items assessing an individual's likelihood of engaging in various risky activities (e.g. 'Betting a day's income at the horse races'; 'Engaging in unprotected sex'). Overall, patients with social phobia (extreme fear of social situations) and generalised anxiety disorder (chronic worry) had lower risk-taking scores than the control group.

One of the most interesting studies was by Raghunathan and Pham (1999). Participants had to decide whether to accept job A (high salary + low job security) or job B (average salary + high job security). Participants in an anxious mood state were much less likely than those in a neutral state to choose the high-risk option (job A): 32 per cent versus 56 per cent, respectively.

We have seen that anxiety or fear can make people cautious and risk-averse, which often impairs their decision-making. That suggests the interesting hypothesis that patients with damage to brain areas associated with emotional experience might actually perform better than healthy individuals on a gambling task.

Shiv *et al.* (2005) tested the above hypothesis in a study involving three groups. One group had brain damage to emotion areas (amygdala, orbitofrontal cortex and insular or somatosensory cortex). The other groups consisted of patients with brain damage in areas unrelated to emotion and of healthy controls. Participants were all given $20 to start with. They had to decide on each of twenty rounds whether or not to invest $1. They lost the money if a coin came up heads but gained $1.50 if it came up tails. Thus, participants gained an average of 25 cents every time they invested, and so the optimal strategy is to invest every time.

What did Shiv *et al.* (2005) find? As predicted, patients with brain damage in emotion regions outperformed the other two groups. The detailed findings are shown in Figure 12.5. As you can see, all groups were willing to invest when they had won on the previous round. However, the groups differed substantially in their investment behaviour if they had lost on the previous round. Patients with damage to emotion areas were far more likely than those in the other two groups to invest in those circumstances. The anxiety created by loss deters individuals from taking risks except in the case of brain-damaged patients who experience very little anxiety.

In a similar study, De Martino *et al.* (2010) studied loss aversion in two women. Both of these women had suffered severe damage to the amygdala, which is of crucial importance in fear and other emotional states. The key finding was that neither of the women showed any

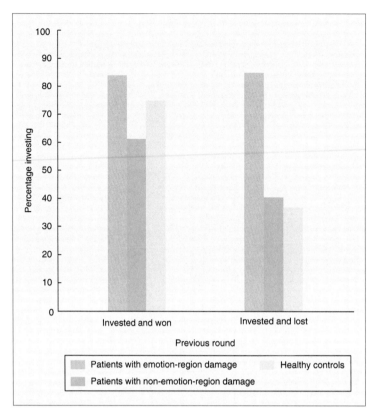

Figure 12.5 Percentage of rounds in which patients with damage to emotion regions of the brain, patients with damage to other regions of the brain, and healthy controls decided to invest $1 having won or lost on the previous round. (Data from Shiv *et al.*, 2005.)

Source: Eysenck (2012).

evidence of loss aversion. As De Martino *et al.* concluded, it seems as if the amygdala acts as a 'cautionary brake'.

It has been established clearly that anxiety is associated with risk aversion. What is somewhat less clear is precisely *why* this is the case. However, we can identify two major factors. First, anxious individuals are reluctant to make risky decisions because they are more pessimistic than non-anxious individuals about the likely outcome.

Second, anxiety is an aversive mood state and so anxious individuals seek ways of reducing their level of anxiety. How can this be achieved? It is known that high levels of situational uncertainty increase anxiety (Frijda, 1986). Sarinopoulos *et al.* (2010) studied brain activity indicative of stress and anxiety in response to aversive pictures. There was greater brain activity when participants were uncertain whether an aversive or neutral picture would be presented next. Reducing uncertainty by making low-risk decisions (e.g. choosing a job with high security) is an effective way of reducing anxiety.

SADNESS

Sadness resembles anxiety in that both are negative mood states. However, there is an important difference. Sadness (which turns into depression when sufficiently intense) is associated with an absence of positive affect to a greater extent than anxiety (Clark and Watson, 1991). As a consequence, sad individuals experience the environment as being relatively unrewarding, and this may motivate them to obtain rewards even if risks are involved.

Decision-making

Studies on the effects of sadness on judgement were reviewed by Waters (2008). Sad individuals regarded the likelihood of health hazards and adverse life events as greater than did happy or positive individuals.

The notion that sad individuals may be motivated to reduce their sadness by obtaining rewards suggests they may be less averse to risk than anxious individuals. That is, indeed, what is indicated by the limited evidence available. Earlier I discussed a study by Raghunathan and Pham (1999) in which participants had to choose between a high-risk and a low-risk job. Anxiety led participants to favour the low-risk job. In contrast, sadness caused participants to select the high-risk job – 78 per cent of sad participants did so compared with only 56 per cent of those in a neutral mood. This finding can be explained on the basis that sad participants were motivated to obtain the reward of high pay associated with the high-risk option.

Some research has focused on the decision-making processes used by individuals in a sad mood. We can distinguish between two major types of processing. First, there is systematic or analytic processing which is relatively slow and consciously controlled. Second, there is heuristic processing which is relatively effortless and involves using heuristics (rules of thumb). The evidence suggests that sad individuals tend to use analytic processing (Andrews and Thomson, 2009). In a literature review, Schwarz (2000) concluded that being in a sad mood causes people to use a processing strategy in which much attention is paid to details. This is in essence analytic processing.

De Vries *et al.* (2008) hypothesised that people are most satisfied with their decision-making when they have made use of their preferred processing strategy. They tested this idea by requiring participants to use heuristic/intuitive or analytic/deliberative processing when making a decision. As predicted, participants put into a sad mood by watching a clip from *Schindler's List* were more satisfied with their decision following analytic/deliberative processing than when following heuristic/intuitive processing. This study is discussed further later in the chapter.

ANGER

It is important not to exaggerate the similarities among negative emotional states. That is especially the case with anger, which differs in several ways from other negative states such as anxiety and sadness. Even though anger is regarded as a negative emotional state, it can be a moderately positive emotion if the individual believes he/she can control the situation and dominate disliked others (Lerner and Tiedens, 2006). However, there are probably important cross-cultural differences here. For example, consider the Machiguenga Indians in the Peruvian Amazon. They are a very peaceful people who regard fear as preferable to anger and who avoid anger at all costs (Johnson *et al.*, 1986).

One example of how anger can lead to a positive emotional state is *schadenfreude*. This involves experiencing pleasure at the misfortune of disliked others. Hareli and Weiner (2002) found that schadenfreude is greater in those who are angry. Leach and Spears (2008) studied a fictitious competition between the participants' own university and a more successful other university. The failure of the successful university created schadenfreude. Much of this schadenfreude occurred because of the participants' anger based on the pain of their university's inferiority.

Of course, anger is very often associated with negative affect as well as positive (Litvak *et al.*, 2010). The events that cause anger are typically remembered as unpleasant. In addition, the consequences of anger (e.g. aggression; violence) can cause very negative emotional states.

What are the effects of anger on judgement? Of interest, the effects are very different from those of anxiety or sadness. Waters (2008), in a review discussed earlier, found that anger was generally associated with fairly optimistic judgements about the likelihood of negative events. In other words, the perceived likelihood of negative events was low. In contrast, both anxiety and sadness were associated with pessimistic judgements. The optimism of angry individuals is surprising in view of the fact that individuals who are characteristically angry are more likely than other people to have cardiovascular problems and to be divorced (Lerner and Keltner, 2001).

Why does anger differ from other negative emotional states in being associated with optimistic judgements? What is important is that anger (unlike anxiety or sadness) is associated with perceived control over others (Litvak *et al.*, 2010). Angry individuals feel in control and thus able to determine their own destiny, which makes them optimistic about the future. In contrast, anxious and sad individuals have much less perceived control and feel themselves at the mercy of fate and of other people. As a result, they are pessimistic about the future.

Decision-making

It is popularly assumed that anger greatly reduces our ability to think rationally and to make sensible decisions. In the words of the American philosopher Ralph Waldo Emerson, anger 'blows out the light of reason'. As we will see, there is reasonable support for this point of view (see Litvak *et al.*, 2010, for a review).

One example of anger impairing decision-making comes in a study by Bright and Goodman-Delahunty (2006). The participants were mock jurors who had to decide on the guilt or innocence of a man who was alleged to have murdered his wife. Some of the jurors were made angry by seeing gruesome photographs taken of the murdered woman. The angry jurors were more than four times as likely as the non-angry ones to return a guilty verdict. Thus, their decision-making was greatly influenced by their anger.

Another example was reported by Coleman (2010). He studied the *sunk-cost effect*, which is an increased tendency to invest resources in an uncertain project following previous failure with that project. Most people show this effect even though it would be preferable on average to accept the loss and invest elsewhere. In other words, the sunk-cost effect involves 'throwing good money after bad.'

Coleman (2010) used a hypothetical problem in which students decided whether to do a course for which they had paid in advance or (at no extra financial cost) switch to a course offering a better chance of success. His key finding was that the sunk-cost effect was greater in angry participants than in those in a sad or neutral mood. Thus, anger increased the tendency for students to make a suboptimal decision.

Why does anger often impair the quality of decision-making? We can address that issue with reference to the distinction discussed earlier between systematic or analytic processing and heuristic processing which is based on heuristics (rules of thumb). According to Litvak *et al.* (2010), anger leads to increased use of heuristic processing and reduced used of analytic processing.

Convincing evidence that anger increases the use of heuristic processing was reported by Small and Lerner (2008). Their participants were given a decision-making task. They had to decide how much welfare assistance should be received by a fictitious Patricia Smith, who was a 25-year-old divorced woman with three children. Angry participants awarded her less assistance than did participants put into a neutral or sad mood state. There was a further condition in which angry participants had to perform an additional cognitively demanding task at the same time as the decision-making task. This condition was designed to force participants to rely mostly on heuristic processing on the decision-making task. The key finding was that the addition of a second cognitively demanding task did not affect the amount of welfare assistance awarded by angry participants. The implication is that angry participants primarily used heuristic processing even in the absence of a secondary task.

There is other evidence that anger causes judgements to be made on the basis of heuristic processing. Ask and Granhag (2007) induced anger in experienced police investigators by asking them to recall (and write about) an event they had encountered in their police work that had caused anger or sadness. After that, the police investigators read the summary of a criminal case together with statements by two witnesses. Finally, they judged the witnesses on several measures (e.g. reliability; trustworthiness) and judged the probability of guilt.

What did Ask and Granhag (2007) find? The key finding was that angry participants engaged in more heuristic or superficial processing of the information about the case than did sad ones. For example, the judgements made by angry participants were less influenced than those of sad participants by the content of the witness statements.

POSITIVE MOOD

There has been much interest in optimistic bias – the judgement that we are more likely than other people to experience positive events (e.g. a pleasant holiday) but less likely to experience negative events (e.g. divorce; serious illness). The obvious prediction is that individuals in a positive or good mood would exhibit a stronger optimistic bias than those in a neutral or negative mood.

The evidence in favour of the above prediction is much weaker than might have been imagined. Drace *et al.* (2009) carried out several experiments on optimistic bias with mood state being manipulated by means of pictures and music. There was much general evidence for optimistic bias. More importantly, however, its extent was very similar across positive, negative and neutral mood states.

The negative findings of Drace *et al.* (2009) contrast with previous research. In that research, it was often found that individuals in a positive mood state perceived themselves as less likely to experience negative events than did sad individuals (Waters, 2008). How can we explain the difference? In many of the studies, the participants' mood states were measured shortly before assessing comparative optimism. Thus, some participants may have guessed that the experimenter was interested in the relationship between mood and comparative judgements and altered their judgements accordingly. In contrast, Drace *et al.* designed their experiments so as to minimise the chance of such distortions occurring.

Decision-making

What are the effects of positive mood states on decision-making? The first point to make is that such mood states are typically associated with a risk-averse approach to decision-making (Blanchette and Richards, 2010). For example, Mustanski (2007) carried out a diary study on men who have sex with other men. The prevalence of HIV risk behaviours was significantly less among men who experienced high levels of positive affect. Cahir and Thomas (2010) studied decision-making involving betting on imaginary horse races. Participants in a positive mood made less risky decisions than those who were in a neutral mood.

Why does being in a positive mood cause people to become risk-averse? The most likely reason is that someone who is happy is motivated to maintain that positive state and so is disinclined to take chances. However, it could be argued that this interpretation is rather post hoc. Suppose it had been found that individuals in a positive mood are less risk-averse. It could plausibly be argued that individuals in a positive mood believe themselves largely immune from danger and so are inclined to take risks (anonymous reviewer).

Much research on mood and decision-making has made use of the distinction between analytic or deliberate processing and heuristic or effortless processing. It has generally been found that being in a positive mood causes people to make more use of heuristic processing and less of analytic processing (see Griskevicius *et al.*, 2010, for a review).

De Vries *et al.* (2008) argued that people who use their preferred processing strategy are more content with the decisions they make that those who use a non-preferred strategy. We saw earlier that that was the case for participants put into a sad mood – they were more satisfied with their decision when required to use analytic/deliberative processing than when required to use heuristic/intuitive processing. In the same study, other participants were put into a happy mood by watching a video clip from *The Muppet Show*, whereas others were put into a sad mood by watching a video clip from the film *Schindler's List*.

The findings obtained by de Vries *et al.* (2008) supported their hypothesis (Figure 12.6). Happy participants were more satisfied with their decision following heuristic/intuitive processing than when following analytic/deliberative processing. The findings for sad participants were precisely the opposite. Thus, people are most content with their decisions when there is a fit between their mood and the decision strategy they have used.

You may have been wondering (or maybe not!) about a strange difference between research on negative and positive mood states. Researchers in the former area have distinguished among *three* different negative mood states (e.g. anxiety; sadness; anger). In contrast, most researchers in the latter area have considered only a *single* positive mood state. This makes sense only if all types of positive affect have comparable effects on cognitive processing.

Griskevicius *et al.* (2010) compared the effects of several kinds of positive affect including attachment love, awe, contentment, anticipatory enthusiasm, amusement and nurturant love. The participants had to assess the persuasiveness of strong or weak arguments relating to the possible introduction of a new examination.

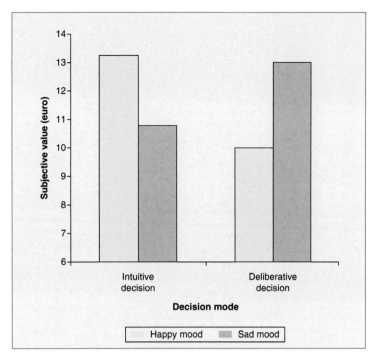

Figure 12.6 Subjective value associated with decision as a function of mood (happy *vs.* sad) and decision strategy (intuitive *vs.* deliberative).

Source: de Vries *et al.* (2008).

The extent to which participants made use of heuristic processing (assessed by persuasiveness of weak arguments) varied across the different positive emotional states (Figure 12.7). Participants who experienced anticipatory enthusiasm, attachment love or

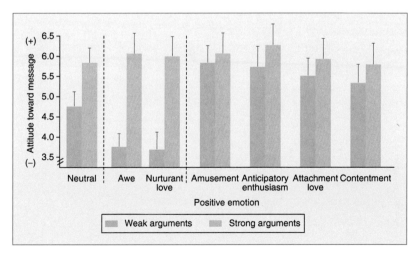

Figure 12.7 Effects of six positive emotions on persuasiveness of arguments (weak *vs.* strong).

Source: Griskevicius *et al.* (2010).

amusement all exhibited heuristic or shallow processing because they were persuaded even by weak arguments. However, awe and nurturant love were both associated with *reduced* heuristic processing compared with a neutral mood state. Thus, positive emotional states vary in their effects on cognitive processing. However, more research is needed to clarify *why* each positive state has the specific effects it does.

SUMMARY AND CONCLUSIONS

The most important finding to emerge from research on the effects of mood state on judgement and decision-making is that each mood state is associated with its own pattern of effects (Figure 12.8). How can we make overall sense of the idiosyncratic pattern of effects associated with each mood state? There is as yet no satisfactory answer to that question. However, the starting point is to recognise that each mood state or emotion fulfils certain functions (Oatley and Johnson-Laird, 1987). It is probable that most moods or emotions fulfil more than one function, but we will focus mostly on the most important one in each case.

What is the main function of anxiety? As discussed earlier, anxiety occurs in threatening situations in which there is uncertainty and unpredictability. It follows that an important function of anxiety is to reduce the aversive anxious state by increasing certainty and predictability. This can often be accomplished by minimising risk-taking and choosing safe options.

Individuals become sad or depressed when they realise that some desired goal cannot be achieved. Sadness or depression leads the individual to abandon the goal that cannot be achieved and to engage in extensive thinking about which goal should replace it. Thus, the function of sadness or depression is to persuade individuals to rethink their goals and priorities.

A theoretical approach along these lines was put forward by Andrews and Thomson (2009) in their analytic rumination hypothesis. They argued that depressed individuals have reduced motivation to engage in distracting activities and so focus on their symptoms and on what to do next (rumination). Such rumination involves analytic processing. This hypothesis helps to explain why sadness is the only mood state associated with analytic rather than heuristic processing.

What is the main function of anger? Anger has the function of overcoming some obstacle to an important goal by direct (and often aggressive) action. This approach is most likely to be taken when the

Figure 12.8 Effects of mood states on judgment and decision-making.

	Anxiety	Sadness	Anger	Positive mood
Judgement	Pessimistic	Pessimistic	Optimistic	Optimistic?
Attitude to risk	Risk averse	Risk taking	Risk taking	Risk averse
Processing	Inefficient	Analytic	Heuristic	Heuristic

individual feels he/she has personal control and is thus optimistic that the goal can be achieved. This sense of personal control also persuades angry individuals to take risks to achieve what they want.

What is the main function of positive moods or emotions? According to Oatley and Johnson-Laird (1987), the main function is to preserve or maintain the current mood. This leads happy individuals to engage in shallow or heuristic processing and to avoid taking risks that might endanger the positive mood state.

LIMITATIONS

What are the main limitations of research on mood states and decision-making? Some of the main ones revolve around the issue of ecological validity or the extent to which the research findings generalise to real life.

First, there is an important distinction between integral emotions and incidental emotions. Integral emotions are those of direct relevance to the situation and to the current task (e.g. decision-making). In contrast, incidental emotions are carried over from a previous situation and so are essentially irrelevant to the current task.

Most of the research we have discussed has involved incidental emotions. For example, participants write about a personal event that made them very sad, anxious, angry or happy. After that, they perform a task that has nothing at all to do with that event. It is undoubtedly the case that some of our decision-making in real life is influenced by incidental emotions. However, it seems likely that we are more often influenced by integral emotions, but research so far has shed relatively light on what happens in such circumstances.

Second, we have seen in studies of decision-making in laboratory conditions that various mood states are associated with shallow or heuristic processing. This may reflect in part the artificial nature of the research, since the decisions made by participants have no implications outside the laboratory situation. For example, individuals in real life deciding which job to take or which decision to make as jurors in a court case are unlikely to make rapid decisions based on heuristic processing.

Third, there has been much emphasis in the literature on the distinction between heuristic or shallow processing and analytic or deliberate processing. This distinction is oversimplified (Keren and Schul, 2009). In practice, many cognitive processes cannot be categorised neatly as heuristic or analytic – they involve a combination of both types.

12.5 JUDGEMENT AND DECISION-MAKING: COGNITIVE NEUROSCIENCE

We have just considered the ways in which various mood states influence judgement and decision-making. Cognitive neuroscience provides an alternative way of understanding the role played by emotional factors in judgement and decision-making.

Much of the research within the cognitive neuroscience approach has focused on very difficult moral problems of a particular type. Consider two related problems. In the trolley problem, you have to decide whether to divert a runaway trolley that threatens the lives of five people onto a side-track where it will kill only one person.

In the footbridge problem, there is also a runaway trolley. This time, however, you have to decide whether to push a fat person over a bridge. This will cause the death of the person pushed but will stop the runaway trolley and prevent five deaths. About 90 per cent decide it is worth diverting the trolley in the trolley problem but only 10 per cent decide to push the person to push the person off the footbridge (Hauser, 2006).

What is going on here? According to Greene (2007), the difference is that the footbridge problem triggers a strong emotional response. This causes us to disapprove of pushing the person to their death even though that would save five lives. More specifically, we respond strongly at an emotional level to the notion of causing *direct* harm to another person (which is not present in the trolley problem). Problems such as the footbridge problem are known as personal moral dilemmas.

Greene *et al.* (2004) studied various personal moral dilemmas including the crying baby dilemma:

> *Enemy soldiers have taken over your village. They have orders to kill all remaining civilians. You and some of your townspeople have sought refuge in the cellar of a large house. Outside, you hear the voices of soldiers who have come to search the house for valuables. Your baby begins to cry loudly. You cover his mouth to block the sound. If you remove your hand from his mouth, his crying will summon the attention of the soldiers who will kill you, your child, and the others hiding out in the cellar. To save yourself and the others, you must smother your child to death. Is it appropriate for you to smother your child in order to save yourself and the other townspeople?*
>
> (Greene *et al.*, 2004: 390)

According to Greene *et al.* (2004), dilemmas such the crying baby dilemma are agonisingly difficult because of the conflicts they create. On the one hand, there is a very powerful emotional imperative not to smother one's own baby (emotional argument). On the other hand, there is the powerful argument that more lives will be saved if you smother your child to death (cognitive argument). The problem is very hard because the emotional and cognitive factors are in direct conflict with each other. This explanation of decision-making with personal moral dilemmas is known as the dual-process theory.

Some people attach more weight to the cognitive argument than to the emotional one. They generally make utilitarian judgements based on saving as many people as possible (e.g. smother your own child). Other people attach more weight to the emotional argument and make non-utilitarian judgements (e.g. do not smother your child).

Suppose people were required to make moral judgements while at the same time performing a task that placed demands on cognitive processing. It would be predicted that this would increase the extent to which emotional considerations influenced moral decision-making and so lead to a reduction in utilitarian moral judgements. Greene (2007) discussed an unpublished study in which precisely this finding was obtained.

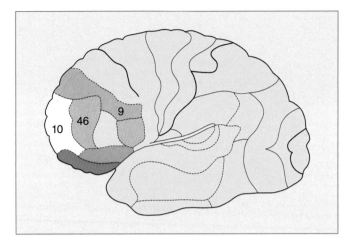

Figure 12.9   The dorsolateral prefrontal cortex is located approximately in Brodmann areas 9 and 46; the ventromedial prefrontal cortex is located approximately in Brodmann area 10.

Source: Ward (2010).

COGNITIVE NEUROSCIENCE RESEARCH

How can cognitive neuroscience clarify what is happening in such decision-making? Two relevant brain regions are the dorsolateral prefrontal cortex (DLPFC) and the ventromedial prefrontal cortex (VMPFC, Figure 12.9). In approximate terms, the DLPFC is involved in cognitive control. In contrast, the VMPFC is (among other activities) important in the processing and generation of emotions.

Suppose we consider activity within the DLPFC for those who make utilitarian (or 'cognitive') judgements and those who make non-utilitarian (or 'emotional') judgements on complex personal moral dilemmas (e.g. crying baby dilemma). We would expect the former individuals to exercise more cognitive control, and so they should show more activity in the DLPFC. Precisely that finding was reported by Greene *et al.* (2004) (Figure 12.10).

Suppose we consider patients who have suffered damage to the VMPFC. Such patients have reduced emotional responsiveness and so should attach less weight than healthy controls to emotional arguments. Accordingly, we would expect such patients to be more likely than healthy controls to make utilitarian or cognitive judgements with personal

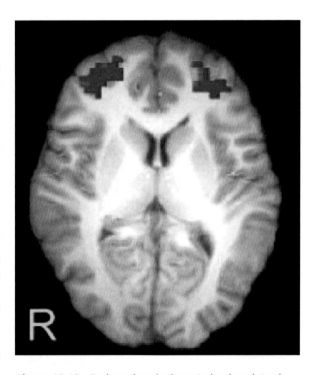

Figure 12.10   Brain regions in the anterior dorsolateral prefrontal cortex that were activated more when utilitarian decisions were made than when non-utilitarian decisions were made.

Source: Greene *et al.* (2004).

moral dilemmas. Koenigs *et al.* (2007) found that VMPFC-damaged patients made more than twice as many utilitarian judgements than healthy controls (45 per cent versus 20 per cent). This did *not* happen because brain damage impaired the patients' ability to think effectively – there were no differences between them and the healthy controls on other judgement tasks.

The limitation in the study by Koenigs *et al.* (2007) is that they did not provide any *direct* evidence that reduced emotional responsiveness in VMPFC patients was responsible for their tendency to make utilitarian judgements. This issue was addressed by Moretto *et al.* (2010). Healthy controls produced a strong emotional response (measured by skin conductance responses) before endorsing violations of personal morality. VMPFC patients approved more moral violations than controls. Of importance, they did not produce an emotional response before endorsing violations of personal morality. These findings support the view that the VMPFC is involved in assessing the emotional consequences of personal moral violations.

The relevance of the VMPFC to emotional processing can be seen in individuals with antisocial personality disorder (popularly known as psychopaths). These individuals have an almost complete absence of empathy (emotional understanding of other people) in spite of having intact cognitive processing. Harenski *et al.* (2010) studied brain activity in criminal psychopaths and other imprisoned individuals in response to pictures showing moral violations. The non-psychopathic prisoners had greater activity in the VMPFC when viewing these pictures than other pictures. In contrast, there was comparable VMPFC in the psychopaths for all types of pictures, indicating that the pictures showing moral violations had no special emotional significance for them.

LIMITATIONS

There is convincing evidence that personal moral dilemmas can cause substantial conflict between cognitive and emotional processes. This is as predicted by dual-process theory, as are the roles of DLPFC and VMPFC in influencing cognitive and emotional processing, respectively.

In spite of the successes of dual-process theory, it is oversimplified in various ways, two of which we will consider here. First, the brain areas involved in decision-making with moral dilemmas are more widespread than is implied by the focus of the theory. Cognitive processing is associated with several brain areas in addition to the DLPFC and emotional processing involves areas additional to the VMPFC.

Second, the account of cognitive processing with personal moral dilemmas is limited. It is assumed that the involvement of cognitive processing increases the tendency to prefer utilitarian judgemenss or decisions. In fact, matters are more complex than that as is discussed below.

Broeders *et al.* (2011) argued that the moral rule that is most accessible to the cognitive system influences moral decisions. Participants were presented with the footbridge problem preceded by information designed to lead them to focus on the moral rule, 'Saving lives' or the rule, 'Do not kill.' Participants for whom the rule 'Saving lives' was more accessible were significantly more in favour of pushing the person off the footbridge than those receiving the rule 'Do not kill.' Thus, focusing cognitive processes on certain moral rules can increase or decrease the tendency to make utilitarian judgements with personal moral dilemmas.

12.6 REASONING

There has been a considerable amount of research on reasoning (see Chapter 8). Much of this research has focused on deductive reasoning, which allows us to draw conclusions that are certain provided that other statements are assumed to be true. One of the most popular deductive-reasoning tasks is syllogistic reasoning. Two premises or statements are presented (e.g. 'All cats are obedient'; 'Lulu is a cat') followed by a conclusion (e.g. 'Therefore, Lulu is obedient'). In this example, the conclusion *must* be valid if we accept the truth of the premises.

It has generally been found that negative emotional states impair deductive reasoning (see Blanchette *et al.*, 2007, for a review). Oaksford *et al.* (1996) used brief film clips to put participants into a negative or a positive mood state. Reasoning performance was impaired to a similar extent by both mood states.

In spite of the general finding that emotional mood states have an adverse effect on reasoning performance, this is not invariably the case. Johnson-Laird *et al.* (2006) asked individuals with many or few depressive symptoms to list as many logical possibilities as they could when presented with various scenarios. The key finding was that high depressives produced many more valid possibilities than low depressives when the scenarios produced depressive feelings. Depressed individuals devote much more time than non-depressed ones in thinking about the causes of their depression, as a result of which they become expert at reasoning about depression.

WORKING MEMORY

Why is reasoning performance impaired by various negative and positive emotional states? Before answering that question, we need to consider the cognitive processes involved in performing reasoning tasks. Of particular important is the *central executive,* which is a limited-capacity, attention-like component of the working memory system (Baddeley, 2007; see also Chapter 5). There is much evidence (e.g. De Neys, 2006) that solving most reasoning problems requires extensive use of the central executive. Thus, one hypothesis as to why emotional states impair reasoning is because they deplete the resources of the central executive.

There is reasonable support for the above hypothesis. Eysenck and colleagues (e.g. Eysenck and Calvo, 1992; Eysenck *et al.*, 2007) have

> **Key Term**
>
> **Deductive reasoning**
> An approach to reasoning in which conclusions can be judged valid or invalid given that certain statements or premises are assumed to be true.

argued that anxiety causes individuals to allocate some of their attention to task-irrelevant thoughts (e.g. 'I am doing this task poorly'). Such thoughts pre-empt some of the resources of the central executive and this reduces performance on many cognitive tasks.

In a study by Derakshan and Eysenck (1998), individuals with high and with low levels of anxiety performed a reasoning task at the same time as a second memory task that required (or did not require) use of central executive resources. The adverse effect of the second task involving the central executive was much greater among the highly anxious participants. This happened because the highly anxious individuals had fewer central executive resources available to perform the reasoning task.

It is possible to explain the effects of sadness or depression on reasoning performance in a similar way. There is much evidence that depressed or sad individuals engage in much rumination (focusing on distress symptoms), which leads to impaired performance on several cognitive tasks (Gotlib and Joormann, 2010). In a study by Channon and Baker (1994), depressed individuals had poorer performance than non-depressed ones on syllogistic reasoning problems. Of most interest, the depressed participants found it hard to integrate information from the two premises, which is demanding of central executive resources.

What about the effects of positive mood state on working memory? Martin and Kerns (2011) found evidence that positive mood state impaired the functioning of the central executive. In a study discussed above, Oaksford *et al.* (1996) found that positive mood impaired reasoning performance. In another experiment, they obtained a comparable impairment when participants had to perform a second task demanding of central executive resources at the same time as the reasoning task. These findings suggest that positive mood depletes central executive resources.

SUMMARY

- Anxiety leads to attentional narrowing, whereas a sad mood leads to attentional broadening. These effects of mood on attention partly explain why memory for peripheral information is greater in a sad mood than an anxious one.
- Mood-congruent memory is greater in positive moods than in negative ones because individuals in a negative mood are motivated to improve their mood state.
- There is more evidence of mood-state-dependent memory when people have to generate their own retrieval cues.
- Memories of childhood abuse initially recalled outside therapy are more likely to be genuine than those initially recalled inside therapy. Freud's notion of repression is an unconvincing explanation of recovered memories.

- Each of the three negative mood states (anxiety; sadness; anger) has an idiosyncratic pattern of effects on judgement and decision-making. These differences reflect the different functions fulfilled by each mood state.
- Angry and positive moods are associated with heuristic or shallow processing, whereas sad mood is associated with analytic processing.
- Angry, sad, anxious and positive moods all lead to impaired reasoning performance. The main reason is that all these mood states deplete the resources of the central executive.
- Personal moral dilemmas produce a serious conflict between emotional and cognitive considerations. The ventromedial prefrontal cortex is involved in emotional responsiveness and the dorsolateral prefrontal cortex is involved in cognitive processing of dilemmas.

FURTHER READING

- Blanchette, I. and Richards, A. (2010). The influence of affect on higher level cognition: A review of research on interpretation, judgment, decision making and reasoning. *Cognition and Emotion*, 24, 561–595. Isabelle Blanchette and Anne Richards provide a reasonably comprehensive account of the effects of several emotional states on human cognition.
- Eysenck, M. W. and Keane, M. T. (2010). *Cognitive Psychology: A Student's Handbook* (6th edn). Hove: Psychology Press. Chapter 15 in this textbook covers the effects of cognitive processes on emotion as well as the effects of emotion on cognition.
- Fox, E. (2008). *Emotion Science: Cognitive and Neuroscientific Approaches to Understanding Human Emotions*. New York: Palgrave Macmillan. Elaine Fox discusses effects of emotion on cognition in a comprehensive way, especially in Chapters 6–8.
- Litvak, P. M., Lerner, J. S., Tiedens, L. Z. and Shonk, K. (2010). Fuel in the fire: How anger impacts judgment and decision-making. In M. Potegal, G. Stemmler and C. Spielberger, (eds) *International Handbook of Anger: Constituent and Concomitant Biological, Psychological, and Social Processes* (pp. 287–310). New York: Springer. This chapter provides a comprehensive overview of the unexpected effects of anger on cognition.

Glossary

Active perception Perception as a function of interaction with the world.

Affordances Represent the interaction of the individual with the environment. Objects afford the use to which the individual can put them.

Agnosia The failure to recognise or interpret stimuli despite adequate sensory function. It is usually classified by sensory modality, so visual agnosia is the failure to recognise objects that are seen.

Alexia/dyslexia Both refer to problems in reading written language. Alexia always refers to acquired difficulties in reading, while dyslexia is used to refer to developmental difficulties in reading. However some specific acquired reading problems – e.g. deep versus surface dyslexia – are used to refer to particular profiles of acquired reading problems.

Alzheimer's disease (AD) A degenerative brain disorder usually (but not always) afflicting the elderly, which first appears as an impairment of memory but later develops into a more general dementia.

Amnesia A pathological impairment of memory function.

Anterograde amnesia (AA) Impaired memory for events which have occurred since the onset of the disorder (contrasts with **retrograde amnesia**).

Aphasia An acquired language disorder, which primarily affects the comprehension of spoken language (a receptive aphasia), or the production of spoken language (expressive aphasia). In global aphasia, both speech production and perception are compromised.

Articulatory suppression A task used to occupy the articulatory control process of the working memory, normally involving the repetition of a sound (such as 'the') which requires articulation but little processing.

Attention conspicuity The interaction of aspects of a stimulus (such as colour, luminance, form) with aspects of an individual (such as attention, knowledge, preconceptions) that determine how likely a stimulus is to be consciously perceived. (See also **sensory conspicuity**.)

Automatic processing Processing that does not demand attention. It is not capacity limited or resource limited, and is not available for conscious inspection (contrasts with **controlled processing**).

Availability heuristic Making judgements on the basis of how available relevant examples are in our memory store.

Base rate fallacy Ignoring information about the base rate in light of other information.

Behaviourism An approach to psychology which constrains psychologists to the investigation of externally observable behaviour, and rejects any consideration of inner mental processes.

Binaural cues Cues that rely on comparing the input to both ears, as for example in judging sound direction.

Binding problem The problem of how different properties of an item are correctly put together, or bound, into the correct combination.

Blindsight The ability of some functionally blind patients to detect visual stimuli at an unconscious level, despite having no conscious awareness of seeing them. Usually observed in patients with occipital lobe lesions.

Boston Aphasia Classification System A systematic classification of aphasic profiles which can be used to identify aphasia and to predict what profiles of damage a patients might be expected to show when assessing their damage. The Boston Classification System builds on the models of aphasia which were developed by Broca, Wernicke and Lichtheim. Implicit in this approach is the concept that language can be localised in the human brain, and that different profiles of language deficits are related to distinctly different patterns of brain damage.

Bottleneck The point in processing where parallel processing becomes serial.

Bottom-up (or stimulus-driven) processing Processing which is directed by information contained within the stimulus (contrasts with **top-down processing**).

Breakthrough The ability of information to capture conscious awareness despite being unattended. Usually used with respect to the unattended channel in dichotic listening experiments.

Broca's area A region of the brain normally located in the left frontal region, which controls motor speech production.

Capture The ability of one source of information to take processing priority from another. For example the sudden onset of novel information within a modality such as an apple falling may interrupt ongoing attentional processing.

Cell assembly A group of cells which have become linked to one another to form a single functional network. Proposed by Hebb as a possible biological mechanism underlying the representation and storage of a memory trace.

Central executive A hypothetical mechanism which is believed to be in overall control of the working memory. It is assumed to control a variety of tasks, such as decision-making, problem-solving and selective attention.

Cognitive interview An approach to interviewing eyewitnesses which makes use of the findings of cognitive psychology, such as context reinstatement.

Cognitive neuropsychology The study of the brain activities underlying cognitive processes, often by investigating cognitive impairment in brain-damaged patients.

Cognitive neuroscience The investigation of human cognition by relating it to brain structure and function, normally obtained from brain-imaging techniques.

Cognitive psychology The study of the way in which the brain processes information. It includes the mental processes involved in perception, learning and memory storage, thinking and language.

Comprehension Refers to the outcome of a range of linguistic processes, from acoustic to semantic and syntactic, which contribute to the way that a linguistic message is understood.

Computer modelling The simulation of human cognitive processes by computer. Often used as a method of testing the feasibility of an information-processing mechanism.

Confabulation The reporting of memories which are incorrect and apparently fabricated, but which the patient believes to be true.

Congenital prosopagnosia This is thought to be present from birth and is thought to occur without any apparent brain injury.

Conjunction A term from feature integration theory of attention that describes a target defined by at least two separable features, such as a red O amongst green O's and red T's.

Consistent mapping A task in which distractors are never targets and targets are never distracters, so that there is a consistent relationship between the stimuli and the responses to be made to them.

Constancy The ability to perceive constant objects in the world despite continual changes in viewing conditions.

Constructivist approach Building up our perception of the world from incomplete sensory input. (See also **perceptual hypotheses**.)

Contention scheduler A component of Norman and Shallice's (1986) model which is responsible for the semi-automatic control of schema activation to ensure that schema run off in an orderly way.

Controlled attention Attention processing that is under conscious, intentional control. It requires attentional resources, or capacity, and is subject to interference.

Controlled processing Processing that is under conscious control, and which is a relatively slow, voluntary process (contrasts with **automatic processing**).

Covert attentional orienting Orienting attention without making any movement of the eyes.

Decision-making This involves making a selection from various options, often in the absence of full information.

Declarative memory Memory which can be reported in a deliberate and conscious way (contrasts with **procedural memory**).

Deductive reasoning An approach to reasoning in which conclusions can be judged valid or invalid given that certain statements or premises are assumed to be true.

Deductive reasoning task A problem that has a well-defined structure in a system of formal logic where the conclusion is certain.

Dementia A persistent impairment in intellectual function due to brain dysfunction, which commonly is associated with a progressive loss of function. It is mainly a disease of ageing, being more common in more elderly populations. Dementias can be relatively focal in their effects (e.g. semantic dementia) or more widespread and 'global' in their effects (e.g. Alzheimer's disease). Some dementias primarily affect subcortical regions (e.g. Parkinson's disease) and other have a more cortical effect (e.g. Pick's disease).

Developmental prosopagnosia This is thought to be a result of early neurological trauma that might be caused by accident or injury

Diencephalon A brain structure which includes the thalamus and hypothalamus. Parts of the diencephalon are involved in processing and retrieving memories, and damage to these structures can cause amnesia.

Digit span A measure of the largest number of digits which an individual can recall when tested immediately after their presentation. Widely used as a test of the capacity of the phonological component of the working memory.

Direct perception Perception without the need for top-down processing.

Disinhibition Impaired response inhibition, an inability to suppress previous incorrect responses observed in patients with frontal lobe epilepsy.

Dorsal stream A pathway which carries visual information about the spatial location of an object.

Double dissociation A method of distinguishing between two functions whereby each can be separately affected or impaired by some external factor without the other function being affected, thus providing particularly convincing evidence for the independence of the two functions.

Dysexecutive syndrome A collection of deficits observed in frontal lobe patients which may include impaired concentration, impaired concept formation, disinhibition, inflexibility, perseveration, impaired cognitive estimation and impaired strategy formation.

Dyslexia Developmental difficulties in reading. (See also **alexia**.)

Early selection Selective attention that operates on the physical information available from early perceptual analysis.

Easterbrook's hypothesis The notion that high levels of arousal or anxiety cause a narrowing of attention.

Ecological validity The extent to which findings in psychology (especially those obtained in the laboratory) generalise to the real world.

Electroconvulsive therapy (ECT) A treatment used to alleviate depression which involves passing an electric current through the front of the patient's head.

Electroencephalography (EEG) Recording the brain's electrical activity via electrodes placed against the scalp. Can be used to continuously record rhythmic patterns in brain function or particular responses to events (**event-related potentials**).

Encoding The process of transforming a sensory stimulus into a memory trace.

Encoding specificity principle (ESP) The theory that retrieval cues will only be successful in accessing a memory trace if they contain some of the same items of information which were stored with the original trace.

Endogenous attention Attention that is controlled by the intention of a participant.

Episodic buffer A hypothetical component of working memory which integrates information from different sense modalities, and provides a link with the long-term memory.

Episodic memory Memory for specific episodes and events from personal experience, occurring in a particular context of time and place (contrasts with **semantic memory**).

Event-related potentials (ERP) Systematic changes in the brain's electrical responses linked to the presentation of a stimulus. Typically the stimulus is presented numerous times with the electroencephalographic (EEG) signals time-locked to its occurrence then being averaged to separate the signal from noise.

Executive functions Meta-abilities necessary for appropriate social functioning and everyday problem-solving, for example the deployment of attention, self-regulation, insight, planning and goal-directed behaviour.

Exogenous attention Attention that is drawn automatically to a stimulus without the intention of the participant. Processing by exogenous attention cannot be ignored.

Experimental psychology The scientific testing of psychological processes in human and animal subjects.

Explicit memory Memory which a subject is able to report consciously and deliberately (contrasts with **implicit memory**).

Extended hippocampal complex A system of interconnected structures within the brain, incorporating the hippocampus, anterior thalamus and mammillary bodies, which is involved in the encoding and storage of new memory traces.

Familiarity The recognition of an item as one that has been encountered on some previous occasion.

Feature detectors Mechanisms in an information-processing device (such as a brain or a computer) which respond to specific features in a pattern of stimulation, such as lines or corners.

Feature overlap The extent to which features of the memory trace stored at input match those available in the retrieval cues. According to the **encoding specificity principle** (ESP), successful retrieval requires extensive feature overlap.

Features Elements of a scene that can be extracted and then used to build up a perception of the scene as a whole. (See also **geons**.)

Fixation When the fovea of the eye dwells on a location in visual space, during which time information is collected.

Flashbulb memory A subject's recollection of details of what they were doing at the time of some major news event or dramatic incident.

Form agnosia This is now the generally accepted term for patients who are unable to discriminate between objects and are unable to copy line drawings of objects (this was previously termed apperceptive agnosia).

Formants Spectral prominences in spoken language, specific patterns of which are associated with particular speech sounds – thus vowels in English are different in how the formants are spaced across the frequency range.

Frontal lobe syndrome The pattern of deficits exhibited by patients with damage to the frontal lobes. These patients are distractible, have difficulty setting, maintaining and changing behavioural goals, and are poor at planning sequences of actions.

Functional fixedness The inability to use an object appropriately in a given situation because of prior experience of using the object in a different way.

Functional magnetic resonance imaging (fMRI) A medical imaging technology that uses very strong magnetic fields to measure changes in the oxygenation of the blood in the brain and thus map levels of activity in the brain. It produces anatomical images of extremely high resolution.

Fusiform face area (FFA) The fusiform area has been shown to be a key structure in face and object processing; numerous studies have shown that the fusiform gyrus contains an area dedicated to face processing – the fusiform face area (FFA).

Galvanic skin response A measurable change in the electrical conductivity of the skin when emotionally significant stimuli are presented. Often used to detect the unconscious processing of stimuli.

Gaze-mediated orienting An exogenous shift of attention following the direction of gaze of a face presented at fixation.

Geons Basically features, but conceived explicitly as being 3-D features.

Gestalt psychology An approach to psychology which emphasised the way in which the components of perceptual input became grouped and integrated into patterns and whole figures.

Gyrus The surface of the brain is formed by the cerebral cortex, and this has its surface area greatly increased by being thrown into folds. A gyrus is the outer surface of one of these folds, and a sulcus is formed when in the depths of a fold. If the fold in the cortex is very deep it is called a fissure, like the lateral fissure which separates the temporal lobe from the frontal lobe.

Haptic perception Tactile (touch) and kinaesthetic (awareness of position and movement of joints and muscles) perception.

Herpes simplex encephalitis (HSE) A virus infection of the brain, which in some cases leaves the patient severely amnesic.

Heuristics Methods or strategies which often lead to problem solution but are not guaranteed to succeed.

Hippocampus A structure lying within the temporal lobes, which is involved in the creation of new memories. Hippocampal lesions usually cause impairment of memory, especially the storage of new memories.

Ideomotor compatibility The compatibility between the stimulus and its required response in terms of, usually, spatial relations.

Illusions Cases in which perception of the world is distorted in some way.

Impasse A sort of mental 'blank' experienced when trying to solve a problem, which is accompanied by a subjective feeling of not knowing what to do.

Implicit memory Memory whose influence can be detected by some indirect test of task performance, but which the subject is unable to report deliberately and consciously (contrasts with **explicit memory**).

Individuation Recognising one specific item from other members of that class of item (e.g. recognising the face of a particular individual).

Inductive reasoning task A problem that has a well-defined structure in a system of formal logic where the conclusion is highly probable but not necessarily true.

Insight The reorganising or restructuring of the elements of the problem situation in such a way as to provide a solution. Also known as productive thinking.

Integrative agnosia This is the generally accepted term for associative agnosia. It refers to patients who can perceive the individual shapes and elements of objects but are unable to integrate these into a representation of the whole object.

Interpolation Using computerised image-processing systems to construct images that are intermediate between two other images.

Judgement This involves an assessment of the likelihood of an event occurring on the basis of incomplete information; it often forms

the initial process in decision-making.

Knowledge Information that is not contained within the sensory stimulus.

Korsakoff's syndrome A brain disease which usually results from chronic alcoholism, and which is mainly characterised by a memory impairment.

Late selection An account of selective processing where attention operates after all stimuli have been analysed for their semantic properties.

Laws of perceptual organisation Principles (such as proximity) by which parts of a visual scene can be resolved into different objects.

Lesion Refers to tissue damage – in the brain this can be a result of a stroke, a tumour, an infectious disease, the effects of a toxin, a direct injury or a progressive disease (a dementia).

Lexical decision task An experiment in which participants are given a target item (typically written), and asked to decide whether it is a real word or not. Lexical decision tasks are used as the amount of time taken to give a response can indicate how the target item is being processed: this response can be used in combination with other tasks, e.g. priming.

Long-term memory Memory held in permanent storage, available for retrieval at some time in the future (contrasts with **short-term memory**).

Long-term potentiation (LTP) A lasting change in synaptic resistance following the application of electrical stimulation to living brain tissue. Possibly one of the biological mechanisms underlying the learning process.

Masking The disruptive effect of an auditory or visual pattern that is presented immediately after an auditory or visual stimulus. This is backward masking, but there are other types of masking.

Means–ends analysis A general heuristic where a sub-problem is selected that will reduce the difference between the current state and the goal state.

Mental model A representation that we construct according to what is described in the premises of a reasoning problem, which will depend on how we interpret these premises.

Mental set A term to describe the rote application of one successful method to solve a problem which makes one 'blind' to an alternative and possibly much simpler method.

Meta-analysis A form of statistical analysis based on combining all the findings in a specific area to obtain an overall picture.

Misinformation effect The contamination of eyewitness testimony by information acquired after the witnessed event.

Mnemonic A technique or strategy used for improving the memorability of items, for example by adding meaningful associations.

Modality The processing system specific to one of the senses, such as vision, hearing or touch.

Modular system A system in which different types of processing are carried out by separate and relatively independent sub-systems.

Mood-congruent memory The finding that learning and retrieval are better when the learner's (or rememberer's) mood state is the same as (or congruent with) the affective value of the to-be-remembered material.

Mood-state-dependent memory The finding that memory performance is better when the individual's mood state is the same at learning and retrieval than when it differs.

Morphemes Units of meaning within words. A word like 'descendant' contains a number of morphemes which contribute to its meaning ('de-' = from, '-scend-' = climb, '-ant' = person with the property of).

Neologisms Non-words which can be used by some neuropsychological patients in place of real words. The patients frequently do not know that they are not using real words. More widely, neologisms are used to refer to new words which are making their way into wider, more commonplace language use.

Neurotransmitter A chemical substance which is secreted across the synapse between two neurons, enabling one neuron to stimulate another.

Numena The world as it really is. (See also **phenomena**.)

Optimistic bias An individual's mistaken belief that he/she is more likely than most other people to experience positive events but less likely to experience negative events.

Organic amnesia An impairment of memory function caused by physical damage to the brain.

Orienting In the spotlight model of visual attention, this is attention to regions of space that does not depend upon eye movements.

Orienting task A set of instructions used to influence the type of cognitive processing employed.

Overt attentional orienting Making an eye movement to attend to a location.

Pandemonium A fanciful but appealing conceptual model of a feature extraction process.

Parallel distributed processing (PDP) approaches Stimuli are represented in the brain, not by single neurons, but by networks of neurons. An approach sometimes used to model cognitive processes.

Perception The subjective experience of sensory information after having been subjected to cognitive processing.

Perceptual hypotheses An element of the constructivist approach, in which hypotheses as to the nature of a stimulus object are tested against incoming sensory information.

Perseveration An inability to shift response strategy characteristic of frontal lobe patients.

Phantom word illusion What we hear may be influenced by what we expect to hear.

Phenomena Numena as we perceive them.

Phenomenological experience Our conscious experience of the world.

Phoneme The smallest unit of speech which contributes to its linguistic meaning: changing a phoneme will change the meaning of a word.

Phonological loop A hypothetical component of working memory, which is assumed to provide brief storage for verbally presented items.

Phonotactics Rules which govern how phonemes can be combined and sequenced in any one language – for example, a syllable can start with 'dw-' in English, but a syllable cannot end '-dw'.

Pop-out An object will pop out from a display if it is detected in parallel and is different from all other items in the display.

Positron emission tomography (PET) A method of imaging structure and function in the human brain by directly tracking blood flow using radioactive tracers. PET can be used to form structural images of blood flow in the brain, as the brain is richly supplied with blood. PET can also be used to look at neural activity by tracking local changes in regional cerebral blood flow, which are seen when there is local increased in neural activity. Because the power of PET is limited by the number of scans, and because the number of scans is limited by the amount of radioactivity which can safely be administered, PET is becoming less commonly used for functional imaging studies.

Pragmatic reasoning schemata Clusters of rules that are highly generalised and abstracted but defined with respect to different types of relationships and goals.

Primal sketch First stage in Marr's model of vision, which results in computation of edges and other details from retinal images.

Problem reduction An approach to problem solving that converts the problem into a number of sub-problems, each of which can be solved separately.

Problem space A term introduced by Newell and

Simon to describe the first stage in problem-solving; represented in the problem space are the initial state, the goal state, the instructions, the constraints on the problem and all relevant information retrieved from long-term memory.

Procedural knowledge Unconscious knowledge about how to do something. It includes skills and knowledge that cannot be made explicit but can be demonstrated by performance.

Procedural memory Memory which can be demonstrated by performing some skilled procedure such as a motor task, but which the subject is not necessarily able to report consciously (contrasts with **declarative memory**).

Production system A computational model based on numerous IF–THEN condition–action rules. IF the rule is represented in working memory THEN the production stored in long-term memory is applied.

Proprioception Knowledge of the position of the body and its parts (arms, fingers, etc.). (See also **haptic perception**.)

Prosopagnosia An inability to recognise faces despite adequate visual acuity.

Prototypes Representations of objects in terms of fairly abstract properties. More flexible than **templates**.

Psychogenic amnesia A memory impairment of psychological origin.

Psychological refractory period The time delay between the responses to two overlapping signals that reflects the time required for the first response to be organised before the response to the second signal can be organised.

Recency and primacy effects The tendency for participants to show particularly good recall for items presented towards the end (recency) or the start (primacy) of a list.

Recollection Remembering a specific event or occasion on which an item was previously encountered.

Reconsolidation The finding that the reactivation of a memory makes it temporarily vulnerable to change.

Recovered memories Childhood traumatic or threatening memories that are remembered many years after the relevant events or experiences.

Re-entrant processing Information flow between brain regions (bidirectional).

Regular orthography Refers to a writing system in which there is a direct correspondence between speech sounds and letters. In irregular orthographies, like English, the relationship between speech sounds and letters is more opaque and variable.

Rehabilitation Strategies used to help patients to cope with an impairment or disability, enabling them to function as effectively as possible within the limitations created by the impairment.

Representativeness heuristic Making judgements on the basis of the extent to which the salient features of an object or person are representative of the features thought to be characteristic of some category.

Repression Motivated forgetting of traumatic or other very threatening events (e.g. childhood abuse).

Retrieval-induced forgetting (RIF) The phenomenon whereby the successful retrieval of a memory trace inhibits the retrieval of rival memory traces.

Retrograde amnesia (RA) Impaired memory for events which occurred prior to the onset of amnesia (contrasts with **anterograde amnesia**).

Reversible figure A figure in which the object perceived depends on what is designated as 'figure' and what is designated as '(back)ground'.

Saccade The movement of the eyes during which information uptake is suppressed. Between saccades the eye makes fixations during which there is information uptake at the fixated area.

Saccadic eye movements Small eye movements which are automatic and involuntary.

Schema A mental pattern, usually derived from past experience, which is used to assist with the interpretation of subsequent cognitions, for example by identifying familiar shapes and sounds in a new perceptual input.

Scotoma A blind area within the visual field, resulting from damage to the visual system (plural = scotomata).

Selection for action The type of attention necessary for planning controlling and executing responses, or actions.

Selection for perception The type of attention necessary for encoding and interpreting sensory data.

Selective filtering An attentional task that requires selection of one source of information for further processing and report in a difficult task such as dichotic listening or visual search for a conjunction of properties.

Selective set An attentional task requiring detection of

a target from a small set of possibilities.

Semantic memory Memory for general knowledge, such as the meanings associated with particular words and shapes, without reference to any specific contextual episode (contrasts with **episodic memory**).

Semantics The meanings of words and the ways that this knowledge is structured and interpreted. Sentences can be ungrammatical but fully semantically comprehensible (e.g. I don't want you to turn me down! I want you to turn me yes!).

Sensation The 'raw' sensory input (as compared with **perception**).

Sensory conspicuity The extent to which aspects of a stimulus (such as colour and luminance) influence how easily it can be registered by the senses. (See also **attention conspicuity**.)

Sensory overload A situation in which there is too much incoming sensory information to be adequately processed.

Shadowing Used in a dichotic listening task in which participants must repeat aloud the to-be-attended message and ignore the other message.

Short-term memory Memory held in conscious awareness, and which is currently receiving attention (contrasts with **long-term memory**).

Sign language A visual language, normally arising in deaf communities, in which the hands are used to express linguistic information. Sign languages are not just sequences of pantomimed gestures, nor are they typically visual forms of existing spoken languages –

for example, British Sign Language has very little in common with spoken British English, having a very different syntax and rules for combining words. In sign language, the face is often used to replace the role of prosody and intonation in spoken language, being used to convey emphasis and emotion.

Size constancy The perceived size of objects is adjusted to allow for perceived distance.

Slips of action Errors in carrying out sequences of actions, e.g. where a step in the sequence is omitted, or an appropriate action is made, but to the wrong object.

Spectral cues Auditory cues to, for example, distance provided by the distortion of the incoming stimulus by (e.g.) the pinnae (ear lobes).

Speech Spoken form of a language: a way of conveying linguistic information with the human voice.

State–action tree A diagram showing all the possible sequences of actions and intermediate states which can be constructed if the problem is well-defined.

Stroke Refers to brain damage which occurs as a result of cardiovascular issues. The brain is an energy intensive organ, using around 20 per cent of the available oxygen circulating in the blood supply. Disruption to blood supply causes brain damage to occur very quickly. The damage can occur due to a blockage in a blood vessel (an ischaemic stroke) or due to a blood vessel rupturing (haemorrhagic stroke). Strokes are associated with sudden onsets of symptoms of brain damage, and the symptoms

can reduce in severity as time passes.

Stroop effect The effect of a well-learned response to a stimulus slowing the ability to make the less-well-learned response; for example, naming the ink colour of a colour word.

Subliminal Below the threshold for conscious awareness or confident report.

Supervisory attentional system A term used by Norman and Shallice to describe a system that can heighten a schema's level of activation, allowing it to be in a better position to compete with other schemas for dominance and thus increasing its probability of being selected in contention scheduling.

Synaesthesia A condition in which individuals presented with sensory input of one modality consistently and automatically experience a sensory event in a different modality (for example seeing colour on hearing musical notes).

Synaesthete A person who has the condition **synaesthesia**.

Synapse The gap between the axon of one neuron and the dendrite of another neuron.

Syntax Grammatical rules of a language. These rules govern the ways that words can be combined (and declined). Syntax can be independent of meaning: a sentence can be syntactically correct but meaningless (e.g. 'colourless green dreams sleep furiously').

Templates Stored representations of objects enabling object recognition.

Testing effect The finding that actively testing a memory improves its subsequent retrievability.

Three-dimensional (3-D) sketch Third stage in Marr's model of vision. This is a viewer-independent representation of the object which has achieved perceptual constancy or classification.

Top-down (or schema-driven) processing Processing which makes use of stored knowledge and schemas to interpret an incoming stimulus (contrasts with **bottom-up processing**).

Transcranial magnetic stimulation (TMS) This technique uses an electrical coil placed near the surface of the head to induce a rapid change in the magnetic field, which, in turn, produces a weak electrical current in underlying brain tissue. This can cause depolarisation or hyperpolarisation. The technique can use single bursts or repetitive stimulation. It can be used to support inferences about the role of that brain region in a particular task (e.g. by showing that repetitive stimulation slows responses in task *a* but not task *b*, that the region is involved in task *a*).

Two-and-a-half-dimensional (2.5-D) sketch Second stage in Marr's theory of vision. Aligns details in primal sketch into a viewer-centred representation of the object.

Unilateral spatial neglect A difficulty in noticing or acting on information from one side of space typically caused by a brain lesion to the opposite hemisphere (e.g. right-hemisphere damage producing lack of awareness for information on the left). Also called hemispatial neglect or hemispatial inattention.

Urbach–Wiethe disease A disease in which the amygdala and adjacent areas are destroyed; it leads to the impairment of emotional processing and memory for emotional material.

Varied mapping The condition in which a stimulus and its response are changed from trial to trial.

Ventral stream A pathway in the brain that deals with the visual information for what objects are.

Visual masking Experimental procedure of following a briefly presented stimulus by random visual noise or fragments of other stimuli. Interferes with or interrupts visual processing.

Visual search Experimental procedure of searching through a field of objects ('distractors') for a desired object ('target').

Visuo-spatial sketchpad A hypothetical component of working memory, which is assumed to provide brief storage for visually presented items.

Weapon focus The finding that eyewitnesses pay so much attention to some crucial aspect of the situation (e.g. a weapon) that they ignore other details.

Wernicke's area A region of the brain normally located in the left temporal region, which is concerned with the perception and comprehension of speech.

Word A word is a lexical unit which can stand alone in terms of its use in a language and its meaning. Words have meanings which map onto things and ideas: words are the level at which languages convey meaning.

Word-length effect The finding that word span in immediate recall is greater for short words than for long words.

Working memory (WM) A hypothetical short-term memory system which serves as a mental workspace in which a variety of processing operations are carried out on both new input and retrieved memories.

Writing A visual system for representing a language. Writing systems can be alphabetic (where one symbol corresponds roughly to one speech sound), syllabic (where one symbol corresponds to one syllable), or ideographic/logographic (where individual symbols correspond to one word).

References

Ackerly, S. (1937). Instinctive, emotional and mental changes following prefrontal lobe extirpation. *American Journal of Psychiatry*, 92, 717–729.

Addis, D. R. and Tippett, L. J. (2004). Memory of myself: Autobiographical memory and identity in Alzheimer's disease. *Memory*, 12, 56–74.

Addis, D. R. and Schacter, D. L. (2012). The hippocampus and imagining the future: Where do we stand? *Frontiers in Human Neuroscience*, 5(article 173), 1–15.

Aggleton, J. P. (2008). Understanding anterograde amnesia: Disconnections and hidden lesions. *Quarterly Journal of Experimental Psychology*, 61, 1441–1471.

Aggleton, J. P. and Saunders, R. C. (1997). Anatomical basis of anterograde amnesia. *Memory*, 5, 49–71.

Aglioti, S., DeSouza, J. F. X. and Goodale, M. A. (1995). Size-contrast illusions deceive the eye but not the hand. *Current Biology*, 5, 679–685.

Albert, M. S., Butters, N. and Levin, J. (1979). Temporal gradients in the retrograde amnesia of patients with alcoholic Korsakoff's disease. *Archives of Neurology*, 36, 211–216.

Alderman, N., Burgess, P. W., Knight, C. and Henman, C. (2003). Ecological validity of a simplified version of the multiple errands shopping test. *Journal of the International Neuropsychological Society*, 9, 31–44.

Allen, G. A., Mahler, W. A. and Estes, W. K. (1969). Effects of recall tests on long-term retention of paired associates. *Journal of Verbal Learning and Verbal Behaviour*, 8, 463–470.

Altmann, E. M. and Schunn, C. D. (2012). Decay versus interference: A new look at an old interaction. *Psychological Science*, 23, 1435–1437.

Altmann, G. M. T. (1998). Ambiguity in sentence processing. *Trends in Cognitive Sciences*, 2(4), 146–151.

Alzheimer, A. (1907). Uber eine eigenartige Erkrankung der Hirnrinde. *Allgemeine Zeitschrift fur Psychiatrie Psychoisch-Gerichliche Medicin*, 64, 146–148.

Amir, N., Badour, C. L. and Freese, B. (2009). The effect of retrieval on recall of information in individuals with PTSD. *Journal of Anxiety Disorders*, 23, 535–540.

Amir, N., Leiner, A. S. and Bomyea, J. (2010). Implicit memory and posttraumatic stress symptoms. *Cognitive Therapy and Research*, 34, 49–58.

Amodio, D. M. and Ratner, K. G. (2011). A memory systems model of implicit social cognition. *Current Directions in Psychological Science*, 20, 143–148.

Anderson, B., Mennemeier, M. and Chatterjee, A. (2000). Variability not ability: Another basis for performance decrements in neglect. *Neuropsychologia*, 38(6), 785–796.

Anderson, J. M., Gilmore, R., Roper, S. *et al.* (1999). Conduction aphasia and the arcuate fasciculus: A reexamination of the Wernicke-Geschwind model. *Brain and Language*, 70, 1–12.

Anderson, J. R. (1980). *Cognitive Psychology and Its Implications*. San Francisco: W. H. Freeman.

Anderson, J. R. (2004). *Cognitive Psychology and Its Implications* (7th edn). New York: Worth.

Anderson, J. R. and Bower, G. H. (1972). *Human Associative Memory*. Washington, DC: Winston.

Anderson, J. R., Fincham, J. M., Qin, Y. and Stocco, A. (2008). A central circuit of the mind. *Trends in Cognitive Sciences*, 12, 136–143.

Anderson, M. C. (2001). Active forgetting: Evidence for functional inhibition as a source of memory failure. *Journal of Aggression, Maltreatment, and Trauma*, 4, 185–210.

Anderson, M. C. (2003). Rethinking interference theory: Executive control and the mechanisms of forgetting. *Journal of Memory and Language*, 49, 415–445.

Anderson, M. C. and Neely, J. H. (1996). Interference and inhibition in memory retrieval. In E. L. Bjork and R. A. Bjork (eds) *Memory: Handbook of Perception and Cognition*. New York: Academic Press.

Anderson, M. C., Bjork, R. A. and Bjork, E. L. (1994). Remembering can cause forgetting: Retrieval dynamics in long-term memory. *Journal of Experimental Psychology: Learning, Memory, and Cognition*, 20, 1063–1087.

Anderson, M. C., Bjork, R. A. and Bjork, E. L. (2000). Retrieval-induced forgetting: Evidence for a recall-specific mechanism. *Journal of Experimental Psychology: Learning, Memory, and Cognition*, 7, 522–530.

Andrewes, D. (2001). *Neuropsychology: From Theory to Practice*. Hove: Psychology Press.

Andrews, B., Brewin, C. R., Ochera, J., Morton, J., Bekerian, D. A., Davies, G. M. and Mollon, P. (1999). The timing, triggers and qualities of recovered memories in therapy. *British Journal of Clinical Psychology*, 39, 11–26.

Andrews, P. W. and Thomson, J. A. (2009). The bright side of being blue: Depression as an adaptation for analysing complex problems. *Psychological Review*, 116, 620–654.

Andrews, S. (1997). The effects of orthographic similarity on lexical retrieval: Resolving neighborhood conflicts. *Psychological Bulletin and Review*, 4, 439–461.

Anolli, L., Antonietti, A., Crisafulli, L. and Cantoia, M. (2001). Accessing source information in analogical problem solving. *The Quarterly Journal of Experimental Psychology*, 54A, 237–261.

Asher, J. E., Lamb, J. A., Brocklebank, D., Cazier, J. B. *et al.* (2009). A whole-genome scan and fine-mapping linkage study of auditory-visual synesthesia reveals evidence of linkage to chromosomes 2q24, 5q33, 6p12, and 12p12. *American Journal of Human Genetics*, 84(2), 279–285.

Ask, K. and Granhag, P. A. (2007). Hot cognition in investigative judgments: The differential influence of anger and sadness. *Law and Human Behavior*, 31, 537–551.

Aslan, A., Zellner, M. and Bauml, K-H. (2010). Working memory capacity predicts listwise directed forgetting in adults and children. *Memory*, 18, 442–450.

Assal, G., Favre, C. and Anders, J. P. (1984). Non-reconnaissance d'animaux familièrs chez un paysan: Zooagnosie ou prosopagnosia pour les animaux. *Revue Neurologique*, 140, 580–584.

Atkinson, R. C. and Shiffrin, R. M. (1968). Human memory: A proposed system and its control processes. In K. W. Spence and J. T. Spence (eds) *The Psychology of Learning and Motivation* (Vol. 2). London: Academic Press.

Auerbach, S. H., Allard, T., Naeser, M., Alexander, M. P. and Albert, M. L. (1982). Pure word deafness: Analysis of a case with bilateral lesions and a defect at the prephonemic level. *Brain*, 105, 271–300.

Avidan, G. and Behrmann, M. (2008). Implicit familiarity processing in congenital prosopagnosia. *Journal of Neuropsychology*, 2(1), 141–164. doi: 10.1348/174866407X260180.

Baddeley, A. D. (1986). *Working Memory*. Oxford: Oxford University Press.

Baddeley, A. D. (1993). Working memory or working attention? In A. Baddeley and L. Weiskrantz (eds) *Attention: Selection, Awareness and Control: A Tribute to Donald Broadbent*. Oxford: Oxford University Press.

Baddeley, A. D. (1995). Memory. In C. C. French and A. M. Colman (eds) *Cognitive Psychology*. New York: Longman.

Baddeley, A. D. (1996). Exploring the central executive. *Quarterly Journal of Experimental Psychology*, 49A, 5–28.

Baddeley, A. D. (1997). *Human Memory: Theory and Practice*. Hove: Erlbaum.

Baddeley, A. D. (2000). The episodic buffer: A new component of working memory? *Trends in Cognitive Sciences*, 4, 417–423.

Baddeley, A. D. (2003). Working memory and language: An overview. *Journal of Communication Disorders*, 36, 189–208.

Baddeley, A. D. (2004). The psychology of memory. In A. D. Baddeley, M. D. Kopelman and B. A. Wilson (eds) *The Essential Handbook of Memory Disorders for Clinicians*. Chichester: Wiley.

Baddeley, A. D. (2007). *Working Memory, Thought and Action*. Oxford: Oxford University Press.

Baddeley, A. D. (2009a). Learning. In A. D. Baddeley, M. W. Eysenck and M. C. Anderson (eds) *Memory*. Hove: Psychology Press.

Baddeley, A. D. (2009b). Working memory. In A. D. Baddeley, M. W. Eysenck and M. C. Anderson (eds) *Memory*. Hove: Psychology Press.

Baddeley, A. D. and Warrington, E. K. (1970). Amnesia and the distinction between long- and short-term memory. *Journal of Verbal Learning and Verbal Behaviour*, 9, 176–189.

Baddeley, A. D. and Hitch, G. J. (1974). Working memory. In G. H. Bower (ed.) *The Psychology of Learning and Motivation* (Vol. 8). London: Academic Press.

Baddeley, A. D. and Lewis, V. J. (1981). Inner active processes in reading: The inner voice, the inner ear, and the inner eye. In A. M. Lesgold and C. A. Perfetti (eds) *Interactive Processes in Reading*. Hillsdale, NJ: Lawrence Erlbaum Associates.

Baddeley, A. D. and Wilson, B. (1988). Frontal amnesia and the dysexecutive syndrome. *Brain and Cognition*, 7, 212–230.

Baddeley, A. D. and Wilson, B. (1994). When implicit learning fails: Amnesia and the problem of error elimination. *Neuropsychologia*, 32, 53–68.

Baddeley, A. D. and Wilson, B. (2002). Prose recall and amnesia: Implications for the structure of working memory. *Neuropsychologia*, 40, 1737–1743.

Baddeley, A. D., Thomson, N. and Buchanan, M. (1975). Word length and the structure of short-term memory. *Journal of Verbal Learning and Verbal Behaviour*, 14, 575–589.

Baddeley, A. D., Lewis, V. J. and Vallar, G. (1984). Exploring the articulatory loop. *Quarterly Journal of Experimental Psychology*, 36, 233–252.

Baddeley, A. D., Gathercole, S. and Papagno, C. (1998). The phonological loop as a language learning device. *Psychological Review*, 105, 158–173.

Baddeley, A. D., Kopelman, M. D. and Wilson, B. A. (eds) (2004). *The Essential Handbook of Memory Disorders for Clinicians*. Chichester: Wiley.

Baddeley, A. D., Eysenck, M. W. and Anderson, M. C. (2009). *Memory*. Hove: Psychology Press.

Bahrick, H. P., Bahrick, P. O. and Wittlinger, R. P. (1975). Fifty years of memory for names and faces: A cross-sectional approach. *Journal of Experimental Psychology: General*, 104, 54–75.

Bahrick, H. P., Hall, L. K. and Da Costa, L. A. (2008). Fifty years of memory for college grades. *Emotion*, 8, 13–22.

Bailey, C. H. and Kandel, E. R. (2004). The synaptic growth and persistence of long-term memory: A molecular perspective. In M. S. Gazzaniga (ed.) *The Cognitive Neurosciences* (3rd edn). Cambridge, MA: MIT Press.

Bailey, P. J. and Summerfield, Q. (1980). Information in speech: Observations on the perception of [s]-stop clusters. *Journal of Experimental Psychology: Human Perception and Performance*, 6, 536–563.

Baizer, J. S., Ungerleider, L. G. and Desimone, R. (1991). Organization of visual inputs to the inferior temporal and posterior parietal cortex in macaques. *Journal of Neuroscience*, 11(1), 168–190.

Balani, A. B., Soto, D. and Humphreys, G. W. (2009). Constraints on task-based control of behaviour following frontal lobe damage: A single-case study. *Cognitive Neuropsychology*, 26, 635–654.

Baldo, J. V., Delis, D. C., Wilkins, D. P. and Shimamura, A. P. (2004). Is it bigger than a breadbox? Performance of patients with prefrontal lesions on a new executive function test. *Archives of Clinical Neuropsychology*, 19, 407–419.

Balota, D. A. and Spieler, D. H. (1998). The utility of item-level analyses in model evaluation: A reply to Seidenberg and Plaut. *Psychological Science*, 9, 238–240.

Balota, D. A., Cortese, H. J. and Pilotti, M. (1999). Item-level analyses of lexical decision performance results from a mega-study. In *Abstracts of the 40th Annual Meeting of the Psychonomic Society* (p. 44). Los Angeles: Psychonomic Society.

Balota, D. A., Cortese, M. J., Sergent-Marshall, S. D., Spieler, D. H. and Yap, M. J. (2004). Visual word recognition of single-syllable words. *Journal of Experimental Psychology: General*, 133, 283–316.

Balota, D. A., Yap, M. J., Cortese, M. J., Hutchison, K. A., Kessler, B., Loftis, B., Neely, J. H., Nelson, D. L., Simpson, G. B. and Treiman, R. (2007). The English Lexicon Project. *Behavior Research Methods*, 39, 445–459.

Bamdad, M. J., Ryan, L. M. and Warden, D. L. (2003). Functional assessment of executive abilities following traumatic brain injury. *Brain Injury*, 17, 1011–1020.

Banich, M. T. (2004). *Cognitive Neuroscience and Neuropsychology*. Boston, MA: Houghton Mifflin.

Banich, M. T. and Compton, R. J. (2010). *Cognitive Neuroscience, International Edition* (3rd edn). Pacific Grove, CA: Wadsworth.

Barceló, F. (1999). Electrophysiological evidence of two different types of error in the Wisconsin card sorting test. *Neuroreport*, 10, 1299–1303.

Barceló, F. and Knight, R. T. (2002). Both random and perseverative errors underlie WCST deficits in prefrontal patients. *Neuropsychologia*, 40, 349–356.

Barceló, F., Sanz, M., Molina, V. and Rubia, F. J. (1997). The Wisconsin Card Sorting Test and the assessment of frontal function: A validation study with event-related potentials. *Neuropsychologia*, 35, 399–408.

Barnett, K. J., Finucane, C., Asher, J. E., Bargary, G., Corvin, A. P., Newell, F. N. and Mitchell, K. J. (2008). Familial patterns and the origins of individual differences in synaesthesia. *Cognition*, 106(2), 871–893.

Barnier, A. J., Conway, M. A., Mayoh, L. and Speyer, J. (2007). Directed forgetting of recently recalled autobiographical memories. *Journal of Experimental Psychology: General*, 136, 301–322.

Baron, J. and Strawson, C. (1976). Use of orthographic and word-specific knowledge in reading words aloud. *Journal of Experimental Psychology: Human Perception and Performance*, 2, 386–393.

Baron-Cohen, S. (1992). The theory of mind hypothesis of autism: History and prospects of the idea. *The Psychologist*, 5, 9–12.

Baron-Cohen, S., Wyke, M. A. and Binnie, C. (1987). Hearing words and seeing colours: An experimental investigation of a case of synaesthesia. *Perception*, 16, 761–767.

Baron-Cohen, S., Harrison, J., Goldstein, L. H. and Wyke, M. (1993). Coloured speech perception: Is synaesthesia what happens when modularity breaks down? *Perception*, 22, 419–426.

Baron-Cohen, S., Burt, L., Smith-Laittan, F. and Harrison, J. (1996). Synaesthesia: prevalence and familiarity. *Perception*, 25, 1073–1080.

Bartlett, F. C. (1932). *Remembering*. Cambridge: Cambridge University Press.

Barton, J. J. S. (2008). Structure and function in acquired prosopagnosia: lessons from a series of 10 patients with brain damage. *Journal of Neuropsychology*, 2(Pt 1), 197–225.

Barton, J. J. S., Cherkasova, M. V. and O'Connor, M. (2001). Covert recognition in acquired and developmental prosopagnosia. *Neurology*, 57, 1161–1168.

Barton, J. J. S., Cherkasova, M. V., Press, D. Z., Intriligator, J. M. and O'Connor, M. (2003). Developmental prosopagnosia: A study of three patients. *Brain and Cognition*, 51, 12–30.

Basden, B. H. and Basden, D. R. (1996). Directed forgetting: Further comparisons of the item and list methods. *Memory*, 4, 633–653.

Basso, A., Spinnler, H., Vallar, G. and Zanobio, M. E. (1982). Left hemisphere damage and selective impairment of auditory-verbal short-term memory. *Neuropsychologia*, 20, 263–274.

Bate, S., Haslam, C., Tree, J. J. and Hodgson, T. L. (2008). Evidence of an eye movement-based memory effect in congenital prosopagnosia. *Cortex*, 44(7), 806–819.

Bauer, R. M. (1984). Autonomic recognition of names and faces in prosopagnosia: A neuropsychological application of the Guilty Knowledge Test. *Neuropsychologia*, 22, 457–469.

Bauml, K-H. and Kuhbandner, C. (2007). Remembering can cause forgetting – but not in negative moods. *Psychological Science*, 18, 111–115.

Bayley, P. J. and Squire, L. R. (2003). The medial temporal lobe and declarative memory. *International Congress Series*, 1250, 245–259. doi: 10.1016/S0531–5131(03)00192–4.

Bearman, C. R., Ball, L. and Ormerod, T. C. (2007). The structure and function of spontaneous analogising in domain-based problem solving. *Thinking and Reasoning*, 13, 273–294.

Bearman, C. R., Ormerod, T. C., Ball, L. and Deptula, D. (2011). Explaining away the negative effects of evaluation on analogical transfer: The perils of premature evaluation. *The Quarterly Journal of Experimental Psychology*, 64, 942–959.

Beck, A. T., Rush, A. J., Shaw, B. F. and Emery, G. (1979). *Cognitive Therapy of Depression*. New York: Wiley.

Beck, D. M., Rees, G., Frith, C. D. and Lavie, N. (2001). Neural correlates of change detection and change blindness. *Nature Neuroscience*, 4(6), 645–650.

Beck, D. M., Muggleton, N., Walsh, V. and Lavie, N. (2005). Right parietal cortex plays a critical role in change blindness. *Cerebral Cortex*, 15, 1736–1741.

Becker, J. T. and Overman, A. A. (2004). The memory deficit in Alzheimer's disease. In A. D. Baddeley, M. D., Kopelman and B. A. Wilson (eds) *The Essential Handbook of Memory Disorders for Clinicians*. Chichester: Wiley.

Behrmann, M., Avidan, G., Giao, F. and Black, S. (2007). Structural imaging reveals anatomical alterations in inferotemporal cortex in congenital prosopagnosia. *Cerebral Cortex*, 7(10), 2354–2363.

Beilock, S. L., Carr, T. H., MacMahon, C. and Starkes, J. L. (2002). When paying attention becomes unproductive: Impact of divided verus skill-focussed attention in novice and experienced performance in sensorimotor skills. *Journal of Experimental Psychology: Applied*, 8, 6–16.

Bellas, D. N., Novelly, R. A., Eskenazi, B. and Wasserstein, J. (1988). Unilateral displacement in the olfactory sense: A manifestation of the unilateral neglect syndrome. *Cortex*, 24(2), 267–275.

Bellugi, U., Wang, P. P. and Jernigan, T. L. (1994). Williams syndrome: An unusual neuropsychological profile. In S. H. Broman and J. Grafman (eds) *Atypical Cognitive Deficits in Developmental Disorders: Implications for Brain Function*. Hillsdale, NJ: Laurence Erlbaum.

Bench, C. J., Frith, C. D., Grasby, P. M., Friston, K. J., Paulesu, E., Frackowiak, R. S. J. and Dolan,

R. J. (1993). Investigations of the functional anatomy of attention using the stroop test. *Neuropsychologia*, 31, 907–922.

Bentin, S., DeGutis, J. M., D'Esposito, M. and Robertson, L. C. (2007). Too many trees to see the forest: Performance, event-related potential, and functional magnetic resonance imaging manifestations of integrative congenital prosopagnosia. *Journal of Cognitive Neuroscience*, 19(1), 132–146.

Benton, A. L. (1991). The prefrontal region: Its early history. In H. S. Levin, H. M. Eisenberg and A. L. Benton (eds) *Frontal Lobe Function and Dysfunction*. Oxford: Oxford University Press.

Benton, T. R., Ross, D. F., Bradshaw, E., Thomas, W. N. and Bradshaw, G. S. (2006). Eyewitness memory is still not common sense: Comparing jurors, judges and law enforcement to eyewitness experts. *Applied Cognitive Psychology*, 20, 115–129.

Beranek, L. L. (1996). *Concert and Opera Halls: How They Sound*. Woodbury, NY: Acoustical Society of America.

Berntsen, D. and Rubin, D. C. (2004). Cultural life scripts structure recall from autobiographical memory. *Memory and Cognition*, 32, 427–442.

Berti, A. and Rizzolatti, G. (1992). Visual processing without awareness: Evidence from unilateral neglect. *Journal of Cognitive Neuroscience*, 4, 345–351.

Besner, D., Davies, J. and Daniels, S. (1981). Reading for meaning. The effects of concurrent articulation. *Quarterly Journal of Experimental Psychology*, 33A, 415–437.

Bianchi, L. (1922). *The Mechanisms of the Brain and the Functions of the Frontal Lobes* (translation by J. H. Macdonald). Edinburgh: Livingstone.

Biederman, I. (1987). Recognition-by-components: A theory of human image understanding. *Psychological Review*, 94, 115–147.

Bishop, D. V. M. (2006). What causes specific language impairment in children? *Current Directions in Psychological Science*, 15(5), 217–221.

Bisiach, E. and Luzzatti, C. (1978). Unilateral neglect of representational space. *Cortex*, 14, 129–133.

Bjork, R. A. (1972). Theoretical implications of directed forgetting. In A. W. Melton and E. Martin (eds) *Coding Processes in Human Memory*. Washington, DC: Winston.

Bjork, R. A. and Bjork, E. L. (1992). A new theory of disuse and an old theory of stimulus fluctuation.

In A. F. Healy, S. M. Kosslyn and R. M. Shiffrin (eds) *From Learning Processes to Cognitive Processes: Essays in Honour of William K. Estes* (Vol. 2, pp. 35–67). Hillsdale, NJ: Erlbaum.

Blackmore, S. (2003). *Consciousness: An Introduction*. London: Hodder & Stoughton.

Blaiss, C. A. and Janak, P. H. (2006). Post-training and post-reactivation administration of amphetamine enhances morphine conditioned place preference. *Behavioural Brain Research*, 171, 329–337.

Blakemore, S. J., Wolpert, D. M. and Frith, C. D. (1998). Central cancellation of self-produced tickle sensation. *Nature Neuroscience*, 1(7), 635–40.

Blanchette, I. and Dunbar, K. (2000). How analogies are generated: The roles of structural and superficial similarity. *Memory and Cognition*, 28, 108–124.

Blanchette, I. and Dunbar, K. (2001). Analogy use in naturalistic settings: The influence of audience, emotion, and goals. *Memory and Cognition*, 29, 730–735.

Blanchette, I. and Richards, A. (2010). The influence of affect on higher level cognition: A review of research on interpretation, judgment, decision making and reasoning. *Cognition and Emotion*, 24, 561–595.

Blanchette, I., Richards, A., Melnyk, L. and Lavda, A. (2007). Reasoning about emotional contents following shocking terrorist attacks: A tale of three cities. *Journal of Experimental Psychology: Applied*, 13, 47–56.

Blank, S. C., Scott, S. K., Murphy, K., Warburton, E. and Wise, R. J. (2002). Speech production: Wernicke, Broca and beyond. *Brain*, 125, 1829–38.

Blesser, B. (1972). Speech perception under conditions of spectral transformation: I. phonetic characteristics. *Journal of Speech and Hearing Research*, 15, 5–41.

Bliss, T. V. P. and Lomo, T. (1973). Long-lasting potentiation of synaptic transmission in the dentate area of the anaesthetised rabbit following stimulation of the perforant path. *Journal of Physiology*, 232, 331–356.

Blix, I. and Brennen, T. (2012). Retrieval-induced forgetting after trauma: A study with victims of sexual assault. *Cognition and Emotion*, 26, 321–331.

Bock, J. K. and Levelt, W. J. M. (1994). Language production: Grammatical encoding. In M. A. Gernsbacher (ed.) *Handbook of Psycholinguistics*. London: Academic Press.

Bodamer, J. (1947). Die Prosopa-Agnosie. *Archiv für Psychiatrie und Nervenkrankheiten*, 179, 6–53.

Bogen, J. E. and Bogen, G. M. (1976). Wernicke's region – Where is it? *Annals of the New York Academy of Sciences*, 280, 834–843.

Bornstein, B., Sroka, M. and Munitz, H. (1969). Prosopagnosia with animal face agnosia. *Cortex*, 5, 164–169.

Bottini, G., Karnath, H. O., Vallar, G., Sterzi, R., Frith, C. D., Frackowiak, R. S. J. and Paulesu, E. (2001). Cerebral representations for egocentric space – Functional-anatomical evidence from caloric vestibular stimulation and neck vibration. *Brain*, 124(6), 1182–1196.

Boucher, V. J. (1994). Alphabet-related biases in psycholinguistic enquiries: Considerations for direct theories of speech production and perception. *Journal of Phonetics*, 22 (1), 1–18.

Boutsen, L. and Humphreys, G. W. (2002). Face context interferes with local part processing in a prosopagnosic patient. *Neuropsychologia*, 40(13), 2305–2313.

Bowen, A., McKenna, K. and Tallis, R. C. (1999). Reasons for variability in the reported rate of occurrence of unilateral spatial neglect after stroke. *Stroke*, 30(6), 1196–1202.

Bower, G. H., Monteiro, K. P. and Gilligan, S. G. (1978). Emotional mood as a context for learning and recall. *Journal of Verbal Learning and Verbal Behaviour*, 17, 573–585.

Bowles, D. C., McKone, E., Dawel, A., Duchaine, B., Palermo, R., Schmalzl, L., Rivolta, D. *et al.* (2009). Diagnosing prosopagnosia: effects of ageing, sex, and participant-stimulus ethnic match on the Cambridge Face Memory Test and Cambridge Face Perception Test. *Cognitive Neuropsychology*, 26, 423–455. doi:10.1080/02643290903343149.

Braine, M. D. S. and O'Brien, D. P. (1991). A theory of *if*: A lexical entry, reasoning program, and pragmatic principles. *Psychological Review*, 98, 182–203.

Braine, M. D. S., Reiser, B. J. and Rumain, B. (1984). Some empirical justification for a theory of natural propositional logic. In G. H. Bower (ed.) *The Psychology of Learning and Motivation* (Vol. 18, pp. 313–371). New York: Academic Press.

Brandt, K. R., Gardiner, J. M., Vargh-Khadem, F., Baddeley, A. D. and Mishkin, M. (2009). Impairment of recollection but not familiarity in a case of developmental amnesia. *Neurocase*, 15, 60–65.

Bransford, J. D. and Johnson, M. K. (1972). Contextual prerequisites for understanding: Some investigations of comprehension and recall. *Journal of Verbal Learning and Verbal Behaviour*, 11, 717–726.

Brewer, N. and Wells, G. L. (2006). Eyewitness identification. *Current Directions in Psychological Science*, 20, 24–27.

Brewin, C. R. (1998). Intrusive memories, depression, and PTSD. *The Psychologist*, 11, 281–283.

Brickner, R. M. (1936). *The Intellectual Functions of the Frontal Lobes*. New York: Macmillan.

Bridgeman, B. (1992). Conscious vs unconscious processing: The case of vision. *Theory and Psychology*, 2(1), 73–88.

Bridgeman, B., Peery, S. and Anand, S. (1997). Interaction of cognitive and sensorimotor maps of visual space. *Perception and Psychophysics*, 59(3), 456–469.

Bright, D. A. and Goodman-Delahunty, J. (2006). Gruesome evidence and emotion: Anger, blame, and jury decision-making. *Law and Human Behavior*, 30, 183–202.

Broadbent, D. E. (1958). *Perception and Communication*. Oxford: Pergamon.

Broca, P. (1861a). Perte de la parole. Ramollissement chronique et destruction partielle du lobe anterieur gauche du cerveau. *Bulletin de la Societe d'Anthropologie (Paris)*, 2, 235–238.

Broca, P. (1861b). Remarques sur le siege de la faculte du language articule, suivies d' une observation d' aphemie. *Bulletin de la Société d'anthropologie (Paris)*, 2, 330–357.

Brockmole, J. R. and Logie, R. H. (2013). Age-related change in visual working memory: A study of 55,753 participants aged 8–75. *Frontiers of Psychology* (29 January). doi: 10.3389.00012.

Broeders, R., van den Bos, K., Müller, P. A. and Ham, J. (2011). Should I save or should I not kill? How people solve moral dilemmas depends on which rule is mostaccessible. *Journal of Experimental Social Psychology*, 47, 923–934.

Broman, M. (2001). Spaced retrieval: A behavioural approach to memory improvement in Alzheimer's and related dementias. *NYS Psychologist*, 13, 35–40.

Brown, A. S. (2002). Consolidation theory and retrograde amnesia in humans. *Psychonomic Bulletin and Review*, 9, 403–425.

Brown, A. S. (2004). *The Déjà Vu Experience*. Hove: Psychology Press.

Brown, A. S. and Murphy, D. R. (1989). Cryptomnesia: Delineating inadvertent plagiarism. *Journal of Experimental Psychology: Learning, Memory, and Cognition*, 15, 432–442.

Brown, C., Lloyd-Jones, T. and Robinson, M. (2008). Eliciting person descriptions from eyewitnesses: A survey of police perceptions of eyewitness performance and reported use of interview techniques. *European Journal of Cognitive Psychology*, 20, 529–560.

Brown, J. (1958). Some tests of the decay theory of immediate memory. *Quarterly Journal of Experimental Psychology*, 10, 12–21.

Brown, R. and Kulik, J. (1977). Flashbulb memories. *Cognition*, 5, 73–99.

Bruce, V. and Young, A. (1986). Understanding face recognition. *British Journal of Psychology*, 77, 305–327.

Bruce, V. and Young, A. (2012). *Face Perception*. Psychology Press: Hove.

Bruce, V., Green, P. R. and Georgeson, M. A. (1996). *Visual Perception, Physiology, Psychology and Ecology* (3rd edn). Hove: Psychology Press.

Bruner, J. S., Goodnow, J. J. and Austin, G. A. (1956). *A Study of Thinking*. New York: Wiley.

Bruyer, R. (1991). Covert face recognition in prosopagnosia – A review. *Brain and Cognition*, 2, 223–335.

Bruyer, R., Laterre, C., Seron, X., Feyereisen, P., Strypstein, E., Pierrard, E. and Rectem, D. (1983). A case of prosopagnosia with some preserved covert remembrance of familiar faces. *Brain and Cognition*, 2, 257–284.

Buckner, R. L. (2000). Neuroimaging of memory. In M. S. Gazzaniga (ed.) *The New Cognitive Neurosciences* (2nd edn). Cambridge, MA: MIT Press.

Budson, A. E. and Gold, C. A. (2009). Flashbulb, personal, and event memories in clinical populations. In O. Luminet and A. Curci (eds) *Flashbulb Memories: New Issues and Perspectives*. Hove: Psychology Press.

Bullier, J. and Nowak, L. G. (1995). Parallel versus serial processing: New vistas on the distributed organization of the visual system. *Current Opinion in Neurobiology*, 5(4), 497–503.

Burgess, M. C. R. and Weaver, G. E. (2003). Interest and attention in facial recognition. *Perceptual and Motor Skills*, 96, 467–480.

Burgess, P. W. and Shallice, T. (1994). Fractionation of the frontal-lobe syndrome. *Revue de Neuropsychologie*, 4, 345–370.

Burgess, P. W. and Shallice, T. (1996a). Response suppression, initiation and strategy use following frontal lobe lesions. *Neuropsychologia*, 34, 263–273.

Burgess, P. W. and Shallice, T. (1996b). Bizarre responses, rule detection and frontal lobe lesions. *Cortex*, 32, 241–259.

Burgess, P. W., Alderman, N., Evans, J., Emslie, H. and Wilson, B. A. (1998). The ecological validity of tests of executive function. *Journal of the International Neuropsychological Society*, 4, 547–558.

Burgess, P. W., Alderman, N., Volle, E., Benoit, R. G. and Gilbert, S. J. (2009). Mesulam's frontal lobe mystery re-examined. *Restorative Neurology and Neuroscience*, 27, 493–506.

Burton, A. M., Young, A. W., Bruce, V., Johnston, R, R. and Ellis, A. W. (1991). Understanding covert recognition. *Cognition*, 39(2), 129–166.

Butterworth, B. (1993). Aphasia and models of language prouction and perception. In Blanken, G., Dittmann, J., Grimm, H., Marshall, J. C., Wallesch, C-W. and de Gruyter, W. (eds) *Linguistic Disorders and Pathologies: An International Handbook*. Berlin: New York.

Byrne, R. M. J. (1989). Suppressing valid inferences with conditionals. *Cognition*, 31, 61–83.

Cahill, L., Babinsky, R., Markowitsch, H. J. and McGaugh, J. L. (1995). The amygdale and emotional memory. *Nature*, 377, 295–296.

Cahir, C. and Thomas, K. (2010). Asymmetric effects of positive and negative affect on decision making. *Psychological Reports*, 106, 193–204.

Camp, G., Pecher, D. and Schmidt, H. G. (2007). No retrieval-induced forgetting using item-specific independent cues: evidence against a general inhibitory account. *Journal of Experimental Psychology: Learning, Memory, and Cognition*, 33, 950–958.

Campbell, D. (1909). Störungen der Merkfähigkeit und fehlenders Krankheitsgefühl bei einem Fall von Stirnhirntumor. *Monatsschrift für Psychiatrie*, 26, 33–41.

Campbell, R. and Conway, M. A. (1995). *Broken Memories*. Oxford: Blackwell.

Campion, J., Latto, R. and Smith, Y. M. (1983). Is blindsight an effect of scattered light, spared cortex, and near-threshold vision? *Behavioural and Brain Sciences*, 6, 423–428.

Caplan, D., Rochon, E. and Waters, G. S. (1992). Articulatory and phonological determinants of word length effects in span tasks. *The Quarterly Journal of Experimental Psychology*, 45(2), 177–92.

Carpenter, S. (2001). Everyday fantasia: The world of synaesthesia. *Monitor on Psychology*, 32.

Carpenter, S. K. and Pashler, H. (2007). Testing beyond words: Using tests to enhance visuospatial map learning. *Psychonomic Bulletin and Review*, 14, 474–478.

Carpenter, S. K., Pashler, H., Wixted, J. T. and Vul, E. (2008). The effect of tests on learning and forgetting. *Memory and Cognition*, 36, 438–448.

Carroll, M., Campbell-Ratcliffe, J., Murnane, H. and Perfect, T. J. (2007). Retrieval-induced forgetting in educational contexts: Monitoring expertise, text integration and text format. *European Journal of Cognitive Psychology*, 19, 590–606.

Cavaco, S., Anderson, S. W., Allen, J. S., Castro-Caldas, A. and Damasio, H. (2004). The scope of preserved procedural memory in amnesia. *Brain*, 127, 1853–1867.

Cavenett, T. and Nixon, R. D. V. (2006). The effect of arousal on memory for emotionally-relevant information: A study of skydivers. *Behaviour Research and Therapy*, 44, 1461–1469.

Cermak, L. S. and O'Connor, M. (1983). The anterograde and retrograde retrieval ability of a patient with amnesia due to Encephalitis. *Neuropsychologia*, 21, 213–234.

Chalmers, D. J. (1995). The puzzle of conscious experience. *Scientific American*, 62–68.

Chang, W., Hwang, W. and Ji, Y. G. (2011). Haptic seat interfaces for driver information and warning systems. *International Journal of Human–Computer Interaction*, 27:12, 1119–1132.

Channon, S. and Baker, J. (1994). Reasoning strategies in depression: Effects of depressed mood on a syllogism task. *Personality and Individual Differences*, 17,707–711.

Chase, W. G. and Simon, H. A. (1973a). Perception in chess. *Cognitive Psychology*, 4, 55–81.

Chase, W. G. and Simon, H. A. (1973b). The mind's eye in chess. In W. G. Chase (ed.) *Visual Information Processing*. New York: Academic Press.

Chen, Z., Mo. L. and Honomichl, R. (2004). Having the memory of an elephant: Long-term retrieval and the use of analogues in problem solving. *Journal of Experimental Psychology: General*, 133, 415–433.

Cheng, P. W. and Holyoak, K. J. (1985). Pragmatic reasoning schemas. *Cognitive Psychology*, 17, 391–416.

Cheng, P. W., Holyoak, K. J., Nisbett, R. E. and Oliver, L. M. (1986). Pragmatic versus syntactic approaches to training deductive reasoning. *Cognitive Psychology*, 18, 293–328.

Cherry, E. C. (1953). Some experiments on the recognition of speech with one and two ears. *Journal of the Acoustical Society of America*, 25, 975–979.

Cherry, K. E., Park, D. C., Frieske, D. A. and Rowley, R. L. (1993). The effect of verbal

Elaborations on memory in young and older adults. *Memory and Cognition*, 21, 725–738.

Chi, M. T. H., Bassok, M., Lewis, M., Reimann, P. and Glaser, R. (1989). Self-explanations: How students study and use examples in learning to solve problems. *Cognitive Science*, 13, 145–182.

Chi, M. T. H., Feltovich, P. J. and Glaser, R. (1981). Categorization and representation of physics problems by experts and novices. *Cognitive Science*, 5, 121–152.

Chomsky, N. (1957). *Syntactic structures*. The Hague: Mouton.

Chronicle, E. P., MacGregor, J. N. and Ormerod, T. C. (2004). What makes an insight problem? The roles of heuristics, goal conception, and solution recording in knowledge-lean problems. *Journal of Experimental Psychology: Learning, Memory, and Cognition*, 30, 14–27.

Chu, S. and Downes, J. J. (2000). Long live Proust: The odour-cued autobiographical memory bump. *Cognition*, 75, 41–50.

Chun, M. M. and Potter, M. C. (2001). The attentional blink within and across the modalities. In K. Shapiro (ed.) *The Limits of Attention: Temporal Constraints in Human Information Processing* (pp. 20–30). Oxford: Oxford University Press.

Cicerone, K., Lazar, R. and Shapiro, W. (1983). Effects of frontal lobe lesions on hypothesis sampling during concept formation. *Neuropsychologia*, 21, 513–524.

Clancy, S. A. and McNally, R. J. (2005/06). Who needs repression? Normal memory processes can explain "forgetting" of childhood sexual abuse. *Scientific Review of Mental Health Practice*, 4, 66–73.

Claparede, E. (1911). Recognition et moiite. *Archives Psychologiques Geneve*, 11, 79–90.

Clare, L., Wilson, B. A., Breen, E. K. and Hodges, J. R. (1999). Errorless learning of face-name associations in early Alzheimer's disease. *Neurocase*, 5, 37–46.

Clare, L., Baddeley, A. D., Moniz-Cook, E. and Woods, R. (2003). A quiet revolution. *The Psychologist*, 16, 250–254.

Claret, P. L., Castillob, J. d. D. L. d., Moleónc, J. J. J., Cavanillasc, A. B., Martínc, M. G. and Vargasc, R. G. (2003). Age and sex differences in the risk of causing vehicle collisions in Spain, 1990 to 1999. *Accident Analysis and Prevention*, 35(2), 261–272.

Clark, L. A. and Watson, D. (1991). Tripartite model of anxiety and depression: Psychometric evidence and taxonomic implications. *Journal of Abnormal Psychology*, 100, 316–336.

Claxton, G. (1998). Knowing without knowing why. *The Psychologist*, 11, 217–220.

Cleary, A. M., Morris, A. L. and Langley, M. M. (2007). Recognition memory for novel stimuli: The structural regularity hypothesis. *Journal of Experimental Psychology: Learning, Memory, and Cognition*, 33, 379–393.

Cohen, G. (1983). *The Psychology of Cognition* (2nd edn). London: Academic Press.

Cohen, L., Jobert, A., Le Bihan, D. and Dehaene, S. (2004). Distinct unimodal and multimodal regions for word processing in the left temporal cortex. *Neuroimage*, 23(4), 1256–1270.

Cohen, N. J. and Squire, L. R. (1980). Preserved learning and retention of pattern-analysing skill in amnesia: Dissociation of knowing how and knowing that. *Science*, 210, 207–210.

Cohen, N. J. and Squire, L. R. (1981). Retrograde amnesia and remote memory impairment. *Neuropsychologia*, 19, 337–356.

Cohen, N. J. and Eichenbaum, H. E. (1993). *Memory, Amnesia, and the Hippocampal System*. Cambridge, MA: MIT Press.

Colchester, A., Kingsley, D., Lasserson, D., Kendell, B., Bello, F., Rush, C., Stevens, T., Goodman, G., Heilpern, G., Stanhope, N. and Kopelman, M. D. (2001). Structural MRI volumetric analysis in patients with organic amnesia, 1: Methods and findings, comparative findings across diagnostic groups. *Journal of Neurology, Neurosurgery, and Psychiatry*, 71, 13–22.

Cole, B. L. and Hughes, P. K. (1984). A field trial of attention and search conspicuity. *Human Factors*, 26(3), 299–313.

Coleman, M. D. (2010). Sunk cost, emotion, and commitment to education. *Current Psychology*, 29, 346–356.

Collette, F. and Van der Linden, M. (2002). Brain imaging of the central executive component of working memory. *Neuroscience and Biobehavioural Reviews*, 26, 105–125.

Collette, F., Van der Linden, M., Laureys, S., Delfiore, G., Degueldre, C., Luxen, A. and-Salmon, E. (2005). Exploring the unity and diversity of the neural substrates of executive functioning. *Human Brain Mapping*, 25, 409–423.

Coltheart, M. (1980). Deep dyslexia: A right-hemisphere hypothesis. In M. Coltheart. K. E. Patterson. and J. C. Marshall (eds) *Deep Dyslexia* (pp. 326–380). London: Routledge and Kegan Paul.

Coltheart, M. T., Davelaar, E., Jonsson, J. and Besner, D. (1977). Access to the internal lexicon. In S. Dornic (ed.) *Attention and Performance VI*. New York: Academic Press.

Coltheart, M., Patterson, K. E. and Marshall, J. C. (1987). Deep dyslexia since 1980. In M. Coltheart, K. E. Patterson and J. C. Marshall (eds) *Deep Dyslexia* (pp. 407–451). London: Routledge and Kegan Paul.

Coltheart, M., Rastle, K., Perry, C., Langdon, R. and Ziegler, J. (2001). DRC: A dual route cascaded model of visual word recognition and reading aloud. *Psychological Review*, 108(1), 204–256.

Conroy, M. A., Hopkins, R. O. and Squire, L. R. (2005). On the contribution of perceptual fluency and priming to recognition memory. *Cognitive, Affective, and Behavioural Neuroscience*, 5, 14–20.

Conway, R. A., Cowan, N. and Bunting, M. F. (2001). The cocktail party revisited: The importance of working memory capacity. *Psychonomic Buletin and Review*, 8, 331–335.

Corbett, F., Jefferies, E., Ehsan, S. and Lambon-Ralph, M. A. (2009). Different impairments of semantic cognition in semantic dementia and semantic aphasia: Evidence from the non-verbal domain. *Brain: A Journal of Neurology*, 132, 2593–2608.

Corbetta, M. and Schulman, G. L. (2002). Control of gaol-directed and stimulus-driven attention in the brain. *Nature Reviews Neuroscience*, 3, 201–215.

Corkin, S. (1968). Acquisition of motor skill after bilateral medial temporal-lobe excision. *Neuropsychologia*, 6, 255–265.

Corkin, S., Amaral, D. G., Gonzalez, R. G., Johnson, K. A. and Hyman, B. T. (1997). H. M.'s medial temporal lobe lesion: Findings from magnetic resonance imaging. *Journal of Neuroscience*, 17, 3964–3979.

Corsi, P. M. (1972). Human memory and the medial temporal region of the brain. Unpublished Thesis, cited in S. Della Sala, C. Gray, A. D. Baddeley, N. Allamano and N. Wilson (1999). Pattern span: A tool for unwelding visuo-spatial memory. *Neuropsychologia*, 37, 1189–1199.

Corteen, R. S. and Wood, B. (1972). Autonomous responses to shock associated words in an unattended channel. *Journal of Experimental Psychology*, 94, 308–313.

Corteen, R. S. and Dunn, D. (1974). Shock associated words in a non-attended message: A test for momentary awareness. *Journal of Experimental Psychology*, 102, 1143–1144.

Cosentino, S., Chute, D., Libon, D., Moore, P. and Grossman, M. (2006). How does the brain support script comprehension? A study of executive processes and semantic knowledge in dementia. *Neuropsychology*, 20, 307–318.

Cowan, N. (2005). *Working Memory Capacity*. New York: Psychology Press.

Cowan, N. (2010). The magical mystery four: How is working memory capacity limited, and why? *Current Directions in Psychological Science*, 19, 51–57.

Cowey, A. (2004). The 30th Sir Frederick Bartlett lecture: Fact, artefact, and myth about blindsight. *The Quarterly Journal of Experimental Psychology*, 57A, 577–609.

Cowey, A. and Azzopardi, P. (2001). Is blindsight motion blind? In B. de Gelder, E. de Haan and C. A. Heywood (eds) *Out of Mind* (pp. 87–103). Oxford: Oxford University Press.

Craik, F. I. M. (1970). The fate of items in primary memory. *Journal of Verbal Learning and Verbal Behaviour*, 9, 143–148.

Craik, F. I. M. (1977). Depth of processing in recall and recognition. In S. Dornik (ed.) *Attention and Performance* (Vol. 6, pp. 679–698). New York: Raven Press.

Craik, F. I. M. (2002). Levels of processing: Past, present ... and future? *Memory*, 10, 305–318.

Craik, F. I. M. (2007). Encoding: A cognitive perspective. In Roediger, H. L. III, Dudai, Y. and Fitzpatrick, S. M. (eds) *Science of Memory: Concepts* (pp. 129–135). New York: Oxford University Press.

Craik, F. I. M. and Lockhart, R. S. (1972). Levels of processing: A framework for memory research. *Journal of Verbal Learning and Verbal Behaviour*, 11, 671–684.

Craik, F. I. M. and Tulving, E. (1975). Depth of processing and the retention of words in episodic memory. *Journal of Experimental Psychology, General*, 104, 268–294.

Craik, F. I. M. and McDowd, J. M. (1987). Age differences in recall and recognition. *Journal of Experimental Psychology: Learning, Memory, and Cognition*, 13, 474–479.

Craik, F. I. M. and Bialystock, E. (2006). Planning and task management in older adult cooking breakfast. *Memory and Cognition*, 34, 1236–1249.

Craik, F. I. M., Morris, L. W., Morris, R. G. and Loewen, E. R. (1990). Relations between source amnesia and frontal functioning in older patients. *Psychology of Ageing*, 5, 148–151.

Creem, S. H. and Proffitt, D. R. (1998). Two memories for geographical slant: separation and interdependence of action and awareness. *Psychonomic Bulletin and Review*, 5(1), 22–36.

Crick, F. (1994). *The Astonishing Hypothesis*. London: Simon & Schuster.

Crick, F. and Koch, C. (1990). Towards a neurobiological theory of consciousness. *Seminars in the Neurosciences*, 2, 263–275.

Crinella, F. M. and Yu, J. (2000). Brain mechanisms and intelligence. Psychometric *g* and executive function. *Intelligence*, 27, 299–327.

Cutler, A. (1981). Making up materials is a confounded nuisance, or: Will we able to run any psycholinguistic experiments at all in 1990? *Cognition*, 10, 65–70.

Dallenbach, K. M. (1951). A puzzle-picture with a new principle of concealment. *American Journal of Psychology*, 64, 431–433.

Damasio, A. R., Damasio, H. and VanHosen, G. W. (1982). Prosopagnosia: Anatomic basis and behavioural mechanisms. *Neurology*, 32, 321–341.

Dando, C. J., Wilcock, R. and Milne, R. (2009). The cognitive interview: The efficiency of a modified mental reinstatement of context procedure for frontline police investigators. *Applied Cognitive Psychology*, 23, 138–147.

Davidson, P. S. R. and Glisky, E. L. (2002). Is flashbulb memory a special instance of source memory? Evidence from older adults. *Memory*, 10, 99–111.

Davies, S. P. (2000). Move evaluation as a predictor and moderator of success in solutions to well-structured problems. *The Quarterly Journal of Experimental Psychology*, 53A, 1186–1201.

Davis, D. and Loftus, E. L. (2005). Age and functioning in the legal system: Perception memory and judgement in victims, witnesses and jurors. In I. Noy and W. Karwowski (eds) *Handbook of Forensic Human Factors and Ergonomics*. London: Taylor & Francis.

Davis, D. and Loftus, E. L. (2007). Internal and external sources of misinformation in adult witness memory. In M. P. Toglia, J. D. Read, D. F. Ross and R. C. L. Lindsay (eds) *Handbook of Eyewitness Psychology*, Vol. 1 (pp. 195–237). Mahwah, NJ: Erlbaum.

Davis, M. H., Marslen-Wilson, W. D. and Gaskell, M. G. (2002). Leading up the lexical garden-path: Segmentation and ambiguity in spoken word recognition. *Journal of Experimental Psychology: Human Perception and Performance*, 28(1), 218–244.

Day, R. H. (1989). Natural and artificial cues, perceptual compromise and the basis of veridical and illusory perception. In D. Vickers and P. L. Smith (eds) *Human Information Processing: Measures and Mechanisms* (pp. 107–109). Amsterdam: Elsevier.

De Fockert, J. W., Rees, G., Frith, C. D. and Lavie, N. (2001). The role of working memory in selective attention. *Science*, 291(5509), 1803–1806.

De Graaf, T. A., Hsieh, P-J. and Sack, A. T. (2012). The "correlates" in neural correlates of consciousness. *Neuroscience and Biobehavioural Reviews*, 36, 191–197.

De Groot, A. D. (1965). *Thought and Choice in Chess*. The Hague: Mouton.

De Haan, E. H. F. and Campbell, R. (1991). A fifteen year follow-up of a case of developmental prosopagnosia. *Cortex*, 27, 489–509.

De Haan, E. H. F. and Cowey, A. (2011). On the usefulness of 'what' and 'where' pathways in vision. *Trends in Cognitive Sciences*, 15(10), 460–466.

De Haan, E. H. F., Young, A. W. and Newcombe, F. (1987). Face recognition without awareness. *Cognitive Neuropsychology*, 4, 385–415.

De Haan, E. H. F., Bauer, R. M. and Greve, K. W. (1992). Behavioural and physiological evidence for covert face recognition in a prosopagnosic patient. *Cortex*, 28(1), 77–95.

De Martino, B., Camerer, C. F. and Adolphs, R. (2010). Amygdala damage eliminates monetary loss aversion. *Proceedings of the National Academy of Sciences*, 107, 3788–3792.

De Monte, V. E., Geffen, G. M. and Kwapil, K. (2005). Test-retest reliability and practice effects of a rapid screen test of mild traumatic brain injury. *Journal of Clinical and Experimental Neuropsychology*, 27, 624–632.

De Neys, W. (2006). Automatic-heuristic and executive-analytic processing during reasoning: Chronometric and dual-task considerations. *Quarterly Journal of Experimental Psychology*, 59, 1070–1100.

De Renzi, E. and di Pellegrino, G. (1998). Prosopagnosia and alexia without object agnosia. *Cortex*, 34(3), 403–415.

De Renzi, E., Gentilini, M. and Barbieri, C. (1989). Auditory neglect. *Journal of Neurology, Neurosurgery and Psychiatry*, 52, 613–617.

De Renzi, E., Faglioni, P., Grossi, D. and Nichelli, P. (1991). Apperceptive and associative forms of prosopagnosia. *Cortex*, 27, 213–221.

De Renzi, E., Perani, D., Carlesimo, G. A., Silveri, M. C. and Fazio, F. (1994). Prosopagnosia can be associated with damage to the right

hemisphere – an MRI and PET study and a review of the literature. *Neuropsychologia*, 32(8), 893–902.

De Ruiter, J. P., Mitterer, H. and Enfield, N. J. (2006). Predicting the end of a speaker's turn; a cognitive cornerstone of conversation. *Language*, 82(3), 515–535.

De Vries, M., Holland, R. W. and Witteman, C. L. M. (2008). Fitting decisions: Mood and intuition vs. deliberative decision strategies. *Cognition and Emotion*, 22, 931–943.

De Zeeuw, C. I. (2007). Plasticity: A pragmatic compromise. In H. L. Roediger III, Y. Dudai and S. M. Fitzpatrick (eds) *Science of Memory: Concepts* (pp. 83–86). New York: Oxford University Press.

Dehane, S. and Naccache, L. (2001). Towards a cognitive neuroscience of consciousness: Basic evidence and a workplace framework. *Cognition*, 79, 1–37.

Delaney, P., Nghiem, K. and Waldum, E. (2009). The selective directed forgetting effect: Can people forget only part of a text? *Quarterly Journal of Experimental Psychology*, 62, 1542–1550.

Delis, D. C., Squire, L. R., Bihrle, A. and Massman, P. (1992). Componential analysis of problem-solving ability: Performance of patients with frontal lobe damage and amnesic patients on a new sorting test. *Neuropsychologia*, 30, 683–697.

Dell, G. S. (1986). A spreading-activation theory of retrieval in sentence production. *Psychological Review*, 93, 283–321.

Dell, G. S. and O'Seaghdha, P. G. (1991). Mediated and convergent lexical priming in language production: A comment on Levelt *et al.* (1991). *Psychological Review*, 98, 604–614.

Dell, G. S., Schwartz, M. F., Martin, N., Saffran, E. M. and Gagnon, D. A. (1997). Lexical access in aphasic and nonaphasic speakers. *Psychological Review*, 104(4), 801–838.

Della Sala, S., Gray, C., Spinnler and Trivelli, C. (1998). Frontal lobe functioning in man. *Archives of Clinical Neuropsychology*, 13, 663–682.

Deloche, G., Andreewsky, E. and Desi, M. (1982). Surface dyslexia: A case report and some theoretical implications to reading models. *Brain and Language*, 15(1), 12–31.

Derakshan, N. and Eysenck, M. W. (1998). Working-memory capacity in high trait-anxious and repressor groups. *Cognition and Emotion*, 12, 697–713.

Desimone, R. and Duncan, J. (1995). Neural mechanisms of selective visual attention. *Annual Review of Neuroscience*, 18, 193–222.

Deutsch, D. (2003). *Phantom Worlds and Other Curiosities*, Audio CD. Philomel Records.

Deutsch, J. A. and Deutsch, D. (1963). Attention, some theoretical considerations. *Psychological Review*, 70, 80–90.

Di Lollo, V., Enns, J. T. and Rensink, R. A. (2000). Competition for consciousness among visual events: The psychophysics of reentrant visual processes. *Journal of Experimental Psychology: General*, 129(4), 481–507.

Dixon, M. J., Smilek, D., Cudahy, C. and Merikle, P. M. (2000). Five plus two equals yellow. *Nature*, 406, 365–365.

Dixon, M. J., Smilek, D. and Merikle, P. M. (2004). Not all synaesthetes are created equal: Projector versus associator synaesthetes. *Cognitive, Affective and Behavioral Neuroscience*, 4(3), 335–343.

Dobler, V. B., Manly, T., Verity, C., Woolrych, J. and Robertson, I. H. (2003). Modulation of spatial attention in a child with developmental unilateral neglect. *Developmental Medicine and Child Neurology*, 45(4), 282–288.

Dobler, V. B., Anker, S., Gilmore, J., Robertson, I. H., Atkinson, J. and Manly, T. (2005). Asymmetric deterioration of spatial awareness with diminishing levels of alertness in normal children and children with ADHD. *Journal of Child Psychology and Psychiatry*, 46(11), 1230–1248.

Dodds, C. M., van Belle, J., Peers, P. V., Duncan, J., Cusack, R. and Manly, T. (2008). Rightward shift in spatial awareness with time-on-task and increased cognitive load. *Neuropsychology*, 43, 1721–1728.

Dodson, C. S. and Krueger, L. E. (2006). I misremember it well: Why older adults are unreliable witnesses. *Psychonomic Bulletin and Revue*, 13, 770–775.

Drace, S., Desrichard, O., Shepperd, J. A. and Hoorens, V. (2009). Does mood really influence comparative optimism? Tracing an elusive effect. *British Journal of Social Psychology*, 48, 579–599.

Driver, J. (2001). A selective review of selective attention from the past century. *British Journal of Psychology*, 92, 53–78.

Driver, J. and Halligan, P. W. (1991). Can visual neglect operate in object-centred co-ordinates? An affirmative single-case study. *Cognitive Neuropsychology*, 8, 475–496.

Driver, J. and Spence, C. J. (1994). Spatial synergies between auditory and visual attention. In C. Umilta and M. Moscovitch (eds) *Attention and Performance XV, Conscious and Nonconscious Information Processing*. Cambridge, MA: MIT Press.

Driver, J. and Spence, C. J. (1998). Cross-modal links in spatial attention. *Philosophical Transactions of the Royal Society of London. Series B, Biological Sciences*, 353(1373), 1319–1331.

Driver, J. and Spence, C. J. (1999). Cross-modal links in spatial attention. In G. W. Humphreys, J. Duncan and A. Treisman (eds) *Attention, Space and Action*. Oxford: Oxford University Press.

Driver, J., Davis, G., Ricciardelli, P., Kidd, P., Maxwell, E. and Baron-Cohen, S. (1999). Gaze perception triggers visuo-spatial orienting. *Visual Cognition*, 6(5), 509–540.

Dronkers, N. F. (1996). A new brain region for coordinating speech articulation. *Nature*, 14, 384(6605), 159–61.

Drosopoulos, S., Wagner, U. and Born, J. (2005). Sleep enhances explicit recollection in recognition memory. *Learning and Memory*, 12, 44–51.

Duchaine, B. (2000). Developmental prosopagnosia with normal configural processing. *Neuroreport*, 11, 79–83.

Duchaine, B. and Garrido, L. (2008). We're getting warmer – characterizing the mechanisms of face recognition with acquired prosopagnosia: A comment on Riddoch *et al.* (2008). *Cognitive Neuropsychology*, 25(5), 765–8. doi:10.1080/02643290802092102.

Duchaine, B., Yovel, G., Butterworth, E. J. and Nakayama, K. (2006). Prosopagnosia as an impairment to face-specific mechanisms: Elimination of the alternative hypotheses in a developmental case. *Cognitive Neuropsychology*, 23(5), 714–47. doi:10.1080/02643290500441296.

Duffy, P. L. (2002). *Blue Cats and Chartreuse Kittens: How Synesthetes Color Their Worlds*. New York: Henry Holt.

Dumay, N., Frauenfelder, U. H. and Content, A. (2002). The role of the syllable in lexical segmentation in French: Word-spotting data. *Brain and Language*, 81, 144–161.

Dunbar, R. I. M., Duncan, N. and Nettle, D. (1995). Size and structure of freely forming conversational groups. *Human Nature*, 6(1), 67–78.

Dunbar, R. I. M., Duncan, N. D. C. and Marriott, A. (1997). Human conversational behaviour. *Human Nature*, 8, 231–246.

Duncan, J. (2006). EPS mid-career award (2004). Brain mechanisms of attention. *Quarterly Journal of Experimental Psychology*, 59, 2–27.

Duncan, J. and Humphreys, G. W. (1989). Visual search and visual similarity. *Psychological Review*, 96, 433–458.

Duncan, J. and Humphreys, G. W. (1992). Beyond the search surface: Visual search and attentional engagement. *Journal of Experimental Psychology: Human Perception and Performance*, 18, 578–588.

Duncan, J., Emslie, H. and Williams, P. (1996). Intelligence and the frontal lobe: The organization of goal-directed behavior. *Cognitive Psychology*, 30, 257–303.

Duncker, K. (1945). On problem solving. *Psychological Monographs*, 58 (Whole No. 270).

Dupoux, E., Kakehi, K., Hirose, Y., Pallier, C. and Mehler, J. (1999). Epenthetic vowels in Japanese: A perceptual illusion? *Journal of Experimental Psychology – Human Perception and Performance*, 25(6), 1568–1578.

Durie, B. (2005). Doors of perception. *New Scientist*, 185(2484), 34–36.

Easterbrook, J. A. (1959). The effect of emotion on cue utilisation and the organisation of behaviour. *Psychological Review*, 66, 183–201.

Ebbinghaus, H. (1885). *Uber das Gedachtnis: Untersuchugen zur Experimentellen Psychologie*. Leipzig: Dunker and Humbolt.

Edgar, G. K., Edgar, H. E. and Curry, M. B. (2003). *Using Signal Detection Theory to Measure Situation Awareness in Command and Control*. Paper presented at the Human Factors and Ergonomics Society 47th Annual Meeting, Denver, Colorado.

Edquist, J., Rich, A. N., Brinkman, C. and Mattingley, J. B. (2006). Do synaesthetic colours act as unique features in visual search? *Cortex*, 42(2), 222–231.

Edworthy, J., Hellier, E. J., Walters, K., Clift-Matthews, W. and Crowther, M. (2003). Acoustic, semantic and phonetic influences in spoken warning signal words. *Applied Cognitive Psychology*, 17, 915–933.

Egeth, H. E. and Yantis, S. (1997). Visual attention: control, representation, and time course. *Annual Review of Psychology*, 48, 269–297.

Eich, E. (1995). Searching for mood-dependent memory. *Psychological Science*, 6, 67–75.

Eichenbaum, H. (2004). Hippocampus: Cognitive processes and neural representations that underlie declarative memory. *Neuron*, 44, 109–120.

Eichenbaum, H., Yonelinas, A. P. and Ranganath, C. (2007). The medial temporal lobe and recognition memory. *Annual Review of Neuroscience*, 30, 123–152.

Eisner, F. and McQueen, J. M. (2005). The specificity of perceptual learning in speech processing. *Perception and Psychophysics*, 67(2), 224–238.

Eisner, F. and McQueen, J. M. (2006). Perceptual learning in speech: Stability over time (L). *Journal of the Acoustical Society of America*, 119(4), 1950–1953.

Ellis, A. W. and Young, A. W. (1996). *Human Cognitive Neuropsychology: A Textbook With Readings*. Psychology Press.

Endler, J. A., Endler, L. C. and Doerr, N. R. (2010). Great bowerbirds create theaters with forced perspective when seen by their audience. *Current Biology*, 20(18), 1679–1684.

Enns, J. T. and Di_Lollo, V. (2000). What's new in visual masking? *Trends in Cognitive Sciences*, 4(9), 345–352.

Eriksen, B. A. and Eriksen, C. W. (1974). Effects of noise letters upon the identification of a target in a non-search task. *Perception and Psychophysics*, 16, 143–149.

Eriksen, C. W. and St. James, J. D. (1986). Visual attention within and around the field of focal attention: A zoom lens model. *Perception and Psychophysics*, 40, 225–240.

Esgate, A. and Groome, D. H. (2005). *An Introduction to Applied Cognitive Psychology*. Hove: Psychology Press.

Eskes, G. A., Szostak, C. and Stuss, D. T. (2003). Role of the frontal lobes in implicit and explicit retrieval tasks. *Cortex*, 39, 847–869.

Eslinger, P. J. and Damasio, A. R. (1985). Severe disturbance of higher cognition after bilateral frontal lobe ablation: Patient E. V. R. *Neurology, Cleveland*, 35, 1731–1741.

Evans, J. St. B. T. (1989). *Bias in Human Reasoning: Causes and Consequences*. Hove: Erlbaum.

Evans, J. St. B. T. (2003). In two minds: dual process accounts of reasoning. *Trends in Cognitive Sciences*, 7, 454–459.

Evans, J. St. B. T. (2009). How many dual-process theories do we need: One, two or many? In J. St. B. T. and K. Frankish (eds) *In Two Minds: Dual Processes and Beyond* (pp. 31–54). Oxford: Oxford University Press.

Evans, J. St. B. T. (2011). Dual-process theories of reasoning: Contemporary issues and developmental applications. *Developmental Review*, 31, 86–102.

Evans, J. St. B. T. and Lynch, J. S. (1973). Matching bias in the selection task. *British Journal of Psychology*, 64, 391–397.

Evans, J. St. B. T. and Over, D. E. (1996). *Rationality and Reasoning*. Hove: Psychology Press.

Evans, J. St. B. T. and Over, D. E. (2004). *If.* Oxford: Oxford University Press.

Evans, J. St. B. T. and Ball, L. J. (2010). Do people reason on the Wason selection task? A new look at the data of Ball *et al.* (2003). *The Quarterly Journal of Experimental Psychology*, 63, 434–441.

Evans, J. St. B. T., Barston, J. L. and Pollard, P. (1983). On the conflict between logic and belief in syllogistic reasoning. *Memory and Cognition*, 11, 295–306.

Evans, J. St. B. T., Handley, S. J. and Over, D. E. (2003). Conditionals and conditional probability. *Journal of Experimental Psychology: Learning, Memory, and Cognition*, 29, 321–335.

Evans, S., Kyong, J. S., Rosen, S., Golestani, N., Warren, J. E., McGettigan, C., Mourão-Miranda, J., Wise, R. J. and Scott, S. K. (2013). The Pathways for Intelligible Speech: Multivariate and Univariate Perspectives. *Cerebral Cortex* (12 April).

Eysenck, M. W. (1979). Depth, elaboration, and distinctiveness. In L. S. Cermak and F. I. M. Craik (eds) *Levels of Processing in Human Memory*. Hillsdale, NJ: Lawrence Erlbaum Associates.

Eysenck, M. W. (1992). *Anxiety: The Cognitive Perspective*. Hove: Psychology Press.

Eysenck, M. W. (1997). *Anxiety and Cognition: A Unified Theory*. Hove: Psychology Press.

Eysenck, M. W. (2012). *Fundamentals of Cognition* (2nd edn). Hove: Psychology Press.

Eysenck, M. W. and Calvo, M. G. (1992). Anxiety and performance: The processing efficiency theory. *Cognition and Emotion*, 6, 409–434.

Eysenck, M. W. and Keane, M. T. (2005). *Cognitive Psychology: A Student's Handbook*. Hove: Psychology Press.

Eysenck, M. W. and Keane, M. T. (2010). *Cognitive Psychology: A Student's Handbook* (6th edn). Hove: Psychology Press.

Eysenck, M. W., Payne, S. and Santos, R. (2006). Anxiety and depression: Past, present, and future events. *Cognition and Emotion*, 20, 274–294.

Eysenck, M. W., Derakshan, N., Santos, R. and Calvo, M. G. (2007). Anxiety and cognitive performance: Attentional control theory. *Emotion*, 7, 336–353.

Farah, M. J. (2004). *Visual Agnosia* (2nd edn). Cambridge, MA: MIT Press.

Farah, M. J. and McClelland, J. L. (1991). A computational model of semantic memory impairment: Modality-specificity and emergent category-specificity. *Journal of Experimental Psychology: General*, 120, 339–357.

Farah, M. J., Hammond, K. M., Levind, D. N. and Calvanio, R. (1988). Visual and spatial mental imagery: Dissociable systems of representation. *Cognitive Psychology*, 20, 439–462.

Farah, M. J., Hammond, K. M., Mehta, Z. and Ratcliff, G. (1989). Category-specificity and modality-specificity in semantic memory. *Neuropsychologia*, 27, 193–200.

Farah, M. J., McMullen, P. A. and Meyer, M. M. (1991). Can recognition of living things be selectively impaired? *Neuropsychologia*, 29, 185–193.

Farah, M. J., Levinson, K. L. and Klein, K. L. (1995). Face perception and within-category discrimination in prosopagnosia. *Neuropsychologia*, 33, 661–674.

Feinberg, T., Gonzalez-Rothi, L. J. and Heilman, K. M. (1986). Multimodal agnosia from a unilateral left hemisphere lesion. *Neurology*, 36, 864–867.

Felleman, D. J. and Van Essen, D. C. (1991). Distributed hierarchical processing in primate visual cortex. *Cerebral Cortex*, 1, 1–47.

Ferrier, D. (1876). *The Functions of the Brain*. London: Smith, Elder.

Fiedler, K., Nickel, S., Muehifriedel, T. and Unkelbach, C. (2001). Is mood congruity an effect of genuine memory or response bias? *Journal of Experimental Social Psychology*, 37, 201–214.

Fillmore, C. J. (1968). The case for case. In E. Bach and R. T. Harms (eds) *Universals in Linguistic Theory* (pp. 1–88). New York: Holt, Rinehart, and Winston.

Fimm, B., Willmes, K. and Spijkers, W. (2006). The effect of low arousal on visuo-spatial attention. *Neuropsychologia*, 44(8), 1261–1268.

Finn, B. and Roediger, H. L. III. (2011). Enhancing retention through reconsolidation: Negative emotional arousal flowing retrieval enhances later recall. *Psychological Science*, 22, 781–786.

Fisher, R. P. and Craik, F. I. M. (1977). Interaction between encoding and retrieval operations in cued recall. *Journal of Experimental Psychology: Human Learning and Memory*, 3, 701–711.

Fisher, R. P., Geiselman, R. E. and Amador, M. (1990). A field test of the cognitive interview: Enhancing the recollections of actual victims and witnesses of crime. *Journal of Applied Psychology*, 74, 722–727.

Fisher, R. P., Milne, R. and Bull, R. (2011). Interviewing cooperative witnesses. *Current Directions in Psychological Science*, 2016–19.

Fitch, G. M., Hankey, J. M., Kleiner, B. M. and Dingus, T. A. (2011). Driver comprehension of multiple haptic seat alerts intended for use in an integrated collision avoidance system. *Transportation Research Part F*, 14, 278–290.

Fitts, P. M. and Posner, M. I. (1973). *Human Performance*. Basic Concepts in Psychology series. London: Prentice Hall.

Fleischman, D. A., Wilson, R. S., Gabrieli, J. D. E., Bienias, J. L. and Bennett, D. A. (2004). A longitudinal study of implicit and explicit memory loss in old persons. *Psychology and Ageing*, 19, 617–625.

Flin, R., Boon, J., Knox, A. and Bull, R. (1992). The effect of a five-month delay on children's and adult's eyewitness memory. *British Journal of Psychology*, 83, 323–336.

Fodor, J. A. (1983). *Modularity of Mind*. Cambridge, MA: MIT Press.

Fornazzari, L., Fischer, C. E., Ringer, L. and Schweizer, T. A. (2011). 'Blue is music to my ears': Multimodal synesthesias after a thalamic stroke. *Neurocase*, 18(4), 318–322.

Forster, S. and Lavie, N. (2007). High perceptual load makes everybody equal: Eliminating individual differences in distractibility with load. *Journal of Experimental Psychology: Applied*, 14, 73–83.

Franz, V. H., Gegenfurtner, K. R., Bülthoff, H. H. and Fahle, M. (2000). Grasping visual illusions: No evidence for a dissociation between perception and action. *Psychological Science*, 11, 20–25.

Frassinetti, F., Angeli, V., Meneghello, F., Avanzi, S. and Ladavas, E. (2002). Long-lasting amelioration of visuospatial neglect by prism adaptation. *Brain*, 125, 608–623.

Frazier, L. (1979). *On Comprehending Sentences: Syntactic Parsing Strategies*. Bloomington: Indiana University Linguistics Club.

Freund, C. S. (1889). Uber optische Aophasie und Seelenblindheit. *Archiv für Psychiatrie und Nervenkrankheiten*, 20, 276–297.

Frijda, N. (1986). *The Emotions*. Cambridge: Cambridge University Press.

Friederici, A. D., Rüschemeyer, S. A., Hahne, A. and Fiebach, C. J. (2003). The role of left inferior frontal and superior temporal cortex in sentence comprehension: Localizing syntactic and semantic processes. *Cerebral Cortex,* 13(2), 170–177.

Friedman, N. P., Miyake, A., Corley, R. P., Young, S. E., DeFries, J. C. and Hewitt, J. K. (2006). Not all executive functions are related to intelligence. *Psychological Science,* 17, 172–179.

Friedman, N. P., Miyake, A., Young, S. E., DeFries, J. C., Corley, R. P. and Hewitt, J. K. (2008). Individual differences in executive functions are almost entirely genetic in origin. *Journal of Experimental Psychology: General*, 137, 201–225.

Friesen, C. K. and Kingstone, A. (1998). The eyes have it! Reflexive orienting is triggered by non-predictive gaze. *Psychonomic Bulletin and Review*, 5, 331–342.

Fromkin, V. (1971). The non-anomalous nature of anomalous utterances. *Language*, 47(1), 27–52.

Fromkin, V. (1973). *Speech Errors as Linguistic Evidence*. The Hague: Mouton.

Fukuda, K., Vogel, E., Mayr, U. and Awh, E. (2010). Quantity, not quality: The relationship between fluid intelligence and working memory capacity. *Psychonomic Bulletin and Review*, 17, 673–679.

Funnell, E. and Sheridan, J. (1992). Categories of knowledge? Unfamiliar aspects of living and nonliving things. *Cognitive Neuropsychology*, 9, 135–153.

Gabbert, F., Hope, L. and Fisher, R. P. (2009). Protecting eyewitness evidence: Examining the efficacy of a self-administered interview tool. *Law and Human Behaviour*, 33, 298–307.

Gable, P. and Harmon-Jones, E. (2010). The blues broaden but the nasty narrows: Attentional consequences of negative affects low and high in motivational intensity. *Psychological Science*, 21, 211–215.

Gabrieli, J. D. E., Cohen, N. J. and Corkin, S. (1988). The acquisition of lexical and semantic knowledge in amnesia. *Society for Neuroscience Abstracts*, 9, 328.

Gaffan, D., Parker, E. and Easton, A. (2001). Dense amnesia in the monkey after transaction of the fornix, amygdala and anterior stem. *Neuropsychologia*, 39, 51–70.

Gainotti, G., Barbier, A. and Marra, C. (2003). Slowly progressive defect in recognition of familiar people in a patient with right anterior temporal atrophy. *Brain*, 126, 792–803.

Gaissert, N. and Wallraven, C. (2012). Categorizing natural objects: A comparison of the visual and the haptic modalities. *Experimental Brain Research*, 216, 123–134.

Gale, M. and Ball, L. J. (2009). Exploring the determinants of dual goal facilitation in a rule discovery task. *Thinking and Reasoning*, 15, 294–315.

Galetta, K. M., Barrett, J., Allen, M. *et al.* (2011). The King-Devick test as a determinant of head trauma and concussion in boxers and MMA fighters. *Neurology*, 76, 1456–1462.

Galfano, G., Dalmaso, M., Marzoli, D., Pavan, G., Coricelli, C. and Castelli, L. (2012). Eye gaze cannot be ignored (but neither can arrows). *The Quarterly Journal of Experimental Psychology*, 65 (10), 1895–1910.

Gallace, A. and Spence, C. (2005). Examining the crossmodal consequences of viewing the Muller-Lyer illusion. *Experimental Brain Research*, 162, 4, 490–496.

Galton, F. (1883). *Inquiries Into Human Faculty and Its Development*. London: Macmillan.

Gardiner, J. M. (2002). Episodic memory and autonoetic consciousness: A first person approach. In A. Baddeley, M. Conway and J. Aggleton (eds) *Episodic Memory: New Directions in Research*. Oxford: Oxford University Press.

Gardiner, J. M. and Parkin, A. J. (1990). Attention and recollective experience in recognition. *Memory and Cognition*, 18, 579–583.

Gardiner, J. M. and Java, R. I. (1993). Recognising and remembering. In R. F. Collins, S. E. Gathercole, M. A. Conway and P. E. Morris (eds) *Theories of Memory*. Hove: Lawrence Erlbaum Associates.

Gardiner, J. M., Brandt, K. R., Baddeley, A. D. Vargha-Khadem, F. and Mishkin, M. (2008). Charting the acquisition of semantic knowledge in a case of developmental amnesia. *Neuropsychologia*, 46, 2865–2868.

Gardner, M. B. and Gardner, R. S. (1973). Problem of localization in the median plane: Effect of pinnae cavity. *Journal of the Acoustical Society of America*, 53, 400–408.

Garrett, M. (1975). The analysis of sentence production. In G. H. Bower (ed.) *The Psychology of Learning and Motivation* (Vol. 9, pp. 133–177). New York: Academic Press.

Garrett, M. (1988). Processes in language production. In F. Newmeyer (ed.) *Linguistics: The Cambridge Survey III. Language: Psychological and Biological Aspects*. Cambridge: Cambridge University Press.

Garrido, L., Eisner, F., McGettigan, C., Stewart, L., Sauter, S., Hanley, J. R., Schweinberger, S. R., Warren, J. D. and Duchaine, B. C. (2009). Developmental phonagnosia: A selective deficit of vocal identity recognition. *Neuropsychologia*, 47(1), 123–131.

Garrod, S. and Pickering, M. J. (2004). Why is conversation so easy? *Trends in Cognitive Sciences*, 8, 8–11.

Gathercole, S. E. and Baddeley, A. D. (1989). Development of vocabulary in children and short-term phonological memory. *Journal of Memory and Language*, 28, 200–213.

Gathercole, S. E. and Baddeley, A. D. (1990). Phonological memory deficits in language disordered children: Is there a causal connection? *Journal of Memory and Language*, 29, 336–360.

Gathercole, S. E., Service, E., Hitch, G., Adams, A. M. and Martin, A. J. (1999). Phonological short-term memory and vocabulary development: Further evidence on the nature of the relationship. *Applied Cognitive Psychology*, 13, 65–77.

Gazzaniga, M. S., Ivry, R. B. and Mangun, G. R. (2009). *Cognitive Neuroscience: The Biology of the Mind* (2nd edn). New York: W. W. Norton.

Geiselman, R. E. (1999). Commentary on recent research with the cognitive interview. *Psychology, Crime, and Law*, 5, 197–202.

Geiselman, R. E. and Fisher, R. P. (1997). Ten years of cognitive interviewing. In D. G. Payne and F. G. Conrad (eds) *Intersections in Basic Memory Research*. Mahwah, NJ: Erlbaum.

Geiselman, R. E., Bjork, R. A. and Fishman, D. L. (1983). Disrupted retrieval in directed forgetting: A link with posthypnotic amnesia. *Journal of Experimental Psychology: General*, 112, 58–72.

Geiselman, R. E., Fisher, R. P., MacKinnon, D. P. and Holland, H. L. (1985). Eyewitness memory enhancement in police interview: Cognitive retrieval mnemonics versus hypnosis. *Journal of Applied Psychology*, 70, 401–412.

Gentner, D. and Gentner, D. R. (1983). Flowing waters and teeming crowds: Mental models of electricity. In D. Genter and A. L. Stevens (eds) *Mental Models*. Hillsdale, NJ: Lawrence Erlbaum Associates.

Gentner, D., Loewenstein, J. and Thompson, L. (2003). Learning and transfer: A general role for analogical encoding. *Journal of Educational Psychology*, 95, 393–408.

George, M., Dobler, V., Nicholls, E. and Manly, T. (2005). Spatial awareness, alertness, and ADHD: the re-emergence of unilateral neglect with time-on-task. *Brain and Cognition*, 57(3), 264–275.

George, M. S., Mercer, J. S., Walker, R. and Manly, T. (2008). A demonstration of endogenous modulation of unilateral spatial neglect: The impact of apparent time-pressure on spatial bias. *Journal of the International Neuropsychological Society*, 14(1), 33–41.

Geraerts, E. (2012). Cognitive underpinnings of recovered memories of childhood abuse. *Nebraska Symposium on Motivation*, 58, 175–191.

Geraerts, E., Schooler, J. W., Merckelbach, H., Jelicic, M., Hauer, B. J. and Ambadar, Z. (2007). The reality of recovered memories: Corroborating continuous and discontinuous memories of childhood sexual abuse. *Psychological Science*, 18, 564–568.

Gernsbacher, M. A. (1984). Resolving 20 years of inconsistent interactions between lexical familiarity and orthography, concreteness and polysemy. *Journal of Experimental Psychology: General*, 113, 256–281.

Geschwind, N., Quadfasel, F. A. and Segarra, J. M. (1968). Isolation of the speech area. *Neuropsychologia*, 6, 327–340.

Gibson, J. J. (1950). *The Perception of the Visual World*. Boston, MA: Houghton Mifflin.

Gibson, J. J. (1966). *The Senses Considered as Perceptual Systems*. Boston, MA: Houghton Mifflin.

Gibson, J. J. (1979). *The Ecological Approach to Visual Perception*. Hillsdale, NJ: Lawrence Erlbaum Associates.

Gick, M. L. and Holyoak, K. J. (1980). Analogical problem solving. *Cognitive Psychology*, 12, 306–355.

Gick, M. L. and Holyoak, K. J. (1983). Schema induction and analogical transfer. *Cognitive Psychology*, 15, 1–38.

Gilhooly, K. J. (1996). *Thinking: Directed, Undirected and Creative* (3rd edn). London: Academic Press.

Gilhooly, K. J., Phillips, L. H., Wynn, V., Logie, R. H. and Della Sala, S. (1999). Planning processes and age in the 5 disk Tower of London task. *Thinking and Reasoning*, 5, 339–361.

Glanzer, M. and Cunitz, A. R. (1966). Two storage mechanisms in free recall. *Journal of Verbal Learning and Verbal Behaviour*, 5, 351–360.

Glenberg, A. M., Smith, S. M. and Green, C. (1977). Type 1 rehearsal: Maintenance and more. *Journal of Verbal Learning and Verbal Behaviour*, 16, 339–352.

Glisky, E. L., Schacter, D. L. and Tulving, E. (1986). Computer learning by memory-impaired patients: Acquisition and retention of complex knowledge. *Neuropsychologia*, 24, 313–328.

Gloning, I., Gloning, K., Hoff, H. (1963). Aphasia: A clinical syndrome. In L. Halpern (ed.) *Problems of Dynamic Neurology* (pp. 63–70). Jerusalem: Hebrew University.

Gluck, J. and Bluck, S. (2007). Looking back over the life span: A life story account of the reminiscence bump. *Memory and Cognition*, 35, 1928–1939.

Godden, D. R. and Baddeley, A. D. (1975). Context-dependent memory in two natural environments: On land and under water. *British Journal of Psychology*, 66, 325–331.

Godden, D. R. and Baddeley, A. D. (1980). When does context influence recognition memory? *British Journal of Psychology*, 71, 99–104.

Goel, V. and Grafman, J. (1995). Are the frontal lobes implicated in "planning" functions? Interpreting data from the Tower of Hanoi. *Neuropsychologia*, 33, 623–642.

Gold, J. M., Hahn, B., Zhang, W. W., Robinson, B. M., Kappenman, E. S., Beck, V. M. and Luck, S. J. (2010). Reduced capacity but spared precision and maintenance of working memory representations in schizophrenia. *Archives of General Psychiatry*, 67, 570–577.

Goldman-Rakic, P. S. (1987). Circuitry of primate prefrontal cortex and regulation of behavior by representational knowledge. In F. Plum and V. Mountcastle (eds) *Handbook of Physiology* (Vol. 5, pp. 373–417). Bethesda, MD: American Physiological Society.

Goldstein, E. B. (2002). *Sensation and Perception*. Pacific Grove, CA: Wadsworth.

Goldstein, E. B. (2009). *Sensation and Perception, International Edition* (8th edn). Pacific Grove, CA: Wadsworth.

Goltz, F. (1892). Der Hund ohne Grosshirn: Siebente Abteilung über die Verrichtungen des Grosshirns. *Pfuger's Archiv für die Gesamte Physiologie*, 51, 570–614.

Gonnerman, L. M., Seidenberg, M. S. and Andersen, E. S. (2007). Graded semantic and phonological similarity effects in priming: Evidence for a distributed connectionist approach to morphology. *Journal of Experimental Psychology: General*, 136, 323–345.

Goodale, M. A. (2008). Action without perception in human vision. *Cognitive Neuropsychology*, 25(7–8), 891–919. doi:10.1080/02643290801961984.

Goodale, M. A. and Milner, A. D. (1992). Separate visual pathways for perception and action. *Trends in Neurosciences*, 15(1), 20–25.

Goodale, M. A. and Milner, A. D. (2004). *Sight Unseen: An Exploration of Conscious and Unconscious Vision*. Oxford: Oxford University Press.

Goodglass, H. and Kaplan, E. (1972). *The Assessment of Aphasia and Related Disorders*. Philadelphia: Lea and Febiger.

Goodwin, D. W., Powell, B., Bremer, D., Hoine, H. and Stern, J. (1969). Alcohol and recall: State dependent effects in man. *Science*, 163, 1358.

Gopie, N., Craik, F. I. M. and Hasher, L. (2011). A double dissociation of implicit and explicit memory in younger and older adults. *Psychological Science*, 22, 634–640.

Gorelick, E. D. and Ross, E. D. (1987). The aprosodias: Further functional-anatomic evidence for the organization of affective language in the right hemisphere. *Journal of Neurology, Neurosurgery and Psychiatry*, 50, 553–560.

Gorman, Michael E. and Gorman, Margaret E. (1984). A comparison of disconfirmation, confirmation and control strategy on Wason's 2–4–6 task. *Quarterly Journal of Experimental Psychology*, 36A, 629–648.

Goswami, U. (2010). A temporal sampling framework for developmental dyslexia. *Trends in Cognitive Sciences*, 15, 3–10.

Goswami, U., Thomson, J., Richardson, U., Stainthorp, R., Hughes, D., Rosen, S. and Scott, S. K. (2002). Amplitude envelope onsets and developmental dyslexia: A new hypothesis. *Proceedings of the National Academy of Sciences of the USA*, 99(16), 10911–10916.

Gotlib, I. H. and Joormann, J. (2010). Cognition and depression: Current status and future directions. *Annual Review of Clinical Psychology*, 6, 285–312.

Gough, P. and Cosky, M. (1977). One second of reading again. In N. Castellan, D. Pisoni and G. Potts (eds) *Cognitive Theory* (Vol. 2). Hillsdale, NJ.: Erlbaum.

Graf, P. and Schacter, D. L. (1985). Implicit and explicit memory for novel associations in normal and amnesic subjects. *Journal of Experimental Psychology: Learning, Memory, and Cognition*, 11, 501–518.

Graf, P., Squire, L. R. and Mandler, G. (1984). The information that amnesic patients do not forget. *Journal of Experimental Psychology: Learning, Memory, and Cognition*, 10, 164–178.

Graham, K. S., Kropelnicki, A., Goldman, W. P. and Hodges, J. R. (2003). Two further investigations of autobiographical memory in semantic dementia. *Cortex*, 39, 729–750.

Graham, K. S., Lee, A. C. H. and Barense, M. D. (2008). Impairments in visual discrimination in amnesia: Implications for theories of the role of medial temporal lobe regions in human memory. *European Journal of Cognitive Psychology*, 20, 655–696.

Greene, J. D. (2007). Why are VMPFC patients more utilitarian? A dual-process theory of moral judgment explains. *Trends in Cognitive Sciences*, 11, 322–323.

Greene, J. D., Nystrom, L. E., Engell, A. D., Darley, J. M. and Cohen, J. D. (2004). The neural bases of cognitive conflict and control in moral judgment. *Neuron*, 44, 389–400.

Greenough, W. T. (1987). Experience effects on the developing and the mature brain: Dendritic branching and synaptogenesis. In N. A. Krasnegor, E. Blass, M. Hofer and W. P. Smotherman (eds) *Perinatal Development: A Psychobiological Perspective*. New York: Academic Press.

Greenspoon, J. and Ranyard, R. (1957). Stimulus conditions and retroactive inhibition. *Journal of Experimental Psychology*, 53, 55–59.

Greenwald, A. G. and Shulman, H. G. (1973). On doing two things at once: II. Elimination of the psychological refractory period. *Journal of Experimental Psychology*, 101, 70–76.

Greenwald, A. G. and Banaji, M. R. (1995). Implicit social cognition: Attitudes, self-esteem, and stereotypes. *Psychological Review*, 102, 4–27.

Gregory, R. (1966). *Eye and Brain*. London: Weidenfield & Nicolson.

Gregory, R. L. (1980). Perceptions as hypotheses. *Philosophical Transactions of the Royal Society of London*, B290, 181–197.

Gregory, R. L. (1997). Knowledge in perception and illusion. *Philosophical Transactions of the Royal Society London B*, 352, 1121–1128.

Grice, H. P. (1975). Logic and conversation. In P. Cole and J. Morgan (eds) *Syntax and Semantics* (Vol. 3, pp. 41–58). New York: Academic Press.

Griffin, Z. M. and Crew, C. M. (2012). Research in language production. In M. J. Spivey, K. McRae and M. Joanisse (eds) *Cambridge Handbook of Psycholinguistics*. Cambridge University Press.

Griffiths, T. D., Rees, A. and Green, G. G. R. (1999). Disorders of human complex sound processing. *Neurocase*, 5(5), 365–378.

Griggs, R. A. and Cox, J. R. (1982). The elusive thematic materials effect in the Wason selection task. *British Journal of Psychology*, 73, 407–420.

Griggs, R. A. and Cox, J. R. (1983). The effects of problem content and negation on Wason's selection task. *Quarterly Journal of Experimental Psychology*, 35A, 519–533.

Grimm, J. L. C. and Grimm, W. C. (1909). *Grimm's Fairy Tales* (trans. E. Lucas). London: Constable and Co. Ltd.

Griskevicius, V., Shiota, M. N. and Neufeld, S. L. (2010). Influence of different positive emotions on persuasive processing: A functional evolutionary approach. *Emotion*, 10, 190–206.

Groome, D. and Grant, N. (2005). Retrieval-induced forgetting is inversely related to everyday cognitive failures. *British Journal of Psychology*, 96, 313–319.

Groome, D. and Sterkaj, F. (2010). Retrieval-induced forgetting and clinical depression. *Cognition and Emotion*, 24, 63–70.

Grossenbacher, P. G. and Lovelace, C. T. (2001). Mechanisms of synaesthesia: Cognitive and physiological constraints. *Trends in Cognitive Sciences*, 5, 36–41.

Habib, R., McIntosh, A. R., Wheeler, M. A. and Tulving, E. (2003). Memory encoding and hippocampally-based novelty/familiaritydiscrimination networks. *Neuropsychologia*, 41, 271–279.

Hall, D. A., Johnsrude, I. S., Haggard, M. P., Palmer, A. R., Akeroyd, M. A. and Summerfield, A. Q. (2002). Spectral and temporal processing in human auditory cortex. *Cerebral Cortex,* 12 (2), 140–149.

Halstead, W. C. (1940). Preliminary analysis of grouping behaviour in patients with cerebral injury by the method of equivalent and non-equivalent stimuli. *American Journal of Psychiatry*, 96, 1263–1294.

Handy, T. C., Grafton, S. T., Shroff, N. M., Ketay, S. and Gazzaniga, M. S. (2003). Graspable objects grab attention when the potential for action is recognized. *Nature Neuroscience*, 6, 421–427.

Happé, F. (1999). Autism: Cognitive deficit or cognitive style? *Trends in Cognitive Sciences*, 3, 216–222.

Harding, A., Halliday, G., Caine, D. and Kril, J. (2000). Degeneration of anterior thalamic nuclei differentiates alcoholics with amnesia. *Brain*, 123, 141–154.

Hareli, S. and Weiner, B. (2002). Dislike and envy as antecedents of pleasure at another's misfortune. *Motivation and Emotion*, 26, 257–277.

Harenski, C. L., Keith, A., Shane, M. S. and Kiehl, K. A. (2010). Aberrant neural processing of moral violations in criminal psychopaths. *Journal of Abnormal Psychology*, 119, 863–874.

Harley, T. (2001). *The Psychology of Language*. Sussex: Psychology Press.

Harlow, J. M. (1848). Passage of an iron bar through the head. *Boston Medical and Surgical Journal*, 39, 389–393.

Harlow, J. M. (1868). Recovery from the passage of an iron bar through the head. *Publications of the Massachusetts Medical Society*, 2, 327–347.

Hart, J. and Kraut, M. A. (2007). *Neural Basis of Semantic Memory*. Cambridge: Cambridge University Press.

Hartley, T., Bird, C. M., Chan, D., Cipolotti, L., Husain, M., Vargha-Khadem, F. *et al.* (2007). The hippocampus is required for short-term topographical memory in humans. *Hippocampus*, 17, 34–48.

Hastorf, A. H. and Cantril, H. (1954). They saw a game: A case study. *Journal of Abnormal and Social Psychology*, 49, 129–134.

Hauser, M. (2006). *Moral Minds: How Nature Designed Our Universal Sense of Right and Wrong*. New York: Ecco.

Hawkins, S. (2003). Roles and representations of systematic fine phonetic detail in speech understanding. *Journal of Phonetics*, 31, 373–405.

Haxby, J. V., Horwitz, B., Ungerleider, L. G., Maisog, J. M., Pietrini, P. and Grady, C. L. (1994). The functional organization of human extrastriate cortex: a PET-rCBF study of selective attention to faces and locations. *Journal of Neuroscience*, 14, 6336–6353.

Haxby, J., Hoffman, E. and Gobbini, M. (2000). The distributed human neural system for face perception. *Trends in Cognitive Sciences*, 4(6), 223–233. Retrieved from http://www.ncbi.nlm.nih.gov/pubmed/10827445.

Hayashi, T., Umeda, C. and Cook, N. D. (2007). An fMRI study of the reverse perspective illusion. *Brain Research*, 1163, 72–78.

Hayes, J. R. and Simon, H. A. (1974). Understanding written problem instructions. In L. W. Gregg (ed.) *Knowledge and Cognition*. Hillsdale, NJ: Lawrence Erlbaum Associates.

Hayman, C. A. G. and Tulving, E. (1989). Is priming in fragment completion based on a "traceless" memory system? *Journal of Experimental Psychology: Learning, Memory, and Cognition*, 15, 941–956.

Haynes, J. D. and Rees, G. (2005). Predicting the orientation of invisible stimuli from activity in human primary visual cortex. *Nature Neuroscience*, 8, 686–691.

Head, H. (1926). *Aphasia and Kindred Disorders of Speech* (Vol. 1, pp. 54–60). Cambridge: Cambridge University Press.

Heathcote, D. (2005). Working memory and performance limitations. In A. Esgate and D. H. Groome (eds) *An Introduction to Applied Cognitive Psychology*. Hove: Psychology Press.

Hebb, D. O. (1949). *The Organisation of Behaviour*. New York: Wiley.

Heilman, K. M. (2006). Aphasia and the diagram makers revisited: An update of information processing models. *Journal of Clinical Neurology*, 2(3), 149–162.

Heilman, K. M., Tucker, D. M. and Valenstein, E. A. (1976). A case of mixed transcortical aphasia with intact naming. *Brain*, 99, 415–525.

Heilman, K. M., Gonzalez-Rothi, L. J., McFarling, D. and Rottman, A. (1981). Transcortical sensory aphasia with relatively spared spontaneous speech in naming. *Archives of Neurology*, 38, 236–239.

Heller, M. A. Brackett, D. D. Wilson, K. Yoneyama, K. and Boyer, A. (2002). The haptic Muller-Lyer illusion in sighted and blind people. *Perception*, 31, 1263–1274.

Helmstaedter, C., Kemper, B. and Elger, C. E. (1996). Neuropsychological aspects of frontal lobe epilepsy. *Neuropsychologia*, 34, 399–406.

Henriques, D. Y. and Soechting, J. F. (2003). Bias and sensitivity in the haptic perception of geometry. *Experimental Brain Research*, 150, 95–108.

Henson, R. N. A., Burgess, N. and Frith, C. D. (2000). Recoding, storage, rehearsal, and grouping in verbal short-term memory: An fMRI study. *Neuropsychologia*, 38, 426–440.

Herrmann, D., Raybeck, D. and Gruneberg, M. (2002). *Improving Memory and Study Skills: Advances in Theory and Practice*. Ashland OH: Hogrefe and Huber.

Hersh, N. and Treadgold, L. (1994). Neuropage: The rehabilitation of memory dysfunction by prosthetic memory and cueing. *NeuroRehabilitaion*, 4, 187–197.

Hickok, G. and Poeppel, D. (2004). Dorsal and ventral streams: A framework for understanding aspects of the functional anatomy of language. *Cognition*, 92, 67–99.

Hickok, G. and Poeppel, D. (2007). The cortical organization of speech processing. *Nature Reviews Neuroscience*, 8(5), 393–402.

Hickok, G., Erhard, P., Kassubek, J., Helms-Tillery, A. K., Naeve-Velguth, S., Strupp, J. P. *et al.* (2000). A functional magnetic resonance imaging study of the role of left posterior superior temporal gyrus in speech production: Implications for the explanation of conduction aphasia. *Neuroscience Letters*, 287, 156–60.

Hill, C., Memon, A. and McGeorge, P. (2008). The role of confirmation bias in suspect interviews: A systematic evaluation. *Legal and Criminological Psychology*, 13, 357–371.

Hill, E. (2004). Executive dysfunction in autism. *Trends in Cognitive Sciences*, 8, 26–32.

Hills, B. L. (1980). Vision, visibility and perception in driving. *Perception*, 9, 183–216.

Hinton, G. E. and Shallice, T. (1991). Lesioning an attractor network: Investigations of acquired dyslexia. *Psychological Review*, 98(1), 74–95.

Hiraoka, K., Suzuki, K., Hirayama, K. and Mori, E. (2009). Visual agnosia for line drawings and silhouettes without apparent impairment of real-object recognition: A case report. *Behavioural Neurology*, 21(3), 187–92. doi:10.3233/BEN-2009-0244.

Ho, C. E. (1998). Letter recognition reveals pathways of second-order and third-order motion. *Proceedings of the National Academy of Sciences of the United States of America*, 95(1), 400–404.

Ho, C. and Spence, C. (2005). Assessing the effectiveness of various auditory cues in capturing a driver's visual attention. *Journal of Experimental Psychology Applied*, 11, 3, 157–174.

Hodges, J. R., Patterson, K. and Tyler, L. K. (1994). Loss of semantic memory: Implications for the modularity of mind. *Cognitive Neuropsychology*, 11, 505–542.

Hofman, P. A. M. Verhay, F. R. J. Wilmink, J. T. Rozandaal, N. and Jolles, J. (2002). Brainlesions in patients visiting a memory clinic with post-concussional sequelae after mild to moderate brain injury. *Journal of Neuropsychiatry and Clinical Neurosciences*, 14, 176–184.

Holland, A. C. and Kensinger, E. A. (2010). Emotion and autobiographical memory. *Physics of Life Reviews*, 7, 88–131.

Horowitz, M. J. (1976). *Stress Response Syndromes*. New York: Aronson.

Howell, P. (2011). Listen to the lessons of *The King's Speech*. *Nature*, 470, 7.

Hubbard, E. M. and Ramachandran, V. S. (2005). Neurocognitive mechanisms of synesthesia. *Neuron*, 48(3), 509–520.

Hubel, D. H. and Wiesel, T. N. (1959). Receptive fields of single neurons in the cat's striate cortex. *Journal of Physiology*, 148, 574–591.

Hulme, C., Maughan, S. and Brown, G. D. A. (1991). Memory for familiar and unfamiliar words: Evidence for a long-term memory contribution to short-term memory span. *Journal of Memory and Language*, 30, 685–701.

Hulme, C., Suprenant, A. M., Bireta, T. J., Stuart, G. and Neath, I. (2004). Abolishing the word-length effect. *Journal of Experimental Psychology: Learning, Memory, and Cognition*, 30, 98–106.

Humphreys, G. W. and Riddoch, M. J. (1987). *To See or Not to See: A Case Study of Visual Agnosia*. London: Lawrence Earlbaum Associates.

Humphreys, G. W. and Riddoch, M. J. (2006). Features, objects, action: The cognitive neuropsychology of visual object processing, 1984–2004.

Cognitive Neuropsychology, 23(1), 156–83. doi:10.1080/02643290542000030.

Hunt, R. R. (2013). Precision memory through distinctive processing. *Current Directions in Psychological Science*, 22, 10–15.

Hunt, R. R. and McDaniel, M. A. (1993). The enigma of organisation and distinctiveness. *Journal of Memory and Language*, 32, 421–445.

Hupbach, A., Gomez, R., Hardt, O. and Nadel, L. (2007). Reconsolidation of episodic memories: A subtle reminder triggers integration of new information. *Learning and Memory*, 14, 47–53.

Hupe, J. M., James, A. C., Payne, B. R., Lomber, S. G., Girard, P. and Bullier, J. (1998). Cortical feedback improves discrimination between figure and ground by V1, V2 and V3 neurons. *Nature*, 394, 784–787.

Hupe, J. M., Bordier, C. and Dojat, M. (2012). The neural bases of grapheme-color synesthesia are not localized in real color-sensitive areas. *Cerebral Cortex*, 22(7), 1622–1633.

Huppert, F. A. and Piercy, M. (1976). Recognition memory in amnesic patients: Effect of temporal context and familiarity of material. *Cortex*, 4, 3–20.

Huppert, F. A. and Piercy, M. (1978). The role of trace strength in recency and frequency judgements by amnesic and control subjects. *Quarterly Journal of Experimental Psychology*, 30, 346–354.

Husserl, E. (1931). *Ideas: General Introduction to Pure Phenomenology* (Vol. 1). New York: Macmillan.

Hyde, T. S. and Jenkins, J. J. (1973). Recall for words as a function of semantic, graphic, and syntactic orienting tasks. *Journal of Verbal Learning and Verbal Behaviour*, 12, 471–480.

Hyden, H. (1967). Biochemical and molecular aspects of learning and memory. *Proceedings of the American Philosophical Society*, 111, 347–351.

Jacobsen, C. F., Wolfe, J. B. and Jackson, T. A. (1935). An experimental analysis of the functions of the frontal association areas in primates. *Journal of Nervous and Mental Disease*, 82, 1–14.

Jacoby, L. L. and Dallas, M. (1981). On the relationship between autobiographical memory and perceptual learning. *Journal of Experimental Psychology: General*, 3, 3006–3040.

Jacquemot, C. and Scott, S. K. (2006). What is the relationship between phonological short-term memory and speech processing? *Trends in Cognitive Sciences*, 10(11), 480–486.

Jacquemot, C., Pallier, C., Lebihan, D., Dehaene, S. and Dupoux, E. (2003). Phonological grammar shapes the auditory cortex: A functional Magnetic Resonance Imaging study. *Journal of Neuroscience*, 23(29), 9541–9546.

James, W. (1890). *Principles of Psychology*. New York: Holt.

Jansma, J. M., Ramsey, N. F., Slagter, H. A. and Kahn, R. S. (2001). Fuctional anatomical correlates of controlled and automatic processing. *Journal of Cognitive Neuroscience*, 13, 730–743.

Janssen, S. M. J., Rubin, D. L. and Conway, M. A. (2012). The reminiscence bump in the temporal distribution of the best football players of all time: Pele, Cruijff or Maradonna? *Quarterly Journal of Experimental Psychology*, 65, 165–178.

Janssen, W. and Nilsson, L. (1993). Behavioral effects of driver support. In A. M. Parkes and S. Franzen (eds) *Driving Future Vehicles* (pp. 147–155). London: Taylor & Francis.

Jared, D., McRae, K. and Seidenberg, M. S. (1990). The basis of consistency effects in word naming. *Journal of Memory and Language*, 29, 687–715.

Jastrowitz, M. (1888). Beiträge zur Localisation im Grosshirn und über deren praktische Verwerthung. *Deutsche Medizinische Wochenschrift*, 14, 81–83, 108–112, 125–128, 151–153, 172–175, 188–192, 209–211.

Jerabek, I. and Standing, L. (1992). Imagined test situations produce contextual memory enhancement. *Perceptual and Motor Skills*, 75, 400.

Jewanski, J., Day, S. A. and Ward, J. (2009). A colorful albino: The first documented case of synaesthesia, by Georg Tobias Ludwig Sachs in 1812. *Journal of the History of the Neurosciences*, 18(3), 293–303.

Joanisse, M. F. and Seidenberg, M. S. (1999). Impairments in verb morphology following brain injury: A connectionist model. *Proceedings of the National Academy of Sciences of the USA*, 96, 7592–7597.

Johnson, A., Johnson, O. and Baksh, M. (1986). The colours of emotions in Machiguenga. *American Anthropologist*, 88, 674–681.

Johnson, J. A. and Zartorre, R. J. (2006). Neural substrates for dividing and focussing attention between simultaneous auditory and visual events. *Neuroimage*, 31, 27–64.

Johnson-Laird, P. N. (1983). *Mental Models*. Cambridge, MA: Harvard University Press.

Johnson-Laird, P. N. and Wason, P. C. (1970). Insight into a logical relation. *Quarterly Journal of Experimental Psychology*, 22, 49–61.

Johnson-Laird, P. N., Legrenzi, P. and Legrenzi, M. S. (1972). Reasoning and a sense of reality. *British Journal of Psychology*, 63, 395–400.

Johnson-Laird, P. N., Byrne, R. M. J. and Schaeken, W. (1992). Propositional reasoning by model. *Psychological Review*, 99, 418–439.

Johnson-Laird, P. N., Mancini, F. and Gangemi, A. (2006). A hyper-emotion theory of psychological illnesses. *Psychological Review*, 113, 822–841.

Johnstone, E. C., Deakin, J. F. W., Lawler, P., Frith, C. D., Stevens, M., McPherson, K. *et al.* (1980). The Northwick Park ECT trial. *The Lancet*, 1317–1320.

Johnstone, L. (2003). A shocking treatment? *The Psychologist*, 16, 236–239.

Joseph, R. (1999). Frontal lobe psychopathology: Mania, depression, confabulation, catatonia, perseveration, obsessive compulsions, and schizophrenia. *Psychiatry – Interpersonal and Biological Processes*, 62(2), 138–172.

Juhasz, B. J. (2005). Age-of-acquisition effects in word and picture identification. *Psychological Bulletin*, 131(5), 684–712.

Jung, R. E. and Haier, R. J. (2007). The parieto-frontal integration theory (P-FIT) of intelligence: Converging neuroimaging evidence. *Behavioural and Brain Sciences*, 30, 135–154.

Kaas, J. H. and Hackett, T. A. (1999). "What" and "where" processing in auditory cortex. *Nature Neuroscience*, 2(12), 1045–1047.

Kahneman, D. (1973). *Attention and Effort*. Englewood Cliffs, NJ: Prentice Hall.

Kahneman, D. and Treisman, A. M. (1984). Changing views of attention and automaticity. In R. Parsuraman and D. R. Davies (eds) *Varieties of Attention*. Orlando, FL. Academic Press.

Kahneman, D. and Frederick, S. (2002). Representativeness revisited: Attribute substitution in intuitive judgement. In T. Gilovich, D. Griffin and D. Kahneman (eds) *Heuristics and Biases: The Psychology of Intuitive Judgment* (pp. 49–81). Cambridge: Cambridge University Press.

Kane, M. J. and Engle, R. W. (2002). The role of prefrontal cortex in working memory capacity, executive attention, and general fluid intelligence: An individual differences perspective. *Psychonomic Bulletin and Review*, 9, 637–671.

Kanwisher, N., McDermott, J. and Chun, M. M. (1997). The fusiform face area: A module in human extrastriate cortex specialized for face perception. *The Journal of Neuroscience*, 17(11), 4302–4311. Retrieved from http://www.ncbi.nlm.nih.gov/pubmed/9151747.

Kapur, N., Ellison, D. Smith, M. McLellan, D. L. and Burrows, E. H. (1992). Focal retrograde amnesia following bilateral temporal lobe pathology. *Brain*, 115, 73–85.

Kapur, N., Thompson, C., Cook, P., Lang, D. and Brice, J. (1996). Anterograde but not retrograde memory loss following combined mammilary body and medial thalamic lesions. *Neuropsychologia*, 34, 2–8.

Kapur, N., Glisky, E. L. and Wilson, B. A. (2004). External memory aids and computers in memory rehabilitation. In A. D. Baddeley, M. D. Kopelman and B. A. Wilson (eds) *The Essential Handbook of Memory Disorders for Clinicians*. Chichester: Wiley.

Karat, J. (1982). A model of problem-solving with incomplete constraint knowledge. *Cognitive Psychology*, 14, 538–559.

Karnath, H. O. (1997). Spatial orientation and the representation of space with parietal lobe lesions. [Comparative Study]. *Philosophical Transactions of the Royal Society of London. Series B, Biological Sciences*, 352(1360), 1411–1419.

Karnath, H. O., Christ, K. and Hartje, W. (1993). Decrease of contralateral neglect by neck muscle vibration and spatial orientation of trunk midline. *Brain*, 116, 383–396.

Katz, R. B. and Goodglass, H. (1990). Deep dysphasia: Analysis of a rare form of repetition disorder. *Brain and Language*, 39, 153–185.

Keane, M. T. G. (1987). On retrieving analogues when solving problems. *Quarterly Journal of Experimental Psychology*, 39A, 29–41.

Keane, M. T. G. (1990). Incremental analogizing: theory and model. In K. J. Gilhooly, M. T. G. Keane, R. H. Logie and G. Erdos (eds) *Lines of Thinking: Reflections on the Psychology of Thought, Vol. 1: Representation, Reasoning, Analogy and Decision Making*. Chichester: John Wiley.

Kelley, L. A. and Endler, J. A. (2012). Illusions create mating success in great bowerbirds. *Science*, doi: 10.1126/science.12124.

Kelly, J. and Local, J. L. (1986). Long-domain resonance patterns in English. In *Proceedings International Conference on Speech Input/Output* (pp. 304–308). London: IEE.

Kenealy, P. M. (1997). Mood-state-dependent retrieval: The effects of induced mood on memory reconsidered. *Quarterly Journal of Experimental Psychology*, 50A, 290–317.

Kensinger, E. A., Addis, D. R. and Atapattu, R. K. (2011). Amygdala activity at encoding corresponds with memory vividness and with memory for select episodic details. *Neuropsychologia*, 49, 663–673.

Keren, G. and Schul, Y. (2009). Two is not always better than one: A critical evaluation of two-system theories. *Perspectives on Psychological Science*, 4, 533–550.

Kertesz, A., Sheppard, A., MacKenzie, R. (1982). Localization in transcortical sensory aphasia. *Archives of Neurology*, 39(8), 475–478.

Kihlstrom, J. F. and Schacter, D. L. (2000). Functional amnesia. In F. Boller and J. Grafman (eds) *Handbook of Neuropsychology* (Vol. 2, pp. 409–427). Amsterdam: Elsevier.

Kimball, J. (1973). Seven principles of surface structure parsing in natural language. *Cognition*, 2, 15–47.

Kimberg, D. Y. and Farah, M. J. (1993). A unified accound of cognitive impairments following frontal lobe damage: The role of working memory in complex, organized behavior. *Journal of Experimental Psychology: General*, 122, 411–428.

King, J. A., Trinkler, I., Hartley, T., Vargha-Khadem, F. and Burgess, N. (2004). The hippocampal role in spatial memory and the familiarity-recollection distinction: A case study. *Neuropsychology*, 18, 405–417.

King, N. S. and Kirwilliam, S. (2011). Permanent post-concussion symptoms after mild head injury. *Brain Injury*, 25, 462–470.

Kinsbourne, M. (1977). Hemi-neglect and hemisphere rivalry. In E. A. Weinstein and R. P. Friedland (eds) *Advances in Neurology* (Vol. 18, pp. 41–49). New York: Raven.

Kintsch, W. (1968). Recognition and free recall in organised lists. *Journal of Experimental Psychology*, 78, 481–487.

Kirdendall, D. T. and Garrett, W. E. (2001). Heading in soccer: Integral skill or grounds for cognitive dysfunction? *Journal of Athletic Training*, 36, 328–333.

Klatzky, R. L. Lederman, S. J. and Metzger, V. (1987). Identifying objects by touch: An "expert" system. *Perception and Psychophysics*, 37, 299–302.

Klauer, K. C. and Zhao, Z. (2004). Double dissociations in visual and spatial short-term memory. *Journal of Experimental Psychology: General*, 133, 355–381.

Klein, D. E. and Murphy, G. L. (2001). The representation of polysemous words. *Journal of Memory and Language*, 45, 259–282.

Knoblich, G., Ohlsson, S., Haider, H. and Rhenius, D. (1999). Constraint relaxation and chunk decomposition in insight problem solving. *Journal of Experimental Psychology: Learning, Memory, and Cognition*, 25, 1534–1556.

Knoblich, G., Ohlsson, S. and Raney, G. E. (2001). An eye movement study of insight problem solving. *Memory and Cognition*, 29, 1000–1009.

Koehnken, G., Milne, R., Memon, A. and Bull, R. (1999). The cognitive interview: A meta-analysis. *Psychology, Crime, and Law*, 5, 3–27.

Koenigs, M., Young, L., Adolphs, R., Tranel, D., Cushman, F., Hauser, M. *et al.* (2007). Damage to the prefrontal cortex increases utilitarian moral judgments. *Nature*, 446, 908–911.

Koffka, K. (1935). *Principles of Gestalt Psychology*. New York: Harcourt Brace.

Köhler, W. (1925). *The Mentality of Apes*. New York: Harcourt Brace.

Kolb, B. and Whishaw, I. Q. (1996). *Fundamentals of Human Neuropsychology* (4th edn). New York: Freeman.

Kopelman, M. D. (1989). Remote and autobiographical memory, temporal context memory and frontal atrophy in Korsakoff and Alzheimer patients. *Neuropsychologia*, 27, 437–460.

Kopelman, M. D. (1995). Assessment of psychogenic amnesias. In A. D. Baddeley, B. A. Wilson and F. N. Watts (eds) *Handbook of Memory Disorders* (1st edn, pp. 427–448). Chichester: Wiley.

Kopelman, M. D. (2002). Psychogenic amnesia. In A. D. Baddeley, M. D. Kopelman and B. A. Wilson (eds) *Handbook of Memory Disorders* (2nd edn, pp. 451–472). Chichester: Wiley.

Kopelman, M. D. (2010). Varieties of confabulation and delusion. *Cognitive Neuropsychiatry*, 15, 14–37.

Kopelman, M. D., Wilson, B. A. and Baddeley, A. D. (1990). *The Autobiographical Memory Interview*. Bury St. Edmunds: Thames Valley Test Company.

Kopelman, M. D., Stanhope, N. and Kingsley, D. (1999). Retrograde amnesia in patients with diencephalic, temporal lobe, or frontal lesions. *Neuropsychologia*, 35, 1533–1545.

Kopelman, M. D., Lasserson, D., Kingsley, D., Bello, F., Rush, C. *et al.* (2001). Structural MRI volumetric analysis in patients with organic amnesia, 2: Correlations with anterograde memory and executive tests in 40 patients. *Journal of Neurology, Neurosurgery, and Psychiatry*, 71, 23–28.

Koriat, A., Goldsmith, M. and Pansky, A. (2001). Towards a psychology of memory accuracy. *Annual Review of Psychology*, 481–537.

Korsakoff, S. S. (1887). Troubles de l'activite psychique dans la paralysie alcoolique et leurs rapports avec les troubles de la sphere psychique dans la vevrite multiple d'origine non alcoolique. *Vestnik Psychiatrii*, 4, 2.

Kousta, S. T., Vigliocco, G., Vinson, D. P., Andrews, M., Del Campo, E. (2011). The representation of abstract words: Why emotion matters. *Journal of Experimental Psychology: General*, 140, 14–34.

Kozak, K., Pohl, J., Birk, W., Greenberg, J., Artz, B., Bloomer, M., Cathey, L. and Curry, R. (2006). Evaluation of lane departure warnings for drowsy drivers. *Proceedings of the Human Factors and Ergonomics Society*, 2400–2404.

Króliczak, G., Heard, P., Goodale, M. A. and Gregory, R. L. (2006). Dissociation of perception and action unmasked by the hollow-face illusion. *Brain Research*, 1080, 9–16.

Kuffler, S. W. (1953). Discharge patterns and functional organisation of mammalian retina. *Journal of Neurophysiology*, 16, 37–68.

Kuhl, B. A., Kahn, I., Dudukovich, N. M. and Wagner, N. M. (2008). Overcoming suppression in order to remember: Contributions from anterior cingulated and ventrolateral prefrontal cortex. *Cognitive Affective and Behavioural Neuroscience*, 8, 211–221.

Külpe, O. (1895). *The Outlines of Psychology: Based Upon the Results of Experimental Investigation*. New York: Swan Sonnenschein and Co.

Kurtz, K. J. and Loewenstein, J. (2007). Converging on a new role for analogy in problem solving and retrieval: When two problems are better than one. *Memory and Cognition*, 35, 334–341.

Kussmaul, A. (1877). *Die Storungen der Sprache*. Leipzig: Vogel.

LaBar, K. S. and Cabeza, R. (2006). Cognitive neuroscience of emotional memory. *Nature Reviews Neuroscience*, 7, 54–64.

LaBar, K. S., Gitelman, D. R., Parrish, T. B. and Mesulam, M. (1999). Neuroanatomic overlap of working memory and spatial attention networks: a functional MRI comparison within subjects. *Neuroimage*, 10, 695–704.

Laberge, D. (1983). Spatial extent of attention to letters and words. *Journal of Experimental Psychology: Human Perception and Performance*, 9, 371–379.

Laird, J., Newell, A. and Rosenbloom, P. (1987). SOAR: An architecture for general intelligence. *Artificial Intelligence*, 33, 1–64.

Lang, A. J., Craske, M. J. and Bjork, R. A. (1999). Implications of a new theory of disuse for the treatment of emotional disorders. *Clinical Psychology; Science and Practice*, 6, 80–94.

Langham, M., Hole, G., Edwards, J. and O'Neil, C. (2002). An analysis of "looked but failed to see" accidents involving parked police vehicles. *Ergonomics*, 45(3), 167–185.

Lashley, K. S. (1950). In search of the engram. *Symposium of the Society of Experimental Biology*, 4, 454–482.

Lavie, N. (1995). Perceptual load as a necessary condition for selective attention. *Journal of Experimental Psychology; Human Perception and Performance*, 21, 451–468.

Lavie, N. (2005). Distracted and confused? Selective attention under load. *Trends in Cognitive Science*, 9, 75–82.

Lavie, N. (2006). The role of perceptual load in visual awareness. *Brain Research*, 1080, 91–100.

Lavie, N. (2010). Attention, distraction and cognitive control under load. *Current Directions in Cognitive Science*, 19(3), 143–148.

Law, R., Groome, D., Thorn, L., Potts, R. and Buchanan, T. (2012). The relationship between retrieval-induced forgetting, anxiety, and personality. *Anxiety, Stress and Coping*, 25, 711–718.

Lawson, I. R. (1962). Visual-spatial neglect in lesions of the right cerebral hemisphere: A study in recovery. *Neurology*, 12, 23–33.

Leach, C. W. and Spears, R. (2008). "A vengefulness of the impotent": The pain of in-group inferiority and schadenfreude toward successful outgroups. *Journal of Personality and Social Psychology*, 95, 1383–1396.

Lederman, S. J. and Klatzky, R. L. (1990). Haptic classification of common objects: Knowledge-driven exploration. *Cognitive Psychology*, 22, 421–459.

Lee, A. C. H., Bussey, T. J., Murray, E. A., Saksida, L. M., Epstein, R. A., Kapur, N., Hodges, J. R. and Graham, K. S. (2005). Perceptual deficits in amnesia: Challenging the medial temporal lobe mnemonic view. *Neuropsychologia*, 43, 1–11.

Lee, A. C. H., Yeung, L-K. and Barense, M. D. (2012). The hippocampus and visual perception. *Frontiers of Human Neuroscience*, 6, 91. doi: 10.3389/fnhum.2012.00091.

Legrenzi, P., Girotto, V. and Johnson-Laird, P. N. (2003). Models of consistency. *Psychological Science*, 14, 131–137.

Lench, H. C. and Levine, L. J. (2005). Effects of fear on risk and control judgments and memory: Implications for health promotion messages. *Cognition and Emotion*, 19, 1049–1069.

Lench, H. C. and Ditto, P. H. (2008). Automatic optimism: Biased use of base rate information for positive and negative events. *Journal of Experimental Social Psychology*, 44, 631–639.

Lerner, J. S. and Keltner, D. (2001). Fear, anger, and risk. *Journal of Personality and Social Psychology*, 81, 146–159.

Lerner, J. S. and Tiedens, L. Z. (2006). Portrait of the angry decision maker: How appraisal tendencies shape anger's influence on cognition. *Journal of Behavioral Decision Making*, 19, 115–137.

Lerner, J. S., Gonzalez, R. M., Small, D. A. and Fischhoff, B. (2003). Effects of fear and anger on perceived risks of terrorism: A national field experiment. *Psychological Science*, 14, 144–150.

Levelt, W. J. M. (1989). *Speaking: From Intention to Articulation*. Cambridge, MA: MIT Press.

Levelt, W. J. M. (1992). Accessing words in speech production: stages, processes and representations. *Cognition*, 42, 1–22.

Levelt, W. (2012). *A History of Psycholinguistics: The Pre-Chomskyan Era*. Oxford: Oxford University Press.

Levelt, W. J. M., Schriefers, H., Vorberg, D., Meyer, A. S., Pechmann, Th. and Havinga, J. (1991). The time course of lexical access in speech production: A study of picture naming. *Psychological Review*, 98, 122–142.

Levelt, W. J. M., Roelofs, A. and Meyer, A. S. (1999). A theory of lexical access in speech production. *Target Paper for Behavioral and Brain Sciences*, 22, 1–75.

Levine, B., Svoboda, E., Hay, J. F., Winocur, G. and Moscovitch, M. (2002). Ageing and autobiographical memory: Dissociating episodic from semantic retrieval. *Psychology and Ageing*, 17, 677–689.

Levine, L. J. and Edelstein, R. S. (2009). Emotion and memory narrowing: A review and goal-relevance approach. *Cognition and Emotion*, 23, 833–875.

Levy, J., Pashler, H. and Boer, E. (2006). Central interference in driving: Is there any stopping the psychological refractory period? *Psychological Science*, 17(3), 228–235.

Lhermitte, F. (1983). "Utilization behaviour" and its relation to lesions of the frontal lobes. *Brain*, 106, 237–255.

Lhermitte, F. (1986). Human autonomy and the frontal lobes. Part II: patient behaviour in complex and social situations: The "environmental dependency syndrome". *Annals of Neurology*, 19, 335–343.

Libet, B. (1985). Unconscious cerebral initiative and the role of conscious will in voluntary action. *Behavioural and Brain Sciences*, 8, 529–539.

Lichtheim, L. (1885). On Aphasia. *Brain*, 7, 433–484.

Liebenthal, E., Binder, J. R., Spitzer, S. M., Possing, E. T. and Medler, D. A. (2005). Neural substrates of phonemic perception. *Cerebral Cortex*, 15(10), 1621–31.

Lief, H. and Fetkewicz, J. (1995). Retractors of false memories: The evolution of pseudo-memories. *The Journal of Psychiatry and Law*, 23, 411–436.

Lien, M. C., Proctor, R. W. and Allen, P. A. (2002). Ideomotor compatibility in the psychological refractory period effect: 29 years of oversimplification. *Journal of Experimental Psychology: Human Perception and Performance*, 28, 396–409.

Lindsay, P. H. and Norman, D. A. (1972). *Human Information Processing*. New York: Academic Press.

Lindsay, D. S. and Read, J. D. (1994). Psychotherapy and memories of childhood sexual abuse: A cognitive perspective. *Applied Cognitive Psychology*, 8, 281–338.

Linton, M. (1975). Memory for real-world events. In D. A. Norman and D. E. Rumelhart (eds) *Explorations in Cognition*. San Francisco: Freeman.

Lisker, L. (1977). Factors in the maintenance and cessation of voicing. *Phonetica*, 34, 304–306.

Lissauer, H. (1890). Ein Fall von Seelenblindheitnebt einem Beitrage zur Theorie Derselben. *Archiv für Psychiatrie und Nervenkrankheit*, 21, 222–270.

Litvak, P. M., Lerner, J. S., Tiedens, L. Z. and Shonk, K. (2010). Fuel in the fire: How anger impacts judgment and decision-making. In M. Potegal, G. Stemmler and C. Spielberger (eds) *International Handbook of Anger: Constituent and Concomitant Biological, Psychological, and Social Processes* (pp. 287–310). New York: Springer.

Liu, X., Crump, M. J. C. and Logan, G. D. (2010). Do you know where your fingers have been? Explicit knowledge of the spatial layout of the keyboard in skilled typists. *Memory and Cognition*, 38(4), 474–484.

Local, J. and Kelly, J. (1986). Projection and silences: Notes on phonetic and conversational structure. *Human Studies*, 9, 185–204.

Lockhart, R. S. and Craik, F. I. M. (1990). Levels of processing: A retrospective commentary on a framework for memory research. *Canadian Journal of Psychology*, 44, 87–112.

Loeb, J. (1902). *Comparative Physiology of the Brain and Comparative Psychology*. New York: Putnam.

Loewenstein, J., Thompson, L. and Gentner, D. (2003). Analogical learning in negotiation teams: Comparing cases promotes learning and transfer. *Academy of Management Learning and Education*, 2, 119–127.

Loftus, E. L. and Palmer, J. C. (1974). Reconstruction of automobile destruction: An example of the interaction between language and memory. *Journal of Verbal Learning and Verbal Behaviour*, 13, 585–589.

Loftus, E. F. and Pickrell, J. E. (1995). The formation of false memories. *Psychiatric Annals*, 25, 720–725.

Loftus, E. F. and Davis, D. (2006). Recovered memories. *Annual Review of Clinical Psychology*, 2, 469–498.

Loftus, E. F., Loftus, G. R. and Messo, J. (1987). Some facts about "weapons focus". *Law and Human Behavior*, 11, 55–62.

Logan, G. D. and Crump, M. J. C. (2009). The left hand doesn't know what the right hand is doing. Disruptive effects of attention to the hands while typewriting. *Psychological Science*, 20, 1296–1300.

Logie, R. H. (1986). Visuo-spatial processes in working memory. *Quarterly Journal of Experimental Psychology*, 38A, 229–247.

Logie, R. H. (1995). *Visuo-Spatial Working Memory*. Hove: Erlbaum.

Logie, R. H. (2011). The functional organisation and capacity limits of working memory. *Current Directions in Psychological Science*, 20, 240–245.

Logie, R. H., Baddeley, A. D., Mane, A., Donchin, E. and Sheptak, R. (1989). Working memory and the analysis of a complex skill by secondary task methodology. *Acta Psychologica*, 71, 53–87.

Logothesis, N. K. (1994). Physiological studies of motion inputs. In A. T. Smith (ed.) *Visual Detection of Motion* (pp. 177–216). London: Academic Press.

Lorayne, H. and Lucas, J. (1974). *The Memory Book*. London: W. H. Allen.

Lorian, C. N. and Grisham, J. R. (2011). Clinical implications of risk aversion: An online study of risk-avoidance and treatment utilisation in pathological anxiety. *Journal of Anxiety Disorders*, 25, 840–848.

Loveday, C. and Conway, M. A. (2011). Using SenseCam with an amnesic patient: Accessing inaccessible everyday memories. *Memory*, 19, 697–704.

Luce, P. A. and Pisoni, D. B. (1998). Recognizing spoken words: The neighborhood activation model. *Ear Hear*, 19(1), 1–36.

Luchins, A. S. (1942). Mechanization in problem solving. *Psychological Monographs*, 54:6, Whole No. 248.

Luria, A. R. (1966). *Higher Cortical Functions in Man*. London: Tavistock.

Luria, A. R. (1973). *The Working Brain: An Introduction to Neuropsychology*. Harmondsworth: Penguin Books.

McCall, W. V. (2004). Quality of life and function after electroconvulsive therapy. *British Journal of Psychiatry*, 185, 405–409.

McCarthy, G., Puce, A., Gore, J. and Allison, T. (1997). Face-specific processing in the human fusiform gyrus. *Journal of Cognitive Neuroscience*, 9, 605–610.

McCarthy, R. A., Kopelman, M. D. and Warrington, E. K. (2005). Remembering and forgetting of semantic knowledge in amnesia: A 16-year follow-up investigation of RFR. *Neuropsychologia*, 43, 356–372.

McClelland, J. L. and Patterson, K. (2002). Rules or connections in past-tense inflections: What does the evidence rule out? *Trends in Cognitive Sciences*, 6(11), 465–472.

McClelland, J. L. and Rumelhart, D. E. (1986). *Parallel Distributed Processing: Explorations in the Microstructure of Cognition* (Vols 1 and 2). Cambridge, MA: MIT Press.

McDaniel, M. A. and Fisher, R. P. (1991). Tests and test feedback as learning sources. *Contemporary Educational Psychology*, 16, 192–201.

McDaniel, M. A., Roediger, H. L. III and McDermott, K. B. (2007). Generalising test-enhanced learning from the laboratory to the classroom. *Psychonomic Bulletin and Review*, 14, 200–206.

McGeoch, J. A. (1932). Forgetting and the law of disuse. *Psychological Review*, 39, 352–370.

McGettigan, C., Warren, J. E., Eisner, F., Marshall, C. R., Shanmugalingam, P. and Scott, S. K. (2011). Neural correlates of sublexical processing in phonological working memory. *Journal of Cognitive Neuroscience*, 23(4), 961–77.

McGinn, C. (1999). *The Mysterious Flame: Conscious Minds in a Material World*. New York: Basic Books.

MacGregor, J. N., Ormerod, T. C. and Chronicle, E. P. (2001). Information processing and insight: A process model of performance on the nine-dot and related problems. *Journal of Experimental Psychology: Learning, Memory, and Cognition*, 27, 176–201.

McIntosh, R. D., Rossetti, Y. and Milner, A. D. (2002). Prism adaptation improves chronic visual and haptic neglect: A single case study. *Cortex*, 38, 309–320.

Macken, W. J. and Jones, D. M. (1995). Functional characteristics of the "inner voice" and the "inner ear": Single or double agency? *Journal of Experimental Psychology: Learning, Memory, and Cognition*, 21, 436–448.

MacLeod, C. M. (1998). Training on integrated versus separated stroop tasks: The progression of interference and facilitation. *Memory and Cognition*, 26, 201–211.

MacLeod, M. D. (2002). Retrieval-induced forgetting in eyewitness memory: Forgetting as a consequence of remembering. *Applied Cognitive Psychology*, 16, 135–149.

MacLeod, M. D. and Macrae, C. N. (2001). Gone today but here tomorrow: The transient nature of retrieval-induced forgetting. *Psychological Science*, 12, 148–152.

MacLeod, M. D. and Saunders, J. (2005). The role of inhibitory control in the production of misinformation effects. *Journal of Experimental Psychology: Learning, Memory and Cognition*, 31, 964–979.

McLeod, P. D. (1978). Does probe RT measure central processing demand? *Quarterly Journal of Experimental Psychology*, 30, 83–89.

Macmillan, M. B. (1986). A wonderful journey through the skull and brains: The travels of Mr Gage's tamping iron. *Brain and Cognition*, 5, 67–107.

McNally, R. J. and Geraerts, E. (2009). A new solution to the recovered memory debate. *Perspectives on Psychological Science*, 4, 126–134.

McNeil, J. E. and Warrington, E. K. (1993). Prosopagnosia: A face-specific disorder. *Quarterly Journal of Experimental Psychology*, 46A, 1–10.

McQueen, J. M. (1998). Segmentation of continuous speech using phonotactics. *Journal of Memory and Language*, 39, 21–46.

Macrae, C. N. and MacLeod, M. D. (1999). On recollections lost: When practice makes imperfect. *Journal of Personality and Social Psychology*, 77, 463–473.

MacSweeney, M., Capek, C. M., Campbell, R. and Woll, B. (2008). The signing brain: the neurobiology of sign language. *Trends in Cognitive Sciences*, 12(11), 432–440.

Maier, N. R. F. (1930). Reasoning in humans I: On direction. *Journal of Comparative Psychology*, 10, 115–143.

Maier, N. R. F. (1931). Reasoning in humans II: The solution of a problem and its appearance in consciousness. *Journal of Comparative Psychology*, 12, 181–194.

Mair, W. G. P., Warrington, E. K. and Weiskrantz, L. (1979). Memory disorders in Korsakoff's psychosis: A neuropathological and neuropsychological investigation of two cases. *Brain*, 102, 749–783.

Majerus, S., Poncelet, M., Elsen, B. and van der Linden, M. (2006). Exploring the relationship between new word learning and short-term memory for serial order recall, item recall, and item recognition. *European Journal of Cognitive Psychology*, 18, 848–873.

Malhotra, P. A., Parton, A. D., Greenwood, R. and Husain, M. (2006). Noradrenergic modulation of space exploration in visual neglect. *Annals of Neurology*, 59(1), 186–190.

Mandler, G. (1972). Organization and recognition. In E. Tulving and W. Donaldson (eds) *Organization of Memory*. New York: Academic Press.

Mandler, G. (1980). Recognising: The judgement of a previous occurrence. *Psychological Review*, 27, 252–271.

Mandler, G. (1989). Memory: Conscious and unconscious. In P. R. Soloman, G. R. Goethals, C. M. Kelley and B. R. Stephens (eds) *Memory: Interdisciplinary Approaches*. New York: Springer-Verlag.

Mandler, G. (2002). Organisation: What levels of processing are levels of. *Memory*, 10, 333–338.

Mandler, G. (2008). Familiarity breeds attempts: A critical review of dual-process theories of recognition. *Perspectives on Psychological Science*, 3, 390–399.

Mandler, G. (2011). From association to organisation. *Psychological Science*, 20, 232–235.

Mandler, G. Pearlstone, Z. and Koopmans, H. S. (1969). Effects of organisation and semantic similarity on a recall and recognition task. *Journal of Verbal Learning and Verbal Behaviour*, 8, 410–423.

Maner, J. K., Richey, J. A., Cromer, K., Mallott, M., Lejuez, C. W., Joiner, T. E. *et al.* (2007). Dispositional anxiety and risk-avoidant decision-making. *Personality and Individual Differences*, 42, 665–675.

Manly, T., Robertson, I. H. and Verity, C. (1997). Developmental unilateral visual neglect: A single case study. *Neurocase*, 3(1), 19–29.

Manly, T., Woldt, K., Watson, P. and Warburton, E. (2002). Is motor perseveration in unilateral neglect 'driven' by the presence of neglected left-sided stimuli? *Neuropsychologia*, 40(11), 1794–1803.

Manly, T., Dobler, V. B., Dodds, C. M. and George, M. A. (2005). Rightward shift in spatial awareness with declining alertness. *Neuropsychologia*, 43(12), 1721–1728.

Mantyla, T. (1986). Optimising cue effectiveness: Recall of 500 and 600 incidentally learned words. *Journal of Experimental Psychology: Learning, Memory, and Cognition*, 12, 66–71.

Marcel, A. J. (1980). Conscious and preconscious recognition of polysemous words: Locating the selective effects of prior verbal context.

In R. S. Nickerson (ed.) *Attention and Performance, VII*, NJ. Erlbaum.

Marcel, A. J. (1983). Conscious and unconscious perception: An approach to the relations between phenomenal experience and perceptual processes. *Cognitive Psychology*, 15, 238–300.

Marr, D. (1982). *Vision: A Computational Investigation into the Human Representation and Processing of Visual Information*. San Francisco: Freeman.

Marr, D. and Nishihara, K. (1978). Representation and recognition of the spatial organisation of three-dimensional shapes. *Philosophical Transactions of the Royal Society, Series B*, 269–294.

Marshall, J. C. and Newcombe, F. (1966). Syntactic and semantic errors in paralexia. *Neuropsychologia*, 4, 169–176.

Marshall, J. C. and Newcombe, F. (1973). Patterns of paralexia: A psycholinguistic approach. *Journal of Psycholinguistic Research*, 2, 175–199.

Marshall, J. C. and Halligan, P. W. (1988). Blindsight and insight in visuo-spatial neglect. *Nature*, 336, 766–767.

Marshall, J. C. and Halligan, P. W. (1993). Visuo-spatial neglect: A new copying test to assess perceptual parsing. *Journal of Neurology*, 240, 37–40.

Marslen-Wilson, W. D. (1973). Linguistic structure and speech shadowing at very short latencies. *Nature*, 244 (5417), 522–523.

Marslen-Wilson, W. D. (1975). Sentence perception as an interactive parallel process. *Science*, 189, 226–228.

Marslen-Wilson, W. D. (1987). Functional parallelism in spoken word-recognition. *Cognition*, 25, 71–102.

Marslen-Wilson, W. (ed.) (1989). *Lexical Representation and Process*. Cambridge, MA: MIT Press.

Marslen-Wilson, W. D. and Zwitserlood, P. (1989). Accessing spoken words: The importance of word onsets. *Journal of Experimental Psychology: Human Perception and Performance*, 15(3), 576–585.

Martin, E. A. and Kerns, J. G. (2011). The influence of positive mood on different aspects of cognitive control. *Cognition and Emotion*, 25, 265–279.

Martin, R. C. (1993). Short-term memory and sentence processing: Evidence from neuropsychology. *Memory and Cognition*, 21, 176–183.

Massie, D. L., Campbell, K. L. and Williams, A. F. (1995). Traffic Accident involvement rates by driver age and gender. *Accident Analysis and Prevention*, 27(1), 73–87.

Mattingley, J. B., Rich, A. N., Yelland, G. and Bradshaw, J. L. (2001). Unconscious priming eliminates automatic binding of colour and alphanumeric form in synaesthesia. *Nature*, 410, 580–582.

Mattson, A. J., Levin, H. S. and Grafman, J. (2000). A case of prosopagnosia following moderate closed head injury with left hemisphere focal lesion. *Cortex*, 36(1), 125–137.

Mattys, S. L., White, L. and Melhorn, J. F. (2005). Integration of multiple speech segmentation cues: A hierarchical framework. *Journal of Experimental Psychology: General*, 134, 477–500.

Maurer, D. and Mondloch, C. J. (2006). The infant as synesthete? *Attention and Performance*, XXI, 449–471.

Mayes, A. R. (2002). Does focal retrograde amnesia exist and if so, what causes it? *Cortex*, 38, 670–673.

Meeter, M., Murre, J. M. and Janssen, S. M. (2005). Remembering the news: Modelling retention data from a study with 14,000 participants. *Memory and Cognition*, 33, 793–810.

Meeter, M., Murre, J., Janssen, S., Birkenhager, T. and van den Broek, W. W. (2011). Retrograde amnesia after electroconvulsive therapy: A temporary effect? *Journal of Affective Disorders*, 132, 216–222.

Melby-Lervåg, M. and Hulme, C. (2013). Is working memory training effective? A meta-analytic review. *Developmental Psychology*, 49 (2), 270–291.

Memon, A. and Wright, D. B. (1999). Eyewitness testimony and the Oklahoma bombing. *The Psychologist*, 12, 292–295.

Memon, A., Zaragoza, M., Clifford, B. R. and Kidd, L. (2009). Inoculation or antidote? The effects of cognitive interview timing on false memory for forcibly fabricated events. *Law and Human Behavior*, 34,105–117.

Mendez, M. F. and Benson, D. F. (1985). Atypical conduction aphasia: A disconnection syndrome. *Archives of Neurology*, 42(9), 886–891.

Meredith, C. and Edworthy, J. (1994). Sources of confusion in intensive care unit alarms. In N. Stanton (ed.) *Human Factors in Alarm Design* (p. 238). London: Taylor & Francis.

Mesulam, M. (1999). Spatial attention and neglect: parietal, frontal and cingulate contributions to the mental representation and attentional targeting of salient extrapersonal events. *Philosophical Transactions of the Royal Society of London Series B-Biological Sciences*, 354(1387, 29 July), 1325–1346.

Michel, F. and Andreewsky, E. (1983). Deep dysphasia: An analog of deep dyslexia in the auditory modality. *Brain and Language*, 18, 212–223.

Middlebrooks, C. J. (1992). Narrow-Band Sound localisation Related to External Ear acoustics. *Journal of the Acoustical Society of America*, 92(5), 2607–2624.

Milders, M. V., Berg, I. J. and Deelman, B. G. (1995). Four-year follow-up of a controlled memory training study in closed head injured patients. *Neuropsychological Rehabilitation*, 5, 223–238.

Miller, E. (1977). *Abnormal Ageing: The Psychology of Senile and Presenile Dementia*. Chichester: Wiley.

Miller, G. A. (1956). The magic number seven, plus or minus two: Some limits on our capacity for processing information. *Psychological Review*, 63, 81–93.

Miller, L. A. and Tippett, L. J. (1996). Effects of focal brain lesions on visual problem-solving. *Neuropsychologia*, 34, 387–398.

Mills, C. B., Boteler, E. H. and Oliver, G. K. (1999). Digit synaesthesia: A case study using a stroop-type test. *Cognitive Neuropsychology*, 16, 181–91.

Milne, R. and Bull, R. (2002). Back to basics: A componential analysis of the original cognitive interview mnemonics with three age groups. *Applied Cognitive Psychology*, 16, 743–753.

Milne, R. and Bull, R. (2003). Does the cognitive interview help children to resist the effects of suggestive questioning? *Legal and Criminological Psychology*, 8, 21–38.

Milner, A. D. and Goodale, M. A. (1995). *The Visual Brain in Action*. Oxford: Oxford University Press.

Milner, A. D. and Goodale, M. A. (2006). *The Visual Brain in Action* (2nd edn). Oxford: Oxford University Press.

Milner, A. D. and Goodale, M. A. (2008). Two visual systems re-viewed. *Neuropsychologia*, 46, 774–785.

Milner, B. (1964). Some effects of frontal lobectomy in man. In J. M. Warren and K. Akert (eds) *The Frontal Granular Cortex and Behavior*. New York: McGraw-Hill.

Milner, B. (1966). Amnesia following operation on the temporal lobes. In C. W. M. hitty and O. L. Zangwill (eds) *Amnesia*. London: Butterworth.

Milner, B., Corkin, S. and Teuber, H. L. (1968). Further analysis of hippocampal amnesia – 14-year follow-up of H. M. *Neuropsychologia*, 6, 215–234.

Miranda, R. and Kihlstrom, J. F. (2005). Mood congruence in childhood and recent autobiographical memory. *Cognition and Emotion*, 19, 981–998.

Misanin, J. R., Miller, R. R. and Lewis, D. J. (1968). Retrograde amnesia produced by electroconvulsive shock after reactivation of a consolidated memory trace. *Science*, 160, 554–555.

Mitchell, D. B. (2006). Nonconscious priming after 17 years. *Psychological Science*, 17, 925–929.

Miyake, A. and Friedman, N. P. (2012). The nature and organisation of individual differences in executive functions: Four general conclusions. *Current Directions in Psychological Science*, 2, 8–14.

Miyake, A., Friedman, N. P., Emerson, M.J, Witzki, A. H., Howerter, A. and Wager, T. D. (2000). The unity and diversity of executive functions and their contributions to complex "frontal lobe" tasks: A latent variable analysis. *Cognitive Psychology*, 41, 49–100.

Mohr, J. P., Pessin, M. S., Finkelstein, S., Funkenstein, H. H., Duncan, G. W. and Davis, K. R. (1978). Broca aphasia: Pathologic and clinical. *Neurology*, 28, 311–324.

Moors, A. and De Houwer, J. (2006). Automaticity: A theoretical and conceptual analysis. *Psychological Bulletin*, 132, 297–326.

Moray, N. (1959). Attention in dichotic listening: Affective cues and the influence of instruction. *Quarterly Journal of Experimental Psychology*, 11, 56–60.

Moretto, G., Ladavas, E., Mattioli, F. and Di Pellegrino, G. (2010). A psychphysiological investigation of moral judgment after ventromedial prefrontal damage. *Journal of Cognitive Neuroscience*, 22, 1888–1899.

Morris, P. E., Gruneberg, M. M., Sykes, R. M. and Merrick, A. (1981). Football knowledge and the acquisition of new results. *British Journal of Psychology*, 72, 479–484.

Morris, R. D. and Baddeley, A. D. (1988). Primary and working memory functioning in Alzheimer-type dementia. *Journal of Clinical and Experimental Neuropsychology*, 10, 279–296.

Morris, R. G., Ahmed, S., Syed, G. M. and Toone, B. K. (1993). Neural correlates of planning ability: Frontal lobe activation during the Tower of London test. *Neuropsychologia*, 31, 1367–1378.

Morris, R. G., Bullmore, E. T., Baron-Cohen, S. and Gray, J. A. (2002). Functional magnetic resonance imaging of synesthesia: activation of V4/V8 by spoken words. *Nature Neuroscience*, 5, 371–375.

Morrison, C. M. and Ellis, A. W. (1995). Roles of word frequency and age of acquisition in word naming and lexical decision. *Journal of Experimental Psychology: Learning, Memory and Cognition*, 21, 116–133.

Morsella, E. and Miozzo, M. (2002). Evidence for a cascade model of lexical access in speech production. *Journal of Experimental Psychology: Learning, Memory, and Cognition*, 28, 555–563.

Mort, D. J., Malhotra, P., Mannan, S. K., Rorden, C., Pambakian, A., Kennard, C. and Husain, M. (2003). The anatomy of visual neglect. *Brain*, 126, 1986–1997.

Mortimer, A. and Shepherd, E. (1999). Frames of mind: Schemata guiding cognition and conduct in the interviewing of suspected offenders. In A. Memon and R. Bull (eds) *Handbook of the Psychology of Interviewing* (pp. 293–315). Chichester: Wiley.

Morton, J. (1969). The interaction of information in word recognition. *Psychological Review*, 76, 165–178.

Morton, J. (1970). A functional model for memory. In D. A. Norman (ed.) *Models of Human Memory*. New York: Academic Press.

Morton, J. (1979). Facilitation in word recognition: Experiments causing change in the Logogen model. In P. A. Kolers, M. E. Wrolstad and H. Bouma (eds) *Processing of Visible Language*. New York: Plenum.

Morton, J. and Patterson, K. (1980). A new attempt at an interpretation, or, an attempt at a new interpretation. In M. Coltheart, K. E. Patterson, J. C. Marshall (eds) *Deep Dyslexia* (pp. 91–118). London: Routledge and Kegan Paul.

Morton, J. and Patterson, K. (1987). A new attempt at an interpretation, or, an attempt at a new interpretation. In M. Coltheart, K. E. Patterson and J. C. Marshall (eds) *Deep Dyslexia* (2nd edn). London: Routledge.

Moscovitch, M. (1989). Confabulation and the frontal system: strategic versus associative retrieval in neuropsychological theories of memory. In H. L. Roediger and F. I. M. Craik (eds) *Variety of Memory and Consciousness: Essays in Honour of Endel Tulving*. Hillsdale, NJ: Lawrence Erlbaum Associates.

Moscovitch, M., Yaschyshyn, M., Ziegler, M. and Nadel, L. (1999). Remote episodic memory and retrograde amnesia: Was Endel Tulving right all along? In E. Tulving (ed.) *Memory, Consciousness, and the Brain: The Tallin Conference*. New York: Psychology Press.

Mulligan, N. W. and Picklesimer, M. (2012). Levels of processing and the cue-dependent nature of recollection. *Journal of Memory and Language*, 66, 79–92.

Murty, V. P., Ritchey, M., Adcock, R. A. and LaBar, K. S. (2010). fMRI studies of successful emotional memory encoding: A quantitative meta-analysis. *Neuropsychologia*, 48, 3459–3469.

Mustanski, B. (2007). The influence of state and trait affect on HIV risk behaviors: A daily diary study of MSM. *Health Psychology*, 26, 618–626.

Muter, P. (1980). Very rapid forgetting. *Memory and Cognition*, 8, 174–179.

Myles, K. M., Dixon, M. J., Smilek, D. and Merikle, P. M. (2003). Seeing double: The role of meaning in alphanumeric-colour synaesthesia. *Brain and Cognition*, 53, 342–345.

Na, D. L., Adair, M. D., Kang, Y., Chung, C. S., Lee, K. H. and Heilman, K. M. (1999). Motor perseverative behaviour on a line cancellation task. *Neurology*, 52, 1569–1576.

Nader, K., Schafe, G. and Ledoux, J. E. (2000). The labile nature of the consolidation theory. *Nature Neuroscience Reviews*, 1, 216–219.

Naeser, M. A., Helm-Estabrooks, N., Haas, G., Auerbach, S. and Srinivasan, M. (1987). Relationship between lesion extent in "Wernicke's area" on computed tomographic scan and predicting recovery of comprehension in Wernicke's aphasia. *Archives of Neurology*, 44, 73–82.

Nairne, J. S. (2002a). The myth of the encoding-retrieval match. *Memory*, 10, 389–395.

Nairne, J. S. (2002b). Remembering over the short term: The case against the standard model. *Annual Review of Psychology*, 53, 53–81.

Naish, P. (2005). Attention. In N. Braisby and A. Gellatly (eds) *Cognitive Psychology*. Oxford: Oxford University Press.

Nakamura, N., Fujita, K., Ushitani, T. and Miyata, H. (2006). Perception of the standard and the reversed Muller-Lyer figures in pigeons and humans. *Journal of Comparative Psychology*, 120(3), 252.

Navarro, J., Mars, F. and Hoc, J.-M. (2007). Lateral control assistance for car drivers: A comparison of motor priming and warning systems. *Human Factors*, 49(5), 950–960.

Navon, D. (1977). Forest before trees: The precedence of global features in visual perception. *Cognitive Psychology*, 9, 353–383.

Neath, I. and Nairne, J. S. (1995). Word-length effects in immediate memory: Overwriting the trace decay theory. *Psychonomic Bulletin and Review*, 2, 429–441.

Neisser, U. (1967). *Cognitive Psychology*. New York: Appleton-Century-Crofts.

Neisser, U. (1976). *Cognition and Reality*. San Francisco: Freeman.

Neisser, U. (1982). *Memory Observed*. San Francisco: Freeman.

Neisser, U. (1994). Multiple systems: A new approach to cognitive theory. *European Journal of Cognitive Psychology*, 6(3), 225–241.

Neisser, U. and Becklen, P. (1975). Selective looking: Attending to visually superimposed events. *Cognitive Psychology*, 7, 480–494.

Neisser, U. and Harsch, N. (1992). Phantom flashbulbs: False connections of hearing the news about Challenger. In E. Winograd and U. Neisser (eds) *Affect and Accuracy in Recall: Studies of "Flashbulb" Memories*. New York: Cambridge University Press.

Nelson, H. E. (1976). A modified card sorting test sensitive to frontal lobe defects. *Cortex*, 12, 313–324.

Nelson, K. and Ross, G. (1980). The generalities and specifics of long-term memory in infants and younger children. In M. Perlmutter (ed.) *Children's Memory: New Directions for Child Development*. San Francisco CA: Jossey-Bass.

Neufeld, J., Sinke, C., Zedler, M., Dillo, W., Emrich, H. M., Bleich, S. and Szycik, G. R. (2012). Disinhibited feedback as a cause of synesthesia: Evidence from a functional connectivity study on auditory-visual synesthetes. *Neuropsychologia*, 50(7), 1471–1477.

Newell, A. and Simon, H. A. (1961). Computer simulation of human thinking. *Science*, 134, 2011–2017.

Newell, A. and Simon, H. A. (1972). *Human Problem Solving*. Englewood Cliffs, NJ: Prentice-Hall.

Newell, A. and Rosenbloom, P. S. (1981). Mechanisms of skill acquisition and the law of practice. In J. R. Anderson (ed.) *Cognitive Skills and Their Acqusition*. Hillsdale, NJ; Lawrence Earlbaum Associates.

Newell, A., Shaw, J. C. and Simon, H. A. (1958). Elements of a theory of human problem solving. *Psychological Review*, 65, 151–166.

Newstead, S. E., Ellis, M. C., Evans, J. St. B. T. and Dennis, I. (1997). Conditional reasoning with realistic material. *Thinking and Reasoning*, 3, 49–76.

Newstead, S. E., Handley, S. J., Harley, C., Wright, H. and Farrelly, D. (2004). Individual differencs in deductive reasoning. *The Quarterly Journal of Experimental Psychology*, 57A(1), 33–60.

Nieuwenstein, M. R., Potter, M. C. and Theeuwes, J. (2009). Unmasking the attentional blink. *Journal of Experimental Psychology: Human Perception and Performance*, 35(1), 159–169.

Nilsson, L. G. and Gardiner, J. M. (1993). Identifying exceptions in a database of recognition failure studies from 1973 to 1992. *Memory and Cognition*, 21, 397–410.

Norman, D. A. (1981). Categorization of action slips. *Psychological Review*, 88, 1–15.

Norman, D. A. and Shallice, T. (1986). Attention to action: Willed and automatic control of behaviour. In R. Davison, G. Shwartz and D. Shapiro (eds) *Consciousness and Self Regulation: Advances in Research and Theory*. New York: Plenum.

Norman, J. (2001). Ecological psychology and the two visual systems: Not to worry. *Ecological Psychology*, 13(2), 135–145.

Norman, J. (2002). Two visual systems and two theories of perception: An attempt to reconcile the constructivist and ecological approaches. *Behavioral and Brain Sciences*, 25(1), 73–96.

Nunn, J. A., Gregory, L. J., Brammer, M., Williams, S. C. R., Parslow, D. M. *et al.* (2002). Functional magnetic resonance imaging of synesthesia: Activation of V4/V8 by spoken words. *Nature Neuroscience*, 4, 371–375.

Nyberg, L. (2002). Levels of processing: A view from functional brain imaging. *Memory*, 10, 345–348.

Nys, G. M., van Zandvoort, M. J. E., Roks, G., Kappelle, L. J., de Kort, P. L. and de Haan, E. H. (2004). The role of executive functioning in spontaneous confabulation. *Cognitive and Behavioural Neurology*, 17, 213–218.

Oaksford, M. (2005). Reasoning. In N. Braisby and A. Gellatly (eds) *Cognitive Psychology*. Oxford: Oxford University Press.

Oaksford, M. and Chater, N. (1994). A rational analysis of the selection task as optimal data selection. *Psychological Review*, 101, 608–631.

Oaksford, M. and Chater, N. (1998). *Rationality in an Uncertain World: Essays on the Cognitive Science of Human Reasoning*. Hove: Psychology Press.

Oaksford, M. and Chater, N. (2001). The probabilistic approach to human reasoning. *Trends in Cognitive Sciences*, 5, 349–357.

Oaksford, M. and Chater, N. (2007). *Bayesian Rationality: The Probabilistic Approach to Human Reasoning*. Oxford: Oxford University Press.

Oaksford, M. and Chater, N. (2009). Precis of Bayesian rationality: The probabilistic approach to human reasoning. *Behavioral and Brain Sciences*, 32, 69–84.

Oaksford, M. and Chater, N. (2010). Conditional inferences and constraint satisfaction: Reconciling mental models and the probabilistic approach. In M. Oaksford and N. Chater (eds) *Cognition and Conditionals: Probability and Logic in Human Thinking* (pp. 309–334). Oxford: Oxford University Press.

Oaksford, M., Morris, F., Grainger, B. and Williams, J. M. G. (1996). Mood, reasoning, and central executive processes. *Journal of Experimental Psychology: Learning, Memory, and Cognition*, 22, 476–492.

Oatley, K. and Johnson-Laird, P. N. (1987). Towards a cognitive theory of emotions. *Cognition and Emotion*, 1, 29–50.

Oberauer, K. (2003). Understanding serial position curves in short-term recognition and recall. *Journal of Memory and Language*, 4, 469–483.

Obleser, J., Boecker, H., Drzezga, A., Haslinger, B., Hennenlotter, A., Roettinger, M., Eulitz, C. and Rauschecker, J. P. (2006). Vowel sound extraction in anterior superior temporal cortex. *Human Brain Mapping*, 27(7), 562–571.

Obleser, J., Wise, R. J., Dresner, M. and Scott, S. K. (2007). Functional integration across brain regions improves speech perception under adverse listening conditions. *Journal of Neuroscience*, 27(9), 2283–2289.

O'Connor, M., Butters, N., Miliotis, P., Eslinger, P. and Cermak, L. S. (1992). The dissociation of retrograde and anterograde amnesia in a patient with Herpes Encephalitis. *Journal of Clinical and Experimental Neuropsychology*, 14, 159–178.

Ogden, J. A. and Corkin, S. (1991). Memories of H. M. In W. C. Abraham, M. C. Corballis and K. G. White (eds) *Memory Mechanisms: A Tribute to G. V. Goddard*. Hillsdale, NJ: Erlbaum.

Ohlsson, S. (1992). Information processing explanations of insight and related phenomena. In M. T. Keane and K. J. Gilhooly (eds) *Advances in the Psychology of Thinking* (pp. 1–44). London: Harvester Wheatsheaf.

Oldfield, S. R. and Parker, S. P. A. (1984a). Acuity of sound localization: A topography of auditory space. I. Normal conditions. *Perception*, 13, 581–600.

Oldfield, S. R. and Parker, S. P. A. (1984b). Acuity of sound localization: a topography of auditory space. II. Pinna cues absent. *Perception*, 13, 601–617.

Olivers, C. N. L. (2007). The time course of attention: It is better than we thought. *Current Directions in Psychological Science*, 16, 11–15.

Öllinger, M., Jones. G. and Knoblich, G. (2006). Heuristics and representational change in two-move matchstick arithmetic tasks. *Advances in Cognitive Psychology*, 2, 239–253.

Öllinger, M., Jones, G. and Knoblich, G. (2008). Investigating the effect of mental set on insight problem solving. *Experimental Psychology*, 55, 269–282.

O'Regan, J. K. (1992). Solving the "real" mysteries of visual perception: The world as an outside memory. *Canadian Journal of Psychology*, 46(3), 461–488.

Ormerod, T. C., MacGregor, J. N. and Chronicle, E. P. (2002). Dynamics and constraints in insight problem solving. *Journal of Experimental Psychology: Learning, Memory, and Cognition*, 28, 791–799.

O'Rourke, T. B. and Holcomb, P. J. (2002). Electrophysiological evidence for the efficiency of spoken word processing. *Biological Psychology*, 60(2–3), 121–150.

Ost, J., Granhag, P., Udell, J. and Hjelmsater, E. R. (2008). Familiarity breeds distortion: The effects of media exposure on false reports concerning media coverage of the terrorist attacks in London on 7 July 2005. *Memory*, 16, 76–85.

Otten, L. J. and Rugg, M. D. (2001). Task-dependency of the neural correlates of episodic encoding as measured by fMRI. *Cerebral Cortex*, 11, 1150–1160.

Owen, A. M., Downes, J. J., Sahakian, B. J., Polkey, C. E. and Robbins, T. W. (1990). Planning and spatial working memory following frontal lobe lesions in man. *Neuropsychologia*, 28, 1021–1034.

Owen, A. M., Roberts, A. C., Polkey, C. E., Sahakian, B. J. and Robbins, T. W. (1991). Extra-dimension versus intra-dimensional shifting performance following frontal lobe excisions, temporal lobe excisions or amygdalo-hippocampectomy in man. *Neuropsychologia*, 29, 993–1006.

Owen, A. M., McMillan, K. M., Laird, A. R. and Bullmore, E. (2005). N-back working memory paradigm: A meta-analysis of normative functional neuroimaging studies. *Human Brain Mapping*, 25, 46–59.

Owen, D. H. (1990). Lexicon of terms for the perception and control of self-motion and orientation. In R. Warren and A. H. Wertheim (eds) *Perception and Control of Self-Motion* (pp. 33–50). Hillsdale, NJ: Lawrence Erlbaum.

Ozonoff, S., Strayer, D., McMahon, W. and Filoux, F. (1994). Executive function abilities in autism and Tourette syndrome: An information-processing approach. *Journal of Child Psychology and Psychiatry*, 35, 1015–1032.

Oztekin, I., Davachi, L. and McElree, B. (2010). Are representations in working memory distinct from representations in long-term memory? Neural evidence in support of a single store. *Psychological Science*, 21, 1123–1133.

Parkin, A. J. (1983). The relationship between orienting tasks and the structure of memory traces: Evidence from false recognition. *British Journal of Psychology*, 74, 61–69.

Parkin, A. J. (1993). *Memory: Phenomena, Experiment, and Theory*. Oxford: Blackwell.

Parkin, A. J. (1996). *Explorations in Cognitive Neuropsychology*. Oxford: Blackwell.

Parkin, A. J. (1997). *Memory and Amnesia*. Oxford: Blackwell.

Parkin, A. J. and Walter, B. (1992). Ageing, conscious recollection, and frontal lobe dysfunction. *Psychology and Ageing*, 7, 290–298.

Parkin, A. J., Reid, T. and Russo, R. (1990). On the differential nature of implicit and explicit memory. *Memory and Cognition*, 18, 507–514.

Parkin, A. J., Gardiner, J. M. and Rosser, R. (1995a). Functional aspects of recollective experience in face recognition. *Consciousness and Cognition*, 4, 387–398.

Parkin, A. J., Walter, B. M. and Hunkin, N. M. (1995b). Relationships between normal ageing, frontal lobe function, and memory for temporal and spatial information. *Neuropsychology*, 9, 304–312.

Parra, M. A., Abrahams, S., Fabi, K., Logie, R., Luzzi, S. and Della Sala, S. (2009). Short-term memory binding deficits in Alzheimer's Disease. *Brain*, 132, 1057–1066.

Parsons, L. M. and Osherson, D. (2001). New evidence for distinct right and left brain systems for deductive versus probabilistic reasoning. *Cerebral Cortex*, 11, 954–965.

Pashler, H. (1990). Do response modality effects support multi-processor models of divided attention? *Journal of Experimental Psychology: Human Perception and Performance*, 16, 826–842.

Pashler, H. (1994). Dual task interference in simple tasks: Data and Theory. *Psychological Bulletin*, 16, 220–224.

Patterson, K. (1982). The relationship between reading and phonological coding: Further neuropsychological observations. In A. W. Ellis (ed.) *Normality and Pathology in Cognitive Functions* (pp. 77–111). London: Academic Press.

Patterson, K., Nestor, P. J., and Rogers, T. T. (2007). Where do you know what you know? The representation of semantic knowledge in the human brain. *Nature Reviews Neuroscience*, 8(12), 976–987.

Pecher, C., Lemercier, C. and Cellier, J.-M. (2009). Emotions drive attention: Effects on driver's behaviour. *Safety Science*, 47, 1254–1259.

Peelen, M. V., Lucas, N., Mayer, E. and Vuilleumier, P. (2009). Emotional attention in acquired prosopagnosia. *Scan*, 4, 268–277. doi:10.1093/scan/nsp014.

Perret, E. (1974). The left frontal lobe of man and the suppression of habitual responses in verbal categorical behavior. *Neuropsychologica*, 12, 323–330.

Perrett, D. I., Smith, P. A., Potter, D. D., Mistlin, A. J., Head, A. S., Milner, A. D., Jeeves, M. A., (1985). Visual cells in the temporal cortex sensitive to face view and gaze direction. Proceedings of the Royal Society B: Biological Sciences, 223, 293–317.

Persaud, N., McLeod, P. and Cowie, A. (2007). Post-decision wagering objectively measures awareness. *Nature Neuroscience*, 10, 257–261.

Peru, A. and Avesani, R. (2008). To know what it is for, but not how it is: semantic dissociations in a case of visual agnosia. *Neurocase*, 14(3), 249–63. doi:10.1080/13554790802269968.

Peterson, L. R. and Peterson, M. J. (1959). Short-term retention of individual items. *Journal of Experimental Psychology*, 58, 193–198.

Phillips, C. E., Jarrold, C., Baddeley, A. D., Grant, J. and Karmiloff-Smith, A. (2004). Comprehension of spatial language terms in Williams syndrome: Evidence for an interaction between domains of strength and weakness. *Cortex*, 40, 85–101.

Piercy, M. F. (1977). Experimental studies of the organic amnesic syndrome. In C. W. M. Whitty and O. L. Zangwill (eds) *Amnesia*. London: Butterworth.

Pillemer, D. B. and White, S. H. (1989). Childhood events recalled by children and adults. In H. W. Reese (ed.) *Advances in Child Development and Behaviour*. San Diego CA: Academic Press.

Pinker, S. (1991). Rules of language. *Science*, 253, 530–535.

Pinker, S. (1997). *How the Mind Works*. London: Penguin.

Pinker, S. (1999). *Words and Rules*. New York: Basic Books.

Pinker, S. (2001). Four decades of rules and associations, or whatever happened to the past tense debate? In E. Dupoux (ed.) *Language, the Brain,* and *Cognitive Development: Papers in Honor of Jacques Mehler*. Cambridge, MA: MIT Press.

Plaut, D. C. and Shallice, T. (1993). Deep dyslexia: A case study of connectionist neuropsychology. *Cognitive Neuropsychology*, 10, 377–500.

Poletiek, F. H. (1996). Paradoxes of falsification. *The Quarterly Journal of Experimental Psychology*, 49A, 447–462.

Polivy, J. (1981). On the induction of emotion in the laboratory: Discrete moods or multiple affect states? *Journal of Personality and Social Psychology*, 41, 803–817.

Poppel, E. Held, R. and Frost, D. (1973). Residual visual function after brain wounds involving the central visual pathways in man. *Nature*, 243, 295–296.

Posner, M. I. (1980). Orienting of attention. *Quarterly Journal of Experimental Psychology*, 32, 3–25.

Posner, M. I. and Boies, S. J. (1971). Components of attention. *Psychological Review*, 78, 391–408.

Posner, M. I. and Petersen, S. E. (1990). The attentional system of the human brain. *Annual Review of Neuroscience*, 13, 25–42.

Posner, M. I. and Badgaiyan, R. D. (1998). Attention and neural networks. In R. W. Parks, D. S. Levine and R. D. Badgaiyan. *Fundamentals of Neural Network Modelling*. Cambridge, MA: MIT Press.

Posner, M. I., Snyder, C. R. R. and Davidson, B. J. (1980). Attention and the detection of signals. *Journal of Experimental Psychology: General*, 109, 160–174.

Potts, R., Law, R., Golding, J. and Groome, D. (2011). The reliability of retrieval-induced forgetting. *European Psychologist*, 1, 1–10.

Power, M. J., Dalgleish, T., Claudio, V., Tata, P. and Kentish, J. (2000). The directed forgetting task: Application to emotionally valent material. *Journal of Affective Disorders*, 57, 147–157.

Praamstra, P., Hagoort, P., Maassen, B. and Crul, T. (1991). Word deafness and auditory cortical function a case history and hypothesis. *Brain*, 114, 1197–1225.

Price, C. J. and Devlin, J. T. (2003). The myth of the visual word form area. *Neuroimage*, 19(3), 473–81.

Price, C. J., Wise, R. J., Warburton, E. A. *et al.* (1996). Hearing and saying: The functional neuro-anatomy of auditory word processing. *Brain*, 119, 919–931.

Prince, S. E., Tsukiura, T. and Cabeza, R. (2007). Distinguishing the neural correlates of episodic memory encoding and semantic memory retrieval. *Psychological Science*, 18, 144–151.

Pujol, M. and Kopelman, M. D. (2003). Korsakoff's syndrome. *Advances in Clinical Neuroscience and Rehabilitation*, 3, 14–17.

Raghunathan, R. and Pham, M. T. (1999). All negative moods are not equal: Motivational influences of anxiety and sadness on decision making. *Organizational Behavior and Human Decision Processes*, 79, 56–77.

Raine, A., Hulme, C., Chadderton, H. and Bailey, P. (1992). Verbal short-term memory span in speech-disordered children: Implications for articulatory coding in short-term memory. *Child Development*, 62, 415–423.

Ramachandran, V. S. and Hubbard, E. M. (2002). Synaesthesia – a window into perception, thought and language. *Journal of Consciousness Studies*, 8, 3–34.

Ranganath, C. (2010). Binding items and contexts: The cognitive neuroscience of episodic memory. *Current Directions in Psychological Science*, 19, 131–137.

Rao, S. C., Rainer, G. and Miller, E. K. (1997). Integration of what and where in the primate prefrontal cortex. *Science*, 276, 821–824.

Räsänen, M. and Summala, H. (1998). Attention and expectation problems in bicycle-car collisions: an in-depth study. *Accident Analysis and Prevention*, 30(5), 657–666.

Rastle, K., Davis, M. H. and New, B. (2004). The broth in my brother's brothel: Morpho-orthographic segmentation in visual word recognition. *Psychonomic Bulletin and Review*, 11, 1090–1098.

Rauschecker, J. P. and Scott, S. K. (2009). Maps and streams in the auditory cortex: nonhuman primates illuminate human speech processing. *Nature Neuroscience*, 12(6), 718–724.

Raymond, J. E., Shapiro, K. and Arnell, K. M. (1992). Temporary suppression of visual processing in an RSVP task: An attentional blink? *Journal of Experimental Psychology: Human Perception and Performance*, 18, 653–662.

Rayner, K. and Bertera, J. H. (1979). Reading without a fovea. *Science*, 206, 468–469.

Read, J. and Bentall, R. (2010). The effectiveness of electroconvulsive therapy: A literature review. *Epidemiologia e Psichiatria Sociale*, 19, 333–346.

Reason, J. T. (1979). Actions not as planned: The price of automatisation. In G. Underwood and R. Stevens (eds) *Aspects of Consciousness: Vol. 1: Psychological Issues*. London: Academic Press.

Reed, J. M. and Squire, L. R. (1998). Retrograde amnesia for facts and events: Findings from four new cases. *Journal of Neuroscience*, 18, 3943–3954.

Reed, L. J., Lasserson, D., Marsden, P., Stanhope, N., Stevens, T., Bello, F., Kingsley, D., Colchester, A. and Kopelman, M. D. (2003). FDG-PET findings in the Wernicke-Korsakoff syndrome. *Cortex*, 39, 1027–1045.

Rees, G. (2007). Neural correlates of the contents of visual awareness in humans. *Philosophical Transactions of the Royal Society B – Biological Sciences*, 362, 877–886.

Reeve, D. K. and Aggleton, J. P. (1998). On the specificity of expert knowledge about a soap opera: An everyday story of farming folk. *Applied Cognitive Psychology*, 12, 35–42.

Regard, M. and Landis, T. (1984). Transient global amnesia: Neuropsychological dysfunction during attack and recovery of two "pure" cases. *Journal of Neurology, Neurosurgery, and Psychiatry*, 47, 668–672.

Renault, B. S., Signoret, J., Debruille, B., Breton, F. and Bolgert, F. (1989). Brain potentials reveal covert facial recognition in prosopagnosia. *Neuropsychologia*, 27, 905–912.

Reverberi, C., Lavaroni, A., Gigli, G. L., Skrap, M. and Shallice, T. (2005a). Specific impairments of rule induction in different frontal lobe subgroups. *Neuropsychologia*, 43, 460–472.

Reverberi, C., Toraldo, A., D'Agostini, S. and Skrap, M. (2005b). Better without (lateral) frontal cortex? Insight problems solved by frontal patients. *Brain*, 128, 2882–2890.

Reyna, V. F. and Brainerd, C. J. (2011). Dual processes in decision making and developmental neuroscience: A fuzzy-trace model. *Developmental Review*, 31, 180–206.

Ribot, T. (1882). *Diseases of Memory*. New York: Appleton.

Riccio, G. E. and McDonald, P. V. (1998). *Multimodal Perception and Multicriterion Control of Nested Systems, 1, Coordination of Postural Control and Vehicular Control* (Technical Report No. NASA/TP-3703): NASA.

Richmond, J. and Nelson, C. A. (2007). Accounting for change in declarative memory: A cognitive neuroscience perspective. *Developmental Review*, 27, 349–373.

Riddoch, M. J. and Humphreys, G. W. (1983). The effect of cueing on unilateral neglect. *Neuropsychologia*, 21, 589–599.

Riddoch, M. J. and Humphreys, G. W. (1987). A case of integrative visual agnosia. *Brain*, 110, 1431–1462.

Riddoch, M. J., Humphreys, G. W., Akhtar, N., Allen, H., Bracewell, R. M. and Schofield, A. J. (2008a). A tale of two agnosias: distinctions between form and integrative agnosia. *Cognitive Neuropsychology*, 25(1), 56–92. doi:10.1080/02643290701848901.

Riddoch, M. J., Johnston, R. A., Bracewell, R. M., Boutsen, L. and Humphreys, G. W. (2008b). Are faces special? A case of pure prosopagnosia. *Cognitive Neuropsychology*, 25(1), 3–26. doi:10.1080/02643290801920113.

Robbins, T. W., Anderson, E. J., Barker, D. R., Bradley, A. C., Fearnyhough, C., Henson, R.,Hudson, S. R. and Baddeley, A. D. (1996). Working memory in chess. *Memory and Cognition*, 24, 83–93.

Robertson, I. H. and Hawkins, K. (1999). Limb activation and unilateral neglect. *Neurocase*, 5, 153–160.

Robertson, I. H., Manly, T., Beschin, N., Daini, R. *et al.* (1997). Auditory sustained attention is a marker of unilateral spatial neglect. *Neuropsychologia*, 35(12), 1527–1532.

Robertson, I. H., Hogg, K. and McMillan, T. M. (1998a). Rehabilitation of unilateral neglect: improving function by contralesional limb activation. *Neuropsychological Rehabilitation*, 8(1), 19–29.

Robertson, I. H., Mattingley, J. B., Rorden, C. and Driver, J. (1998b). Phasic alerting of neglect patients overcomes their spatial deficit in visual awareness. *Nature*, 395, 169–172.

Robertson, I. H., McMillan, T. M., MacLeod, E., Edgeworth, J. and Brock, D. (2002). Rehabilitation by limb activation training reduces left-sided motor impairment in unilateral neglect patients: A single-blind randomised control trial. *Neuropsychological Rehabilitation*, 12(5), 439–454.

Roca, M., Parr, A., Thompson, R., Woolgar, A., Torralva, T., Antoun, N., Manes, F. and Duncan, J. (2010). Executive function and fluid intelligence after frontal lobe lesions. *Brain*, 133, 234–247.

Rock, I. (1977). In defense of unconscious inference. In W. Epstein (ed.) *Stability and Constancy in Visual Perception: Mechanisms and Processes* (pp. 321–377). New York: Wiley.

Rock, I. (1983). *The Logic of Perception*. Cambridge, MA: MIT Press.

Rogers, A., Pilgrim, D. and Lacey, R. (1993). *Experiencing Psychiatry: Users Views of Services*. London: MacMillan.

Rogers, T. B., Kuiper, N. A. and Kirker, W. S. (1977). Self-reference and the encoding of personal information. *Journal of Personality and Social Psychology*, 35, 677–688.

Rose, D. (1996). Guest editorial: Some reflections on (or by?) grandmother cells. *Perception*, 25(8).

Rose, N. S. and Craik, F. I. M. (2012). A processing approach to the working memory/long-term memory distinction: Evidence from the levels-of-processing span task. *Journal of Experimental Psychology: Learning, Memory, and Cognition*, 38, 1019–1029.

Rosenbaum, R. S., Kohler, S., Schacter, D. L., Moscovitch, M., Westmacott, R., Black, S. E., Gao, F. and Tulving, E. (2005). The case of K. C.: Contributions of a memory-impaired person to memory. *Neuropsychologia, 43*, 989–1021.

Rosenbaum, R. S., Gilboa, A., Levine, B., Winocur, G. and Moscovitch, M. (2009). Amnesia as an impairment of detail generation and binding: Evidence from personal, fictional, and semantic narratives in K. C. *Neuropsychologia*, 47, 2181–2187.

Ross, E. D. (1980). Left medial parietal lobe and receptive language functions: Mixed transcortical aphasia after left anterior cerebral artery infarction. *Neurology*, 30, 144–151.

Ross, E. D. (1981). The Aprosodias: Functional-anatomic organization of the affective components of language in the right hemisphere. *Archives of Neurology*, 38, 561–569.

Ross, E. D. (2000). Affective prosody and the aprosodias. In M. M. Mesulam (ed.) *Principles of Behavioral and Cognitive Neurology*. New York: Oxford University Press.

Ross, E. D. and Mesulam, M. M. (1979). Dominant language functions of the right hemisphere? Prosody and emotional gesturing. *Archives of Neurology*, 36, 144–148.

Ross, E. D. and Monnot, M. (2008). Neurology of affective prosody and its functional-anatomic organization in right hemisphere. *Brain and Language*, 104(1), 51–74.

Rossetti, Y., Rode, G., Pisella, L., Farne, A., Li, L., Boisson, D. and Perenin, M. T. (1998). Prism adaptation to a rightward optical deviation rehabilitates left hemispatial neglect. *Nature*, 395, 166–169.

Rossi, S., Caverni, J. P. and Girotto, V. (2001). Hypothesis testing in a rule discovery problem: When a focused procedure is effective. *The Quarterly Journal of Experimental Psychology*, 54A, 263–267.

Roth, H. L., Nadeau, S. E., Hollingsworth, A. L., Marie Cimino-Knight, A. and Heilman, K. M. (2006). Naming concepts: evidence of two routes. *Neurocase*, 12, 61–70.

Rouw, R., Scholte, H. S. and Colizoli, O. (2011). Brain areas involved in synaesthesia: A review. *Journal of Neuropsychology*, 5(2), 214–242.

Rubenstein, H., Lewis, S. and Rubenstein, M. A. (1971). Evidence for phonemic recording in visual word recognition. *Journal of Verbal Learning and Verbal Behavior*, 10, 645–657.

Rubin, D. C. and Wenzel, A. (1996). One hundred years of forgetting: A quantitative description of retention. *Psychological Review*, 103, 734–760.

Rubin, D. C., Wetzler, S. E. and Nebes, R. D. (1986). Autobiographical memory across the life span. In D. C. Rubin (ed.) *Autobiographical Memory*. Cambridge: Cambridge University Press.

Rubin, D. C., Rahhal, T. A. and Poon, L. W. (1998). Things learned in early adulthood are remembered best. *Memory and Cognition*, 26, 3–19.

Rubin, E. (1915). *Synoplevde Figurer*. Copenhagen: Gyldendalske.

Rueckert, L. and Grafman, J. (1996). Sustained attention deficits in patients with right frontal lesions. *Neuropsychologia*, 34, 953–963.

Ruggeri, M., Guariglia, C. and Sabatini, U. (2009). Amnesia after right frontal subcortical lesion, following removal of a colloid cyst of the septum pellucidum and third ventricle. *Minerva Psichiatrica*, 50, 93–97.

Rumelhart, D. E. and McClelland, J. L. (eds) (1986). *Parallel-Distributed Processing: Explorations in the Microstructure of Cognition* (Vol. 1). Cambridge, MA: MIT Press.

Russell, W. R. (1971). *The Traumatic Amnesias*. London: Oxford University Press.

Rusting, C. L. and DeHart, T. (2000). Retrieving positive memories to regulate negative mood: Consequences for mood-congruent memory. *Journal of Personality and Social Psychology*, 78, 737–752.

Sabey, B. and Staughton, G. C. (1975). "Interacting roles of road environment, vehicle and road user." Paper presented at the 5th International Conference of the International Association for Accident Traffic Medicine, London.

Sacks, H., Schegloff, E. A. and Jefferson, G. (1974). A simplest systematics for the organization of turn-taking for conversation. *Language*, 50, 696–735.

Saffran, E. M., Bogyo, L. C., Schwartz, M. F. and Marin, O. S. M. (1987). Does deep dyslexia reflect right hemisphere reading? In M. Coltheart, K. E. Patterson and J. C. Marshall (eds) *Deep Dyslexia* (2nd edn). London: Routledge and Kegan Paul.

Saffran, J. (2003). Statistical language learning: Mechanisms and constraints. *Current Directions in Psychological Science*, 12(4), 110–114.

Salame, P. and Baddeley, A. D. (1982). Disruption of short-term memory by unattended speech: Implications for the structure of working memory. *Journal of Verbal Learning and Verbal Behaviour*, 21, 150–164.

Saliba, A. (2001). *Auditory-Visual Integration in Sound Localisation*. University of Essex, Colchester.

Saling, L. L. and Phillips, J. G. (2007). Automatic behaviour: Efficient not mindless. *Brain Research Bulletin*, 73, 1–20.

Salmaso, D. and Denes, G. (1982). The frontal lobes on an attention task: A signal detection analysis. *Pereptual and Motor Skills*, 45, 1147–1152.

Salthouse, T. A. (1994). Ageing associations: influence of speed on adult age differences in associative learning. *Journal of Experimental Psychology: Learning, Memory, and Cognition*, 20, 1486–1503.

Salthouse, T. A. (2011). Effects of age on time-dependent cognitive change. *Psychological Science*, 22, 682–688.

Samuelsson, H., Hjelmquist, E., Jensen, C., Ekholm, S. and Blomstrand, C. (1998). Nonlateralized attentional deficits: An important component behind persisting visuospatial neglect? *Journal of Clinical and Experimental Neuropsychology*, 20(1), 73–88.

Sander, D. (2009). Amygdala. In D. Sander and K. R. Scherer (eds) *The Oxford Companion to Emotion and the Affective Sciences* (pp. 28–32). Oxford: Oxford University Press.

Sarinopoulos, I., Grupe, D. W., Mackiewicz, K. L., Herrington, J. D., Lor, N., Steege, E. E. *et al.* (2010). Uncertainty during anticipation modulates neural responses to aversion in human insula and amygdala. *Cerebral Cortex*, 20, 929–940.

Sayer, T. B., Sayer, J. R. and Devonshire, J. M. H. (2005). Assessment of a driver interface for lateral drift and curve speed warning systems: mixed results for auditory and haptic warnings. *Proceedings of the Driving Assessment 2005: 3rd International Driving Symposium on Human Factors in Driver Assessment, Training, and Vehicle Design* (pp. 218–224).

Schacter, D. L., Harbluk, J. L. and McLachlan, D. R. (1984). Retrieval without recollection: An experimental analysis of source amnesia. *Journal of Verbal Learning and Verbal Behaviour*, 23, 593–611.

Schachter, D. L., Savage, C. and Rauch, S. (1996). Conscious recollection and the human hippocampal formation: Evidence from PET. *Proceedings of the National Academy of Sciences*, 93, 321–325.

Schacter, D. L., Wagner, A. D. and Buckner, R. L. (2000). Memory systems of 1999. In E. Tulving and F. I. M. Craik (eds) *The Oxford Handbook of Memory*. New York: Oxford University Press.

Schaeken, W., Vandierendonck, A. Schroyens, W. and D'Ydewalle, G. (2007). *The Mental Models Theory of Reasoning: Refinements and Extensions*. Mahwah, NJ: Lawrence Erlbaum.

Schank, R. C. and Abelson, R. P. (1977). *Scripts, Plans, Goals, and Understanding*. Hillsdale, NJ: Lawrence Erlbaum Associates.

Scheerer, M. (1963). Problem solving. *Scientific American*, 208, 118–128.

Schenk, T., Franz, V. and Bruno, N. (2011). Vision-for-perception and vision-for-action: Which model is compatible with the available psychophysical and neuropsychological data? *Vision Research*, 51(8), 812–818.

Schiller, D., Monfils, M. H., Raio, C. M., Johnson, D. C., Ledoux, J. E. and Phelps, E. A. (2010). Preventing the return of fear in humans using reconsolidation update mechanisms. *Nature*, 463, 49–53.

Schindler, B. A., Ramchandani, D., Matthews, M. K. and Podell, K. (1995). Competency and the frontal lobe. *Psychosomatics*, 36, 400–404.

Schindler, I., Kerkhoff, G., Karnath, H.-O., Keller, I. and Goldenberg, G. (2002). Neck muscle vibration induces lasting recovery in spatial neglect. *Journal of Neurology Neurosurgery and Psychiatry*, 73, 412–419.

Schlesinger, I. M. (1995). *Cognitive Space and Linguistic Case: Semantic and Syntactic Categories in English*. Cambridge: Cambrige University Press.

Schmida, M., De Nunzioa, A. M. and Schieppatia, M. (2005). Trunk muscle proprioceptive input assists steering of locomotion. *Neuroscience Letters*, 384, 127–132.

Schneider, G. E. (1967). Contrasting visuomotor functions of tectum and cortex in the golden hamster. *Psychologische Forschung*, 31, 52–62.

Schneider, G. E. (1969). Two visual systems. *Science*, 163, 895–902.

Schneider, W. X. and Deubel, H. (2002). Selection for perception and selection for spatial motor action are coupled in visual attention: A review of recent findings and new evidence from stimulus driven saccade control. In W. Printz and B. Hommel (eds) *Attention and Performance XIX: Common*

Mechanisms in Perception and Action. Oxford: Oxford University Press.

Schneider, W. and Shiffrin, R. M. (1977). Controlled and automatic human information processing: 1. Detection, search, and attention. *Psychological Review*, 84, 1–66.

Schnur, T. T., Schwartz, M. F., Kimberg, D. Y., Hirshorn, E., Coslett, H. B. and Thompson-Schill, S. L. (2009). Localizing interference during naming: Convergent neuroimaging and neuropsychological evidence for the function of Broca's area. *Proceedings of the National Academy of Sciences of the USA*, 106(1), 322–327. doi: 10.1073/pnas.0805874106. Epub 2008 Dec 31.

Schott, B. H., Henson, R. N. A., Richardson-Klavehn, A., Becker, C., Thoma, V. *et al.* (2005). Redefining implicit and explicit memory: The functional neuroanatomy of priming, remembering, and control of retrieval. *Proceedings of the National Academy of Sciences of the USA*, 102, 36–71.

Schroyens, W. and Schaeken, W. (2003). A critique of Oaksford, Chater, and Larkin's (2000). Conditional Probability Model of Conditional Reasoning. *Journal of Experimental Psychology: Learning, Memory, and Cognition*, 29, 140–149.

Schulz, K. P., Fan, J., Tang, C. Y., Newcorn, J. H., Buchsbaum, M. S. Cheung, A. M. and Halperin, J. M. (2004). Response inhibition in adolescents diagnosed with attention deficit hyperactivity disorder during childhood: An event-related FMRI study. *American Journal of Psychiatry*, 161, 1650–1657.

Schwarz, N. (2000). Emotion, cognition, and decision making. *Cognition and Emotion*, 14, 433–440.

Scotko, B. G., Kensinger, E. A., Locascio, J. J., Einstein, G., Rubin, D. C., Tupler, L. A., Krendl, A. and Corkin, S. (2004). Puzzling thoughts for H. M.: Can new semantic information be anchored in old semantic memories? *Neuropsychology*, 18, 756–769.

Scott, J. J. and Gray, R. (2008). A comparison of tactile, visual, and auditory warnings for rear-end collision prevention in simulated driving. *Human Factors: The Journal of the Human Factors and Ergonomics Society*, 50(2), 264–275.

Scott, S. K., Blank, S. C., Rosen, S. and Wise, R. J. S. (2000). Identification of a pathway for intelligible speech in the left temporal lobe. *Brain*, 123, 2400–2406.

Scoville, W. B. and Milner, B. (1957). Loss of recent memory after bilateral hippocampal lesions.

Journal of Neurology, Neurosurgery, and Psychiatry, 20, 11–21.

Sedda, A., Monaco, S., Bottini, G. and Goodale, M. A. (2011). Integration of visual and auditory information for hand actions: Preliminary evidence for the contribution of natural sounds to grasping. *Experimental Brain Research*, 209(3), 365–374.

Segall, M. H., Campbell, D. T. and Herskovits, M. J. (1963). Cultural differences in the perception of geometrical illusions. *Science*, 139, 769–771.

Sehm, B., Frisch, S., Thone-Otto, A., Horstman, A., Villringer, A., Obrig, H., de Beeck, H. P. (2011). Focal retrograde amnesia: Voxel-based morphometry findings in a case without MRI lesions. PLoS ONE, 6, doi: 10.1371journal.pone. 0026538.

Seidenberg, M. (2012). Computational models of reading. In M. J. Spivey, K. McRae and M. Joanisse (eds) *Cambridge Handbook of Psycholinguistics*. Cambridge University Press.

Seidenberg, M. S. and McClelland, J. L. (1989). A distributed, developmental model of word recognition and naming. *Psychological Review*, 96 (4), 523–568.

Selfridge, O. G. (1959). Pandemonium: A paradigm for learning. In *Symposium on the Mechanisation of Thought Processes*. London: HMSO.

Selfridge, O. G. and Neisser, U. (1960). Pattern recognition by machine. *Scientific American*, 203, 60–68.

Seligman, M. E. P., Railton, P., Baumeister, R. F. and Sripada, C. (2013). Navigating into the future or driven by the past. *Perspectives on Psychological Science*, 8, 119–141.

Sellal, F., Manning, L., Seegmuller, C., Scheiber, C. and Schoenfelder, P. (2002). Pure retrograde amnesia following a mild head trauma: A neuropsychological and metabolic study. *Cortex*, 38, 499–509.

Sergent, J. and Signoret, J. L. (1992). Varieties of functional deficits in prosopagnosia. *Cerebral Cortex*, 2, 375–388.

Service, E. (1992). Phonology, working memory, and foreign language learning. *Quarterly Journal of Experimental Psychology*, 45A, 21–50.

Shaffer, L. H. (1975). Multiple attention in continuous verbal tasks. In P. M. A. Rabbitt and S. Dornic (eds) *Attention and Performance V* (pp. 157–167). New York: Academic Press.

Shallice, T. (1982). Specific impairments of planning. *Philosophical Transactions of the Royal Society of London*, B298, 199–209.

Shallice, T. (1988). *From Neuropsychology to Mental Structure.* Cambridge: Cambridge University Press.

Shallice, T. and Warrington, E. K. (1974). The dissociation between long-term retention of meaningful sounds and verbal material. *Neuropsychologia,* 12, 553–555.

Shallice, T. and Evans, M. E. (1978). The involvement of frontal lobes in cognitive estimation. *Cortex,* 13, 294–303.

Shallice, T. and Warrington, E. K. (1980). Single and multiple component central dyslexic syndromes. In M. Coltheart, K. E. Patterson and J. C. Marshall (eds) *Deep Dyslexia* (pp. 119–145). London: Routledge.

Shallice, T. and Burgess, P. W. (1991a). Deficits in strategy application following frontal lobe damage in man. *Brain,* 114, 727–741.

Shallice, T. and Burgess, P. W. (1991b). Higher-order cognitive impairments and frontal lobe lesions. In H. S. Levin, H. M. Eisenberg and A. L. Benton (eds) *Frontal Lobe Function and Dysfunction.* Oxford: Oxford University Press.

Shallice, T., Burgess, P. W., Schon, F. and Baxter, D. M. (1989). The origins of utilization behaviour. *Brain,* 112, 1587–1598.

Shapiro, K. L., Raymond, J. and Arnell, K. (2009). Attentional blink. *Scholarpedia,* 4(6), 3320. Retrieved from http://www.scholarpedia.org/w/index.php?title=Attentional_blink&action=cite&rev=91007.

Shapley, R. (1995). Parallel neural pathways and visual function. In M. S. Gazzaniga (ed.) *The Cognitive Neurosciences* (pp. 315–324). Cambridge, MA: MIT Press.

Shaw, J. S., Bjork, R. A. and Handal, A. (1995). Retrieval-induced forgetting in an eyewitness-memory paradigm. *Psychonomic Bulletin and Review,* 2, 249–253.

Shepard, R. N. and Metzler, J. (1971). Mental rotation of three-dimensional objects. *Science,* 171, 701–703.

Sheppard, D. M., Bradshaw, J. L., Mattingley, J. B. and Lee, P. (1999). Effects of stimulant medication on the lateralisation of line bisection judgements of children with attention deficit hyperactivity disorder. *Journal of Neurology, Neurosurgery and Psychiatry,* 66(1), 57–63.

Shiffrin, R. M. and Schneider, W. (1977). Controlled and automatic information processing: II. Perception, learning, automatic attending and a general theory. *Psychological Review,* 84, 127–190.

Shimamura, A. P., Jernigan, T. L. and Squire, L. R. (1988). Korsakoff's syndrome: Radiological (CT) findings and neuropsychological correlates. *Journal of Neuroscience,* 8, 4400–4410.

Shimamura, A. P., Janowsky, J. and Squire, L. R. (1990). Memory for temporal order of events in patients with frontal lobe lesions and amnesic patients. *Neuropsychologia,* 28, 803–813.

Shiv, B., Loewenstein, G., Bechera, A., Damasio, H. and Damasio, A. R. (2005). Investment behaviour and the negative side of emotion. *Psychological Science,* 16, 435–439.

Siebert, M., Markowitsch, H. J. and Bartel, P. (2003). Amygdala, affect and cognition: Evidence from 10 patients with Urbach-Wiethe disease. *Brain,* 126, 2627–2637.

Sierra, M. and Berrios, G. E. (2000). Flashbulb and flashback memories. In G. E. Berrios and J. R. Hodges (eds) *Memory Disorders in Psychiatric Practice.* New York: Cambridge University Press.

Simcock, G. and Hayne, H. (2003). Age-related changes in verbal and non-verbal memory during early childhood. *Developmental Psychology,* 39, 805–814.

Simon, H. A. and Reed, S. K. (1976). Modelling strategy shifts on a problem solving task. *Cognitive Psychology,* 8, 86–97.

Simon, S. R., Khateb, A., Darque, A., Lazeyras, F., Mayer, E. and Pegna, A. J. (2011). When the brain remembers but the patient doesn't: Converging fMRI and EEG evidence for covert recognition in a case of prosopagnosia. *Cortex,* 47, 825–838.

Simons, J. S., Graham, K. S., Galton, C. J., Patterson, K. and Hodges, J. R. (2001). Semantic knowledge and episodic memory for faces in semantic dementia. *Neuropsychology,* 15, 101–114.

Simons, J. S., Peers, P. V., Hwang, D. Y., Ally, B. A., Fletcher, P. C. and Budson, A. E. (2008). Is the parietal lobe necessary for recollection in humans? *Neuropsychologia,* 46, 1185–1191.

Singh-Curry, V. and Husain, M. (2009). The functional role of the inferior parietal lobe in the dorsal and ventral stream dichotomy. *Neuropsychologia,* 47(6), 1434–1448.

Skinner, B. F. (1938). *The Behaviour of Organisms.* New York: Appleton-Century-Crofts.

Slobin, D. I. (1966). Grammatical transformations and sentence comprehension in childhood and adulthood. *Journal of Verbal Learning and Verbal Behaviour,* 5, 219–227.

Small, D. A. and Lerner, J. S. (2008). Emotional policy: Personal sadness and anger shape judgments about a welfare case. *Political Psychology*, 29, 149–168.

Smilek, D., Dixon, M. J. and Merikle, P. M. (2005). Synaesthesia: Discordant male monozygotic twins. *Neurocase*, 11, 363–370.

Smith, C., Frascino, J., Kripke, D., McHugh, P., Treisman, G. and Squire, L. (2010). Losing memories overnight: A unique form of human amnesia. *Neuropsychologia*, 48, 2833–2840.

Smith, E. E. and Jonides, J. (1999). Working memory: A view from neuroimaging. *Cognitive Psychology*, 33, 5–42.

Smith, E. E., Jonides, J. and Koeppe, R. A. (1996). Dissociating verbal and spatial working memory using PET. *Cerebral Cortex*, 6, 11–20.

Smith, M. L. and Milner, B. (1984). Differential effects of frontal-lobe lesions on cognitive estimation and spatial memory. *Neuropsychologia*, 19, 781–793.

Smith, M. L. and Milner, B. (1988). Estimation of frequency of occurrence of abstract designs after frontal or temporal lobectomy. *Neuropsychologia*, 26, 297–306.

Smith, S. M. (1986). Environmental context-dependent memory: Recognition memory using a short-term memory task for input. *Memory and Cognition*, 14, 347–354.

Smith, S. M. and Vela, E. (2001). Environmental context-dependent memory: A review and meta-analysis. *Psychonomic Bulletin and Review*, 8, 203–220.

Snowling, M. (1998). Dyslexia as a phonological deficit: Evidence and implications. *Child Psychology and Psychiatry Review*, 3(1), 4–11.

Song, Z., Wixted, J. T., Hopkins, R. O. and Squire, L. R. (2011). Impaired capacity for familiarity after hippocampal damage. *Proceedings of the National Academy of Sciences of the United States of America*, 108, 9655–9660.

Soon, C. S., Brass, M., Heinze, H. J. and Hayes, J. D. (2008). Unconscious determinants of free decisions in the human brain. *Nature Neuroscience*, 10, 257–261.

Sorger, B., Goebel, R., Schiltz, C. and Rossion, B. (2007). Understanding the functional neuroanatomy of acquired prosopagnosia. *Neuroimage*, 35(2), 836–852.

Spence, C. (2010). Cross modal spatial attention. *Annals of the New York Academy of Sciences*, 1191, 182–200.

Spence, C. and Driver, J. (1996). Audiovisual links in covert spatial attention. *Journal of Experimental Psychology: Human Perception and Performance*, 22, 1005–1030.

Spence, C. and Read, L. (2003). Speech shadowing while driving: On the difficulty of splitting attention between eye and ear. *Psychological Science*, 14, 251–256.

Sperber, D. and Wilson, D. (1986). *Relevance: Communication and Cognition*. Oxford: Blackwell. (2nd edn 1995.)

Sperling, G. (1960). The information available in brief visual presentations. *Psychological Monographs*, 74, 1–29.

Spieler, D. H. and Balota, D. A. (1997). Bringing computational models of word naming down to the item level. *Psychological Science*, 8, 411–416.

Spiers, H. J., Maguire, E. A. and Burgess, N. (2001). Hippocampal amnesia. *Neurocase*, 7, 357–382.

Spitsyna, G., Warren, J. E., Scott, S. K., Turkheimer, F. E. and Wise, R. J. (2006). Converging language streams in the human temporal lobe. *Journal of Neuroscience*, 12, 26(28), 7328–7336.

Sprague, J. M. (1966). Interaction of cortex and superior colliculus in mediation of visually guided behaviour in the cat. *Science*, 153, 1544–1547.

Squeri, V., Sciutti, A., Gori, M., Masia, L., Sandini, G. and Konczak, J. (2012). Two hands, one perception: How bimanual haptic information is combined by the brain. *Journal of Neurophysiology*, 107(2), 544–550.

Squire, L. R. (1982). Comparisons between forms of amnesia: Some deficits are unique to Korsakoff's syndrome. *Journal of Experimental Psychology: Learning, Memory and Cognition*, 8, 560–571.

Squire, L. R. (1992). Declarative and nondeclarative memory: Multiple brain systems supporting learning and memory. *Journal of Cognitive Neuroscience*, 4, 232–243.

Squire, L. R., Slater, P. C. and Miller, P. L. (1981). Retrograde amnesia and bilateral electroconvulsive therapy. *Archives of General Psychiatry*, 38, 89–95.

Squire, L. R., Cohen, N. J. and Nadel, L. (1984). The medial temporal region and memory consolidation: A new hypothesis. In H. Weingartner and E. Parker (eds) *Memory Consolidation*. Hillsdale, NJ: Erlbaum.

Squire, L. R., Ojeman, J. G., Miezin, F. M., Petersen, S. E., Videen, T. O. and Raichle, M. E. (1992). Activation of the hippocampus in normal humans: A functional anatomical study of memory. *Proceedings of the National Academy of Sciences of the USA*, 89, 1837–1841.

St Jaques, P. L. and Schacter, D. L. (2013). Modifying memory: Selectively enhancing and updating memories for a museum tour by reactivating them. *Psychological Science*, published online, doi: 10.1177/0956797612457377.

Stanovich, K. E. and West, R. F. (2000). Individual differences in reasoning: Implications for the rationality debate? *Behavioural and Brain Sciences*, 23, 654–664.

Starcke, K., Wolf, O. T., Markowitsch, H. J. and Brand, M. (2008). Anticipatory stress influences decision making under explicit risk conditions. *Behavioral Neuroscience*, 122, 1352–1360.

Starcke, K., Pawlikowski, M., Wolf, O., Altstotter-Gleich, C. and Brand, M. (2011). Decision making under risk conditions is susceptible to interference by a secondary executive task. *Cognitive Processing*, 12, 177–182.

Starr, A. and Phillips, L. (1970). Verbal and motor memory in the amnestic syndrome. *Neuropsychologia*, 8, 75–88.

Stefanacci, L., Buffalo, E. A., Schmolk, H. and Squire, L. R. (2001). Profound amnesia after damage to the medial temporal lobe: A neuroanatomical and neuropsychological profile of patient E. P. *Journal of Neuroscience*, 20, 7024–7036.

Steinvorth, S., Levine, B. and Corkin, S. (2005). Medial temporal lobe structures are needed to re-experience remote autobiographical memories: Evidence from H. M. and W. R. *Neuropsychologia*, 43, 479–496.

Steven, M. S. and Blakemore, C. (2004). Visual synaesthesia in the blind. *Perception*, 33, 855–868.

Stevenson, R. J. and Over, D. E. (2001). Reasoning from uncertain premises: effects of expertise and conversational context. *Thinking and Reasoning*, 7, 367–390.

Stewart, F., Parkin, A. J. and Hunkin, N. M. (1992). Naming impairments following recovery from Herpes Simplex Encephalitis: Category specific? *The Quarterly Journal of Experimental Psychology*, 44A, 261–284.

Stone, S. P., Halligan, P. W. and Greenwood, R. J. (1993). The incidence of neglect phenomena and related disorders in patients with an acute right or left-hemisphere stroke. *Age and Ageing*, 22(1), 46–52.

Storandt, M. (2008). Cognitive deficits in the early stages of Alzheimer's disease. *Current Directions in Psychological Science*, 17, 198–202.

Storm, B. C. (2011). The benefit of forgetting in thinking and remembering. *Current Directions in Psychological Science*, 20, 291–295.

Storm, B. C. and White, H. A. (2010). ADHD and retrieval-induced forgetting: Evidence for a deficit in inhibitory control of memory. *Memory*, 18, 265–271.

Strayer, D. L. and Drews, F. A. (2007). Cell-phone induced driver distraction. *Current Directions in Psychological Science*, 16, 128–131.

Stroop, J. R. (1935). Studies of interference in serial verbal reactions. *Journal of Experimental Psychology*, 18, 643–662.

Stuss, D. T. (2006). Frontal lobes and attention: Processes and networks, fractionation and integration. *Journal of the International Neuropsychological Society*, 12, 261–271.

Stuss, D. T. and Alexander, M. P. (2000). Executive functions and the frontal lobes: A conceptual view. *Psychological Research*, 63, 289–298.

Stuss, D. T. and Alexander, M. P. (2007). Is there a dysexecutive syndrome? *Philosophical Transactions: Biological Sciences*, 362, 901–915.

Stuss, D. T., Floden, D., Alexander, M. P., Levine, B. and Katz, D. (2001). Stroop performance in focal lesion patients: dissociation of processes and frontal lobe lesion location. *Neuropsychologia*, 39, 771–786.

Styles, E. A. (1997). *The Psychology of Attention*. Hove: Psychology Press.

Suprenant, A. M. and Neath, I. (2009). The 9 lives of short-term memory. In A. Thorn and M. Page (eds) *Interactions Between Short-Term and Long-Term Memory in the Verbal Domain* (pp. 16–43). Hove: Psychology Press.

Suslow, T., Konrad, C., Kugel, H., Rumstadt, D., Zwitserlood, P., Schöning, S. *et al.* (2010). Automatic mood-congruent amygdala responses to masked facial expressions in major depression. *Biological Psychiatry*, 67, 255–160.

Talarico, J. M. and Rubin, D. C. (2003). Confidence, not consistency, characterises flashbulb memories. *Psychological Science*, 14, 455–461.

Talarico, J. M. and Rubin, D. C. (2009). Flashbulb memories result from ordinary memory processes and extraordinary event characteristics. In O. Luminet and A. Curci (eds) *Flashbulb Memories: New Issues and Perspectives*. Hove: Psychology Press.

Talarico, J. M., Berntsen, D. and Rubin, D. C. (2009). Positive emotions enhance recall of peripheral details. *Cognition and Emotion*, 23, 380–398.

Talland, G. A. (1965). *Deranged Memory*. New York: Academic Press.

Tandoh, K. and Naka, M. (2007). Durability of retrieval-induced forgetting. *Shrinrigaku Kenku*, 78, 310–315.

Tanenhaus, M. K., Spivey-Knowlton, M. J., Eberhard, K. M. and Sedivy, J. C. (1995). Integration of visual and linguistic information in spoken language comprehension. *Science*, 268, 1632–1634.

Taylor, F. K. (1965). Cryptomnesia and plagiarism. *British Journal of Psychiatry*, 111, 1111–1118.

Taylor, R. and O'Carroll, R. (1995). Cognitive estimation in neurological disorders. *British Journal of Clinical Psychology*, 34, 223–228.

Theeuwes, J. and Hagenzieker, M. P. (1993). Visual search of traffic scenes: On the effect of location expectations. In A. G. Gale (ed.) *Vision in Vehicles IV* (pp. 149–158). Amsterdam: Elsevier.

Thomas, J. C. (1974). An analysis of behaviour in the hobbits-orcs problems. *Cognitive Psychology*, 6, 257–269.

Thomas, N. J. T. (1999). Are theories of imagery theories of imagination? An active perception approach to conscious mental content. *Cognitive Science*, 23(2), 207–245.

Thompson, L. A., Williams, K. L., L'Esperance, P. R. and Cornelius, J. (2001). Context-dependent memory under stressful conditions: The case of skydiving. *Human Factors*, 43, 611–619.

Thompson, V. A. (2009). Dual process theories: A metagcognitive perspective. In J. St. B. T. and K. Frankish (eds) *In Two Minds: Dual Processes and Beyond* (pp. 171–198). Oxford: Oxford University Press.

Thompson, V. A., Evans, J. St. B. T. and Handley, S. J. (2005). Persuading and dissuading by conditional argument. *Journal of Memory and Language*, 53, 238–257.

Thorndike, E. L. (1898). Animal intelligence: An experimental study of the associative processes in animals. *Psychological Monographs*, 2, No. 8.

Thorndike, E. L. (1914). *The Psychology of Learning*. New York: Teachers College.

Tipper, S. P. (1985). The negative priming effect: Inhibitory effects of ignored primes. *Quarterly Journal of Experimental Psychology*, 37A, 571–590.

Tipper, S. P. and Cranston, M. (1985). Selective attention and priming: The inhibitory and facilitatory effects of ignored primes. *Quarterly Journal of Experimental Psychology*, 37A, 591–611.

Tippett, L. J., Miller, L. A. and Farah, M. J. (2000). Prosopamnesia: A selective impairment in face learning. *Cognitive Neuropsychology*, 17, 1–3.

Tisserand, D. J. and Jolles, J. (2003). On the involvement of prefrontal networks in cognitive ageing. *Cortex*, 39, 1107–1128.

Toffalo, M. B. J., Smeets, M. A. M. and van den Hout, M. A. (2012). Proust revisited: Odours as triggers of aversive memories. *Cognition and Emotion*, 26(1), 83–92.

Tomson, S. N., Avidan, N., Lee, K. *et al.* (2011). The genetics of colored sequence synesthesia: Suggestive evidence of linkage to 16q and genetic heterogeneity for the condition. *Behavioural Brain Research*, 223(1), 48–52.

Treisman, A. (1960). Contextual cues in selective listening. *Quarterly Journal of Experimental Psychology*, 12, 242–248.

Treisman, A. (1964). Verbal cues, language and meaning in selective attention. *American Journal of Psychology*, 77, 206–219.

Treisman, A. (1986). Features and objects in visual processing. *Scientific American*, 255, 106–115.

Treisman, A. (1988). Features and objects: The fourteenth Bartlett memorial lecture. *Quarterly Journal of Experimental Psychology*, 40A, 201–237.

Treisman, A. (1993). The perception of features and objects. In A. Baddeley and L. Weiskrantz (eds) *Attention: Selection, Awareness and Control. A Tribute to Donald Broadbent* (pp. 5–35). Oxford: Clarendon Press.

Treisman, A. M. (1999). Feature binding, attention and object perception. In G. W. Humphreys, J. Duncan and A. Treisman (eds) *Attention Space and Action: Studies in Cognitive Neuroscience* (pp. 91–111). Oxford: Oxford University Press.

Treisman, A. M. and Gelade, G. (1980). A feature integration theory of attention. *Cognitive Psychology*, 12, 97–136.

Troscianko, E. (2013). Cognitive realism and memory in Proust's madaleine episode. *Memory Studies*, published online, doi: http://dx.doi.org/10.1177/1750698012468000.

Trueswell, J. C. (1996). The role of lexical frequency in syntactic ambiguity resolution. *Journal of Memory and Language*, 35, 566–585.

Tsuruhara, A., Nakato, E., Otsuka, Y., Kanazawa, S., Yamaguchi, M. K. and Hill, H. (2011). The hollow-face illusion in infancy: Do infants see a screen based rotating hollow mask as hollow? *i-Perception*, 2, 418–427.

Tuckey, M. R. and Brewer, N. (2003). How schemas affect eyewitness memory over repeated retrieval attempts. *Applied Cognitive Psychology*, 17, 785–800.

Tulving, E. (1972). Episodic and semantic memory. In E. Tulving and W. Donaldson (eds) *Organisation and Memory*. New York: Academic Press.

Tulving, E. (1976). Ecphoric processes in recall and recognition. In J. Brown (ed.) *Recall and Recognition*. New York: Wiley.

Tulving, E. (1979). Relation between encoding specificity and levels of processing. In L. S. Cermak and F. I. M. Craik (eds) *Levels of*

Processing in Human Memory. Hillsdale, NJ: Lawrence Erlbaum Associates.

Tulving, E. (1983). *Elements of Episodic Memory.* Oxford: Clarendon Press.

Tulving, E. (1985). How many memory systems are there? *American Psychologist*, 40, 385–398.

Tulving, E. (1989). Memory: Performance, knowledge, and experience. *The European Journal of Cognitive Psychology*, 1, 3–26.

Tulving, E. (2001). The origin of autonoesis in episodic memory. In H. L. Roediger and J. S. Nairne (eds) *The Nature of Remembering: Essays in Honour of Robert G. Crowder.* Washington, DC: American Psychological Association.

Tulving, E. (2002). Episodic memory: From mind to brain. *Annual Review of Psychology*, 53, 1–25.

Tulving, E. and Thomson, D. M. (1971). Retrieval processes in recognition memory: Effects of associative context. *Journal of Experimental Psychology*, 87, 116–124.

Tulving, E. and Thomson, D. M. (1973). Encoding specificity and retrieval processes in episodic memory. *Psychological Review*, 80, 352–373.

Tulving, E., Schacter, D. L. and Stark, H. A. (1982). Priming effects in word fragment completion are independent of recognition memory. *Journal of Experimental Psychology: Learning, Memory, and Cognition*, 17, 595–617.

Turner, M. L. and Engle, R. W. (1989). Is working memory capacity task-dependent? *Journal of Memory and Language*, 28, 127–154.

Tweney, R. D., Doherty, M. E., Worner, W. J., Pliske *et al.* (1980). Strategies of rule discovery in an inference task. *Quarterly Journal of Experimental Psychology*, 32, 109–123.

Ucros, C. G. (1989). Mood state-dependent memory: A meta-analysis. *Cognition and Emotion*, 3, 139–167.

Underwood, B. J. and Postman, L. (1960). Extra-experimental sources of interference in forgetting. *Psychological Review*, 67, 73–95.

Ungerleider, L. G. and Mishkin, M. (1982). Two cortical visual sysems. In D. J. Ingle, M. A. Goodale and R. J. W. Mansfield (eds) *Analysis of Visual Behaviour.* Cambridge, MA: MIT Press.

Vallar, G. and Baddeley, A. D. (1982). Short-term forgetting and the articulatory loop. *Quarterly Journal of Experimental Psychology*, 34A, 53–60.

Vallar, G. and Baddeley, A. D. (1984). Fractionation of working memory: Neuropsychological evidence for a phonological short-term store.

Journal of Verbal Learning and Verbal Behaviour, 23, 151–161.

Vallar, G., Bottini, G., Rusconi, M. L. and Sterzi, R. (1993). Exploring somatosensory neglect by vestibular stimulation. *Brain*, 116, 71–86.

Vallar, G., Di Betta, A. M. and Silveri, M. C. (1997). The phonological short-term store rehearsal system: Patterns of impairment and neural correlates. *Neuropsychologia*, 35, 795–812.

Vallée-Tourangeau, F. and Payton, T. (2008). Graphical representation fosters discovery in the 2–4–6 task. *The Quarterly Journal of Experimental Psychology*, 61, 625–640.

Van Leeuwen, T. M., den Ouden, H. E. and Hagoort, P. (2011). Effective connectivity determines the nature of subjective experience in grapheme-color synesthesia. *The Journal of Neuroscience*, 31(27), 9879–9884.

Varley, R. and Siegal, M. (2000). Evidence for cognition without grammar from causal reasoning and "theory of mind" in an agrammatic aphasic patient. *Current Biology*, 15(10), 723–726.

Varley, R. A., Klessinger, N. J., Romanowski, C. A. and Siegal, M. (2005). Agrammatic but numerate. *Proceedings of the National Academy of Sciences of the USA*, 102(9), 3519–3524. Epub 2005 Feb 15.

Velten, E. (1968). A laboratory task for induction of mood states. *Behaviour Research and Therapy*, 6, 473–482.

Verfaillie, M. and Roth, H. L. (1996). Knowledge of English vocabulary in amnesia: An examination of premorbidly acquired semantic memory. *Journal of the International Neuropsychology Society*, 5, 443–453.

Verfaillie, M., Koseff, P. and Alexander, M. P. (2000). Acquisition of novel semantic information in amnesia: Effects of lesion location. *Neuropsychologia*, 38, 484–492.

Verhaeghen, P. (2011). Ageing and executive control: Reports of a demise greatly exaggerated. *Current Directions in Psychological Science*, 20, 174–180.

Verschueren, N., Schaeken, W. and d'Ydewalle, G. (2005). A dual-process specification of causal conditional reasoning. *Thinking and Reasoning*, 11, 239–278.

Victor, M., Adams, R. D. and Collings, G. H. (1989). *The Wernicke-Korsakoff Syndrome and Related Neurologic Disorders due to Alcoholism and Malnutrition* (2nd edn). Philadelphia: Davis.

Vitevitch, M. S. and Luce, P. A. (1998). When words compete: Levels of processing in perception of spoken words. *Psychological Science*, 9, 325–329.

Vitevitch, M. S. and Luce, P. A. (1999). Probabilistic phonotactics and neighborhood activation in spoken word recognition. *Journal of Memory and Language*, 40, 374–408.

Vitevitch, M. S. and Luce, P. A. (2005). Increases in phonotactic probability facilitate spoken non-word repetition. *Journal of Memory and Language*, 52, 193–204.

Vlahovic, T. A., Roberts, S. and Dunbar, R. (2012). Effects of duration and laughter on subjective happiness within different modes of communication. *Journal of Computer-Mediated Communication*, 17(4), 436–450.

Voeller, K. K. S. and Heilman, K. M. (1988). Attention deficit disorder in children: A neglect syndrome? *Neurology*, 38, 806–808.

Vroomen, J. and de Gelder, B. D. (1997). Activation of embedded words in spoken word recognition. *Journal of Experimental Psychology: Human Perception and Performance*, 23, 710–720.

Vroomen, J. and de Gelder, B. D. (2000). Sound enhances visual perception: Cross-modal effects of auditory organization on vision. *Journal of Experimental Psychology: Human Perception and Performance*, 26(5), 1583–1590.

Vroomen, J., Bertelson, P. and de Gelder, B. D. (2001). The Ventriloquist Effect does not depend on the direction of automatic visual attention. *Perception and Psychophysics*, 63(4), 651–659.

Wada, Y. and Yakamoto, T. (2001). Selective impairment of facial recognition due to a maematoma restricted to the right fusiform and lateral occipital region. *Journal of Neurology, Neurosurgery and Psychiatry*, 71, 254–257. doi:10.1136/jnnp.71.2.254.

Wagenaar, W. A. (1986). My memory: A study of autobiographical memory over six years. *Cognitive Psychology*, 18, 225–252.

Wagenaar, W. A. (1994). The subjective probability of guilt. In G. Wright and P. Ayton (eds) *Subjective Probability*. Chichester: John Wiley.

Wager, T. and Smith, E. E. (2003). Neuroimaging studies of working memory: A meta-analysis. *Cognitive, Affective, and Behavioural Neuroscience*, 3, 255–274.

Wagner, G. P., MacPherson, S. E., Parente, M. A. M. P. and Trentini, C. M. (2011). Cognitive estimation abilities in healthy and clinical populations: The use of the Cognitive Estimation Test. *Neurological Sciences*, 32, 203–210.

Walker, B. N. and Kramer, G. (2004). Ecological psychoacoustics and auditory displays: Hearing, grouping and meaning making. In J. G. Neuhoff (ed.) *Ecoloical Psychoacoustics*. London: Academic Press.

Ward, J. (2010). *The Student's Guide to Cognitive Neuroscience* (2nd edn). Hove: Psychology Press.

Ward, J. (2013). Synesthesia. *Annual Review of Psychology*, 64, 49–75.

Ward, J., Li, R., Salih, S. and Sagiv, N. (2007). Varieties of grapheme-colour synaesthesia: A new theory of phenomenological and behavioural differences. *Consciousness and Cognition*, 16(4), 913–931.

Warren, E. W. and Groome, D. H. (1984). Memory test performance under three different waveforms of ECT for depression. *British Journal of Psychiatry*, 144, 370–375.

Warren, J. E., Wise, R. J. and Warren, J. D. (2005). Sounds do-able: Auditory-motor transformations and the posterior temporal plane. *Trends in Neurosciences*, 28(12), 636–643. Epub 2005 Oct 10.

Warrington, E. K. (1986). Memory for facts and memory for events. *British Journal of Clinical Psychology*, 25, 1–12.

Warrington, E. K. and Weiskrantz, L. (1968). A new method of testing long-term retention with special reference to amnesic patients. *Nature*, 217, 972–974.

Warrington, E. K. and Shallice, T. (1969). The selective impairment of auditory-verbal short-term memory. *Brain*, 92, 885–896.

Warrington, E. K. and Weiskrantz, L. (1970). Amnesic syndrome: Consolidation or retrieval? *Nature*, 228, 628–630.

Warrington, E. K. and Shallice, T. (1972). Neuropsychological evidence of visual storage in short-term memory tasks. *Quarterly Journal of Experimental Psychology*, 24, 30–40.

Warrington, E. K. and Shallice, T. (1979). Semantic access dyslexia. *Brain*, 102, 43–63.

Warrington, E. K. and Shallice, T. (1984). Category specific semantic impairments. *Brain*, 107, 829–853.

Wason, P. C. (1960). On the failure to eliminate hypotheses in a conceptual task. *Quarterly Journal of Experimental Psychology*, 12, 129–140.

Wason, P. C. (1968). Reasoning about a rule. *Quarterly Journal of Experimental Psychology*, 23, 63–71.

Wason, P. C. and Shapiro, D. (1971). Natural and contrived experience in a reasoning problem. *Quarterly Journal of Experimental Psychology*, 23, 63–71.

Waters, E. A. (2008). Feeling good, feeling bad, and feeling at risk: A review of incidental affect's influence on likelihood estimates of health hazards and life events. *Journal of Risk Research*, 11, 569–595.

Watson, J. B. (1913). Psychology as the behaviourist views it. *Psychological Review*, 20, 158–177.

Wearing, D. (2005). *Forever Today*. London: Transworld.

Weeks, D., Freeman, C. P. L. and Kendell, R. E. (1980). ECT: II. Enduring cognitive deficits? *British Journal of Psychiatry*, 137, 26–37.

Wegner, D. M. (2003). The mind's best trick: How we experience conscious will. *Trends in Cognitive Sciences*, 7, 65–69.

Weinberg, J., Diller, L., Gordon, W., Gertsman, L. *et al.* (1977). Visual scanning training effect on reading -related tasks in acquired right brain damage. *Archives of Physical Medicine and Rehabilitation*, 58, 479–486.

Weisberg, R. W. and Alba, J. W. (1981). An examination of the alleged role of "fixation" in the solution of several "insight" problems. *Journal of Experimental Psychology: General*, 110, 169–192.

Weiskrantz, L. (1986). *Blindsight: A Case Study and Implications*. Oxford: Clarendon Press.

Weiskrantz, L., Warrington, E. K., Sanders, M. D. and Marshall, J. (1974). Visual capacity in the hemianopic field following a restricted occipital ablation. *Brain*, 97, 709–728.

Weiss, P. H. and Fink, G. R. (2009). Grapheme-colour synaesthetes show increased grey matter volumes of parietal and fusiform cortex. *Brain*, 132, 65–70.

Weiss, P. H., Zilles, K. and Fink, G. R. (2005). When visual perception causes feeling: Enhanced cross-modal processing in grapheme-color synesthesia. *NeuroImage*, 28, 859–68.

Welford, A. T. (1952). The psychological refractory period and the timing of high speed performance: A review and a theory. *British Journal of Psychology*, 43, 2–19.

Welt, L. (1888). Über Charakterveranderungen des Menschen infolge von Läsionen des Stirnhirns *Deutsche Archiv für Klinische Medizin*, 42, 339–390.

Wernicke, C. (1874). *Der Aphasiche Symptomkomplex: Eine Psychologische Studie Aufanatomischer Basis*. Breslau: Cohn and Weigert.

Wernicke, C. (1881). *Lehrbuch der gehirnkrankheiten fur aerzte und studirende*, Vol. 2 (pp. 229–242). Kassel Theodor Fischer.

Wertheimer, M. (1912). Experimentelle studien uber das sehen von bewegung. *Zeitschrift fur Psychologie*, 61, 161–265.

Wertheimer, M. (1923). Untersuchungen zur Lehre von der Gestalt. *Zeitschrift Forschung*, 4, 301–350.

Wessinger, C. M., Fendrich, R. and Gazzaniga, M. S. (1997). Islands of residual vision in hemianopic patients. *Journal of Cognitive Neuroscience*, 9, 203–221.

West, M. J., Coleman, P. D., Flood, D. G. and Troncoso, J. C. (1994). Differences in the pattern of hippocampal neuronal loss in normal ageing and Alzheimer's disease. *The Lancet*, 344, 769–772.

Westwood, D. A. and Goodale, M. A. (2003). Perceptual illusion and the realtime control of action. *Spatial Vision*, 16, 243–254.

Westwood, D. A. and Goodale, M. A. (2011). Converging evidence for diverging pathways: Neuropsychology and psychophysics tell the same story. *Vision Research*, 51(8), 804–811.

Wetherick, N. E. (1962). Eliminative and enumerative behaviour in a conceptual task. *Quarterly Journal of Experimental Psychology*, 14, 129–140.

Whitlow, S. D., Althoff, R. R. and Cohen, N. J. (1995). Deficit in relational (declarative) memory in amnesia. *Society for Neuroscience Abstracts*, 21, 754.

Whitty, C. W. M. and Zangwill, O. L. (1976). *Amnesia*. London: Butterworths.

Wickelgren, W. A. (1968). Sparing of short-term memory in an amnesic patient: Implications for strength theory of memory. *Neuropsychologia*, 6, 235–244.

Wilkins, A. J., Shallice, T. and McCarthy, R. (1987). Frontal lesions and sustained attention. *Neuropsychologia*, 25, 259–365.

Williams, S. J., Wright, D. B. and Freeman, N. H. (2002). Inhibiting children's memory of an interactive event: The effectiveness of a cover-up. *Applied Cognitive Psychology*, 16, 651–664.

Wilson, B. A. (1987). *Rehabilitation of Memory*. New York: Guilford.

Wilson, B. A. (2004). Management and rehabilitation of memory problems in brain-injured adults. In A. D. Baddeley, M. D. Kopelman and B. A. Wilson (eds) *The Essential Handbook of Memory Disorders for Clinicians*. Chichester: Wiley.

Wilson, B. A. and Wearing, D. (1995). Amnesia in a musician. In R. Campbell and M. Conway (eds) *Broken Memories*. Oxford: Blackwell.

Wilson, B. A., Kazniak, A. W. and Fox, J. H. (1981). Remote memory in senile dementia. *Cortex*, 17, 41–48.

Wilson, B. A., Baddeley, A. D. and Kapur, N. (1995). Dense amnesia in a professional musician following herpes simplex virus encephalitis. *Journal of Clinical and Experimental Neuropsychology,* 17, 668–681.

Wilson, B. A., Gracey, F., Evans, J. J. and Bateman, A. (2009). *Neuropsychological Rehabilitation: Theory, Models, Therapy and Outcome.* Cambridge: Cambridge University Press.

Wilson, C. E., Palermo, R., Schmalzl, L. and Brock, J. (2010). Specificity of impaired facial identity recognition in children with suspected developmental prosopagnosia. *Cognitive Neuropsychology,* 27(1), 30–45.

Wilson, D. and Sperber, D. (2002). Truthfulness and relevance. *Mind,* 111, 583–632.

Wilson, M. and Wilson, T. P. (2005). An oscillator model of the timing of turn-taking. *Psychonomic Bulletin and Review,* 12(6), 957–968.

Wingate, M. E. (1976). *Stuttering: Theory and Treatment.* New York: Irvington.

Winograd, E. (1976). Recognition memory for faces following nine different judgements. *Bulletin of the Psychonomic Society,* 8, 419–421.

Wise, R. J., Greene, J., Büchel, C. and Scott, S. K. (1999). Brain regions involved in articulation. *Lancet,* 27, 353(9158), 1057–1061.

Witthoft, N. and Winawer, J. (2013). Learning, memory, and synesthesia. *Psychological Science,* 24, 258–65. doi: 10.1177/0956797612452573.

Wolters, G. and Goudsmit, J. J. (2005). Flashbulb and event memory of September 11, 2001: Consistency, confidence and age effects. *Psychological Reports,* 96, 605–619.

Wolters, G. and Raffone, A. (2008). Coherence and recurrency: Maintenance, control, and integration in working memory. *Cognitive Processing,* 9, 1–17.

Wood, N. and Cowan, N. (1995). The cocktail party phenomenon revisited: How frequent are attention shifts to one's name in an irrelevant auditory channel? *Journal of Experimental Psychology, Learning Memory and Cognition,* 2, 255–260.

Wright, D. B., Self, G. and Justice, C. (2000). Memory conformity: Exploring misinformation effects when presented by another person. *British Journal of Psychology,* 91, 189–202.

Wright, D. B., Loftus, E. F. and Hall, M. (2001). Now you see it, now you don't: Inhibiting recall in the recognition of scenes. *Applied Cognitive Psychology,* 15, 471–482.

Yaro, C. and Ward, J. (2007). Searching for Shereshevskii: what is superior about the memory of synaesthetes? *Quarterly Journal of Experimental Psychology,* 60(5), 681–695.

Young, A. W. and Burton, A. M. (1999). Simulating face recognition: Implications for modelling cognition. *Cognitive Neuropsychology,* 16, 1–48.

Young, M. J., Tiedens, L. Z., Jung, H. and Tsai, M.-H. (2011). Mad enough to see the other side: Anger and the search for disconfirming information. *Cognition and Emotion,* 25, 10–21.

Zacher, W. (1901). Über ein Fall von doppelseitigem, symmetrisch gelegenem Erweichungsherd im Stirnhirn und Neuritis optica. *Neurologisches Zentralblatt,* 20, 1074–1083.

Zanetti, O., Zanieri, G., Giovanni, G. D., de Vreese, L. P. *et al.* (2001). Effectiveness of procedural memory stimulation in mild Alzheimer's disease patients. In L. Clare and R. T. Woods (eds) *Cognitive Rehabilitation in Dementia: A Special Issue of Neuropsychological Rehabilitation.* Hove: Psychology Press.

Zaragoza, M. S. and Lane, S. M. (1998). Processing resources and eyewitness suggestibility. *Legal and Criminological Psychology,* 3, 294–300.

Zeki, S. (2003). The disunity of consciousness. *Trends in Cognitive Sciences,* 7, 214–218.

Zevin, J. D. and Seidenberg, M. S. (2002). Age of acquisition effects in reading and other tasks. *Journal of Memory and Language,* 47, 1–29.

Zevin, J. D. and Seidenberg, M. S. (2004). Age of acquisition effects in reading aloud: Tests of cumulative frequency and frequency trajectory. *Memory and Cognition,* 32, 31–38.

Zhu, B., Chen, C., Loftus, E. F., Lin, C., He, Q., Chen, C. *et al.* (2010). Individual differences in false memory from misinformation: Cognitive factors. *Memory,* 18, 543–555.

Zihl, J. (1994). Rehabilitation of visual impairments in patients with brain damage. In A. C. Koijman, P. L. Looijjjeesijn, J. A. Welling and G. J. van der Wildt (eds) *Low Vision* (pp. 287–295). Amsterdam: IOS Press.

Zihl, J. (1995). Eye movement patterns in hemianopic dyslexia. *Brain,* 118, 891–912.

Zola-Morgan, S. and Squire, L. R. (2000). The medial temporal lobe and the hippocampus. In E. Tulving and F. I. M. Craik (eds) *The Oxford Handbook of Memory.* Oxford: Oxford University Press.

Zwitserlood, P. (1989). The locus of the effects of sentential-semantic context in spoken-word processing. *Cognition,* 32(1), 25–64.

Author index

Subject index

An Introduction to Cognitive Psychology companion website

The companion website for *An Introduction to Cognitive Psychology* offers an array of supplementary materials for both students and lecturers.

Student resources

- A comprehensive glossary
- Interactive exercises, animations and simulations of key phenomena
- Links to related websites and further reading
- Chapter summaries and flash cards to aid revision.

Lecturer resources

- A testbank of multiple-choice questions
- PowerPoint slides containing figures from the book.

Access to lecturer resources is restricted to lecturers through password protection. All resources are available free of charge to qualifying lecturers. Please visit the website: **www.psypress.com/cw/groome** and follow the instructions to request access.